Savu

Savu

History and Oral Tradition on an Island of Indonesia

Geneviève Duggan and Hans Hägerdal

NUS PRESS
SINGAPORE

© 2018 Geneviève Duggan and Hans Hägerdal

Published by:

NUS Press
National University of Singapore
AS3-01-02, 3 Arts Link
Singapore 117569

Fax: (65) 6774-0652
E-mail: nusbooks@nus.edu.sg
Website: http://nuspress.nus.edu.sg

ISBN 978-981-4722-75-9 (case)

National Library Board, Singapore Cataloguing in Publication Data

Names: Duggan, Geneviève. | Hägerdal, Hans, authors.
Title: Savu: history and oral tradition on an island of Indonesia / Geneviève Duggan
    and Hans Hägerdal.
Description: Singapore: NUS Press, [2018]
Identifier(s): OCN 1024231438 | ISBN 978-981-47-2275-9 (hardcover)
Subject(s): LCSH: Sawu Islands (Indonesia)--History. | Sawu Islands
    (Indonesia)--Civilization. | Sawu Islands (Indonesia)--Politics and government. |
    Sawu Islands (Indonesia)--Social conditions.
Classification: DDC 959.868--dc23

Unless otherwise stated, all the illustrations in this volume are the private collections of Geneviève Duggan.

Cover image: A traditional priest (Apu Lod'o Muhu of Mesara) in his customary attire mounted on his sacred Savunese horse. He and the young woman, Danga, are both wearing traditional Savunese ikat. The structure in the background is the founding house of Ledetadu village, Mesara (est. 1760s/1770s). Photograph by Geneviève Duggan.

Typeset by: Ogma Solutions Pvt Ltd
Printed by: Markono Print Media Pte Ltd

Contents

List of Figures

List of Maps

Key for all maps

Features	Examples of lettering style and symbols
Country, island, regency and district	SAVU
Present-day village and town	● Bolou
Place of historical importance; ancient settlement	● *Raenalai*
Bay River Mountain	*Uba Ae* *Liu* ▲ Pemulu

List of Photographs

List of Plates

(between pages 326 and 327)

Foreword by Professor James Fox

This is a book of exceptional scope and consummate scholarship focused on the small island of Savu, located between the larger islands of Sumba and Timor in eastern Indonesia. A 19th century Dutch visitor described it as "a lump of stone in an immense sea". Yet Captain James Cook, who happened upon Savu in 1770, heading home after his voyage across the Pacific and along the coast of Australia, was entirely taken by the beauty of the island: "At the time the *Endeavour* lay there it was the end of the dry season, when it had not rained for almost seven months, nor was there a running stream of fresh water to be seen … yet even in this dry season, the appearance of the island was beautiful."

Joseph Banks, who accompanied Cook, was even more fascinated by the Savunese themselves and he used his brief time on the island to interrogate Johann Christopher Lange, a native of Saxony, who had been stationed in Savu as an officer of the Dutch East India Company for over ten years. Lange appraised Banks of Savu's five "principalities", each with its own raja; the island's produce, particularly its palm juice which cooked to syrup was the mainstay of the population—an "immense quantity" of which, "several hundred gallons" was purchased to supply the *Endeavour*; the Savunese "marshal prowess" and "warlike disposition" whose only sign Banks could see was in a "refuse of old armories"—spears, lances and rusted muskets; and most notably, Savunese "pride of descent, particularly of being sprung from a family which has for many years been respected". Cook was equally explicit on this point: "The chief object of pride among these people … is a long pedigree of respectable ancestors."

Significantly Banks recognised Savu's comparative linguistic connections. On the basis of a list of some 66 words in Savunese, which he carefully recorded, Banks concluded of the language: "The genius of it seems much to resemble that of the South Sea Isles; in several instances words are exactly the same and the numbers are undoubtedly from the same source."

As Banks was the first to recognise, the Savunese, as an Austronesian-speaking population, possessed many features in common with the Polynesian populations whom Cook and Banks had met— in particular, a society of status and precedence, an elaborate priesthood and an obsession with genealogies linked to the creation of the cosmos, thus assigning each individual a specific place in the formation and unfolding of their past.

This book is an examination of these key features of Savunese life. It is a work of meticulous fieldwork and extended archival scholarship—a fusion of anthropological and historical research. It is a work of long and significant collaboration by its two authors. Geneviève Duggan, who has been doing field research in Savu for almost three decades, has gained an almost encyclopedic knowledge of its traditions. She relies on the elaborate scaffolding of the island's oral genealogies to present the Savunese conception of their past: the ordered succession of the deeds of their ancestors and the conflicted development of the island's constituent social and religious divisions. In a similar vein, Hans Hägerdal, who has laboured, over two decades, in the archives of the Dutch East India Company to gain an unparalleled understanding of the recorded history of eastern Indonesia, presents a detailed account of developments on Savu from the time of early contact with the Dutch. This combination of special skills provides a unique portrait of a remarkable society.

The confluence of these two perspectives—from within and without—offers a valuable opportunity to assess what each of these perspectives provides. The overlap between these perspectives, for which there is neither complete coincidence nor entire dissimilarity about the past, is itself revealing. Interestingly, for example, Cook provided a clear description of Ama Doko Lomi Jara, the raja of Seba, and of Manu Jami whom Cook referred to as his "Prime Minister". He and Banks dined and dealt with both men to obtain the supplies the *Endeavour* needed for its onward voyage. The names of these Savunese figures are thus recorded in the annals of 18th century exploration. They are also documented in the archival records of the Dutch East India Company but, notably as well, these same names are still remembered in current oral genealogies and their descendants who live on in Savu continue to take pride in the pedigrees that join them to their ancestral past.

This book, however, goes well beyond the imaginings of Cook and Banks. In Savu, genealogies reckoned through women are as extensive and as comprehensive as those through men. Male genealogies assign individuals to clans (*udu*) and lineages (*kerogo*) while female genealogies assign these same individuals to 'blossoms' (*hubi*) and their various 'seeds' (*wini*). While there are many clans and even more lineages on Savu, there only two 'blossoms' across the whole of the island—a Greater Blossom (*Hubi Ae*) and a Lesser Blossom (*Hubi Iki*)—each with its distinctive 'seed' groups. This female affiliation is coded through complex textile patterns that are personally displayed by participants at rituals.

Nowhere in the Austronesian-speaking world is there this level of genealogical elaboration. This double genealogical specificity for all members of society is what gives Savu its local grounding. The ethnographic attention to these dual identities and their historical significance is a critical feature of the detailed social evidence compiled, analysed and presented in this volume.

This book is a monument of research scholarship to be appreciated and studied with care and attention. Despite Savu's relative isolation and previous lack of ethnographic attention, this small island society—as this book demonstrates—provides historical case study of fundamental relevance to the on going comparative examination of the Austronesian-speaking populations arrayed across more than half the world, from Madagascar to Hawai'i, and from Taiwan to Timor.

James J. Fox
The Australian National University

Acknowledgements

Since we began to work seriously on the book in around 2012, we have benefited from the help and support of a large number of persons and institutions whom we want to thank. Perhaps the most important person is our copy-editor Emma Coupland, working from Dili, Timor-Leste, who managed the impressive job of scrutinising hundreds of pages of text and never failed in giving important feedback. Thanks also go to the staff at NUS Press, particularly Paul Kratoska and Lena Qua. James Fox in Canberra has been a great inspiration along the way as has Robert Barnes in Cambridge, Massachusetts. We also wish to make the following individual acknowledgements.

I would like to thank Professor Roxana Waterson who was a precious source of inspiration as I wrote my thesis and Professor James Fox for his valuable advice over the years as well as for his careful review of my manuscript. Thanks also to our friend, Emilie Wellfelt, who passed on my thesis to Hans Hägerdal, with whom I then exchanged knowledge and confronted sources until we decided to write this book together.

All this would not have been possible without the generosity and openness of many Savunese who let me take part in their rituals and ceremonies, sharing happy gatherings and sad family moments. I sincerely thank my hosts in Seba, the late Bernardus Lado and his wife, the late Ina Mina Raja. Their son, Elo Lado (Malobo), was for years my assistant and facilitator in the field, translator and *ojek* (motorbike taxi [In]) driver until he chose a path in politics after the creation of the Savu Raijua regency. My most vivid memories are certainly the evenings on the veranda of my host family in Mesara. I sat while the late *Bapak* (title for a respected older man [In]) Zadrak Bunga and his neighbours commented on current events or recounted stories, passing around a bottle of local arak, and his wife Ina Nara—the best cook on the island—worked next to the oil lamp spinning cotton or tying yarns together. It was there on the veranda that I gathered many of my leads for interviews. My thanks go to the elders who entrusted me with their knowledge as they realised that their children and grandchildren were only looking to the future and were no longer interested in things of the past. They are mentioned throughout the chapters and I apologise if I have not managed to retain all the knowledge they entrusted to me. Finally, my thanks go to my husband, Tony, who from the very beginning has supported my research on Savu both morally and financially.

Geneviève Duggan (known as Ina Dope Jena in Savu)
Singapore, February 2018

My interest in the past of eastern Indonesia dates back to a postdoc at the International Institute for Asian Studies (IIAS) in Leiden in the late 1990s. I am much obliged to its one-time director Wim Stokhof for his encouragement, as well as to the grand organiser of the International Convention of Asian Scholars (ICAS) conferences, Paul van der Velde. I also wish to express my thanks to a number of people with whom I have had the opportunity to discuss eastern Indonesian matters over the years, such as Arend de Roever, Donald P. Tick, Antoinette Schapper, James Fox, Robert Barnes, Ruth Barnes, Steven Farram, and Douglas Kammen. Usif Leopold Nisnoni, Kupang, generously helped my research through his extensive network of contacts in the NTT area. The Linnaeus University Center for Concurrences in Colonial and Postcolonial Studies has supported and generously funded my research on Savu since 2012. Here, I also take the opportunity to thank the participants of the Center who have provided constructive feedback on the way. I especially want to mention Emilie Wellfelt, presently at Stockholm University. Furthermore, thanks go to the staff of the Koninklijk Instituut voor Taal-, Land- en Volkenkunde (KITLV), Leiden, Nationaal Archief, The Hague, Arsip Nasional Republik Indonesia (ANRI), Jakarta, and the Faculty of Arts and Humanities (FKH), Linnaeus University, Växjö-Kalmar. Finally, I wish to thank my family which has put up with all my travelling to far-away archives, conferences and sites of investigation.

Hans Hägerdal
Lund, Sweden, February 2018

1. Map of NTT (Nusa Tenggara Timur, the Eastern Southeast Islands) (credit Jeroen Toussaint)

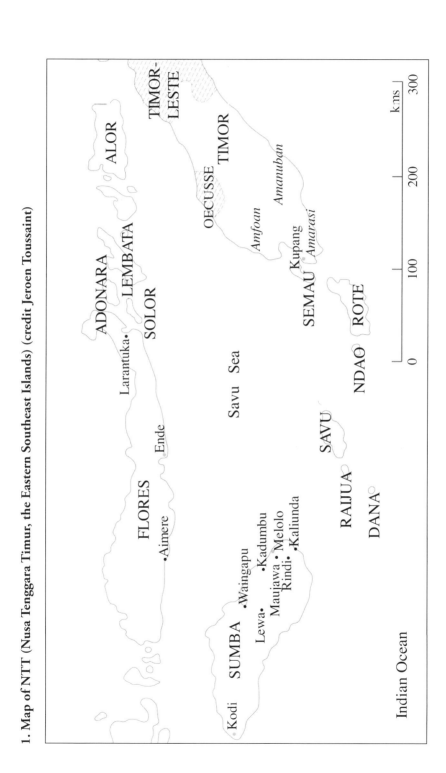

2. Map of Savu; its five districts and places of historical importance (credit Jeroen Toussaint)

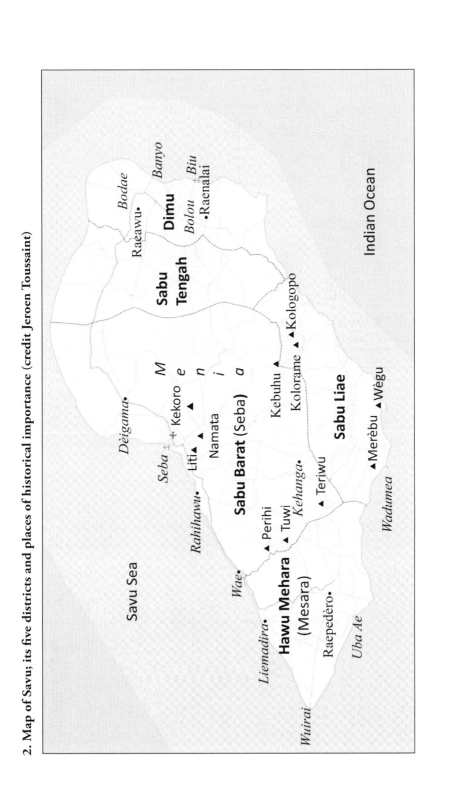

3. Map of Sabu Liae (credit Jeroen Toussaint)

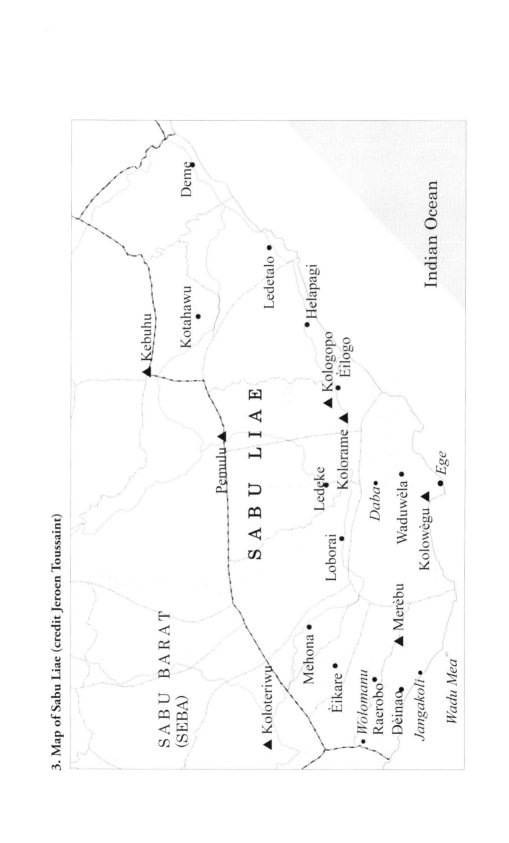

**4. Map of Sabu Tengah (Central) and Sabu Timur (Dimu)
(credit Jeroen Toussaint)**

5. Map of Hawu Mehara (Mesara) (credit Jeroen Toussaint)

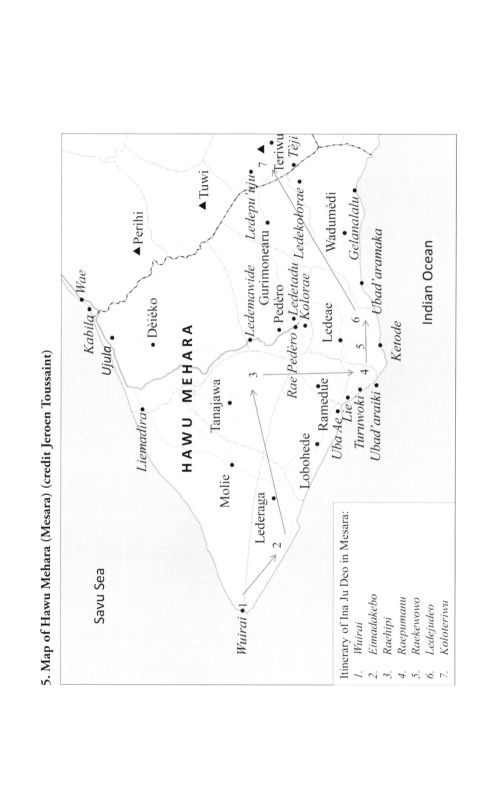

Itinerary of Ina Ju Deo in Mesara:

1. *Wuirai*
2. *Eimadakebo*
3. *Raehipi*
4. *Raepumanu*
5. *Raekewowo*
6. *Ledejudeo*
7. *Koloterivu*

6. Map of Sabu Barat (Seba) (credit Jeroen Toussaint)

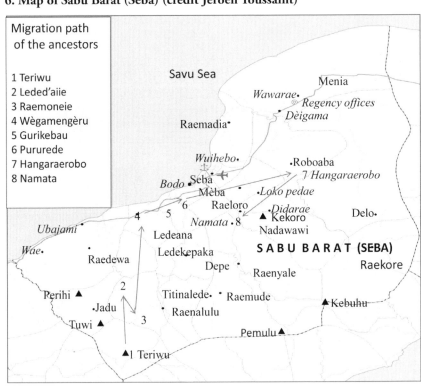

Migration path
of the ancestors

1 Teriwu
2 Leded'aiie
3 Raemoneie
4 Wègamengèru
5 Gurikebau
6 Pururede
7 Hangaraerobo
8 Namata

Savu Sea

Menia

Wawarae·

Regency offices

Dèigama

Raemadia·

Wuihebo·

·Roboaba

7 Hangaraerobo

Bodo ·Seba

Mèba ·

·Loko pedae

6

Raeloro

·Didarae

Delo·

4

5

Namata ·8

▲ Kekoro

Ubajami·

Ledeana

Nadawawi

Wae·

SABU BARAT (SEBA)

Raedewa

Ledekepaka

Depe ·

Raekore

2

Raenyale

Perihi ▲

Titinalede· · Raemude

·Jadu

▲Kebuhu

3

· Raenalulu

Tuwi ▲

Pemulu▲

▲l Teriwu

7. **Map of Raijua (credit Jeroen Toussaint)**

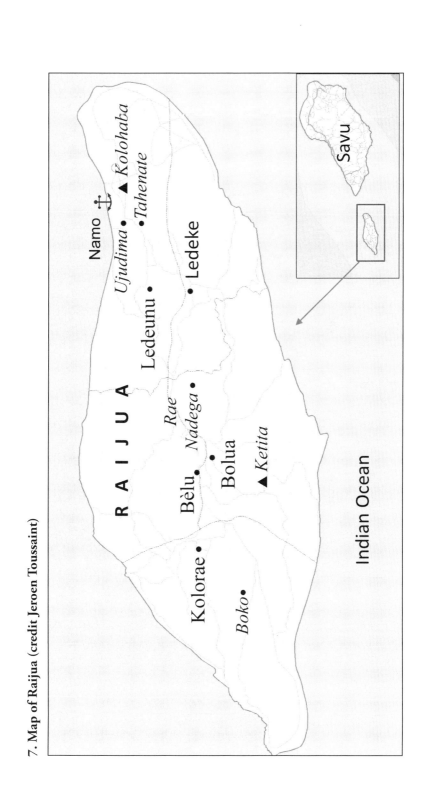

Introduction: Methods and Sources

Savu, or Rai Hawu to use the indigenous name, is not a big place by any standard. Together with the nearby islands of Raijua and Dana, it only encompasses 460 square kilometres, being considerably smaller than Singapore. Its somewhat isolated position between Timor, Sumba and Flores does not make it a frequently visited place. Exceedingly few tourists make it to Savu, even in comparison with the other islands of the seldom-visited Nusa Tenggara Timur (NTT [the Eastern Southeast Islands]) province.

However, Savu cannot be considered a forgotten island. Modern anthropological work—especially by James J. Fox—has highlighted the unique ritual and ecological system of local society and has probably engendered more interest in Savu than the Sula Islands (North Maluku), Bonerate (South Sulawesi), Buru (Maluku), Pantar (NTT) and so on. Readers of historical travel literature might know it from the engaged eyewitness account of Captain Cook. The common perception is usually to pair Savu with Rote with which it shares important features in terms of economic bases and traditional territorial division. Both islands have acquired some fame for their basic means of nutrition, the sugar juice tapped from the lontar palms, which gave their inhabitants the reputation of being "the non-eating people" (cf. Fox 1977: 1). Eastern Indonesia often suffers from a lack of rainfall and less fertile soil compared to the western and central parts, but its inhabitants have developed ingenious ways of making a living from scarce resources; Savu is a prime example. In addition, the activities of the Savunese and Rotenese have influenced a much wider geographical and professional area than suggested by their tiny home islands. Their fearsome reputation as Dutch auxiliaries in the old days and their prominence as politicians and urban professionals in more recent times have given migrating Savunese a certain standing in the larger context of eastern Indonesia.

The present work blends anthropological and historical analysis in order to trace the past of a very special island people. There are several reasons to undertake such a project. Like many other societies in eastern Indonesia, Savu has developed a comprehensive socio-religious system where political hierarchy, genealogical affiliation, territoriality and ritual functions are intimately intertwined. The society is classified as bilineal; from the day s/he is born, everyone belongs to a male clan (*udu*) through the father and to a female moiety[1] (*hubi*) through the mother (Fox 1972: 78–9). This double identity cannot be changed throughout life, not even through marriage.

In the course of time clans have formed lineages (*kerogo*). The two female moieties, descended from two sisters, are known as Greater Blossom (*hubi ae*) and Lesser Blossom (*hubi iki*); throughout time they too created subgroups called 'seeds' (*wini*). A man should marry in the same *wini* or at least in the same *hubi* as his mother (Kana 1978: 241). Consequently, the marriage rule from the moiety point of view is endogamy, while on the paternal side it is irrelevant if the groom marries within his own clan or lineage, or outside it. *Hubi* and *wini* are highly relevant to the life-crisis ceremonies, especially traditional baptism (*daba*), marriage (*kenoto*) and funerals. *Hubi* and *wini* are not localised and may be scattered over Savu and Raijua. In contrast, the *udu* and *kerogo* are localised groups which own the land. Residence being patrilocal, the male genealogies of one *kerogo* can sometimes be traced in one hamlet or in one village only. One *udu* is generally to be found in just one area, sometimes in one or two villages. Therefore, exceptions reveal either marriage and war alliances or how clans overruled others.

Most clans are represented in the councils of priests of the ancestral religion Jingi Tiu, which in everyday language is called *agama suku* (Indonesian [In]) or 'religion of the clans'. The exact meaning of Jingi Tiu is complex. According to Allan Walker and James Fox, the term *jingi* derives from the Portuguese, *gentio*, meaning pagan, and *tiu* comes from *Deo*, God, thus designating people who are not God's children. It is interesting that the word *jingi* already existed in Savunese, meaning to destroy, sack or pillage (*rampas* [In]).[2] In the moiety Lesser Blossom, a subgroup is called Jingi Wiki and is associated with black magic.[3] It is puzzling that council of priest members accepted the label 'destructive' to describe their

---

[1] Moiety refers to a society which is divided into halves. In the case of Savu, the moieties are female and encompass female genealogies; they express precedence in relation to birth but not a hierarchy.

[2] Jingi Tari was the paternal uncle of Kore Rohi, the first raja of Portuguese times (Figure 17). It cannot, however, be stated if the name is a coincidence or related to encounters with the Portuguese, if it underwent changes during his life or after death, to become part of his mantra name.

[3] It is *swangi* in Indonesian. *Wiki* means more, thus more destructive, which is then appropriate for the negative power Jingi Wiki people can exercise.

religion.[4] The second term, *tiu*, is not known outside the expression Jingi Tiu and *Deo* constitutes half the names of the two highest priest positions: Deo Rai (Lord of the Earth) and Deo Mengèru (Lord of Prosperity).

Membership of a council of priests (*Mone Ama*) is hereditary. The number and composition of the councils have evolved over time with the increasing power of certain clans. A council cannot exist without a high priest or Deo Rai. For the other positions, the ranking among the priests varies according to the diverse ceremonial domains. One priest position, Apu Lod'o (Descendant of the Sun) ranks relatively highly and is always filled by someone from the ruler's clan. The various priest positions concern either agricultural activities (fertility and prosperity for plants and, consequently, for humans too) or are related to war matters (safety of the warriors). One priestly position, Rue, is related to when disasters strike the community and it is in his power to re-establish the cosmic balance. He may also prevent disasters; therefore, all the other priests need him, so he occupies a very special and high position. Priests are in command of secret and sacred recitations, *li pana* (Savunese [Sa]). This powerful and poetic language is referred to as *bahasa mantra* by Indonesian speakers on the island. This expression also deserves attention. While Dutch missionaries generally called the local religion Jingi Tiu, it was sometimes labelled 'Hindu'. The equation of *bahasa mantra* with *li pana* might have been inherited from this time and left traces to the present.[5]

Gathering anthropological data in Savu entails the use of two analytical tools; one is the concept of temporal and spatial precedence. For example, each of the five ceremonial domains of the Savu Raijua archipelago has a specific number for determining the dates of rituals and the number of offerings to be made. Seba has the highest number, nine, and is thus attributed the highest ranking, Mesara and Liae are number seven while Dimu and Raijua have the lowest position, six. The

---

[4] There is a second word for designating the ancestral religion – *nuhe* – which means to bow or bend over and describes the movement of the body when praying and before placing offerings at the foot of pillars inside a house or on top of stones (Zadrak Bunga, personal communication; 24.04.2011).

[5] It might also derive from locally produced school books for teaching local traditions. Teachers explained that Savu society has a caste system, and they see a link between India and Savu. However, most clans have priests (see for instance Figure 1 for Upper Mesara); the raja's clan too is represented with at least a priest (Apu Lod'o) on the council, *Mone Ama*. Besides, Savu society is not really hierarchical, with marriages between members of all clans being possible.

lunar calendar also reflects this precedence in a temporal manner.[6] The year starts in April–May in Seba, in May–June in Mesara and Liae, and in June–July in Dimu and Raijua. The names of the months related to major agricultural events or ceremonies often carry the same name in all domains.[7] Spatial precedence concerns dualistic classifications either in complementary gendered pairings present in rituals as well as in everyday life, or it forms a spatial oppositional pair as, for example, up/down, inside/outside, front/back, hot/cold. Most essential are binary gendered associations guaranteeing fertility and reproduction. Such pairings are found at all levels of the society. Therefore, the combination of oral accounts and practices form a coherent and useful system for anchoring events in memory.

Genealogies and names

"All Austronesian societies make in varying degrees use of precedence as a means of social and individual differentiation" (Fox 1995: 226). Temporal precedence is not based solely on the lunar calendar but also on genealogies and this entirely oral knowledge covers tens of generations. Genealogies form the backbone of the local chronology and indicate how far in the past something happened (Vansina 1985: 24). The recitation of names conveys a chronological sense of temporal representation. The recitation of genealogies is referred to as *huhu kebie*, which literally means 'to pile up beams' and evokes the construction of a building, each generation supporting the next one. This terminology recalls an ancient form of architecture which could be seen in some regions of Indonesia until recently.[8] In Savu 'piling the beams' is a particular form of narrative organising an essential social 'memory scape'. The complete expression is *huhu raiti d'a'i, huhu d'èi dida* and means 'pile up from the bottom, pile up to the top'.

Genealogies are of direct relevance to today's social structures. In addition, male and female genealogies exist side by side and are remembered separately,

---

[6] *Kalendar adat* (In). For the ceremonial systems in the various domains of Savu, see Appendix II. For early publications on this subject see Jeanne Cuisinier (1956: 11–9); James. J. Fox for the domains of Seba and Liae (1979: 145–73); and Nico Kana for the domain of Mesara (1978: 353–420; 1983:75–104).

[7] For instance, the names of the months Ko'o ma (month of preparing the fields for planting), Daba (traditional baptism) and Bangaliwu (thanksgiving) are shared by all domains. The name Wèru a'a (month of the elder [sibling]), which marks the first month of the year, is the same in all parts of Savu while Raijua has the variant Wèru wadu a'a (month of the elder stone).

[8] 'Block-buildings' are constructed with interlocking beams in the style of a log cabin. They existed in Sumatra among the Batak people and in Sulawesi (Tana Toraja). On the Trobriand Islands such architecture is still used for yam store houses. See Waterson (1990: 25).

which is of importance for cross-checking information; marriage alliances build horizontal links between both groups. Most people remember their own paternal and maternal genealogy over a dozen generations, whereas some specialists are in command of entire genealogies. Female genealogies are surrounded by more secrecy and a man refrains from disclosing the genealogy of his female ancestors even if he is well informed. Contrasting with other societies, such as Sumba, Rote or Toraja (South Sulawesi), where genealogical knowledge is the prerogative of the aristocracy, in Savu everybody has a genealogy irrespective of his/her social status.[9] Savu offers a unique case for confronting oral and written sources because of the extent of the male and female genealogical data.

As genealogies are crucial in tracing the Savu people's past, it is necessary to provide some explanations about the way names are given. A person has at least three or four names generally loaded with meaning: a 'formal-personal' or 'real' name; a pet name; a teknonym; and a sacred name. Some names are gendered while others are not. The formal-personal name is binomial, and is given during a ceremony for cutting the first hair and piercing the ears. This ceremony called *hapo* (to adopt) takes place three to seven days after birth; the newborn is presented to the close family and his/her 'real' name is disclosed. The first half of the formal name is a specific personal identifier; the parents or grandparents choose it from an open repertoire of names. The first half of the formal-personal name can be changed if it appears inauspicious to its owner, especially during childhood if the child is often sick or does not develop normally.

The second half of the personal name is drawn from the first half of the father's name and can be labelled as a surname or family name as it is shared by all siblings. Nevertheless, the surname is valid for one generational level only, forming a unique link in a chain of names. The formal-personal or 'real' name can be meaningful or it might equally make no particular sense at first. When reciting genealogies certain combinations of sounds are easier to memorise, using alliterations and assonances as mnemonic tags. The second half of the personal name can also change during the course of a person's life, such as in the case of an adoption. An adult's personal name is normally unique to an individual and is remembered in genealogies. For memory purposes, genealogical homonymy is the exception in Savu, although cases were found in all districts. Such cases can be resolved as, if necessary, the father and grandfather's names are then disclosed.[10]

---

[9] See Fox (1971); Geirnaert-Martin (1992); Waterson (1997: 67).

[10] For example, a certain Manu Jami lived in Seba and a man of the same name lived in Menia about the same time. However, the first one is Manu Jami Lobo Tuka and the other is Manu Jami Tèro Weo (Ch. 6). For further information about the analysis of people's names, see Duggan (2011c: 32–4).

When they become parents, people are addressed with a teknonym; the term *Ama* or *Ma* (Father [of]) or *Ina* or *Na* (Mother [of]) is followed by the name of the first born child. It is necessary here to point out the differences between the names of married men and women. Both take the name of their first-born child, placing *Ama* or *Ina* in front. However, when reciting male genealogies, men tend to give the name of the first born son even when the first born child is a daughter. Accordingly, when reciting female genealogies the name of a supposed first born daughter preceded by *Ina* is given, even if she is not the first born child. A number of men and women marry several times in their lives. In such cases, a man's teknonym does not change with successive marriages while the teknonym of a woman changes each time bridewealth is received. Fortunately, such complications could be disentangled during interviews.

In the case of conversion to a modern religion, a Christian or Muslim name is given. This is not normally used on the island, except during religious rituals and at meetings with outsiders and foreigners. The Christian name usually presents some homophony with the personal first name. For the last three to four generations, personal names tend to be repeated, breaking up the traditional pattern. This is particularly obvious in the ruling families of Dutch times, possibly in order to fulfil the administrative wishes of the colonial power.[11]

Equally important for tracing the Savu people's past is the fact that each person has also a secret and sacred name to protect him/her throughout life; it belongs to *li pana* (Sa) (*mantra* name [In]). The recitation of the mantra name starts with the personal name and can swell into poetic stanzas. This powerful and coded name may embody characteristics of its bearer, such as a trait of his/her personality, or refer to particular events in his/her life, for instance, the circumstances of an unnatural death. Created first by the parents or grandparents during the *hapo* ceremony shortly after birth, it is not even known to all the guests present. Consisting of metaphors, it can expand during the person's life. It is disclosed on at least two occasions: upon marriage and at the funeral during the nights when genealogies are recited. The poetic verses act as a short biography of the deceased who is then remembered by his/her descendants through both personal and mantra names.

---

[11] G. Duggan's host family in Seba shows how names are given and how they may change. The father, Beha Lado, attended Dutch Volksschool from the age of 12 and converted to Christianity shortly after, receiving the name Bernardus Lado as it sounded close enough to Beha. He became a teacher and, following the administrative recommendations, called his son Elo Lado, not Elo Beha. As a young adult, the son changed his name to Elo Huma Lado, Huma being the name of an ancestor. When Beha Lado passed away in 2007, another son, Weo Lado, changed his name by introducing Beha as middle name, thus Weo Beha Lado.

Verses of an early ancestor's mantra name can also become part of ritual chants in public ceremonies. Consequently, events fixed in a mantra name are not only part of the social memory of a lineage but belong as well to collective memory. It is actually through the knowledge of mantra compositions that it is possible to reconstruct a more detailed and possibly more accurate history of the island. Such compositions still contain information which might have been left out of oral narratives and other vernacular texts. Mantra names are poetic texts which are too powerful to be easily manipulated by subsequent generations. Adoptions, for example, are not traceable in the genealogies. However, an adoption is remembered in a mantra name.

People's names are associated with places; indeed visual and auditory memories are the most pervasive forms of remembering. Therefore, temporal and spatial precedence are often complementary and visually represented in the layout of villages and ritual places as, for instance, in the traditional villages of Namata in Seba or Raepedèro in Mesara. Places, too, have genealogies. Not only have the names of people been transmitted from generation to generation but also the name of the founding settlement or village of origin (*rae kepue*). The names of settlements created one after another form a chronology of places or a genealogy of settlements, or "topogenies" (Fox 1997). The same phenomenon can be observed in the succession of houses the ancestors inhabited, forming a genealogy of houses or "domogenies" (figure 43). Furthermore, patterns created on hand-woven cloths are remembered in connections to female ancestors so that there are genealogies of patterns (or "textilogenies") (figure 44) as there are female genealogies. It is remarkable how Savunese people use genealogical constructs as mnemonic devices and as stable references for various aspects of their society. Topogenies, domogenies and more general spatial precedence are important means for cross-checking contemporary oral sources; for filling the blanks where memory has faded; or for challenging oral sources. Places are loaded with personal and social meaning; language and practices are combined and form essential memory markers.

Indigenous versus external sources

The social system, the peculiarities of remembering practised in Savunese society and expressing the local or emic point of view are all significant factors in describing Savu's past. Another consideration is how to analyse the indigenous, non-written sources as well as the external written material in light of each other. In itself, this is an issue of much wider interest than Savu; it relates to Gayatri Spivak's well-known question—"Can the Subaltern Speak?" (Spivak 1988). Can a thorough investigation of data about a limited region, such as Savu, yield more positive answers than those of Spivak? The circumstances suggest they can.

While the advances of colonialism, Christianity and the postcolonial bureaucratic state have led to the erosion of the old ways of life in the region, it has proven surprisingly resilient in Savu where the old Jingi Tiu religion still has its adherents and oral tradition is strong. Meanwhile, written documents relating to Savu exist from the 17th century onwards and are sometimes quite detailed. As a historical case study, Savu is therefore of great interest. A picture emerges of a local-island society potentially adapting to the pressures of colonialism over a period of several hundred years.

Savu before 1870 may be considered a non-literate island, although there are hints in the old documents that the written word was not totally unfamiliar to the elite. It was only with the installation of missionary schools that a few people learned to read and write; as in the rest of Indonesia, mass education only became more widespread from 1949, after independence. However, history is also transmitted in forms other than written documents—through place names, heritage objects, archaeological remains, linguistic data and, not least, oral tradition. When the British expedition of Captain James Cook visited Savu in 1770, the visitors noticed the people's extraordinary interest in the past. They compared the Savunese to Welsh genealogists who could tell the ancestry of individuals innumerable generations back in time. Recent research has confirmed the mnemotechnical capacity of the islanders who are often still able to recount their pedigree from memory. When gathered together, the lines of descent are grouped into patrilinear clans (*udu*) and female kinship groups (*hubi*). These, in turn, form the branches of a gigantic genealogical tree that goes back to mythical ancestral figures. It is to be noted that not only is the elite involved in this but also the general population. Savunese tell stories of key figures in the genealogies, some of which are long accounts of considerable literary interest.

The occurrence of a lively oral tradition is not unique to Savu. Stories of the past are recounted in Timor, Flores, Solor, Alor and so on, obviously the natural means of conveying information in a society where writing is rare or unknown. Anthropologists have long recognised the value of such traditions for mapping the culture and social structure of local societies. However, their usefulness for actually mapping the past has been a moot issue. While narratives were sometimes uncritically used in premodern historiography, the historical-critical trends prevalent in the West in the late 19th and early 20th centuries regarded them as unusable. Modern historical writing has normally leant on contemporary or near-contemporary texts while interdisciplinary attempts to assess other sources have been relatively rare in the West. However, the independence of nations with a non-literate history—in particular those of sub-Saharan Africa—necessitated new ways of uncovering the past. In 1960, Jan Vansina presented a set of methodological devices to work with oral materials. Vansina downplayed the differences between written and oral sources; they must both be studied methodically and critically. It is necessary to compare versions, establish possible inter-dependence and undertake comparisons with other types of materials. Most essentially, one has to analyse the circumstances of the performer and performance: who is telling the story and in what circumstances does s/he tell it?

While some attempts to write pre colonial African history in the 1960s and 1970s might have been over-optimistic in their use of non-written data, the importance of oral tradition and interdisciplinary approaches in African studies is now generally acknowledged. For some coastal areas, such as Benin, Nigeria, Kongo and Angola, the traditions can be checked against European documents. The result varies greatly from case to case. Strongly organised kingdoms, such as Ashanti (in present-day Ghana) and Dahomey (in what is now Benin), have preserved a biased but factually reliable corpus of data about rulers and basic events while others, such as Allada in Benin, have a traditional history that bears little resemblance to written records. A weak central tradition, abrupt breaks or crises may contribute to a factually distorted version of the past (Finnegan 1996). Still, this needs some qualification: a 'traditional' group may have other purposes for the stories of the past than to convey precise fact. Orally transmitted history frequently explains the origins and position of a polity, thereby legitimising the current or recent order. In such an endeavour, it may be essential to commemorate matters other than conventional historical data.

How does the material gathered in the field meet the written text? The enormous record-producing apparatus of the Dutch East India Company (VOC) and, to a lesser extent the Portuguese *Estado da Índia*, provide us with a rare opportunity to follow a set of non-literate polities over several hundred years (Hägerdal 2015). The Dutch established a post for trade and military surveillance in Kupang in westernmost Timor in 1653 at the height of VOC expansion, some months after the first settlement in South Africa (De Roever 2002: 253). Like all the VOC posts, it was strongly expected to document its existence in detail. The post normally dispatched two longer reports to the hub of the company in Batavia each year. VOC Batavia also received copies of a further number of important documents—economic accounts, letters, minutes of legal proceedings and *dagh-register*s (daily journals), with annotations from the post's head resident (*opperhoofd*). Luckily, there are a considerable number of *dagh-register*s which company representatives kept from tours of inspection to Savu. These provide some insight into political conditions on the island during the 17th and 18th centuries, and even hint at cultural and social processes. One advantage of the material is that it was not meant for publication; rather it was for employers who wanted facts and not fancies, in order to make strategic decisions and allocate resources. The texts are, therefore, presumably less prone to embellishments than published accounts. This is also their weakness: the reports tell of matters of importance for VOC activities and tend to ignore other aspects.

The VOC material becomes less detailed in its coverage of indigenous conditions towards the late 18th century. The source situation is even worse for the transitional period in 1800–16 and the new Dutch colonial state after 1816. It is only from the 1830s that regular colonial reports about the Timor area reappear in the archives. For much of the 19th century there is meagre information about Savu, but after 1870 another category fills in the void. This is the verbose corpus of reports and letters from the Protestant missionaries. While they usually did not possess a scholarly education, the missionaries wrote extensively about the local society they encountered. The clerical observers are actually the first ones to attempt to map the Savunese mindset, an endeavour that was necessary in order to convert them to the Christian creed. Comparison with anthropological data suggests that they ignored or misunderstood many fundamentals of Savunese life, but they still depict many aspects of society before the onset of tighter colonial rule in the early 20th century.

A comparison between the archival and the oral stories yields fascinating results. The VOC documents give ample information about the succession of local leaders and the details usually fit precisely with the inherited genealogies as far back as the 17th century. The exactitude is much greater than in Timor and comparable to some of the *nusak* (domains) in Rote. Oral narratives of specific dramatic events, such as the exile of a rebel, the war between two local princedoms or the murder of a prince, are also often confirmed by the colonial archive. Nevertheless, these episodes of history have taken on their own dynamics in the oral tradition. Basic particles or 'facts' are preserved over the centuries in a relatively faithful way but are given new significations. This phenomenon can also be studied in other parts of the region—in Timor, Rote and Solor. Even so, it would not be fair to treat oral stories as merely second-best sources to apply when the archival ones disappear. It should be recalled that the colonial (and, for that matter, the missionary) archive is constituted according to a set of rules on selection and inclusion. It is not just a repository of information that happened to survive but a highly ideological institution (Prescott 2008; Stoler 2009). What was significant for the VOC or the Dutch colonial state, or for the missionary societies, did not correspond to what was important for Savunese self-understanding. The colonial reports, written by officials who mostly stayed in the Timor area for a few years, convey fragments of information, often but not always lacking in context. The Savunese tradition, conveyed by spokesmen (and spokeswomen) of lineages, sees the past from a deeper perspective that the colonial officials obviously lacked. For the non-literate peoples of eastern Indonesia, tradition plays an important role in the way people interact and order their lives, which suggests a great deal of care in the process of transmission.

It would be wrong to assume that the Timor area is neglected in academic research. There is a significant output in history, anthropology, material culture, economics and politics. *A Bibliography of Timor* (1980), Kevin Sherlock's exemplary research, lists close to 3,000 works on the region. The period since 1980 has seen an increasing interest, not least in the wake of East Timor's struggle for independence which brought this part of the world to international attention. While much of this has been political and development studies, the region's historical past has caught the attention of several scholars such as Arend de Roever, René Pélissier, Steven Farram and Frédéric Durand.

As for Savu, however, relatively few studies have been published to date. A classic work intersecting anthropology and history is *Harvest of the Palm* by James Fox (1977), which makes sense of oral data and written sources in tracing the ecological and social changes in Rote and Savu from the proto-historical period until the 20th century. Nico Kana's doctoral thesis, *Dunia Orang Sabu* (*The World of the Savunese*) (1978), is a structural analysis of the Mesara domain and the most in-depth work written in Indonesian. Further work includes Jakob Detaq's brief study *Memperkenalkan kebudayaan suku bangsa Sabu* (*Introducing the Culture of the Savu People*) (1973) and Robert Riwu Kaho's survey *Orang Sabu dan budayanya* (*The Savunese and their Culture*) (2005). However, there is still a need for a historical-anthropological synthesis based on a thorough survey of the available archival materials and oral tradition. It is hoped that the present work goes some way towards filling this need, and serves as an illustration of how a minor Indonesian island has developed and interacted with colonial and other external forces over the centuries.

The present text thus represents the efforts of an anthropologist and a historian to apply the above-mentioned considerations to a detailed study of a small, but in many respects, remarkable island's past. The chapters follow the political, cultural and social developments of Savu in a roughly chronological way. While such a layout may be perceived as traditional, it is important to remember that much of the story is uncharted territory; it has simply never been told before. Therefore, arranging the analysis chronologically puts it into the context of Indonesian and Southeast Asian history. The first three chapters are mainly concerned with the Savunese collective memory of the island's origins, clans, ritual systems and territorial divisions. Chapter 4 studies the comparatively vague evidence of Majapahit and Portuguese influences in the period up to the early 17th century. Chapters 5 and 6 deal with the VOC era in the 17th and 18th centuries, when written sources become available and sometimes provide circumstantial details. These chapters present the processes from a colonial and indigenous perspective, and discuss the contrasts between the two. Chapters 7 and 8 discuss Savu's inclusion in the new Dutch colonial state in the 19th century; the Savunese migrations to Timor and Sumba; and the efforts of Christian missionaries whose verbose writings give a detailed but biased view of Savunese society. Chapter 9 studies the society in the late colonial period and describes events during the Japanese occupation and the Indonesian revolution. Although the remainder of the study approaches modern times, it is still often dependent on oral history due to the paucity of archival data. The tenth and last chapter surveys developments in the postcolonial era, up to the challenges that the Savunese presently face.

<table>
<tr><td>Chapter
1</td><td></td></tr>
</table>

Chapter 1 | From the Base of the World

"[More myths] turn out to stem from actual events and real observations
of the world than twentieth-century scholars have commonly believed"
(Barber and Barber 2004: 3).

This chapter examines the cosmogony of the Savunese people which starts at 'the
base of the world', tracing early ancestors of the secret and sacred genealogies.
This poetic and coded knowledge (*li pana* [Sa] or *bahasa mantra* [In]) is not part
of collective memory but is held by the priests of the ancestral religion Jingi Tiu.
The publicly known genealogies start with the ancestor Kika Ga, whose arrival
questions the local ideas of indegenous and foreign discussed in the chapter. The
discourse names only the key ancestors and closes after considering a series of
cockfights during which the ancestor Dida Miha lost everything to the 'people
of the sea'.

It is a common feature of Austronesian societies to remember the
cosmological past as a genealogy. In Savunese cosmogony, the beginning is at
the base of the world or the universe and emerges out of darkness, *d'a'i nata
woro ei*.[1] 'Bubbles of water' were formed, followed by 'bubbles of blood' which
turned into 'red blood', then into 'red copper'; then came *Muri mara*. *Muri*
means life, but Savu people refuse to give *mara* the meaning copper in this case
though do not provide any other meaning. Then appeared Deo Muri (God of
Life)—the Supreme Being—who is called Deo Muri Mara in rituals, a very
sacred and powerful name. Thus, people do not use the name except during such
ceremonies as funerals when genealogies are recited so, in everyday conversation,
people simply say Deo Muri. People in Seba say Deo Muri Mada; *mada* meaning

---

[1] *D'a'i* means down; *nata* (bottom, base); *woro* (foam, bubble, also form); *ei* (water, also
liquid). To explain the spelling of Savuense words, the language has implosive and explosive
consonants (/b'/, /d'/, /g'/ and /j'/ and /b/, /d/, /g/ and /j/). The text distinguishes between the
consonant groups only in cases where the sole differentiation is through such consonants; for
example, *dai* (winnow), *d'ai* (to arrive) and *d'a'i* (down, below); *d'ara* (inside) and *dara* (mark);
d'ue (two) and *due* (lontar sap); *lod'o* (sun) and *lodo* (to go). The spelling in the glossary is
according to modern linguistic conventions respectful of these distinctions.

eye or source (God Source of Life). Thus, the first steps in the creation of the world are seen as a genealogy.

Figure 1: From the base of the world[2]

Deo Muri	God of Life
↑	↑
Muri Mara	Life [Copper]
↑	↑
Mara Mea	Copper Red
↑	↑
Mea Ra	Red Blood
↑	↑
Ra Woro	Blood Bubble
↑	↑
D'a'i Nata Woro Ei	From the Bottom of the World Bubble [of] Water

In collective memory Deo Muri is 'the one who makes our body (*ngi'u*), who holds our spirit (*hemanga*) and breath (*henga*)'. The other name for Deo Muri, the Supreme Being, is Apu Lod'o Liru (God in the Sky) or (God in Heaven). In Liae, Deo Muri is also called Deo Woro (God who gave form to beings) and Deo Mengèru. *Mengèru* means green and, by extension, growth and prosperity, so Deo Mengèru is 'God who makes every plant, animal and human'. Savunese believe that Deo Woro formed humans out of earth. The different names are various manifestations of the Supreme Being. The marker Deo Mengèru is given to a certain category of priest up to the present day and this name appears in several chapters.

There was no explanation for the origin of the word *Deo*, which prompts some questions. If it was adopted after contact with Christian missionaries, one may wonder about the name of the Supreme Being prior to this. People say Apu Lod'o Liru in everyday speech, yet this does not fit in the genealogical charter about the origin of the world. The same question concerns both the high priests Deo Rai and Deo Mengèru. People address them with *Ama Deo*, using Christian vocabulary for non-Christian priests while they use the Indonesian *Tuhan* or

---

2 The diagram demonstrates the idea that genealogies start at the bottom and evolve through to the top. As noted earlier, the recitation of genealogies is rendered with the expression 'pile up from the bottom, pile up to the top'. However, in order to make the genealogical figures easily accessible to the reader, other genealogies start at the top of the page.

Allah for God. This practice has been so well absorbed into Savunese culture that the name *Deo* is used as though it existed since the beginning.

Deo Muri (God in Heaven) had five siblings who are mainly related to bad spirits associated with sickness. They have negative influences on humans as they are seen to be responsible for people losing control, becoming emotional, violent or losing consciousness. They existed before humans were created and formed a category, *Wango*. One of them, Maja Muri, so affected people's imaginations that a priest is dedicated to this unpredictable and invisible spirit.[3] Christian missionaries have misrepresented Wango as Satan but, in the traditional view, Wango is not essentially negative; it can be good or bad for humans without the systematic intention of temptation or betrayal. Wango is intrinsically erratic and is associated with the sea where it resides. It can be placated with offerings, which are of a different kind to those given to the ancestors and involve spilling blood. It is notable that the only other sacrifice which includes 'blood flow' is when the earth has been 'wounded'.[4] In their ritual chants, the priests can call Wango to carry away what is bad for humans. The followers of the ancestral religion, Jingi Tiu, have neither a concept of Satan trying to lure, deceive or trap people, nor a concept of hell. Christians are now so used to identifying Wango as Satan that they have little understanding of its concept in Jingi Tiu.

The creation of the world then expands further as the genealogy carries on, generating the cosmos. The tiered division of the world, creating the continents (*rai* [ground, land also realm]), the sky (*liru*) and the oceans (*dahi*) took place at the time of Bèla Bako's children, one of whom is Liru Bèla. Every subsequent step of the creation divides it from a previous stage which creates a chronological distinction, a diversification. Parts of the names are found in later genealogies, all referring to male names. In Mesara, during the thanksgiving ceremony called *hole*, the genealogies are recited backwards three times for each of the key ancestors of the three-tiered world: Liru Bèla (Great Sky), Dahi Bèla (Great Sea) and Rai Bèla (Great Earth) (*rai* refers to a spatial category and the English

---

[3] The name of the spirit called Maja might have merged with the same name associated with the kingdom of Majapahit. Maja is a key figure in narratives and ceremonies in Raijua and is considered later. See also Akiko Kagiya (2010).

[4] The throat of the young animal is cut before its body is thrown in the air or into the sea. Humans do not consume any part of its body. For example, sacrifices for the wounded earth take place when clearing the fields and digging holes in the ground for planting or building, as it is the case for the ritual *pepèhi* (*lempar batu* [In]). Underground spirits might escape from below and have to be calmed by blood flow. Sources for Savu: interviews with Leba Alu (Ma Medo), Ama Bawa Iri, Deo Rai's helper (Ama Lai Helu). Source for Seba: interview with Dida Bèngu (the priest Maukia). Sources for Mesara: interviews with Ama Tape Rike and Ama Pela (the priest Apu Lod'o Wadu).

translation varies with the context).[5] The order is that the sky has precedence over the sea and the sea over the land, which was created last.

The ancestor D'ara Dunga had more than one hundred children. Two of whom, Hila D'ara and Ngada D'ara, are referred to as giants, *hila* and *ngada* meaning high, tall.[6] The brothers pushed the sky away from the earth because it was too hot—everything was burning and nothing could grow. The heat of the earth at the beginning is a recurrent theme in the area.[7] In the domain of Seba, two stones are said to be the petrified marks the brothers left on the ground when they pushed the sky away. It is commonly believed in Savu that the sky and earth are connected by two threads which have to be of the same width, the same length and the same strength so that the world is balanced. It is reminiscent of the vine that connects the earth to the sky in many societies of the region.[8]

The many children of D'ara Dunga are responsible for the elements in nature. The names of these ancestors in the mantra genealogies are mostly different from the element names in everyday language, so only those in command of the hundreds of mantra names are fully able to understand ritual chants. In the following examples, the names in brackets are currently used for the elements in Savunese. While for D'ara Dunga's son Lod'o D'ara, who became the sun (*lod'o*), and his daughter Biri D'ara, who became the moon (*wèru biri* being the 'halo of the moon'), the meanings are accessible to the uninitiated, it is not possible to guess the name Langi D'ara, who is the wind (*ngèlu*) or O D'ara, the rain (*èji*), without prior knowledge. These mantra names allude to the coded and poetic language of ritual, so that even in a public prayer the full meaning is only accessible to insiders—the priests themselves and their close relatives. The vast majority of the people have only a general understanding of the ritual texts. This becomes evident when translating ritual chants. Although there are variations in Savunese cosmological names as well as discrepancies in the siblings' birth order, there is a consensus on most of their names and on the distinctions they created.[9]

---

[5] The most common meaning is land. However, it also translates as island, realm and earth. For example, Rai Hawu is the island of Savu, and *Rai Dahi* is the realm of the sea. *Rai Bèla* translates best as Great Earth and the office of Deo Rai as Lord of the Earth, although it has been rendered as *Tuan Tanah* in Indonesian.

[6] The name of Hila D'ara appears again in the Seba genealogies as a son of D'ara Wai. Another son is called Naga D'ara (instead of Ngada D'ara in the cosmology).

[7] Hoskins (1993: 62); Kuipers (1990: 54); Forth (1998: 217).

[8] Erb (1987: 77, 79, 116); Forth (1998: 236).

[9] There are also some minor discrepancies with the genesis genealogy Kana gave (1978: 101–9). See also Duggan (2001: 24) for the genesis and the origin of vegetable dyes.

Before creating humans, plants and animals, the Supreme Being created those who became his helpers, Deo Heu Holo, seen as various manifestations of Deo Muri. Among them is Deo Ga'i Hèku Luji (God who takes care of life and cuts the breath or God who measures life); Deo Woro, Deo Penyi is responsible for the formation of the foetus; and there is Deo Kekara Kabu Die (God the source of energy or God who takes care of producing the mother's milk). One of D'ara Dunga's descendants, A Wonga, is at the origin of humanity.[10] Other descendants mark the beginning of animals: for example, Oe Wonga, the buffalo (*kebau*); Ke Wonga, the horse (*jara*); Rau Wonga, the chicken (*manu*); and Kengo Wonga, the dog (*ngaka*). People consider that these animals, so essential to their everyday life, must have existed since the beginning. The reality, however, is that on a small and isolated island, such as Savu, settlers must have introduced all the domesticated animals.[11]

A succession of names in the genesis is like a succession of generations—each creating a division, a principle of causation. People tell of a flood during this early period of Savu's past that changed the ancestors into plants, especially those essential for vegetable dyes. They were male as well as female ancestors, and those responsible for the tie or binding technique (*ikat*) and weaving process are found in the cosmogony around this time. There is a reason or a logical cause for everything existing in Savu, which is in the genealogy. Ancestors who did not have descendants and those who had a violent death have a stone carrying their name. Some were changed into stones which became the island's petrified past; the stone is a memory tag of tragic events. Everything that has a name is anchored in the genealogies. Other ancestors who disappeared are said to have changed into animals. For example, two children of a key ancestor for Seba genealogies, Hana Aba and Lai Aba, became respectively an owl and a tokay (big gecko).[12]

Seven generations after the original human, the first branching occurs for Rede Moto (Full Star) and Weo Moto (Bright Star). Rede Moto's son, Babo Rede married his father's brother's daughter, Dila Weo. They had four children: a boy, Wunu Babo, and three daughters, Muji Babo, Lou Babo and Re

---

[10] See Detaq (1973: 20–3) Kana (1978: 101–9) for minor variations in the cosmogony. See R.H. Barnes for a common ancestry of humans and animals (1974: 30).

[11] See Vansina for how the Europeans' introduction of the horse to the Assiniboine of Canada dramatically changed their life style. As the Assiniboine consider the horse so significant that it belongs to the creation myths, having always been present, there are no narratives about its arrival. (1985: 119). See also Bankoff and Swart (2007) for the introduction of the horse to Indonesia.

[12] There is a food taboo either for animals which helped an ancestor (crocodile for the Kekoro clan; beef for the female lineage *wini* Jèwu; whale for *wini* Waratada) or because someone was changed into an animal (turtle for members of the Kekoro clan).

Figure 2: Early mantra genealogies

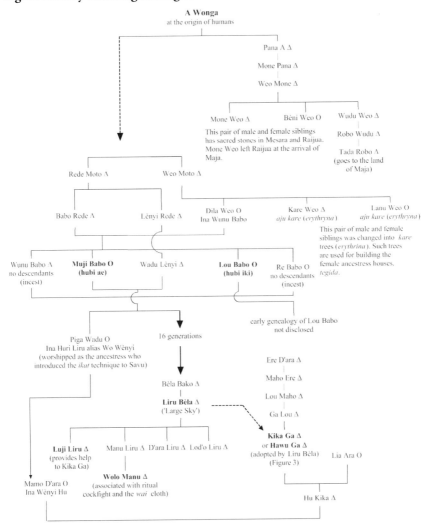

Babo. Wunu and Re broke Savu taboo by having an incestuous relationship, provoking their mother's wrath, so they were changed into two stars which never appear in the sky at the same time — hence, Wunu and Re can never meet again. Wunu is Wunu Pidu, the Pleiades, and Re is the double star, Antares, in the constellation of Scorpio.[13] Reference to the relationship appears in today's common response to two children arguing—'you are like Wunu and Re; you never should meet again'.

The two remaining daughters, Muji Babo and Lou Babo, start the two maternal lines or female moieties, Greater Blossom (*hubi ae*) and Lesser Blossom (*hubi iki*). It is noteworthy that the names of these two key ancestors at the origin of the female lines appear very early in the genealogies. People only disclose this knowledge, of course, when considering the female mantra genealogies. The formation of two female moieties is directly relevant to the structure of Savu society right up to the present. It means that the society's division into two distinct social groups, based on an early maternal line, precedes the formation of male clans. Of Muji and Lou Babo's female descendants, the only genealogies completely disclosed were the important names related to the development of the island's weaving traditions. In contrast, tradition revealed instead the genealogy of Muji Babo's husband, Wadu Lèngi. It is part of the male sacred genealogies (*silsilah mantra* [In]) and uttered only in rituals; for example, at the *hole* (thanksgiving) harvest ceremony. The island recorded 17 generations between Wadu Lèngi and Liru Bèla.

The children of Liru Bèla were Luji Liru (*luji* [portion also eagle]),[14] Manu Liru (*manu* [chicken]), D'ara Liru (*d'ara* [inside]) and Lod'o Liru (*lod'o* [sun]). Collective memory relates this time to a big flood or a tsunami (*lale dahi*).[15] The ancestors fled in a boat and those who later returned are said to be either the same ancestors or their descendants. A constant principle is to maintain the monolithic view of Savu society through the genealogies; all Savunese are tied to each other through genealogical links and the present is connected to the ancestors from the very beginning. While as a general rule researchers see

---

[13] See Kana (1978: 360) for the role of Pleiades and Antares in the Savu agricultural cycle. See Arndt (1951: 62–5) about the same myth in Flores and R.H. Barnes for Kedang (1974: 117–9).

[14] *Luji* has different meanings—also a 'portion' of food—but Luji Ae is the mythological great eagle, so the translation of Luji Liru is open to various interpretations.

[15] Almost every mythology has the concept of a flood (Oppenheimer 1998). For references in the region see Forth (1998: 218) about a primeval flood; Therik (2004) and the idea of the first dry land. The flood at the time of D'ara Liru must have been the second flood in Savu's early history.

a "floating gap"[16] between the mythological past and the history of a society, in Savu there is no such gap; the idea of continuity prevails. However, where there is a break is between the sacred and secret (mantra) genealogies, and those accessible to everyone.

The arrival of Kika Ga

Kika Ga is the first ancestor of the publicly known male genealogies. These are fixed in time, generating a ranking among the people. Therefore, the unique position an individual occupies is remembered by reciting long lists of names. From the local point of view, Kika Ga was the first Savunese to return after the island had been flooded. The idea of flood and return is important because his comeback establishes his anteriority, thus his precedence, and his identity as an original inhabitant. It also highlights the concept of the island's purification through flood: the island was cleansed and everything started anew.

"The capacity of human memory being limited, the addition of details or certain episodes often implies that others are deleted" (Barber and Barber 2004: 3). Indeed, a range of versions emphasising or deleting certain aspects of Kika Ga's arrival exist which Detaq (1973), Kana (1978; 1983) and Duggan (1997; 2001) recorded, so the chapter only gives the most relevant episodes for the social organisation and historical developments.

In collective memory, Kika Ga came from a country far away in the west and stayed on a rock, *Wadu Mea* (Red Rock), which is in today's district of Liae at the foot of Mount Merèbu (Plate 1). People believe that at the time the island of Savu did not exist as it is today. There were only two mountains—Merèbu and Kebuhu—emerging out of the sea. One day when Luji Liru, the son of the deity Liru Bèla, was fishing from the sky he noticed a boy and a girl. They were Kika Ga and his sister Male Ga. With his fishing hook he only pulled Kika Ga up to the sky, leaving his sister behind. She went into the sea where she became Iwa Lungi, the mythical whale.

In the sky (or in heaven) Liru Bèla adopted Kika Ga and, thus, he became Luji Liru's stepbrother. In some sources Kika Ga married in the sky. He and his wife came back to earth and lived on Mount Merèbu. In other sources, he came back and went overseas where he married Lia Ra (or Lia Ara) a 'woman from the sea' before returning to Savu. In one version recorded in Namata (Seba), when Kika Ga came back to earth, Liru Bèla gave him a spear and a spindle.

After Kika Ga and his wife settled on Mount Merèbu, Luji Liru helped his stepbrother Kika Ga to carry earth from Raijua to connect Merèbu to Kebuhu,

---

[16] Vansina 1985: 23.

Figure 3: Kika Ga's descendants

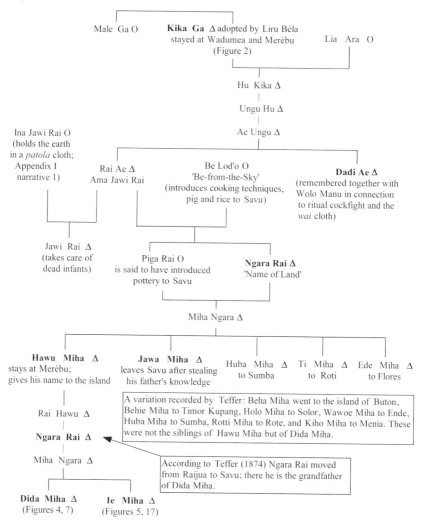

the other mountain, to create Savu. They stole soil again and again from under the house of the siblings Mone Weo and Bèni Weo[17] in a sacred cloth called *patola lai rede*. *Patola* is a highly valued Indian silk cloth; *lai rede* means full sail or full matter. In the Mesara version, they were caught stealing the soil, so they reached an agreement with Raijua whereby Kika Ga and Luji Liru had to pay a food tribute every year after the harvest: *terae* (sorghum) and *kebui* (mung beans) in *kedue* (small containers made of plaited palm leaves). They also had to bring some soil to represent the soil that they had taken. So in the Mesara collective representation, Raijua is the mother island of Savu. Interestingly, people in Raijua do not know this version for reasons the next chapter reveals.

The brother-sister pair, Mone Weo and Bèni Weo, play a small role in Kika Ga's story. They are among the early ancestors (see Figure 2) which is in concordance with the idea of founding pairs of siblings in ancient Austronesian societies. However, while people in Savu and Raijua remember them well and positively, there is no geneology for Mone Weo and Bèni Weo: their lines are said to have vanished. In Raijua, there is a ritual house called Mone Weo to worship him. Mone Weo and Bèni Weo might stand as generic names for true autochthons while a later settler, such as Kika Ga, also became an indigenous ancestor.

The Kika Ga myth is informative in several respects. Firstly, the mention of Kika Ga's sister, Male Ga, is reminiscent of Austronesian traditions where a brother and a sister are the original ancestors of a community. However, collective remembering does not follow this pattern as Male Ga went into the sea and became the mythical whale Iwa Lungi. She is said to help sailors in trouble at sea. This is a recurrent theme in ancient Asian stories (Mazu in Daoism or Ratu Kidul in Java). A second aspect is that people in Raijua know the tales about a golden fishing hook.[18] There it is linked to a crucial moment in the division of socio-religious tasks and the creation of male clans. However, in Savu the fishing hook is only important as a means of lifting Kika Ga up to the sky or heaven.

The myth's relevance is also that Liru Bèla's giving of a spindle to Kika Ga only makes sense if he came back to Savu as a married man; all activities related to spinning and weaving are exclusively female tasks in Savu as they are elsewhere in Indonesia. A spear and a spindle do not only have male and female connotations; both are symbols for prayers. Kika Ga could use the spear if he was

---

[17] Bèni Weo in Mesara and Raijua, and Bèni Baku in other domains. Vischer recalls a similar action "where the primordial ancestors brought a stone and some earth" to create the island of Palu'e (2003: 60).

[18] On the fish-hook tale, see chapter 2 as well as Kagiya (2010: 48).

desperate, as by plunging the spear into, for example, a tree trunk, the ground or a pillar inside the house, Liru Bèla would come to his aid. Ever since, when a man addresses a prayer to his ancestors, he places his spear (*kepoke*) against the male pillar of his house, remembering Liru Bèla's gift and his promise to assist the people. The spindle is used in a number of prayers women address to the ancestors. During the ritual cockfight, by spinning cotton thread to channel their prayers women establish a vertical link to their ancestors, allowing them to descend and help their husbands to win (Fox 1979: 158). Also important is the fact that collective remembering places the use of metal—a spear—at the very beginning of the island's history. The same is true of the spindle. Both cases recognise the tools' foreign or divine origins. Thus, people place the knowledge of spinning and weaving right at the start of the male genealogies. However, the weaving tools as well as the plants for indigo and red dyes were already present in the mantra genealogies.

Savu's beliefs around the spear and the spindle show some similarities with Kodi on the island of Sumba where the spear used in divination is called *mone haghu* (Savunese man) (Hoskins 1993: 52). In the domain of Toda, also in Sumba, there is an "heirloom spindle that once connected the heaven to the earth by a line of cotton" (ibid.: 121). In Kodi, people said the tradition of spinning, dyeing and weaving was imported from Savu. The use of cotton thread or of a spear in ritual is common to both cultures.

An element derived from the myth is informative about the origin of an essential tradition after harvest. Every year a ceremony takes place to launch a boat loaded with offerings (*kowa hole*) to send back to the ancestors. In Mesara, it is seen as a tribute to Raijua; in other domains, the prayer, addressed to the ancestors who are somewhere in the west, asks for prosperity and fertility.[19] In the ceremony's ritual recitations, Kika Ga is mentioned with his mantra name—*Hawu lèba jara, mone ia jari rai* (Hawu, the crowned horse, the man able to start the land). People remember two carvings in a cave located at the foot of Mount

---

[19] In all domains, the *hole* ceremony takes place in the month of Bangaliwu; see Kana (1978: 417, 418). In Liae and Dimu, no boats are launched into the sea as it is already the southeast monsoon. In Seba and Menia, a boat (really a raft) is launched to the ancestors' world in the west but not to Raijua. In Raijua, the Ketita inhabitants launch a raft loaded with offerings (*kowa Mone Weo*) to remember an ancient ancestor, Mone Weo, who fled at the arrival of Maja. The rafts with their offerings have reached the south coast of Sumba.

Merèbu dedicated to Kika Ga.[20] One wood carving apparently represented a horse rider. However, this cannot be confirmed as the statues are no longer there. In the cave a flat stone known as the 'seat of Kika Ga' (*wowadu mejèd'i Kika Ga*) remains.

Finally, Kika Ga is presented as the first ancestor to settle in Savu, as before him the island did not exist. Savunese left the land, which would later become the island of Savu, because of the flood and lived at sea or in other countries. He is considered to be the first ancestor to return to Savu after the flood and his story is placed at the turning point between mythology and reality. Being taken to heaven confers supernatural powers on him. The formation of Savu from stolen soil is reminiscent of a category of creation myths known as 'Earth diver': someone descends from the sky or a deity descends from heaven and dives to the bottom of the sea to take soil or mud to form the land.[21] The Kika Ga story resonates also with the tradition widely spread in the Austronesian world of the 'stranger', a foreigner who establishes himself in another country, marrying an indigenous woman, and becomes the ruler. In Raijua and in Mesara, his four immediate ancestors are known and are said to be 'people of the sea'.[22] However, none of these names appear in Savunese mantra texts or in the mantra genealogies. The link is created through Liru Bèla's adoption of Kika Ga. The names of his stepbrothers Luji Liru and Lod'o Liru, who belong to the 'people of the sky', are part of the mantra genealogies discussed above.[23] The mantra genealogies are indirectly informative about Kika Ga, a foreigner constructed as an indigenous Savunese. This is not the way collective memory should remember this stage of Savu's early history. The secrecy surrounding the female and the mantra genealogies contains a different truth.

People with large feet

At the time of Kika Ga, Mone Weo and Bèni Weo were already living in Raijua. In Savu the Seba priests know mantra texts and chants mentioning

---

[20] When French anthropologist Jeanne Cuisinier visited Savu in 1955, she heard of inscriptions and carvings in a cave at Mount Merèbu but was unable to reach the place (Cuisinier 1999). People are aware of inscriptions only at Wadumea where Kika Ga landed. However, these 'inscriptions' are actually incised lines in the rocks and were created through erosion, not by humans.

[21] Leeming and Leeming 2009: 6, 79–80.

[22] They are Ere Dara, Maho Dara, Lou Maho and Ga Lou (Kana 1978: 127). In his genealogy, Kika Ga is also known as Hawu Ga and gave his name to the island. These ancestors are the direct descendants of A Wonga, bypassing more than 20 generations of the mantra genealogies.

[23] See Sahlins (1985); Therik (2004); Fox (2008); Lewis (2010).

ancient settlers called Jola who have specific charateristics: they had no fixed location, and they were small in size (*dou do baba*) with large feet and large ears (*do bèla jèla, bèla dilu*). In 1874, the missionary Matheus Teffer collected the names of nine villages in Savu in existance prior to the arrival of Kika Ga: "Jerroe, Torri, Kokki, Dikki, Bellajella in the east, and Kedoewa, Doewa, Taja, Oewa in the west".[24] Some of these names resonate with verses of a mantra text recorded in Seba:[25]

Do era ne li	There is a saying that there were
Do bèla jèla bèla dilu,	People with large feet and large ears,
Do Tèka Ledejèru,	People at Tèka, Jèru hill,
Do Kedua d'èimada,	People at Kedua [harbour] near a spring
Do Napae pai huru	People at Napae fishing with torches

Tèka and Jèru hill are names of two places in modern Nadawawi village. Dèki (Dikki in Teffer) is located between the Namata and Kekoro hills. Kedua (Keduwa in Teffer) is a small landing place in today's village of Ledeana; it has a spring nearby. Napae is near Seba's harbour. *Pai huru* refers to the activity of fishing at night while using a torch made of a lontar palm leaf, twisted and soaked in the oil obtained from the *kepaka* tree (*nitas* [In], *Sterculia foetida*). This traditional way of fishing is still practised today from dugout canoes using kerosene lamps instead of oily torches.[26] The priests explained that Kika Ga and his descendants coexisted with these authochtonous people for a number of generations, but they disagree about their disappearance; either the Jola were expelled at the time of Hawu Miha (see below) or later at the time of the three ancestors of Seba.[27] Alternately, the Jola were exterminated. In Liae a place scattered with stone flakes and called Gurijola (Murdered Jola) seems to corroborate this view. A ceremonial chant, *hod'a kelila* Jola, is still partly remembered by people who learnt it as children as it has a joyful rhythm; however, the lines have been so corrupted that it is impossible to render a full translation. And yet, two lines mention the vanished Jola people:[28]

---

[24] Raad voor de Zending der Nederlandse Hervormde kerk (Council for the Mission of the Dutch Reformed Church), 1102–1: 1411, M. Teffer, report 1874.

[25] Recording of Ama Bawa Iri (Ama Lai Helu), helper of the priest Deo Rai in Namata (02.05.2000); he said they were the first inhabitants of Savu after the great flood. Interviews with Leba Alu and the priest Apu Lod'o, Seba (07.05.2000); Deo Megènru, Kekoro (04.10.2000); and Ama Bèhi Mene (Raja Pono) (17.11.2017).

[26] See Duggan (2008: 368–75) and Appendix II.

[27] Taga Nyela, Ote Horo and Mata Lai. See chapter 3 and Figure 23.

[28] See Appendix I.

Ele Jola, ele Jola ya pa ne	The Jola have disappeared, the Jola from here
Ele ana, ana tudi Jola bèlo	The blade has disappeared, the blade [of] the knife [of] the Jola [who] have vanished.

The second line about the blade and the knife does not suggest a peaceful departure. The Jola's expulsion from the island might not have happened at once. Place names identified in Teffer as well as in mantra texts are all located in today's district of Seba. There are more names of ancient people examined later; for instance, in east Savu. Remembrance of authochtonous people is vague and at best they have survived in fixed chants. As they fade in collective memory, only the names of people and places continue to exist.

Early key ancestors descended from Kika Ga

As collective memory presents Kika Ga as the first ancestor on a virgin land, his descendants can claim landownership using the principle of precedence known through the genealogies.[29] Consequently, all narratives related to developments on the island have to be placed accordingly among his descendants. These include, for example, knowledge of fire making, slash-and-burn techniques, pottery making and cooking processes, the introduction of essential plants, such as the lontar tree or wet rice cultivation, as well as the creation of the female moieties.[30]

Hu Kika is Kika Ga's son. *Hu* refers to the tip or point of a knife. Hu Kika married an indigenous woman, known as Ina Wènyi Hu, a descendant of Muji Babo (of the mantra genealogies). For the next two generations, there is no specifically remembered story.

Rai Ae (Great Land) and Ngara Rai (Name [of the] Land) lived respectively four and five generations after Kika Ga. On both islands their names are sung in chorus for ritual recitations.[31] In Mesara, Rai Ae had three brothers, two of them had no descendants—Jawa Ae (Great Foreigner) and Hina Ae (Great Chinese)—with Rai Ae living in Ledepukai (Mesara), Hina Ae in Ketode

---

[29] However, one member of the very secretive clan, *udu* Gopo of Liae, disclosed a different genealogy, claiming to be direct descendants of Lod'o Liru, son of Liru Bèla, not recognising Kika Ga as their ancestor. This knowledge is, of course, rejected by other clans.

[30] At the start of fieldwork in Savu in 1994, the creation of the female moieties was placed at the time of Dida Miha's grandson, Babo Rede Dida.

[31] For example, during the thanksgiving ceremony, *hole* or the ritual cockfight *daba ae*. Inserting Jawa Ae and Hina Ae as siblings in the early genealogies justifies the emergence of the personal names Jawa and Hina in the generations immediately preceding or contemporary to early European presence in the region.

(southern coast) and Jawa Ae at the western tip of the island, Wuirai. Mesara narratives remember Jawa Ae as the contemporary ruler of Raijua—though this is not known in Raijua—and a number of stones commemorate him.

Rai Ae's third brother, Dadi Ae, is remembered collectively through a narrative about a cockfight and a sacred cloth called a *wai*. His name is also associated with an ancestor of the mantra genealogies, Wolo Manu (Figure 2). In these early times, the sky was still near the earth and people used to go back and forth to the sky where they took part in cockfighting. However, the main place for cockfights was called Nadawolomanu[32] which is today in Liae, not far from the former polity of Teriwu. At that time, many people were victims of black magic and died. Dadi Ae and Wolo Manu also fell victim to black magic. The Supreme Being (Apu Lod'o Liru [God in the Sky]), feeling sorry for all these casualties, decided to call them all back to life. However, only Dadi Ae and Wolo Manu who were wearing a *wai*, small narrow belt-like indigo cloth, came back to life. Since that time, it is compulsory for members of the ancestral religion to wear a *wai* cloth when they pass away. It is believed that the weaving has the power to bring the wearer back to life in an unspecified future. The *wai* cloth is still woven today during a special ceremony (*mane wai*), following the most ancient weaving techniques used on the island.[33]

Rai Ae had many children. If it is possible to acredit some truth to the story of Rai Ae, alias Ama Jawi Rai, he married twice.[34] His first wife, Ina Jawi Rai, had such long breasts that she carried them on her back over her shoulders which her son, Jawi Rai, said was disgusting. Offended by her son's remark, Ina Jawi Rai went back to her parents, leaving her husband and son on their own. There she has been ever since, holding the earth in a *patola* cloth.

Ama Jawi Rai's second wife was Be Lod'o (Be from the Sun). She was expelled from heaven by Apu Lod'o Liru (God in Heaven), the Supreme Being. By having Be Lod'o land in Savu in the shape of a pig (and bringing the knowledge for making fire and cooking techniques), God in Heaven used her as an intermediary to give pigs and rice to the Savunese.[35] Again Jawi Rai (the son of the first marriage) caused offence, referring to Be Lod'o's pig origins, so she too left, returning to heaven with her children, Ngara Rai and Piga Rai. Ama

[32] *Nada* means arena; *wolo* (verdict, also to judge); *manu* (chicken, here rooster); the name Wolo Manu possibly refers to his position in the society as an arbiter in cockfights (see Figure 2).

[33] See Duggan (2001: 65).

[34] See the narrative of Ama Jawi Rai and Be Lod'o in Appendix I.

[35] In return, Savunese have to cook Deo Muri a certain type of rice and sacrifice a pig during a ceremony called *kelila*, offering them first to the Supreme Being before being able to eat them (see Appendix II).

Jawi Rai begged God in Heaven to help him to get his wife and children back. However, Ama Jawi Rai had to accomplish several tasks before being allowed to take them back to earth.

Ama Jawi Rai and Be Lod'o's daughter, Piga Rai (Plate Land), in collective memory is responsible for introducing the skill of making pottery—her name refers to earthenware. In a ritual chant for a *tao leo* funeral Piga Rai is mentioned as *Piga Rai, Bèni Raja Lai Lulu* (Piga Rai, the noble woman who rolls/unrolls the sail).[36] As an important figure, her name is also part of mantra texts related to the ceremonial cockfight.

Ama Jawi Rai's second son, Ngara Rai (Name of the Land) is, like his father, often invoked in rituals. He is said to have married his sister Piga Rai, thus committing incest, and they produced a son called Miha Ngara. This view is widely shared in the archipelago. Jawi Rai, from Ama Jawi Rai's first marriage, did not have descendants. Killed by his father, he is said to 'take care' of all young children who die before the traditional baptism (*daba*). In ordinary speech, *Ana Jawi* refers to an infant in its first year.

In Savu, people generally believe that the ancestors stayed on Mount Merèbu until the time of Miha Ngara who moved to Mount Teriwu.[37] For this reason Teriwu is known as *Rai ie bangi Hawu* (the good land that dominates Savu). The expression is significant on two levels. The first is that Teriwu is one of the highest hills in Savu overlooking the north and the south coasts, and does indeed dominate the rest of the island. The second meaning is that the people of Teriwu are the traditional rulers of Savu: they 'dominate' in the sense of precedence. The second interpretation is interesting as the polity of Teriwu had already disappeared by precolonial times.

Miha Ngara had a number of children, of whom only one stayed on the island. A story records a struggle between indigenous and foreign people represented by two brothers, Hawu Miha and Jawa Miha. This is the first acknowledged case of rivalry and betrayal between siblings in collective memory (Duggan 2001: 81–2). Hawu Miha stayed on the island while Jawa Miha went abroad. Before leaving, Jawa Miha took a branch of the tree in which his placenta was hung at birth, but the tree never grew abroad. This detail implies that someone cannot change or transplant his/her origin. What is considered 'foreign' on the island is thus attributed to the ancestor Jawa Miha and the idiom is accompanied by *jawa*. Every sacred site has a stone dedicated to Jawa Miha. Other children went to Sumba, Rote and Flores. For this reason, Savunese consider their island to be the point from which the region was populated. Of note here is that the Reformed

---

[36] This refers to the sail of the boat the deceased boards to reach the place of the ancestors.
[37] Raijuanese claim their island is the residence of these early ancestors.

Protestant missionary Mattheus Teffer in the 1870s recorded seven full brothers for Dida Miha (instead of Hawu Miha) who were ancestral figures for a number of geographical places. Thus, Beha Miha went to the island of Buton, Behie Miha to Timor Kupang, Holo Miha to Solor, Wawoe Miha to Ende, Hoeba Miha to Sumba, Rotti Miha to Rote, and Kiho Miha to Menia.[38]

Hoskins reports that in Sumba people remember the story of two brothers, in which the elder stayed in Sumba while the younger moved to Savu.[39] Savu people do not know the story and do not acknowledge the precedence of the Sumba people over the Savunese. They cannot envisage anyone ranking higher than they do in the area. Of interest is that a number of East Sumba clans acknowledge Savu as their origin (Umbu Pura Woha 2008: 24–6). Savunese are also mentioned among the "fathers of Timor" (Middelkoop 1957: 54, 108) and they are referred to in ancient verses:

> … Sails made to shelter the house yard,
> Made for the attention of the people of Savu,
> The people of Savu who are above,
> Whose feet do not break and shatter.[40]

As seen previously, Hawu Miha might have chased away the authochtonous Jola people of Savu. Jingi Tiu followers believe that the Jola people were the first people to celebrate a large cycle of ceremonies called *kelila* and consider that the present-day Savunese adopted the principle of *kelila* rituals from them around the time of Hawu Miha. Apparently, Savunese had to promise the Jola that they would celebrate *kelila jola* so that they would be remembered.[41] These ancient people left the Savunese a variety of sorghum known as *terae hika* (dotted sorghum) because the grains appear black and white when the ears open.

For the next four generations names of ancestors repeat themselves but Savunese insist on the accuracy of this list. When Detaq recorded Savu's main genealogies he simply deleted one of these two blocs of names, which

---

[38] (Raad voor de Zending, 1102–1: 1411, M. Teffer, report 1874). In Teffer's account, Dida Miha belonged to the ninth generation after Kika (Ga) instead of the eleventh generation (Figure 3). There he is the grandson of Ngara Rai who had first left Raijua for Savu. The name Ngara Rai appears twice in the genealogies and he is indeed the grandson of the second Ngara Rai (Ngara Rai Hawu Miha).

[39] See R.H. Barnes about Kedang for a reverse case. The younger brother stayed in Kedang while the older brothers left and founded the rest of the world's population (1974: 30).

[40] Lewis 2010: 306, 308.

[41] Interview with Ama Bawa Iri (Ama Lai Helu) (2.10.2000). For the *kelila* rituals see Appendix II.

caused resentment in Savu. However, one or two sets of those names do not have major implications for the Savu genealogies. Nevertheless, the missing ancestors are among those who migrated to other islands, and this is of importance to Savunese collective memory as later settlers are seen as early ancestors who returned to Savu.[42]

The care Savu people take in remembering their genealogies, even in early times, emphasises their sense of a chronology—their desire to establish a kind of ranking or precedence. In this matter, Savu shares common features with other Austronesian societies of the region. Precedence establishes "some form of superiority and/or priority between people" (Fox 1996: 131), and this works inside a clan as well as between them. The origin of a group is conceptualised as a path traceable from the first ancestor to the final settlement occupied by the present generation, using an order of events which then defines and justifies social differences. In the following section it is clear how the idea of precedence is expressed in various situations.

First division of the land in Savu

Dida Miha (Up Alone) is generally accepted as being the elder son of Miha Ngara and has at least one brother, Ie Miha (Good Alone). The time of Dida Miha is a major juncture in Savu's past. A number of narratives exist which all relate the same key elements, though they differ from each other in some of the episodes or details. The narrative below invokes the major moments of Dida Miha's life, combining details of various accounts.[43]

> Dida Miha first married Wěnyi D'ara Dahi, a 'woman from inside the sea'. While she was pregnant he had to go to the island of Raijua. However, before he left he told his wife that if she had a son, she was to make a fire in a coconut shell and place it on the ridge of their house so that he could see it from Raijua. Wěnyi D'ara Dahi did in fact give birth to a son, but she did not make fire on the ridge of her house. She did not want to

---

[42] In Raijua, four generations of the genealogy have been compressed into one. There Jua Miha replaces Hawu Miha who leaves Raijua after he found out that he had been betrayed. Around this time, three branching groups are remembered in Dimu: the Nabe'e, Hai'iki and Wolo people, and they are recognised as the original settlers of Dimu.

[43] Sources for Mesara: interviews with Ama Jula Lede (27.01.2001), (20.04.2002); and Ama Jo Haba (26.04.2002). Source for Seba: interview with Leba Alu (25.09.2000). Source for Liae: interview with Nguru Nape (31.03.2002). The same story is known in Raijua but takes place there and not in Savu; this results in minor changes in the narrative's place names. In Portuguese Timor, the Tetum people of Viqueque had a narrative recounting how a son defeated his father and later everyone in the kingdom in a series of cockfights. (Hicks 1982: 102–5).

inform her husband as she had heard that he had taken another wife in Raijua. She sent her son Dari Wènyi to the 'people inside the sea'.

Dida Miha must have spent years in Raijua as he fathered several children there including Jua Dida, who gave his name to the island of Raijua, and Hu'e Dida, who himself or his descendants later settled in Dimu, East Savu.

> When Dida Miha returned from Raijua he asked Wènyi D'ara Dahi about the child born after he left. She replied that she gave birth to something that looked like 'buffalo shit' (*tai kebau*) and that she threw it into the sea.[44]

> [Years passed]. Dida Miha organised a cockfight and, for the first time in his life, he lost. After losing several times, he grew suspicious and came to the conclusion that only his own son could have defeated him. He thought of ways to meet his son. He organised festivities with dances and cockfights to which he also invited the 'people from inside the sea'. He organised *pedoa*[45] dances at Jangakoli, but Dari Wènyi did not come.[46] Then he organised a cockfight at Nadawolomanu using hens and not roosters, and a particular kind of spur called a *hi*.[47] Dida Miha won the cockfight as usual. However, when more 'people from inside the sea' came [with Dari Wènyi], Dida Miha started to lose. Then he changed the place for the cockfight from Nadawolomanu to Marau, but still he kept losing. He then went to Kèjiwoka with the same outcome; he changed the cockspur for a *woka*, a hook,[48] but still he lost. He moved to Pudièta and called his sons living in Raijua for help. They also lost. There were no more roosters, no chickens and hens, and no more eggs on the island. Dida Miha had lost everything to the 'people inside the sea'.[49]

> Dida Miha went to his wife and asked her about their son. She denied having a son, and repeated what she had told him. Then Dida Miha asked Dari Wènyi to come and to sit by the male pillar of their house (*tèru duru*)

---

[44] A variant from Liae: *anaknya lahir mati* (still born [In]).

[45] *Pedoa* is a circle dance accompanied by chanting and performed at night during the last two months of the ceremonial year; baskets attached to the dancers' feet provide the rhythm.

[46] In the village of Dèinao, at the bottom of Mount Merèbu.

[47] *Hi* is made from a segment of a lontar leaf. *Nada* means arena and Wolomanu is the name of an ancestor, previously mentioned. The place is also known as Lariwolomanu or Raewoloma, in today's village of Wadumèdi, Mesara, near the border to Liae. All places named are either in Liae or near current borders between Liae and Mesara or Liae and Dimu.

[48] *Woka* is the tip of a metal hook. A fishing hook is also called a *woka*.

[49] In a variant from Mesara, Dida Miha went to consult his younger brother, Ie Miha, who told him that he was clearly the last one not to know that he had lost everything to his own son. He said, "You have a 'son from inside the sea'. I stayed in Savu all the time while you were in Raijua, so I know. Your son is hiding in the sea." Dida Miha asked his younger brother to bring Dari Wènyi to his house. Interview with Zadrak Bunga (02.06.2000).

and to open his mouth while his wife had to sit by the female pillar (*tèru wui*) and press her breast. Milk spurted out of her breast and went directly into Dari Wènyi's mouth.[50] Then Dida Miha decided to *hapo* (adopt) Dari Wènyi, giving him his own name. However, the younger brother, Ie Miha, told him that he could not organise the *hapo* ceremony because he also had children in Raijua. Dida Miha went first to Raijua to the priest Rue—able to re-establish the balance after wrongdoing (*mai hala*). He paid a fine—*manu bèla, manu mokèla, ngaka modaka, wawi mokode*—the mantra names of insects, symbolically representing, respectively, a chicken, a dog and a pig, which he no longer had. He compensated also with the red threads from the fringe of his loincloth (*wurumada buda mea*), symbolising gold.[51] Then the *hapo* ceremony took place and Dari Wènyi became Rede Dida.[52]

Dida Miha sent the 'people inside the sea' back to the sea and forbade them ever to return to the land. He decided also that the 'people inside the land' should never go to the sea. If the 'people of the land' went to the 'people inside the sea' they would die, and if the 'people inside the sea' came on land, they too would die. In order to put a border between the land and sea, Dida Miha planted a thorny plant, *lakai*, along the beaches so those of the sea would die on the thorns if they tried to come on to the land.

"Before writing", Barber and Barber remark (2004: 2), "myths had to serve as transmission systems for information deemed important". Therefore, people had to sieve and select what was worth passing on and narratives needed to be encoded in vivid and extraordinary ways to ensure correct remembering and transmission; hence, the 'people inside the land' and the 'people inside the sea', as well as the spurting milk and the mock payment with insects to compensate for adultery.

The story of Dida Miha combines realistic elements, referring to places in Savu, and extraordinary aspects, offering two levels of reading—either as a true event or as a legend. In the Savunese narratives about ancient times, the particular

---

[50] Storytellers who want to give a more extraordinary dimension to the story say that Wènyi D'ara Dahi was on Mt Merèbu while her son Wènyi D'ara was on the hill of Wègu (now Waduwèla village) standing on a large stone, which has since carried his name.

[51] Interview with Ama Jo Haba (15.11.2002). All these elements have been used until today in rituals to remember how Dida Miha paid for his sins. The insects are varieties of locusts, crickets and grasshoppers; the red threads from the loincloth fringe, or the threads left after sewing a woman's tubular cloth, are called *wurumada buda* and are constantly used in rituals because they are considered powerful. When purchasing an old loincloth it is not uncommon to see some missing red fringe threads, a sign that the cloth has been used for ritual purposes.

[52] *Rede* means literally full, expressing the idea that he is the last or youngest child from the socio-political point of view. Dida Miha did not have other children after Rede Dida.

terminology 'people inside the sea' and 'people inside the land' is constantly used instead of 'people of the sea' and 'people of the land' in order to transform an ordinary and plausible event into a legend, ensuring that remembering is surer.[53] At the time of the ancestor Kika Ga, another category of people is mentioned; the people in heaven or 'people inside the sky'. Another reading of these ancient narratives considers the various groups of Savunese people as being from the land, the sea or the sky. Such symbolic labels are recurrent themes in oral accounts as well as in expressions used in rituals all over the island. They correspond to categories which are considered in later chapters.

Cockfighting is an essential element of social life in Savu and Raijua; moreover, ritual cockfights still take place every year in all domains. Men continue to use the mantra words uttered by Dari Wènyi in order to win against Dida Miha at cockfights in Savu. These words show that Dari Wènyi's dominance lies in his personal aura, in the superiority of his character. Mentioning the different types of blades used in cockfights shows how important this knowledge is even to today's Savunese. Dida Miha successively tried all four blade types known to the present in his competition with Dari Wènyi, but still his son defeated him. In at least male collective memory, there is a known historical chronology for the use of cockspurs in Savu. *Hi* or *lidi* is made from a segment of a lontar leaf, forming a loop, which does not result in a bird dying. *Hi* was replaced later by *teri*, a bamboo knife as sharp as a blade which, in turn, was replaced by *woka*, the tip of a fishing hook (or harpoon). The latest development is *kepoke*, a straight metal blade used for cockfights if accompanied by gambling.[54] Dida Miha's supposed application of all types of cockspurs has to be taken with some reservation with regards the use of metal in contemporary Savunese history. For instance, why use palm leaves and bamboo blades if people already knew about metal blades? The narrative's description of cockfighting techniques ensures the transmission of important knowledge to the present.

Fights between indigenous peoples and newcomers are a recurrent theme in the region. For the Ema of North Central Timor, the newcomers' victory led to the disappearance of the first settler who went to the sky, taking the sun with him (Clamagirand 1982: 120–1). In Raijua, ancient settlers, such as Mone Reu and Mone Weo, are said to have disappeared upon the arrival of a

---

[53] For simplification, these groups are referred to as the 'people of the land' and the 'people of the sea', although the correct expressions always contain the word 'inside'.

[54] Interviews with Leba Alu of Seba (25.09.2000); Ama Jo Haba of Mesara (26.04.2002). For example, *hi* or *lidi* is used today for ceremonial cockfights in Seba while *woka* is used for ceremonial cockfights in Mesara. In Raijua, *kepoke* is used for the first round of a ritual cockfight and *woka* for all other confrontations.

foreigner called Maja. Mone Weo is remembered through a priest position and a ceremony *kowa Mone Weo*. About the Bali Aga people, Reuter remarks that "powerful newcomers may usurp the authority of the original settlers and put the existing order of precedence into question so that 'origin' can be retrospectively defined rather than being a simple reflection of 'actual history'" (2002: 23). The same probably happened in Savu with the arrival of Kika Ga, an outsider retrospectively constructed as an indigenous ancestor to justify later claims of land ownership; all male genealogies are then derived from him. Vansina writes that "one cannot reconstruct what has been eliminated or disentangle what has been telescoped through time" (1985: 122). For this reason, narratives place a flood in Savu's past to delete what existed before, creating a blank sheet for a new start.

However, as Vansina argues, what is suppressed leaves traces somewhere else. It is interesting to note that the two female moieties and ancestors worshipped in relation to the dyeing and weaving processes appear prior to Kika Ga's arrival, the first 'official' ancestor of today's male genealogies. Moreover, the powerful male ancestors invoked during the *hole* ritual are also found in these early or mantra genealogies. It is now clear why the first part of the genealogies is deliberately secret and considered sacred, while the second part is public knowledge and in the collective memory. "An order of precedence", Reuter writes, "does not just happen nor is it imagined in retrospect; it is made" (2002: 24). The precedence derived from Kika Ga was made *a posteriori* and certain aspects in the story, such as Dida Miha's cockfight against his son, have been imagined in retrospect. The cockfight might have been a metaphor for a war, with ancient times constructed to "become congruent with the present" (Vansina 1985: 118). Nevertheless, narratives have carried elements of the account up to the present and serve as a reference for today's social organisation in the domain of Liae. For example, the participation or exclusion of a clan in the ceremonial cockfight is derived from Dida Miha's defeat. A number of ritual texts contain knowledge kept in the mantra genealogies. Without these data, especially about the female genealogies, it would not have been possible to reconstruct this early time of Savu's history.

It is possible to derive two pivotal ideas from the chronology of ancestors' names and the branching of groups. One is the essential concept of a shared origin, a recurrent idea in the area (Fox 1996: 132; McWilliam 2002: 17). It implies that newcomers have been indigenised and taken up in a group's genealogy to fit the general pattern, so it is no longer possible to trace them as newcomers or outsiders. However, an external origin can sometimes be traced by knowing the individual's mantra name, though the start is hard to pinpoint as his/her descendants do not speak the mantra name. The narratives acknowledge that, in some cases, the ancestors left Savu and returned a few generations later; they are treated as descendants of Savu people and generally form a new lineage. The second essential message carried in the Dida Miha narrative is the idea of precedence derived from chronological order as a fundamental organising principle, connecting the past and the present.

There are over 40 generations between Kika Ga and the present, and some 30 generations between the two brothers, Dida Miha and Ie Miha, and Savunese today. Calculations for the average length of a male generation in Savu, by locating names mentioned in VOC manuscripts and in their respective genealogies, give an average of 25 years.[55] If 25 years is the considered length of a male generation, it places the time of Kika Ga at the beginning of the second millennium and of Dida Miha in the 13th century.

There has been little archaeological research so far in the Savu archipelago. Excavations in the Lie Madira cave in Mesara show that the site has been inhabited for at least 3,000 years. There is a hill located between Merèbu and Teriwu where the ground is covered with stone flakes or tools. The name of this place is not fortuitous—Gurijola (Murdered Jola people)—mentioned earlier on and does not indicate a peaceful fate for the inhabitants. The Jola, considered the ancient inhabitants of Savu, did not have a fixed place to live and are said to have left the island a long time ago. In folk imagery, they are small people with large feet and large ears (do bèla jèla, do bèla dilu). There is another reference to the Jola people in the domain of Seba, but more archaeological work is needed. The coded language about the people of the sky, the land and of the sea might also refer to various groups of settlers in Savu.

To summarise the way Savu people envision the stages of development since the time of the Supreme Being Deo Muri, it can be asserted that the cosmogony recounted as a genealogy does not give an a-temporal account of mythical times. It is, on the contrary, a logical, precise, chronologically growing, expanding time with no floating gap between mythical and historical times. Elements in nature were created before humans and animals. There are two periods in early Savu times. One is before Kika Ga that contains the sacred and secret (mantra) genealogies during which at least one flood occurred. During this period, two female moieties (hubi) were created, but no male clans had yet emerged; this fact reveals a matrifocal structure of the society at its origin. Identification according to the moieties is still known today and carried on through the female genealogies. The second epoch starts with Kika Ga's arrival after another flood. From this point, Kika Ga is indigenised and part of the category 'people of

---

[55] With variations, there are between 22 to 30 years per generation, depending on the clan and the domain (Duggan 2011c: 62).

the land' while his wife is 'people of the sea' However, the male clans had not developed before the time the land was divided between the two brothers, Dida and Ie Miha. The next two chapters consider what collective memory has passed on about the descendants of the two brothers in Savu and Raijua, examining the male genealogies, the creation of clans and their branching into lineages, and comparing the oral texts from each domain.

Figure 4: Clans descended from Dida Miha

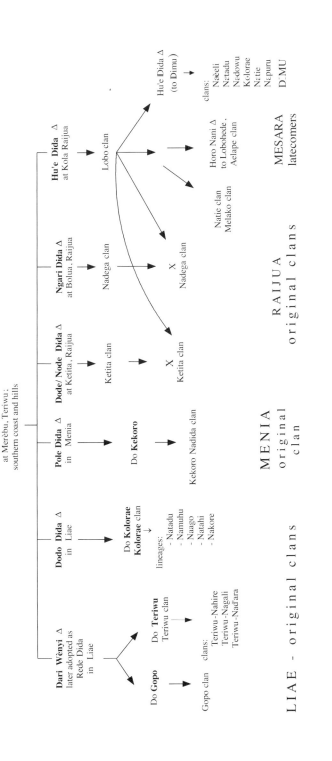

Figure 5: Clans descended from Ie Miha

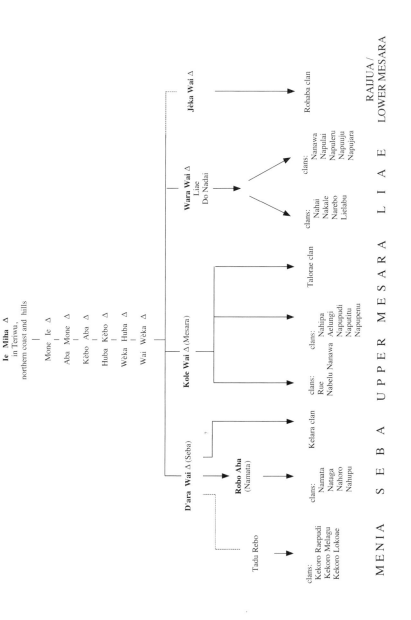

Figure 6: Moieties, *hubi* and the formation of *wini*

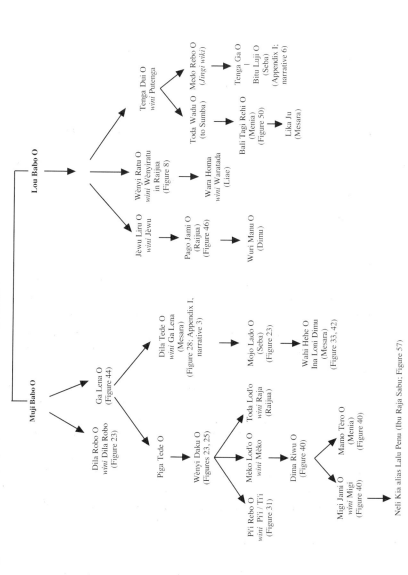

Muji Babo O

Dila Robo O
wini Dila Robo
(Figure 23)

Ga Lena O
(Figure 44)

Piga Tede O

Dila Tede O
wini Ga Lena
(Mesara)
(Figure 28: Appendix I,
narrative 3)

Mojo Lado O
(Seba)
(Figure 23)

Wahi Hehe O
Ina Loni Dimu
(Mesara)
(Figure 33, 42)

Wenyi Daku O
(Figures 23, 25)

Pi'i Rebo O
wini Pi'i / Ti'i
(Figure 31)

Toda Lod'o
wini Raja
(Raijua)

Meko Lod'o
wini Meko

Dima Riwu O
(Figure 40)

Mamo Tero O
(Menia)
(Figure 40)

Migi Jami O
wini Migi
(Figure 40)

Neli Kia alias Lalu Penu (Ibu Raja Sabu; Figure 57)

Lou Babo O

Jewu Liru O
wini Jewu

Wenyi Ratu O
wini Wenyiratu
in Raijua (Figure 8)

Tenga Dui O
wini Putenga

Pago Jami O
(Raijua)
(Figure 46)

Wara Homa
wini Waratada
(Liae)

Toda Wadu O
(to Sumba)

Medo Rebo O
(*Jingi wiki*)

Wuri Manu O
(Dimu)

Bali Tagi Rehi O
(Menia)
(Figure 50)

Tenga Ga O

Lika Ju
(Mesara)

Bitu Luji O
(Seba)
(Appendix I;
narrative 6)

Chapter 2 | The Descendants of the Elder Brother

This chapter traces the descendants of the elder of the two brothers, Dida Miha and Ie Miha, and the development of the most ancient proto-clans and clans of Savu, examining how the concept of precedence applies to them. A socio-political and religious organisation called a *ratu* (council) developed in parallel with the clans. The chapter follows the *ratu*'s development and uncovers the struggles to control it.

The domain of Liae

A range of hills running roughly in an east-west direction naturally divides the island of Savu into two areas. The idea of Savu's territorial division at the time of the two brothers Dida Miha and Ie Miha is widely accepted. Dida and his descendants lived on the Teriwu hills along the southern coast, while his younger brother Ie moved to the hills' northern slopes, further down towards the northern coast.

Dida Miha's descendants, found today in all of Savu and Raijua's domains, lived first in the domain of Liae and are associated with the Merèbu and Teriwu settlements. Teriwu is known in poetic recitations as 'the good land that rules over Savu'. Located on top of a hill overlooking both the Indian Ocean and the Savu Sea, it occupies a strategic position. In collective memory, people acknowledge that in the past the priests of the various ritual domains 'went to Teriwu to fetch the seeds' for planting. They believe the fertility contained in the seeds is channelled to them through the ancestors who settled in Teriwu and through the great ancestress Bèni Ae. The idea of Teriwu's precedence over the other domains is explicit in such statements and practices, and it is generally accepted.

When these two brothers lived the order of precedence was established in two ways: first was the precedence of Dida Miha over Ie Miha on the island; and second was a ranking between the children of Dida Miha, who had offspring from two marriages. The number and names of his children vary according to place and sources, a sign that groups of people have been retrospectively included as descendants of the elder brother. There is a general agreement about the names Dari Wènyi alias Rede Dida, Dodo Dida, Pole Dida, Jua Dida and Hu'e Dida.[1]

The case of Rede Dida requires closer examination because people remember the rules derived from his specific circumstances. As Dida Miha adopted Rede Dida after more children carrying their father's name had been born, he is considered of lower rank. First impressions suggest that the marriage between Dida Miha and Wènyi D'ara Dahi was not a 'proper' marriage, otherwise Dari Wènyi would have carried his father's, not his mother's, name. However, it can be argued that Dida Miha was not in Savu when his son was born. Therefore, he could not have conducted the *hapo* ceremony that takes place three days after the birth of a child, during which the father gives his name to the newborn. In the absence of the biological father, the mother's brother becomes the social father and the child enters the mother's clan. As the child was known as Dari Wènyi, he received his mother's name and belonged to her origin group the 'people of the sea' with whom, according to the story in the previous chapter, he grew up. As Rede Dida's adoption took place after more children were born, he was not recognised as the first son in the local order of precedence. His name Rede, meaning full, provides an explanation: being the last of the children to carry the father's name, the Miha family was then *rede* (complete)—completed by the action of his adoption. *Rede* is undeniably a mnemonic tag. Rede Dida also means full up or top end, as expressed, for example, through the metaphor of a growing plant when the youngest leaf is *ru dida*. Reconsidering the name Dodo Dida, the second of Dida Miha's sons, becomes semantically significant if it is pronounced Dod'o Dida, meaning 'who is not at the top end'. Rede Dida's adoption marked the position reflected in the brothers' names—with Rede Dida at the 'top end' and Dod'o Dida 'who is not at the top end'. It is not over-speculating to say that these names were given later and that they encapsulate some historical clues as the following paragraph explains.

In the domain of Liae, from which come the lines of Dida Miha's sons, Rede Dida and Dodo Dida, people repeat the following phrases in order to cut short any contestation:[2]

Apu do Teriwu   The ancestor of the people of Teriwu [Rede Dida]

---

[1] Less-mentioned names are Node Dida and Pojo Dida. Of Rede Dida's descendants, the name Dida Miha repeats; thus it is possible that some of the children attributed to the first Dida Miha are in fact descendants of the second Dida Miha.

[2] Interview with Nguru Nape (30.08.2006).

| *mone a'a ne metana,* | is the elder brother by birth |
| *tapulara mone ari pa hapo.*[3] | but the younger by adoption. |

Apu do Kolorae	The ancestor of the people of Kolorae [Dodo Dida]
mone ari ne metana,	is the younger brother by birth
tapulara mone a'a pa ngara.	but the elder by name.

The principle of precedence is thus governed by the order in which the name is received, not by the birth order; ranking is not based on the son who receives the father's blood first.[4] *Do* means people, so *do* Teriwu and *do* Kolorae designate respective groups of people not yet organised as clans, which would otherwise be called *udu* Teriwu and *udu* Kolorae. These are proto-clans with their settlements on the top of hills overlooking loosely defined territories. However, these phrases explaining precedence cannot be complete. They consider only the respective ranking of the descendants of Rede Dida (*do* Teriwu) and those of Dodo Dida (*do* Kolorae). The ranking of their other siblings is much less certain.

Rede Dida had two sons, Lod'o Rede and Babo Rede. The latter began *do* Teriwu, while Lod'o Rede's son, Gopo Lod'o, formed *do* Gopo and the settlement of the same name on Gopo hill. Logically, *do* Gopo should have a lower position than *do* Teriwu and *do* Kolorae, as the group formed two or three generations later. In fact, the Gopo people dispute the official genealogy of Savu and claim to be directly descended from Lod'o Liru Bèla, thus being from the category 'people of the sky' and not from the adopted son Kika Ga (Detaq 1973: 59).

At this stage of history, the ancestors did not reside in exactly defined territories and yet they organised their politico-religious tasks through councils (*ratu*) and formed the *Ratu Mone Tèlu* (Council of Three Men). The complete title is *Ratu Mone Tèlu Aji Mone D'ue* (Council of Three Men Two Priests). *Aji* refers to a priest position and the word appeared in Javanese texts of the first millennium.[5] In Savu, Aji is also a personal name found in genealogies from early times to the present. The existence of a council (*ratu*) is indicated in the name

---

[3] *Hapo* is a noun here. The complete expression is *hapo ana* (to adopt a child). See the explanation for adoption on the previous page. Duggan's adoption in Ledetadu village in November 2002 was also called *hapo ana*.

[4] Similar cases were recorded in Seba for the children of Haba Jami and Mojo Lado (see chapter 4).

[5] See de Grave (2001) who defines *aji* as a 'spiritual force' or a 'charismatic quality', which also refers to those who possess these qualities.

of Gopo Lod'o's son, Ratu Gopo.[6] The council's 'three men' are from the groups Gopo, Teriwu and Kolorae, while the two priests were from Gopo (bearing the title Deo Gopo) and Kolorae (Deo Mengèru). These two religious positions still exist today. Deo Gopo is also called Deo Rai (Lord of the Earth) who is the highest priest in any council of priests. *Mengèru* means green, nature and growth so, by extension, Deo Mengèru is the priest of prosperity for plants and humans. The tasks of both priests are similar and work in parallel as is clearly displayed in the adat calendar (knots of the land) of Liae in Appendix II.

The system of forming priest positions and clans (*udu*) in Liae continued for up to 17 generations. It deserves closer examination as research in Liae yielded the most detailed information. Gopo did not split into further lineages while Teriwu and Kolorae did.

Babo Rede and the Teriwu people

Teriwu is also remembered as the 'great land' with a 'sweet scent', the idea of sweetness being linked to luck, fertility and prosperity. A common phrase referring to the split of Teriwu is *tèlu wue kerogo ma haka ngati udu Teriwu* (the Teriwu clan fractured into three lineages). *Haka* suggests violence, conflict, indicating it was not a smooth division. This happened at the time of the ancestor Wunu Babo who lived eleven generations after Dida Miha.[7] In fact, the resulting branches did not form lineages (*kerogo*) but independent clans: *udu* Teriwu-Nahire, *udu* Teriwu-Nagali and *udu* Teriwu-Nad'ara. It is certain that *udu* Teriwu lost land to Seba and possibly to other domains surrounding it, such as Liae and Mesara. Teriwu has long been associated with the turmoil in the early stages of Savu's history.

Wunu Babo had two sons, Hire Wunu and Gali Wunu, and a daughter, Mare Wunu. People in Seba remember her marriage to D'ara Jami of Seba, a descendant of D'ara Wai.[8] D'ara Jami, adopted as D'ara Wunu, joined Teriwu to form *udu* Teriwu-Nad'ara. Mare Wunu Babo of Teriwu lived twelve generations

---

[6] Unfortunately, the *udu* Gopo genealogy received so far is made up of groups of names that repeat four times over 50 generations, so it is of no use for comparisons with other male and female genealogies. As *udu* Gopo is not mentioned in the Liae clans' order of precedence, it points to discrepancies which now cannot be untangled.

[7] See Figure 8. The names Dida Miha and Wunu Babo repeat in the Teriwu genealogy.

[8] See Figure 8. D'ara Jami Kore Naga D'ara Wai: see D'ara Wai's genealogy, descendant of Ie Miha. Some sources give Riwu instead of D'ara Jami as the first part of the name 'Kore Naga D'ara Wai', explaining that the domain name Teriwu is derived from his name. However, there are several factors to indicate that Teriwu existed and was so named before the arrival of the Seba ancestor.

Figure 7: Council of Three Men

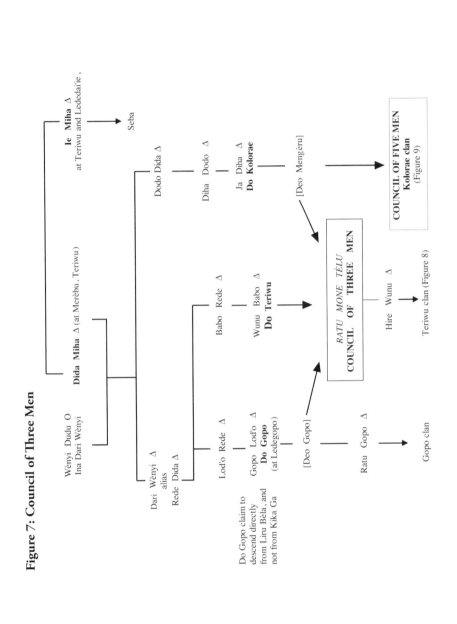

Ie Miha △
at Teriwu and Lededaʼie .
→ Seba

Wěnyi Dudu O
Ina Dari Wěnyi

Dida Miha △ (at Merěbu . Teriwu)

Dodo Dida △

Diha Dodo △

Ja Diha △
Do Kolorae

[Deo Mengěru]

Dari Wěnyi △
alias
Rede Dida △

Babo Rede △

Wunu Babo △
Do Teriwu

RATU MONE TÈLU
COUNCIL OF THREE MEN

Hire Wunu △

Teriwu clan (Figure 8)

Lodʼo Rede △

Gopo Lodʼo △
Do Gopo
(at Ledegopo)

[Deo Gopo]

Ratu Gopo △

Gopo clan

Do Gopo claim to
descend directly
from Liru Bêla. and
not from Kika Ga

COUNCIL OF FIVE MEN
Kolorae clan
(Figure 9)

Figure 8: Early times of Teriwu and Haba Dida

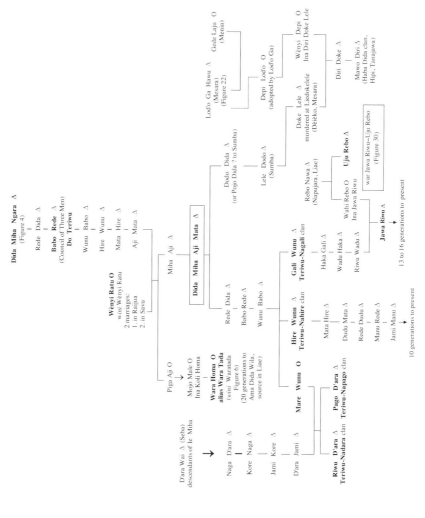

after Dida Miha, and D'ara Jami (Wunu), ten generations after the younger brother Ie Miha, which makes their marriage genealogically plausible. The creation of *udu* Teriwu-Nad'ara dates from this time and is remembered in relation to a loss of land. Given these facts, the marriage between Mare Wunu of Teriwu and D'ara Jami of Seba is plausible. This is the second time (after Dida Miha and his adopted son Rede Dida) in Liae's history that an adoption compensated for a loss of land. The loser 'adopts' the winner in order to protect his name and save face. It might also suit the winner to form a new clan. This is how knowledge is transmitted through the generations and composed in a way more favourable to the genealogies.

Originally, people of *udu* Teriwu were descendants of the elder brother, but after losing land to Seba and marrying the younger brother's descendants, at least one branch became part of contemporary Seba. It has to be noted that Teriwu's ritual cockfighting arena was located at Raemoneie, which became Seba's territory, the latter recognising only Namata for ritual cockfights. However, in religious matters Teriwu belongs to Liae's priest system with the position of Doheleo (Overseer) and Rue (Priest of Misfortune). At the time of this war, Ie Miha's descendants in Seba might have formed or were about to form clans as D'ara Jami is at the same generational level as Robo Aba of Seba, who founded Namata and formed clans for some of his children.

Kolorae and the Council of Five Men

Twelve generations after Dida Miha the sudden death of Lumu Lutu caused a crisis of succession in the Kolorae clan. It occurred at the same generational level as Teriwu's split. However, counting generations gives only a rough temporal estimation and it does not mean that both events took place at the same time.

There are two narratives about Lumu Lutu. The first is a short popular folktale that tells the story of how he visited his lover, Hana Mata of *udu* Namata in Seba, in a magical boat which was able to cross over land at night. One night he was late leaving his lover and daybreak caught him as he was sailing back to Liae in his 'land-boat'; he and his boat were petrified at a place called Nauru, now located in Raenalulu village. A second and more elaborated version also mentions Hana Mata of the Namata clan as his beloved mistress; however, he was not petrified but murdered at Nauru, without having a son to carry on his name. A stone was placed there as his memorial.

Without a descendant to perform rituals, Lumu Lutu's line might have lost the priest position of Deo Mengèru to another group. Apparently, the rituals could not be held for two years. However, Lumu Lutu had a son out of wedlock with Hana Mata called Mèngi Mata, who was then adopted by the Kolorae clan as D'ara Lumu. This solved the problem of succession. As compensation, the people of Seba (Namata clan) received a piece of land called Kehanga, located in Racnalulu village, comprising the memorial stone of Lumu Lutu, the so-called petrified boat. However, the land compensation is not mentioned in the narratives.[9]

In the area, it is commonly accepted that Kolorae also 'gave' land to *udu* Nanawa—a group newly arrived in Liae—owing to the fact that it had been unable to perform the rituals over a certain period of time. The new group then assumed the position of Apu Lod'o (Descendant of the Sun).[10] Again this underlines the struggle for power which must have been going on for generations. For a while there was a Council of Three Priests (*Aji Mone Tèlu*) with one position held by Gopo, Teriwu and Kolorae respectively, though there are no further details. Fixed phrases, transmitted from generation to generation, have survived a long span of time, but their precise meaning has been lost. Four generations after Lumu Lutu at the time of Lele Re *udu* Kolorae split into five lineages (*kerogo*), and formed *Ratu Mone Lèmi* (Council of Five Men) with five positions corresponding to its five lineages.

Lele Re had many children with three different wives. Five sons survived and have descendants.[11] Tahi Lele and Muhu Lele's mother is said to be from the 'people of the sea'; Kore Lele's mother is from the Kekoro clan of Menia. Ago Lele and Tadu Lele's mother is from Ende, Flores.[12] Lele Re created the Council of Five Men for his five sons: three of the five positions related to warfare. There is no doubt that it was a time of turmoil and that the new council, replacing the Council of Three Men, aimed at weakening the power of Gopo and Teriwu, and possibly of Nanawa too.[13] A narrative relates the situation at that time:

---

[9] Main sources: interviews with Leba Alu (27.09.2000); Ama Koro Ga (28.03.2002); and Nguru Nape (14.05.2006).

[10] According to some sources, the position of Apu Lod'o was created at that time; it did not exist before. There is no further information to sustain or refute this argument.

[11] There is a narrative about a daughter, Hana Lele, who was changed into a turtle, and a son, Woe Lele, who became a crocodile. People of the Kolorae clan thus do not consume either turtle or crocodile meat, though there are no longer crocodiles in Savu. A hill in Waduwèla, between Wègu and Merèbu, is shaped like a turtle and is associated with Hana Lele. As Hana Lele's mother was from Kekoro, members of this clan do not consume turtle meat either.

[12] She is known as Kewawo Lede Meja; *Kewawo* means the island of Flores and *Lede Meja* is the name of a mountain in Flores. Thus, the title refers to her birthplace and is not her actual name.

[13] Teriwu had already lost some power four generations before.

> As the Council of Five Men was not able to make the system work, the
> Council of Three Men was formed again because the ceremonial cooking
> place already had three stones, so it was already strong because of Rai
> Bèla, Dahi Bèla and Liru Bèla.

The three stones refer to the ceremonial hearth. Each stone represents an ancestor
(or a deity): Rai Bèla (Great Earth), Dahi Bèla (Great Sea) and Liru Bèla (Great
Sky), mirroring the tripartite division of the cosmos and the cosmological
balance. In their coded narratives about this war, Liae people have a retrospective
interpretation which uses the metaphor of the ritual cooking place, explaining
that at the time of the Council of Five Men, only Dahi Bèla and Liru Bèla
formed the ceremonial hearth. It means that at a practical level the cooking place
had only two stones on which it was unfeasible to place a pot; as a consequence,
it was impossible to cook food for the ancestors and make offerings. The rituals
could no longer be performed properly. It means also that essential tasks in the
priest system were no longer carried out. On an abstract level, the cosmos was
not balanced, so war and diseases ruled the island.

> As [it was] not strong, a war started called 'enemies on land, broken land'.
> People from the land went to the sky, people from inside the sea came
> onto the land and people from the land went to the bottom of the world.
> Because of all of this, they made a meeting and formed the Council of
> Seven Men inside *udu* [*do*] Nadai.[14]

The war is remembered through the image of a broken, open land that let diseases
invade the country and destroy everything. These vivid images give an idea of the
size of the disaster. It is very possible that Teriwu's fate was related to the terrible
war that took place in Liae, referred to as a war between land, sky and sea.

The Council of Three Men was never revived. From this point onwards, two
parallel priest systems existed in Liae. One is the Council of Five Men in the
Kolorae clan under the leadership of Deo Mengèru. His ritual house is located
on a perfectly conical hill, Ledewègu, not far from Merèbu, so he is also known
as Deo Wègu. The council incorporated two important ritual positions from the
Teriwu members—that of Doheleo (Overseer) and Rue (Priest of Misfortune).
It is not clear when the clans became associated; it might have taken place after
the terrible war and the dissolution of Teriwu as the most ancient ritual domain.

The second system is the Council of Seven Men formed mainly by descendants
of the younger brother, Ie Miha. As they moved to Liae, these ancestors first
formed a proto-clan, *do* Nadai, before creating seven clans. Today the council
is led by Deo Gopo, renamed Deo Rai (Lord of the Earth). A council of priests
cannot exist without either Deo Mengèru or Deo Rai. It is very likely that the

---

[14] Interview with Nguru Nape (30.08.2006).

Figure 9: Kolorae and the Council of Five Men

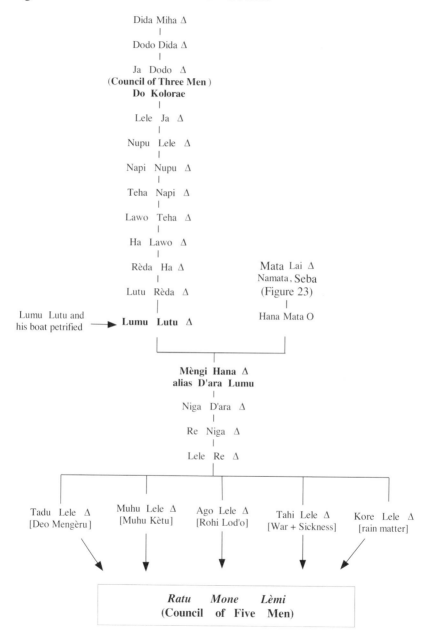

Gopo people were invited by (or allied with) the newcomers so that the Council of Seven Men could be established under the leadership of Deo Gopo. Apu Lod'o of the Nanawa clan held the second highest position in the council.

Today, people feel, speak of and even contest the consequences of the two sets of divisions contemporaneous to Dida Miha and Ie Miha. Ie Miha's descendants, who settled later in Liae, have a lower rank in ceremonies than any descendant of Dida Miha, although they formed the largest number of clans and occupy most of the Liae territory. The precedence is reflected in the last two months of rituals closing the Liae ceremonial year. Dida Miha's descendants hold their rituals first in the month Bangaliwu (April). The following month, Bangaliwu rame (May), the Nadai people descended from Ie Miha may celebrate the end of the year. The priest positions of this group are accompanied with the label *rai* (land or earth), showing that they have descended from the 'people of the land'. The tags 'people of the sea' and 'people of the sky' are now associated with Dida Miha's descendants. Retrospectively, Dida Miha, who adopted Dari Wènyi, became one of the 'people of the sea'. The precedence of the clans, labelled 'people of the sea' and 'people of the sky', is spatially and temporally demonstrated in the two months of high rituals in Liae.[15]

Contestation and the struggle for power shaped Liae's history and led to the domain of Teriwu's disappearance. Ceremonial cockfights, most people believe, replaced warfare in Savu. The traditional domain of Liae is certainly where ceremonial cockfights are still well attended and the rules are highly respected (Plate 6). At both annual ceremonial cockfights, the Gopo and Teriwu clans, descended from the winner at Dida Miha's cockfight, always take part in ritual Liae cockfighting, while Kolorae (from the ancestor Dodo Dida) is absent from this ceremony. Dodo Dida helped his father Dida Miha against Rede Dida; therefore, his descendants are excluded from taking part in the ritual cockfight. The absence of the Kolorae clan at Liae's ritual cockfights is used as a mnemonic tag. The rule for attending or not attending the ritual cockfight has been observed since Dida Miha's time, some 700 years ago. It is noteworthy that the Kolorae clan lost its right to have gongs in rituals, apparently also since the time of Dida Miha. However, the Teriwu clan has the right to hold gongs and, since it joined forces with Kolorae for rituals, Teriwu members' gongs can be used in the Council of Five Men rituals.

It was only possible to trace the Liae ancient priest system prior to the Council of *Mone Ama* as it is still practised today. This ancient organisation called *ratu* with its priests called *aji* could be reconstructed combining geographical elements

---

[15] The mantra name of Deo Mengèru's taboo horse is reminiscent of these categories; it is called Jara Liru (Sky Horse).

and observation of ritual cockfights, genealogical knowledge and narratives as well as rich ritual recitations. The willingness of Liae people to share cultural information deserves recognition here. Other societies of the region consider that the original settlers are the 'people of the land' while newcomers are the 'people of the sea'. The reverse situation occurs in Liae where the 'people of the sea' have precedence over the 'people of the land'. It is neccessary to examine how the sea-land dichotomy is expressed in the other domains of Savu and Raijua.

The descendants of Dida Miha in Dimu

One of Dida Miha's children is Hu'e Dida who lived in Raijua. Seven generations later a second Hu'e Dida moved to Savu where he is considered to be the founding ancestor of Dimu, the most eastern domain of Savu. However, he might not have arrived in unoccupied territory as the Nabe'e, Hai'iki and Wolo people, descended from an earlier branching group, had settled at the north-eastern end of Savu. They are generally recognised as Dimu's original settlers. The Nabe'e occupied the northern part of Dimu (Bodae) and the Wolo the southern part (Bolou), while the Hai'iki lived in Menia. The descendants of Hu'e Dida and Paha Hama occupied the southern part (Bolou), thus sharing the space with the Wolo. Muhu Hama settled in the northern part, Kolodihe, later renamed Kujiratu which was originally the land of the Nabe'e.[16]

People in Dimu claim the same Dida Miha cockfight story as Liae people. They declare that they descended from the famous Dari Wènyi who defeated Dida Miha and was adopted as Rede Dida. To interpret the dual claim to the Dida Miha story, it is helpful to consider some pragmatic aspects. Liae's hilly and rugged terrain offers better protection against enemies than the flat land of Dimu. Therefore, it is strategically better suited as a location for the early ancestors. The formation of clans in Dimu occurred later in comparison with Liae where the same time saw the creation of three clans organised in the Council of Three Men. Why were the Dimunese slower to become organised? Is it because they had to share the territory with other groups?

A key Dimu ancestor is Hama Dole whose grandmother married respectively in Seba, Mesara and lastly in Liae where she became Ina Alu Lai. Alu Lai then married in Dimu. When she passed away, people of all the domains came to Dimu as they were closely related. People remember Ina Hama Dole's death in connection with a war between Dimu and all the other domains. Each domain has its own narrative regarding this war. Nguru Nape (March 2002) narrated the following from Liae:

---

[16] Interviews with Na Laike, Miha Lulu and Lado Bèngu (23.05.2014).

Figure 10: Early times in Dimu

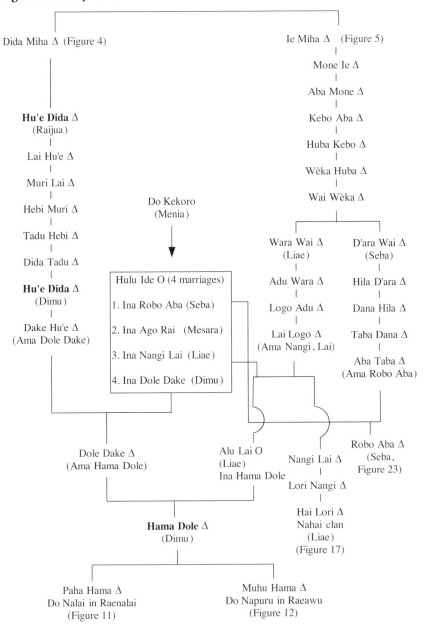

After Hulu Ide became Ina Robo Aba in Seba, she became Ina Ago Rai in Mesara. Then she became Ina Nangi Lai, Alu Lai in Liae. After that she went to Dimu and there became Ina Dole Dake. … As Alu Lai married Dole Dake, she became Ina Hama Dole.[17] Alu Lai and Dole Dake had the same mother, so it was a marriage between siblings. So is the saying in Savu.

Alu Lai's funeral in Dimu led to a war between Liae and Dimu. People of Dimu came to Liae to inform Nangi Lai [of the death of his sister]. Nangi Lai said "I cannot come today. I have to go first to the garden to pick betel and a whole bunch of areca nuts. I will only go tomorrow." This is the saying. After this the people of Dimu left. Then Nangi Lai went to his two friends the priests Maja and Kenuhe, and they conferred. They left [in the evening] for Dimu carrying a mortar wrapped in a Savunese sarong.

When they arrived, they decided to proceed according to the following plan. Nangi Lai stayed outside so his relatives in Dimu, old and young, came out to greet him, while the corpse was left alone inside the house. The Kenuhe and Maja priests entered the house to exchange the corpse for the mortar. They placed the mortar against the wooden sticks and carried the corpse away.[18] When Nangi Lai's friends were already far away Nangi Lai entered the house. Once inside, he opened the cloth to give his sister's body a kiss, but what he kissed was not a human being. "This is a mortar – this is how you make a fool of me!" This is what he said.

Nangi Lai returned to Liae. There he made a hole at the foot of a tree at the *herèti* place [this is where all the tools used for a funeral are discarded]; he buried the corpse there because no one would look for a body [in such a place]. After that he decided to make war against Dimu. He went to Mesara to tell the people of the war against Dimu. This is how the people of Mesara and Laie came to be called *hekene hi'i* [a blanket woven in one piece with no seam], one piece of weaving since the time of Kole Wai who came to stay in Liae. This was the war caused by the death of Ina Hama Dole who was Alu Lai. This is what is said in Liae.

Details in the narrative are known to insiders, but a general audience requires some explanation. The priests Kenuhe and Maja can travel underground and remain invisible to people. During the meeting with Nangi Lai, undisclosed to the listener, the three friends decided to steal Ina Hama Dole's body; however, only later in the narrative does the listener understand that Nangi Lai wanted to retrieve his sister's body. It is unclear if his intention to cause a war by acting

[17] Ina Hama Dole is her tecknonym, so Alu Lai/Ina Hama Dole is the same person. As seen in the introduction, parents are named after their firstborn with *Ina* (mother) or *Ama* (father) placed in front.

[18] The deceased is wrapped in a number of weavings and placed sitting in a foetal position against five or seven branches which reach from the floor to the loft.

in such a way was premeditated. The use of a mortar to replace a corpse might appear odd to an outsider, but it is possible to mistake a mortar draped in a textile for the deceased in a foetal position, wrapped in a number of cloths. As Ina Hama Dole was to be buried in the foetal position—an ancient practice for all Jingi Tiu people who die naturally, replicating their time in the womb—it is clear that she was not murdered; only people who suffer a violent death are buried horizontally. The *herèti* place where all the tools used for a funeral are discarded is an unlikely place to bury a highly respected human as bad spirits may wander there from time to time. It shows Nangi Lai feared someone might try to steal the body.

Finally, the word *hekene hi'i* refers to a blanket. It is entirely woven with the same weft thread; the metaphor underlines the special close relationship between Liae and Mesara. As later chapters show, the descendants of the two apical brothers, Dida Miha and Ie Miha, who eventually settled in Mesara lived first in Liae. Nguru Nape sees the origin of the close relationship between the two domains in the Ina Hama Dole narrative.

This female ancestor is a key figure in collective memory. People believe in Ina Hama Dole's charismatic power: in Seba, some men go to Kekoro hill—where she originated and is believed to be buried—to pray for her blessing before attending a cockfight. The strength of Ina Hama Dole's aura influenced her brother's decision to bury her where no one would find her. Each domain claims to have kept something of hers—either her body (whole or part thereof) or an adornment. From other narratives recorded in Mesara and Seba, Ago Rai and Robo Aba also wanted to retrieve their stepsister's body. People in Dimu do not want to lose face when hearing other versions of the story. They declare that they had anticipated the kidnapping of the corpse and had buried it in a secret place. The narrative about Ina Hama Dole is important to show people's way of thinking. They already consider that they all have the same male ancestors; the successive marriages of Hama Dole's mother (whose unmarried name was Hulu Ide) in four domains of Savu give many of them the same ancestress, providing a valuable mnemonic tag for connecting male ancestors throughout Savu.

However, close blood relations did not deter the domains from fighting each other. Hama Dole declared war on Seba during which Hama Dole's son, Muhu Hama, was killed. *Muhu* means war or enemy. The following phrase, taken from a ritual chant, gives details about his tragic death:

Ina Lai Paha's necklace was taken off her neck
to put in the place of the head of Muhu Hama
who was decapitated by the people of Seba.

Figure 11: *Do* Nalai in Dimu

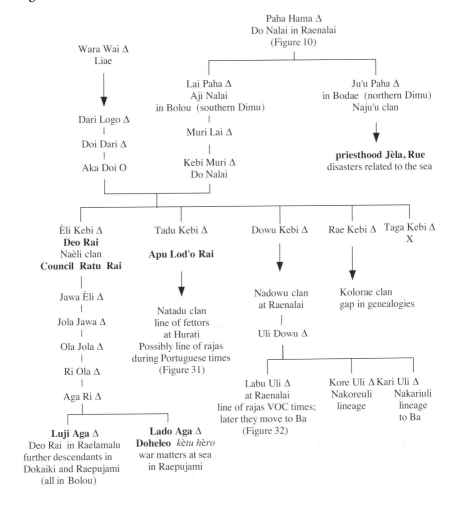

In Hama Dole's time, the clans had not yet been created nor was the territory clearly defined. His sons Paha Hama, the firstborn, and the unfortunate Muhu Hama were the first to divide the land in Dimu between them. The previous division of the island had occurred on each side of the hills into a southern and a northern part—Dida Miha's descendants occupied the southern hill slopes. Those who settled in Dimu created centres roughly in a north-south axis, creating proto-clans.

The descendants of Paha Hama

Paha Hama established himself in the southern part, Bolou (*lou* meaning south). His descendants are known as *do* Nalai (Nalai people) named after the place they lived (Raenalai is derived from the ancestor Lai Paha) and seem to have shared the place with earlier settlers, the Wolo people. The biggest site has three groups of large megaliths—some in the form of tables or dolmens supported by standing stones. The stones might indicate the presence of different settler groups; however, it was not possible to obtain further information. Raenalai is the only place in Savu with dozens of megaliths. One group of ceremonial stones is shaped as the bow of a boat, oriented roughly towards the west, and its head stone is intentionally placed to form a boat prow. There are only two such sites in Savu; at the second place on Kekoro hill (Menia) a megalith symbolises the bow.

The descendants of Paha Hama formed a council of priests known as *Ratu Rai* (Council of the Land). The acting priest in the ritual was also known as *Aji* Nalai. He must have been responsible for a position similar to the priest Deo Rai while his younger brother, Ju'u Paha, began *udu* Naju'u and the position of Rue (Priest of Misfortune). The position is also known as Jèla as it deals with specific disasters and diseases related to the sea. Ju'u Paha seems to have had only daughters, so the position of Rue was in female hands at the beginning.

Later in the line, a descendant's name appears in a narrative related to Portuguese times: he is Lado Aga. His elder brother, Luji Aga, held the position of Deo Rai and lived in Raeiki.[19] Lado Aga received the same position and established himself in Raepujami. To outsiders, Lado Aga is commonly translated as Doheleo (Overseer) known to insiders as Lado Aga Lou—*lou* meaning south but also sea (*laut* [In]) or as Lado Aga Hèro (*hèro* is bitter), a position related to warfare at sea. Thus the Nalai people's priest system has at least two positions

---

[19]   This is still in the southern part of Dimu. His descendants are in the hamlets of Raelamalu, Dokaiki and Raeiki. Information for Dimu's priest positions comes from interviews with Ama Lilo Wadu (11.11.2002); Ama Luka Lena (09.11.2002), and Ama Tada Talo (15.07.2007).

Photo 1. Sacred stones – some in the shape of mini dolmens; Raenalai, Dimu (2017)

Photo 2. A ritual place in the shape of a boat bow; Raenalai, Dimu (2017)

related to the sea: Jèla and Lado Aga Lou. These are reminders of the ancient wars in Dimu between the 'people of the land' and the 'people of the sea'.

Four generations after Paha Hama clans were created for Kebi Muri's four sons: *udu* Naèli for Èli Kebi, in charge of most ritual tasks, and *udu* Natadu for Tadu Kebi, which provided the line of Apu Lod'o in the council of priests and of the *fettors* (executive regents) for political matters.[20] *Udu* Nadowu was created for Dowu Kebi, which is the line of rajas, and *udu* Kolorae for Rae Kebi, a clan which did not rise to power. A fifth son, Taga Hebi, did not have descendants. The Nadowu clan formed lineages, Nakoreuli and Nakariuli for Kari Uli, whose grandson founded the Ba settlement, which was where the Dimu rajas resided during Dutch times.

The descendants of Muhu Hama

The tragic death of Muhu Hama during a war between Dimu and Seba is related to Raeawu village, burned down during the same war.[21] Muhu Hama must have died without having a male descendant as a ritual chant mentions that Paha Hama gave Hire Ao to be adopted as Hire Muhu in order to provide Muhu Hama with a male descent line.[22] The saying is as follows:

> The idea came to Paha Hama
> to take Hire Ao to become Hire Muhu,
> taking the child, leaving the mother.

Such a phrase prevents any contestation of precedence between the brothers. After someone has been adopted, it is not possible to distinguish between biological and adopted children in the genealogies. However, ritual chants trace the events, transmitting the knowledge during ceremonies, especially funerals in which chants recount the happenings of ancient times. Muhu Hama—or the line descended through Hire Muhu—settled in the northern part of Dimu, Bodae (*dae* is north) and formed the proto-clan *do* Napuru (*puru* to come down). The village of Raeawu was rebuilt next to the ancient settlement. Hire Muhu's

---

[20] The term *fettor*, used in Timor and adjacent islands, is probably from the Portuguese *feitor* (overseer).

[21] Raeawu is located west of Kujiratu. *Rae* designates a fenced settlement. Names of settlements and villages are written in one word, although they are often made of several meaningful words such as Raeawu (*Rae Awu* [Village of Ashes]) and Raemoneie (*Rae Mone Ie* [Village of the Ancestor Mone Ie]). *Rae* should not be mixed up with the word *rai* which has several meanings, the most common being land, and refers to a spatial category.

[22] There is no explanation for Hire Ao's origins.

only known descendant is a daughter, Wènyi Hire, indicating the lack of a son to continue the line. Paha Hama's descendants, known first as *do* Nalai with the position of *Aji* Nalai for rituals before the creation of clans, are similar to the descendants of Muhu Hama, *do* Napuru, who created a priest system with *Aji* Dopuru before establishing the Napuru clan. Thus, as seen in Liae, the two parallel priest systems in Dimu have survived until now.

Wènyi Hire had three sons; Raga, Dari and Be'e—the latter mentioned only in some sources as a way to construct the Nabe'e people in Dimu's official genealogies. There was also a daughter, Medo, who married in Belu (West Timor) where she had descendants. The eldest son, Raga Wènyi was Deo Rai. His line created the Natie clan, responsible for most of the Napuru people's ritual positions. The second son, Dari Wènyi, kept the main line of *udu* Napuru at Raeawu and held only one ritual position, Leo Kodo, for taking the heads of enemies. Wènyi Hire as a woman did not have the right to hold land, so land was divided between her sons Raga Wènyi and Dari Wènyi. The act is remembered in an oath stipulating that the brothers could never fight each other, placing a curse on them and their descendants should this ever happen.[23] The third son, Be'e Wènyi, received no share of the land. Later, during Portuguese times, some of Dari Wènyi's descendants shared a site called Kolodihe with the Nabe'e, renaming it Kujiratu with the mantra name *Kujiratu udu ga, ngara ne pejau* (Kujiratu, the good clan whose name is much talked about). The Nabe'e do not have a house of origin at Kujiratu but own part of the site where they have two stones for worship. They kept the right of precedence in rituals which is remembered to the present. In this case, earlier settlers were neither expelled nor exterminated but were gradually pushed aside, losing their land and retaining a symbolic role in rituals without being part of either one of Dimu's two councils of priests. In official genealogies, the Nabe'e lineage descended from Wènyi Hire; however, their descendants remember a divergent past, offering a counter-memory to the official discourse.[24]

Dimu developed a specific terminology for the priest position of Doheleo; these are Lado Aga Hèro for *do* Nalai established in the southern part, Bolou, and Lado Aga Nèta for *do* Napuru in the northern part, Bodae. The months or parts of the months in Dimu's ritual calendar are divided into *nèta* (sweet) and *hèro* (bitter) phases. The domain is also divided in a 'sweet' northern part, Bodae, and a 'bitter' southern part, Bolou. Dimu uses the number six for calculating propitious days in rituals, the lowest number used for rituals on the entire island.

---

[23] Interview with Ama Tada Talo (12.05.2007).

[24] Interviews with Miha Lulu and Lado Bèngu, Nabe'e (23.05.2014).

The same number is used for calculating the ritual days in Raijua, which is not surprising as the people who ruled Dimu originated in Raijua.

When comparing the genealogies of Dimu and Liae, descended from the same ancestor, it appears that the Dimu clans and the councils of priests were created much later. The Seba clans, descended from the younger brother, were formed at about the same time. In Dimu, the clans which rose to power during Portuguese and Dutch times—taking the positions of *fettor* (executive regent) and raja—were shaped seven generations before the first contacts with the Portuguese, later than those of Liae and Seba.

Pole Dida and the Kekoro clan in Menia

In Savu, people attribute another son, Pole Dida, to Dida Miha. Little is known about this ancestor or his son, Wui Pole, and his grandsons Manu Wui and Mone Wui. The famous ancestress Hulu Ide, who married in four domains of Savu, is a descendant of Manu Wui. However, both names repeat and a second Wui Pole appears five generations after the ancestor of the same name. Six of his sons met a violent death. Stones and springs carrying their names form a trail along today's border between Seba and Liae as well as in Sabu Tengah. These tragic deaths took place before the clans were created and the locations act as mnemonic places for these ancestors; each one has a stone for ancestral worship.

People remembering these place names are the descendants of the two surviving children, Manu Wui and Mone Wui, who began the Kekoro-Nadida clan. This clan was not established in Liae, as were the three other clans directly descended from Dida Miha, but on the Kekoro hill, facing the north coast, where the ritual centre is reminiscent of a roughly shaped boat. Not far from the summit there is a large banyan tree and a spring and, halfway down, three segments of a large menhir lie on the ground.[25] Although the place is now deserted, it used to be a significant settlement. One priest position filled by the Kekoro-Nadida clan is that of Deo Mengèru.[26] This area became known later as the domain of Menia whose rulers are descended from the younger brother Ie Miha.

---

[25] Interview with Ama Raja Lele (30.07.2001). The places are known as Kepokewui (the spear of [Wuru] Wui), Èimadakekèli (the spring of Kèli Wui), Jamike (the forest of Ke Wui), Jamiraedète (the forest at the fenced settlement of Dète Wui), Raekai (the fenced settlement of Kai Wui) and Delo (for Delo Wui). One son, Toe Wui, left for Sumba and helped the local raja in warfare. Then he settled in Sumba and joined the Matolang clan.

[26] This position is part of the ritual cycle of Seba and is considered later. See also Table 6 'Large knots of the land' in Appendix II.

Figure 12: *Do* Napuru in Dimu

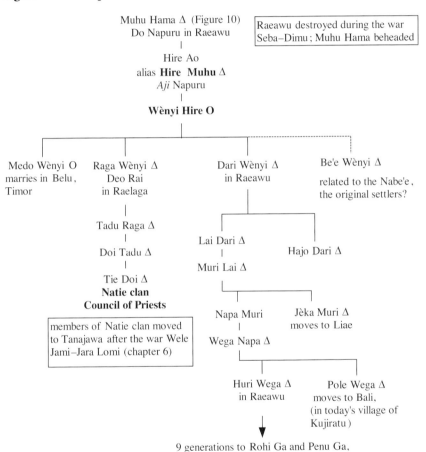

Muhu Hama Δ (Figure 10)
Do Napuru in Raeawu

Raeawu destroyed during the war
Seba–Dimu; Muhu Hama beheaded

Hire Ao
alias **Hire Muhu** Δ
Aji Napuru

Wènyi Hire O

Medo Wènyi O
marries in Belu,
Timor

Raga Wènyi Δ
Deo Rai
in Raelaga

Tadu Raga Δ

Doi Tadu Δ

Tie Doi Δ
Natie clan
Council of Priests

members of Natie clan moved
to Tanajawa after the war Wele
Jami–Jara Lomi (chapter 6)

Dari Wènyi Δ
in Raeawu

Be'e Wènyi Δ

related to the Nabe'e,
the original settlers?

Lai Dari Δ

Hajo Dari Δ

Muri Lai Δ

Napa Muri

Jèka Muri Δ
moves to Liae

Wega Napa Δ

Huri Wega Δ
in Raeawu

Pole Wega Δ
moves to Bali,
(in today's village of
Kujiratu)

9 generations to Rohi Ga and Penu Ga,
the founders of Kujiratu (Figure 33)

Some sources indicate that a certain Tanu Leslo of West Timor arrived in Savu and was adopted as Tadu Rebo, replacing an ancestor who had vanished. This narrative seems to be a construction in the younger brother's genealogy. The descendants of Tadu Rebo formed a new Kekoro clan with three branches: Kekoro-Melagu, Kekoro-Lokoae and Kekoro-Raepudi for the rajas of Menia, absorbing parts of the Kekoro-Nadida traditional land. However, an ancient group of settlers, the Hai'iki people (already mentioned – *hai* meaning landing place and *iki* is small) had occupied the flat land of Menia; they lived near the sea from which they derived their living. After they disappeared, the Nabe'e people of Dimu settled in the area. When the Kekoro clan later moved from the hills to the Menia flat land, they did not settle in a virgin territory; they shared the land with the Nabe'e.[27] In the 19th century, Seba absorbed Menia, so it is difficult to reconstruct Menia's past.

The descendants of Dida Miha in Lower Mesara

Dida Miha's descendants, who established themselves in Lower Mesara, possibly originated from the Teriwu clan of Liae, or from Tadu Rebo's descendants of Menia's Kekoro clan, or from the Lobo clan of Raijua. They are considered latecomers in Mesara.

One of Dida Miha's children is Pojo Dida. People say he went to the island of Flores where he apparently helped a local ruler, Ara Kia, in a war against another leader, Raja Ara Boro. Pojo Dida married Wènyi Ara, Ara Kia's daughter, and stayed in Flores.[28] Sometimes settlers coming from Flores are said to be the descendants of Pojo Dida. Doke Lele is one of them. As he returned to Savu, Lod'o Ga Hawu of Mesara was at war and asked Doke Lele for help. After Lod'o Ga was victorious, Doke Lele received land in Hipi in Tanajawa village. Later he was killed at a rock shelter, Liedokelele, which has since carried his name. Lod'o Ga Hawu had no male heir but his adopted daughter, Depi Lod'o, received a plot of land from him known as Hipi. This land became part of a new clan, Haba Dida, established in Tanajawa.[29]

---

[27] Interviews with Miha Lulu and Lado Bèngu, Nabe'e (23.05.2014). According to interviewee Nguru Nape (18.05.2014), the Gopo clan of Liae has a lineage called Hai'iki whose members live in the flat land of Helapaji, along the coast.

[28] Interviews with Ama Jula Lede (27.07.2001) and Ama Raja Lele (30.07.2001). *Arakia* is a generic name for rulers in Flores (Stefan Dietrich, personal communication; 1996). However, the Kekoro clan also claims an ancestor called Pojo Dida. Some sources say Pojo Dida's descendants stayed in Lederaga in the domain of Mesara. A certain Doke Lele Dodo Dida is part of Mesara's history.

[29] See Figure 8.

Figure 13: Early Kekoro clan genealogies in Menia

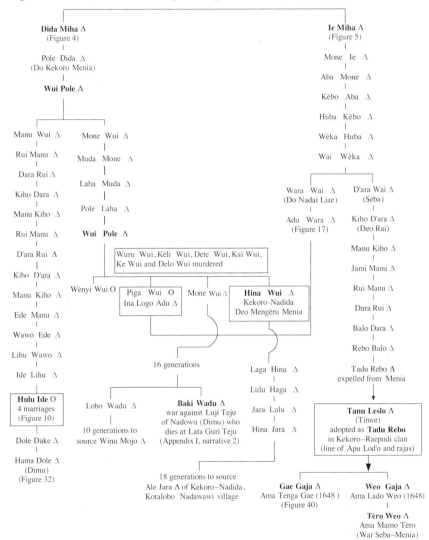

Figure 14: Tadu Rebo; relationships between clans in Menia, Mesara and Seba

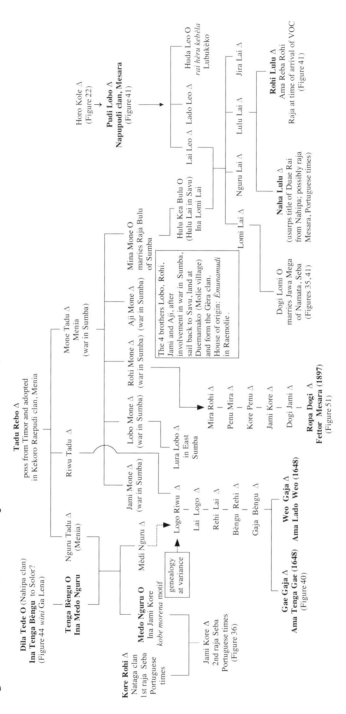

Some of the sons and grandsons of Tadu Rebo from Menia left for east Sumba. Of interest is that a clan (*kabihu*) called Mehara (Mesara) was created in the area of Mangili, showing an ancient relationship between Savu and Sumba. Some of Tadu Rebo's sons or grandsons moved to Mesara and founded the Gèra clan in the villages of Molie and Tanajawa.[30] Two more groups of settlers came to Lower Mesara; one was the Rohaba clan which exists on both sides of the Raijua Strait; the second was the Aelape clan, a branch of the Lobo clan of Raijua. Contemporary to Mata Lai of Seba, Horo Nani of the Lobo clan in Raijua helped the Namata clan in a conflict with Dimu. As is often mentioned about ancient wars, it was not a violent fight—the conflict was won through trickery.[31]

The descendants of Dida Miha in Raijua

Raijuanese refer to themselves *Do* Hawu or Savu people; in Savu they are also known as *Niki-niki Maja, niki* being a shorten form of *ana iki* (small child). Maja is the name of an enigmatic figure connected with Wango spirits. As mentioned above, the Raijua people claim that the story of Dida Miha took place at the western end of their island, near the seashore where they worship at flat stones associated with him and his younger brother Ie Miha. The area also has caves which could have offered shelter to these early ancestors. One might wonder why Dida Miha stayed in unprotected low-lying land near the sea instead of establishing himself on one of Raijua's steep hills such as Kolohaba, Kolorae or Ketita. Were these hills already occupied by earlier migrants?

Nevertheless, Raijuanese concede that Dida Miha's son, Rede Dida, lived in Savu while his other children lived in Raijua. Indeed, the quality of information gathered about Rede Dida and his descendants in Liae fully sustains this view. Dida Miha's children in Raijua received a variety of names. Three are considered here: Dode (or Node) Dida from the Ketita clan, Ngari Dida for Nadega and Hu'e Dida whose descendants formed the Lobo clan. The clans formed by the elder brother Dida Miha's descendants are in Upper Raijua and the west of the island while those descended from the younger brother, Ie Miha, settled in Lower Raijua and in the island's eastern part. In popular memory, Upper and Lower Raijua were continuously at war until Wore Baha reconciled them. In Savu, while the two brothers divided the island into north and south, geographical features were decisive for the organisation of settlements. And yet in both Savu

---

[30] See Figure 14.

[31] See Appendix I, Narrative 2 recounted by Ama Nico Ratu of Lobohede, a descendant of Horo Nani.

Figure 15: Clans descended from Dida Miha in Raijua

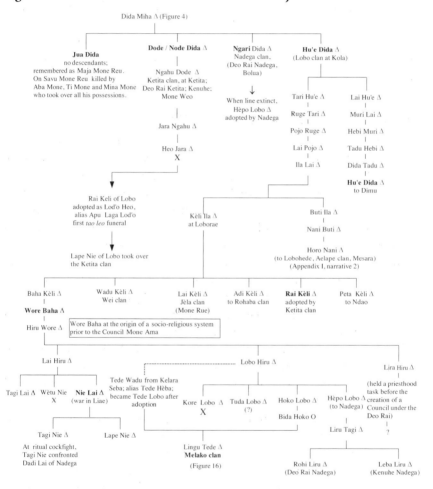

and Raijua an east-west axis corresponds to the layout of fenced villages (*rae*) and their houses. It seems that in Savu there was enough space for all inhabitants so the two groups were not constantly at each other's throats, as the Raijua narratives seem to indicate.

Ketita

The steep hill of Ketita is considered the most ancient and revered location in Raijua, located in today's Bolua village. The Ketita line became extinct only four generations after Dode Dida, at the time of Heo Jara (Nine Horses). Rai Kèli of the Lobo clan took over the Ketita clan's line under the name Lod'o Heo (Nine Suns). However, when comparing genealogies, Rai Kèli lived eight generations after Dida Miha, revealing a discrepancy of four generations, which is odd for such a short time span. The most elaborate form of funeral known as *tao leo* was first held for Apu Laga Lod'o (Lod'o Heo) at Ketita.[32] At that time, gongs were not yet known. Instead, people beat stone slabs which when struck give different frequencies; these might be similar to stone chimes found in tombs in Ancient China. Sources from the Lobo clan assert that today's members of the Ketita clan are descended from their ancestors.

The Ketita site provides interesting information and raises questions. Today only four houses remain, built as in Savu, on an east-west axis. When entering Ketita through the northern gate there is only one house left on the right side, *èmu* (house) Bèni Dèla, and the remnant of another house unrelated to any ritual role. On the left side, first in a line is *èmu* Maja then *èmu* Rato where the priest Kenuhe resides today. The next house has only the foundation stones left; it belonged to a lineage of the Nadega clan. The fourth house is for the priest position of Mone Weo. The fifth and most southern house (*èmu* Kehale) is no longer standing. Of interest is that the present links to the narratives of the past: at the same location is the house of Mone Weo, an ancient and revered ancestor, and the house of turbulent Maja, who caused Mone Weo to leave the island.[33]

A major difference is immediately noticeable regarding Maja's house: the direction it faces. As all sacrifices made to Maja serve the purpose to calm him, he is associated with Wango spirits and is feared in the archipelago. It is the reason why Maja's ritual house was built to face the opposite direction; away from the

---

[32] In other sources, he is Ama Laga Lado Weo (Magnificent Crown). The story of the first *tao leo* funeral at Ketita is also remembered in connection with Mau Alo (*udu* Nadaibu) who brought a red buffalo for the funeral. However, there are discrepancies in the genealogies. Various narratives about Ketita may have been compressed into one story.

[33] According to Kagiya (2010: 86), Mone Weo was the ruler of Raijua when Maja arrived.

centre of the village. In contrast, Mone Weo is remembered through the ritual role of the same name and through the annual ceremony that launches a boat loaded with offerings after harvest (*kowa Mone Weo*), said to sail to wherever he resides so he has enough food. People show opposite attitudes towards Maja and Mone Weo.

Nadega

Either one of Dida Miha's sons or one of his grandsons is at the origin of the Nadega clan. Raenadega is located in today's Bolua village near the limits between Upper and Lower Raijua. Twelve generations after Dida Miha this line too became extinct; Weo Ai (Great Fire) was killed and Hèpo Lobo of the Lobo clan was adopted (*hapo*) by the Nadega clan. Therefore, members of the Lobo clan controlled both the Ketita and Nadega clans which then avoided extinction.

Lobo

The Lobo clan thrived for most of the twelve generations following Dida Miha with the Hu'e Dida line, his members strengthening other clans. A descendant of his, carrying the same name, is at the origin of most of Dimu's clans. A key ancestor, Wore Baha who lived nine generations after Dida Miha, organised Raijua's customary law and established a priest system that ruled the island prior to the Council *Mone Ama*, as it is known today. A series of linking narratives recounts events referring to Wore Baha's time: the first narrative involves tapping the sap of the lontar tree; the second, the search for a golden fishing hook which ends with the new social organisation in Raijua, introduced by the comment *lagu pana uku rai d'i* (the sacred chant about our customary law).

Wore Baha and Ama Lado Ga[34]

Wore Baha's narrative of the golden fish hook:

> Pedi derived his living from tapping the sap of lontar trees.[35] One day he had already collected the sap of several trees and each time left the bucket containing the harvested sap at the foot of each tree while he climbed.

---

[34] Interview with Ama Mau Hude (23.04.2013). In the Indonesian version of the story, Ama Lado Ga (Great Crown) is also mentioned as *Raja Laut* (King of the Sea [In]).

[35] Pudi Tie in Kagiya (2010: 48) recounts a similar version of the golden fishing hook story. Pedi is considered the elder. There are narratives about a golden fishing hook in various societies of eastern Indonesia; for instance, in Bima, Flores, Alor, Timor and Kei islands. See Hicks (2017: 260–7).

When he came down the bucket had been kicked over by a goat which wanted to drink the sap. He held Pehuhu, a shepherd who was nearby, responsible for the spillage and requested that he replace the sap. Pehuhu started to dig at the place and found a spring at the foot of the tree, so he replaced the sap with water. As water is scarce in Raijua, Pedi was lucky that Pehuhu had found a spring for him and they became friends.

Sometime later Pedi and Pehuhu went fishing. Pehuhu had a golden hook (*kai mela*) and used pork meat as bait. Pedi used a silver hook (*kai mela pudi*) and used a squid. Alas, a fish ate the squid and the hook, and broke the line, so Pedi asked Pehuhu for his golden hook. Pehuhu told him that if he lost the hook he had to replace it. Again a fish ate the hook breaking the line. Pedi went to the sea looking for a way to replace the golden hook. He could find neither a golden hook nor gold to replace it. He stayed at the seashore full of sadness and feared meeting Pehuhu.

One day Wore Baha of the Lobo clan came by and asked Pedi why he was at the seashore, and why he was so sad. Pedi told him his story and Wore Baha told him to stay there and wait for him. Wore Baha went home, took his fishing hook, met Pedi again and asked him to follow him to sea to look for the golden fishing hook. They went to sea and spent a long time looking for the fish that ate the golden hook. Finally, they met Ama Lado Ga (Great Crown). Wondering about the two men's presence he asked what was the trouble on land that his visitors were roaming the seas. They told him that there was no particular trouble on land, but that they were looking for a lost fishing hook. Ama Lado Ga knew nothing about it, but said that his daughter had been sick for quite some time—she could no longer eat—and asked his visitors if they could do something for her. Wore Baha was willing to try and entered the house, examined the girl, felt the hook and took it out of her stomach, immediately hiding the golden hook in the knot of his hip cloth. He came out showing his own hook and announced that the girl was cured. Indeed, soon after the daughter recovered and was eating again. Ama Lado Ga asked Wore Baha what he wanted for his help. Wore Baha did not want anything. Ama Lado Ga asked them if there were *kepaka* trees on land.[36] They said no. Ama Lado Ga gave them a branch of *kepaka* and a kind of drum filled with all sorts of things, among them pieces of bamboo.

They came back to Raijua pulling the drum with the branch of *kepaka*. Wore Baha told all the clans to come together. The *kepaka* branch was planted upside down at a place called Ngararai (Name of the Land). Then a fire was made and the drum and its contents burned. Inside the container were all sorts of metal tools. Wore Baha asked each 'clan' to take one tool, but nobody did so because the tools were hot. Finally, Wore Baha gave a tool to each of the 'clans' and each was assigned a religious and political task at the same time. Since this time, warfare between the

---

[36] *Sterculia foetida*, also known as *nita/nitas* (In) and as Java olive.

clans was forbidden and replaced by a ritual cockfight. Each clan brings
the tool it received from Wore Baha to the annual ritual cockfight which
takes place in the month Daba Ae (April).

The verb *woro/wore* means 'to bring together', 'to assemble' and *baha* means
peaceful. Thus, Wore Baha is remembered as the person who brought all the
groups of people together (proto-clans) and united them peacefully. It shows that
all the clans in Raijua accepted Wore Baha's choice; it explains the foreign origin
of metal tools, that is, new categories of weapons in Raijua. The narrative about
the replacement of inter-clan wars with ritual cockfights is linked to protagonists
of the widely known tale of the golden fishing hook. From a local point of view,
the technique for tapping the sap of the lontar palm tree was already known and
practised on the island. Wore Baha lived nine generations after Dida Miha and
about 22 generations before the present.

Although in an idealised discourse the conflicts between Upper and Lower
Raijua ended with Wore Baha, another tale about his great grandson, Nie Lai,
recounts a violent confrontation between the Lobo and Nadega clans. It means
the end of Raijua's inter-clan wars and the creation of a ritual cockfight as a war
substitute must be placed later in Raijua's history. As Nie Lai of Raijua's story
interferes with the history of Liae, the narrative is recounted below:

> One night Wètu Nie was murdered. Nobody knew who killed him. After
> his funeral, his father, Nie Lai, wanted to find out who murdered his son.
> First, he asked the spirit Wango but did not receive an answer. Then he
> went to the sky and asked Apu Lod'o Liru, who told him that his son had
> been decapitated (*lore*) by Weo Ai.[37] Nie Lai asked Apu Lod'o Liru to give
> him the necessary sacred knowledge to seek revenge for his son's death.
> Apu Lod'o told him to go back to Raelobo, his village of origin, and to
> sacrifice a number of animals—a black boar and a red sow, a red rooster
> and a red dog, a red goat and a sheep—and to go to the warriors' house
> and sleep there.
>
> The next morning on the sacrificial stone there was a lance (*kepoke*) with
> the mantra name *ladole*, a sword (*hemala*) with the mantra name *pungèlu*,
> and a shield (*tami*). Besides, Nie Lai's horse received the mantra name
> *winga le li ta j'ège, li ta b'ole rohe* (Looked after with great care, can't be
> disturbed).
>
> The lance had the power to pierce eight people at once and return to
> its owner. Nie Lai went to Weo Ai and declared him his enemy. They
> confronted each other, Weo Ai standing high on a flat stone [dolmen] at
> the eastern gate of Nadega village and Nie Lai standing on a stone in the

---

[37] Weo Ai is from the Nadega clan, but his genealogy could not be recorded. There are 18
generations between Tagi Nie and the present.

village of Lobo. First, Weo Ai threw stones at Nie Lai, but they did not hit him; the stones hit the hill next to him which then collapsed. As Nie Lai threw his lance, Weo Ai tried to find a shelter and entered the space under his stone, but the lance pierced him from the rear to the head. Then the spear came back to Nie Lai. As a consequence, the Lobo clan received half of the space in Nadega village.[38] Weo Ai's defeat marked the end of the war between the Lobo and Nadega clans, as well as that between Upper and Lower Raijua.

Then Nie Lai left for Liae in Savu which was at war with Seba. There the raja of Lielabu asked for his help. Nie Lai asked for a red pig and a red goat, and returned to Raijua to take his spear and sword, pray and carry out the necessary ritual that would enable him to win against his enemies.

Back in Liae, Nie Lai threw his spear which on the first day of the fight immediately killed eight people in Seba and returned to his hand. He successfully threw his spear three times. On the second day he threw his spear twice and on the third day once with the same success; it was enough for the Seba people to disband. Nie Lai asked for Bèni Migi, the raja of Lielabu's daughter in Liae. Then Nie Lai stayed in Liae until his son, Lape Nie, was big enough to follow him to Raijua. The mother, Bèni Migi, stayed in Liae.

There is a saying in Raijua that the name of Ledeke village in Liae was derived from the name of Ledeke village in Raijua and that the name is linked to Nie Lai. However, this is not remembered in Liae. Later, Lape Nie was adopted by Tua Kai, the younger brother Ie Miha's descendant; thereafter, Tua Kai had two sons, Lape Tua and Lai Tua.

The most important message of both narratives is the fact that warfare was replaced by two ritual cockfights organised on two consecutive days at the limits between Upper and Lower Raijua (Plates 11, 12). The arena chosen for the first day is called Daba ae, in the centre of which a large flat stone supported by short standing stones acts as a memorial for those who died a violent death. In Savu and Raijua, such mini-dolmens act as memorials and do not necessarily carry the name of the person(s) remembered there but have a generic name, *wowadu turu*. On the second day, the cockfight takes place at Dèiwei, in the same vicinity as Daba ae and Ngararai. At the cockfight arena, clans in their order of formation and each *kebihu* (temporary grouping) bring offerings to the sacred stone in the centre of the arena. The first confrontation has to take place between the *kebihu*

---

[38] Raelobo and Raenadega are not far from each other. For certain rituals, members of the Lobo clan do not assemble in their village of origin but in Raenadega before marching to the ceremonial place (for example for *nau'u ruju* [harpooning a manatee] two days before a full moon in the month Daba Ae).

of the Deo Rai from the Nadega clan (Upper Raijua) and the *kebihu* of the Apu Lod'o from the Nadaibu clan (Lower Raijua) as a reminder of past wars.

For ritual cockfights, participants are not organised according to their clans but according to temporary groupings or *kebihu*. The term is reminiscent of *kabisu* in Sumba where it is the general word for clan. *Kebihu* is a grouping of people, smaller than a clan, shaped for cockfight purposes only. Each kebihu has an *ada manu* (small hut) newly built every year. There, holding their paraphernalia and their roosters, men address prayers to their ancestors before departing as a group, marching one behind the other to the cockfight arena. Later the group has to disband from the same place. During the fights, female relatives of the leader stay at the *ada manu* spinning cotton threads, channelling prayers to the ancestors for the success of their *kebihu*. Every few years new *kebihu* are formed in order to avoid tensions between the clans. After two days of ritual cockfights, recreational cockfights, involving money, take place each day until the end of the month, changing location every day, alternating places in Upper and Lower Raijua, each time confronting *kebihu* of Upper Raijua with *kebihu* of Lower Raijua.[39]

Melako

Wore Baha's grandson, Lobo Hiru, is remembered as having four sons: Kore Lobo, Tuda Lobo, Hoko Lobo and Hèpo Lobo (who was adopted by the Nadega clan, as seen above). Lobo Hiru had 'lost' a son to another clan but gained one from Savu. One day a man called Tede Wadu from the Kelara clan of Seba appeared in Raijua.[40] He had fled Savu by swimming to the shores of Raijua where he was hiding in a cave when Tuda Lobo found him and brought him to his father. Tede Wadu married Hoko Lobo's daughter, Bida Hoko, and was adopted into the Lobo clan. Their son, Lingu Tede, decided to break away and created a new clan called Melako. In popular memory, Melako is said to have been formed by four 'brothers'. These are in fact the grandchildren and great grandchildren of Lingu Tede. They are Lele Gai, for the lineage Nalele, Talo Gai for Natalo, Dedi Raba for Nabèlu and Lai Lulu for Nawèli.

The name of the clan and that of some of its founding members raise questions. Melako is a reminder of Malaka, and Talo of the former kingdom of Talo in South Sulawesi. The formation of clans in Raijua is clearly linked to adoptions and very possibly to foreign additions. The Melako clan and the Kekoro clan of Menia both identify with either the elder brother's line because of

---

[39] See Table 2 'The knots of the land in Liae' in Appendix II.

[40] In the narratives he is also known as Tede Hèba – Hèba meaning Seba.

Figure 16: Lingu Tede and the Melako clan in Raijua

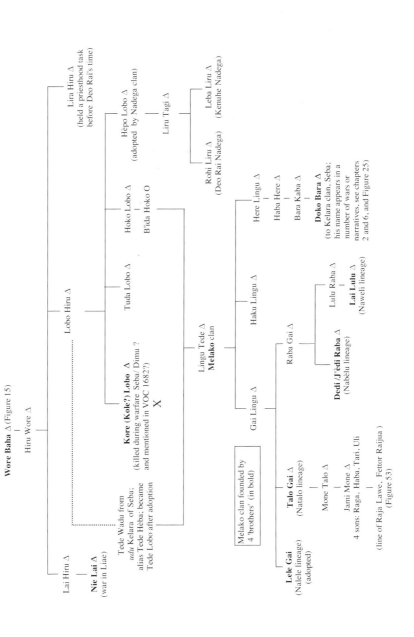

Tede Hèba's adoption by the Lobo clan or the line of the younger brother, as Tede Hèba was originally from Seba's Kelara clan but separated from the Lobo clan.

To conclude, the chapter makes a number of important points. The genealogy for Dida Miha's descendants (Figure 8) diverges from the genealogy Detaq published (1973: 53). There the matrifocal groups (*hubi ae* and *hubi iki*) were created about twelve generations after the apical ancestor Kika Ga, at the time of Babo Rede, Dida Miha Ngara's grandson. In such a case, the formation of clans coincides with the creation of female moieties. In the 1990s, Detaq's booklet *Meperkenalkan kebudayaan orang Sabu* (Introducing Savunese Culture) was accessible on the island, so in official discourse people explained that Muji Babo and Lou Babo were the daughters of Babo Rede Dida of Teriwu in Liae.[41] It is common knowledge that the moieties *hubi ae* and *hubi iki* divided the society into two matrifocal groups. Consequently, one may wonder about the moiety status of women over the twelve generations between Kika Ga and Babo Rede Dida. It prompted the question several times during fieldwork until knowledgeable elders in different groups revealed the moieties' creation as belonging to the mantra genealogies prior to the arrival of the ancestor Kika Ga (Figure 2). The start of the two maternal lines contemporary with Dida Miha's grandson seems to be a construction. Here is one more element to demonstrate today's desire to position everything in Savu's history after Kika Ga arrived, as he has to be the first ancestor.

Most narratives highlight male cultural figures; however, women's names occur from time to time providing precious information when male and female genealogies are compared. For instance, Hulu Ide, who married in all four domains of Savu, established an important connection or time marker in Savu thought, linking important figures at one generational level throughout the island. It is not a matter of whether the story is true or constructed; this is how Savu people see and remember their past. For them, it is a fact used for building the genealogical 'scaffolding' of all domains. They are concerned with having a coherent structure which is reasserted at different stages of their history; they are all one people, constantly connected.

The first council of priests, *Ratu Mone Tèlu* (Council of Three Men), coincides with the formation of proto-clans with the label *do* (people). At that point, the clans did not yet exist, but areas were identified with the different proto-clans. During this time, it is remarkable that no foreign personal names, such as Jawa, Mega, Talo, Nguru (Guru) or Hina (China), appear in the genealogies while later

---

[41] The name Babo Rede exists in the mantra genealogies where he is Babo Rede Moto (Figure 2) as well as in genealogies descended from Kika Ga (Babo Rede Dida Miha Ngara and Babo Rede Dida Miha Aji Mata) as shown in Figure 8. In Detaq he is Babo Rede Dida Miha Ngara.

they become common. The only names of possible foreign origin were *ratu* for the councils and *aji* for their acting priests.[42] *Ratu* underwent changes, revealing the struggle for power and the exercise of active counter-power. It is clear that there was no single priest system for each domain, contrary to what has been stated so far by Detaq (1973: 19), Fox (1977: 85) and Kaho (2005: 67–70). It is a common saying in Savu which does not find confirmation through observation, and attendance at rituals and ceremonies.

The formation of clans occurred first in Liae. It implies that other descendants of Dida Miha were not strong enough to establish their own clans and they shared the space with earlier settlers who were gradually pushed aside. The landscape is divided into east and west in all domains except in Dimu where for topographical reasons the spatial organisation on a north-south axis prevails. In chapter 3, after following the younger brother Ie Miha's descendants, further analysis compares all of the clans and councils of priests. However, it is already clear that the study of how Raijua's clans formed contradicts two widespread ideas. First of all, Raijua's precedence over Savu cannot be confirmed. The tale about the theft of soil from Raijua to create Savu, uniting two Savunese mountains, is not known in Raijua and is not widely shared in Savu either; it is only heard in Mesara. Secondly, the reason for the nickname 'Niki-Niki Maja' when referring to the Raijuanese is unclear. The term, descended from members of the Majapahit Empire which ruled over Indonesian seas until the 15th century, has no validation through observation and analysis of the genealogies except if either Wore Baha, who is at the origin of the social organisation in Raijua, or Lado Ga (Raja Laut [King of the Seas]) is from the Majapahit Empire. Although Raijuanese are comfortable with the name 'Niki-Niki Maja', they fall short of justifying the label; it was never clearly stated during interviews or while recording genealogies. Raijuanese acknowledge the same origin as the Savunese. In fact, they call themselves '*Do* Hawu' and their customary or *adat* law is *uku rai Hawu*. Chapter 4 considers the possible Majapahit connections.

---

[42] *Ratu* might be as well related to the Austronesian word *datu* (James Fox, personal communication; 25.02.2017).

Chapter 3

The Descendants of the Younger Brother

The descendants of Dida Miha's younger brother Ie Miha also settled across the Savu islands, forming clans and priest positions before the arrival of Europeans. The chapter examines two key aspects: the concept of precedence and the categories 'people of the sea' and 'people of the land'.

While Dida Miha's descendants organised a council (*ratu*) there is no similar memory for the descendants of his younger brother Ie Miha. At that stage of their history, little is known about the first generations. The lack of evidence questions collective memory and the claim that Dida Miha and Ie Miha were uterine brothers. Nevertheless, without external contemporary substantiation, the past presented thus far in the book is from the indigenous point of view and considers local assessments.

Like Dida Miha, his younger brother Ie Miha married a 'woman from the sea' named Huri Ga. He left Teriwu, where a sacred stone placed in a cave commemorates him, and went to Lededai'ie (the hill where Ie arrives) a safe and strategically well-located place with good access to water. Irrigation works were conducted in the area in 1974. The construction process unearthed two bronze axes, a sign that the location had long been inhabited. Unfortunately, as the site had been disturbed, archaeological research was no longer possible, so the bronze tools remain undated.[1] Halfway down the hill an important spring runs through limestone, leaving a narrow passage between the rocks to Lededai'ie. One of the pools that formed in the limestone is said to have been the 'bathtub' of Mamo Miha. *Mamo* means shady, hiding and cool. The name is eminently female and associated with clouds and rain. There was no further explanation about her or how she is related to Ie Miha.[2] Where Ie Miha's son, Mone Ie

---

[1] The farmer's son, who found one of the axes, explained that it was in a white stone which then opened to release the axe. This alludes to the mould in which the bronze was cast. One axe is in Kupang's provincial museum; the second axe could not be located.

[2] According to Leba Alu, Seba (27.03.1999), she was Dida Miha's sister. However, her name does not appear in the female genealogies. Rain worship is often associated with Mamo Hina (*Hina* is Chinese). By extension, Mamo Miha is also associated with rain.

(Good Man), went is not clear, though a hamlet called Raemoneie (Mone Ie's Village), halfway between Teriwu and Lededai'ie, is apparently named after him.[3] Further downhill, near the northern coast, a sacred stone commemorates him at Gurikebau (Dead Buffalos), near Wègamengèru (Prosperous Banyan Tree) and Pururede (Come Down Full). These locations were the settlements for a number of Ie Miha's descendants until the time of Robo Aba, eleven generations later; they contain sacred stones worshipped at various times of the year.

People remember Mone Ie and his children in several stories. They killed an ancient settler, Mone Reu, who gave them a number of domesticated animals before he died. One son, Ti Mone, migrated to Rote and another, Bune Mone, to the south coast of Sulawesi. Sources in Mesara, Dimu and Raijua claim that Mone Ie had a no biological descent line and that his son Aba Mone was adopted. One story refers to an eagle piercing Aba Mone's eyes and heart when he was still a child.[4] The eagle was caught and only set free after promising to give Aba Mone's sight back. The eagle then went to the sea and took the eyes of a shark, which has since been called 'the blind shark'.[5] In exchange, the eagle requested that Mone Ie and his descendants build their houses with extended roof ridges on either end, as they are today.[6] Finally, rats killed the eagle. In another narrative, when Aba Mone was born his mother's relatives arrived, bringing a dog with them. While the mother and the newborn were asleep, they exchanged the baby for the dog. The relatives took Aba Mone to a cave, placed him in a giant clam, covered his mouth and ears, and said prayers. Ama Jo Haba, whose Seba ancestors moved to Mesara, connects this story with a common phrase. When a child is born Ie Miha's descendants say *metana ana ngaka* (a puppy is born).[7] It is probably no longer possible to decode these messages except to confirm that Aba Mone was Mone Ie's adopted son. This clearly excludes Ie Miha's line from any claim for precedence. *Aba* means to protect or to provide shelter and Aba Mone is considered the first priest for Ie Miha's descendants. The time of Mone Ie and his children is linked to a religious leader, domesticated animals and new architecture for houses, all of which point to external influences.

For the next three generations, there are no memories of particular events. Apparently, people stayed near the northern coast and dedicated stones to the

---

[3] However, the Teriwu people named Raemoneie as their ancient arena for ritual cockfights until they were defeated by Seba (chapter 2).

[4] See Detaq (1973: 47–8); Duggan (2001: 83).

[5] In Indonesian, *hiu buta* is the common name for the leopard shark (James Fox, personal communication; 25.02.2017).

[6] See Plate 5 for an example of a roof ridge.

[7] Interview with Ama Jo Haba (15.11.2002).

contemporary ancestors. People still worship there today. It seems they were not scared either by the possibility of invasions from the sea or by tsunamis, the place being much more exposed to danger than, for example, Lededai'ie where Ie Miha lived. One reason or why Ie Miha's descendants moved to an unprotected location might be that other settlers were already occupying the hills.

Four buffalos

The story of the four buffalos is a mnemonic tag for explaining the first division of the land in Savu between Ie Miha's descendants. It is linked to the ancestor Wai Wèka (Old Belt) who had four sons, D'ara Wai, Kole Wai, Wara Wai and Lèki Wai, and possibly another son, Jèka Wai. The latter did not take part in the land division: instead he went to Raijua and married there.[8] In collective memory, when Wai Wèka was old (*wèka*) or after he passed away, the land was divided into four parts according to the paths taken by his four buffalos. Each son chose an animal and the four buffalos were set free at midnight from the top of Ledeperihi, an important mountain in early narratives. Each son followed his respective buffalo and, wherever the buffalo went, that land then belonged to him. D'ara Wai's buffalo walked to Seba, Kole Wai's to Mesara, Wara Wai's to Liae and Lèki Wai's buffalo to Dimu. It explains why descendants of these ancestors are there today.

From other narratives about this time, the buffalos must have walked towards Seba as three of the sons ended up in Mèba (Seba). D'ara Wai, whose buffalo arrived at Mèba, sent his brother Wara Wai away. Nguru Nape of Liae, a descendant of Wara Wai, recounted these details in the following narrative:

"Au ri we na kebau au ri we la bira Dimu haku owe" ane D'ara Wai. Haku ta d'ae tange d'e ne kebau ne, do ju mèke la lete ngèlu bahagia bira Dimu pewata Hèba nga Liae, èi mili Liae nga Hèba.	"Let's exchange our buffalos and you go towards the east" D'ara Wai said. Wara Wai hardly looked at the buffalo. He agreed and went in the direction of the east wind to the border of Seba and Liae where the rain water flows towards Liae as well as towards Seba.

After building a village on a hill where the water flows towards the south and the north coast, Wara Wai held a ceremony. While pouring coconut water (*ta luna*) on his head for purification, he named the new village

---

[8] According to Ama Jo Haba's interview (19.04.2006), Jèka Wai was a later settler; he appears in a narrative recounted in chapter 4.

Maluna. Two stones are memorials for the two brothers; one on the east side for D'ara Wai and one on the west side for Wara Wai. The place is uninhabited now.[9] Wara Wai's descendants in Liae are mainly in the villages of Ledeke, Raewiu, Èilogo, Daba and Deme. In Deme, the first settlers lived near the Èimada Ae spring but later moved to Kolorame hill. It is the ritual place for Wara Wai's descendants in Liae, with one of the domain's two ritual cockfight arenas.

The descendants of Wara Wai and the Council of Seven Men in Liae

Wara Wai's descendants in Liae are known as *do* Nadai.[10] There is no explanation for the origin of the name Nadai. *Na* means child and is often used to name a clan or a lineage, but no name is linked to *dai*.[11] *Do* Nadai refers to a first grouping of people before the formation of clans, similar to cases seen in Liae, Dimu and Raijua for Dida Miha's descendants. Of importance is that one of Wara Wai's sons, Adu Wara, married Piga Wui, descended from Pole Dida Miha. The alliance cemented relations between descendants of the two apical brothers in Liae. Piga Wui is known as Ina Kore Adu and a spring in Deme—Èimadanakore—bears her name. Piga Wui, alias Ina Kore Adu, lived eight generations after Dida Miha and her husband lived eight generations after Ie Miha.[12] Out of the union seven sons were born: three of them, Logo Adu (Nahai, Narega and Narebo clans), Tiga Adu (Nanawa clan) and Ngara Adu (Napujara clan) stayed and thrived in Liae, while Pia Adu moved to Raijua, Bèlu Adu to Mesara and Jèka Adu to Seba. Kore Adu did not have descendants.

The Nanawa clan was formed contemporary to Nawa Radi, five generations after Adu Wara; in local memory the clan provided the rajas during Portuguese times. It received the priest role of Apu Lod'o (Descendant of the Sun) from Deo Mengèru of the Kolorae clan, as well as a piece of land, and a copper stove (*tungku dari tembaga* [In]), attributed to his assignment. Considering that rituals should use only objects and plants indigenous to the island, the existence of

---

[9] Maluna is often mentioned in narratives. Now it is part of Raenalulu village, not far from Kehanga and Nauru, which has Lumu Lutu's 'petrified boat' (Kolorae clan of Liae).

[10] Main sources for Liae are Nguru Nape (alias Ama Uju Nguru), Migu Lutu, Ama Jari, Ama Koro Ga and Hege Wila.

[11] *Dai* is a winnow; *d'ai* means to arrive. This meaning would be convenient as it designates a newly arrived group. However, the pronunciation and meaning are rejected locally. See Figure 17.

[12] In the genealogies she is also known as Ina Logo Adu as Kore Adu did not have descendants.

a stove of foreign origin is unusual.[13] Knowing the rivalries recounted in the previous chapter between the different councils and the 'sky-sea-earth war', one might question the authenticity of one group's 'gift' of a ritual position and land to another. It is very plausible that *udu* Kolorae lost the position of Apu Lod'o to Nanawa, which in turn lost it in the 17th century to the Napujara clan. For generations, each position handover was accompanied by the transfer of the copper stove. When the last Apu Lod'o, Jara Lado, passed away in 2001, the succession was open. A potential candidate declined to take on the role when he realised that the copper stove was missing; he did not want to assume a task without its symbolic attribute. Since then, the role has been offered once again to members of the Nanawa clan who declined for the same reason.[14]

Today, the Nanawa clan only holds the position of Gerao (responsible for rituals related to eclipses). The first Liae rajas of Portuguese times were from the clan, 14 generations after Wara Wai. There are two narratives involving Nida Dahi who is remembered as the first raja in Liae. One is the consequence of a war at Liti in the domain of Seba; there he rescued his niece Bitu Luji. The second narrative recalls a confrontation with Sumbanese after Nida Dahi had stolen golden objects from a grave in Sumba.[15] The Sumbanese chased him up to Kolowègu without success. Nida Dahi did not have descendants.

The clans did not form at the same generational level but one after the other. Nanawa and Nahai formed five generations after Wara Wai and two sub-clans, Narega and Narebo, were created three generations later. Napujara formed ten generations after Wara Wai and eight generations before the first mention of a Liae ruler in VOC records (Riwu Manu in 1688; see chapter 6). Napujara is the youngest clan in Liae, but it became the most powerful clan providing rajas in Dutch times, as chapter 5 shows.

The formation of the Council of Seven Men (*Ratu Mone Pidu*) by Wara Wai's descendants is remembered in the phrase *Rai pidu lai, pidu uli, pidu dara, pidu kewèhu* (The land with seven ceremonial offices, seven rudders, seven marks, seven knots). *Uli* refers both to the rudder and to the helmsman. The name Uli is often found in the genealogies, indicating the role of particular ancestors. The knots refer to fixed rituals of the ceremonial calendar and the seven positions

---

[13] However, local heirloom baskets sometimes contain foreign textiles; their external origin made them more sacred, so they are kept in different baskets.

[14] The ritual stove might be now in a private collection (or in a museum). It is unlikely that the owner is aware of his/her part in the disappearance of Apu Lod'o and the related rituals in Liae!

[15] The narrative about the war at Liti and Bitu Luji's rescue is recounted in Appendix I, Narrative 6.

correspond to seven clans or allied clans: Nanawa, Nahai, Nakale, Narega-Narebo, Napulai, Napuleru-Napuuju and Napujara. The number seven is specific to Liae's propitious days for rituals. The original ceremonial cycle was based on a multiple of seven years but underwent some modifications in the 19th century.[16]

There is another phrase about *Ratu Mone Pidu. Mone Do Nadai, pidu udu, lèmi dou, èpa ama* (The men of Nadai [who formed] seven clans [were] five men [and] four fathers) seems to be an *a posteriori* explanation of the council's composition as field observations do not corroborate it. The 'five men' of *do* Nadai are Adu Wara's five sons—Ngara Adu, Tiga Adu, Bèlu Adu, Logo Adu and Jèka Adu—omitting Kore Adu and Pia Adu. The 'four fathers' are the same men without Jèka Adu, who is said to have no descendants, although he has descendants in Seba. Clans have been combined to share a priest position: Narega and Narebo, Napuuju and Napuleru in order to obtain the obligatory number seven for Liae's socio-political organisation.

Kole Wai and the origins of Mesara

Like his brother Wara Wai, Kole Wai followed his buffalo to Seba. The narrative recounting four buffalos walking to Savu's four domains serves to justify the present situation and sustains the main lines of the ancestors' migratory paths while erasing the details. According to collective memory in Mesara, Kole Wai did not go directly there. Starting from Wègamengèru on the northern coast, he went to Tedida, a place near Liti hill in Depe, and later joined Wara Wai in Liae who stayed at Nauru, near Maluna. Ama Jo Haba of Mesara adds one step to the ancestors' migration on the island. Wara Wai and Kole Wai moved to Teriwu and asked the descendants of Dida Miha for land on which to stay. Then Kole Wai or his descendants moved to Ledepu'uju near Teriwu, which is also near Wolomanu, an important place for ritual cockfights (as noted in chapter 1 for Dida Miha's famous cockfights). Every year, people construct a small sacred building (*ada manu*) there before the ritual cockfights start. One expression recalls the time when Wara Wai and Kole Wai were staying together in Liae. Their descendants are called *mi hekene hi'i*, which refers to a loincloth woven as one piece without a seam. The image of a single cloth woven with the same yarn means that they were very close brothers, perhaps helping each other through hard times; they were as one.[17]

---

[16] See Table 2 'The knots of the land in Liae' in Appendix II.

[17] The main sources for early times in Mesara: Ama Jo Haba, Ama Tape Rike, Ama Raja (Mèngi Lino) and the priests Apu Lod'o Wadu (Ama Pela) and Deo Rai (Mada B'iri). See Map 5 for Mesara.

Figure 17: Clans descended from Ie Miha in Liae and the Council of Seven Men

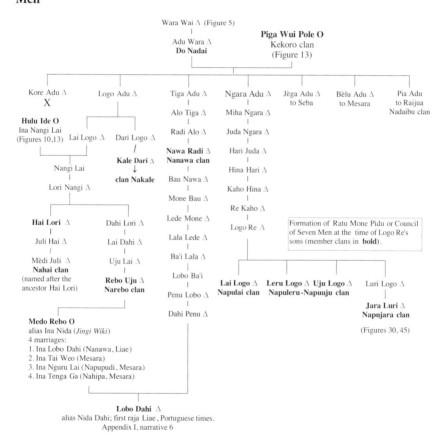

Each settlement had a place for the annual launch of the ceremonial boat (*kowa hole*) for the thanksgiving ceremony after harvest.[18] When the ancestors stayed at Ledepu'uju, they launched the ceremonial boat from Ubad'aramaka (Maka harbour). After Kole Wai moved to Tèji at Ledekolorae, which is at the boundaries of Teriwu/ Liae and today's Wadumèdi village, the arena for cockfights was still in Wolomanu, but the boat was launched from Ubad'araiki (Small Harbour). Later, Kole Wai (or his descendants) moved to Kolorae-Pedèro, the place presently known for rituals. Since this time, the *kowa hole* launching place has been in Uba Ae (Large Bay) and the ensuing cockfight nearby at Turuwoki. The diagram below gives the chronology, and the settlement genealogies (topogenies) for the ritual cockfight arenas and for launching *kowa hole*. Notably, for the early stage of Mesara's history people remember a combination of elements anchoring the time in collective memory: firstly, a succession of settlements; secondly, a chronology of places for ritual cockfights; and thirdly, the sites where the ceremonial boat, *kowa hole*, was launched after harvest—during the most essential ceremony of the year—thus significant enough to be carried in collective memory right up to the present. Surprisingly, for this stage of their history people remember ceremonial place names but not the name of each settlement's founding house.

Figure 18: Chronology of settlements, ritual cockfight arenas and ceremonial places for *kowa hole*[19]

Settlement	Ritual place for cockfights	Location for *kowa hole*
Ledepu'uju (Teriwu)	Adamanu/Wolomanu	Ubad'aramaka
Tèji at Ledekolorae (Teriwu/Liae)	Adamanu/Wolomanu	Ubad'araiki
Kolorae at Pedèro (Upper Mesara)	Turuwoki	Uba Ae

Halfway up the steep hill to Kolorae, today's ceremonial centre in Upper Mesara, is the small hamlet of Tedida. It has a large megalith around which people perform the ceremonial *pedoa* dances. The place is called Nadawoe (Arena of the Crocodile). The large, round, flat megalith is said to have been brought there after settlers moved from a place of the same name in the domain of

---

[18] *Hole* is the thanksgiving ceremony which takes place over several days and ends with the ceremonial boat launching. There are one or more ceremonies each day. *Kowa* means boat. *Kowa hole* refers to the last day of the ceremony during which a boat or raft is built and launched out to sea. See Plates 8 and 15.

[19] Interview with Zadrak Bunga (25.11.2002).

Seba (Liti). Of note is that the three names, Kolorae, Tedida and Nadawoe, are reminders of previous ancestor settlements.[20] While on the move, ancestors also 'moved' the name of the place as a way of reproducing the previous location. It is unlikely that they moved the large megalith up and down hills from Liti. They transferred the name to another large stone. It is within the priests' power to transfer the sacredness of a stone to another. People recall the ancestors' journey as if it took place within one generation, but it might have taken more time. Horo Kole is remembered in Wolomanu as well as Due Horo (the Lontar Tree of Horo), not far from Tedida in Liti, which is now in the domain of Seba. He was buried under his brother Jua Kole's house at Adamanu (Wolomanu) in today's Liae. His grandson, Lele Wila, died at the same place from a cockspur injury. When asked why the *kowa hole* launch constantly changed places, the response was that those launching places did not bring prosperity. "The harvest was too meagre," Ama Pela explained and the ancestors were not happy with the offerings sent to them.[21] The previous settlements linked to these places did not bring prosperity either and were probably not safe. In contrast, the group's final settlement in Upper Mesara with the ritual place on top of Kolorae hill overlooking the sea and Uba Ae bay is a good strategic location.

The migration of the Upper Mesara ancestors from Seba to Mesara over Liae does not cover more than 20 to 25 kilometres and yet every move is remembered. It is a feature common to Austronesian societies. The origin of a group is conceptualised as a path traceable from the apical ancestor to the final settlement occupied by the present generation in an order of events that justifies current differences (Fox 1995: 221). It is very possible that the migration path of Kole Wai and his descendants took a long time because the area was inhabited by other groups. Mesara's seven year ceremonial cycle mentions two years without rituals because the people in charge of the rituals had vanished. These years are called *lu* (forgotten). It raises the question of whether previous settlers occupied Kolorae's strategic locations and the surroundings.

The clans of Upper Mesara descended from Kole Wai are called *udu ahli* (original clans). When asked about an order of precedence, people in Upper Mesara assert that Ie Miha and Kole Wai's descendants were the original settlers

---

[20] It was a common practice among migrants to North America and Australia to name new places after their European towns of origin.

[21] There are no more than five kilometres between Ubad'aramaka (Kelako near Tanjung Ketode) and Uba Ae, the actual launching place for Upper Mesara. However, these details are important enough to Mesara people to be remembered until today.

of Mesara. This might be true for Upper Mesara. However, observing the rituals reveals a different situation, as explained by Ama Jo Haba:[22]

> When Kole Wai arrived at Teriwu, he asked Dida Miha [for permission to stay on his land].[23] When they celebrate *kelila*, the large ritual of the ceremonial calendar every seven years, those who prepare the ritual food and make the heaps of offerings are the descendants of Kole [Wai] because he asked Dida Miha to stay on their land. Those who perform the ceremony and place the meat on top of the [ritual] stone are the descendants of Dida Miha, not of Kole Wai. Those who put the seeds on the ritual stone for the fields and the gardens are the descendants of Dida Miha. The descendants of Kole Wai who live in Mesara hold their ceremonies on land which belongs to Dida Miha.

Dida Miha's descendants are in Lower Mesara, in Molie, Lobohede and Tanajawa. There used to be one priest system for Upper Mesara and another for Lower Mesara. While that for Upper Mesara is still strong, there are no longer priests for Lower Mesara and there is an economic explanation. People's standard of living there has increased remarkably over the last few decades owing to seaweed farming. People built concrete houses with corrugated roofs, neglecting their traditional fenced villages (*rae kepue*) and their houses of origin, which are in dire need of repair. They also embraced a world religion which has deleted the ancestors from memory.[24] The last priest in Lower Mesara was Apu Lod'o Dahi. The mnemonic tag *dahi* (sea) identifies Dida Miha's descendants.

Kole Wai had three sons: Jua Kole, Horo Kole and Talo Kole. Jua Kole's descendants formed the clans of Nabèlu (seven generations later), Nanawa (eight generations later) and Rue, the latter being the name of the priest of misfortune which started with Jua Kole's granddaughter. The name of a clan usually carries its founder's name, but in the case of the Rue clan which does not refer to a specific ancestor, it is not clear when it was created. In collective memory, a woman, Rika Maji, held the first position of Rue, an exception for a priest system usually in the hands of men. This is not the only case where a woman was at the origin of a priest position. There are also female ritual leaders for all things related to life crisis ceremonies and, more generally, to both female moieties (*hubi*) and their branching groups, *wini* (Duggan 2008: 451–7). This shows that Savu society had from the beginning a strong female orientation and in a number of cases the first

---

[22] Interview (19.04.2006).

[23] Kole Wai actually asked the descendant of Dida Miha. In his recount, Ama Jo Haba (23.11.2002) uses Kole Wai and Dida Miha as generic names for both groups of people.

[24] Notably, these include the new Christian sects of the Seventh Day Adventists and the Bethel Church.

priest in the line was a woman (Deo Rai, Rue). None of the priests can perform fertility rites without the participation of their wives, Bèni Deo or Bèni Aji.

Clans descended from Jua Kole

Of Jua Kole's descendants, there is an important ancestor, Ago Rai, with the priest role of Deo Rai and a contemporary of a key Sebanese ancestor, Robo Aba. They are remembered as stepbrothers (see Figure 10 and chapter 2). However, the name Ago Rai repeats: the first Ago Rai lived three generations after Jua Kole and did not have descendants; the second Ago Rai lived ten generations after Jua Kole. Name repetition is always a source of confusion in narratives wrongly attributed to one or the other ancestor. Narratives recounting struggles between Ago Rai and Robo Aba give the upper hand to Ago Rai, if recorded in Mesara, and to Robo Aba, if recounted in Seba.

One narrative recalls how the contemporary border between Seba and Mesara was moved further west, thus reducing Mesara's territory. Previously set at Rahihawu (today in Ledeana village), the border was moved to Wae Uba Jami (Want the estuary at the forest) where Ago Rai stood on his stone *dèjarai* and Robo Aba on the other side of the river Wae.[25] The limits then followed the summits of Perihi, Tuwi, up to Teriwu and then downhill towards Merèbu. Both ancestors were chanting mantra texts still remembered today—a snippet is translated below:

> Like a sacred belt[26]
> Sacred land, land from the base [of the world]
> Straight land, border land,
> The boundary cutting at the river
> The boundary adopted at the river.

A second account involving Ago Rai and Robo Aba is possibly the consequence of the new limits set between the stepbrothers at Wae Uba Jami. In this narrative, Robo Aba is accused of stealing a ritual house newly built by Ago Rai. When Ago Rai, accompanied by Maja, arrived at Namata claiming ownership of the ritual house, Robo Aba invited them to a food contest which ended in a competition

---

[25] *Dèja rai* (to stamp the ground) is a reminder of the process through which the limit was set. Although the border between Seba and Mesara moved westwards, some ritual and recreational cockfights organised by the Mesara people still take place at this stone, so the Seba people do not have to enter Mesara's territory for the occasion. Sources: Ama Jo Haba and Ama Wila Laka of Mesara.

[26] *Wai* is also the name of a narrow sacred cloth worn around the waist (Duggan 2001: 65–7).

of mantra chants. The priest of Mesara failed in the end to retrieve his house and the following agreement was reached, sealed with an exchange of objects. Ago Rai was told to build his future ritual house with Robo Aba's body measurements while the Seba people would build their ritual house with the measurements of Ago Rai which they already had.[27] As a consequence of this symbolic exchange of houses, an important memory marker of the event, the ritual house belonging to Deo Rai—the highest priest in both domains—carries the same common name, Bèni Deo (also the name of Deo Rai's wife—*bèni* means woman or female), but they have different mantra names.[28] The numbers used in rituals for Mesara and Seba are said to have been defined on this occasion: nine for Seba and seven for Mesara.[29] Robo Aba also gave a type of sorghum, thus far unknown in Mesara, to plant there.

The reason why Robo Aba stole the ritual house was apparently because the trees used for its construction belonged to him: he had the building dismantled and carried to his place in Namata.[30] It is possible, knowing both narratives—one about the boundary changes and the second about the stolen ritual house—to connect them. The ownership of the trees had changed when the domain boundaries shifted, although Ago Rai, the previous land owner, continued to claim rights over its resources. This narrative carries an important message: long before Europeans came to the area people in Savu had a sense of landownership with defined borders, using stones, trees, rivers and summits as visual mnemonic markers.[31]

The descendants of Jua Kole hold three key positions in the Council of *Mone Ama*. To the present, the highest ritual position—Deo Rai (Lord of the Earth)—has been in the hands of the Nabèlu clan. The clan also had the role of

---

[27] It is common to build a house using the owner's body measurements. Ago Rai built his house in Mesara with his measurements; after Robo Aba stole it, the house was in Seba (Namata). Therefore, Roba Aba already had Ago Rai's measurements when he needed to rebuild the house.

[28] Interview with Ama Ju Rihi in Seba (13.10.2000).

[29] In popular memory, the number eight not seven is important for Mesara. As proof, Mesara people say that the launching of the ceremonial boat, *kowa hole*, takes place eight days after the ceremony at full moon in the same month. However, if the ceremony at full moon takes place on a Tuesday, *kowa hole* takes place the following Tuesday, seven days later (or on the eighth day).

[30] Ama Jo Haba (22.04.2002) telling the Mesara and the Seba versions of the stolen house story gave his personal view. The reason for his insider knowledge is that twelve generations ago his ancestor, Jawa Mega (see Figure 23), moved from Seba to Mesara where he received land, established himself and married.

[31] The problem of landownership and usufruct is discussed in chapter 7.

Figure 19: Descendants of Jua Kole in Mesara

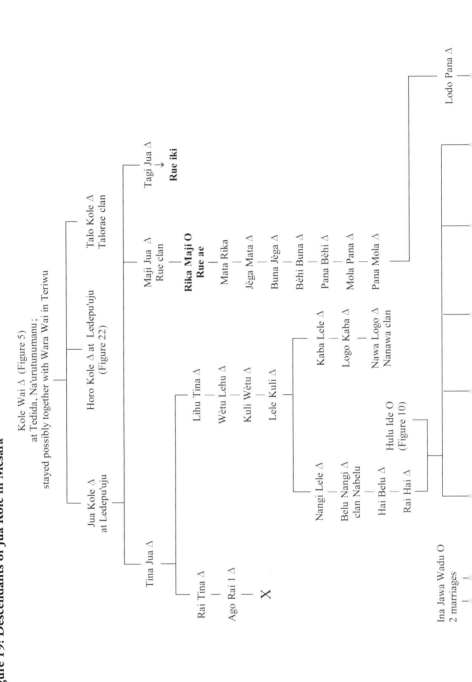

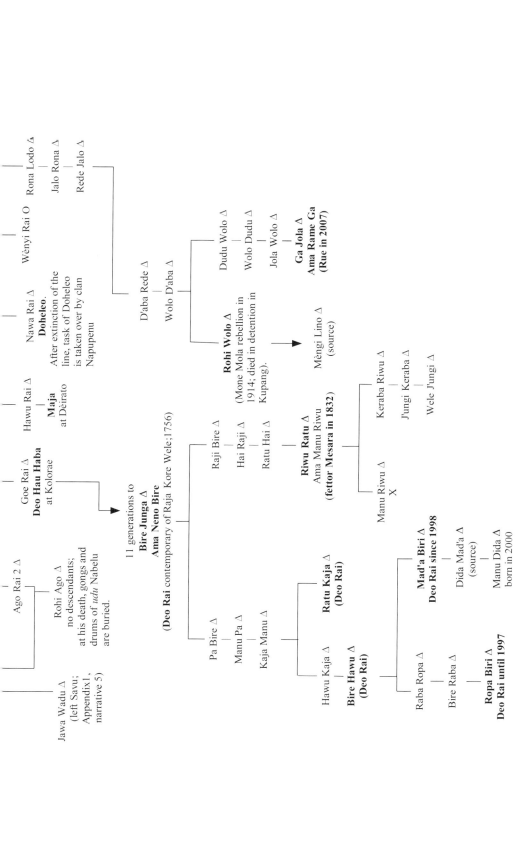

Rona Lodo △

Jalo Rona △

Rede Jalo △

Wenyi Rai O

Nawa Rai △
Doheleo.
After extinction of the line, task of Doheleo is taken over by clan Napupenu

D'aba Rede △

Wolo D'aba △

Dudu Wolo △

Wolo Dudu △

Jola Wolo △

**Ga Jola △
Ama Rame Ga
(Rue in 2007)**

Rohi Wolo △
(Mone Mola rebellion in 1914; died in detention in Kupang).

Mengi Lino △
(source)

Hawu Rai △
Maja
at Dèirato

Goe Rai △
Deo Hau Haba
at Kolorae

11 generations to
**Bire Junga △
Ama Neno Bire**
(**Deo Rai** contemporary of Raja Kore Wele:1756)

Raji Bire △

Hai Raji △

Ratu Hai △

**Riwu Ratu △
Ama Manu Riwu
(fettor Mesara in 1832)**

Manu Riwu △
X

Keraba Riwu △

J'ungi Keraba △

Wele J'ungi △

Ago Rai 2 △

Rohi Ago △
no descendants; at his death, gongs and drums of *udu* Nabelu are buried.

Jawa Wadu △
(left Savu; Appendix I, narrative 5)

Pa Bire △

Manu Pa △

Kaja Manu △

Hawu Kaja △

**Ratu Kaja △
(Deo Rai)**

**Bire Hawu △
(Deo Rai)**

Raba Ropa △

Bire Raba △

**Ropa Biri △
Deo Rai until 1997**

**Mad'a Biri △
Deo Rai since 1998**

Dida Mad'a △
(source)

Manu Dida △
born in 2000

Doheleo or Overseer of the Council, while the Rue clan had a similar position which split into Rue Ae, dealing with catastrophes and major accidents, and Rue Iki, in cases of breaching taboo.

Clans descended from Horo Kole

Horo Kole is remembered through the place name Due Horo (Lontar Tree of Horo), indicating that people were already cultivating the lontar palm tree as a precious agricultural item. Horo Kole is at the origin of the largest number of clans in Mesara: Nahipa (four generations after Horo Kole), Aelungi (five), Napupudi (seven), Naputitu (eight) and Napupenu-Napuhina, nine generations after Horo Kole. However, things were certainly not smooth at the beginning: Horo Kole's son was buried at Wolomanu under his brother Jua Kole's house revealing that he had not founded his own house and, a generation later, Wila Horo was killed by a cockspur at the same place.

Nahipa is collectively remembered as the oldest clan and the uppermost rulers of Mesara (*Duae Rai*), also holding the priest role of Deo Rai (Lord of the Earth). The name of the clan is derived from Hipa Hungu who did not have descendants. The clan had several misfortunes in its history, so it is not easy to reconstruct. However, a few events serve as time markers. First, land was given away at the time of the ancestress Depi Lod'o, alias Ina Wěnyi Depi. She lived six generations after Horo Kole and is Lod'o Ga Hawu's daughter. As Lod'o Ga did not have male descendants, she inherited the rights over his land. A female line does not own land but can receive the right to cultivate it. The land was never returned to other male lines of the group as there are still female descendants who have the right to cultivate it. The daughter, Wěnyi Depi, became Ina Diri Doke Lele. Her husband (Doke Lele) provides some clues about early connections between Savu and neighbouring islands. He was the descendant of Pojo Dida from the Teriwu clan who went to Sumba to help the local raja in a war and married there. A descendant of his moved to Savu and, for helping the Nahipa clan, he received two plots of land: Tanah Ja and Ngaba near Dènirai. He is remembered as a *ketadu haba* player,[32] a popular music instrument in Savu and Rote.[33]

Nahipa was repeatedly allied to the Nataga clan of Seba, as seen during Portuguese and Dutch times, and both clans exchanged their houses of origin

---

[32] Interviews with Ama Mara Ha, Nahipa clan (19.11.2002) and (21.11.2004); and Ama Keraba Wila (19.11.2002). Some sources say that he was killed in Liedokelele, Mesara, others that he was killed in Dènipadalere, Dimu holding his music instrument.

[33] *Ketadu haba* is a kind of cither; its resonance body is made of a large lontar palm leaf. It might have been the novelty that stuck in popular memory.

Figure 20: Upper Mesara; relationships between priest position and clan formation

Ranking according to priest position; Description of tasks	Precedence according to clan formation
1. Deo Ha'u Haba/Deo Rai (on the hill top and eastern side of Raepedèro): rituals for plants, e.g. sorghum and mung beans, and human wellbeing	7. Nabèlu-Nanawa clan

2. Rue
    Rue Ae: rituals for re-gaining cosmic harmony after disaster, violent death and accidents
    Rue Iki: rituals for repairing human wrongdoing
	2. Rue clan

3. Kenuhe and Maja: rituals related to warfare
    Kenuhe: travels underground and aids warriors in battle (in the past also took the heads of enemies)
    Maja: rituals to prevent wrongdoing by the Maja spirit
	4. Aelungi clan
	
	8. Napupenu-Napuhina clan

4. Doheleo (now under Deo Rai): oversees activities for Deo Rai when the priest has to stay secluded	7. Nabèlu-Nanawa clan (earlier Napupenu clan)

5. Apu Lod'o Muhu: rituals related to warfare
    Apu Lod'o Wadu: rituals for the lontar palm tree
	6. Naputitu clan
	
	    Naputitu clan

6. Bawa iri Apu Lod'o: helper of Apu Lod'o Muhu
    Bawa iri Deo Rai: helper of Deo Rai
 	
    Bawa iri Rue: helper of Rue
	5. Napupudi clan
	1. first under the Talorae clan; as the role is now redundant it is under the Bèlu clan
	    Bèlu clan

7. *Pehere jara mokebara* (horse dance to prevent locusts destroying crops)	3. Nahipa clan (absent from Raepedèro)

Figure 21: Diagram of Raepèdero

Raepedèro is situated on a gentle slope at the bottom of Kolorae hill where the high priest Deo Rai (Nabèlu clan) has his ritual house. Raepedèro consists of five low terraces and each clan occupies one level. All the houses in Raepedèro are the *èmu rukoko* style with extended ridges.

A. Area of the Rue clan on the highest terrace
  1. Rue ritual house
  2. Rue residential houses
  3. Nadahari (Arena for All) with sacred stones
  4 South gate
  5. East gate to Kolorae and Uba Ae
 	
B. Area of the Aelungi clan
  6. Maja ritual house
  7. & 8. Aelungi's former ancestral houses
  9 West gate
 	
C. Area of the Napupudi clan
  10. Napupudi house of origin: Bèni Bala
 	
D. Area of the Naputitu clan
  11. Former Naputitu house of origin, *èmu kepue*, with a trunk of *aj'u kola* (*Bischofia javanica*) for hanging offerings; stones of the ceremonial hearth
  12. Present house: Bèni Patu
  13. Nada Ae (Big Arena) for Apu Lod'o Wadu and Apu Lod'o Muhu
  14. Ritual house of Apu Lod'o Muhu: Muri Deo
 	
E. Area of the Napupenu clan on the lowest terrace
  15. & 16. Napupenu's former houses; J'ole Wila, the Napupenu house of origin, no longer exists.
	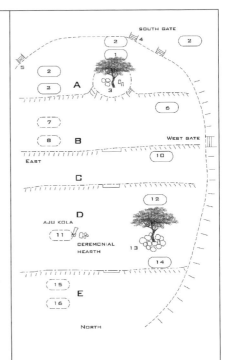

Figure 22: Descendants of Horo Kole in Mesara

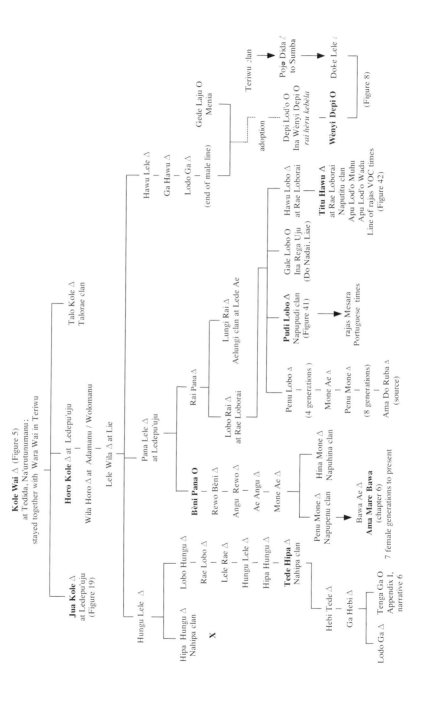

(*èmu kepue*). The Hinge Haba house of Nataga was brought to Raemèdi village in Mesara and the Bèni Keka house of Mesara was moved to Nadawawi on Namata hill. While Hinge Haba still exists, Bèni Keka was destroyed by fire in 1946 and never rebuilt.

Twelve generations after Horo Kole, his descendant Lod'o Ga Hebi lost to the Nabèlu clan his ritual position of Deo Rai, a ceremonial spear (*kepoke*), a ceremonial drum (*dere*) and land located near Raemèdi. Sources are at variance about the Deo Rai position. According to some, Lod'o Ga Hebi usurped the position of Deo Rai from Nabèlu but had to give it back after a severe drought, a sign of the ancestors' discontent. According to others, Nahipa had the role of Deo Rai from the beginning while the Nabelu clan had the position of Deo Hau Haba (for agricultural rituals) which is very similar in its tasks to the Deo Rai. Nabèlu had lost the right of ceremonial drums during Ago Rai's time; thus it regained this right with the transfer of the ceremonial drum from the Nahipa clan.[34]

The Aelungi clan derived its name from the ancestor Lungi Rai. *Lungi* means whale, so the name forms connections between the land and sea. The clan has the priest role of Maja for placating the possible misdeeds of the Maja spirit. There are no specific recorded narratives about this clan; however, it is remembered that at some point the clan rose to the position of raja, although no specific name was given. Interestingly, in 1682, VOC documents name two figures of Mesara: Ama Weo (Dahi Lulu) and Manu Dahi. Both can be traced in the Aelungi genealogies.[35]

The Napupudi clan seems to have thrived during the Portuguese period. Social memory is very precise about this time; it recalls that the ancestor Naha Lulu usurped the ruling position from the Nahipa clan. This possibly coincided with the arrival of Portuguese in the area who were recruiting local rulers. Collective memory names four rajas (see Figure 41) and a number of marriage alliances between clans in Mesara as well as with clans in Seba and Raijua. Chapter 7 describes how the Napupudi clan lost the raja title to the Naputitu during Dutch times (see Figure 41).

Other clans descended from the ancestor Horo Kole, but their genealogies are less certain. Talo Kole, a younger brother of Horo Kole, formed the Talorae clan. His descendants allied with Bèlu Adu of Liae; after Bèlu Adu received land, the clan was renamed Bèlu. They achieved only helper positions in the *Mone Ama*

---

[34] Later, during early VOC times, Nahipa sided with Seba in a war between Mesara and Seba at the time of Wele Jami (Naputitu clan of Mesara) and Jara Lomi (Nataga clan, Seba), and lost land to Mesara's Aelungi clan.

[35] Interview with Ama Jo Haba (22.04.2002). See also Duggan (2011c: 52–7) and chapter 6.

Council. The Napupenu clan had a woman at its origin and, therefore, did not own land but a key figure, Bawa Ae (Great Helper), left memories in Mesara; he might have occupied the position of Overseer for a while. Chapter 6 discusses his deeds. The Napuhina clan, named after Hina Lobo, has obvious foreign connotations and did not have any religious tasks; it allied to Napupenu.[36]

Naputitu, one of the youngest clans of Mesara, rose to power during Dutch times. It shows a trajectory similar to Napujara in Liae. An interesting narrative recounts how the Naputitu clan was formed by Titu Hawu who undertook a journey similar to a quest for knowledge.[37]

> Titu Hawu was suffering from illness and his body was covered with suppurating sores. One day he started to prepare flour to cook a meal for his children. While the flour was cooking, it disappeared. He looked everywhere until he came to the seashore. Then he suspected that he had been a victim of black magic, and thought of the spirits of the sea (Wango) and their [unpredictable] power. There he met an octopus. Yes, the octopus knew [who had taken what he was seeking], but Titu Hawu had to compensate the octopus with something. He gave it 'chicken shit'. Ever since this event, the octopuses eject black ink. "Yes, it is with 'God inside the Sea'" the octopus replied.
>
> Titu Hawu continued his journey along the shore and met a sea urchin to whom he asked the same question. Yes, the urchin knew [who had taken what he was seeking], but Titu Hawu first had to give him something. Titu asked, "What do you want?" He answered, "The pus from your wounds." Ever since, the sea urchins have had inside them a whitish substance that reminds one of sores. The urchin told him that what he was looking for was with 'God inside the Sea'.
>
> Titu Hawu went deeper into the sea and met a large crab to whom he addressed the same question. The crab first wanted something from Titu Hawu. He gave him a generous quantity of betel spit; hence, it is the reason the crab now has three red dots on its shell. The crab also told Titu Hawu that 'God inside the Sea' was in possession of what he was looking for. Titu Hawu continued his journey and finally met 'God inside the Sea' who instructed him to carry out a specific task for the dry season because there was too often hunger on the island. Deo Para Dahi gave him the role of Apu Lod'o Rai for the time of the dry season and this role would belong to the clan *Naputitu pa d'ara Nada Ae* (Naputitu inside the Big Arena). He told him to 'plant' stones at three sacred places: Nada Ae,

---

[36] Hina Lobo might be the same person as Wila Lobo of the Kelara clan. See below for the mysterious Kelara clan of Seba.

[37] Interview with Apu Lod'o Wadu (08.04.2002). Kodi has a tradition of tales which end with a lesson and moral comments for the Kodi people (Middlekoop 1957: 157). The story of Titu Hawu belongs to the same category of narratives.

Nadamudi, and Nadahari. 'God inside the Sea' also told Titu Hawu to mark his cattle with three incisions in both ears.

The story contains a moral lesson and a code of conduct. 'God inside the Sea' gave Titu Hawu the divine role of Apu Lod'o Rai, the mnemonic tag *rai* (earth) identifying him as a descendant of the younger brother Ie Miha. The big arena is in the ritual village of Raepedèro. The priest role split into two further offices; one of Apu Lod'o Muhu (*muhu* is war) corresponding to the position of Maukia (priest of war) in other domains. The second position, Apu Lod'o Wadu, is dedicated to tapping the lontar palm tree, which indeed became essential for the Savu people. *Wadu* (stone) is synonymous with the dry season when no grass is left and all the stones on the island become visible. One might wonder why 'God in the Sea' gave instructions for rituals related to the land. Talo Nawa (Talo the Wave), who is not part of the Savu genealogies, apparently brought the lontar palm tree to Savu. His foreign origin is stressed in the name Talo, reminiscent of a South Sulawesi kingdom. The story recounted as a divine command legitimises the position of Apu Lod'o Wadu in the domain. Today's ritual place for Apu Lod'o Wadu is in Ledelo where Kana Mone, Titu Hawu's grandson, established himself. The house of origin, *èmu kepue*, is called Bale Ara (Plate 4). For names or expressions containing the word *ara*, people refer either to the title of Flores rulers, such as Arakia, or translate it as Arab. With names such as Talo Nawa and Bale Ara, a link to Makassar and to the west seems plausible. The ceremonial hearth *rao ae* of Mesara has four cooking holes and is larger than any other ceremonial hearth in Savu and Raijua which all have a maximum of three holes. This is a visual marker of Mesara's precedence over all the other domains in matters related to the lontar palm.[38]

The creation of the Naputitu clan acknowledged a higher rank or precedence for the 'people of the sea' over 'people of the land'. In Mesara, there are priests of the land: Deo Rai and Apu Lod'o Rai descended from the younger brother Ie Miha complementing the 'Priest of the Sea', Apu Lod'o Dahi, residing in Lower Mesara and descended from the elder brother Dida Miha.

Examining the genealogies, orally transmitted from generation to generation, and a number of narratives and chants makes it possible to reconstruct the chronology of the clans' formation and early Upper Mesara history. The main focus of narratives and genealogies concerns justifying the division of religious and political tasks, and validating land ownership. The possession of certain heirlooms, such as a ceremonial spear or drums and gongs, serve as "memory

---

[38] See the ceremonial calendar of Apu Lod'o Wadu for ceremonies related to the lontar in Appendix II, Table 4.

boxes" (Hoskins 1998: 5). People have transmitted the narratives about how people acquired the objects or, on the contrary, when and how the right of their use was lost over generations. As shown in Liae, the memory of a vanished group is marked by the absence of rituals in certain years which are labelled *lu* (forgotten). One more element can be added to this analysis: the plan for the ritual centre of Upper Mesara provides us with a peculiar understanding of Mesara's past. It reflects a rule of precedence for the Upper Mesara clans after they were created. It is noteworthy that the Nahipa clan is not represented there (see Figure 21). A key moment in Mesara's past is certainly Ago Rai's time, important enough to be kept in collective memory. It included the contemporary movement of boundaries between Seba and Mesara, and that the ritual houses for the priests Deo Rai in Upper Mesara and in Seba have since been built with measurements of the other. This is a remarkable memory tag. Propitious numbers for rituals were defined for both domains (seven for Mesara and nine for Seba) and the former benefited from a new type of sorghum which had not yet reached the domain.

The descendants of D'ara Wai and the formation of the Seba clans[39]

In Seba, as in Mesara, the ancestors did not settle immediately at the place their descendants occupy today. D'ara Wai's descendants, who lived eleven generations after Ie Miha, are generally considered Seba's first settlers. In fact, most sources give for all of Seba's clans a genealogy derived from Ie Miha only and acknowledge Namata as the sole ritual place in the domain.

The path of Ie Miha and his descendants from Teriwu to Lededai'ie and from there to the northern coast is mentioned above. A number of places, all located near each other, are remembered in association with the contemporary ancestors: Wègamengèru (The Green [prosperous] Banyan Tree), Gurikebau (Dead Buffalos) and Pururede (Come Down Full). The first airstrip built in Savu, now part of the road from Seba to Mesara, cuts the former site of Wègameneru/ Gurikebau into two, the larger area being between the road and the sea. On the southern side of the road, there is a sacred stone dedicated to Mone Ie. People who live there interpret the stones scattered over one hundred meters of ground as the twelve pillars of Aba Mone's house.[40] Next to the old trees of Wègamengèru

---

[39] Main sources for Seba: Leba Alu (Ma Medo), Ama Obi Nale, Ama Ju Rihi, Priest Maukia (Dida Bèngu), Bawa Iri.

[40] A 100 metre long house would have more than twelve pillars and the position of the stones does not seem to support the long house argument. However, Joseph Banks, who visited Savu in 1770, mentions long houses of 300 to 400 feet (1770: 330).

is a small yellow stone, partly hidden in limestone, and dedicated to Re, the constellation of Antares. Near the beach is a stone dedicated to Jawa Ae (The Great Foreigner), who is repeatedly mentioned in the chant for the *hole* ceremony in relation to Piga Hina Mamo Deo (Chinese Plate, Priestess Mamo). The name of the place, 'Come Down Full' refers to the hope that the tapped sap will flow in great quantity. A dozen stones scattered at Pururede are part of the rituals related to tapping lontar sap. In 2001, during a ritual dedicated to the lontar blossom (*hubi due*) a priest noted that one stone was missing from a group of seven small stones placed in a sort of circle and dedicated to Wunu Pidu, the Pleiades. The priest looked around and found a suitable stone to replace it. It is not clear if this was the missing stone; it seemed as if any suitably sized stone was appropriate. It is often the case that a sacred stone is buried because it is too 'hot' and that small stones on the surface are only meant to mark the place.

In the story of the four buffalos, D'ara Wai arrived in Mèba along the river of Seba. All these locations are near each other. For some twelve generations, the descendants of Ie Miha apparently resided there near the sea, in an area unprotected from invaders and giant waves. This is puzzling as slave traders raided the coasts of the eastern archipelago, as they did in other parts of Southeast Asia over the centuries.[41] There are two possible answers to this enigma; one is that the coast is partly protected by a reef only passable at high tide, so that people could flee to the hills and safely hide in their earlier settlements. The other explanation is that when the ancestors lived there, 20 to 27 generations or 500 to 600 years ago, the slave trade had not developed to the extent known in early Portuguese accounts.

Robo Aba

Four generations after D'ara Wai, his descendant Aba Taba married Hulu Ide of *udu* Kekoro, a 'woman of the sea'. Chapter 2 shows that she married in four domains of the island. Hulu Ide lived 15 generations after Dida Miha, while Aba Taba lived 11 generations after his brother Ie Miha which makes the situation plausible.

---

[41] (Reid 2000: 210–2; Fox 2000b: 246–62).

Robo Aba married Mare Ga who also belonged to the 'people of the sea'.[42] Robo Aba moved further east from Wègamengèru to Hangaraerobo, which was on the Kekoro clan's traditional land in Menia. The site is strategically better located than that on the northern coast—at the edge of a deep valley oriented towards the island's interior. Banyan trees, some dead, some alive, and a number of stones whose names were not disclosed show that it was a site of worship. The place was inhabited for a long time and is still considered sacred. In severe drought situations, the Seba priests come to the place and propitiate the stones, calling their earliest ancestors as they are expected to provide a better outcome. Before he left, a stone—*wowadu Robo Aba*—was placed near Seba's present harbour, where priests still worship. Covered with sand and sediments this menhir-shaped stone is not normally visible. However, a heavy storm in February 2002 washed away much of the beach nearby, exposing it. People knew of the stone's existence and location, although it can remain invisible for decades.

Robo Aba is credited with a number of children; 'children of the sea'—as he is said to have spent time at sea, some were born there—and 'children of the land'. Two children did not have descendants; they are said to have changed into animals—Hana Robo into an owl and her brother Lai Robo into a tokay. Such an interpretation is common in collective memory for someone who disappeared without a burial place or without leaving a trace. The other two have descendants. The daughter Dila Robo is at the origin of a subgroup *wini* Dila Robo in the female moiety, Greater Blossom. Haba Robo is Haba Mare, who was adopted by Robo Aba. People in Seba are reluctant to disclose the narrative about Haba Mare, although it is widely known. Haba Mare was born of an incestuous relationship between Mare Ga and Lod'o Mare, her son who did not grow up with her. Robo Aba killed Lod'o Mare who was then beheaded. His skull was buried at Ledewolodo, between Namata and Depe, at a sacred place to ask for rain. His body was cut into two halves: one half was buried at the bottom of Namata, along the Seba River; the other half was thrown into the sea. Haba Robo's son, Radi Haba, formed a lineage called Nataga-Naradi.[43] Robo Aba later

---

[42] In Raijua, the women of the Greater Blossom moiety worship an important figure called Marega (Kagiya 2010: 78). She was the daughter of Ama Lado Ga, a ruler from overseas. See also the narrative about Wore Baha and Ama Lado Ga (chapter 2). Marega has no descendants in Raijua while Mare Ga has descendants in Seba. A link between both characters is not excluded as Mare Ga is known as a 'woman from the sea' and belongs to the same moiety, Greater Blossom.

[43] For details about Dila Robo, see Duggan (2001: 39-41). For the Nataga genealogies, see Figures 23, 28 and 36.

Figure 23: Descendants of D'ara Wai in Seba

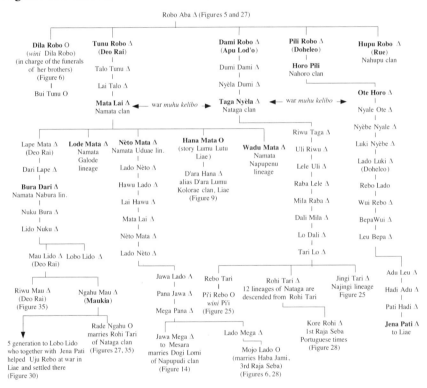

had four more children, known as the 'children of the land' because they were born in Savu. They are Tunu Robo, Dami Robo, Pili Robo and Hupu Robo.

Robo Aba, already mentioned in two narratives involving Ago Rai of Mesara, appears in another popular story. Regarding his move from Hangaraerobo to Namata, the story recalls a wild pig hunt. For this Robo Aba forged a spear for each of his sons, but the four sons returned from the hunt empty-handed and with broken weapons.[44] With new spears on a second attempt, they were victorious. The father looked at the soil on the pig's feet and declared the area fertile; they moved to the place which they called Namata – *mata* means to wait (for the wild pig).[45] In the rainy season, a pond forms in Namata; it is called Nadawawi (the arena of the pig). The wild pig hunt in Namata, comprising first a defeat and finally a victory, recalls in reality a battle against a group of autochthonous people which led to Robo Aba establishing himself in Namata. In informal conversations, people say the reason why only thorny plants (*lakai*) grow in Namata is because Robo Aba set the place on fire before moving in. Furthermore, fire destroyed Namata three times in its history; to some people this is the ancestors' curse as Robo Aba burned the place before settling there. The last conflagration was in September 1946 and most of the houses were never rebuilt. The people no longer living in Namata but who kept their founding houses in the ritual village, including Bèni Keka of Mesara (mentioned previously), lost their heirlooms.

Comparing Namata's strategic location with the settlements of Robo Aba's ancestors along the north coast, it becomes clear that they were not in a position to conquer the hill. If the hill had not already been inhabited, they would have established themselves in Namata earlier. The distance between Wègamengèru and Namata is no more than four kilometres. When following the Seba riverbed, which is dry for most of the year, one easily arrives at the bottom of Namata hill, protected by a double bend of the river. At some points, the river has cut vertical ridges in the hill creating a natural fence for the village. Seba's ritual chants do not often mention ancestors earlier than Robo Aba. In some cases, he is mentioned immediately after the first ancestor, Kika Ga, whose ritual coded name is Leba Jara (Large Horse), building a parallel between both Leba Jara building Savu,

---

[44] *Kepoke woka* is a spear with a hook. A spur with a hook for cockfighting is also called *woka*. There are similarities in the names for the weapons of war and for cockfights.

[45] Interview with Leba Alu, Namata clan (27.03.1999). Namata's ritual place was divided into two parts; the eastern side belongs to the Namata clan and the priests under Deo Rai (Lord of the Earth). The western side, Nadawawi, belongs to the Nataga clan with the priest position of Apu Lod'o (Descendant of the Sun); it was also the residence of Seba's rajas in early European times. See Figure 45.

and Robo Aba building Namata; hence, the chant gives Robo Aba the qualities similar to those of the first ancestor.

...	...
Hawu Leba Jara,	Hawu Leba Jara
Mone ia tao kaba kèro rai	The man who was able to form the hard coconut shell, [Savu]
do mejed'e d'e	The land he is sitting on [ruling over]. Ya, because of this, You, Great
b'oke wèta mèke ou Robo Aba Ae	Robo Aba
Mone ia hèro rae	[are] the man who was able to create the village.
pemejed'e	You are ruling [over Namata]
Rai eeee Rai Ae....	Land, Great Land........(chorus)[46]

As Mesara people tend to start the history of their domain with Kole Wai, so people in Seba believe their history starts with Robo Aba. There are six generations from D'ara Wai to Robo Aba and six generations from Kole Wai to Ago Rai. In D'ara Wai and Kole Wai's time, Seba and Mesara people were still moving. With Robo Aba, the younger brother Ie Miha's descendants become sedentary in Seba and with Ago Rai, the ancestors settled permanently in Upper Mesara.

There are no memories of major events regarding the four ancestors preceding Robo Aba. As discussed in chapter 1, people consider that the ancestor Kika Ga was Savu's first settler, which prevents the questioning of land rights; similarly, narratives present Robo Aba as the first ancestor of Seba for the same reasons. Following this logic, there is no need to remember occurrences prior to Robo Aba's founding of Namata and Seba in great detail. Events which might not have served Seba's formal discourse either fell into oblivion or were deleted from collective memory. The land the group lived on before Robo Aba's time was a small area which now has the villages of Ledeana, Raeloro and Mèba. Collective thought considers that Seba's development started with Robo Aba, whose ritual place has since been in Namata. In most narratives, this does not appear as the end of the migratory journey, but as the beginning of Seba's history.[47]

The place where the first house was built in Namata is called Raja Mara (*raja* is to hammer; *mara* means copper). This house of origin—called *Rahihawu* (meeting place of Hawu)—was destroyed in 1946 and the owner Leba Alu rebuilt

---

[46] Recounted by Leba Alu (27.03.1999).

[47] See Lewis (1988: 76).

it in 1998 in exactly the same place. Located on the northern side of the ritual site, it is slightly smaller than the other houses. In order for the house's pillars to stand in their original positions, it was necessary to conduct a ceremony to find them.[48] It is remarkable that the use of spears as well as the name Raja Mara in Namata's early days indicates that Savu's inhabitants knew how to forge tools out of metal; this knowledge surrounded by magical practices was the prerogative of a ruler such as Robo Aba.

The story of the pig hunt is not only a coded way to recount a war; it is also convenient to explain the division of positions attributed to Robo Aba's sons. The pig was cut into four parts. Tunu Robo who received the front left quarter became Deo Rai (Lord of the Earth).[49] Dami Robo had the front right quarter and became Apu Lod'o (Descendant of the Sun); Hupu Robo, who received the part of the back with the tail, took the role of Rue for re-establishing the cosmological balance after accidents or wrongdoing. Pili Robo had the remaining back quarter and became Doheleo (the Overseer). The line of the adopted brother Haba Robo, who did not receive a portion of meat, later became Apu Lod'o's helper. Haba Robo must have been compensated with some land as his branch is known as *kerogo* Nataga-Naradi, after Haba Robo's son, Radi Haba. The four brothers are at the beginning of the four religious roles and their descendants, two to four generations later, creating Seba's four original clans. Placing the distribution of the pig's four quarters between Robo Aba's sons at a time when clans in Seba had not yet formed meant nobody could later contest their landownership. An inspection of the ritual place, Nada Ae in Namata, reveals that the position of sacred stones and ritual houses spatially reproduces the manner in which the pig carcass was divided. Deo Rai, with precedence over all other priests, occupies the eastern part while Apu Lod'o and the Nataga clan are on the western side (Nadawawi). As in other parts of Savu, east has precedence over west.

An intriguing detail evokes the ancient settlers. The ceremonial cycle, called *kelila*, is shared between the Council of *Mone Ama* of Seba for 27 years and Deo Mengèru of Kekoro, Menia for nine years, the latter replacing the Jola, ancient settlers who had vanished. In a mantra chant, the Jola people are described as small people (*dou do baba*) with large ears (*bèla dilu*) and large feet (*bèla kae*).

---

[48] The Department of Tourism in the 1980s directed the construction of concrete steps leading to Namata, which cut through Leba Alu's land (probably prompting him to rebuild the house). The concrete path is right at the edge of his house; Leba Alu may have wanted to emphasise where the house of origin stood.

[49] See Detaq for some variations on the narrative (1973: 26–7). For precedence and ritual tasks associated with parts of a sacrificial animal (a goat instead of a pig), see the people of Marobo, north central Timor (Clamagirand 1982: 122–3).

Figure 24: Ritual centre of Namata

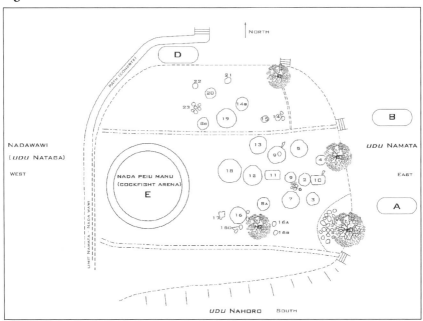

Names of priests and their ritual stones	A: House of Deo Rai and Bèni Deo
	B: House of Maukia and Heo Kèni
Deo Rai: 1 (rectangular flat stone + upright stone); 2, 3, 9 (a small stone on top of a large stone); 11 and small stones as part of 6	C: Trees – *Ziziphus jujuba*
	D: House of Bèka Pahi and Rahi Hawu at Raja Mara
	E: Arena for ritual cockfighting, *peiu manu*

Maukia: 5, 13, 14 a, 14 b

Doheleo: 7

Bèka Pahi: 4, 18, 19, 20

Latia: (helper of Maukia) 8a, 8b, (8c as part of 6)

Tutu Dalu: (helper of Maukia) 12

Rue: 16, 16a, 16b, 16c

Deo Rae Nada: 19

No information was available for 15, 17, 22 and 23.

Photo 3. Sacred stones; Namata, Seba (Sabu Barat) (2012)

Photo 4. *Kerogo*, a basket to hold sacrificial meat to be shared with members of the same lineage; Ledetadu, Mesara (2006)

They are reminiscent of *Homo floresiensis*, the small hairy humanlike creatures who lived in Flores.[50]

Namata

Unlike Liae and Mesara, where the creation and transformation of priest positions are traceable over a long period, in Seba Robo Aba's sons were each given a ritual task that was carried out until recently. The clans (*udu*) were all formed no more than four generations after the division of ritual positions. Mata Lai, a descendant of Tunu Robo (Lord of the Earth), started *udu* Namata. He is remembered for his brutality and the bloody wars he waged in many locations.[51] He tried to claim land with help from Horo Nani from the Lobo clan of Raijua. After Mata Lai fought for and won in Dimu, Horo Nani apparently refused the land Mata Lai offered him and established himself in Lobohede, Lower Mesara where he started the Aelape clan.[52] Mata Lai's brother, Nèto Lai, received the religious role of Bèka Pahi for holding rituals to prevent lontar trees from being struck by lightning. The tradition of tapping the lontar tree for sap must have existed at this time.

A Dutch missionary report from 1874 recorded a curious tradition about Mata Lai. In this version, the descendants of Kika Ga did not encounter an uninhabited land when they moved to Savu. Rather, there was a peaceful and industrious autochthonous population settled in nine villages: Jerroe, Torri, Kokki, Dikki and Bellajella in the east; and Keddoewa, Doewa, Tadja and Oewa in the west. There are few traces of these place names today. The newcomers and the old population coexisted for several generations, but rivalry over land eventually led to violent conflicts. Mata Lai first befriended the populations of the western villages, which were opposed by the eastern ones. Those in the east were exterminated through his intervention. However, Mata Lai turned out to be an unreliable ally, for he likewise attacked and eradicated the western villages after a period. At the beginning, the villagers stayed on as workers, but later Mata Lai sold them as slaves to buyers from outside Savu, so the original population entirely disappeared. Nevertheless, Mata Lai could not master the entire island

---

[50] See Gregory Forth (2010). See Seba's ceremonial cycle in Appendix II, Table 6. Alterations in this cycle are discussed in chapter 6.

[51] Interviews with Ama Obi Nale (09.10.2000) and Leba Alu (09.10.2001). Wars contemporaneous to Mata Lai of Namata, Taga Nyela of Nataga and Ote Horo of Nahoro depict the three clans joining forces to fight against groups considered to be living too near Namata.

[52] See Narrative 2 about Horo Nani in Appendix I.

as the various domains went their separate ways.[53] Modern recorded stories have no clear reference to Teffer's account and it is likely that the missionary—who did not master the Savunese language—refers to the vanished Jola people (chapter 1). However, chapter 5 has a Dutch account from 1648 which refers to a population in the interior subjected to slave raids by the coastal rajas (Tiele and Heeres 1886–95, III: 426).

Mata Lai's daughter, Hana Mata, had a son out of wedlock with Lumu Lutu of the Kolorae clan in Liae.[54] Mata Lai's four sons formed four lineages: Nèto Mata kept the main Namata line and was called Namata Uduae. The line from Lape Mata formed Namata-Nabura; the role of Deo Rai stayed with this line. Lode Mata formed Namata-Nalode and Wadu Mata's line created Namata-Napupenu.

Seven generations after Mata Lai, the position of Deo Rai was given to the firstborn son, Riwu Mau. The younger brother Ngahu Mau assumed the war-related role of Maukia. Maukia corresponds to the role of Apu Lod'o Muhu in Mesara or Rohi Lod'o for the Kolorae clan in Liae. To put a time marker beside the creation of the position, Ngahu Mau's daughter, Rade Ngahu, married Rohi Tari of the Nataga clan and became Ina Kore Rohi, the mother of Seba's first raja in Portuguese times. The marriage places the first priest of war in the late 15th or early 16th century.

In Seba, the clear distinction between ritual leadership, mainly in the hands of *udu* Namata, and political power, exclusively held by *udu* Nataga, became obvious four generations after Robo Aba. The Namata clan held further religious positions: for instance, Latia and Bèka Pahi, Maukia's helpers, were in charge of war matters and thunder; Tutu Dalu was responsible for taking the scalps of enemies, belonging to the same line as Maukia, and corresponded to the position of Kenuhe in other domains. The number of priest roles related to war coincided with the Portuguese presence in the area. About this time is the appearance of a number of foreign names such as Jawa, Mega, Nguru, Pana, Talo and Hina (Duggan 2011c: 35).

Nataga

One line of Dami Robo's descendants held the ritual role of Apu Lod'o; another line (Nataga Naluluweo) became Seba's political rulers, from which came the rajas of Portuguese and Dutch times. Nataga was formed at the same generational level as Namata, but it was two generations after Nahoro and three after Nahupu. Here is the same pattern as in Liae and Mesara, where the lines holding

---

[53] Raad voor de Zending, 1102–1: 1411, M. Teffer, report, 1874.

[54] See the Kolorae clan of Liae in the previous chapter (see Figure 9).

essential ritual positions form their clans later. Wars contemporary with Mata Lai (Namata), Taga Nyela (Nataga) and Ote Horo (Nahoro) are remembered as *muhu kelibo* (encircled by enemies), which in fact was merely an excuse to justify Seba's expansionist wars to the detriment of the surrounding domains. However, the people of Seba do not like to be reminded of the conflict. If they recount the events, they give the upper hand to their clan or to their domain through the use of magic as seen in the chant below:

> The descendants of Kole Wai were waiting, ready to fight
> The people of Mesara from Ledetedida,
> From Raeraga at Ledetedida.
> The people of Seba obtained a sword from Raijua:
> The sword was called Ledole.
> The spear from here [Seba] was called Rear Wind.
> They were hung in a jujube [*Ziziphus jujuba*] at the house of Bèni Ke.
> A pig was killed and the people were expelled towards Mesara.
> The spear stuck eight times.
> For the ninth time, the statue [made of *erythrina* wood] struck.
> There is a saying that then the people ran to Gurimoned'ue, Gurimonearu,
> The people of Mesara fled to Mesara.

Nataga people obtained help from Raijua. The sword named *ledole* appears in a narrative about Nie Lai of Raijua. The spear that attacked eight times on its own harks back to previous narratives where, after striking several enemies at once, the weapon returns to its owner. It was in the statue's power also to strike once. Such a small anthropomorphic statue is made of *aju kare* (*erythrina* wood). The belief in Savu is that during a flood in cosmological times humans changed into *kare* trees: thus its wood is sacred in Savu because of its close relationship to humans, particularly the female moieties. It can represent or act in place of a priest in a ritual. The Maukia priest in Namata kept such a statue in his house and used it during his mother Ina Bèngu Jungu's funeral in 1999 (Duggan 2001: 71, fig. 134).

For 12 generations, there is no record of special events or groups branching from the main line. A possible reason for the amnesia is that the future line of rajas in Seba was not credited with any deeds relevant to today's perspective.[55] Tari Lo created lineages (*kerogo*) for his four sons, Rebo Tari, Rohi Tari, Jingi Tari and Uli Tari. The first son, Rebo Tari, is remembered through his marriage with

---

[55] The next chapter follows the Nataga clan during Portuguese times.

Wènyi Daku, a descendant of Piga Tede Hipa of Mesara.[56] After her husband's death, Wènyi Daku married her brother-in-law, Jingi Tari. Her three daughters formed the *wini* Pi'i, Mèko and Raja lines (Figure 6). Jingi Tari formed the lineage of *udu* Nataga called Najingi and never assumed a position either in the priest system or as a political ruler. Uli Tari went to Sumba and six generations later his descendant, Lèdi Ke, returned to Savu to form Nataga-Wa; *wa* means west and, by extension, Sumba. Tari Lo had a brother, Kana Lo, whose grandson Dewa Dida Kana provided the name for Raedewa village in the domain of Seba. Altogether 13 lineages—the highest number for Savu clans—originated from the Nataga clan. According to genealogical knowledge, the sudden creation of male lineages (*kerogo*) and female lines (*wini*) either predated the Portuguese in the area by a generation or coincided with it.

Nahoro

The Nahoro clan, associated with the Doheleo (the Overseer), was formed one generation after the role's creation. Altogether four *kerogo* formed from Nahoro. Nine generations after Robo Aba, Kahu Rebo created *kerogo* Nakahu while his brother, Wui Rebo, kept the main Nahoro line and the role of Doheleo. Twelve generations after Robo Aba, Nawa Logo formed *kerogo* Nahoro-Nanawa. Jèga Adu from Liae had a descendant called Lai Wadu who created the third *kerogo*. While there is no record of Jèga Adu's descendants in Liae, they are traceable in Seba, eleven generations later. Lai Wadu formed Nahoro-Napawa and Haga Bara created the fourth *kerogo*, Nahoro-Napuhaga.

The position of Overseer no longer exists. Doheleo was responsible for agricultural rituals related to sorghum. Nowadays, Deo Rai conducts these ceremonies and those related to mung beans. Doheleo also represented the Deo Rai and the Apu Lod'o in the outside world when these priests had to stay secluded for weeks or months to meditate or perform rituals in their houses.[57] The Nahoro clan's house of origin still can be seen on Namata hill on the southern side, but it is not visible from the ritual arena. It is in dire need of repair.

Nahupu

The Nahupu clan, which has the position of Rue or Priest of Misfortune, did not split into further branches. Rue is a full member of the *Mone Ama* and participates

---

[56] Figure 6, see also Duggan (2001: 44, 104).

[57] The period of seclusion is a time related to heat and danger; therefore, the priests cannot have contact with the outside world. In the traditional kingdom of Wehali (Timor), the highest priest also stayed secluded for months in his ceremonial house performing rituals.

in all council of priest rituals. Previous scholarship minimised the position of Rue in the *Mone Ama*, stating his clan did not have land.[58] However, *udu* Nahupu's land is in Raedewa, not far from Lededai'ie where the ancestor Ie Miha lived. As seen in all other domains, Rue is an essential part of the *Mone Ama* and he holds three large stones at the Namata ritual centre. People might be reserved when talking about Rue's tasks because of a superstition attached to tragedies. In fact, he is highly respected by priests and the population alike because of his ability to prevent harm to humans and animals. It is in his power to send 'bad' things out to sea, even before they manifest themselves in the form of diseases.[59] Therefore, Rue accompanies other priests who conduct rituals because they need him. For the ceremony *kowa hole* in Mesara, Rue is the most essential priest after Deo Rai. When people ask for fertile seeds they also request that the ancestors remove bad, infertile grains. One of Rue's roles is to mediate in this matter.

The mysterious Kelara clan

The Kelara clan is said to have descended from the ancestor Lèki D'ara. However, in pre-European times his genealogy shows serious gaps. There is a legend about Kelara people that everybody in Savu knows. They are invisible to humans and, according to the Maukia priest, only visible to priests in their dreams. They are very industrious people, working at night, and live on the invisible island of Kelara.[60] They occasionally return from to Savu at night to worship at their ancestors' sacred sites. The root *lara* in *kelara* is yellow. It has two interpretations according to the context. In the case of sickness, *lara* has the negative meaning of purulence. In other contexts, *lara* refers to the yellow threads (dyed with turmeric) in the weavings of raja family members and, by extension, means gold.

The priests in Namata acknowledge that Mata Lai, Robo Aba's great-grandson, chased away two groups of people from Savu—the Jola and the Kelara.[61] Names can be traced in Hutankelara (Kelara forest), not far from Namata, Ledekelara (Kelara hill), near Tuwi, and the Kelara people's village of origin is Raetuleika, near

---

[58] Fox (1979: 159). According to Leba Alu (05.09.2001) the position of Rue in Namata existed before the ancestors moved there. It was not created for one of Robo Aba's sons but was taken over.

[59] Rue has an important role in the three-day ceremony of *keboko pèda* (to gather diseases), which is held from the seventh to the ninth day of the new moon in the first month of the year, Wèru a'a (May–June). On the last day, the priests Maukia, Latia and Rue send the potential diseases out to sea in a small boat (Duggan 2001: 139, fig. 97).

[60] Interview with Dida Bèngu (25.05.2000). This is common knowledge in Savu. The legend about the Kelara people has been printed several times in local newspapers.

[61] The Jola were mentioned regarding the *kelila* cycle in Seba.

Raebodo.[62] Ama Dubu Wadu is the keeper of his ancestors' fenced settlement. Asked about the mysterious Kelara people and their invisible island, he smiled but said nothing. Later he recounted the following:[63]

> The people of Kelara were in competition with the people of Namata. One day they decided to find out who was richer and stronger. They organised a *tao leo* ceremony during which buffalos were slaughtered.[64] The people of Namata, instead of killing the buffalos and roasting them, burned copra and other rubbish. The Kelara people, seeing the smoke, thought that people were roasting buffalos in Namata. They also heard the banging of the rice mortar and thought that people were pounding rice. In fact, they only pounded coconut husks. The Kelara people slaughtered buffalos one after the other, roasted them and pounded rice until they did not have any more cattle or rice. Meanwhile, there was still smoke coming from Namata and they could still hear the banging mortars; they were tricked. Kelara people had lost and, to avoid losing face, they left the island and went to the mysterious island of Kelara.

It is common knowledge in Seba that the Kelara people were chased away. The real story might have been more violent than the group vanishing after losing face in a competition. A descendant Wila Holo travelled from mysterious Kelara Island to worship at his ancestors' stones in the forest of Kelara. He left his boat in Mesara and, while walking through the night to the forest, he fell into an exhausted sleep. When people from Mesara found him he acknowledged his identity. They said he could stay in Mesara where his descent line still exists. Wila Holo's descendants have been incorporated into *udu* Napuhina in Mesara. In Savunese, Holo—an older pronunciation—means Solor, the small island near Flores.[65] Thus Solor, or the wider area of Lamaholot, indicates Wila Holo's foreign origin. However, there is no Wila Holo in Napuhina's genealogies, but there is Hina Holo. Here again Hina refers to a foreign origin, so Wila Holo and Hina Holo might be the same person.

---

[62] In a list of villages established by the Dutch in 1851 (see Appendix IV), Raetuleika is given as Tulan Ikan, which is also the name of a settlement found on the south coast of Timor. Therefore, a link between both cannot be excluded, although it is unknown in group social memory.

[63] (03.05.2008). Figure 25.

[64] This is not the actual meaning of *tao leo*. A *tao leo* ceremony is performed only at a funeral for charismatic people or people of a certain rank. Ama Dubu Wadu's narrative is a reminder of Potlatch ceremonies performed by the indigenous people of North America's Pacific north-west coast.

[65] Robert Barnes, personal communication; March 2016.

Figure 25: Kelara clan

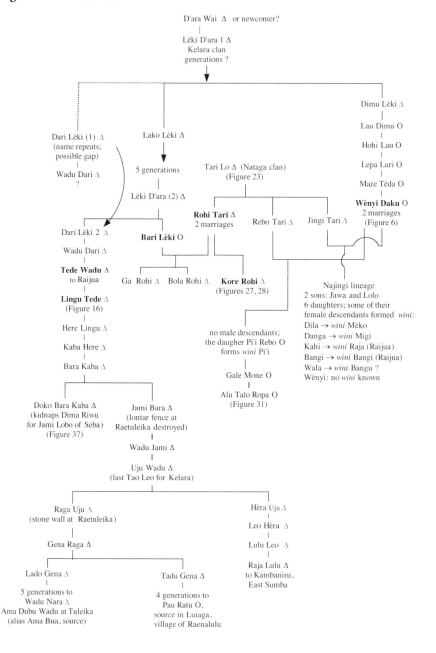

An important ancestor of the Kelara clan, Tede Wadu, swam from Savu to Raijua and was adopted by the Lobo clan. However, his son Lingu Tede is at the origin of the Melako clan. A descendant of Lingu Tede, Doko Bara Kaba, appears four generations later in the Kelara clan genealogy; he played a part in Seba's history around 1700.[66]

The Kelara people were not invisible people living on an invisible island. They were a group of people, possibly newcomers, who failed to become indigenised. Although Kelara women married local rulers, the group has been discriminated against or banned several times in its history. As seen in later chapters, Kelara men helped several rulers at war with other domains but were merely considered mercenaries. Although physically present, the Kelara people became socially invisible. They were an ostracised group; they became the brutalised victims of ruling Nataga clan members in the late 18th century. The story of *udu* Kelara as recounted by Ama Dubu Wadu is a clear case in which facts and events were turned into a tale; where history was transformed into legend.

The descendants of Pia Adu in Raijua

All of Ie Miha's descendants in Raijua originated in Savu. Pia Adu of Liae created one of the links between Savu and Raijua. In Raijua, Ie Miha is said to have no descendants and the Savu story says his son Mone Ie, without a male descendant, adopted a baby boy called Aba Mone.

Pia Adu, who has vanished from memory in Liae, is traceable in Raijua; his son Gèla Pia went to Lamakera on the island of Solor near the eastern end of Flores.[67] A generation later Ngari Gèla first moved to Ledeke in Liae, his grandfather's original domain, before establishing a line in Raijua. The line descended from his son Alo Ngari is sometimes referred to as *udu* Naalo. More generally, the line is known as *udu* Nadaibu, named after the arena in its original village, Wuirae.[68] Six generations later there were three new lineages: Wètu Kai formed *kerogo* Wuirae; Bèpa Kai is at the origin of the raja line in Raijua; and Tua Kai began *kerogo* Natua.

---

[66] See chapter 6 and the war between Jami Lobo and Tèro Weo.

[67] *Gèla* refers to a boat mast as well as a social task in the community.

[68] Wuirae means literally 'stern village'. The younger brother's descendants' second-place ranking is once more confirmed; the elder brother occupied the 'bow' or 'head' position. *Nada* (arena) and *ibu* is the root of the verb *peibu* (to bring together, to assemble).

Figure 26: Descendants of Pia Adu in Raijua

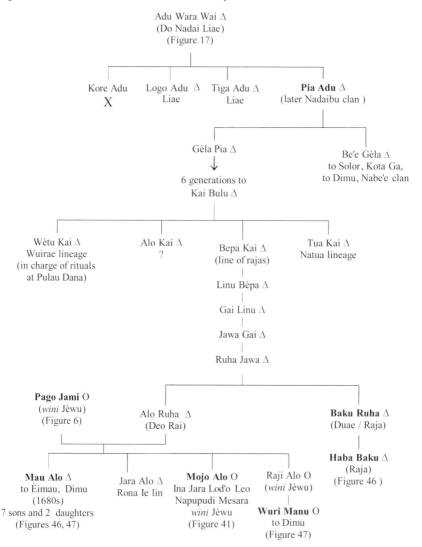

Savu before 'history'; a preliminary reflection

The first section of the book can rely only on local oral recollections and observations as there are no existing external written sources. Before following the development of the society through a combination of local sources and the subsequent external documents, it is useful to reflect on recurrent themes encountered in these first chapters as well as on essential cultural categories shared by all the domains.

The sea-land dichotomy and foreign versus indigenous

A number of the narratives about early times in Savu evolved into myths. These resonate with the myths from other parts of the world that deal with the arrival of a foreigner or an outsider who becomes indigenous.[69] Chapter 1 discusses, for instance, how the outsider Kika Ga, coming from the sea, was adopted by 'God in the sky' and made an autochthon. As he became an insider, he entered the category 'people of the land'. Interestingly, his wife belonged to a different category as she is labelled 'women of the sea'. Kika Ga is not an isolated case: other important ancestors married 'women of the sea'—Dida Miha, Robo Aba— thus expressing a different cultural category. The sea-land dichotomy takes an interesting twist with the two brothers Dida Miha and Ie Miha. As descendants of Kika Ga, both are 'people of the land'. The former lost all his possessions in a series of cockfights, after which he was adopted by the 'people of the sea' and consequently was classified as 'sea', leaving his younger brother Ie Miha (who was not involved) in the 'land' category.

Narrative analysis clearly identified a succession of settlers. However, a number of ancient settlers merely left names in collective memory. They are Mone Reu and the Jola in Seba, Mone Weo in Raijua, the Nai'iki, Nabe'e and Wolo in east Savu. The ceremonial cycles of Liae and Mesara have years with no rituals marking those people who vanished. Nevertheless, the absence of ritual serves as a memory tag. The precious knowledge retained in the genealogies helps to trace personal names and gives clues about indigenous people and when later settlers arrived. In early genealogies, there are names like Gèla (mast), Uli (rudder) and Wui (stern) referring to parts of a boat, as well as names such as Ratu (council) and Aji (priest). They refer to the socio-religious positions of these ancestors. Names, such as Hina, Jawa, Mega, Guru, Hili or Talo, only appear in the 15th or 16th century and some of their descendants became rulers or were members of ruling clans.

---

[69] See, for example, Fox about founding myths in which an "outsider is installed inside" (2008: 201–18).

In *The Stranger Kings of Sikka* (2010), Douglas Lewis links a tradition of 'stranger-kings' to continuous Portuguese contacts in societies of the Lesser Sunda Islands and questions the case of Savu (2010: 197). For Savu, it is possible to look back into a past more distant than the 16th century. The sudden emergence of foreign male names in the genealogies would corroborate observations made about other Austronesian societies. While analysing the tradition of 'stranger-kings' on Fijian islands, Marshall Sahlins (1985: 89) notes the following corresponding categories "the chief is to the people as foreign is to native, the sea is to the land, the wife-takers to the wife-givers". Among the Marobo and the Wehali of Timor, and the Tana Ai of Sikka the 'people of the land' are autochthon, the elder siblings are insiders and at the centre; consequently, others are younger siblings at the periphery and outsiders.[70] In Sumba, Stephen Lansing argues for a small number of new male settlers marrying local women and traces them through linguistics and genetics.[71]

Subsequent chapters reveal that the arrival of the Portuguese in Savu did not lead to the sudden nomination of an outsider as 'stranger-king'; the pedigree of these rulers can be verified through their genealogies and those of their siblings. To summarise the discussion of outsiders and the 'stranger-king' it can be said that Kika Ga was a stranger—his descendants methodically either cleared the area of previous settlers or assimilated them—but at the time of European contact there is no obvious case of a 'stranger-king' taking over positions in Savu. Conversely, they have been so discreetly integrated into the local discourse and the genealogies that it is not possible to trace them. For Savunese identity, it is important not to be ruled by an outsider. Genealogies undeniably structure Savunese thought and its terminology reveals the type of mental images Savu people construct for their genealogical 'sites of memory'. From the local point of view, no place is accredited to any possible 'stranger-king'.

Another foundation myth, the pig hunt, in association with beginning a new settlement is shared with several societies in the region. For example, the "History of the Hunters" (Lewis 1988: 53–7) recounts how two brothers conquered the Tana Ai land in eastern Flores. After overcoming a number of obstacles, the hunt following the wild animal trails, was finally successful. The elder brother cleared his path to a new settlement while hunting a deer; the younger brother made his way to the new place after successfully hunting a wild pig. Geirnaert-

---

[70] See Clamagirand (1982) about the Marobo, Lewis about Sikka (2010: 77–8) and Therik on Wehali (2004: 55) See a range of journal articles in *Stranger-kings in Indonesia and beyond*, edited by Caldwell and Henley (2008). See also Lansing et al. (2011) and more specifically on Sumba (2007), Tumonggor et al. on Timor (2014).

[71] Lansing et al. (2007).

Martin (1992: 43–4) narrates how the Sumbanese ancestors roamed for a long time and finally reached Laboya (West Sumba) while hunting a wild pig. After they caught the wild pig, they realised that "[i]t was not a usual pig, it was really a woman who belonged to the people of the forest (that is, the autochthonous people of Sumba)". The Manggarai of western Flores have a mythical narrative recounting a deer hunt in which the deer is also a woman (Erb 1987: 95). In another narrative about an immigrant from Minangkabau, the newcomer took a local pregnant sow which ran away several times. Each time the man followed the run-away animal and his journey to a number of settlements is remembered today through the sow's path (Erb 1999: 71–5). All these narratives show similarities and have the same purpose. They share the theme of a journey and the wild animal is female; it transforms into a woman after being caught and is synonymous with indigenous people. They lead to a new political organisation of the society (Lewis 1988: 76). In Laboya too, the autochthonous people, whose female connotation is metaphorically the wild pig-woman, retained ritual power while the newcomers took political power. One of the Manggarai people, the "true aborigine woman", gave her land to the clan of her newly arrived husband as well as providing a direct link to supernatural power (Erb 1999: 75).

The sea-land dichotomy is important. An investigation of the Jingi Tiu belief system and its rituals reveals on both islands the ceremonial precedence of the 'people of the sea' (the elder brother) over the 'people of the land' (the younger brother), which is the reverse of other societies in the area. What are the implications of such a situation? The sea-land opposition serves to build socio-cultural categories. Relevant here is the fact that while changing categories, the elder brother maintained precedence over his younger brother and this is in concordance with other societies. The sea and land idioms still express the essential binary opposition known in Austronesian societies and this dichotomy should not be taken too narrowly. Moreover, in Savu people never say 'men of the sea' as the sea is imminently female; water and the darkness 'inside the sea' refer to women. The Savunese word for water—*ei*—sounds similar to the name of the tubular cloth women wear. Cultural categories are not static but have evolved according to situations. Yet the labels 'sea' and 'land' remain mnemonic tags for identifying two lines of settlers—the elder and the younger brothers—without the inherent opposition that the labels foreign versus indigenous carry in other societies in the region.

Oral accounts not only provide details about various groups of settlers, they also show that Savu society had from the beginning a strong female orientation; in a number of cases, the first priest in the line was a woman (Deo Rai, Rue). However, the society evolved towards a more patriarchal society after the formation of male clans and their councils of priests *Ratu* and *Mone Ama*. And yet none of the priests can perform fertility rites without the participation of their wives, Bèni Deo or Bèni Aji. For example, in Seba during agricultural rites, the physical act of mixing sorghum and mung bean seeds, as well as planting them, have to be carried out by Bèni Deo.

The genealogical knowledge and the social memory of certain clans are essential in tracing the circumstances of events. Such transformations of facts into myths or legends have been observed elsewhere.[72] It is remarkable that the Savu people already had a sense of territoriality in precolonial history. Researchers have found that among the people of Southeast Asia the sense of territory was linked to people, not to a fixed land area, so that the 'territory' moved as people migrated. In Mesara people moved the names of places and stones to their final settlements. However, the boundaries between Seba and Mesara were already defined when Robo Aba and Ago Rai lived, a long time before any European interference. Savu people had from early on a sense of territory. There is no doubt that the clans (*udu*) were linked to named places delimited through natural features of the landscape to founding houses, *èmu kepue*, as well as to named stones and trees. They fought each other for the control of their land; thus, they had a sense of territoriality. This is not a western or colonial import but was born out of spatial limitation.[73]

Councils of priests and ceremonial cycles

When looking closely at societal development in all domains, Dida Miha's descendants have the right of precedence. In Liae, they organised themselves rapidly into proto-clans called *do* and in the specific socio-politico-religious organisation of *ratu* and *aji*. In collective memory the first ancestors lived in Liae (in Merèbu and Teriwu). After turbulent times and the restructuring of positions, the 'people of the sea' gained representation in the Council of Five Men (Kolorae and Teriwu clans) while the descendants of the younger brother, the 'people of the land', organised themselves first in the proto-clan *do* Nadai; they shaped the Council of Seven Men. In Dimu, too, people organised themselves first as proto-clans, though it was later than in Liae. There the descendants of both brothers had the label *do*: *do* Nalai and *do* Napuru. In all other domains, the younger brother's descendants did not seem to have formed proto-clans, and

---

[72] Barber and Barber (2004: 6).

[73] Thongchai Winichakul (1985) argues in *Siam Mapped: A History of the Geo-Body of a Nation* that the idea of exact boundaries and fixed borders in Southeast Asia did not develop before colonialism when mapping started as a means to control natural resources and manpower. Continental Southeast Asia might not be comparable to the tiny island of Savu where the sea forms a natural boundary and where land might have become limited even in early days.

several generations were necessary for them to shape clans (*udu*) and councils of priests (*Mone Ama*). All councils shaped by the younger brother's descendants carry the mnemonic tag *rai*.[74]

In all domains there is not one but at least two systems—council of priests—either working in parallel (Seba, Mesara, Liae) or complementing each other (Dimu). In Raijua, five priest positions called Deo Rai were identified, meaning that each clan had its own council of priests. As this is no longer the case, it is impossible to trace each of them. In Mesara, the councils of priests correspond to the two apical ancestors. For Lower Mesara, the roles have the identifier *dahi* corresponding to Dida Miha the elder brother and the 'people of the sea', while in Upper Mesara the roles are labelled *rai* to denote descendants of the younger brother. In Dimu, both councils of priests stem from the elder brother Dida Miha. Each council is identified with spatial markers: 'north' for Bodae which has retained the priest position of Rue; and 'south' for Bolou and the Council *Ratu Rai* in the Naèli clan. The Apu Lod'o Rai is from the Nadowu clan, which provided the rajas during Dutch times. In Dimu, the calendar is divided into sweet (*nèta*) and bitter (*hèro*) months. In other domains, the balance between sweet and bitter is expressed in the first two months of the year: Wèru a'a (month of the elder sibling) and Wèru ari (month of the younger sibling), which is a silent month dedicated to the dead. In Mesara, sweetness is incorporated in the name Penèta, the month which corresponds to the blooming of the mung beans (February). Raijua and Dimu show a number of similarities, which is not surprising as both domains are linked through their genealogies; Dimu's ancestors originated in Raijua. They also share the number six for auspicious rituals. However, all domains have the same principle for rituals which take place at fixed times of the adat calendar. They are referred to as *kewèhu rai* (knots of the land), to tie the communities together through ceremonies and festivals. Furthermore, each domain has larger ceremonial cycles called *kelila* which combine the tasks of both councils. The meaning of the word *kelila* is not clear; it contains the root *lila* which is to fly. In Seba's collective memory, the Jola passed *kelila* on to the community and they have since vanished.[75]

When analysing and comparing the various councils in each domain, the common rule is that a council of priests cannot exist without the high priest Deo Rai. He is linked to the east, the left side, and has female characteristics.

---

[74] In Dimu, where the younger brother's descendants are not represented in a council, one council derived from the elder brother carries the mnemonic tag *rai* as if it is imperative that the dichotomy of complementarity sea-land always be present in the councils of the domain (see Figure 11).

[75] See Appendix II for the adat calendars in the various domains and the large *kelila* cycles.

He is associated with secrecy and seclusion in the ritual months, which echoes situations in other Austronesian societies. Clans of the Deo Rai never provided rajas or fettors in Portuguese and Dutch times. Ritual authority presides over political power. For the other positions, each domain or even each council inside a domain developed its own hierarchy. After the Deo Rai, the Rue appears to be the most essential priest—his presence at all rituals can prevent unwanted or dangerous situations that can spoil the performance—and he is able to re-establish a harmonious and balanced state. In Mesara, he occupies Raepedèro's highest terrace. In Seba, Rue holds three large stones at the ritual centre of Namata.

Research raises questions regarding the role and the rank of the Apu Lod'o. The role existed before the Europeans came in the 16th century and the political ruler (raja) under the Portuguese and the Dutch was always recruited from the Apu Lod'o's clan. He too has to stay secluded during certain months. Being from the same clan as the ruler might have helped him to reach a higher position in some councils of priests. For instance, in public talks in Seba and Liae the Apu Lod'o has second ranking. However, it is remarkable that at the Seba ritual centre the sacred stones for which the Apu Lod'o is responsible are not located at the big arena (*Nada ae*) but outside, at Nadawawi, the cradle of the Nataga clan. The Apu Lod'o does not share ceremonial meals with the Deo Rai and his helpers, even if they share the same sacrificial animal. Later in Liae's history, the Nanawa clan, which provided rajas during Portuguese times, held the Apu Lod'o role, but with the VOC's arrival the positions of Apu Lod'o and raja went to the Napujara clan. Neither does the situation in Mesara satisfactorily explain the status of the Apu Lod'o role. Mesara has three Apu Lod'o; Apu Lod'o Dahi is part of the council of priests of Lower Mesara while for Upper Mesara there are Apu Lod'o Muhu (corresponding to the role of Maukia in Seba, Lado Aga in Dimu and Kètu Muhu in Liae) and Apu Lod'o Wadu who is in charge of rituals dedicated to the lontar palm tree during the dry season. However, both are from the Naputitu clan which provided the rajas during Dutch times.

The formation of clans and lineages was closely related to the creation of ritual roles, especially for those clans linked to war under the Maukia's leadership. The prevalence of war and how much power the clans gained tended to dictate the creation of ritual positions. They have different names in the various parts of the islands, mirroring the independence of the councils in each domain; for example, in Seba the priest roles were all under the Maukia and were recruited from the lineages of the Namata clan. While the main priest of war, the Maukia, stayed secluded in his ritual house, his helper the Kenuhe was able to travel clandestinely to where the battles occurred. Together with the Tutu Dalu, he took the heads of enemies and the latter also had to strip the skin from the skulls.[76] The Latia, whose primary task was to deal with thunder and lightning, also became involved in war matters—the link being the noise produced by canons, muskets and rifles.

Metaphors

Recorded interviews, narratives and ritual chants provided a good part of the exegesis for the book thus far. Also essential were observations made in the field during ceremonies and rituals where opposed or complementary categories were exposed; for instance, between the categories elder and younger, male and female, front and back, hot and cold, upper and lower, bitter and sweet, and inside and outside. To learn and remember people construct "apparatuses for the efficient handling and packaging of specific domains of knowledge" (Bloch 1998: 10–1). The mapping of these "apparatuses" appeared useful to uncover the concepts underlying the knowledge. The participation in or the exclusion of certain groups in rituals, the presence or absence of drums, gongs, daggers and textiles in heirlooms, the prescriptions and the prohibitions in the use of certain objects or specific food during rituals, the types of offerings, their numbers and colours, not forgetting the gender of sacrificed animals, were precious tools in revealing an internal social coherence and in reconstructing a plausible past for the island. An outstanding mnemonic device is the memory of an event or ritual's absence.

The overall coherence in the concept of precedence at all levels and on both islands is one of the most striking findings. The primary metaphor expressing precedence is the botanical image of a growing plant, from the roots to the tip, with lower (older) and upper (younger) leaves. The botanical idiom of growth is embedded in all aspects of the society. This can be observed in ritual practices when sacrificial animals are blessed from the rear to the neck. It applies to humans too who receive a gentle rub from the feet, along the spine to the top of the head. The notion of roots has a special significance for people who should walk barefoot to have direct contact with their underground 'roots'.[77]

The botanical idiom of growth serves as a matrix for the genealogical knowledge. The primary mental structure for remembering is in the form of a genealogy, providing people with a shared origin, a sense of chronological time and of precedence as organising principles, connecting the past and the present.

---

[76] In Savu, the skulls of enemies were buried and not exhibited on 'skull-trees' at the village entrance as was the case in Sumba.

[77] Nowadays, very few people aside from the priests of *Mone Ama* walk barefoot or ride their horses bareback.

Photo 5. Rebuilding the priest Maukia's ritual house; the beams supporting the loft, carved in the shape of ancestors, are reminiscent of a catamaran's hull; Namata (2011)

Photo 6. Discarded damaged beams representing ancestors; Namata (2011)

People bear in mind a genealogical construct from the time of the world's creation to the present in which every element, every being finds its place, so the Savu world is ordered.

A mental representation of a cosmic order is present in every society. In Savu, it is expressed in genealogies for which a second metaphor is added, the image of a building's construction, *huhu kebie* (piling up beams or logs); thus the building is continuously developing. The images of a growing plant or of an ever-increasing building used for the genealogies imply a sense of a growing world, a swelling universe, a notion of an ever-expanding time which is in fact a very modern concept. 'Piling up beams' or 'logs' is a reminder of how a wooden building similar to a log cabin is constructed, although such architecture probably never existed in Savu. There are two reasons as to why: one is that the hot climate does not require tight constructions, which are better adapted for mountainous areas than for tropical lowlands; secondly, such architecture would require a large amount of timber and trees do not grow fast on a dry island like Savu. It is more likely that migrants brought with them the terminology derived from this architectural concept, and that they had already transferred this idiom into their genealogy terminology. According to local memory, the typical Savunese house style was introduced in Seba while Aba Mone lived and in Raijua at the time of Wohe Bara. There are differences between the houses—especially those for ritual purposes—on the islands. In Raijua, houses are smaller, built on wooden pillars or placed on stones and, unlike in Savu, the sides at the base are closed with stones (Plates 3 and 10).[78] The wooden pillars are of lontar trees (instead of *kola* [*Bischoffia javanica*] in Savu) while the roof is thatched with pandanus leaves instead of lontar leaves. While in Savu the veranda (*kelaga*) is located on the longest side of the house with a male and female part, in Raijua it runs along the gable side, thus the male part of the house. These details might indicate the different origins of the Raijua and Savu house builders.

With the fundamental principles for Savu and Raijua's politico-religious organisation in place, it is time to consider how they evolved when confronted by major external shocks such as the arrival of Europeans in the region.

---

[78] This type of construction is reminiscent of Micronesian houses. See Waterson (1990: 7).

Chapter	Foreign Influences:
4	Majapahit and the Portuguese

Savu and the wider Southeast Asian Archipelago

Genealogical tradition asserts that the Portuguese established affiliated rajas in various domains in a period that corresponds to the 16th century. As collective memory assigns some significance to this foreign element, the chapter considers the context in which foreign ships arrived in the Savu Sea. It is possible that the Hindu-Buddhist Majapahit Empire had a degree of influence in Savu. Scrutinising fragmentary but suggestive evidence for the early Portuguese presence shows that it may have served as a template for the later and better-documented Dutch impact.

Anthony Reid's well-known study posits a Southeast Asian "age of commerce" from the 15th century (Reid 1988, 1993). A comprehensive network of seaborne routes developed after 1400 with Malacca as an important emporium.[1] At the eastern end of the network lay the spice sultanates Ternate and Tidore, which adopted Islam sometime in the 15th century, and had wide regional influence as far as the Savu Sea. The Maluku spices were a lucrative commodity that found its way as far as Europe and encouraged the early Iberian voyages of 'discovery'. However, the main spice trade route went north of Flores and the Solor Islands: the Savu Sea was dangerous and Savu itself was, therefore, not the port of call that its centrality between Flores, Sumba and Timor might suggest.[2] The Flores-Timor region had less to offer than Maluku in terms of natural products, but sandalwood was an obvious attraction. Sandalwood carried religious significance as it was used for incense and was indispensable to Buddhist and Daoist

---

[1] This, of course, does not mean that Southeast Asia was without extensive commercial networks before 1400. Kenneth Hall identified four overlapping trade networks in what is now Indonesia from 1000 to 1400: in the Melaka Straits, the South China Sea, the Java Sea and one in the Sulu Sea/eastern Indonesia. The latter two included the Savu Sea (Hall 2011: 67).

[2] Compare, however, Roy Ellen's investigation of sea routes used by the early-modern traders of Southeast Ceram, who went to Java with the monsoon winds, returning via the Savu Sea (Ellen 2003: 55).

ceremonies. Like spices, sandalwood linked the eastern archipelago to larger, ultimately global commercial connectivities. The sandalwood island *par preference* was Timor whose resources were exploited on a grander scale from about the late 16th century (De Roever 2002: 35–59). There was only limited access to the valuable wood in Sumba and it is possible that it was the same for the Solor Islands in the remote past.

There is no evidence for a Savunese sandalwood trade. However, three elements require mentioning here: first of all, a few sandalwood trees can be seen on the island today; secondly, the sweet scent of sandalwood makes it a compulsory component of offerings; and thirdly, the rule for Savu and Raijua rituals is to use exclusively indigenous ingredients. There are aromatic roots growing on the island which can replace sandalwood if it is not available. This practice suggests the presence of sandalwood trees in the past; the production was certainly small and the stands might have been depleted even before the Portuguese arrival. Chinese geographical descriptions mention Timor and sandalwood from time to time, although sea travel was discouraged during part of the Ming Dynasty (1368–1644).[3] One may recall the name element Hina (*Sina* is China) that occurs as part of a Savunese name, pointing at possible early visits.

It should be noted that the contemporaneous politically fragmented nature of Savunese society corresponded to conditions in the larger region. Although the Chinese asserted in 1350 that there was "a local chieftain" of Timor, this is almost certainly not true.[4] The eastern parts of the archipelago were divided into small-scale polities and do not seem to have developed larger, durable realms before Islam and Christianity—the Ternate and Tidore sultanates would have been the first of that kind. On the other hand, there could quite possibly have been realms from the central and western parts of the archipelago that achieved influence in these quarters.[5] Europeans in the 19th century heard stories in Savu which referred to the Majapahit Empire (circa 1293–1520) as the origin of the present society. The authoritative naturalist and ethnographic account by Salomon Müller from 1829 says the following:

> As told us by a number of grandees of this people, the island received its first inhabitants from Java; they supposedly consisted of a host of refugees

[3] Ptak (1983) has translated and discussed these early travels. For the first European travel account in the region (1522), see Pigafetta (1923: 234–7).

[4] However, it could allude to the Liurai of Wewiku-Wehali, the highest ranking lord in Timor in olden times. For the hierarchy of traditional polities in Timor, especially West Timor, see Schulte Nordholt (1971); for the symbolic and ritual position of Wewiku-Wehali, see Therik (2004).

[5] The previous chapter refers to foreign names appearing suddenly in the genealogies two or three generations before the first remembered Portuguese contacts; cf. Duggan (2011c).

who saved themselves on ships together with a prince of the royal house of Modjopahit, when this kingdom was overcome by the Mohammedan troops (AD 1478). They subsequently roamed from one island to another until they finally arrived to the uninhabited Savu and settled there … However that may be, people from Rote, Timor, Flores, and other neighbouring islands, as well as a number of Bugis from Celebes and people from Buton, would have mixed with the first settlers. As a consequence of that, the physical appearance as well as the customs and usages necessarily underwent a number of changes (Temminck 1839–44: 291–2).

While centred in Java the kingdom enjoyed an extensive influence across the archipelago. According to the renowned panegyric poem *Nagarakertagama* from 1365,[6] Solor, Timor and Galiyao (Pantar and parts of Alor) were under Majapahit suzerainty, although philologists and historians have strongly debated the veracity of these claims (Robson 1995: 34). On the other hand, there are traditions from other places in the area, such as Ende in Flores and the Alor Islands, which point to a Majapahit or Javanese presence in the distant past. It is possible that this aspect was toned down in 20th-century Savunese tradition, though there are still hints of the Majapahit influence. Nevertheless, it must be stressed that Müller's story of a Majapahit settlement cannot be literally correct; Savu was definitely inhabited before 1478, as seen in the previous chapters, and the language is not derived from Javanese.[7] The missionary W.M. Donselaar surveyed Savunese culture in the early 1870s, but he could not confirm any tradition that the first settlers were Javanese from Majapahit. However, he did record the ancestral figures Maja Pai and Maja Mada who lived in Raijua.[8] Immigrants from Raijua would have subsequently populated Savu itself. Like Müller, Donselaar believed that the first settlers were a mix of Timorese, Rotenese and Endenese from Flores, and migrants from Buton off Sulawesi (Donselaar 1872: 292–3).[9]

---

[6] Written while at the court of King Hayam Wuruk, Prapanca's poem portrays life in the Javanese kingdom. The original title was *Desa warnana* (Description of the Country).

[7] As is now well known, Majapahit did not actually fall in 1478, thus contradicting Müller who followed Javanese historiography. The capital of the Hindu-Buddhist realm moved to Kediri after 1486 and the state eventually collapsed in the 1520s (Ricklefs 2001: 41).

[8] There is no Maja Mada known in Raijua today. It is Gajah Mada (circa 1290–1364), the Majapahit Empire's great military leader. As his birthplace is unknown, some people in Savu and Raijua assert that he was born in Raijua!

[9] Raad voor de Zending, 1102–1: 1411, M. Teffer, report, 1874.

Another missionary, Mattheus Teffer, asserts that King Maja Pahit was expelled from Java by his son and went to settle in Raijua and later Savu. He tried to secure his position as the lord over the islands, but his ambitions were frustrated in Robo Aba's time. A 'Robo Aba' is known to the genealogies of the Nataga clan (Figure 23). There are 12 generations or some 300 years between Robo Aba and Kore Rohi, known as the first raja of Portuguese times. The same can be said if considering the genealogies of the Namata clan (Figure 23). There are eleven generations between Robo Aba and Ngahu Mau, whose daughter Rade Ngahu married Kore Rohi. This places the time of Robo Aba around 1250, before the establishment of the Majapahit Empire, not towards the end. It is puzzling that early connections with the Majapahit Empire did not generate further contacts with Savu and Raijua, and did not influence religious practices, political organisation or the arts, as there is no wooden carving tradition or stone sculpture in Savu and Raijua.

However, modern oral traditions recorded in Raijua reveal that the inhabitants of Raijua are called *Niki-niki Maja* (the children of Maja). And yet, it is not possible to trace someone called Maja in any of the Raijua clans, neither among Dida Miha's descendants nor those of Ie Miha. Nor is there a precise link to the Majapahit Empire in the narratives, which have references to *Raja Laut* and to 'God inside the Sea', whoever they might be.

Nevertheless, a number of narratives relate to a certain Maja. In recent years, there has been a polemic discussion around the character Maja whose deeds and spatial markers have suddenly increased. In order to clarify this case, there are excerpts below reproduced from chants involving Maja. As seen in the mythological part, Maja is known as Maja Muri Lai, an unpredictable spirit best kept at bay through offerings. He is said to reside on the uninhabited island of Dana, as mentioned in a ritual chant about gods descending to the ceremonial place:

.... Coming through the island of Dana
Battered by the waves ...
Passing through the village of Maja Muri Lai
Who can turn everything upside down
Who is changing continuously.[10]

The erratic Maja cannot be trusted and his name pops up in various narratives. Some versions of the story involve Ago Rai of Mesara and Robo Aba of Seba, and are about a stolen ritual house. Ago Rai built the house with Maja—he

---

[10] Deo Rai, Mesara (05.2004).

then accompanied him to Seba in order to confront Robo Aba, who they accuse of stealing it. However, Maja plays no further role in the narrative; he did not employ any tricks against Robo Aba to retrieve the house. On the contrary, Robo Aba out tricked them both.

In Raijua, an ancient settler, Mone Weo, is said to have fled when Maja arrived. Since this time, an annual ceremony takes place: a boat loaded with offerings is launched out to sea in order to compensate Mone Weo. Mone Weo's flight alludes to the arrival of a powerful newcomer, perhaps during Majapahit times. In Mesara and Raijua, there is a priest position called Maja. Like the priest Kenuhe, Maja is able to travel underground and is invisible to humans. In Ketita, Raijua's most revered ceremonial centre, Maja has a ritual house. What is striking is that his house turns its back to the settlement's centre while all the other priestly houses, including the house for Mone Weo, face inwards. There was no explanation for this fact, which implies a visually acknowledged difference for the Maja priest.

Maja in Raijua is possibly the companion of Bèni Kedo, likewise feared and revered. She is the subject of female worship by members of the Lesser Blossom moiety and associated with a sacred rice field for producing red rice for rituals (Kagiya 2010: 76–8). Maja left without leaving a descent line.

Like other societies in the region, the Savu islands have a megalithic tradition: however, it is not clear when the large stones arrived at the ritual places. Among them are stones dedicated to Maja; they are found in as well as outside villages. Flat stones supported by four upright stones look like mini-dolmens and carry various names: *wowadu kebèli* (stone overturned) or *wowadu Maja* (Maja stone) or even *wowadu mèja* (table stone) (from *meja* [In], a descriptive term). They offer a sheltered cavity which occasionally contains a stone of a different nature and colour, and where people place offerings. These stones may serve as memorials for people who died in accidents on the island or overseas. As it is not possible to state the age of Savu's megalithic tradition, it is left to personal interpretation if these stones are actually related to the Majapahit era.

The Majapahit time in Savu is shrouded in mystery; it is only occasionally possible to find allusions to the era. However, it does not seem that the Majapahit age had any direct impact on the political, social or religious organisation in Savu. The exception is perhaps the introduction of red rice, as a sacred rice field is linked to Bèni Kedo, who was allegedly Maja's sister.

Of the numerous principalities in the eastern region (allegedly) subject to Majapahit, Bima in east Sumbawa was one of the more durable. It appears from the geographical account of Tomé Pires circa 1515 that it was a well-populated kingdom with Javanese commercial contacts as well as with Banda and North Maluku (Cortesão 1944: 202). Interestingly, it seems to have taken over some of Majapahit's territorial claims in Nusa Tenggara (the Lesser Sunda Islands). The Bimanese chronicles relate that the grand uncle of Bima's first Muslim sultan (who ascended the throne in 1620) extended his power eastwards to Komodo, Manggarai, Sumba, Ende, Savu and the Solor Islands (Tajib 1995: 164–5). In a letter to the Dutch authorities in 1673, the sultan asserted that his dependencies had been extensive in the days before the Makassar Empire of Sulawesi subordinated his kingdom (1618–26). The realm had previously included "Mangay [Manggarai], Sumba, Solor, the two islands Poulo Sauwa".[11] The latter could mean either Savu/Rote (alias Lesser Savu) or Savu/Raijua. While there is some evidence for Bimanese interests on Sumba's north-west coast, there are no independent sources or local traditions about influence from that direction in Solor or Savu. As the Bimanese tradition on the matter is so persistent, it is nevertheless possible that there was a short-lived connection, perhaps more in terms of diplomatic or commercial relations than concrete dependency.

Early Portuguese influences

Portuguese expansion into maritime Asia added a new dimension to the trading system: the foreign sea power had ambitions to monopolise important commodities incorporating a strong proselytising agenda. The Portuguese conquest of Malacca in 1511 was very quickly followed by the first expedition to Maluku in 1512; the fabled Spice Islands were one of the principal motivations for their seaborne enterprise. Three years later a small fleet may have encountered the north coast of Timor (Leitão 1948: 54). In his well-known commercial geographic study, *Suma Oriental*, Tomé Pires mentions that Timor had the reputation among Southeast Asian merchants for being the place God made for sandalwood. From a letter written in 1523, it is clear that Portuguese traders were already operating in Timor but did so outside the auspices of the official colonial apparatus in Asia, the *Estado da Índia* (Newitt 2005: 122). As a matter of fact, the *Estado* bases in major ports, such as Goa and Malacca (and Macão after 1557), had few resources to spare for the inaccessible Savu Sea. The lucrative sandalwood trade was in effect the prerogative of enterprising private traders.

After 1512, the Portuguese gained influence over the Ternate Sultanate, the most important polity in northern Maluku.[12] The relationship between the white

---

[11] G.J. Held, 'Sumbawa—geschiedenis' (Sumbawa—History), unpublished manuscript, 1955, KITLV Archive, Leiden.

[12] (Van Fraassen 1987 I: 34–45). In the second half of the 15th century, Ternate gained a degree of influence in the Solor and Alor Islands, though its connections with Savu are not specifically recorded (De Roever 2002; Hägerdal 2010).

foreigners and the local inhabitants had its ups and downs, but the Portuguese retained their position in Maluku until the early 17th century when the Dutch appeared on the scene.[13] From Maluku it was comparatively easy to reach the Flores-Timor area. Due to the unofficial nature of these visits there is not much knowledge about them. However, in the 1550s there are references to traders from Portugal who stayed in Solor over the winter (rainy season), going back to their home bases when the monsoon wind changed. In the same decade, Catholic missionaries began expanding their influence in the Solor Islands and on the north coast of Timor.

There is no written record that tells when and how the Portuguese first approached Savu. The genealogies of the various domains do, however, provide unambiguous data about the introduction of Portuguese-affiliated rajas within the context of other significant events considered later in the book. The Seba genealogy states that the first of these rajas was Kore Rohi who lived nine generations before Jara Lomi (established dates, circa 1687–1700). That would place Kore Rohi, at the latest, very early in the 16th century; however, two generations might have later been inserted into the genealogy, suggesting the time at which Kore Rohi flourished is about 1525. In Dimu, according to one version, the second Portuguese raja, Tuka Hida, lived five generations before Ama Rohi Rani (who died 1678), which indicates a similar date.

Stories recorded in modern time assert that the Portuguese had a direct role in the elevation of rajas. According to Ama Bèhi of the Nataga clan the Portuguese first arrived in Dimu, which by implication means the harbour at Banyo, a name supposedly derived from 'Spanyol' (Spaniard).[14] Banyo is historically known as Savu's rainy season harbour while Seba is used during the dry season. This is certainly consistent with the early pattern of Iberian presence in the region, as they stayed over the winter on the well-protected north coast of Solor. In Dimu, the Portuguese stayed at Hurati where a stone fortress still exists (Plate 9). Before their arrival there were only *duae udu* (clan leaders). However, the foreigners asked the new raja of the domain to send a mission to Seba with the intention of choosing a raja. Two priests called Lado Aga and Te Naba went there, and so Kore Rohi was appointed. It has to be noted that Lado Aga is a personal name as well as the name of a ritual role while Te Naba is just the name of a priest position in

---

[13] For the early European seafarers in North Maluku, see in particular Andaya (1993).

[14] Banyo is the harbour the Portuguese used, while Biu was used by the Dutch; the current harbour in Dimu is Biu. According to the *Peta administrasi jaringan air* (the Water Network Adminstration Map), *Teluk* Banyo (Banyo 'Bay' [In]) is north of Bolou—between Bolou and Bali—while the Biu river and the *Teluk* Biu are south of Bolou.

Dimu, so it is pointless to trace these names in the genealogies.[15] While stories recorded almost 500 years later cannot be taken at face value, they do indicate that people felt the raja institution was foreign to Savunese social organisation. The lords of the land, the Deo Rai and the Apu Lod'o, were ritual figures with a role in the agricultural cycle and may not have been suitable as counterparts to the Portuguese traders in their negotiations, prompting the Portuguese demand for a political and commercial spokesman in each domain.

Photo 7. The harbour, Banyo (derived from 'Spanyol'), is an ancient landing place in Dimu used in Portuguese and VOC times. The giant clams in the foreground were traditionally used for sea-salt production (2015)

In general, the early Portuguese phase in this part of the archipelago is not well documented. The most verbose reports are those emanating from the Dominican priests, active since about 1556. The Timor region was not a major priority of the *Estado da Índia* and there was no João de Barros to chronicle the exploits

---

[15] F. Djara Wellem (2005: 331) relates a version of this story. A Portuguese ship anchored off Banyo and the crew visited Hurati, the main residence of eastern Savu. They then sailed to Seba and Raijua. In Raijua, there is a story that the Portuguese landed at Jawa Kela and tried to spread the teachings of Jesus Christ. As Wellem notes, the story stretches the imagination given that Malay was probably not understood in Raijua.

of the white foreigners.[16] What is known is that the Portuguese established a fort in Solor in 1566 under Dominican supervision (Leitão 1948: 79). The newcomers had a hard time defending their position against Javanese Muslims and discontented locals, but they managed to thrive on the sandalwood trade with the north coast of Timor, in the process gaining fundamental information about the region's geography. On maps from the 16th centuries it is possible to chart the progress; they show a gradual evaporation of diffuse ideas about a massive land form south of Maluku and name the main islands. The Portuguese nomenclature did not necessarily correspond to local usage. For example, the name Solor, "Solot", originally applied to all the Solor Islands and easternmost Flores.[17] The maps often categorised regions as more important geographical features than individual islands.

However, for Savu the Portuguese adopted the indigenous name Rai Hawu (the Land of Savu) and, moreover, used it for two different islands. They called the original Savu *Sabo Grande* (Greater Savu) while Rote was *Sabo Pequeno* (Lesser Savu). Rote has some parallels to Savu in terms of economic foundations and culture, but it has a different language (or language cluster) and a largely different historical experience. Also, as it is closer to Timor, it is less isolated. Above all, it is a much larger island than Savu. The curious Portuguese nomenclature is more symbolic than physical: Savu was the 'primary' Savu and therefore 'greater' while Rote was farther away from the Portuguese bases, thereby 'secondary' or 'lesser'. Moreover, there was no self-evident indigenous name for the island of Rote which, by implication, had to be invented when increased contacts made a geographical nomenclature necessary.[18] The nomenclature is not easily understood, however. Some of the earliest Dutch records in Savu—from the 1650s—speak of *Groot Sabo* (Big Savu) and *Cleyn Sabo* (Lesser Savu) *and* Rote in the same reports. The geographical details in these texts are too vague to draw secure conclusions, but here it seems that *Cleyn Sabo* could allude to Raijua rather than Rote.[19]

On the European maps, both Savu and its lesser component Raijua appear either in the late 16th or early 17th century. Flamand Christian Sgrooten's rather confusing map of the East Indies (1588) depicts a small group of islands with

---

[16] Portuguese historian João de Barros (1496–1570) wrote *Decades of Asia*, published from 1522 in four volumes. It is one of the first accounts of European exploration.

[17] This is obvious from the ethnic denomination *Lamaholot* (the land of Solot or the land of the united), which encompasses the populations from easternmost Flores to Lembata.

[18] The name *Nusa Dahena* (the Isle of Man) is sometimes an indigenous name for Rote (James Fox, personal communication; February 2017). However, outsiders hardly ever used it.

[19] (VOC 1193, f. 740–1). A further possibility is that the early Dutch seafarers heard Rote being referred to by two different names and believed it was two islands.

the name "Zabam", which could be either Sumba or Savu. The maps by the Portuguese *mestizo* Manuel Eredia de Godinho, a geographer based in Malacca, are much better informed. A map from 1602 shows "Rajoan" to the south-west of Sumba. In spite of the wrong location, it points to a certain prominence for Raijua as it is mentioned instead of the Savunese main island. Another map by the same author, drawn in 1615, indicates "Sabo" and "Rajoan" some distance to the south of Rote.[20] Maps are not only disinterested assemblies of topographical and geographical facts, they are also a strategic means to master and wield authority over territories. From that point of view, the belated and haphazard way of representing Savu and Raijua in Iberian cartography shows that they were of limited interest for European penetration.

Unfortunately, there are no 16th-century sources about Savu, but in the early 17th century there is Manuel Godinho de Eredia's text 'Concerning Meridional India'.[21] Eredia retold various stories and rumours about a southern continent. He speaks of this southern land as *Luca Veach* (from *Lusa /Nusa*, 'island', and Veach/Beach, a mutilated form of Marco Polo's *Luchak/Lohu*, southern Siam). Apparently, most of what Eredia reported is mariners' tales. Luca Veach is here a land with enormous quantities of gold, very enticing for European adventurers.

Eredia refers to an account by old men in Ende (Flores) who told of an Endenese ship that made a voyage to Luca Veach:

> When they had got as far as the island of Sabbo, they encountered a storm and violent winds ('Tuphon') which prevented them from putting in at Sabbo, nor were they able to make the islands of Rajoam and Lucachancana [*Nusa Cendana* is Sumba] which are in sight of each other. Being compelled by the storm to run before the hurricane, they lost sight of all these islands. When the weather cleared, the winds moderated, and they were becalmed for three days drifting from one place to another: it was during this stage that they discovered Luca Veach.

This island was eight Spanish leagues in circumference.[22] It had small-statured inhabitants of white or brown colour living in very basic conditions but with some agriculture. "All speak the same language, which is that of Rajoaó and Sabbo." There was much gold to be found and the Endenese took on board a quantity which they had bought for *sivallas*, fruit coveted by the locals. On the

---

[20] (Durand 2006: 67, 75, 77). Up to the present it is common for the Raijuans to call Savu *Sabu Besar* (Greater Savu) which would be *Sabo Grande* in Portuguese.

[21] Translated in Mills (1930: 59–73).

[22] A league is approximately 4.23 kilometres.

way back, they encountered another storm and were forced to jettison some of the gold:

> [T]hen with calm weather they made the port of Sabbo where they discharged the gold: even this was so considerable in quantity that it amazed all the people of Sabbo. Actuated by greed for these riches, they proposed to make a second voyage from Sabbo to Luca Veach: but this did not eventuate owing to the ignorance of the people of Sabbo, for they did not know the latitude or appearance of the islands of Luca Veach. The island is so-called because among the natives of Ende and Sabbo and Java, 'Luca' means 'Island' and 'Veach' means 'of Gold'.[23]

Eredia also quotes a text by Pedro de Carvalhaes, captain of Ende's Portuguese fortress from 1601. The captain, referring to some trustworthy local Christians, says that:

> … [A] small boat from Sabbo with some merchants aboard encountered a storm and violent winds, and being driven out of its course by furious currents lost sight of land. Continuing their voyage with the bows pointing to the south for a little less than 30 leagues [127 km], they came to the uninhabited Pulo Cambin, 'island of goats'; thence travelling south about as far again they discovered another island, Polonhior, 'island of coconuts'; further on they discovered the island of Pulo Tambini, 'island of women': then catching sight of Luca Veach they particularly noticed the fortunate mountain of gold. The men from Sabbo disembarked at the port and found on the island such an immense quantity of gold that they were amazed. So they loaded as much gold as they wanted until the boat could bear no greater weight; then with south and austral winds the boat returned to their original port of Sabbo, bringing riches to a country which was ill provided with them: for from the cargo of this boat is derived all the gold which is found in Sabbo today (Mills 1930: 69).

These enticing tales of Savunese argonauts in the southern ocean are interesting to compare with the slightly later Portuguese material. Missionary letters issued from Melaka and Cochin around 1620 speak about the opportunity of starting a new missionary enterprise on the "Islands of Sabbo or Savo". A Spanish priest called Juan de Velasco visited in 1620 but, regrettably, there is no surviving report.[24] The first substantial account is probably a narrative about missionary progress in the region, written after 1641. Being the earliest text to give details of Savu, it is quoted here:

---

[23] (Mills 1930: 67–8). There is no word similar to *Veach* in any regional language meaning gold.

[24] (Jacobs 1984: 408). It should be noted that Spain and Portugal had the same king from 1580 to 1640.

This island, although it is called Savo Grande, is not done so because it is bigger than the other [Savo, that is Rote], but because it is longer, being 25 leagues. It is entirely heathen. The people is very uncultured and neither sail nor trade since the soil gives them all that they need. These natives are, still, whiter than those on the island Savo [Rote]. They have many slaves and turtles, and two brothers of [the order of] Saint Dominic who were there for some months made no fruits [converts]. However, they [the Savunese] made signs of receiving our Catholic faith, since they asked if they [the Dominicans] wanted to stay, or turn back; and since it is very far and outlying they were not disposed to do so. Some who go to Savo Grande find many of these natives, especially the chiefs, in great abundance and served with gold, so that even the parasols with which they guard against the sun, and the mats, have hammered gold. And when one asks from where it has come, since the land does not yield [gold], they refer to it being brought from other small islands which are not far away. They are called Islands of Palm Trees, of Goats, and other names, and they are inhabited by the dwarf people who do trade. They bring nothing but gold. However, when a ship has once been there, it disappears and another one returns. If one approaches someone from these islands and asks about news of the first one, he will answer that he does not know and that, making his trip, he goes loaded with gold as the others. However, all those who have anchored there [on the small islands] at this occasion have become so swollen that the greater part die, and because of that they are so afraid that no-one wants to go back (Sá 1956: 493–4).[25]

The account might be hearsay, especially as it greatly inflates Savu's size and perhaps mixes it up with Sumba. The information is imprecise and sometimes unclear, but it repeats some of the details in Eredia's stories—a Goat Island and small-statured people in a land full of gold.[26] There are two *Pulau Kambing* (Goat Island [In]) in the region; one in Kupang Bay and the other north of Dili, Timor-Leste, officially called Ataúro. The story reinforces the impression from later sources of an economically self-sufficient society that did not actively participate in trade, although slaves were a commercial item. The turtle population presumably decreased early on as turtle shell (*karet*) is not mentioned as a trading item in later accounts. Nevertheless, the account of Joseph Banks in 1770 confirms that he saw turtles and that their meat was considered a delicacy. Actually, turtles are still captured today. The gold imported by the mysterious 'dwarf people' would

[25] A parallel and derivative passage is in the *História de S. Domingo* (Santa Catharins 1866: 279–80). The Savunese who went to the smaller islands to trade in gold were scared to go as they returned swollen and deformed, and mostly died.

[26] There is a small amount of gold found in Timor and rumours of the precious metal could easily have been inflated to enormous proportions—*auri sacra fames* (the accursed greed for gold, in reference to St Paul's teachings).

have been enticing for gold-thirsty Europeans, but it is quite likely the account is exaggerated. As Gregory Forth (2008) recently established, the 'dwarf people' theme is very common in Indonesian lore—known, for example, in nearby Flores. In general, however, these small people are known as wild men, unlikely to conduct civilised pursuits such as trade. Florenese stories of small people received some attention at the time of the *Homo floresiensis* discovery, with speculations that they might have survived into the early-modern period, although the present scholarly consensus is that they died out some 50,000 years ago.

Seba in oral tradition

As Portuguese reports about their contacts with Savu are so few, it is necessary to consider what collective memory has carried with it. Critically reading the narratives prompts certain conclusions on contemporaneous practices. The best place to start is with Savu's first Portuguese-appointed rajas—Tuka Hida in Dimu and Kore Rohi in Seba—considering the latter first.

Some details about Kore Rohi's father, Rohi Tari, echo the Portuguese text above. Rohi Tari is said to have expelled the people of a marginal clan, *udu* Kelara, from Seba. Among its members was a Dari Lèki, whose sister, Bari Lèki, Rohi Tari married. As the previous chapter outlines, there are extraordinary stories about the obscure Kelara clan whose members stayed on an invisible island after leaving Savu, working at night and sleeping during the day. *Lara* means yellow and, by extension, gold. In Raijua, the head of the Kelara people is said to have had a golden table and chair, something unheard of then. This raises the question of the Kelara incorporating groups who roamed the region after the fall of the Majapahit Empire, settling briefly in Savu and Raijua. Furthermore, the village where the Kerala people originated in Seba is called Tuleika, rendered *Tulang Ikan* (Fish Bone [In]) in a Dutch village list of 1832; this is also the name of a settlement on Timor's north coast. From Rohi Tari's union with Bari Lèki, two sons were born. Then Rohi Tari married Rade Ngahu from the Namata clan of Seba. She was the daughter of the domain's Priest of War (Maukia), making it a strategically motivated marriage. Kore Rohi, the first of Seba's rajas, was a child of his father's second marriage. Rade Ngahu is said to have become involved in intrigues so that her son was chosen as raja.[27]

There are also stories of early connections to Sumba. Uli Tari, a brother of Rohi Tari mentioned above, is said to have migrated to Sumba. Seven generations later his descendant Ledi Ke travelled to Savu and founded the

---

[27] In another version, however, the wrong dress code eliminated Bola Rohi, the son of the first marriage, as the Portuguese choice (Duggan 2001: 57).

lineage Nataga Wa (*wa* means west and by extension Sumba; thus his origin is remembered in the lineage name). Another figure, Ama Piga Kaja, was expelled from Sumba and established himself in Dimu; he is remembered as the third raja of Portuguese times.

Photo 8. Banyan trees at Tuwi – Kore Rohi's settlement after his wife expelled him from Nadawawi (2013)

Like his father, Kore Rohi had two marriages. He first married Medo Nguru, whose mother originated from the same clan and the same lineage as Tuka Hida, the raja of Dimu. Female genealogies reveal politically motivated alliances. Then Kore Rohi fell for his niece, Mojo Mone. As she had grown up in his and his wife's household, Medo Nguru, who viewed Mojo Mone as a daughter, strongly objected to her husband's relationship with her sister's daughter, causing him to leave and establish himself on Tuwi hill on the border with Mesara. There a dramatic event occurred. While with his second wife in Tuwi, one of his young sons, Hagu Kore, suddenly disappeared. Kore Rohi was convinced that his son had been murdered.[28] In order to avenge the death or disappearance of his son, Kore Rohi conducted a ritual to identify his son's murderer. This

---

[28] Some sources say that he was killed by his uncle (mother's brother), others that his relatives in Liae kidnapped him and changed his name. This narrative was recounted by Raja Pono (Ama Bèhi Meno) from the Nataga clan, Seba (22.04.2006).

ritual, called *hoiwe*, consists of cutting off a chicken's head and letting the body run; thus indicating the direction where the problem originates. The procedure is repeated three times. Each time the beheaded chicken ran towards Mesara, so Kore Rohi conducted a war against Mesara.[29] The village of Gurimonearu (Eight Dead Men) commemorates the death of eight Mesara men. When asked about it, Mesara people do not recall the massacre but rather name another place, Rarimoned'ue, where two Seba men were killed.[30] What is interesting here is that an oral culture's attitude to the past is not necessarily different from a society with written history. The oral tradition remembers victories, but losses fall into oblivion. The difference is that the overall picture is more nuanced; the losers keep records of intermediate moments in which they won.

During this war, Kore Rohi received support from several clans. The position of Mesara's Nahipa clan, considered a traditional ally of Seba, is not clear in this war as Seba extended its territory towards the west and took part of the Nahipa's land. Nataga and Nahipa also made a pledge that they would never fight each other. The two clans exchanged their founding houses—Bèni Kèka of *udu* Nahipa and Hinge Haba of *udu* Nataga—as a reminder of the oath. Hinge Haba is still standing in Raemèdi in Upper Mesara while Bèni Kèka, which was carried to Namata's ritual place, was destroyed by fire in 1946 and never rebuilt.[31] Besides, both clans decided to use the same branding marks for their cattle. Also of note is that Kore Rohi's first wife, Medo Nguru, is the granddaughter of the famous Dila Tede from the Nahipa clan. Dila Tede created the branching group *wini* Ga Lena in the maternal line (Greater Blossom moiety). Further alliances between Seba and Mesara are known; Kore Rohi's son, Jami Kore, married Lena Rebo from the Napupudi clan, Mesara.

Women who married into ruling lineages must have been strong minded. One generation after Jami Kore, Medo Nguru's granddaughter, Mojo Lado (Namata clan) chose to live with Haba Jami, though he was meant to marry another woman from the Nakalu lineage. This liaison was against cultural rules.[32] However, after she had given birth to two of the couple's children, they formally married. Haba Jami, remembered as Seba's third raja in Portuguese times,

---

[29] Places called Ha'owa and Baribake, in the present-day villages of Pedèro and Kemubu, are remembered in connection with this war.

[30] Gurimonearu is located between Pedèro and Teriwu, in the newly created village of the same name. Rarimoned'ue is in Wadumèdi village.

[31] The next chapter reveals the role of the house Hinge Haba in a war opposing Seba's ruler (Jara Lomi) and Mesara's ruler (Wele Jami).

[32] She was the father's brother's daughter (FBD), while the marriage rule is mother's brother's daughter (MBD). See Figures 6, 28 and 44.

Figure 27: Marriage alliances in Seba before Portuguese times

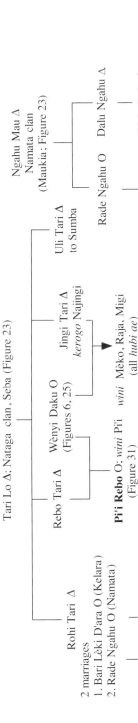

Figure 28: Rulers of Seba in Portuguese times

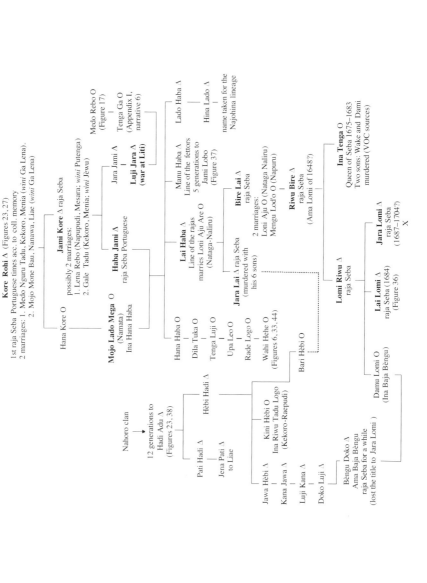

Kore Rohi ∧ (Figures 23, 27)

1st raja Seba Portuguese times acc. to coll. memory
2 marriages: 1. Medo Nguru Tadu, Kekoro, Menia (*wini* Ga Lena).
2. Mojo Mone Bau, Nanawa, Liae (*wini* Ga Lena)

Jami Kore ∧ raja Seba
possibly 2 marriages:
1. Lena Rebo (Napupudi, Mesara; *wini* Putenga)
2. Gale Tadu (Kekoro, Menia; *wini* Jewu)

Hana Kore O

Medo Rebo O
(Figure 17)

Tenga Ga O
(Appendix I,
narrative 6)

Hina Lado ∧

name taken for the
Najohina lineage

Haba Jami ∧
raja Seba Portuguese

Jara Jami ∧

Luji Jara ∧
(**war at Liti**)

Lado Haba ∧

Mojo Lado Mega O
(Namata)
Ina Hana Haba

Lai Haba ∧
Line of the rajas
marries Loni Aju Are O
(Nataga-Naliru)

Manu Haba ∧
Line of the fettors
5 generations to
Jami Lobo
(Figure 37)

Hana Haba O

Dila Tuka O

Tenga Luji O

Upa Leo O

Rade Logo O

Wahi Hehe O
(Figures 6, 33, 44)

Bari Hebi O

Jara Lai ∧ raja Seba
(murdered with
his 6 sons)

Bire Lai ∧
raja Seba
2 marriages:
Loni Aju O (Nataga Naliru)
Mengu Lodo O (Napuru)

Riwu Bire ∧
raja Seba
(Ama Lomi of 1648?)

Ina Tenga O
Queen of Seba 1675–1683
Two sons: Wake and Dami
murdered (VOC sources)

Lomi Riwu ∧
raja Seba

Lai Lomi ∧
raja Seba (1684)
(Figure 36)

Jara Lomi ∧
raja Seba
(1687–1704?)
X

Naboro clan

12 generations to
Hadi Adu ∧
(Figures 23, 38)

Hebi Hadi ∧

Pati Hadi ∧

Jena Pati ∧
to Liae

Jawa Hebi ∧

Kana Jawa ∧

Luji Kana ∧

Doko Luji ∧

Kini Hebi O
Ina Riwu Tadu Logo
(Kekoro–Raepudi)

Bengu Doko ∧
Ama Baja Bengu
raja Seba for a while
(lost the title to Jara Lomi)

Damu Lomi O
(Ina Baja Bengu)

Figure 29: War alliances in Kore Rohi's time

Alliances at the time of Kore Rohi, Nataga clan of Seba and the first raja of Seba in Portuguese times involve the war against Mesara when he was victorious. The role of the Nahipa clan (Mesara), a traditional ally of Nataga clan of Seba, is not clear in this war. Both clans had exchanged their founding houses: the house Hinge Haba of Seba was brought to Mesara while Bèni Kèka of Mesara was carried to Nadawawi, Nataga clan land (chapter 3). The Nahipa clan does not seem to have been rewarded with land at the end of this war.

Allies of Kore Rohi, Nataga clan	Comments	Source
Jote Robo, Nabe'e clan, Dimu	He is Kore Rohi's sister's son; the lineage Nataga-Nabe'e was created. This is a mother's brother-sister's son relationship (*makemone-nakebèni*). The Nabe'e people are said to be the indigenous people of Dimu who had not organised themselves as clan.	Ama Bèhi Meno, Nataga clan, Seba
Ama Banga Wolo Dalu, Namata clan, Seba	He is Kore Rohi's mother's brother and son of the priest of war (Maukia). He was rewarded with land near Tuwi. Again this is a *makemone-nakebèni* relationship.	Ama Bèhi Meno, Nataga clan, Seba
Ama Robo Aji Mata, Teriwu-Nahire clan, Seba.	The domain of Teriwu had disappeared and was part of Seba.	Nata Mita, Napupudi clan, Mesara
Ama Haba Lai Danu of Teriwu-Nad'ara clan, Seba	Same as above	Nata Mita, Napupudi clan, Mesara
Riwu Tadu, Rohaba clan, Lower Mesara	He was rewarded with nine plots of land near Seba; this allowed him to form the lineage Nataga-Rohaba. The nine plots of land are still in the hands of this lineage. The Rohaba clan acted as a mercenary clan in the early time of its existence	Ama Obi, Nataga clan, Rohaba lineage, Seba

recognised all the children of their union. To keep the broken taboo in mind, Mojo Lado created the branching group of *wini* Ga Lena with the heraldic motif *Kobe molai* or male Kobe for the primary sarong of her line.[33] Haba Jami had to compensate the Nakalu for breaking a promise to marry.

In the time of Luji Jara, Haba Jami's nephew, a war took place at Liti, a hill in the domain of Seba. As the conflict raged, he, his wife and their eldest daughter were murdered.[34] His wife was the stepsister of Liae's first raja, Nida Dahi (Nanawa clan). While four generations of rajas in Seba had ruled by this time, it was the first generation of Portuguese rajas in Liae. Nida Dahi did not have descendants.[35] The group's heirloom basket (*kepepe*) is known as *kepepe Nanida*, which is a reminder of Medo Rebo alias Ina Nida Dahi.

Haba Jami's grandson Hina Lado (*Hina* is Chinese; *Lado* is crown) reportedly went to sea and did not have descendants. However, his name is part of the Najohina lineage which provided the line of Seba fettors during colonial times. It is possible that the Portuguese engaged Hina Lado and, as he did not come back, he was remembered in the lineage name. Although it is not possible to ascribe precise dates to these events, several elements point to a Portuguese presence or interference.

There are a few more details about marriage alliances in the Nataga clan in Portuguese times. Stories exist about three of the women mentioned in Figure 28 above. One is Mojo Lado whose marriage to Raja Haba Jami breached taboo. The second is Medo Rebo from the Napujara clan of Liae. She came from the Lesser Blossom moiety and the female Putenga lineage She married four times, supposedly using black magic to achieve her goals. Her daughter Tenga Ga, said to have used similar ploys, moved in with Luji Jara, Haba Jami's nephew, thereby forcing out the first wife. This apparently caused a war that Hede Luij, a son from the first marriage, later conducted against his own father. Bitu Luji, the sole survivor of the massacre, became the keeper of her mother and grandmother's heirloom basket. Her descent line is said to practice black magic and the group called Jingi Wiki has specific motifs on their textiles.[36]

The third woman is Medo Rebo's sister, Wahi Rebo, who married into the Teriwu-Nagali clan. Her son, Jawa Riwu, declared war against his mother's

---

[33] This pattern is obtained through the warp ikat technique as are all Savu textiles that identify a female descent line. For the *kobe molai* motif, see Duggan (2001). See Figure 44.

[34] See Narrative 6 in Appendix I.

[35] Nida is the name of a medicinal plant (*Anamirta cocculus* or levant berry), the seeds of which are used to treat epilepsy. This plant is remembered as having cured Nida Dahi when he was a child; therefore his name reminds people of the cure. See Figure 17.

[36] Duggan (2001: 48, 51).

brother Uju Rebo from the Napujara clan of Liae. The latter obtained help from Lobo Lido (Namata clan) and Jena Pati (Nahoro clan) of Seba. After Jawa Riwu was defeated, Lobo Lido and Jena Pati received pieces of land, *rai kohu muhu*, from Uju Rebo who was known as *duae* (Big Man) in Liae.[37] The event can be dated to Portuguese times as Uju Rebo's grandson appears in a 1682 VOC document and his great-grandsons respectively in others from 1688 and 1689. The war might therefore have taken place in the early years of the 17th century.

Ju Deo and early Catholic influence

As this book attempts to analyse, compare and combine written and oral sources, it is important to examine in some detail the events regarding Ju Deo and his mother Ina Ju Deo. These figures have interesting mythic properties that may relate to early Catholic influences. Here, a 19th century written source meets narratives recently recorded in Savu and Raijua.

In a letter from 1876, the Protestant missionary Mattheus Teffer recalls the life of Ju Deo.[38] His father, the divine being Deo, sent him out of compassion to teach the Raijuanese how to derive a living from their land. He also performed miracles, much appreciated by some, such as turning a rock by the seashore into a well with good drinking water that never ran dry, and he walked on water.[39] Ju Deo left Raijua for a while but later returned as the gods remained compassionate towards the Raijuans. In spite of his good works, he was eventually murdered by hostile islanders, but people still saw him walking in the clouds.

The versions recorded in Mesara and Raijua hardly mention Ju Deo himself. Instead, they mostly deal with his mother's efforts to retrieve his body and bring him back to life. Savu sources reveal nothing about Ju Deo's possible good deeds; on the contrary, Raijua's local ruler killed him for being a troublemaker. In the Raijua narrative, he had an affair with the wife of the Nadega clan's Deo Rai (Lord of the Earth) in Bolua. Deo Rai caught Ju Deo and took him to his house in Nadega village where he was crucified at the crossing of two beams. Ju Deo's

---

[37] Lobo Lido and Jena Pati received the following plots of land in Liae: Madeki'i and Wara in Ledetalo village, and Raemanu in Waduwèla village (interview with Ama Dida Wila, a descendant of Lobo Lido in Liae [19.05.2006]). The term *duae* (*Dou Ae*: lit. Big Man) is also used in Melanesia. A 'Big Man' was the head or leader of a group of people and predates the title raja, introduced by Europeans (though sometimes people still say *duae*).

[38] Raad voor de Zending, 1102–1: 1411, M. Teffer, letter, 29 October 1876.

[39] One of these wells is located near Raijua harbour; its opening is in the shape of a mouth. Of interest is that Maja of Majapahit's times was also said to have created this well.

Figure 30: Napujara clan and the Jawa Riwu–Uju Rebo war

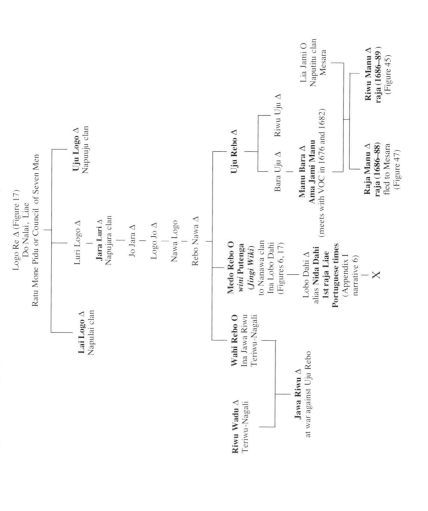

mother, Ina Ju Deo, is also known as Wènyi Muri (Living Woman). The Deo Rai priest of Mesara recounted the following narrative:[40]

> Accompanied by Maja and the priests Apu Lod'o and Kenuhe, Ina Ju Deo started to look for her son in Savu and reached the western end of the island where the group met a man, Jèka Wai, who was working in his garden. Showing some resistance to the requests of the group, Jèka Wai was challenged by Kenuhe and Maja and lost his land to them. Then he was forced to follow the group. When they arrived to Raijua they met near the beach a goat shepherd from the Rohaba clan. Not answering Ina Ju Deo's question to her satisfaction, she decided that the Rohaba clan would only be allowed to gather sea salt and would be forbidden to own land in Raijua.[41] Ina Ju Deo continued to walk inland towards Wuditèngu where she met a buffalo shepherd from Ledetalo. She asked him the same question as to the Rohaba man. Receiving a positive answer this time she rewarded the man with fish traps: *kena'a* and *holo kodo*.[42]

> The group continued to walk towards Liurae and Ina Ju Deo repeated her question. There she was told that the person she was looking for had been crucified at Nada Roju'u in Raenadega. Before entering Raenadega, Ina Ju Deo pressed her left breast and collected her milk in a bottle. Then she sprinkled the milk over the people assembled in the village and all those on whom the drops of her milk landed then died. Since this time there is a stone called *wowadu lakati* (cholera stone) here. She entered the village arena, went to the house of Deo Rai and saw her dead son tied to the house cross beams; she took him from the cross and left immediately.

> Ina Ju Deo, Maja, Apu Lod'o, Kenuhe and Jèka Wai went back to Savu [crossing the Strait on Maja's boat]. In Lederaga, Ina Ju Deo was given cloths for her son's body. She went to the Èimadakebo spring where the group was welcome by the community who performed *ledo* and *pedoa* dances. Later they went to D'ara Raehipi in the village of Tanajawa where the dances continued. They carried on to D'ara Raepumanu in the village of Ledeae, then to D'ara Raekewowo. At each place the dances were performed and little by little Ju Deo started to show more and more signs of life. When they reached Lede-Deo-Ju-Deo hill, Ju Deo had returned to life. They went to Koloteriwu, the most revered settlement of Savu, known in mantra texts as *Rae Pulu Pa Lobo Pulu Ewa Ana Deo Pulu*

---

[40] Deo Rai of Mesara (26.04.2011).

[41] In both versions, Jèka Wai lost either his land or his right to land as a result of Ina Ju Deo's punishment.

[42] *Holo* means generally Solor; thus, the origin of this particular fish trap is linked to the island of Solor where Savunese and Raijuanese have maintained good relations throughout the centuries.

Kati.[43] At Koloteriwu Ina Ju Deo, Ju Deo and their followers climbed to the sky because in early times the sky and the earth were near each other. Then together with her son, Ina Ju Deo ascended to heaven. People saw them in the clouds.

Jèka Wai did not stay in the sky but went back to earth and used Maja's boat, claiming it as his own, which angered Maja. From then on, life was no longer safe on earth because wherever Jèka went, there was continuous lightning and thunder. Once, Jèka took refuge under a *kepaka* tree where Denga lived.[44] Denga told Jèka that he was wrong taking Maja's boat. Therefore, he would be continuously plagued by lightning and thunder until he apologised. Jèka went back to the sky and apologised to Maja who then decided that all people and their descendants would have to sacrifice a pig to Maja once a year and this tradition lasts until today. Jèka kept the boat called *Ama Dèki Lomi*. However for this, his descendants have to launch a ceremonial boat loaded with offerings called *kowa Jèka* once a year from the western end of Mesara.

This narrative contains obvious similarities to biblical texts: Ju Deo, his mother the 'Living Lady', the crucifixion, resurrection and the ascension to heaven are elements on both islands. Teffer's 19th-century text is very brief compared to the versions recently recorded. It raises the question of the tale's age in Savu and Raijua. Is this tale linked to Portuguese missionaries preaching in the 16th and 17th centuries or did biblical texts travel to the area with seafarers, adventurers and traders? After brief contacts with the Portuguese in the 16th century, Christianity had no impact in Raijua until the 20th century. It seems most likely that the narratives stemmed from Portuguese contact in the 16th century and that the Protestant missionary simply omitted any reference to Ina Ju Deo.[45]

The fact that sky and earth were near each other, allowing people to go back and forth between the two, places the narrative in mythical and not historical times. Maja, staying in the sky, occupies an intermediary position between humans on earth and heaven, the realm of gods. When Christianity came to Savu, the theme of the resurrection was not new to local people. The previous chapter shows how a specific cloth, *wai*, allowed ancestors to be called back to

---

[43] This phrase refers to the prosperity and fertility of plants for which the sacred place of Teriwu is revered. *Pulu pa* (planting in a planting hole), *lobo* (field) and *Ewa Ana Deo* (Ewa, child of God).

[44] *Sterculia foetida* or the Java olive. Note: the name Denga does not appear in the genealogies and sounds like a nickname. He is known only as someone living there.

[45] That there were stories of Ina Ju Deo in Raijua (where Protestantism had not yet gained a foothold) by 1885 is clear from archival material (Raad voor de Zending, 1102–1: 1408, J.F. Niks, travel report, 5–29 June 1885). Catholicism arrived again in Raijua in the 1970s through Pastor Franz Lackner's work.

life. A *wai* textile is the first cloth the deceased wears precisely because it allows him/her to live again. While for followers of the Jingi Tiu religion, people today still carry a *wai* cloth when travelling overseas in case of sudden death, Christians believe that being buried with a cross enables them to rise from the dead in a distant future.

The narrative confers extraordinary powers on Ina Ju Deo which enable her to administer divine punishment: poisoning people has more of black magic and sorcery than of Christianity. Over the centuries, the narrative might have been conflated with other events and situations. In the 19th century, smallpox devastated the island twice and cholera once. The sudden death of the Raijuan people who had come into contact with Ina Ju Deo's milk may allude to such epidemics.

The narrative anchors in the local tradition a number of practices specific to both islands: the ceremonial dances *ledo* and *pedoa*; the yearly sacrifice of a pig to Maja; and launching the ceremonial boat, *kowa Jèka*. It explains the introduction of fish traps imported from the Solor archipelago and gives the reason why the Rohaba clan does not own land in Raijua—its members indeed derive their living from the sea (fishing, sea salt production and, more recently, seaweed farming). Teffer's text attributes the well with a rocky mouth to Ju Deo; however, other narratives say Maja, linked to a figure of the Majapahit Empire, created the well. Some sources even name the famous Gajah Mada (circa 1290–1364)—a great military leader in the Majapahit Empire—as the well's creator. Others attribute the well to Jèka Wai, the founder of the Rohaba clan, whose members live on both sides of the Raijua Strait. The narrative has evolved according to circumstances and the narrators' particular purpose.

The biblical narrative is embedded in local practices and beliefs, and several stories are linked. Local protagonists, such as Jèka Wai, Apu Lod'o and Maja, feature in other stories. In another narrative, Jèka Wai married Maja's sister. When their son, Rohu Jèka,[46] was born Maja was not in Raijua, but the ceremony for the new baby took place, keeping aside Maja's portion of sacrificial meat.[47] As the newborn's mother's brother (*Makemone*), he was entitled to a large portion of meat. When he returned he refused the meat, which already smelt foul, so another pig had to be slaughtered especially for him. For this reason, at every *hapo* ceremony one *wawi Maja* (pig for Maja) has to be slaughtered and one piece of the pork meat has to be offered to the Maja spirit. In collective thought,

---

[46] Rohu Jèka appears as the son of Jèka Wai in the Rohaba clan genealogy of Mesara, between 17 and 25 generations from the present, depending on the sources.

[47] *Hapo ana* is the ceremony three days after birth when a newborn baby is presented to the family and 'adopted' or recognised by his/her father.

the purpose is to prevent Maja from disturbing the newborn. The story explains Maja's specific requests to Savu and Raijua people, and justifies offerings and ceremonies dedicated to him.

The variety of place names helps the listening audience to visualise the situation, to anchor the event in a natural local landscape and give consistency, thus, 'truth' to the episode: the place and its name become the proof, the witnesses of the event in time. The description of the journey Ina Ju Deo and her followers took from village to village in Raijua and later in Mesara builds a trail in the story, helping the audience to memorise the places they already know. Listeners can follow the story better—the names build a mental map. The names of sites are mnemonic pegs for the story's various sequences. They give and confer truthfulness to a narrative, as the domains and some places are common knowledge. The mnemo-techniques used here are visual and auditory perceptions (see map 5).

Whatever the remaining Catholic influences, the political position of the Portuguese in these waters was not destined to last long. The Portuguese fortress in Solor was attacked in 1613 by an armada from the Dutch East India Company or VOC, founded in 1602. The fledgling Dutch republic was the declared enemy of the Spanish king, Philip II, who was also the king of Portugal from 1580. Being a profit-driven shareholding company, the VOC had more forceful management than the *Estado da Índia* and began to attack Portuguese strongholds in maritime Asia from 1605. The aim was to drive the Catholic enemy from Asian waters and establish monopolies of important trading commodities; though later the company adopted a more economically diverse approach. The Portuguese proved resilient against the first Dutch onslaught but a few posts, including Solor, did fall to the enemy. After 1613, the base of Portuguese power moved to Larantuka at the eastern end of Flores where a Catholic Eurasian population, the 'Black Portuguese', who referred to themselves as Larantuqueiros, maintained itself.[48] Their intermediate position, encompassing both colonial and indigenous traits, allowed them to build up a wide sphere of influence during the 17th century, which the Dutch tried in vain to stop. Lands from central Flores to easternmost Timor were loosely dependent on Larantuqueiros rule and certain cultural influences were clear even in areas tied to the VOC. James Cook's 1770 expedition documented that Portuguese was occasionally still spoken in Savu and the Britons heard that the Portuguese extended their influence there soon after their arrival in the eastern region

---

[48] The story is related in great detail in De Roever (2002). For the Black Portuguese (sometimes known as the Topasses), see also Boxer (1947) and Andaya (2010).

(Hawkesworth 1773: 698). This gives some colour to the princely Seba and Dimu genealogies referred to above.

To sum up this chapter, the lack of written documents makes it hard to reach definite conclusions about the island up to the early 17th century, but there are interesting tendencies in the oral record that cannot easily be discounted. The accounts about the early legendary figure Maja in Raijua may point to the Majapahit Empire. There are numerous traditions in princedoms of the eastern archipelago that point to Majapahit or Javanese origins. This goes for such diverse places as Ende in Flores and Pandai in Pantar (Hägerdal 2012: 26). The Javanese of Hindu-Buddhist times appeared as archetypical foreign rulers, though the reality of the ancestral stories is debatable. More to the point is the collective memory of the Portuguese. They are clearly remembered in the various Savunese domains as newcomers several generations before the Dutch arrival and promoters of a bona fide raja institution to deal with the foreigners. The scattered Portuguese data reveal that Catholic missionaries were periodically at work and possibly gave rise to the legend of the Jesus-like Ju Deo and his Mary-like mother. Nevertheless, it is likely that any early Javanese and Portuguese visitors found what their successors from the Low Countries did: the frugal flow of life and the elaborate ritual system on the little island gave little reward to those who were searching for profits or souls.

<table>
<tr><td>Chapter
5</td><td># Enter the Company</td></tr>
</table>

The foregoing period detailed in the previous chapters is, in the strict sense of historical criticism, proto-history. While it is possible to deduce a number of probabilities from the genealogies and stories, there are no means to anchor names and events chronologically. In the ensuing period, the situation changes radically. In one of history's many anomalies, a sturdy seafaring people from north-western Europe developed an organisation that described small and illiterate communities on the shores of the Savu Sea, in often circumstantial reports unmatched by indigenous sources in the major Asian kingdoms and empires.

The Dutch set out for what was then known as the East Indies in 1595 in an early scramble for riches, organising the trade east of the Cape of Good Hope a few years later through the *Vereenigde Oost-Indische Compagnie* (Dutch United East India Company) or the VOC. Although its root was a share-holding trade company, the VOC soon took on early colonial features by establishing permanent possessions and a comprehensive diplomatic network. The idea was to use the possibilities of the Asian maritime trade routes and to try to control them rather than merely bringing cargoes to and from Asia (Tarling 1992 I: 359–60). During the 17th century, the VOC systematically explored every possibility to trade east of the Cape—including the famed sandalwood of Timor—which made this otherwise unprofitable island a bone of contention with the company's Iberian rivals. It was just a question of time before the company's *fluyten* (sailing ships used to transport cargo) and *chialoupen* (flat-bottomed boats) approached the Savu coast, as is detailed in the present chapter.

Early Dutch contacts

After 1613, the Dutch stayed intermittently in the Portuguese-built fort at Lohayong in eastern Solor, renamed Fort Henricus. Lohayong, well protected from the natural elements, ensured that Dutch ships could easily reach the sandalwood ports of Timor (De Roever 2002: 169–208). From their second stay in Solor, 1618 to 1629, there is a list of marriages and baptisms by the priest Alonce Bourgois. The list is of considerable interest as it clearly shows the enormous ethnic mix characterising early colonial outposts in Asia. While organisations, such as the Estado da Índia and VOC, are usually referred to as 'European', this is only partly true. While European leadership and organisation may have been the ultimate referent of power, the early colonial enterprises were always based on Asian counterparts who had an interest in supporting the enterprise to gain protection or advantage. The early colonial presence in the Flores-Timor region offers particular examples of this syndrome. Of the personnel and their spouses at Fort Henricus, there were 12 persons from Timor, 37 from the Solor Islands, 10 from Ende (Flores), and a variety of people from Banggai, Malacca, the Philippines and India, among others. There was a Marika Franandes from "Savou", who married two VOC officials in succession—the second man an *adelborst* (naval cadet) from Schiedam, named Joop Adriaenszoon. There were also two women called Isabelle and Notien Pietres from "Sava", probably denoting Savu. The typically Iberian names Franandes (Fernandes), Isabelle and Pietres (Pieres) may strengthen the local Savunese tradition of an early Portuguese influence on the island. How they ended up in Solor is impossible to say—perhaps they were slaves.[1]

Savu appears to have taken no active role in the back-and-forth struggle between the Dutch and the Portuguese to control the region in the following decades. There are irregular VOC and Estado reports about conditions in the Flores-Timor area after 1613, but they make no mention of the small island. Later, local tradition suggests a lingering attachment to Portugal. However, as the chapter explains, the swiftness of the subsequent VOC takeover speaks against a deep local commitment to the Iberian sea-lords. Unlike Rote, there is no direct indication that the Catholic missionary effort produced converts, though the presence of expatriates with Iberian names in neighbouring Solor may contradict that.

After a lengthy break, the Dutch returned to the area in 1646 and this time they stayed until the 1940s. They installed a garrison in Fort Henricus and took steps to counter the Portuguese presence in Flores, West Solor, Adonara and Timor (De Roever 2002: 243–6). Portugal had detached itself from the Spanish king in 1640, but warfare soon flared up between the two seaborne powers.[2] It was therefore a vital matter for the VOC to establish a network of allies in the

[1] Bourgois, 'Memorije van de personen…' (Memorandum of the persons…). Transcript from ANRI, Jakarta, provided by Diederick Kortlang, Nationaal Archief, The Hague.

[2] As the Spanish and the Dutch were enemies of old, one might have expected that Portugal's new-found freedom led to an improvement in relations with the Netherlands. However, this was not the case and peace was only negotiated in 1663.

region that could thwart any Portuguese ambitions. Savu was one of the first places they approached after Solor. There is not much detail regarding Dutch considerations, but what is known is that the Dutch ship *Maria* was wrecked off Savu's coast in 1636. Some of the crew climbed aboard a sloop and managed to reach Bali after 19 terrible days, from whence they could then return to Java. However, the others remained in Savu (De Roever 2002: 224). There does not seem to be any account of their stay, but it appears that they prepared the way for the official contacts that followed. A Pieter de Burggraff, held for years by the local Savunese ruler Talo as a captive of sorts, finally impelled a Dutch squadron in 1645 to arrange for his release from this "motley crew" (*gebroetsel*).[3] Another factor was slaves. The Dutch commander of Solor, Hendrick ter Horst, heard from the Solorese princes that it was possible to purchase a lot of slaves in Savu; for example, the people of Lamahala (in Adonara, a small island east of Flores) went there and bought human cargoes who they sold to Portuguese Larantuka (in eastern Flores) in obvious defiance of the VOC regulations. Savu's central situation between Flores, Timor and Sumba probably gave it a potential strategic importance, especially with the continuing rivalry between the European powers. Peace between the Netherlands and Portugal was not established until 1661–63, by which time only part of the Flores-Timor area remained attached to the Portuguese (Hägerdal 2012: 141).

An expedition led by Hendrick ter Horst departed from Solor in 1648 with the intention to conclude an alliance with the Savunese. Fortunately, the Dutch captains and commanders were required to keep a log of their travels and experiences, the so called *dagh-registers* (daily journals). A fragmentary *dagh-register* from the 1648 trip has been preserved and presents an interesting vignette of early Savu. It deserves quoting in full.

> On 18 [October] in the morning we were about 1/2 a [Dutch] mile[4] from the roadstead, before Menia and Relettij…. We sent the sloop *Den Orangienboom* to the shore to see if some of the foremost grandees might be on land, giving knowledge of our arrival. The [crew of the] sloop came back on board at noon. The steersman reported to us that, in the *negeri* [settlement][5] of Menia, Raja Ammatenga and his brother Ammalanda, being informed about our arrival, seemed very amazed. They asked if

---

[3] VOC 869 (1645), f. 92. The name Talo points to the Dimu domain, especially as Dimu had a position of precedence in Savu when it came to relations with Europeans. The genealogies mention a Talo Uju as the father of the later Dimu ruler Ama Rohi, who flourished from 1648 to 1676.

[4] A Dutch mile is approximately 5 kilometres.

[5] The term *negorij* (*negeri* [In]) is used in VOC texts for settlements, major villages or, occasionally, larger realms.

we would come ashore to discuss trade. At once I went there together with the bookkeeper Bacrent Hunnius. When I arrived I found that the shore was black with people … with … cutlasses and assegais[6] in their hands … they seemed to be a party of barbarian people, very cruel to behold. I found the aforementioned raja and his brother sitting among the common people, who could not be distinguished from the others as they wear the same habit. They are people of a beastly disposition. I can do no better than compare them to the Hottentotts at the Cape of Good Hope, who also all devour any filthy stuff as their food. They have very little speech among them. After they had listened (?) to each other for about a short hour, and … having partly understood our … [manuscript illegible] the raja himself dispatched us on board. The next morning we should let him see some samples of merchandise on the shore … which we promised them. Thus we bade farewell and were transported aboard. The Raja Ammatenga bestowed on us a grilled pig which we thankfully received….

On 19 [October] in the morning we went ashore with the samples of *longebatten* [cloth] and fine Chinese gold to show the rajas who yesterday promised to be on the shore. After having waited for two hours without any of the rajas having appeared, I told their people to go and tell them to come as we sat waiting for their arrival. At noon the aforementioned raja and his brother appeared. The old Raja Ammalumij excused himself [saying] that he was sickly and sent his oldest son Ammamelano (?) in his stead. After the samples had been displayed, which pleased them, I asked them to tell the raja that we would be ashore again the next day, so that we could then discuss trade… We bestowed some nuts, spices, mace and cinnamon, which they very much liked to have, as well as a cayon-goulongh [a textile] and a few cutlasses and axes to each one, which seemed to be very pleasing for them, in order to gain their favourable disposition….

On 20 [October], we appeared on the shore but did not yet find anyone. We went to the *negeri* Menia in order to visit Raja Ammatenga and his brother and also to apprehend what result the discourse of the day might have. They seemed to be pleased by our arrival, and ordered … their people to bring the gongs and drums at once, in order to do us some [manuscript illegible]… manner. They also asked that we would eat with them as a token of friendship and not decline their food. At once they put a living buck with hide and hair, intestines and everything, on the fire. It was half grilled, and prepared as house pot and long soup (?), which seemed to be mixed up with a *warmoes* herb….[7] We did not in any part, in the interest of the Noble Company, refuse it, but tasted a bit of it … eating it with long teeth [that is devouring it] which seemed very

---

[6] An assegai (or assagai) is a small hardwood spear.

[7] It is not clear from other sources what *warmoes* is.

pleasing to the aforementioned raja.… At last the matter was brought so far as they said that the merchandise displayed yesterday did not appeal to them, so they could not resolve to begin trade. They said that if we had red cloth, there would be no lack of commerce. We replied that we did possess that on board. We were thereby inclined to go on board and show him this and still other goods that we trusted they would like. He excused himself that he was inclined to go on board but that the old raja himself had expressly forbidden him to do so. He suggested in a friendly way that I would bring it ashore in the morning, which I promised him, as then commerce would no doubt be initiated. We said goodbye. … As it seems, this nation is tardy in trading … which is sad.…

On 21 [October] in the morning, supposedly after the first quarter of the day (?), we went ashore with a piece of carmoisine[8] red cloth and some patola,[9] and sent our under-steersman to the *negeri* of Raja Ammatenga to announce our arrival, having brought the merchandise [spoken of] yesterday, which they would presently find on the beach. He asked for the cloth. I first showed him some patola that he did not want to see … [unclear sentence] I [He?] said in our Low German tongue, 'That is good' [*dats goet*]. He asked at once how many fathoms[10] I would trade for one slave. I replied that these were not sold by the fathom, but by the 'elle' [69 centimetres] which I showed him. Finally we agreed on 2½ ellen after much difficulty, to deliver for males or half-grown up boys, who were said to serve the older rajas. Again, they promised to show us a sample of a slave on the shore the next day. … [*Tiele's summary of the next section:* The slaves must first be caught among the 'mountain people', to which end not only 'foot soldiers' but also the 'cavalry' were dispatched. The trade proceeded quite poorly; 'it is sad to be so put on the shovel by this Indian nation'].[11]

On 29 [October] … This nation [in the 'negeri Diemo', which was in a state of war with the abovementioned villages] seems to be a very loveable and friendly people … however, the slaughter of the horses will continue among them.…[12] (Tiele and Heeres 1886–95, Vol III: 24)

---

[8] The colour is a deep mulberry shade of red.

[9] A patolu (plural – patola) is an expensive, silk, double-ikat woven sari from Patan, Gujarat in western India.

[10] A fathom is approximately half a metre in metric measurement.

[11] The idiomatic expression apparently reflects the Dutch view that they were less than properly treated.

[12] The comment refers to the sacrifice of horses, known in Savu from other contexts.

This first image of the Savunese is far from flattering, and is somewhat reminiscent of Babur's castigation of the Indians[13] and Anson's denouncement of the Chinese.[14] Despite all the remarks about barbarity in this "Indian nation", the writer displays a certain ethnographic curiosity: he draws comparisons with the Khoisan of South Africa, thereby incorporating the Savunese in a mental geography of civilisation and non-civilisation.

The previous chapters explained the dynamic of Savunese oral tradition in detail. When at last archival material surfaces an essential question is obviously how the data compare to the non-written record. There are interesting confluences here—two of which are the Dutch ship anchored off Menia and a place that might be interpreted as Rai Liti. This place is a fenced village situated on a hill in the domain of Seba, west of the present port. It was destroyed in a war during Portuguese times. However, the elevated place continued to be a marker for navigation. The Menia chiefs named in the Dutch account are readily identified in the genealogies of the raja clan which mention two brothers called Ama Tenga Gae and Ama Lado Weo. The latter was the father of the first official raja under the VOC. There is also an elderly raja called Ammalumij whose place of residence is not clearly indicated. The Seba genealogies reveal a ruler named Ama Lomi Riwu, grandfather of a raja known to have commenced his reign in 1684 (Figure 28). However, the name of his son is obscure and might be corrupted.[15] The notion of a coastland-hill dichotomy and slave raiding inland is more puzzling because the modern tradition presupposes an early division into five domains with no outsider population in the interior.[16]

As seen in the dagh-register account, the Dutch proceeded to the eastern Dimu domain which was described in considerably brighter tones. Local traditions hint that Dimu was the point at which the Portuguese ceased their advances in Savu, possibly as a result of the approaching Dutch. The Dutch signed a contract with Dimu in its alleged position as the power centre of the island, formally inaugurating a period of Dutch dependency that lasted with

---

[13] Babur (tiger in Arabic)—1483–1530—was the first Mughal emperor, founding his empire in northern India. A writer as well as a great military leader, his autobiography was translated and published in the 1920s in two volumes as *Memoirs of Babur*.

[14] Admiral (later Baron) George Anson's four-year voyage around the world (1740–44) started with six warships ending with one, the *Centurion*, which became the first British warship to sail into Chinese waters.

[15] The son of Ama Lomi was Ama Lai Lomi, who much later became raja after his father's death. "Ammamelano" could possibly be a badly corrupted form of Ama Lai Lomi.

[16] Van Lijnden (1851: 405) remarks that there was no difference between the communities of the coast and inland by the mid-19th century. They all belonged to one tribe.

brief interruptions until 1949. It is therefore a good reason to quote the contract in full.

> Revised points and paragraphs between the *coopman* [trader] Hendrick ter Horst, *opperhoofd* [head resident] of Fort Henricus in Solor with the ship's council of the yacht *De Zeemeeuw*, and the most powerful Savunese rajas, aiming at a continuous confirmation of an eternal alliance.
>
> First, the Rajas Ammarossij, Amma Cilli and Ammatallo shall take responsibility for the subjects and merchandise that are left here, in case they suffer loss due to theft or conflagration. Their duty is to see to it that the Noble Company does not suffer damage from this nation.
>
> Also, that the rajas do not permit any landings by Portuguese, Javanese, Malay, Makassarese, Endenese or other ships, without the knowledge of our remaining resident Hendrik Bijlaagh, and not allow the trade of slaves, sicer [turtle shell] or other items that the Noble Company may purchase without passes, so that the newly concluded friendship is not broken through such matters but may continue.
>
> That the aforementioned rajas, following decree, shall push their subjects to collect a good requisition of turtleshell in the west monsoon, and after the collection bring to the aforementioned resident without siphoning anything, for the optimal service of the Noble Company.
>
> That the rajas or inhabitants shall keep the slaves that were traded by the resident Hendrik Bijlaagh under their protection so they do not escape until our yachts or small vessels can bring them off, and bring them aboard without any fraud so that there will be no loss for the Noble Company.
>
> And finally, that the Savunese rajas may maintain the remaining subjects with foodstuff and necessities. With this the rajas and the Savunese vassals are all content.
>
> (undersigned:) Thus done and concluded on the yacht *De Zeemeeuw* lying at anchor at the east of the island Grand Savu, before the negeri Dimu, on 21 November 1648.
>
> Hendrick ter Horst, Jacob Janse Bol, Baerent Hunnius, Micheijl Jochemsen.
>
> With three crosses and appended marks by Rajaje Amma Rossij, Rajaje Ammadocke Cilli, and Ammatallo.[17]

The contract appears to reserve most of the advantages for the so-called "Noble Company"; however, the rajas may well have expected valuable income from otherwise inaccessible trading goods. This is paralleled by the situation in Timor where the alliances between Europeans and local rajas resulted in the import of

---

[17] *Contractenboek* 1616–1759, 1aE ANRI.

textiles, arms and similar items for the elite but few visible advantages for the people. Of the three rajas, in normalised spelling Ama Rohi, Ama Doko Hili and Ama Talo, one is readily identifiable. The Dimu genealogies mention Ama Rohi Rani as a high-born ancestor while the VOC records show that he ruled Dimu up to his demise from smallpox in 1676. He was the son of Talo Uju, perhaps the ruler Talo who kept the Dutch castaways after 1636. The identities of the two others are less clear, but Ama Talo might correspond to Ama Talo Leo from the line of fettors, that is, the domain's seconds-in-command.[18]

The Dutch probably considered the contract conclusion as a decisive moment in which they included the island in their expanding regional diplomatic network. The Dutch signed contracts all over the Southeast Asian archipelago, with literate as well as illiterate rulers, great and small, Muslim and 'heathen'. Often the contracts were combined with local ritual practices such as blood oaths. For local princes, they frequently meant something other than the textual content, namely a moral undertaking of protection and deference.

In his well-known historical-anthropological work on Rote and Savu, James Fox analyses the identity of the 'rajas' who the Dutch encountered in the mid-17th century. The highly ritual position of the Deo Rai (Lord of the Earth) would have made him unsuitable to meet the white strangers. Rather, official contacts were made through the representatives of the Apu Lod'o lineages. However, as the activities of the Apu Lod'o were also too circumscribed for effective governance, other members of their clans eventually became rajas (Fox 1977: 87). Fox does not seem to take into account the tradition of early Portuguese-affiliated rajas, which would have made the Estado da Índia-VOC transition less abrupt when it came to political representation. The various princely genealogies do not entirely confirm Fox's reconstruction, but the Apu Lod'o and raja tended to belong to the same *udu*. An essential act defining the ruler was the reception of a VOC flag which embodied great cultural capital—the same pattern is seen in the other Dutch- and Portuguese-allied territories in the eastern archipelago. The indigenous denomination for a raja, apart from the more general *duae* (leader), would therefore be *Mone Paji*, the 'Man with the Flag' (Heyligers 1920: 27).

Rebels and slaves

Unfortunately, it is not clear exactly how the 1648 contract was concluded. In the first decades of the VOC presence in the Savu Sea, the reports only give

---

[18] The term *fettor*, used for executive regents in Timor and adjacent islands, is likely derived from the Portuguese *feitor* (overseer). VOC sources usually speak of 'second regents' or something similar (see Figures 31 and 32).

patchy information about the island. Savu was clearly not the most urgent priority of the company, which was also working hard to establish a foothold in Timor. From remarks in the Dutch missives, it appears that the Savunese leaders were disappointed at the lack of substantial VOC assistance to defeat rebels in their land.[19] A brief hostile encounter took place in 1650, but the "grand lord of the place" was quick to assure the company that it was no more than an unhappy incident and that his alliance with the white foreigners endured. The rajas, apparently the elite of Dimu, were so hard pressed by the rebels that they dared not stay at their settlement but retreated to "the other rock", perhaps the fortified Hurati inland. Apart from indigenous rebels, they feared inroads by the Portuguese and Sonba'i.[20] The latter was an expansive Atoni kingdom in West Timor which was at that time allied with the Portuguese. The Timorese were not seafarers but could be taken to Savu on Portuguese ships to wreak havoc on the islanders. Sonba'i became a VOC ally in 1655, and their troops were occasionally taken to neighbouring islands to fight rebels and defecting allies. Savu would suffer just such a fate several decades later.

VOC reports illustrate how vulnerable and lacking in political cohesion Savunese society was at the time; it fully explains their leaders' hopeful attitude towards the VOC as a potentially ordering force. In exchange for their active support, Savu leaders promised to gift the Dutch with half the number of any rebels captured and the opportunity to buy the other half as slaves. Slaving had a long and sombre history across the eastern archipelago and the Europeans certainly did not try to restrict the phenomenon—quite the contrary. VOC forces eventually took action between September and October 1651. After visiting Kupang, Hendrik ter Horst went on to "Greater Savu", where the rajas were receptive as his visit occurred at a critical time. As it transpired, the rebels there had gone by ship to "Lesser Savu", which may mean Rote or perhaps Raijua. There they gathered fighters to assist them in attacking the rajas. A rebel ship arrived in Savu after four days, with 30 men and 4 women on board. The company force promptly seized it. Another ship managed to escape from the clutches of the company force in the night and a third ship was stranded on a reef off the "*negeri*", probably that of Dimu. During the flight, the Dutch cut down one of the rebels and destroyed the ship. As the Dutch proudly declared, this inspired great fear in the rebels, so they would be careful in the future not to engage the company in such a way. The grateful rajas seemed devoted to

---

[19] VOC 1180 (1650).

[20] Coolhaas 1964: 499; VOC 1187 (1651), f. 633–4.

maintaining the contract and asked for more company assistance for the "entire extermination of the rebels".[21]

In early 1653, the Dutch built Fort Concordia in Kupang, establishing a small garrison. Four years later the fortress in Solor was abandoned and Fort Concordia instead became the base of Dutch activities in the region until 1949. The VOC's early years were not auspicious. The Dutch and their allies suffered a series of disastrous defeats at the hands of the Portuguese and their Timorese dependents (Hägerdal 2012: 102–26). The area under Dutch control was therefore restricted to a small area along the Kupang Bay (the *sespalen gebied* [an area of six miles]), while Portuguese influence expanded over west and east Timor. The five Muslim Solorese princes remained more or less committed to the company, Rote was drawn into VOC affairs in the 1650s, and the small polities in Alor and Ende in Flores were also indirectly associated, though there was little actual contact. As for Sumba, an island where the Savunese had certain interests, it was in effect a no-man's-land loosely claimed by the Bima sultanate in Sumbawa and, in turn, a VOC vassal after 1667.[22]

From indications here and there in the colonial reports, it appears that Savu was not isolated from the outside world. By expressly forbidding that they land, the 1648 contract suggests that trading ships from Java, Makassar, the Malay world, Ende and Portuguese strongholds regularly traversed the sea and frequented the island. A 'sea' can be seen as interaction between various human and physical factors rather than just a geographical entity. Leonard Andaya discerned two trade-oriented groups who created overlapping 'seas' in eastern region: the Topasses Sea and the Sea of Makassar. The Makassarese were especially important in bringing rice, textiles and iron to the eastern archipelago in exchange for items such as sandalwood, slaves and tortoiseshell (Andaya 2016: 70–80; Duggan 2015: 78). Both 'seas' have some relevance to Savu, though the supply of products for trade was apparently limited. There were a substantial number of horses in Savu by 1648, but whether they were intended for export, as they were in later times, is doubtful. As for the Topasses Sea, a document from 1667 mentions a certain Don Jan who was born in Savu but was ethnically Rotenese and stayed in Lifau, the base of Portuguese power in Timor. The Dutch strongly suspected that he instigated Rotenese people of the Ringgou domain to leave their homes and migrate to Lifau, in other words to defect from the company.[23] Whether it is true or not, his career is a display of geographic

---

[21] Coolhaas 1964: 620–1; VOC 1193 (1652), f. 740–1. The details in the account are too vague to determine whether 'Lesser Savu' (*Cleyn Sabo*) was Raijua or Rote.

[22] Tange 1689, f. 1, H 49v, KITLV Archive.

[23] VOC 1264 (1667).

mobility. One of the four traditional *suco*s (settlements) of the Oecusse kingdom, heir to the Black Portuguese polity, is called Sabos. Local tradition asserts that people expelled from Rote and Savu went to the Lifau-Oecusse area where they took on a Catholic identity and joined the multi-ethnic community.[24] Several Dutch and Portuguese documents from the 17th and 18th centuries explicitly refer to Rotenese or Savunese immigrants in Lifau.[25]

Savu was clearly of interest as a strategic rather than a commercial location. In 1649, the Dutch captain found that the VOC representative in Dimu, Hendrik Bijlaagh, had not been able to purchase more than five slaves, a small number even by the modest expectations that applied to VOC enterprises in the Flores-Timor area. A decade later a short report illustrates the VOC's growing irritation with their Dimu ally.

The then *opperhoofd* Joseph Margits sailed from Kupang in the fall of 1659. After arriving in Dimu on 18 October, he confronted the few Dutch representatives on the island. They alleged that they had continuously asked the elite for slaves, but the elite answered that they could only deliver them if they had gold and textiles to bargain with. Margits and his following went up to the place where Raja Ama Hili (Ama Doko Hili) lay sick. However, when he heard that the whites brought high-quality textiles he was hurriedly on his feet. He excused himself by asserting that some people in his domain had risen against him and so there were no slaves. However, the raja suggested that if Margits accompanied him to Raijua Island he could capture some slaves. Margits agreed and the next day proceeded to Raijua on the company sloops with the raja on board. When Ama Hili went to the main settlement of the small island domain he found a few cannons (possibly from a shipwreck) but was not able to lay hands on any Raijuanese. At this stage Margits' bad temper began to show itself.[26] He complained that the raja fed him daily with lies. Back in Dimu, Ama Hili assured the Dutchman that he would bring some prisoners from the rebel side within four or five days. After having spent half a month in Savu, Margits had not procured more than four slaves of both sexes. "These rascals and liars always promise things" was his comment and proceeded to Rote where there was more trade in human flesh and blood.[27] From the VOC report, it appears that the Dutch were pawns in a local power game and there was limited interest in

---

[24] Interviews with the Salu and Da Costa families, Oecusse (09–11.02.2013).

[25] Matos 1974: 309; VOC 1566 (1694–95), dagh-register, dated 28 October 1694.

[26] Margits was a known alcoholic and presumably not the best-suited person to deal with the Savunese.

[27] VOC 1229 (1659), missive, 26 November 1659.

providing the white foreigners with human cargo. An interesting detail is that the Dutch paid for the salvaged artillery from the shipwreck with 200 *parangs* (machetes)—at this stage, the elite may still have had to import metal weapons. Another highly coveted import was foreign textiles, perhaps originating from South Asia.

The 1676 expedition to Savu

The insatiable Dutch demand for slaves led to a series of confrontations that wrecked the island. Batavia was the company hub and the governor-general and his council allocated resources to the various outposts in maritime Asia on the basis of the reports it received. In the 1660s, as the military strength of the Acehnese sultanate shrank, the Dutch gained a foothold in West Sumatra where they found valuable goldmines (De Klerck 1938 I: 272–3). As the local Minangkabaus were considered "too lazy" to use as workforce, the Dutch wanted slaves for the heavy work in the mines. VOC Batavia expected the otherwise unprofitable post in Kupang to meet their needs.[28] Slave raiding initially occurred in small and vulnerable societies, such as those in the eastern islands, and political crises gave the opportunity to capture people for the slave market. Some Timorese slaves were sent to West Sumatra but, as most of Timor was off-limits to the VOC, it was not enough.

The attempts by Savunese leaders to use the company as a tool against their adversaries converged with the demand for slaves. In 1672, Dimu promised to deliver slaves if the Dutch assisted them in defeating their long-term enemies in the domain of Mesara. The company therefore sent the official Reynout Wagenburgh to Savu with the two sloops *De Carper* and *Timor* and a very small detachment of soldiers, numbering seven or eight men. When Wagenburgh arrived in Dimu he found the elite keen on a peaceful conclusion to the dispute. He and his men therefore marched with some Dimunese towards the main settlement of Mesara. The first reactions to the Dutch arrival were not unfavourable, or so it seemed. Mesara was committed to a settlement, but the chiefs first had to convene to deliberate on the issue.

It is possible that this was no more than a common tactic employed by minor regional polities—to pretend willingness to negotiate in order to win more time. Thus, the very next day the men of Mesara sallied out from the village and proceeded to surround the VOC-Dimu detachment. Finding themselves under attack, the Dutch responded with a musket salvo. Firearms had presumably been in Savu since the Portuguese times, but at this stage they were still awe-inspiring

---

[28] Coolhaas 1968: 845, dated 31 January 1673.

weapons in the region. The Mesara warriors, presumably armed only with lances and cutlasses, hastily withdrew to the village. They were pursued by the company soldiers and their Dimu allies who set fire to the village and burnt some minor settlements in the vicinity. They then withdrew to Dimu; however, the hostilities cost two Dutch lives. The Dimu elite gratefully pledged to have between 100 and 150 slaves ready for the next Dutch visit to Savu.[29]

As it turned out, the Dimu leaders had promised too much. As is usual in the small-scale polities of the eastern region, the population of a Savunese domain only consisted of a few thousand people, meaning that the loss of 100 to 150 persons would have a sizeable impact. Dissatisfaction with the Dutch procurement of human flesh and blood manifested itself in two persons called Talo and Liwu Kone.[30] The former was probably the son of Ama Talo—named in the 1648 contract—from the fettor line of Dimu's ruling clan. However, there are several people called Talo in the pedigrees. The name has a possible foreign connection, as Tallo' was the junior partner in the twin kingdom of Makassar (the other being Gowa) and Tallo' rulers made expeditions to the east of the archipelago in the 17th century. The second figure is not clearly identified in the genealogical accounts. Possibly the patronymic element should be read Kome rather than Kone, as a Kome belonging to the ruling clan seems to have flourished in this era. Names aside, what is certain is that the vengeful actions of these two men had major consequences.

In 1673, the Dutch fort in Kupang dispatched a diplomatic mission to the south coast of Timor. The mission head was the same Reynout Wagenburgh on the same sloop *De Carper* that had been in Savu the previous year. The aim was to parley with the Black Portuguese leader of the day, António Hornay, who had just ousted a rival in Lifau, and was in the process of subjugating all of Timor except Kupang. The meeting never took place as Hornay had his hands full dealing with treachery from within the Portuguese ranks. On its way back, adverse winds blew the sloop past Timor and it was wrecked off shore between Dimu and Kolo Alo.[31] The accident took place in the middle of the night, and most of the crew seems to have survived and got to shore. In the early morning, a local went down to the seashore, discovered the wreck and immediately ran to Dimu to tell the news.

---

[29] Coolhaas 1968: 845–6, dated 31 January 1673.

[30] It is usually spelt 'Lyffkone' in the Dutch documents. Liwu Kone would be Riwu Kone in normalised spelling. See Figures 31 and 32.

[31] Kolo Alo, in the original text Coloalo, situated between Dimu and the river Liu estuary, nowadays in the district of Sabu Tengah (Central Savu).

What follows shows the intense resentment that Dutch actions had generated among some local groups, of which the company seems to have been only dimly aware. A band of Dimunese went to the place and with them was Liwu Kone. In the bushland above the coast, he came across two whites and two Timorese, and immediately had them killed. Meanwhile, Wagenburgh and another Dutchman had been rescued by a local called Ama Lai who took them to his house. However, as he was afraid of the Dimunese he eventually had to turn his guests over to them. The warriors then attacked and killed the foreigners they found at or close to the wreck. Wagenburgh himself was tied up and brought to Dimu. The next day he was murdered in cold blood together with a European boy who always accompanied him. The murder was carried out by Liwu Kone, with the approval of the fettor Talo, and two other grandees called Ama Dami and Ama Doko. The complicity of the Raja Ama Rohi in all this is not apparent from the documents.

The murder of the *De Carper* crew shows the animosity towards the covetous Dutch and their never-ending hunger for human cargo. However, there were also material prizes that attracted the inhabitants of resource-scare Savu. Witnesses later told the Dutch authorities how some Dimu women were clad in *sarassen*, many-coloured silk cloths which made up part of the *De Carper* cargo. Wagenburgh's *rotting* (rattan cane) with a silver knob was also displayed in the settlement, as were his trousers and jacket. People eagerly took various iron objects and even the ship's mast. In one version of the story, Liae people also participated in the murders and shared the spoils with Dimu.[32]

When news about the massacre reached Kupang there was outrage, not least from the Timorese allies who had contributed to the mission. They stated that they would not only burn Dimu to the ground but carry out a general slaughter, not even sparing unborn children in their mothers' wombs. The first idea was to take a sufficient number of Kupang, Sonba'i and Amabi troops on a *fluyt* (cargo ship) and three sloops that were at their disposal. However, instead the *opperhoofd* decided to wait for orders from Batavia.[33] With the small resources at hand in Kupang, expeditions were costly and risky. Dimu therefore had a respite of more than two years, perhaps giving it a false sense of security: the Dutch seemed too few and far away to exact revenge.

The company, however, did not forget; there were a number of unsettled scores in the Timor-Flores area. The society of Rote, deeply divided, had 12 to 15 domains, some of which resisted Dutch domination. The domains Dengka

---

[32] VOC 1311 (1675).

[33] Ibid.

and Lole, and three minor units, stood in open "rebellion" against the VOC. And in Solor, some villagers had murdered a Muslim priest and his followers, which in this context was a violation of company interests. The VOC therefore resolved through a concentrated effort to move against these various hotspots. The enterprise coincided with a period of strong VOC political expansion, having crushed the Makassar Empire in 1667 and 1669, with the impending subjugation of Mataram, Banten and Ternate a few years later (De Klerck 1938 I: 276–7, 288–98).

Thus, in March 1676, no fewer than 220 Dutch soldiers in five companies and 1,100 Timorese auxiliaries massed in Kupang to chastise the enemies in Rote, Savu and the Solor Islands. The expedition movements are fairly well known as the commander kept a scrupulous dagh-register leaving a circumstantial record of events. The opportunity for booty and the wish for blood revenge were so great among the Timorese that they had to be held back by force upon embarking. Among the participants was the king of Kupang in person. The fleet first sailed to nearby Rote where Termanu was the leading princedom and the main prop of Dutch authority on the island. After a war council in Termanu, the forces divided and moved against the recalcitrant places. Fighting tended to comprise besieging stone fortifications with subsequent massacres where sometimes not even women were spared. After four gory weeks, the eerie calm of death ruled in Rote with the main resistance leader Raja Sode of Lole having been slain. The wounded and sick, some of the auxiliaries and the extracted slaves, were sent back to Kupang while the rest of the expedition proceeded to Savu. With them went Minggu,[34] the raja of a small island of Ndao off Rote's west coast. The language of Ndao was similar to that of Savu, so Minggu could be useful as a go-between in negotiations. The ships were not able to drop anchor off Dimu due to the rough breakers and instead anchored at Seba on 2 May 1676. The Sebanese were in no mood to support Dimu or impede the arrival of the company. As amply shown in Rote, shared ethnicity was seldom a unifying factor in insular Southeast Asia, and Seba was only too happy to support the white foreigners against Dimu. While the Dutch saw Dimu as the paramount power of Savu, it is not at all certain that the Sebanese endorsed this perspective.[35]

From Seba the troops marched on to Dimu. Nobody expected it to be a military promenade, for the Dimunese could muster about 1,500 horsemen, actually more than the VOC forces. Raja Ama Rohi came in person with an entourage to meet the troops and asked to negotiate. However, it soon became

---

[34] It could possibly be spelt 'Mingga'.

[35] VOC 1319 (1675–76), dagh-register, dated 2 May 1676.

evident that it was a strategy to win time to prepare the resistance. In the meantime, the Dimunese left their main settlement and flocked inside a fortress that lay about one hour's travel away. The fortress was formidable with three concentric walls made of stone. Although it is not named in the dagh-register, there is little doubt that it is Hurati (Surati) which is situated on an inland hill (Plate 9). Today, the inner wall is in a good state of preservation, and traces of the second and outer walls are still evident. Its origins are hidden in the mist of legends. It was reportedly constructed by "foreigners from the sea" who originally planned to build six to ten concentric walls. However, as the construction apparently took place during one single night, the final structure had a mere three walls. Legends aside, a foreign connection is indeed possible. Hurati or Surati is reminiscent of Surat in Gujarat in India. Another fortified settlement nearby, Kujiratu, is explicitly associated with the Portuguese in local tradition, so it could be named after Gujarat which was an important Indian centre of commercial activities in the early modern era where the Portuguese maintained a presence.

As the VOC expedition approached Dimu, Ama Rohi reappeared, now with a backing of 1,400 to 1,500 armed men. This time there was no real attempt to reach a settlement and the Dimunese withdrew after a while. For the Dutch, it only remained to continue the march to the main settlement of Dimu which was empty. Just outside was a square-shaped fortification. The troops attacked it and occupied the spot after meeting very little resistance. However, this first show of force did nothing to deter the defenders who rashly declared that they would not hear of peace and awaited the company troops in their Hurati stronghold. The expeditionary force attacked the stone walls; however, the fury of the defenders brought the Dutch to a standstill on the first day. During the night the company troops scouted around the fortifications, preparing for the final assault. The account of the battle's climax deserves quoting:

> On Saturday the 9th [of April] the shipper Jan van der Wall and the sailors at hand, with hand grenades, fire jars and pikes, were commanded, together with the lieutenants Tielman and Casper and their companies, to violently attack the side where they began yesterday, under the cover of the hand grenades and fire pikes. Meanwhile, the brave Captain Harmen Egbertsz and the two other companies under the lieutenants Bremer and Kelck drew attention on the other side. The aforementioned shipper and the lieutenants Tielman and Casper easily entered the first and the second *pagger* [fortification], but Tielman was not properly followed by his soldiers. Lieutenant Arent Bremer came to his relief, which was good, since Lieutenant Tielman was wounded, although not fatally. His place was bravely taken by Ensign Frans, who was also wounded. The brave Captain Harmen Egbertsz with the company of Lieutenant Kelck came with relief

close to the place where our men stormed [the fortification], intending to use the necessary means. However, after an hour of skirmishing they were in front of the last pagger, and due to the continuous shooting, our men ran out of gunpowder, bullets and matches. They were ordered not to shoot so much. The brave captain took advantage of the lull to speak to the enemy. Upon that the main regent of Dimu, Ama Rohi, showed up on the pagger with a white flag and shouted 'Sudah berkelahi' [enough fighting].

The quotation indicates that by this time some of the elite were able to speak Malay, the main language of inter-ethnic communication in the East Indies. Negotiations immediately followed and the Dimu elite had to agree to extradite the main culprits—Talo and Liwu Kone. They were also to deliver 300 slaves; men, women and children. Finally, they would have to pay 150 *tael*s of gold and 150 *tael*s of beads to the auxiliaries.[36] If they did not fulfill all the conditions, the forces would burn down the village. After the settlement, the company troops marched back to Seba, as it was not possible to receive all the items at once. Once again, however, this was a device to gain time. Ama Rohi was fully aware that the Dutch position was vulnerable. Large assemblies of troops were always at risk both from the continual need to keep them supplied with food and water, and the poor health conditions at the time; far more troops succumbed to illness than to enemy attacks, no matter where they were. Of the 200 Dutchmen, only 80 were able to march for more than a few hours and sickness raged in the auxiliary ranks. The expedition would soon have to leave Savu.

The Dutch captain Harman Egbertsen resolved to settle the matter once and for all. With 20 men and a lieutenant he entered the settlement of Dimu on 16 May. They proceeded to round up all the adult men, together with those who stayed in the vicinity, and deprived them of their weapons. On a plain outside the settlement, surrounded by the VOC allies, they were thus at the mercy of the invaders. Egbertsen ordered them to pick out the persons regarded as slaves and turn them over to the Dutch. Fearing the worst, the Dimunese picked out 50 men, 62 women, 33 boys, 58 girls and 37 small children, then declaring that there were no more slaves left, only free people. Although this was not quite the number requested, the Dutch considered it unwise to pursue the matter further; after all, an excessive demand for slaves had caused the crew's massacre in 1674. The assembled people seemed relieved to be allowed back into the village, as they had expected nothing less than being taken to the slave market. The gold and bead necklaces were not fully paid either, but the Dimunese provided hostages

---

[36] A *tael* was both a unit of weight (approximately 37.5 g) and a currency used in Southeast Asia.

as surety and promised to deliver the riches later. Nor were the culprits Talo and Liwu Kone extradited as they were hiding in the countryside.

Glad to have the matter settled the Dutch expedition weighed anchor and left Savu, never to return. The vessels proceeded to the Solor Islands where the troops burnt down the priest-slaying village of Wollor (Wolo) and the coastal settlement Lamahala. From an official point of view, the expedition had been reasonably successful in chastising the VOC's perceived enemies and enhancing Dutch prestige. But did this correspond to local perceptions of the event?

Given the detailed genealogical memory of Savunese society, one would perhaps expect a distinct set of stories about the punitive expedition in collective memory. After all, this was the only major Dutch expedition to the island in the course of three centuries of Dutch-Savunese relations. However, memories of the 1676 events are vague and elusive at best. In Dimu, an account has survived of a conflict that was not exactly portrayed as a Dutch triumph. According to the story, a Dutch delegation once arrived in Dimu bringing the Christian religion. They tried to instruct the locals on how to bow before the clerical authority. The Savunese saw this as a trick: if they bowed before the whites, the foreigners would kill them off easier. It was better to kill the strangers first and this is what they did.

A Dutch military expedition to the island was the result of this incident. Ama Bala Nguru, a relative of the raja line, led the Dimunese against the Dutch. He relied on tactics. When the Dutch left their ship and marched up to the main settlement, Ama Bala Nguru had already told the people to evacuate, so the Dutch soldiers found an empty village. Meanwhile, Ama Bala Nguru had posted some of his men close to the beach. While the Dutch troops were still in the interior, they suddenly attacked the ship and took everything of value. Thus the Dutch were worsted. As for the plundered ship, the people subsequently buried it inside a hill called Bukit Kuburan Kapal (Ship's grave hill) at Banyo beach. There it remains.[37]

Another account centres on a woman called Ga Lena. There are several versions of her story, but the one retold here was related by Teffer, the missionary, in the late 19th century.[38] Under a Seba chief called Riwu Ropa, a conflict ensued where Seba tried to subjugate Dimu, but instead Seba was badly defeated. A descendant of D'ara Wai, Ga Lena (or Dila Nawa), used trickery to help Seba's cause. She dressed up as a man and was allowed on a trading ship belonging to a

---

[37] Interview with Ama Dubu (alias Djawa Gigih), Dimu (29.06.2012). If the story is true and took place in the 1670s, it is clear that this Ama Bala Nguru is a different person from Ama Bala Nguru of 1759 (chapter 6).

[38] For another version of the Ga Lena narrative, see Appendix I, Narrative 3.

certain Hadu Kiu. Hadu Kiu took her to Lohayong in Solor where she met the *sengaji* (raja). She revealed her true gender and displayed some bones of a dead dog, pretending they were the remains of people massacred by the gruesome Dimu people. The *sengaji* believed her and, furthermore, fell in love with Ga Lena. They married and had a daughter together called Putri. The fort Kotta Ga was named after Ga Lena.

Photo 9. The Ga Lena stone; Rae Ja, Mesara (2013)

In Solor, Ga Lena was acquainted with the company—in other words the VOC. The enterprising woman took her baby and sailed to Kupang, where she contacted the Dutch administration. She actually received a company flag and a *tongkat* (cane [In]) from the Dutch. After that, she gathered auxiliaries consisting of Solorese, Kupangese, Rotenese and Ndaoese and moved against Dimu. She first arrived in Raijua and left her daughter Putri there. With the flag and *tongkat* in hand, by implication she returned to Savu as the ruling princess of Seba.

However, she was less successful back on Savunese soil. The auxiliaries returned home without having fully carried out their task. Ga Lena consoled herself by marrying a new husband (it is not mentioned whether the *sengaji* was still alive). This was Bèngu Tari (Tagi), the raja of Menia. When the company eventually sent a commission to Savu ten years later, Ga Lena was already dead and her daughter in Raijua did not continue the line. Instead, the Dutch befriended Dimu, which was made the chief village and they also appointed its headman as Dimu's raja. A *posthouder* (company representative), and later on an indigenous teacher, settled there. Through these events, Dimu obtained the pre-eminent position on the island and Seba became, according to adat, Dimu's servant.[39]

It seems likely that Teffer's account is in fact an amalgamation of various elements, some of which can still be found in oral tradition. If the two narratives actually refer to the historical VOC invasion, they view matters in an entirely different light to the Dutch commander. Both oral versions emphasise that Dimu was not really defeated and the second one basically regards the episode as an internal Savunese affair. Dimu's first-ranking position on the island was the result of Dutch interference in local affairs and was not associated with the adat principles described in previous chapters. Historical names related to the 1676 expedition appear here and there. Hadu Kiu or Sadu Kiu was in fact a fettor in Termanu in Rote who supported the Dutch in their dealings with Savu in the late 17th century and joined the expedition. In Dimu, the raja of Ndao, Mingga, is from an Ndaoese-Savunese marriage. Bèngu Tagi was indeed the name of two members of Menia's ruling lineage, although neither of them lived at the time of these events. The name Kotta Ga has no other known reference. The fort at Lohayong is usually known as Fort Henricus.[40] However, what about Ga Lena herself? In current tradition she is occasionally known under the name Ina Tenga, which may link her to a ruling Seba princess with that name who lived in the 1670s and 1680s.

The company as a peacemaker

The expedition of 1676 may well reveal the company at its very worst—a rapacious, violence-prone entity that was essentially driven by the prospect of

---

[39] Raad voor de Zending, 1102–1: 1411, M. Teffer, letter, 7 March 1874. Riwu Ropa could not be identified in the Dimu genealogies. However, the name Ropa exists; there was a Ropa Riwu and his sons Lai Ropa and Talo Ropa who lived in early Portuguese times (before 1600; Figure 31). There is no Raja Bèngu Tari in Menia, but there is a Bèngu Tagi who lived 200 years after Riwu Ropa (Figure 40). See also Figure 44.

[40] Robert Barnes traces the early history of Fort Henricus (1987: 208–36).

tangible profit. However, the picture may be more nuanced. Recent historical research notes that the VOC also played a balancing, mediating role in politically fragmented societies.[41] There was frequent infighting between ethnic groups in the East Indies, such as the Minahasa, Bugis-Makassarese, Minangkabau, Timorese, Rotenese and Savunese, though these groups shared the same language, social structure, material culture and religious beliefs. As subordinate allies of the company, they presented their case to the local Dutch resident and his council for arbitration. The resident and most of the other officials only stayed at a VOC post for a few years and were less likely to be attached to either side, unlike a local man of authority.

As for Savu, the years following the expedition illustrate the VOC's mediator role. The severe decline of the Dimu population and the ensuing weakening of its power apparently prompted aggression from the other Savu polities. In 1682, the *opperhoofd* of Kupang heard worrying news of internal fighting and sent company official Willem Tange there on the ship *D'Battavise Coopman* to mediate. No Dutch ship had been to Savu for two years at that point. Tange picked up the regent Sadu Kiu of Termanu in Rote, who had a good command of the intricacies of Savunese affairs, and reached the island on 4 June. When the Dimunese became aware of their arrival they immediately hoisted the VOC flag and provided some regents to follow Tange to Seba. In Seba, Tange ordered the Seba regents to gather with those of Mesara and Liae to discuss the ongoing conflict.[42] The participants sat in a circle in a tent to confer as the background to the violence was disclosed. The relative dearth of details regarding local Savunese affairs in this era makes the case interesting. It is therefore worth having a closer look at the circumstances.

The Sebanese and Dimunese disputed the origins of the conflict. The Seba version said that people from their domain had been invited to a feast in Liae sometime previously, as there was to be cockfighting. The Sebanese arrived in festive mood and had a merry time. Suddenly, a party of fully armed Dimunese arrived. The Sebanese had no idea what their intention was but took up position, assisted by the Liae people. The Dimu troops made an unprovoked attack and pushed their adversaries back into their domain at the cost of two lives. In the Dimu version, the Sebanese were not so innocent: they had not only come for

---

[41] The idea of the company as a 'stranger-king' with an important mediating function in politically fragmented societies was put forward in Henley (2002). See also the various essays on the 'stranger-kings' theme in *Indonesia and the Malay World* 36 2008; and Hägerdal (2012) for a discussion in the context of early-modern Timor.

[42] VOC 1375 (1681–82), dagh-register, dated 4–7 June 1682.

the cockfighting but intended to kill a Dimu regent called Ama Doko. He was visiting Liae at that time but was warned in advance by a Liae friend.

The Dimu and Seba grandees were in agreement about the rest of the story, quoted here:

> Shortly afterwards those from Dimu came with a raiding party in the night and took a horse with them. When [the Sebanese] realised this, the regent Dami pursued them with a force within a short distance [of Dimu]. They could not however catch them and beheaded a girl from Dimu carrying [the head] with them. When the Dimunese understood this, they again followed after them until not far from Seba, by the river. There [the Sebanese] took up a defensive position and asked the Dimunese why they had stolen the horse at night from their *negeri*. They replied that the horse belonged to them six years ago when the company ruined their domain and was used by the Rotenese regent Sadu. They therefore took custody of it again. They then parted from each other.[43]

Some days afterwards ten Sebanese went to the nearby reef to catch fish. Wagenburgh's murderer, Talo, hid in the forest nearby with a strong mounted force. One of the Sebanese on the shore spotted Talo and approached him. A fight occurred and Talo injured the Sebanese with his lance. The injured man had enough strength to strike Talo's horse with his pike, mortally wounding the animal. Talo then beheaded the wounded Sebanese and took his head as booty. The other nine men, witnessing this, swam out to sea and managed to escape. They told their superiors who summoned a posse to follow the perpetrator. However, they did not find him and returned.

Now Seba, Mesara, Liae and Raijua united to crush Dimu once and for all. The ruling queen of Seba, Ina Tenga, objected, believing the enterprise was inadvisable. However, she was overruled and troops including her son Dami marched against Dimu. They were met by the enemy and a bitter fight ensued. Nineteen men from Raijua and Seba were killed with only two Dimunese deaths, so the allied troops fled, pursued by the victors for some distance. The Dimunese returned with the heads of their enemies which included several regents; one of them was Dami. When the queen heard about her son's death she and her entourage immediately went to the place of slaughter. There she found his corpse lying on the ground. She encountered a gruesome scene: Dami's decapitated body was slashed open and the intestines had been pulled out. The left arm had been cut off, and the legs and the rest of the body were cut asunder. Such was also the state of two other regent corpses. The queen was very distressed by the grisly sight. They carried the three persons back to Seba and buried them there.

---

[43] VOC 1375 (1681–82), dagh-register, dated 8 June 1682.

The hostilities wore on for some time. Apart from a minor skirmish involving Liae, it was hardly warfare in the European sense of the word. Raiding parties beheaded individuals found in the wilderness and stole cattle when the opportunity arose.[44] The interviews Tange conducted with various Savunese grandees present a reasonably genuine idea of the consequences of political fragmentation in the eastern islands in this era. Headhunting was a widespread practice which had its own ritually laden dynamics and the victims were not confined to fighting men. Pitched battles were rare and probably deemed too risky. With perhaps no more than a few thousand souls, it was simply not logical to launch a full-scale assault; Queen Ina Tenga's objections were well founded. As with many small societies, warfare did not entail military heroism but rather tried to minimise the risk of loss by conducting opportunistic raids.[45]

Under these circumstances the role of the company as a 'stranger-king' was functional, as seen in Willem Tange's detailed annotations on his mission. Tange admonished the local regents, saying that the company saw their internal squabbles with great displeasure, the more so as the hostilities had cost the blood of the innocent. He threatened the Savunese, telling them that they had recently seen with their own eyes how the company treated troublemakers and assured them they could count on the VOC's paternalistic benevolence if they ended the conflict peacefully. After a few days of deliberations, the hostile parties declared they were willing to keep the peace, expressing their gratitude to the company which had settled the matter. The peace was formally concluded and confirmed "with the usual ceremonies".[46]

Tange did not expand on the nature of these ceremonies. However, some of the officials who visited Savu in the following decades made extensive notes on what they saw. In July 1717, the Dutch representative convened with the leaders of Dimu, Seba, Mesara and Liae in order to settle a tricky issue between the grandees of Dimu. Although the domains constituted ritual entities with a deep local significance, political cohesion was weak. Serious clashes and thefts of slaves and cattle were common within the domains, and the rajas were sometimes disadvantaged. Raja Rohi Rani of Dimu argued that the sub-regent Danka[47] owed him 57 buffalos, 9 horses, 110 pigs, 380 sheep, 26 slaves, and an assortment of items such as axes and kettles. Eventually, the Dutch managed to arrange an exchange of the stolen goods and the agreement was greeted with loud

---

[44] VOC 1375 (1681–82), dagh-register, dated 8 June 1682.

[45] The point has been made in a global context by Keegan (1994).

[46] VOC 1375 (1681–82), dagh-register, dated 9–13 June 1682.

[47] The name should presumably be 'Daga' in current spelling.

cheering from the troops who accompanied the respective chiefs. On 4 July, a *pemali* (taboo) ceremony was held, as related at length in the dagh-register:

> We came to the small mountain Amaratten and asked the rajas to commence. Then Luji Talo [fettor of Dimu] and the *pemali* seer took a small hog and placed it on an elevated stone. After having mumbled over it for a while according to the way of their land, they stood up and cut off part of the right ear. They put it in a coconut shell with water with which they sprinkled their people. Then they cut its throat with the same cutlass and threw it to the ground where it died with the blood sputtering. When they had done so much, the sub-regent Danka came with a pig of the same size which was handled in the aforementioned manner. Thus this activity came to an end. Then the Resident bade the sub-regent farewell, adding that he would come to Danka's *negeri* in the evening to abide there. He withdrew with the regents in the same manner as he came. We had not yet arrived to the *negeri* of Luji Talo when we saw all his people standing in a ring. He took a young chicken and pulled out some feathers from the right wing after mumbling something, put them in the water and sprinkled all the bystanders. He then cut its throat, as he asserted, to confirm the *pemali* regarding the peace with a good heart that his subjects should consider. We then returned to his house and shared a drink for success and ate a midday meal with them. When we were content we politely bade farewell under condition that they would come to Seba before my departure. Thus we mounted our horses and headed for the aforementioned *negeri* [Seba] where we arrived even before the sun had set.[48]

The next day the Dutch discovered that the stipulations of the peace agreement had not quite been fulfilled and that the rituals were incomplete. The errands told the Dutch Resident that one party "could not accept it as their *pemali* of crops, trees, rivers and sea had not yet been carried out". Eventually, however, all the parties declared that the dispute was over—for now.[49] The peace rituals correspond very closely to similar rituals in Timor, testifying to the cultural interactions taking place.[50]

Dutch sources seldom mention the names of local deities, but there is a case from 1719 when a Dutch official brokered peace after fighting had broken out again:

---

[48] VOC 7979 (1717), dagh-register, dated 4 July 1717.

[49] In fact, the Kupang authorities, at the behest of the Savunese elite, eventually removed Danka or Daga Lai and dispatched him to Batavia in 1727. He was subsequently placed in Edam, an island north of Batavia (Coolhaas 1985: 134–5).

[50] VOC 1346 (1678–79), dagh-register, dated 12 October 1678; summarised in Hägerdal (2012: 213).

> After I had heard each of the parties, and found the [original] matter
> being of such small importance, I pacified these fickle people by friendly
> words by making them join hands and invoke Olla Tallo, with promises
> that they would not undertake any more hostilities against each other,
> so that all of this island is once again in complete peace, and the *pemali*
> [taboo] of ratification has been carried out in our presence. With this, the
> gathering came to an end.[51]

Sacrificing Calvinist purity on the altar of peace, the official seems to induce the
Savunese lords to invoke a powerful spirit. There is no mention of an Ola Talo in
modern religious tradition.

Did the Dutch efforts to make peace have any lasting consequences? There
is no recognisable reminiscence today of the peace agreement in 1682, although
this era is still very much within living memory. Tange's account lists scores of
local rajas and chiefs, and many of these can be found in the orally preserved
pedigrees. However, the spate of warfare in 1681–82 was but one of many similar
incidents in the island's turbulent history, and there is no Savunese Thucydides or
Tacitus to document and comment on the period. The same goes for the Dimu
dispute in 1717 and innumerable other incidents. While there are a number of
oral stories about Dutch interference, these tend to be connected with events of
dynastic consequence such as the change of a raja. The VOC records indicate that
internal clashes flared up in Savu again and again, though they might have spilt
less blood than in Rote or Timor. Nevertheless, the six domains of Savu-Raijua
continued their existence until the late 19th and early 20th centuries. For most
of the time, there was not one single Dutch representative on the island; however,
the absent 'stranger-king', the VOC, was always there as a last resort. After 1676,
the VOC needed no major expedition to retain Savu in the alliance system and,
unlike Rote, the Savunese seem to have made no effort whatsoever to bring the
Portuguese back.

The foregoing chapter has shown several sides of evolving Dutch-Savunese
relations. There seems to have been no initial resistance to the bonding of
the local elite with the VOC. This was highly contingent on their sense of
security: the main rajas on the island had latent problems with other groups,
castigated as "rebels", and regarded the company as a useful ally. A few decades
after initial contact in 1648, the company slid into a role of 'stranger-kings',
outsiders whose foreignness made them suitable to mediate in conflicts between
the domains or between factions within the domains. In that respect, the VOC
presence in the neighbourhood was functional, even indispensable. However,
being a profit-driven organisation with a pragmatic or even cynical view of its

---

[51] VOC 8318 (1719), f. 75–6.

clients, the company had no qualms in exploiting the divisions on the island for their own purposes, whether for trade or political domination. While the Europeans approached Dimu as the foremost domain, this is not matched by local Savunese understandings of history, as they refer to the defunct Teriwu realm as a site of precedence. In fact, the colonial order often underpinned rather than soothed local conflicts. This 'divide et impera' policy was a common way for numerically small European groups to maintain hegemonic rule or at least suzerainty in various parts of Africa and Asia. It is an open question whether the island societies of the eastern archipelago generally improved or deteriorated under Dutch suzerainty, but it is clear enough that there were disadvantages, such as restrictions on shipping and trade, and widespread inter-regional slavery. Thus the VOC squeezed its allies to satisfy its demand for slave labour. The ensuing discontent and the brief war of 1676 demonstrated the vulnerability of the relationship but also the difficulties the Dutch had in maintaining large contingents of troops on a faraway and disease-ridden island. Thus, the bond was cemented in a way that would not be fundamentally changed until the 20th century.

Chapter 6 | The Six Domains Under the Company Flag

Dimu

In the previous chapter, the VOC incorporated the six Savunese-Raijuan domains—probably in existence well before the arrival of the first Europeans—into its strategic network. The Dutch did not expect tangible profits from the arrangement as the association was mainly of a political nature. Unlike some other outlying places, such as Ambon, the Banda Islands and Ternate, Savu was largely left to its own devices. Nevertheless, the Dutch arrival had an impact on the island's power relations. The genealogies of the raja families in some of the domains suggest a change in the ruling clans or lineages in early VOC times. The raja appointments may have only been a response to the Portuguese presence in the 16th century in order to carry out functions unsuitable for the Apu Lod'o and Deo Rai. The Dutch also insisted on upholding Dimu's position of precedence over the other domains, even dubbing its raja the "regent of Savu".

The chapter traces the development of the six domains during the VOC era, beginning with Dimu. Historical data suggest that its precedence began with the Portuguese. The previously analysed contract of 1648 is conspicuous because it only seems to involve Dimunese chiefs, two of whom can be identified in the genealogical tradition. The most prominent was Ama Rohi. He was a fifth-generation descendant of Tuka Hida from Portuguese times, but whether all the intervening generations were ruling rajas is not clear.[1] In spite of its historical importance, the traditions pertaining to Dimu tend to be less explicit than for the other domains. Ama Rohi is mentioned at irregular intervals in the VOC records from 1648 to his death in 1678.

Ama Rohi's son and successor was Rohi Rani who was merely a boy at his accession.[2] His reign, as documented by archival sources, covered the extended period from 1678 to 1731. The VOC missives depict snippets of the rajas' personal lives; they are figures who otherwise appear rather indistinct in the

---

[1] As noted previously, his father Talo Uju might have been Raja Talo, mentioned in VOC 869 (1645), f. 92.

[2] VOC 1338 (1678).

documents. In 1700, for example, Rohi Rani travelled to Kupang on a VOC sloop. His daughter's arm was seriously disabled and he hoped that people in Kupang would be able to cure her: other documents reveal that they had good knowledge of herbal medicine which also interested the VOC.[3] On this occasion, Rohi Rani seems not only to be a good father but also a faithful friend. He specifically asked the company to release a slave who worked in the artisan quarter of Kupang as he was a friend. The raja arranged that he would deliver two good male slaves to the company in his stead.[4] To Europeans or Asians of the day there was nothing cynical about the barter; the institution of slavery was rarely questioned by anyone.

Nevertheless, there is some uncertainty regarding Rohi Rani's exact position within the ruling Dimu hierarchy. As outsiders, the Dutch did not have a good grasp of the internal workings of the domains and what they said was often ambiguous. It is clear that the Dutch never caught or punished Talo, Wagenburgh's murderer; on the contrary, he held a high position in the domain for many years and was referred as the "uncle" of Rohi Rani.[5] From 1688, there is also mention of a Luji Talo, presumably Talo's son, who appears in the documents as "the main regent of Dimu". The later pedigrees suggest that he was the grandson of Ama Talo referred to in the 1648 contract and a member of the fettor lineage which was only distantly related to the raja line.

From Savu it is easy to reach Sumba, so it is by no means surprising that there were early contacts between the two islands. An incident in 1692 clearly indicates that the neighbouring peoples recognised Dimu's position of supremacy. Sumba was even more politically fragmented than Savu, Rote and Timor as it was divided into a large number of small communities, with their *maramba* (chiefs) sometimes known by the Dutch as rajas. Political weakness made Sumba vulnerable to seaborne neighbours who held pretensions towards it. Since at least 1662, the Sumbawan sultanate of Bima had laid claim to the island and the sultan also demanded suzerainty over Manggarai in western Flores (De Roo van Alderwerelt 1906: 189). Both these territories were known as potential sources of slaves as the people were neither Muslim nor Christian and thus prey to slavers.[6] Sumba also had some sandalwood, though difficult to reach, as is

---

[3] VOC 1497 (1691), f. 714–6. See chapter 4 for example – seeds from a plant called *nida* (*Anamirta cocculus* or levant berry) were known to treat epilepsy.

[4] VOC 1637 (1700).

[5] Another of Rohi Rani's uncles, mentioned in the VOC records between 1682 and 1693, was "Ammachezy". He is possibly Ama Hij'i of the genealogies, which present him as the grand-uncle of Rohi Rani and Talo Uju's brother.

[6] Coolhaas 1971: 2, dated 31 January 1675.

Figure 31: Natadu clan

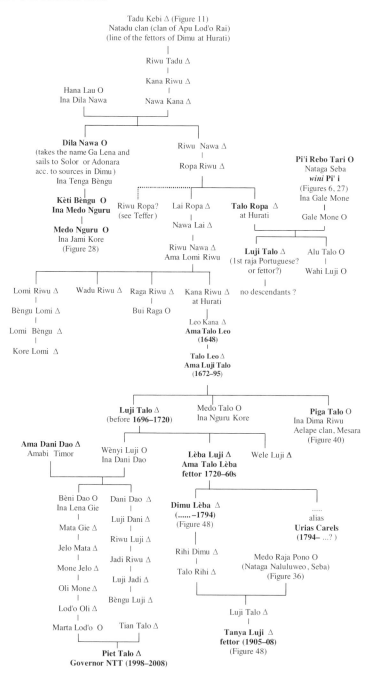

Figure 32: Nadowu clan

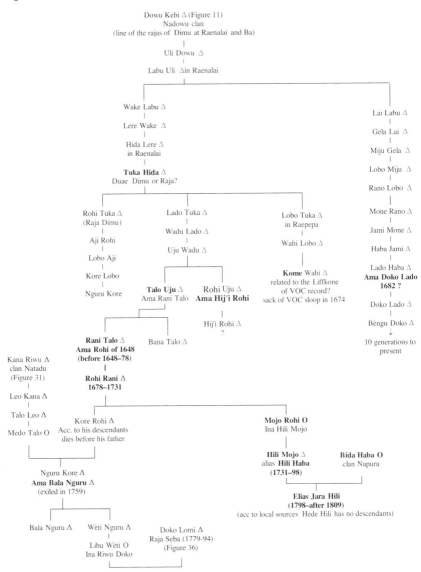

indicated by its alternative name *Sandelbosch*. There were other contenders for Sumba's resources: the Muslim people from the Ende region on the south coast of Flores—a mixture of locals and Makassarese—went there and at least one Endenese raja was killed on the island.[7]

Melolo, one of the small domains of Sumba, approached Dimu in December 1692. After a brief Dutch visit the previous year, the local raja Sama Taka decided to use the VOC as a buffer against the incessant and increasing raids from the Makassarese, Bimanese, Malays and Endenese. He sent his co-regent Leko on a ship to Savu where the grandees of Dimu strongly encouraged him to seek the company's protection. However, the story did not end well. On his way back to Melolo, Leko landed in Raijua where the inhabitants murdered him and his crew.[8] Tying Sumba to Dutch interests was a long slow affair that only became viable in the late 19th century. Savunese connections with the island were to play a great role in this process.

Internally, Dimu's precedence did not provide it with any real power over the other domains. The succession of local conflicts in the late 17th and parts of the 18th centuries clearly shows its lack of influence. Alliances shifted and the enemies of yesterday could very well turn into brothers-in-arms. Thus in 1692, Rohi Rani gathered 100 men and proceeded to join the old enemies in Seba to fight Mesara. As his so-called "uncles" Talo and Luji warned him against it, he eventually backed out. Dimu did not have a good reputation with either the Savunese or the Dutch. There were accusations of cattle rustling against Dimu from all around the island which involved the sale of stolen cattle to the likewise troublesome Raijua. In Raijua, Makassarese people without VOC passes bought the animals, to the obvious detriment of the economic monopoly and regulated trade that the Kupang post tried to maintain.[9]

Nor was the internal political structure of Dimu entirely stable. The raja and his fettor's authority in the Savunese domain was quite limited, an aspect that the Dutch may have had difficulties grasping. Offensive conduct by rulers or persons close to them could result in serious rupture, and there were even outright wars fought between raja and fettor. In December 1707, Rohi Rani unexpectedly arrived in Kupang on a Helong boat with his colleague Wadu Lai of Seba. The two rulers had been unceremoniously expelled from their domains by their respective fettors Luji Talo and Weo. They wanted the VOC to arrange for Timorese auxiliaries to restore them to power. Considering the well-

---

[7] VOC 1335, 1677–78, dagh-register, dated 8 August 1677.

[8] VOC 1531, 1692–93, dagh-register, dated 17 December 1692.

[9] Coolhaas 1975: 525–7, dated 11 December 1692.

known pursuits of Timorese troops in foreign lands—headhunting, slaving and plundering—the request indicates the rajas' desperation. The *opperhoofd* deemed such an expedition unrealistic as there were no means to transport a large number of troops and the war-torn land would not be able to support the auxiliaries.[10] However, he sent a man from Ndao, close to Rote, to the fettors who promised to await company mediation. The *opperhoofd* made his regular tour around the Dutch-aligned areas in June 1708 and intensive deliberations quickly resulted in a general declaration of peace. Rohi Rani and Luji Talo declared that they were close kin, took each other's hand and embraced. This was followed by *pemali* (taboo) acts. The rajas and fettors met between the village of Rohi Rani and Luji Talo, observed by the *opperhoofd*, and accompanied by their 'soothsayers' and armed retainers. The rituals of peace were duly performed, followed by great shouting from the bystanders. Shortly after, Luji Talo went to Rohi Rani's residence, bringing *sirih* (betel leaves [In]), *pinang* (areca nuts [In]) and tobacco. The raja in turn visited his fettor.[11]

The year 1716 and the year after were deeply troubling for Luji Talo. The fettor had a much-trusted slave who watched over his personal security. Some people thought that the slave was in fact a sorcerer who had bewitched the wife of a common "coolie" (a derogatory term used by the VOC writer). Belief in *suangi* (witches, sorcerers [In]) was widespread across the eastern islands and colonial sources give many examples of *suangi* in Timor being killed on the orders of rulers. In Savu the same perception applied: the sorcerer must be executed according to the "law of the land", the prescriptions of adat. A number of Dimunese gathered and demanded that Luji Talo hand over the slave, which he flatly refused to do. An armed and enraged crowd threatened the fettor, forcing an agreement with the customary bestowal of cloth. However, Luji Talo immediately broke the pact, repulsed the onslaught and withdrew to a stone fortress, presumably Hurati, where he gathered provisions. The Dutch *opperhoofd*, hearing about the trouble, hastened to Savu where he managed to reconcile the parties. The solution was pragmatic: the so-called 'sorcerer' was handed over to the *opperhoofd* as a gift and taken back to Kupang where he laboured in chains for VOC public works.[12]

In 1719, there was further conflict between the raja and various lesser chiefs.[13] Here the VOC once again performed its role as 'stranger-king' and settled the

---

[10] VOC 1759 (1708), f. 11–2.

[11] VOC 1759 (1708), dagh-register, dated 28 June–2 July 1708.

[12] Coolhaas 1979: 231–3, dated 30 November 1716; Coolhaas 1979: 265–6, dated 15 January 1717.

[13] Coolhaas 1979: 420–1, dated 30 November 1719.

matter, but the solution was only temporary. In 1724 the violence flared up again, and Seba, Liae and Mesara were quick to interfere.[14] Matters came to a head in early 1731, in circumstances detailed in VOC documents as well as oral tradition. The old and infirm Rohi Rani believed he was unable to carry on as raja. He therefore planned to transfer his position to Hili Haba (Sili Saba), his daughter's son, who was born around 1701–03.[15] He was about 75 years old in 1778, according to the French engineer Jean-Baptiste Pelon, who worked for the company in Kupang (2002: 63), but in 1782 *opperhoofd* Willem Adriaan van Este said he was 81 years old.[16] The choice of heir is understandable because the paternal line was broken; the paternal blood is normally passed on through the sons while the maternal blood is carried by the daughters. This, however, was disputed by a chief called Ama Ratti, son of Rohi Rani's brother, who regarded himself as the more obvious successor.[17] Together with Leba, another chief, he rose against the enfeebled raja while Hili Haba acquired a boat and hastened to Kupang to plead for his cause.[18] Leba is presumably the fettor Leba Luji whose brother-in-law Ama Dani Dao was briefly the regent after 1678, during Ama Rohi's minority. Hili Haba, however, was successful in gaining company support. The *opperhoofd* Gerardus Visscher undertook a trip to Savu in June in the same year to negotiate a peaceful solution.

Visscher arrived in Dimu on 8 June 1731 with the regents of Seba, Liae and Mesara and witnessed a ceremony that confirm the peace. When everything was ready in the morning a puppy and a piglet were brought to a spot outside Rohi Rani's village. Ama Ratti stepped forward from the rival party. He first cut a hair from the puppy, put it in water and sprinkled the former enemies. Subsequently, he cut the puppy's throat. Rohi Rani's followers then opened a young coconut with a knife. They cut off one of the dog's ears and placed it in the coconut. Both parties received sprinkles of coconut water. After that they cut off the tails of the puppy and the piglet. Those standing around began shouting loudly, which was their way to wish for successful peace. The Dimu

---

[14] VOC 2012 (1724).

[15] There is only one other example of the raja or fettor title being inherited through the female line; this is Kore Loni in Liae (r. 1757–64). The name Hili Haba (Sili Saba) is reminiscent of a Sili Saba (or Ama Sili) who was a prince in Ade (Vemasse) in East Timor, who fled before the Portuguese onslaught in 1669 and carved out a new mini-princedom in Iliwaki in Wetar (Hägerdal 2012: 171–3).

[16] VOC 8305 (1782).

[17] VOC 2073 (1727) makes it clear that Ama Ratti (or Ama Ratto) was the nephew and heir of the decrepit Rohi Rani.

[18] VOC 2192 (1730–31), dagh-register, dated 11 March 1731.

elite thanked the *opperhoofd* in a sincere and polite way as he had concluded the matter so speedily.[19]

It is possible that Visscher exaggerated his own role, but it fits the position of mediating neutral outsiders that the whites were expected to play. Ethnographic data classify the dog as male and the pig female. The presence of these two animals reflected the necessary ritualistic complementarity to ensure harmony. It is possible that the people had borrowed parts of the ceremony from Timor where very similar customs existed, described as early as the 17th century (Hägerdal 2012: 213). Timorese culture was likewise imprinted with a symbolic male-female complementarity. It is another example of the inter-island exchange of ideas that only surfaces here and there in the written sources.

Later tradition remembered the transition of 1731. The raja family of Dimu told a story which mentions a certain Kore Rohi, son of Rohi Rani, who was also raja.[20] While Kore Rohi was in charge, the Dutch arrived in Savu. They took his nephew Hili Haba to raise and educate in Batavia. When he later returned to Dimu, Raja Kore Rohi asked Hili Haba what food the Dutch preferred to eat in case they were later to visit Savu. Hili cunningly replied that the Dutch had a culinary preference for dog, served without its head and legs. When the Dutch representatives arrived in Dimu, the unsuspecting raja ordered those preparing the meal to put the dog's head and legs in a separate basket, and to cook and serve them the body. When the Dutch returned from Dimu, Hili Haba asked what they had eaten. They replied that they had no idea. Then Hili Haba disclosed that the raja had served them dog meat. The Dutch, infuriated at their host's perceived lack of civility, quickly turned the kingship over to Hili Haba. He had outwitted his uncle Kore Rohi who was forced to step down.[21]

Ama Ratti is possibly the same person as the otherwise unknown Kore Rohi, although he never actually ruled in his own name. The story obviously reflects the mostly good and constructive relationship between Hili Haba and the Dutch administration in Kupang, who indeed elevated him to raja in 1731. However, VOC documents have not so far confirmed his visit to Batavia and the dog trick is in fact a tale associated with at least one other Savunese domain, namely Mesara. While building on certain basic elements of actual historical names and events fixed in local memory, the setting is dramatised by the addition of a trickster tale. James Fox writes that such trickster tales are also in Rotenese tradition and are in the same way attached to historical successions of power (Fox 2011).

---

[19] Ibid., dated 8 June 1731.

[20] The name repeats in the Savunese aristocratic pedigrees. Thus Kore Rohi was the first raja of Seba under the Portuguese and there was Raja Kore Rohi of Liae in 1751–57.

[21] Interview with Godlief Talo, Bodae (28.06.2012).

Hili Haba married Bida Haba of the Napuru clan. She was the great-granddaughter of one of the founders of Kujiratu, where she grew up. The following verse preserves the circumstances of their marriage:

Banana leaves formed a canopy
Above the path taken by
Bida Haba Jami
As she left Kujiratu,
A lontar grove in Jiwuwu
Was given to her brother.[22]

The wedding procession went from Kujiratu to the nearby raja settlement in Ba. In Savu, the bride's mother's brother (her uncle) is entitled to a large share of the bridewealth; however, if he no longer lives the bride's brother receives his uncle's share, in this case a lontar grove.

Hili Haba had a long though not particularly harmonious political career. Of interest is that his reign lasted longer than that of any other known regional ruler. Indonesian history abounds with allegedly lengthy reigns, including the 104-year tenure of the Pajajaran king Prebu Niskala Wastu Kencana (Atja 1981) and, strangely enough, accepted as fact by some Indonesian historians. However, these reigns are, without exception, poorly chronicled and often depend on modern speculation, such as the alleged 90-year reign of Dalem Baturenggong in Bali from 1460 to 1550 and the 80 years attributed to Panembahan Ratu of Cirebon, circa 1570 to 1650. The other competitor for the title would be I Kumala of Gowa in Sulawesi (who was said to be king from 1826 to 1893), but he did not actually reign until 1844 (Taniputera 2013: 970).

Only when his son asked for investiture in 1798 did Kupang learn of Hili Haba's death. His 67 years are at least fragmentarily documented in the VOC records and show him as an active leader in politics as well as in the few economic opportunities offered by the VOC system. The French engineer Jean-Baptiste Pelon wrote in 1778 that the ruler of Dimu, "being the principal of the island has many privileges when he visits his neighbours. The one who presently reigns is a brave man aged about 75 years. He has governed for 50 years with much fidelity. His name is Sialia [Sielie, that is, Hili]" Pelon (2002: 63). The *opperhoofd* Willem Adriaan van Este, an unheroic but canny administrator who knew the Timor Islands from decades of experience, likewise wrote about the raja in respectful terms. In 1782, the company felt that its position in Timor was threatened by the Amanuban prince Tobani, and asked for Rotenese and Savunese auxiliaries

---

[22] Interview with Ama Tada Talo, Napuru clan (2008; 2010).

Figure 33: Napuru clan in Kujiratu

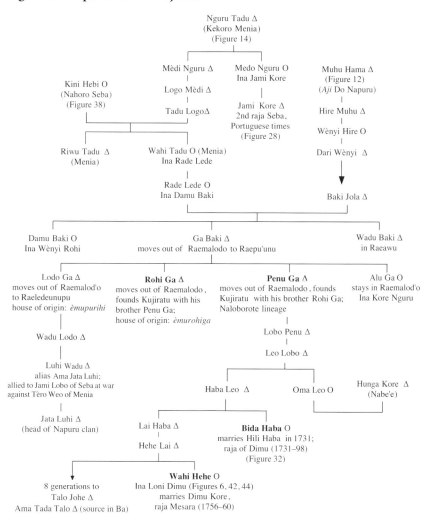

to come to Kupang where they would be provided for by the Timorese regents. The rajas promised to dispatch six *perahu*s (sailing boats [In]) with troops; only one actually appeared but with Hili Haba on board:

> The aforementioned Savunese main regent Hili Haba, a man of 81 years who has been regent since 1728 [recte: 1731] and is still as strong and healthy and has always remained a loyal ally to the Noble Company, had the bad luck to be afflicted by a serious illness shortly after his arrival here. He was therefore afraid to pass away when still that young. He speedily returned to his land again, after promising the *opperhoofd* that if he came back alive, he would take care that the requested Savunese warriors were kept ready.[23]

Hili Haba visited Kupang repeatedly, sailing in his own *perahu*, and took an interest in the slave trade. In 1741, his unnamed brother appeared before the *opperhoofd* and asked that the Savunese be excused from paying duties on the export of slaves to Kupang.[24] However, the Dutch authorities would hear nothing of this as their Timorese allies had already made and been refused the same request.[25] It is possible that the company, notwithstanding its cynicism in such matters, wanted to prevent abuses; if the allied king began to declare subjects as slaves in order to sell them to the Dutch, it might have negative consequences for the fragile system.

Whether he had actually been educated by Dutch tutors in Batavia or not, Hili Haba must have understood the importance of keeping good relations with the company in order to enhance his own position. Other rajas in Savu seldom visited Dutch strongholds during the 18th century and were thus at a disadvantage. Opponents to his governance in Dimu could conveniently be castigated as anti-VOC. In 1746, Hili Haba reported that one of his *temukung*s[26] (genealogical chiefs of villages or settlements) called Ama Bala Nguru stole cattle and other items on the island. Incidents such as this were commonplace, but the raja added that the *temukung* also burnt a *perahu* belonging to the raja which was loaded with slaves for the company. Ama Bala had the temerity to

---

[23] VOC 3505 (1782).

[24] In 1765, VOC archives mention a Zacharias Talo, son of Hili Haba's brother, perhaps a son of the unnamed brother (VOC 3135 [1765], report, 20 June 1765). A certain Maru, junior raja of Dimu, is mentioned in 1760. He commanded Savunese auxiliaries on a VOC expedition to Noimuti (Timor Tengah Utara Regency) in the Timorese highlands, but he withdrew his troops: the enraged *opperhoofd* Hans Albrecht von Plüskow temporarily imprisoned him with Lomi Jara from Seba (s'Jacob 2007: 521).

[25] VOC 8334 (1740–41), dagh-register, dated 20 March 1741.

[26] The term comes from the Malay and Javanese title *tumenggung*, used in the Timor area since the 17th century.

appropriate the slaves and sell them for his own profit. Hili Haba thus required company assistance to pacify his realm.[27] The request probably went unheeded; the *opperhoofd* Meulenbeek was killed shortly afterwards in an incident in Rote and the situation in Dutch Timor descended into a state of confusion.

What happened during the next decade is not well known, but Hili Haba was unable to eliminate Ama Bala Nguru.[28] In 1758, he complained bitterly that Ama Bala sought to deprive him of his domain as well as his life. The indefatigable rebel attracted a lot of people to his cause and built a fortification (see Photo 10 below), creating much mischief in Dimu.[29] What was more worrying was that Mesara interfered in the troubles. The new *opperhoofd* Hans Albrecht von Plüskow was an active and restless German who strove to bring truly VOC-led governance to the Timor Islands. He supported Hili Haba by organising an expedition that managed to subdue both Mesara and the Ama Bala faction in 1759.[30] The profit-driven company did not commit to anything for free: in order to cover the costs of the expedition, the VOC declared 50 rebels as company slaves. The company immediately transported the rebel-slaves to the Banda Islands to work on the Dutch nutmeg plantations, where they probably had short and miserable lives. The VOC also took Ama Bala prisoner, transported him to Batavia and put him at the disposition of the authorities there.[31]

An official Dutch investigation from 1765 discloses a shabby side of the long-lived ruler, who seemed to have had few scruples about reducing tribesmen to slavery. He condemned one of his temukungs to exile in Banda in 1760 for bad behaviour, alluding to Ama Bala. Hili Haba granted Von Plüskow control over Ama Bala's wife and seven children, although they were legally still free people. They were with the *opperhoofd* at the time of his murder by the Black Portuguese (or Larantuqueiros) during an abortive mission to Oecusse in 1761 (Hägerdal 2012: 390). Under Von Plüskow's exceedingly corrupt successor, Ter

---

[27] VOC 8339 (1746), f. 12.

[28] In a letter to the VOC in 1752, Hili Haba mentions that two of his temukungs were constantly at each other's throats in spite of VOC mediation. One of these may have been Ama Bala Nguru (VOC 8345 [1752], f. 73–4).

[29] VOC 8352 (1758), missive, 5 October 1758, f. 59. For the ruins of the fortification located near the river Liu estuary see Photo 10 below, p. 188.

[30] Details of the expedition are vague; there is no suggestion that VOC soldiers fought in Savu, so it may have been that Savunese forces gathered under VOC leadership to defeat Mesara and Ama Bala Nguru.

[31] VOC 8353 (1759), missive, 5 October 1759, f. 18–9. Von Plüskow evidently kept a number of Savunese as slaves. After his sudden demise, an inventory of part of his estate listed 24 persons of Savunese origins or ancestry (VOC 3251 [1769], f. 522–4).

Herbruggen, the woman and her children then became slaves, with Hili Haba's full knowledge. The raja was content to have his enemy's family out of the way. Ter Herbruggen praised Hili Haba as the most valiant of allies, but according to the investigation, the raja was known all over Timor, Rote and Savu as a notorious cheat (*loerendraijer*).[32] It appears that the investigation resulted in the family eventually being released from slavery.

Photo 10. Ruins of Ama Bala Nguru's stronghold by the *Liu* river estuary; Sabu Tengah (2015)

Local tradition remembers Ama Bala Nguru but in a different light. In the social memory of a Nadowu lineage,[33] Rohi Rani had not only a daughter, Mojo Rohi, but also a son, Kore Rohi, who apparently Hili Baba outwitted. Kore Rohi had a son called Nguru Kore, known as Ama Bala Nguru, who could stake a claim to Rohi Rani's succession in the 1730s but never actually took the throne. VOC documents detail the struggle for power and record some genealogical details; this can be compared with the various locally recorded traditions, which show a lack of consensus on the Nadowu genealogies. The line of Nadowu rajas obviously tried to rearrange its genealogies; however, not everyone adhered to the manipulation.

At some stage, Ama Bala briefly managed to supplant Hili Haba and apparently possessed one or more Portuguese cannons and rifles.[34] He hid these weapons in a cave, since known as Lie Ama Bala, suggesting that Ama Bala was

---

[32] VOC 3135 (1765), report, 20 June 1765.

[33] Interview with Godlief Talo (28–29.06.2012).

[34] Interview with Marthen Heke Medo (22.05.2014).

seeking Portuguese help to overthrow Hili Haba.[35] The company declared this was '*sangat jahat*' (extremely wicked [In]) and therefore Ama Bala was first exiled to Madagascar. Oral tradition has kept a chant performed during ceremonial dances (*pedoa*) about the exile of Ama Bala:[36]

> As the time has arrived for us people
> To recite the genealogies of the four traditional domains of Savu.[37]
> Do not hesitate any longer, do not think twice anymore
> Do not let your thoughts vacillate; follow what God has made for us.
> Endure the recitation of the verses since the origin of our ancestors
> Of our large and united family.[38]

> A big crowd follows from behind Nguru Kore Rohi.
> Many people with the same mark [for their cattle] have come together.[39]
> They walk towards the sandy beach, towards the harbour Matiki.[40]
> As the time has arrived they cannot stop tears flowing from their eyes;
> Tears are trickling from the eye lashes of his female relatives.
> They all wipe their eyes, sincere and virtuous women of Dimu.

> Because he wants to go abroad to search for a living
> Looking for ivory adornments until he gets them
> To give to Bala Raja Manu, strengthening him,[41]
> Holding power over Savu and over the sea.[42]

---

[35] In the early 20th century, one cannon was moved to the Skaber military-administrative installation after it was built; when the Skaber site closed in 1965, the cannon left for a private house near Seba's airstrip.

[36] The translation is based on two sources: interviews with Ama Ju Rihi of Seba (2010) and Mojo Lihu of Mesara, a singer at *pedoa* dances (12.05.2014). They do not remember further details about Ama Bala's wrongdoings.

[37] This is seen from today's point of view; in the mid-18th century there were five domains in Savu as Menia still existed. As an independent domain, Menia disappeared in the late 19th century.

[38] The Savunese people are described as a big family.

[39] *Rote* refers to a mark for identifying the cattle of each clan. Those who come together have the same mark for their cattle, that is, they are from the same clan.

[40] Near Banyo in Dimu.

[41] His son.

[42] The text says 'who holds power' which is not possible; the popular song takes dreams for reality. The deportation is disguised as a trip abroad to seek his fortune.

Then he has to leave in a hurry.
Cut the anchor in the shape of a nail
Deeply trapped in the ground, like a spur stuck in the flesh of a rooster.
The crew returns turning the sail,
The crew of the foreign boat which has been in the harbour for a long time.

He wants to receive a large woven belt to roll tightly around his waist,
Ready to accept with tears in his eyes a large foreign patola cloth from Ina
Migi Jami Kore.[43]
The obscure written words reach Ama Bengu Bela Raja Ratu Dima[44]
As decided by the mighty General, the powerful man of the Centre.[45]

A story meant to be suppressed has left traces in the social memory of a supplanted group and in a ceremonial chant; these are two mechanisms of counter-memory for transmitting oral knowledge. Collective memory recalls just a name, Ama Bala, loosely placed in the genealogies. And yet, the chant has kept only traces of Ama Bala's life; there is no reason given for his exile and his departure, described so vividly, is recounted as a fortune-seeking voyage. The line "he has to leave in a hurry" alludes to the fact that he had been arrested, though only an informed audience would know that. It is unlikely that the singer, Mojo Lihu, understood the verse in that way. However, the weeping relatives and the "obscure written words" refer to the punishment meted out by VOC officials. The majority of people were unable to read or understand the language used if it was spoken. The "obscure written words" and "mighty general" show people's powerless against the "powerful man of the Centre" and contribute to portraying Ama Bala Nguru as a sympathetic figure and cultural hero, with little concern for the actual truth.

Ama Bala returned from exile bringing knowledge of a new technique for assembling beams. Called *tuki* in Savunese, it is the method of making a hole in one beam and shaping the end of another so that it fits into the first one. Until that time, people joined beams by tying them together with ropes made of lontar palm leaves. Later, he was exiled for a second time to Ceylon. Hili Haba suspected the raja of Seba, Ama Doko Lomi, of supporting Ama Bala. However, the suspect cleared his name during a meeting attended by all the Savu rajas and received a piece of land in Dimu called Èimadake to compensate for the affront.

---

[43] It is not clear who she is; she cannot be his mother, but she could be his sister or his mother's sister.

[44] Ama Bala also has a son called Bèngu, thus he too can be called Ama Bèngu.

[45] The 'General' is called *Mone Pana*, building a parallel between the power of the VOC and that of a Jingi Tiu priest.

In the 20th century, the Nadowu clan bought back the land, which is now part of the Central Savu subdistrict, and there is a village called Èimadake after the historical area.[46]

Once again Ama Bala was able to return. This time he brought a technique for drawing water from a well. It consists of a forked pole anchored in the ground next to the well with a lever (*wuki*) positioned horizontally between the two arms—the fulcrum; the lever has a stone attached to one end, and a rope and a bucket to the other; lifting the stone allows the bucket to descend into the well and fill with water; lowering the stone raises the bucket. He is also remembered for having introduced a type of mudfish able to survive at the bottom of dried-out ponds during the dry season. While Ceylon was a common destination for exiles from the Dutch East Indies, Madagascar is a very unlikely place as it had not yet been colonised by a European power. The Ama Bala character is interesting as a rogue who is also a cultural hero and it is unfortunate there are not more details about him in Dutch sources.

Savu and the VOC system

It is necessary to have a closer look at the political context of 18th-century Savu. After concluding a peace agreement with Portugal in 1661, only made public two years later, the VOC dependencies in the region were limited to five minor kingdoms in the hinterland of Kupang, Rote, Savu, two domains in eastern Solor and three in Adonara. By extension, certain areas in Lembata, Pantar and Alor, and Ende and Tanjung Bunga in Flores were loosely bound to the VOC sphere, although this had limited impacts at best. As noted earlier, there were various claims to Sumba. The number of company officials in Kupang was small and the other islands had only one or two representatives at the most. Being a commercial company at the core, the VOC did not provide any education for its European staff but rather let the employees serve their way up to more responsible positions. This made for great fluctuations in the competence of those assigned to Timor. The islands of the east were not attractive to most Europeans and the high mortality from malaria or 'Timorese fever' was no doubt an additional deterrent.

Under these circumstances, the community in and around Kupang became more 'local' than Dutch. Early European trading posts in eastern waters were always characterised by a relative dearth of white men and a marked absence of white women. The sources often mention Savunese and Rotenese slaves, and Dutch burghers and company officials regularly formed relationships with

---

[46] Interview with Ama Bèhi Meno (09.05.2014).

women of non-free or dependent status. The Kupang baptismal book has been preserved for the years from 1669 to 1732, and names the fathers and mothers of baptised children. The data show that the Dutchmen preferred to marry Rotenese women who constitute nearly half of the listed mothers. Liaisons with Savunese women were much less frequent; 9 mothers out of the 119 with a stated origin came from Savu.[47] An interesting case of familial relations at a high social level was Dangka Lai (Daga Lai), an under-regent in Dimu who wielded significant political influence in the early 18th century. He was the son of a Savunese father and a Rotenese mother, Martha from Thie. She married the Dutchman Frans Brockaerd who thus became his stepfather. Dangka Lai was baptised in Kupang in 1720 under the name Cornelis at the age of 31.[48] Marriages between Dutch and indigenous aristocrats in the Timor area were not uncommon, although the authorities sometimes tried to prevent it. The early VOC period was a modest beginning for Savunese Christianity (or maybe a new start considering the early Portuguese efforts). The first recorded convert was Sabina from Dimu—presumably a servant or a slave—who was baptised in April 1675. She was followed by a further dozen converts, mostly in the years between 1716 and 1724.[49] How many of these people lived permanently in Kupang is unclear. The numbers are not staggering, but then religious propagation was not a priority for the VOC.

The state of near-siege that afflicted Kupang for long periods added to its unattractive image. The ethnic mix of Portuguese, Lamaholot, Timorese, Dutch deserters and Larantuqueiros was an important factor in Timor during the 17th and 18th centuries. Although outwardly adhering to the Portuguese king and guarding a strong Catholic identity, the Larantuqueiros formed a vigorous polity of their own and dominated most of Timor, with the exception of the lands by the Kupang Bay. Their extensive political and economic network, stretching from Sikka in Flores to the eastern tip of Timor, flourished in the late 17th century thanks to the indiscriminate felling of sandalwood that was loaded onto Portuguese, Chinese, Siamese and Dutch ships, and transported to other parts of Asia. Although they were seldom open enemies of the VOC, the Larantuqueiros allowed their Timorese affiliates to intimidate the five VOC allies in the Kupang hinterland. It was a drawn out and quite bloody affair. The depletion of the available sandalwood and the arrival of a white Portuguese governor in Lifau in 1702 temporarily weakened their position and led to periodic hostilities between

---

[47] *Doopboek* Timor, 1669–1732, ANRI, Jakarta. Transcript kindly provided by Diederik Kortlang, NA, The Hague.

[48] *Doopboek* Timor, 1669–1732, ANRI, Jakarta, dated 26 May 1720.

[49] *Doopboek* Timor, 1669–1732, ANRI, Jakarta.

the two Portuguese factions (neither of which was predominantly 'white' from a literally racial point of view) which went on until 1785 (Hägerdal 2012: 316–20).

While the VOC had been politically dominant in maritime Southeast Asia since the period of the 1660s to 1680s, its main *raison d'être* was profit. With the sandalwood almost inaccessible, there was only sporadic interest in developing the economy in the Timor area. A limited supply of beeswax and slaves was insufficient incentive to invest resources, and the Kupang post was kept mostly for strategic reasons. The Savunese princes provided irregular gifts to Batavia; for example, deliveries of beeswax and green gram (mung bean), but these were not economically significant. In 1764, for example, Dimu delivered six piculs of beeswax while the other four domains each contributed two piculs.[50] A decade earlier Hili Haba of Dimu bestowed one picul of beeswax on the company, demanding one patola cloth, a bundle of paper and 300 pens in return. Apart from the fact that beeswax was rare in Savu in the 19th century (and Dimu may have bought it from the Timorese to give to Batavia), the choice of exchange goods is interesting as Savu was otherwise not a literate society; perhaps the correspondence with Kupang engendered a small production of documents.[51]

A series of events in the mid-18th century suddenly opened up new perspectives and the Savunese had their role in the story. The aforementioned death of *opperhoofd* Meulenbeek in Termanu, Rote in 1746 triggered an unsettled state of affairs on the island where the Larantuqueiros intervened unsuccessfully. A letter from the rajas of Savu, dictated in May 1747, reflects the situation:

> With these few words, we five kings of the *negeri* Savu communicate to the Governor-General and the Noble Councillors of the Netherlands and India, that on 12 October 1746 the *opperhoofd* Jan Anthony Meulenbeek and his wife and several people, both Company servants and burghers, went to the island Rote and Termanu to pay a visit after the example of his predecessors. We five kings of Savu do not know the truth of how things happened there. However, we understand that the people of aforementioned Termanu killed the *opperhoofd*, his wife and the aforementioned people, and took possession of all that these people had brought along, such as drums, muskets and artillery. All these matters Your Excellencies are the better to investigate and consider … Whether we die or live, we shall remain attached to the Noble Company.

---

[50] One picul is about 61 kilograms. The weight measurement was formerly used in Southeast Asia and comes from the Javanese word *pikul*, referring to the load a man can carry across his shoulders.

[51] VOC 8358 [1764], f. 66; VOC 8345 [1752], f. 75. Noimuti and Maucatar in the Timorese highlands yielded a substantial number of old written records where the climate had not ruined the paper (Tefa Sa'u 2013: 107–26; Hägerdal 2012: 346). It is therefore clear that local groups who came into contact with Europeans sometimes kept written texts.

We are also, on one hand, troubled as we do not know if the hearts of the kings of Rote are with the Noble Company. On the other hand, we have heard that the kings of Rote and Termanu want to leave the Noble Company and take refuge with the Portuguese and acknowledge them as their father and mother. To that end we five kings of Savu apply to the merciful judgement of the Noble Company, that they send some men hither in order to offer a helping hand. Meanwhile, we long for them with sorrowful hearts. With this we wish with pure hearts that the almighty God bestow all sorts of blessings on Their Excellencies, in this world as in eternity; and we remain with deep reverence and all submissiveness, the servants Hili Haba, Jara Wadu, Jami Tero, Mone Bengu ... Written in the *negeri* Savu, 27 May 1747.[52]

The letter, written in the polite and submissive style that was a standard discourse in correspondence with the VOC, indicates that the Savunese elite was well aware of events in the region and was keen to assert that they had nothing to do with the Rotenese rebellion. The rajas seem to fear that the violence might spill over to Savu and asked the VOC to dispatch a symbolic force—the mere presence of a few Europeans could have a deterrent effect. However, the tide soon turned against the pro-Portuguese domains in Rote, defeated by a VOC expedition in early 1749 (Hägerdal 2012: 360). Even before that, three important Atoni domains of West Timor, namely Amfo'an, Amanuban and Greater Sonba'i, revolted against Larantuqueiros domination and approached the VOC in Kupang in 1748.[53] By then it seemed obvious that their leader Gaspar da Costa acted without regard for the royal Portuguese authorities and Batavia encouraged the post in Kupang to weaken his position.

The result was the renowned Larantuqueiros expedition against the Dutch stronghold in November 1749. When the enemy was drawing close to the *opperhoofd*, his council decided to dispatch a small army to meet them. It consisted of 24 European soldiers, 130 Mardijkers,[54] 250 Savunese, 60 Solorese, 30 Rotenese and a few volunteers from the local burgher community.[55] Thus, the Savunese contingent constituted about half the force and it appears from the report that there were Savunese regents present in Kupang at the time. When they marched out of Kupang they were followed at some distance by

---

[52] VOC 8340 (1747), f. 9–10. Hili Haba of Dimu, Jara Wadu of Seba, Jami Tèro of Menia and Mone Bèngu of Liae.

[53] VOC 8342 (1749), f. 28–33; Schooneveld-Oosterling 1997: 652, 779.

[54] *Mardijker* (meaning 'freeman' in Dutch) people were, in a Timorese context, mainly Christians of indigenous origins who were under Dutch jurisdiction. In other parts of maritime Asia they were often descendants of freed slaves from former Portuguese-held areas.

[55] VOC 8343 (1750), f. 115–7.

the hesitant Timorese allies who were not used to pitched battles. The force approached the fortifications of the Portuguese and their Timorese affiliates at Penfui, close to the present El Tari Airport, and a remarkable event followed. The enemy was reportedly 20,000 strong, but their motivation to fight in an extended campaign of this kind was not great—some Timorese groups fled at the very beginning of the battle. The battle soon turned into a rout where the defending forces entirely defeated the Portuguese side which suffered enormous losses (the Timorese VOC allies took 1,200 heads and VOC troops killed a substantial number).[56] The cataclysmic encounter was the decisive step towards a rough division of Timor between the Dutch and the Portuguese with political implications to this day.

While the Savunese had a mixed to poor reputation with VOC administrators in the early Dutch period, the battle of Penfui changed everything. The fighting qualities of the Savunese won Dutch admiration whose skins they had largely saved through their prominent role in the battle. The *opperhoofden* lauded the islanders as brave as well as faithful, thus resulting in the Dutch attempts to draw auxiliaries from Dimu to serve in Kupang in the following years.[57] The *opperhoofd* Daniel van der Burgh deemed that the Timorese allies were not able to carry out military campaigning without support and that Savunese assistance was important to expel the Portuguese from western Timor. Unfortunately, the domains of Savu were no more cohesive than they were before: Hili Haba still had to deal with internal conflicts in Dimu and few troops were forthcoming at first.[58] Nevertheless, their presence in VOC affairs increased from this time. In 1751, a few rajas from Savu were present when Daniel van der Burgh landed in Sumba and obtained the formal submission from some of the many chiefs of the island.[59] In the same year, about 1,000 auxiliaries from Rote and Savu arrived in Kupang, and participated in an abortive campaign against the anti-Dutch highland stronghold of Noimuti (in today's regency of Timor Tengah Utara).[60] An impediment to using Savunese warriors was the lack of boats on the island to transport troops and horses, "since these islanders are the hussars of the Noble Company and never want to serve in the war on foot".[61] The Dutch observer drew a parallel here with hussars of Europe, light cavalry that was used for raiding

---

[56] Haga 1882: 391–402; VOC 8343 (1750), f. 132–5.

[57] VOC 2892 (1756), f. 1362–3.

[58] VOC 8343 (1750), f. 76–7.

[59] VOC 8322 (1751), f. 9–11.

[60] VOC 8322 (1751), f. 17–9.

[61] VOC 8347 (1754), f. 43.

and skirmishes. When the British expedition of James Cook visited Savu in 1770 they heard about the martial prowess of the islanders:

> We were informed by Mr. Lange [the European interpreter and representative on Savu], that the chiefs who had successively presided over the five principalities of this island, had lived for time immemorial in the strictest alliance and most cordial friendship with each other; yet he said that the people were of a warlike disposition, and had always courageously defended themselves against foreign invaders. We were told also, that the island was able to raise, upon very short notice, 7300 fighting men, armed with muskets, spears, lances, and targets. Of this force, Laai [Liae] was said to furnish 2600, Seba 2000, Regeeua [Raijua] 1500, Timo [Dimu] 800, and Massãrã [Mesara] 400. Besides the arms that have already been mentioned, each man is furnished with a large pole-ax, resembling a wood-bill, except that it had a strait edge, and is much heavier: this, in the hands of people who have the courage to come to close quarters with an enemy, must be a dreadful weapon; and we were told that they were so dexterous with their lances, that at the distance of sixty feet they would throw them with such exactness as to pierce a man's heart, and such force as to go quite through his body.[62]

To assert there was a close friendship between the rajas of Savu may be an exaggeration, but the time of internal war had indeed receded since the early 18th century. The numbers of fighting men given are debatable; in contrast to the quoted British figures, VOC employee Jean-Baptiste Pelon asserted in 1778 that the five rajas were able to call upon around 4,000 men to fight. (Pelon 2002: 61). The British visitors also found that the warlike traits of the Savunese were something completely different to the military discipline of their homeland:

> How far this account of the martial prowess of the inhabitants of Savu may be true, we cannot take upon us to determine, but during our stay, we saw no appearance of it. We saw indeed in the town-house, or house of assembly, about one hundred spears and targets, which served to arm the people who were sent down to intimidate us at the trading place; but they seemed to be the refuse of old armories, no two being of the same make or length, for some were six, and some sixteen feet long: we saw no lance among them, and as to the muskets, though they were clean on the outside, they were eaten into holes by the rust within; and the people themselves appeared to be so little acquainted with military discipline, that they marched like a disorderly rabble, everyone having, instead of his target, a cock, some tobacco, or other merchandise of the like kind, which he took the opportunity to bring down to sell, and few or none of their cartridge boxes were furnished with either powder or ball, though a piece of paper was thrust into the hole to save appearances. We saw a few swivel

---

[62] Hawkesworth (1773: 692).

guns, and pateraros at the town-house, and a great gun before it; but the swivels and pateraros lay out of their carriages, and the great gun lay upon a heap of stones, possibly to conceal its size, which might perhaps be little less than that of a bore (Hawkesworth 1773. 693).

In 1829, the naturalist Salomon Müller observed that the lances (*kepokeh*) were two and a half meters long, thin and suitable for throwing rather than thrusting. A mounted fighter often had six to twelve lances with him. The British account fails to mention the shields, which were either round and made of ox hide, or rectangular and made from wood (Temminck 1839–44: 294; Plate 14). Several sources mention the Savunese as excellent stone-slingers.

An event of decisive importance, at least from the Dutch point of view, was the large contract between the VOC, and the various rajas in and around Timor who acknowledged the company's suzerainty. The commissioner Johannes Andreas Paravicini was dispatched to Timor in 1756 to bring order to the rather unsettled VOC possessions and avert possible interference from France—this was on the eve of the Seven Years' War.[63] On 9 June, the Dutch held a solemn assembly in Kupang in the presence of no less than 92 aristocrats from Timor, Rote, Savu and the Solor Islands. All signed a verbose contract (with crosses as the rajas generally could not read or write) that mixed rhetorical superlatives about Dutch moral and economic superiority with various practical concerns. Hili Haba was there with his fettor Leba Luji, acting as a representative for the rajas of Mesara and Menia. Also present were Jara Wadu of Seba and Kore Rohi of Liae. Raijua was conspicuously absent.[64]

The text of the contract may not have meant much to the local princes. Probably more important to them was that the contract was a symbol of closer ties with the white 'stranger-kings'. Thus, some traditions identify Hili Haba and Jara Wadu as the very first VOC rajas which, although literally speaking is incorrect, relates to their inclusion in a tighter network. Confirmation of this was a request that the Savunese rajas lodged two months after the conclusion of the contract. To date there had been no European representation on the little outlying island, but they asked for an interpreter, just as Rote and Solor already had. Such an interpreter would serve as a general representative of the VOC. Paravicini approved this and appointed Corporal Christiaan Becker.[65]

---

[63] The war from 1756 to 1763 was the last pan-European conflict before the French Revolution. The war encompassed various colonial regions as Britain, in alliance with the Austrian Netherlands, sought to prevent French expansion.

[64] VOC 2941 (1756), f. 602–12.

[65] VOC 2941 (1756), f. 683.

The Dutch thus officially acknowledged the Savunese rajas as mini-monarchs on par with the more powerful kings of Sonba'i, Wehali and Amanuban, and so on. But did they receive royal treatment when away from Savu? The verbose diary of Paravicini suggests that this was not necessarily so. He related an incident at a feast at the residence of the Mardijker chief in Kupang where the *opperhoofd* and a number of rajas were present. The notorious burgher David Schrijver, who frequently bullied local aristocrats, disturbed the order of the event by verbally battering Hili Haba in an "unacceptable manner". Though Paravicini punished Schrijver for his overbearing attitude towards the rajas, the brawl indicates that the dignity of the minor rulers was not always respected.[66] Paravicini considered unnecessary intercourse between the burghers of Kupang, and the rajas and regents harmful to the stability of company possessions. He issued a decree to this effect, and sent around an errand with drums and bells to announce it to the townsfolk. In his diary he tells of his anger when, in the evening of 27 April 1756, the same day he issued the decree, he came across the Second Lieutenant Oehle who sat over a mug of strong drink fraternising with Hili Haba. In order to make an example of him, Paravicini had Oehle arrested, although he was released the next day with a severe warning.[67]

Seba

While Dimu held the position of precedence in the VOC system, its part-time rival Seba tended to be the more active protagonist. The historical traditions give a much fuller picture of Seba than the other domains. In part this is due to its hegemony over the island in the late colonial period, as seen in chapter 7 and 9. But Seba also has a prominent role in the VOC records. Its roadstead on the northern coast was more convenient for visiting ships than Banyo in the east.

The pedigrees mention nine generations of rajas before the incontestably historical Lai Lomi (who reigned circa 1684 to 1687) and Jara Lomi (r. 1687–04). However, as the first raja Kore Rohi would have been appointed via Portuguese influence, the genealogy does not make sense. The pedigree includes the sequence Lomi—Jara—Lomi—Jara which probably means that two generations were doubled in the orally transmitted list. While the genealogies as they are today tend to fit rather well with archival data in most cases, they are after all the results of social interaction. There are a number of cases where the

<hr>

[66] VOC 2941 (1756), legal proceeding, dated 3 May 1756.

[67] VOC 2941 (1756), diary, dated 27–28 April 1756. In the 1760s, an Adam Bender was interpreter. He was transferred to Rote in 1765 and Jan van Nimweegen took his place (VOC 3115 [1765], meeting, dated 1 August 1765). By 1770, Johann Christopher Lange was in charge as testified by the Cook expedition's account (Hawkesworth 1773: 698).

order of generations has been altered, which might have happened for a number of reasons, consciously or inadvertently. It should be noted that insertions as well as omissions of names are extremely common in Indonesian historiography, including in written chronicles and genealogies.

An elderly raja called Ama Lomi, apparently from Seba, was governing when the Dutch first arrived in 1648. The name indicates he was the father of a Lomi and a Lomi Riwu occurs in generation seven (Figure 28). Nothing is known of him from written documents as the company was not very active in Savu in the 1650s and 1660s. If this Lomi ever ruled Seba in his own name, he must have been succeeded by a sister, the aforementioned Ina Tenga. She headed the polity by 1675 at which time she is said to have stayed inexplicably in Rote and let her sister Inyalo represent her when the Dutch visited the island.[68] She and her chiefs were staunchly pro-company and, when the VOC troops invaded the island the next year, they received active assistance from the Sebanese. As apparent from the expedition's dagh-register, it was understood that she only led Seba until her son Wake had grown up. The commander provided the young Wake with a new company flag to confirm his loyal stance, and encouraged the Sebanese to capture the murderers Talo and Liwu Kone if possible, dead or alive.[69] From the snippets provided by Willem Tange in 1682, it appears that this reigning queen was honoured but not always obeyed. Ina Tenga is also unique in a Savunese context because no other woman ruler appears in either local tradition or archival pieces.

Ina Tenga's position falls well into the pre-modern pattern of maritime Southeast Asia where ruling queens were quite common in Muslim as well as non-Muslim areas. In her era, there were queens of Aceh, Patani and various states in Sulawesi, and there was an entire host of female leaders in Solor and Timor (Hägerdal 2013). Tange tells us that she had little involvement in the actual decision-making, reinforcing the pattern found in other parts of the archipelago: females might enjoy a high position in pre-modern society but were in the first place accorded roles in the inner, ritual sphere. Female rule could nevertheless be functional and successful, as shown by recent studies on the Acehnese queens (Khan 2017). Strangely, there is no clear trace of Ina Tenga in local tradition which is otherwise detailed when it comes to the genealogies of leading clans. The name 'Ina Tenga' occurs a couple of times—once as the mother of Lomi Jara who by inference would be the brother of the historical queen. The active Ga Lena of Seba, who brought an army to Savu to fight Dimu, is known as Ina

---

[68] VOC 1311 (1675), dagh-register 1674–75, dated 3 May 1675.

[69] Ibid., dated 18 May 1676.

Tenga Bèngu in at least one account.[70] Therefore, Ga Lena is also a queen about whom it would be helpful to know more.

Seba's pedigrees indicate that Ama Lomi's son Lomi Riwu had a daughter, Damu Lomi, who married Bèngu Doko of the Nahoro clan (Figures 28 and 36). She is known as Ina Baja Bèngu. Her husband is remembered for having briefly held the position of Seba's raja, but Jara Lomi (his brother-in-law) attacked him and regained the raja position for the Nataga clan. If Damu Lomi had a daughter named Tenga, she would have been known as Ina Tenga Bèngu, thus corresponding to the name Teffer recorded. However, this is speculation as it is not supported by collective or social memory. Ina Tenga passed away in 1683.[71] One cannot escape the suspicion that her son Dami's horrible death the preceding year hastened her own end. Her eldest son Wake was probably dead already as there is nothing more about him. The next year Seba acknowledged Lai Lomi, her brother's son, as raja of the domain. He was not in power for long; in 1687 his brother Jara Lomi was already battling for control of the domain. By this time Savu's previous infighting had resumed again, involving Seba, Liae and Mesara. It seems as if the VOC intervention in 1682 had very little effect. In a sense it was even worse than before as some of the domains had since split into factions. Jara Lomi, in favour of the VOC, had to defend himself against two chiefs called "Amma Tsingo" and "Landonnavo" who wished to keep the company out.[72] To add to the complicated picture, he was at war with Liae which had killed one of his men.

While Jara Lomi managed to stay in power for about a decade and a half, his tenure was punctuated by incessant petty wars. Seba was relatively successful in the continuing play for power. In 1698 or 1700 it attacked the neighbouring domain of Mesara, destroyed the main settlement and subdued the surrounding land after a hard-contested fight.[73] There is no suggestion that the VOC considered chastising its unruly vassal. On the contrary, when Seba asked the same year to replace their worn company flag, the Dutch *opperhoofd* promised to provide a flag on the next possible occasion.[74] By this time, the authorities in Kupang

---

[70] This is also indicated in an observation by the missionary Wijngaarden in 1890; Ga Lena was the mother of a certain Tenga Bunga, which by implication made her Ina Tenga (Raad voor de Zending, 1102–1: 1416, J.K. Wijngaarden, notebook, 1890).

[71] Narrative 3, about Ga Lena alias Ina Tenga as recorded by her descendants, is in Appendix I.

[72] VOC 8310 (1687). The two names "Amma Tsingo" and "Landonnavo" (possibly Lado Nawa) cannot be traced in the Seba genealogies.

[73] The destruction of Mesara occurred about six years before 1704, according to VOC 1691 (1704), f. 25.

[74] Coolhaas 1976: 122–3.

were somewhat disillusioned with Savu. As noted in an official memorandum, the island was too far for quick dispatches and provided the company with few advantages—including slaves to purchase. When VOC ships visited the island it was mostly to check on the state of relations between the local princes and, above all, to ensure that no Makassarese or other foreigners meddled in these troubled waters.[75] Under these circumstances local disturbances could continue without intervention; that is, as long as nobody questioned the VOC-led system and invited in outsiders.

Jara Lomi probably passed away between 1700 and 1704. According to Savunese tradition, it was not a peaceful demise. Jara Lomi molested the niece of the Mesara ruler Wele Jami and demanded that she become his wife. When Wele Jami refused a war commenced between Seba and Mesara. Jara Lomi killed Wele Jami's nephew, Leba Haba, his wife's brother. At some stage, Seba forces captured Wele Jami and confined him to a house in Seba—this detail seems to refer to the defeat in 1700. However, the subjugation of Mesara was only a temporal matter, for Wele Jami found a flask of oil and smeared his body so that he slipped out of Jara Lomi's grasp and escaped. A series of detentions and successful escapes followed where each time Wele Jami was able to get away through luck and cunning. There followed a dramatic duel between the two lords as quoted from the narrative:

> The Sebanese came again to take hold of Wele Jami, but Wele Jami would not go. As a result, there was war. Wele Jami did not communicate this to the people of the family. He only told Ama Mare Bawa who stayed in his house. Meanwhile, Jara Lomi arrived with all his troops. Made Dudu Wawi was the name where the Sebanese were placed. They sat under a *kesambi*[76] tree at Lede Wila Kole. While they sat there, Wele Jami himself sat at the foot of the Kolorae mountain. Meanwhile, only Ama Mare Bawa stayed at home and not one Mesara person appeared. After half a day Wele Jami came forward bringing a blowpipe. Ama Mare Bawa saw that the shadow of the spirit had not yet come to the point of the blowpipe. After some time Ama Mare Bawa went to see the blowpipe and at its point was the shadow of the spirit. Then Wele Jami delivered a shot, but as he did not use the blowpipe correctly, he shot Jara Lomi in the side. Then Ama Mare Bawa said "This is the wrong way; you must shoot towards the sun." Wele Jami followed the advice of Ama Mare Bawa and the arrow flew down again and hit Jara Lomi above the knee.
>
> And so Jara Lomi died. At once he fell from the chair. The Sebanese followed [the corpse of] Jara Lomi back to Seba, and no one from Mesara greeted them. In Seba there was a *tao leo* ceremony. While the *tao leo* was

---

[75] VOC 1826 (1712), f. 32.

[76] *Schleicera oleosa* (gum-lac tree).

in progress, Wele Jami went to Seba on a mare followed by a child. The
horse had bells. Arriving in Seba he cut some grass close to the house and
stuffed the bells so they did not make any sound. The horse was tied to
the the fence near the gate and Wele Jami went into the house. When he
entered all the people were asleep and it was dark. Wele Jami cut out the
eyes, lips, nose and fingers of Jara Lomi and left the corpse in this state.
Wele Jami went back on the horse whose bells now sounded again. In
Mesara Wele Jami gave the spoils from Seba to Ama Mare Bawa, who
buried the body parts of Jara Lomi in a circular form. Thus ended the war
between Jara Lomi and Wele Jami.[77]

According to Seba sources, Jara Lomi did not die immediately.[78] His kinsmen
first carried him to the Hinge Haba house, which at that time belonged to the
Nahipa clan, trusted allies of the Nataga in Seba. Then they placed Jara Lomi
on a buffalo hide tied to two branches of a *kepaka* tree (*nitas* [In]) and took him
to Nadawawi on Namata hill. They later planted the two branches of *kepaka*
upside down; one at Nadawawi—which became the tree where Apu Lod'o of
Seba sat when presiding over ritual cockfighting—and the second in Raepana at
the bottom of the hill. The location became the second settlement of the Seba
rajas before they moved to Mèba in the 19th century.

VOC reports testify to the reconstruction of Mesara in about 1704, although
it was not possible to confirm the duel.[79] There is no suggestion in either
Savunese or Dutch sources that the slain ruler had children, and his successor
was the son of his brother and predecessor. This was Wadu Lai, who was also
known as Ama Medo Wadu (or Ama Jara Wadu). His nephew's reign, which
lasted until after 1740, was of such importance that collective memory says
he was the first VOC-affiliated raja of Seba. A tradition retold by the Dutch
gezaghebber (administrator) Heyligers in 1920 stated that the Apu Lod'o was
the actual 'prince' in olden days, managing questions about planting, sickness,
warfare, corvée labour and so on. When the Dutch company first arrived in Seba,
the commander asked for the prince of the place. As the Apu Lod'o was afraid
to meet the commander, he told his second son Wadu Lai to go in his place. The
Dutchman took it for granted that Wadu Lai was the raja and treated him with
the appropriate honour, handing over a flag. Wadu Lai became known as "the
man with the flag", Mone Paji, equivalent to a raja. His elder brother assumed
the Apu Lod'o title (Heyligers 1920: 27). This story may seem strange as the
company acknowledged several rulers before him, including his father Lai Lomi.
However, the raja institution as such was a foreign import or rather introduced

[77] Interviews with Ama Tapa Rike (17.08.2001); Ama Jula Lede (17.08.2001).
[78] Interviews with Ama Ju Rihi (15.10.2000); Ama Obi Nale (09.10.2000).
[79] VOC 1691 (1704), f. 25.

as a result of foreign influences. Also, the general rule for successions in later times was that a new raja must be chosen from the descendants of Wadu Lai, a restriction that made it less necessary to keep track of his antecedents.[80] While the pedigrees were usually faithfully remembered, the order of succession was sometimes less definite. It did not matter to Savunese society in the same way as for many other especially literate polities of the region.[81]

Oral tradition discloses details about Seba religious affairs in the early 18th century. The account is partly legendary, but it highlights the importance of maintaining the right rituals in local society to avert danger. The priest who held the highest position of the realm, Deo Rai in Namata, passed away without having a legitimate son. However, he sired a natural son—Kore Mojo—with a woman of Liae's Nanawa clan. The son was adopted under the name Kore Rohi while the Nanawa clan received land as compensation for the loss of a son. Kore Rohi became Deo Rai in Namata, but this was not popular with other members of the group who believed they could have provided Seba with a suitable Deo Rai too.

One day Deo Rai's wife, Bèni Deo, was accused of stealing indigo dye out of a vat belonging to *udu* Nataga in Nadawawi on Namata hill. Deo Rai and Bèni Deo were enraged by the accusation and went back to the priest's place of birth in Liae. For a number of years the rituals were no longer held in Seba and no one renewed the layers of lontar palm leaves on the ridge of Deo Rai's house. A terrible drought struck the island. The excessive heat was caused by the sun's rays shining through the ridge of Deo Rai's house. As the rays fell on the ceremonial knife, it became too hot and therefore generated danger. Finally, the population became angry with the *Mone Ama* council of Namata and held them responsible for the drought. The council then had to reconcile with Kore Rohi and his wife, and asked them to return to Namata in order to hold the rituals. They accepted but not without requesting a piece of land from *udu* Namata; this was Rao Ae (great cooking place). It has been the location for the ceremonial hearth, *rao pana*, for making syrup from lontar sap up to the present; it is not located in Namata but is downhill in a north-east direction, 20 minutes away on foot.[82]

Like his predecessor, Wadu Lai sometimes interfered in the troubles besetting his neighbours, but he also had a wider outlook. Dutch and Savunese sources mention that he had at least eight children and a few stayed away from

---

[80] Raad voor de Zending, 1102–1: 1415, J.K. Wijngaarden, letter, 1 April 1890.

[81] However, it should be noted that the order of succession is often simplified or obscured in Indonesian historiography. European sources can often disclose a much more complicated succession than indigenous written chronicles may suggest.

[82] Source: Leba Alu of the Namata clan (for illustrations, see Duggan 2008: 106).

Figure 34: Alliances during the Wele Jami–Jara Lomi war

This war, comprising various episodes, took place around 1700. According to Mesara sources, Jara Lomi, Seba's raja, was not only defeated but also died, which is denied by Seba sources. Jara Lomi's successor and nephew, Wadu Lai, is first mentioned in 1704. Jara Lomi's opponent in this war, Wele Jami, is first documented as raja of Mesara in 1708; a VOC source states his reign ended in 1751. Alliances with the winner are well remembered; it is not the case for alliances with the loser.

There was no information about the role of the Nahipa clan in this war. It usually allied with Seba.

Allies of Wele Jami, Naputitu clan (Mesara)	Comments	Source
Ama Mare Bawa, Napupenu clan (Mesara)	He is a cultural hero in Mesara; his modern descendant Ama Do Ruba still cultivates the plot his ancestor received seven generations earlier.	
Ama Dadi Luji, Napupudi clan (Mesara)	He is Luji Lèru of 1682. He received a plot of land called Mado Ruba Penu. He is also remembered for supporting Dimu in warfare against Seba and received a plot of land called Èilobo Èimada in Matèi.	
Male Luji Penu and Koli Luji alias Ama Dimu Koli, Nanawa clan (Liae)		Ama Jari (2006) and Wila Hege, Liae (2010)
Riwu Manu alias Ama Jami Riwu Manu, Napujara clan (Liae)	He received land in Tanajawa, Lower Mesara.	Ama Jo Haba, Mesara (2010)
Ama Jata Luhi and Ama Hunga Kore, Napuru clan (Dimu)		Ama Tada Talo, Napuru clan, Dimu (2008)
Bèdi Jami and Ama Hara Bèdi, Natie clan (Dimu)	He received land in Tanajawa.	Ama Mako Nara, Gèra clan
Allies of Jara Lomi, Nataga clan (Seba)		
Doke Bara, Kelara clan (Seba)		Ama Jo Haba, Mesara (2010)

Figure 35: Namata clan

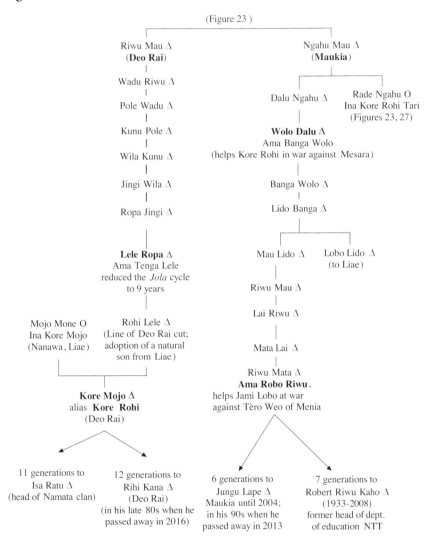

(Figure 23)

Riwu Mau Δ
(**Deo Rai**)

Ngahu Mau Δ
(**Maukia**)

Wadu Riwu Δ

Dalu Ngahu Δ

Rade Ngahu O
Ina Kore Rohi Tari
(Figures 23, 27)

Pole Wadu Δ

Kunu Pole Δ

Wolo Dalu Δ
Ama Banga Wolo
(helps Kore Rohi in war against Mesara)

Wila Kunu Δ

Banga Wolo Δ

Jingi Wila Δ

Lido Banga Δ

Ropa Jingi Δ

Mau Lido Δ

Lobo Lido Δ
(to Liae)

Lele Ropa Δ
Ama Tenga Lele
reduced the *Jola* cycle
to 9 years

Riwu Mau Δ

Lai Riwu Δ

Mojo Mone O
Ina Kore Mojo
(Nanawa, Liae)

Rohi Lele Δ
(Line of Deo Rai cut;
adoption of a natural
son from Liae)

Mata Lai Δ

Riwu Mata Δ
Ama Robo Riwu,
helps Jami Lobo at war
against Tèro Weo of Menia

Kore Mojo Δ
alias **Kore Rohi**
(Deo Rai)

11 generations to
Isa Ratu Δ
(head of Namata clan)

12 generations to
Rihi Kana Δ
(Deo Rai)
(in his late 80s when he
passed away in 2016)

6 generations to
Jungu Lape Δ
Maukia until 2004;
in his 90s when he
passed away in 2013

7 generations to
Robert Riwu Kaho Δ
(1933-2008)
former head of dept.
of education NTT

Figure 36: Nataga clan and the rulers of Seba in VOC times

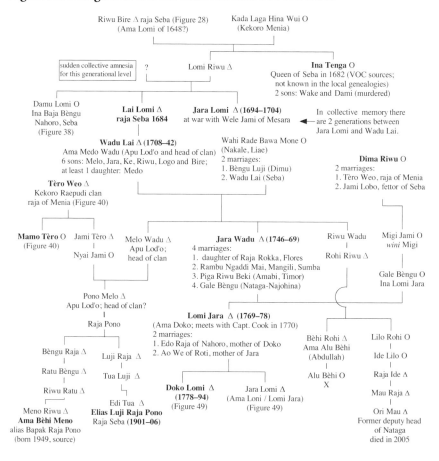

Figure 37: Fettors of Seba

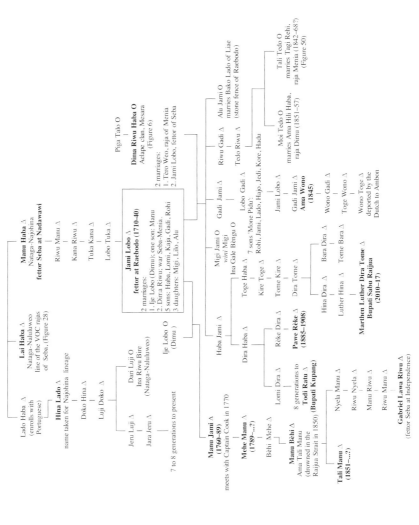

Figure 38: Nahoro clan

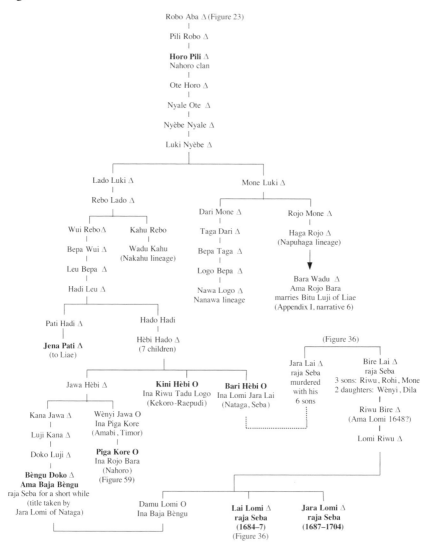

Savu. A son called Bire Wadu lived for some time in Kupang, presumably as a contact person for the company. His end was tragic, however. In 1738, he was murdered by a slave and, in turn, the Savunese in Kupang stoned the slave to death. One year afterwards, his brother-in-law Hili Haba of Dimu arrived in Kupang by ship bringing a number of hogs for a feast to remember the slain prince.[83] According to Savunese tradition, another son, Jara Wadu, quarreled with his father who banished him to Flores. There he assisted the VOC by guarding Ende (Duggan 2008: 342). Although VOC sources do not mention this particular information, it suggests that the Kupang authorities used Savunese aristocrats to monitor areas they had claimed but could not closely control. The Ende area on the south coast of Flores consisted of several small settlements, such as Barai and Tongo, which had a vague connection with Solor. When areas of the Solor Islands became part of the Dutch sphere in 1613, Ende (and Galiyao in Alor-Pantar) followed suit (Tiele and Heeres 1886: 19). The Endenese were a mixed group of Florenese and immigrants from Sulawesi, and were nominal Muslims. Unlike most of the peoples in the region they were good sailors and, as there were no Dutch representatives in the area and the Kupang base had limited resources, they could do as they pleased. There is little doubt that the Dutch benefited from the presence of the comparatively "loyal" Savunese in Ende. According to a note from 1754, Makassarese seafarers plied the waters of the Savu Sea beyond the company's reach, selling cloth to Alor, Solor, Ende and Sumba. The VOC in Batavia and Kupang viewed the activities of these adventurers with increasing concern.[84]

Wadu Lai also met a violent end. Increasing contacts with Europeans had introduced firearms to Timor as well as the adjacent islands. A missive from 1694 states that Raja Jara Lomi possessed a somewhat damaged cannon that he kept in his house purchased from Makassarese traders.[85] Oral sources describe an occasion, probably in early 1742, when Wadu Lai was watching his men cleaning his cannon—perhaps the same one his uncle had owned. Suddenly the cannon went off, killing the raja, and his body was virtually obliterated.[86] There was little left to bury, so the priests consulted the ancestors by thrusting a spear into the main pillar of his residence. Interpreting the signs from the ancestors, the priests arranged a taboo horse to commemorate the deceased raja by conducting *pehere jara* which is a ceremonial horse dance performed at specific occasions. Here the

---

[83] VOC 8332 (1738–39), dagh-register, dated 4 March 1739.

[84] VOC 8347 (1754), f. 19.

[85] Generale Missiven V: 685, dated 30 November 1694.

[86] Interview with Manu Ke (1999/2000); (Duggan 2008: 342). See Figure 36.

Apu Lod'o, who is from the same clan as Raja Wadu Lai, mounts his taboo horse and circles the *kepaka* tree in Raepana nine times in one direction and circles nine times in the reverse direction while reciting a ritual text. This ceremony is repeated every year in the rainy season. The cannon attributed to Wadu Lai's death was left untouched at Nadawawi, on the western side of Namata hill; a landslide caused it to fall into a ravine where it was mostly covered by soil. In 2015, the Department of Tourism retrieved the cannon which is now at the entrance of the Namata site.

Photo 11. A section of old cannon that according to collective memory caused the death of Raja Wadu Lai in c.1742; Namata hill (2016)

Jara Wadu was still in Flores at the time of the accident but returned to Seba and assumed his father's position. According to a recently recorded story, he had a nephew   the son of his elder brother—called Pono Melo. Jara Wadu's nephew was initially appointed raja, but because he already held the title Apu Lod'o and was the Bèngu Udu, chief of the clan, Pono Melo therefore bestowed the title on his returning uncle.[87] Jara Wadu is mentioned from 1746 until his demise in 1769 and was one of the signatories of the Paravicini contract in 1756.[88]

Although VOC records reveal little, indigenous sources describe Jara Wadu as a man who carefully established a network of contacts across the eastern islands, as seen from his many marriages. Savunese men are normally monogamous, but the raja consummated at least four marriages during his long reign. His betrothal to a daughter of the raja in Rokka stemmed from his time in Flores.[89] Rokka is a fertile land in the northern part of Ngada in Central Flores, an area loosely claimed by the Larantuqueiros at the time. In the mid-18th century it produced quality cinnamon, was also known as a place for slaves, rice, vegetable oil and rice, and purveyed foodstuff to Sumba and other nearby lands. It was unsurprising that the VOC sought to gain influence in Rokka and Ende, and oust their Larantuqueiros and Makassarese rivals.[90] Jara Wadu had two children with the Rokka princess—Pati Bupu and Goe Bupu—who stayed in Flores where they had descendants.

Jara Wadu's second marriage was to a Sumbanese woman called Rambu Nggadi Mai who belonged to the *kabisu* (clan) Lukunara in Mangili. This particular information is from Sumbanese not Savunese oral sources.[91] Sumbanese and Savunese aristocrats had maintained relations since at least the 17th century. Parts of Sumba were drawn into the VOC orbit under the leadership of the energetic *opperhoofd* Daniel van der Burgh in 1751, but there was still a lack of any real VOC control over or representation on the politically fragmented island. Considering Jara Wadu's pro-VOC stance, any influence he may have had in Sumba was probably welcomed by the Kupang authorities.

---

[87] Interview with Ama Bèhi (30.06.2012).

[88] Jara Wadu is probably the "Young King of Seba" who waited for an official VOC appointment in 1742 (VOC 8335 [1742], missive, 21 May 1742, f. 9).

[89] In Flores Jara Wadu is remembered in a number of settlements: Borong (in Manggarai), Aimere, Mau Mbawa, Watu Pèsa, Bo'a Nage and Wudhi where he is attributed with a number of offspring. In Keo, residents in a village called Sawu (Sawu clan) claim descent from Jara Wadu (Forth 2001: 33).

[90] VOC 8346 (1753), f. 22–5.

[91] Kapita and Umbu Pura Woha 2008: 46–8.

Mangili was a fertile area in south-eastern Sumba that had been in contact with the VOC on and off since the late 17th century.

Raja Jara Wadu bonded Savu to one of the staunchest VOC allies in Timor, the Amabi princedom.[92] The Amabi people had arrived in Kupang with the Sonba'i in 1658 and settled close to the port. A woman with a Savunese or Savunised name Piga Riwu Beki married Jara Wadu who was actually her second cousin. According to a somewhat confusing pedigree compiled by Kupang Savunese, Piga was the sister of Raja Dao in Amabi and a certain Kana whose son Captain Kana served in the Dutch military and cleared land for rice fields in Oesau east of Kupang. While Dao is otherwise unknown, a Captain Jozef Kana appears in the European sources. He led a Mardijker company into Timor's interior in 1767, but he was killed by the Sonba'i who resented the Dutch enforcement of corvée labour on local people to pan for gold in the highlands (Müller 1857: 138–9). Kana actually seems to be a Savunese name, similar to many Mardijker names that occur in the Dutch records.

Stories pertaining to Jara Wadu tell of a fourth marriage to a Savunese woman, Gale Bèngu. There were at least five children from his manifold liaisons and, at his death in 1769, one of them—Lomi Jara or Ama Doko Lomi, born around 1735—inherited his title. While Ama Doko's rule was relatively short, he is the only Savunese raja who has attracted notice from people other than Savu scholars. Ama Doko features in the accounts of a remarkable visitor to the Seba roadstead on 17 September 1770. The British explorer James Cook and his crew aboard the *Endeavour*, after having gathered geographical data on Australia, arrived in Savu without having called at Kupang. The brief stay, lasting no more than four days, accumulated a substantial amount of information in a number of accounts from the journey. The data are particularly valuable as VOC reports do not usually include ethnographic details and general impressions.

The famous naturalist Joseph Banks travelled with the *Endeavour* on Cook's first voyage from 1768 to 1771. He went ashore with an officer on 18 September and met 20 or 30 Savunese armed with muskets who escorted them to the raja. The "town" of Seba, which lay about a mile from the anchorage, had numerous houses, sometimes sizeable, which were all covered with thatched roofs and had floors constructed on pillars three or four feet above the ground. The officer spoke to Ama Doko via a Portuguese-speaking interpreter, explaining that their ship was a man-o'-war which had made a long journey and carried several sick men. They therefore wished to purchase provisions from the islanders.

---

[92] According to Liae social memory, Hari Juda (Figure 17), a descendant of Ngara Adu of Liae, founded a branch of the Amabi clan in West Timor. See also footnote 150 in this chapter.

He [Ama Doko] answerd that he was willing to supply us with every thing we should want, but being in alliance with the Duch East Indian Company he was not allowd to trade with any other people without their consent, which however he would Immediately apply for to a Duchman belonging to that Company who was the only white man residing upon the Island. A letter was accordingly dispatchd immediately and after some hours waiting answerd by the man in Person, who assurd him with many Civilities that we were at liberty to buy of the natives whatever we pleasd. He express'd a desire of coming on board, as well as the King and several of his attendants, provided however that some of our people might stay on shore, on which two were left and about 2 they arrivd. Our dinners were ready and they readily agreed to dine with us. At setting down however the King excusd himself, saying that he did not imagine that we who were white men would suffer him who was black to set down in our company. A complement however removd his scruples and he and his prime minister sat down and eat sparingly.[93]

The raja's reference to a racial hierarchy is very surprising. While racialism was still ideologically vague and depended on the situation, the idea of the white man's prerogatives seems to have been enforced by a few centuries of European contact. On 19 September, Cook and his men went ashore and met Ama Doko and his grandees in an assembly hall built by the VOC. They deliberated about the barter of goods against domestic animals for consumption. The raja then invited the Britons to a dinner which was gratefully accepted:

About 5 O'Clock dinner was ready, consisting of 36 dishes or rather baskets containing alternately Rice and Boild Pork, and 3 earthen ware bowls of Soup or rather the Broth in which the Pork had been boild; these were rangd on the floor and matts laid round them for us to set upon. We were now conducted by turns to a hole in the floor near which stood a man with a basket of water in his hand; here we wash'd our hands and then rang'd ourselves in order round the victuals waiting for the King to set down. We were told however that the custom of the countrey was that the entertainer never sets down to meat with his guests, however if we suspected the victuals to be poisoned he would willingly do it; we suspected nothing and therefore desire'd that all things might go as usual; all then sitting down we eat with good appetites, the Prime Minister and My[n]heer Lange partaking with us. Our wine passd briskly about, the Radja alone refusing to drink with us saying that it was wrong for the master of the feast to be in liquor. The pork was excellent, the Rice as good, the broth not bad, the spoons only which were made of leaves were so small that few of us had patience to eat it: every one however made a hearty dinner and as soon as we had done removd, as the custom it

---

[93] Banks, dated 18 September 1770. Note that the Britons' visit did not leave memories on the island.

seems was to let the Servants and seamen take our Places. These could not dispach all, but when the women came to take away they forcd them to take away with them all the Pork that was left.[94]

In spite of complaints about excessive prices for the purchased animals, the British visit ended in a friendly mood. The British represented a rival power, particularly in the decade before the fourth Anglo-Dutch war (1780–84), so the Dutch interpreter in Seba took precautions that the *Endeavour* did not stay overly long. In the end, however, he developed considerable sympathy for the rare white guests and provided useful bits of information. During the few precious days of British-Savunese intercourse, the expedition noted a remarkable number of details about the culture and society of the little island which impressed them favourably.

The Britons described Ama Doko as the fattest man they saw on the island. Perhaps his obesity helped put him in an early grave. He passed away in November 1778 at which time he would have been a little over 40.[95] His eldest son and heir Doko Lomi succeeded him and reigned until some time after 1794. In general, the VOC reports become less attentive to details about local polities in the second half of the 18th century. The central VOC authorities gave orders to the various posts to omit information about local matters that were not deemed necessary for the central decision-making process; therefore it is harder to follow developments in Savu in these decades. Local accounts give some details that do not entirely match the colonial archive. Ama Doko Lomi was married twice; first to a Savunese woman and then to a princess from Rote called Aofe. The new Raja Doko Lomi had a half-brother called Jara Lomi, later known as Ama Loni Jara, and there was intense rivalry between the two. The infighting propelled Jara Lomi to take his belongings and sail over to Rote where he obtained protection and assistance from his uncle who was raja there. After some time, he returned to Savu and landed at the Banyo port in Dimu. A relative who was Apu Lod'o met him in Banyo and took him to the Nadawawi village. Later, Seba people accepted him as their raja, although it is not clear what happened to the elder brother.[96] The problem is that Dutch official records show that Ama Loni Jara's reign was from 1830 to 1858, which makes for a very long generation of 80 years for the two brothers. Moreover, in 1803 the records refer

---

[94] Banks, dated 19 September 1770.

[95] VOC 3553 (1779). If Captain Cook was right in his estimate, he was born about 1735.

[96] Interview with Ama Behi (30.06.2012). Marthen Heke Medo from Seba also mentioned the enmity between the two brothers in an interview (30.06.2012). The latter source, however, says that Jara Lomi was the eldest son and succeeded his father directly after his demise. The VOC records gainsay this.

to a raja called Ama Dima, probably from Seba, but he has no confirmed place in the pedigrees. In spite of the general reliability of the genealogical tradition, there are some obscure points and perhaps missing generations.

The VOC records are rich in information regarding the Nataga Naluluweo lineage of the Seba rajas but much less so about other clans and lineages. Neither do the VOC documents have much detail about the Seba fettors. The fettors are from the same clan but from the Najohina lineage. Long before the rajas moved out of Nadawawi on Namata hill, the fettors had established themselves in Bodo near the sea. The stone wall around Bodo must have been a novelty as collective memory records it. Traditional villages had lontar palm stalk fences, a vulnerable defence during warfare. The VOC presence led to new forms of construction, a fact not featured in the company reports. Raebodo village replaced its fence in the late 17th century with a stone wall using dead coral with shooting holes facing inland, reminiscent of European fortresses. This was the work of Ama Bako Lado (*udu* Teriwu-Nahire) who had previously built a similar stone wall for Ege village in Liae.

After finishing the work at Raebodo, Ama Bako Lado did not want a payment. Instead he asked for *manu muri ae* (a great living chick), a metaphor to say that he wanted to marry Alu Jami, the daughter of the fettor Lobo Tuka. She was the sister of a popular character in the early 18th century called Jami Lobo, who became fettor before 1707.[97]

Near Raebodo is Tuleika, the traditional village of the Kelara clan. Tuleika also replaced its fence with a stone wall some time after Raebodo. A fire had destroyed the lontar fence during the lives of two brothers, Jami Bara and Doko Bara. Their father was contemporary with the fettor Jami Lobo (circa 1707–40). These characters play a role in Menia's fate later in the chapter. Lobo Gara of Mesara's Kelara people replaced the Raetuleika fence with a stone wall, also with shooting holes. Muskets had slowly been spreading among indigenous populations in the Timor area since the 17th century.

Instead of payment for working on the wall Jami Bara asked to marry a young woman from Raijua who was staying there. The event is remembered with the expression *Rubi dodo galo, galo dei niki Maja* (One large ceramic pot of lontar syrup, to be brought by the Raijua woman). *Niki Maja* means child of Maja, as Raijuanese are called in Savu. *Rubi* is the largest size for a pot of lontar syrup. In fact, it is so big that it is not possible to carry and its contents have to be transferred into smaller containers. *Do d'o galo* means not yet used, that is, still full of syrup. It is not explicit in the saying, but the text also implies that the woman who brought the pot of lontar syrup was included in the exchange.

---

[97] Interview with Nguru Nape (18.05.2006).

Later, during the 18th century, *udu* Kelara lost its ceremonial rights, including the right to perform a *tao leo* ceremony at a funeral. The story says that *Mone Pidu* (Seven Men of Bodo) were performing a *tao leo* ceremony.[98] While conducting the *ledo* dance, their party left Bodo village and went to the gate of Raetuleika village. There a man was playing the drum. He intentionally made mistakes in the rhythm (*wèba èki*) causing the dancers to lose their timing and they were furious. They destroyed the drum sticks, smashed the drums and cut off the drummer's fingers. They buried the drums on the Ledepuriwu slope towards Namata, at a place now covered with cactus.[99] Since that time, the entire *udu* Kelara has been banned from holding *tao leo*, *pehere jara* or *pedoa* ceremonies and dances. Neither is the Kelara clan allowed to enter Namata's ritual place nor to perform rituals for calling the rain. The ban also prevents them from approaching the Sebanese people's sacred stones. This dramatic story shows the power the ruling clans had over the population during Dutch rule. The Seven Men of Bodo are the sons of Lobo Gadi (Figure 37)—the fettor lineage. Bodo is the centre of the Najohina lineage in the Nataga clan, from which the Seba rajas came.

Menia

Menia was situated to the east of Seba and bordered Dimu territory on the other side. The raja of Menia was often no more than a subregent under the more powerful Seba. In spite of this, a number of significant stories involve Menia, which illuminate the history-making processes of a non-literate society and are interesting comparisons with the colonial archive.

Concurrent to the initial VOC contract in 1648, outlined in chapter 5, Ama Tenga Gae and his brother Ama Lado Weo ruled Menia.[100] Tradition describes them as members of the Kekoro clan. Ama Lado's son Ama Mamo Tèro (or Tèro Weo) was the first raja under the company; however, he is not in the VOC documents. The archives only begin referring to Menia in the 18th century.

---

[98] The Seven Men are the grandsons of Jami Lobo Tuka. Thus, the event might have taken place in the second half of the 18th century. This happened seven generations before Ama Dubu Wadu of Kelara, the source of the narrative. Raetuleika and Raebodo are not more than 200 metres apart.

[99] It is between Raetuleika and Namata. The cactus might serve two purposes: to mark the place and to hinder people from digging up the drums.

[100] Kekoro Raepudi clan. Raepudi refers to a village fenced with white stones (generally coral), a later development in village fencing techniques. Prior to this, a village was fenced with stalks of sorghum or lontar palm trees. See the narrative about Nida Dahi and the magic cloth in Duggan (2001: 57–9).

Nevertheless, Ama Mamo Tèro had a dramatic and far from auspicious reign, according to oral history.

Seba absorbed Menia. The beginning of this was as follows:

> The young Dima Riwu of the Ae Lape clan in Lobohede, Lower Mesara had been promised in marriage to Jami Lobo of the clan Nataga-Najohina, which provided the fettors during Portuguese and Dutch times in the domain of Seba. The marriage had been arranged before Dima Riwu was born. Therefore, as a child she grew up with the Seba fettor's family in Raebodo. Alas, she fell ill with framboesia,[101] a tropical skin disease, and was sent back to her family in Mesara. Later Jami Lobo[102] married Ije Lobo of the domain of Dimu; they had one son: Manu Jami.[103]
>
> Dima Riwu eventually recovered and Tèro Weo asked to marry her. Thus the marriage took place. Two children were born: Mamo Tèro and Jami Tèro. Therefore, Dima Riwu became known as Ina Mamo Tèro and Tèro Weo in turn was given the teknonym Ama Mamo Tèro.
>
> Someone passed away in Kekoro and so there was a funeral. During the funeral feast, there was a dance performance.[104] As nobody wanted to dance with Ama Manu Jami, Ama Mamo Tèro asked his own wife to dance with the guest. Ama Manu Jami was so surprised to see the woman that he was unable to proceed with the dance.[105] He thus left the dancing mat. When outside the dancing area, he asked a follower, Ama Doko Bara Kaba of the Kelara clan, whom the lady might be. Ama Doko Bara replied "How come you do not recognise her? She is the leftover of your *sirih* [betel leaves]. Do you not recognise your own betel chew?"
>
> When they went back to Seba, Ama Manu Jami asked Ama Doko Bara Kaba to bring Ina Mamo Tèro back to him, in other words, to kidnap her. Ama Doko Bara went to Kekoro and told Ama Mamo Tèro that the mother of Ina Mamo was seriously sick. Ama Mamo Tèro replied that his wife was at Èiloe bathing as she had just given birth to a son, Jami Tèro. Ama Doko Bara Kaba went down to the river where the woman was

---

[101] Otherwise known as yaws and previously common in tropical regions, it is a highly contagious bacterial infection which begins as a red skin lesion, hence the name framboesia (raspberry [French]).

[102] Jami Lobo, fettor of Seba, documented in 1707–40. Thus he was known as Ama Manu Jami.

[103] Documented as fettor of Seba in 1760–70.

[104] Ledo during a *tao leo* funeral is a ceremonial dance that has to be performed day and night to attract the ancestors who will take the deceased with them to their realm. People come from all over the island to perform this popular dance.

[105] This is somewhat at variance with other versions of the story. There is no explanation why Jami Lobo should not be able to perform the *ledo* dance; it has to be performed at each *tao leo* funeral and is very well known.

bathing. Upon hearing the news, she immediately followed Ama Doko Bara Kaba who took her not to Mesara but to Seba.

Subsequently, Ama Tèro Weo also departed for Mesara and arrived at the place of Ina Mamo's parents [Lobohede]. However, he found that she was not there. He told the people at the place that he had got a message that his wife's mother was seriously ill. But they revealed that this was not the truth.

Ama Tèro then went to Seba to look for his wife. When he was there he heard the news that Ina Mamo was in the house of Ama Manu Jami. Ama Mamo Tèro returned to his village. He called on everybody, family and other people, telling them that Ina Mamo must be brought back. For Ama Manu Jami this induced him to go to war. He decided that if he lost the war, the land between Tenihawu and Hairawu to the west would belong to Kekoro. If, on the contrary, he won the war, the land of Ama Mamo Tèro Weo [from Tenihawu up to Dèigama in the east] would belong to Ama Manu Jami.

As it turned out, Ama Mamo Tèro Weo was defeated, so [an area of] the Kekoro land came to belong to Seba. This area of land started from the river Loko Pedai, stretching to Hanga Manu Deba, then to the river Dèigama. Ama Mamo Tèro moved to Wawarae.[106]

Before Ama Mamo Tèro arrived in Wawarae, the Hai'iki clan owned the land of Newa. Later on, as there was no one of the Hai'iki clan left, the Nabe'e, another Dimu clan, took ownership of the land. But then the people did not live there anymore. Therefore, Ama Mamo Tèro claimed it as his land. His people possessed all of it up to the border of Dimu. When Ama Mamo Tèro's subjects arrived there, the Nabe'e moved towards the north-east, to other places. They settled near what is nowadays Hotel Rai Hawu, where there were no people. The area extended from Dèigama to Jaminyebo. Thus they took over the land easily.[107]

As in previous narratives, people do not remember those who were allies of the loser or they remain mute as there is nothing heroic to remember. The defeated did not receive plots of land as their reward, which is the main reason for keeping a memory of a war. In Savu, this war was not only a male affair; it had an impact on the maternal lines. From Dima Riwu's second marriage with Jami Lobo, a new branch in the female moiety *hubi ae* or Greater Blossom was created; this is *wini* Migi, named after their daughter Migi Jami. This female line has a humorous ikat weaving pattern: a rooster looking backwards, a reminder of Jami

---

[106] Lokopedai and Hanga Loko Pedae in Mery Kolimon's text, where 34 Savunese were executed in 1966, refer to the same place (Kolimon and Wetangterah 2012).

[107] Interview with Marthen Heke Medo (30.06.2012).

Lobo's second thoughts when he decided to marry Dima Riwu (Duggan 2001: 130, Fig. 69; Plate 17).[108]

Figure 39: Alliances during the Jami Lobo–Tèro Weo war

The war, in the early years of the 18th century, took place between Jami Lobo, from the Nataga clan, Najohina lineage and Seba's fettor (1710–40), and Tèro Weo, the raja of Menia.

As per Figure 34, alliances with the loser are not remembered; hence, there are no details for Tèro Weo.

Allies of Jami Lobo	Clans
Doko Bara Kaba	Kelara (Raijua)
Ara Jana	Napupenu (Mesara)
Bire Kole	Aelungi (Mesara) He received land in today's Raenalulu village.
Riwu Mata alias Ama Robo Riwu	Nahoro (Seba)
Ama Jata Luhi	Napuru (Dimu)

From Dima Riwu's first marriage to Tèro Weo, their daughter Mamo Tèro started a new line. However, the line does not carry a proper name other than *keturunan* Mamo Tèro (descendant of Mamo Tèro), also with a humourous ikat pattern—*kaki bèngku* (feet on a bench), reminiscent of a couple sitting in a love seat (Duggan 2013: 72). Both lineages have small buildings for worshipping Mamo Tèro and Dima Riwu, respectively. These are the youngest female lineages (*wini*) created in Savu. Most if not all of the *wini* began during Portuguese and early VOC times. This is similar to the numerous male lineages (*kerogo*).

It is not just the oral traditions and the position of lineages that mark these changes. This dramatic shift in land ownership indirectly appears in VOC materials. In 1718, the *opperhoofd* in Kupang heard about a dispute in Savu that required attention:

> On the Island of Savu things are in such rest and peace as we found at our visit last year and left it at our departure, as far as the under-regent Danka, the burgher Jan Schroev and the upper steersman Jacob Stovin [manuscript illegible] have told me; except that Jami, the second regent of Seba, has taken some agricultural land or paddy-fields from Tagi, chief of the *negeri* Menia (the same who concluded peace on 1 July last year), for

---

[108] Migi Jami is the maternal grandmother of Lomi Jara, alias Ama Doko Lomi, raja of Seba 1769–78 mentioned earlier on. See Figure 36.

Figure 40: Menia rulers in Portuguese and VOC times; genealogies of *wini* Migi and Mamo Tèro

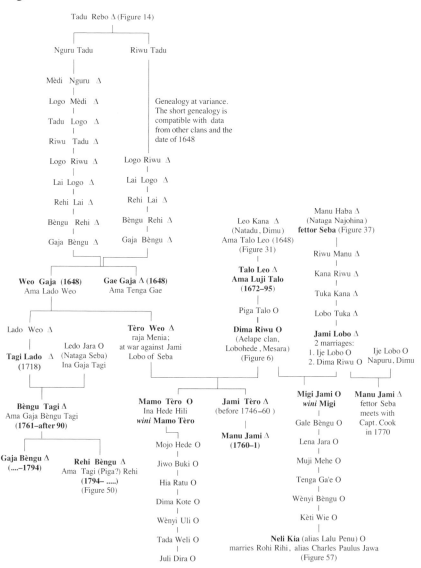

what reason I do not know. He had added that he would not return them unless Tagi took it back from him with the help of weapons. Nay, apart from this, when he [Tagi] had gone down to the seashore to welcome the arriving regent of Deuw [Ndao?], the aforementioned Jami attacked him with his men in order to force him to fight. However, Tagi was not intent to do that and could not be brought to fight. The aforementioned Jami said: "You may be assured that you will never again possess your agricultural lands unless you force me with your weapons". From this it sufficiently appears that this arrogant and outrageous nation is always keen to rob, the one from the other (although it happens in an unjustified way), and know warfare as their game. However I hope that, if in good health, I shall settle it when I come over there, and establish them again as friends and allies of the Company and unite them with Your Excellency.[109]

A dagh-register then relates a Dutch visit to Savu later in 1718, the same year. On 19 June, the *opperhoofd* asked Jami of Seba why he had deprived the under-regent Tagi from Menia of paddy-fields or agricultural land with a weapon in hand, while uttering threats that Tagi was never again to possess them unless he took to arms. Jami replied that he had never had such an intention, let alone to carry it out. Three days later the Dutch resident raised the issue in a grand meeting with the various rulers on the island. He summoned and questioned Tagi as to why he had complained before the burghers from Kupang last year. He replied, in a changed voice, that the Dutch Captain Bladt had handed over these fields to him, of which Jami had taken possession. This was not at all true from what the *opperhoofd* could apprehend. All the rajas confirmed that Jami had taken these lands in a war many years ago. When they had concluded peace, he had kept them as his own. Tagi could not demonstrate the slightest right of ownership. The *opperhoofd* said that in the future Tagi should beware of launching unjustified pretensions and complaints.[110]

The Tagi of the text is Tagi Lado, a nephew of Ama Mamo Tèro. He is not specifically mentioned as raja in the pedigrees, but the dagh-register confirms Jami Lobo's land grab at an unspecified time. It seems that the Kekoro clan lost any right to claim the land when they lost the war.

The succession later went to the other main branch of the Kekoro, to Jami Tèro, son of Ama Mamo Tèro. There is no recorded narrative to explain whether this was by usurpation or regular transfer. However, it is clear that Jami Tèro's status was different to that of his predecessor. After 1746, the VOC reports unexpectedly begin referring to tiny Menia as one of the officially recognised domains which in turn suggests a weakening of Seba's claim to overlordship.

---

[109] VOC 1910 (1718), missive, dated 30 May 1718.

[110] VOC 1910 (1718), dagh-register, dated 19–22 June 1718.

Menia was still not important enough to sign the Paravicini contract in 1756, as Hili Haba of Dimu undersigned for "his regents of Mesara and Menia".[111] The remaining VOC rajas are little more than names for archival readers several hundred years later. Jami Tèro died in 1760 and was briefly survived by his only son Manu Jami, after whose demise in 1761 the junior line took over power again. Tagi Lado's son Ama Gaja Bèngu (r. 1761–90) and his two sons Gaja Bèngu (r. 1790–94) and Ama Piga Rehi (r. 1794–?) are not known to have been in trouble with either of their neighbours or the Dutch. It might be important here that Ama Gaja Bèngu's mother was a Seba princess.

The Dutch sources focus mainly on political matters; and yet they are vague about any change of borders. The VOC obviously considered border demarcation a Savunese internal affair. Oral tradition is valuable to map the altercations; new attributions of land often allowed the creation of a new lineage and, therefore, a new settlement on recently acquired land. Similarly, the Dutch sources have little to report on developments in regard to traditional religion. In this regard, Menia is notable for the various branches of the Kekoro clan and changes in priestly tasks.[112]

Seba and Menia used to share responsibilities in the ceremonial cycle of Seba. According to tradition, this was instigated after ancient settlers (the Jola people) had left the island and the Kekoro-Nadida clan replaced them in the ritual. Seba must hold a cycle of 27 years of rituals (3 x 3 x 3 years) followed by a cycle of 21 years (7 x 3 years) under the leadership of Deo Mengèru from the Kekoro-Nadida. However, the cycle changed under Deo Mengèru's leadership as the Deo Rai of Namata, Lele Ropa alias Ama Tenga Lele, reduced its length from 21 to 9 years (3 x 3 years), so Seba's total cycle was 36 instead of 48 years. The reason for the alteration is unclear, but the result was that Menia had less responsibility in rituals shared with Seba—it meant Menia had less ritual power and fewer links to worshipping ancestors. This occurred despite the fact that Menia had an independent council of priests (*Mone Ama*), which eventually became obsolete after all the potential priests converted to a world religion in the late 20th century.

There is a second significant element. Some 12 to 13 generations ago Deo Mengèru of Kekoro-Nadida failed to perform the ceremonies. The Kekoro Lokoae clan, which has held the position of Deo Mengèru to the present, therefore took over the task. It is not clear if this happened at the same time as the reduction of the Seba ceremonial cycle.

---

[111] VOC 2941 (1756), f. 602–12.

[112] The following detail is based on two sources: interviews with Ama Bawa Iri, Namata clan, Seba (2004) and the priest Deo Mengèru (Ha'e Kale alias Ama Tali Ha'e), Kekoro Lokoae clan, Menia (30.04.2008). See Duggan (2008: 95–9).

A third event is related to the rivalry between Jami Lobo and Tèro Weo. Deo Mengèru of Kekoro Lokoae and his party fled to Dimu and stayed at Èilobololo (today's village of Èimadakc) for a few years. Consequently, Deo Mengèru could not perform rituals at the prescribed sacred stones; a drought occurred which, of course, people attributed to the lack of rituals. Finally, Deo Rai of Namata Seba went to Èilobololo and begged Deo Mengèru to come back and perform the rituals. Deo Mengèru accepted under the condition that he could have his homeland (Kolorato) back as well as a number of rice fields.

Kekoro people do not link their ancestors' move to the well-irrigated lowland with Jami Lobo defeating Tèro Weo. Doko Bara Kaba of the Kelara clan, an ally of Jami Lobo in the narrative, is attributed a role in the Kekoro people's move towards the present Menia territory. A buffalo ran loose in the Kekoro paddy fields and destroyed a lot of the harvest. The Kekoro people caught the animal, killed it and consumed its meat. However, people fell sick and many died, prompting the decision to leave their original settlement and move downhill near the sea. Having arrived there, they built new settlements called Wawarae and Didarae. Today, the lowland of Menia enjoys abundant water and people cultivate the paddy fields all year round. The Kekoro explain that when they moved to the lowland, they relocated the source of water at the same time. It is likely that the water potential in the lowland was untapped until the Kekoro moved there. With this move, the clan gained economically, compensating for the religio-political losses.

Another element sees a measure of restitution in status for the weakened Menia with regards dominant Seba. Each domain in Savu and Raijua is represented by a number for conducting rituals based on the lunar calendar. Seba claims to have the highest number, nine. However, when attending rituals in Menia it becomes obvious that their ritual calendar is calculated on the number ten, thus the highest number in Savu. Ten is not a ritual number normally used by ancient societies; more usual is to use the numbers seven, eight or nine for calculating the number of offerings and the days of rituals. Interviews with the priests of Seba showed that they were not aware of this 'anomaly'. It is very likely that the number ten for Menia's rituals was chosen after the move to the lowland.

These remarkable events in Menia's history are hard to put in chronological order; however, they are evidence of Menia's weak position compared to Seba and show how limited it was in response to Seba's growing political power. A ritual task helped in part to regain lost territory. The memorised genealogies situate the first two events in late Portuguese times and point to the first decades of the 18th century for the last two.

Mesara

Both Mesara and Liae have a secondary role in relation to Dimu and Seba. Although they were never able to act as major players in the fight for power, they remained autonomous domains until the early 20th century. Mesara's history mentions at least three different ruling clans, a further indication that the Savunese domains were not primarily dynastic but rested on a system of official political and ritual functions and clan alliances. Mesara, consisting of the western-most part of Savu, was drawn into the early Portuguese system like the other domains and appointed a raja from the Nahipa clan called Lod'o Ga Hebi. The Nahipa were not long in power but surrendered their prerogatives to two other clans. The ritual power through Deo Rai went to *udu* Nabèlu while the political raja title was appropriated by *udu* Napupudi. Counting the number of generations to datable figures suggests that this took place in the 16th century. The Napupudi line provided some Portuguese-affiliated rajas, namely Naha Lulu, Lodo Leo, Lai Lomi and Rohi Lulu alias Ama Reba Rohi. Although unmentioned in the VOC sources, Ama Reba Rohi must have ruled in the mid-17th century as tradition specifies that he was the leader of Mesara when the company's ships appeared off Savu's shores.

There follows an anecdote that explains why the raja dignity went from Napupudi to a third clan, the Napatitu. When Dutch representatives appeared in Mesara, Ama Reba Rohi served them a meal of dog's meat, much to the dislike of the visitors. His cousin Ria Lado, more aware of European tastes, then invited the VOC officials to a meal of forest pig. Their culinary satisfaction led them to dismiss Ama Reba Rohi and appoint Ria Lado's son Jami Riwu as the new raja. His clan *udu* Napatitu then governed almost uninterruptedly until 1914. This is very similar story to the previously related accession of Hili Haba in Dimu and, as discussed, it must not be regarded as anything more than an archetypical trickster tale that can be applied to different circumstances.

Another important Mesara figure is Ama Mare Bawa (Bawa Ae) from *udu* Napupenu, who is not mentioned in VOC records. He probably lived in the late 17th and early 18th centuries, and his name appears in a number of narratives. For instance, he plays a role in the story of a woman called Mahi Dole who has links to Sumba. The young Mahi Dole was married in Raebodo (in Seba) but was subsequently expelled from Savu after being accused of black magic. She was put out to sea in a drum made from buffalo hide. The elements eventually carried the drum to the shores of Sumba. The son of the Kadumbu raja found her on the beach and, as happens in folktales, she was beautiful and the prince fell in love with her. Out of the ensuing marriage at least one daughter was born—Wènyi Duku who married in Raijua and became Ina Rade Jadi. After

Figure 41: Rulers of Mesara in Portuguese times

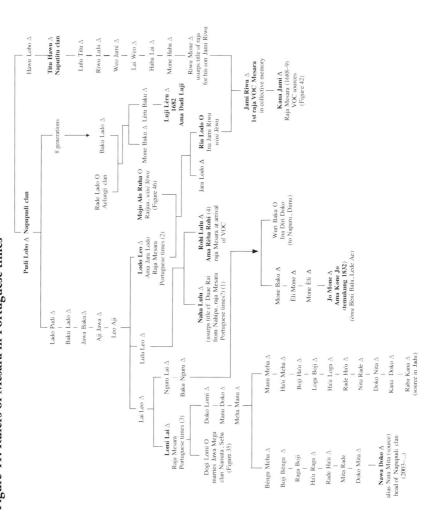

Figure 42: Rulers of Mesara in VOC times

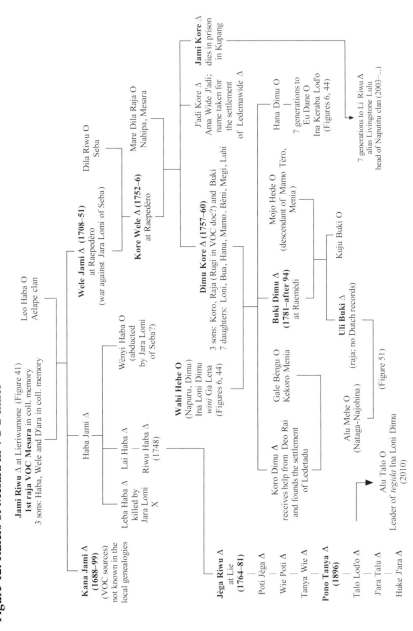

Figure 43: Domogenies of Upper Mesara

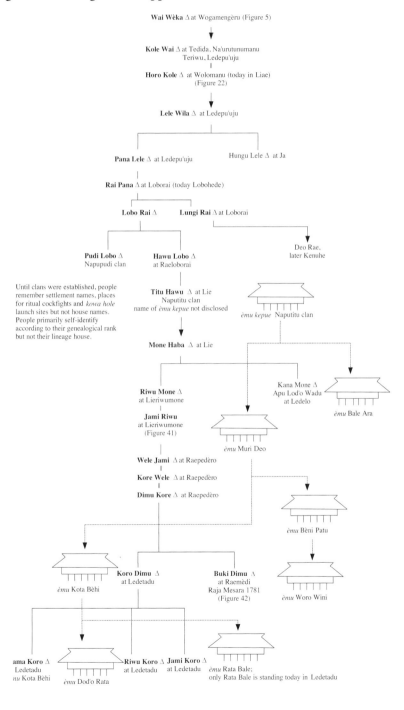

Wai Wèka Δ at Wogamengèru (Figure 5)

Kole Wai Δ at Tedida, Na'urutunumanu
Teriwu, Ledepu'uju

Horo Kole Δ at Wolomanu (today in Liae)
(Figure 22)

Lele Wila Δ at Ledepu'uju

Pana Lele Δ at Ledepu'uju

Hungu Lele Δ at Ja

Rai Pana Δ at Loborai (today Lobohede)

Lobo Rai Δ   **Lungi Rai** Δ at Loborai

Deo Rae,
later Kenuhe

Pudi Lobo Δ
Napupudi clan

Hawu Lobo Δ
at Raeloborai

Until clans were established, people
remember settlement names, places
for ritual cockfights and *kowa hole*
launch sites but not house names.
People primarily self-identify
according to their genealogical rank
but not their lineage house.

Titu Hawu Δ at Lie
Naputitu clan
name of *èmu kepue* not disclosed

èmu kepue Naputitu clan

Mone Haba Δ at Lie

Riwu Mone Δ
at Lieriwumone

Kana Mone Δ
Apu Lod'o Wadu
at Ledelo

èmu Bale Ara

Jami Riwu
at Lieriwumone
(Figure 41)

èmu Muri Deo

Wele Jami Δ at Raepedèro

Kore Wele Δ at Raepedèro

Dimu Kore Δ at Raepedèro

èmu Bèni Patu

èmu Kota Bèhi

Koro Dimu Δ
at Ledetadu

Buki Dimu Δ
at Raemèdi
Raja Mesara 1781
(Figure 42)

èmu Woro Wini

ama Koro Δ
Ledetadu
nu Kota Bèhi

èmu Dod'o Rata

Riwu Koro Δ
at Ledetadu

Jami Koro Δ
at Ledetadu

èmu Rata Bale;
only Rata Bale is standing today in Ledetadu

Wěnyi Duku's death, her daughter Rade Jadi and son Baki Jadi left for Mesara with their maternal uncle (*makemone*). However, the uncle drowned in the narrow but notoriously rough Raijua Strait and the children became stranded on the shore of Mesara. Two hunters called Ama Mare Bawa and Ama Dadi Luji helped the children. Ama Mare Bawa is found in collective memory among the allies of Wele Jami, thus around 1700. Of the rescued children, the boy Baki Jadi lived on a piece of land—'Èilobo, Èimada' in the present village of Matei— that Ama Mare Bawa received in Dimu after helping the Dimunese in warfare against Seba. Furthermore, Ama Mare Bawa provided assistance to a certain Ama Piga Kaja who had been expelled from Sumba and came to Dimu where the hunter had become raja. Later, a descendant of the boy Baki Jadi became the fettor of Dimu.[113]

So far no trace of the first VOC raja, Jami Riwu, has surfaced in archival sources which tell of some dramatic incidents involving the domain. As related in chapter 5, in 1672 joint Dimu and VOC forces made Mesara their object of chastisement and the domain was involved in a general internal upsurge of warfare ten years later. The first "uppermost regent of Mesara" who appears by name in the colonial archive is Ama Weo in 1682.[114] The pedigrees show that he belonged to the Aelungi, a related but distinct clan. A few years later Kana Jami is documented as raja in the years 1688 to 1699. He was the son of Jami Riwu, meaning that the *udu* Napatitu came to the fore again, for unexplained reasons. The Dutch notes about Mesara in the late 17th century are mostly connected to the disturbed state on the island in these years. Mesara was periodically at war with the others princedoms; however, conflict mostly occurred with Seba, which managed to defeat and occupy Mesara between 1698 and 1700.[115] Kana Jami disappears about this time. As discussed earlier, tradition reserves a heroic role for his resourceful brother Wele Jami who managed, after many adventures, to kill the Seba ruler in a duel with blowpipes. The detail is interesting because blowpipes were not used in later Savunese history; as in Timor, they disappeared with the dissemination of firearms.

VOC sources have yet to confirm that Wele Jami killed his opponent, but Mesara indeed appears in the documents as autonomous again by 1704. At that time, the people from Mesara, who Seba had captured, were set free and allowed to resume residence in their old lands.[116] In 1708 the records mention Wele Jami

---

[113]   However, the full genealogical details for this could not be obtained in Dimu.

[114]   VOC 1375 (1682), dagh-register, dated 7 June 1682. "Ampheo" in the Dutch spelling.

[115]   Generale Missiven VI: 122–3.

[116]   VOC 1691 (1704), f. 25.

as a company vassal. His reign lasted until 1751 by which time he must have been very old, according to contemporary standards. The colonial archives have little information about his direct descendants Kore Wele (r. 1752–56), Dimu Kore (r. 1756–60) and Rugi Dimu (r. 1760–64). Dimu Kore was not in Kupang when the respective parties agreed on the Paravicini contract and Hili Haba of Dimu undersigned in his name. His brother and regent Jami Kore interfered in the internal troubles afflicting Dimu in 1758, and therefore evoked the company's displeasure. The VOC eventually arrested Jami Kore and imprisoned him in Kupang while the fettor Jèga Riwu took care of affairs.[117] The raja died in prison in 1760 and his young son Rugi Dimu, who assumed the position, disappeared without a trace in the rough waves of the Savu Sea when sailing home from Kupang in 1764.[118] Jèga Riwu governed Mesara in the absence of an adult heir but also possibly because there was dissent in the raja line. In 1781, when he was old and blind, the original line regained the dignity in the person of Buki Dimu (r. 1781 to after 1794).[119]

Collective memory in Mesara is rich and compensates for the scant VOC records. Interestingly, Wahi Hehe, married to Dimu Kore (d. 1760), made a lasting impression on her posterity and became the object of their ritual worship in Mesara. Wahi Hehe (a descendant of Ga Lena) came from Dimu. After the marriage negotiations, the bride rode on horseback from her parents' house in Kujiratu to Mesara. During the progress, a group of people from Tanajawa—who might have been drunk as they were returning from a funeral—harassed the bride's party. Wahi Hehe (who became Ina Loni Dimu) received a piece of land in Tanajawa as a compensatory gift, which has ever since been transmitted from mother to daughter to the present day. Wahi Hehe also created the pattern *wue jara* (carried on horse back) for female sarongs as a reminder of the aggression. It has been part of the heirloom kept in her *tegida* (the ancestress house in the female line) in Ledetadu and her descendants have the exclusive right to this pattern.[120]

There were three sons and six daughters from Wahi Hehe's marriage to Raja Dimu Kore. When a quarrel flared within the ruling family, her son Koro Dimu fled and received help from Bèngu Ratu of the Aelungi clan, who took him to safety at the border to Teriwu (Tanikoro) where he stayed for a while. The highest

---

[117] VOC 2291 (1760); VOC 8353 (1759), f. 18–9.

[118] VOC 8358 (1764), f. 66.

[119] VOC 3598 (1781).

[120] Interview with Ina Keraba Lod'o (1999/2000). See Figure 44 for the genealogy of *wini* Ga and how it is related to a number of textiles created by several ancestresses of the group throughout time.

Figure 44: Textilogenies or genealogies of *wini* Ga Lena textiles

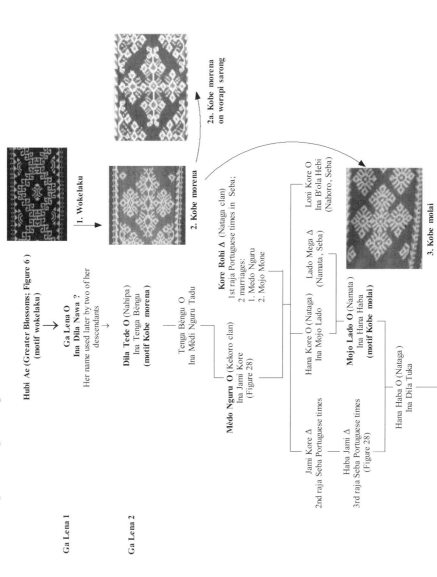

Ga Lena 1

Hubi Ae (Greater Blossoms; Figure 6)
(motif wokelaku)

Ga Lena O
Ina Dila Nawa ?
Her name used later by two of her
descendants →

1. Wokelaku →

Ga Lena 2

Dila Tede O (Nahipa)
Ina Tenga Bèngu
(motif Kobe morena)

2. Kobe morena →

2a. Kobe morena
on worapi sarong

Tenga Bèngu O
Ina Mèdi Nguru Tadu

Mèdo Nguru O (Kekoro clan)
Ina Jami Kore
(Figure 28)

Kore Rohi Δ (Nataga clan)
1st raja Portuguese times in Seba;
2 marriages:
1. Mèdo Nguru
2. Mojo Mone

Jami Kore Δ
2nd raja Seba Portuguese times

Haba Jami Δ
3rd raja Seba Portuguese times
(Figure 28)

Hana Kore O (Nataga)
Ina Mojo Lado

Lado Mega Δ
(Namata, Seba)

Mojo Lado O (Namata)
Ina Hana Haba
(motif Kobe molai)

Loni Kore O
Ina B'ola Hebi
(Nahoro, Seba)

3. Kobe molai

Hana Haba O (Nataga)
Ina Dila Tuka

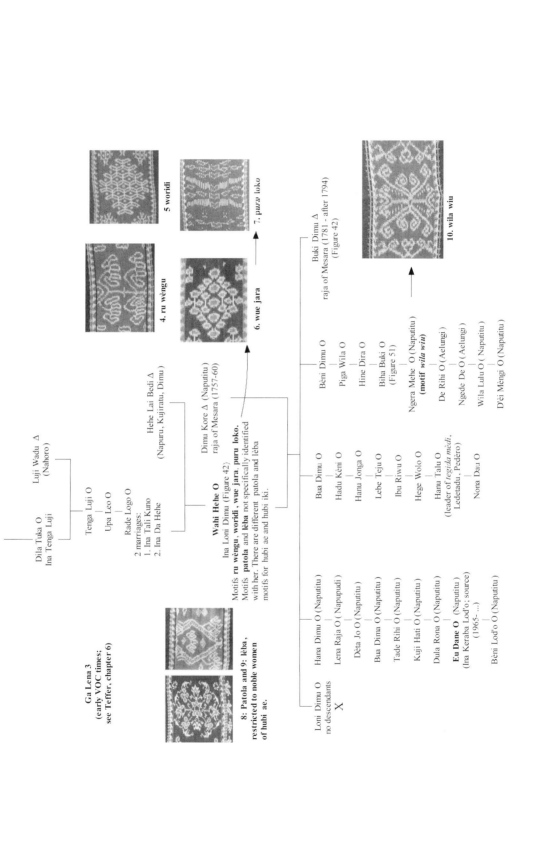

Ga Lena 3
(early VOC times;
see Teffer, chapter 6)

5 woridi

4. ru wèngu

7. puru loko

6. wue jara

10. wila wiu

Luji Wadu △
(Nahoro)

Dila Tuka O
Ina Tenga Luji

Tenga Luji O

Upa Leo O

Rade Logo O

Hehe Lai Bedi △
(Napuru, Kujiratu, Dimu)

2 marriages:
1. Ina Tali Kuno
2. Ina Da Hehe

Dimu Kore △ (Naputitu)
raja of Mesara (1757-60)

Wahi Hehe O
Ina Loni Dimu (Figure 42)

Motifs ru wèngu, woridi, wue jara, puru loko.
Motifs patola and lèba not specifically identified
with her. There are different patola and lèba
motifs for hubi ae and hubi iki.

Buki Dimu △
raja of Mesara (1781 - after 1794)
(Figure 42)

Bèni Dimu O

Piga Wila O

Hine Dira O

Biha Buki O
(Figure 51)

Ngera Mehe O (Naputitu)
(motif wila wiu)

De Rihi O (Aelungi)

Ngede De O (Aelungi)

Wila Lulu O (Naputitu)

D'èi Mèngi O (Naputitu)

Bua Dimu O

Hadu Kèni O

Hanu Jonga O

Lebe Teju O

Ibu Riwu O

Hege Wolo O

Hanu Talu O
(leader of *fegida mèdi*,
Ledetadu, Pedèro)

Nona Dau O

8: Patola and 9: lèba,
restricted to noble women
of hubi ae.

Loni Dimu O
no descendants
X

Hana Dimu O (Naputitu)

Lena Raja O (Napupudi)

Dèta Jo O (Naputitu)

Bua Dima O (Naputitu)

Tade Rihi O (Naputitu)

Kuji Hati O (Naputitu)

Dula Rona O (Naputitu)

Eu Dane O (Naputitu)
(Ina Keraba Lod'o; source)
(1965- ....)

Bèni Lod'o O (Naputitu)

priest of Mesara, the Deo Rai held by Bire Junga, came to Koro Dimu's rescue and offered him land in Ledetadu, thus placing Koro Dimu directly under his protection. As a reminder of the event, the Ledetadu people received the right of precedence over other villages in the annual ritual *kowa hole*; this functions as a mnemonic tag in collective memory. The priest's support for Koro Dimu points to an enmity between the council of priests and the raja, and the reason might be over a religious matter. The name of his brother Buki Dimu—who became the raja of Mesara in 1781—evokes a conversion to Christianity, although the VOC records do not mention this. *Buki* refers to a book and literacy, the book being the Bible. The fact that Koro Dimu received help from the followers of the traditional religion reveals that the priests discerned a change of affiliation in the VOC rajas, which impinged on their power.

The priest Bire Junga also arranged Koro Dimu's marriage with Gale Bèngu of Menia who became Ina Lena Koro. She did not want to use the well in Ledetadu because there had been too many deaths in the village. The precise reason is not clear; perhaps she thought the well water was contaminated. The villagers dug a new well for her outside the village. This detail is a reminder of the violent clashes that took place in Ledetadu and Raepedèro, and cost many lives. Ina Lena Koro brought rice grains and the knowledge of wet-rice cultivation to Mesara.[121] This is plausible as Menia is well known for its wet-rice fields. Koro Dimu had three sons and each of them built a named house (*èmu*) in Ledetadu: Pama Koro (*èmu* Kota Bèhi); Jami Koro (*èmu* Rata Bale); Riwu Koro (*èmu* Dod'o Rata). However, only Rata Bale is standing today (Figure 43).

Dimu Kore was possibly the last raja to reside at Raepedèro. There was a new residence in nearby Raemèdi for his son and indirect successor Buki Dimu. Later, the rajas moved to Ledemawide. Except for a short time when Raja Ama Tenga Doko (Figure 51) moved to Ligu nearby the sea, the Mesara rajas resided there until the end of colonial times. Wila Buki, fettor at national independence, resided there too. At the site there is still an old banyan tree and a primary school, as well as the graves of the rulers from the 19th and 20th centuries.

Liae

Like Mesara, Liae had a secondary role in Savu's political landscape. Situated in the southern part of the island, Liae did not have a harbour of consequence and so European ships bypassed the domain, heading for Dimu or Seba. Nevertheless, it was not inconsequential. After the fall of the old Teriwu domain (at a time unspecified)—"the good land that rules over Savu"—two of the three

---

[121]   Interview with Ina Keraba Lod'o (17.11.2002).

clans deriving from Teriwu settled in Liae. Later, oral data indicates that the *udu* Kolorae was important in the land for a long time. Later, however, as there was a time when they were unable to perform the right rituals, they approached a newly arrived clan called Nanawa and handed over land to them. The Nanawa line carried out the functions of Apu Lod'o while their distant relatives, the *udu* Gopo, secured the role of Deo Rai. Tradition suggests that the division was based on rivalry rather than any ritual dialectic.

Udu Nanawa also provided Liae with its first raja—Nida Dahi—under Portuguese influence. If the pedigrees are reliable, he ruled around 1600, three generations before the late 17th century, so Liae appointed a raja later than Dimu, Seba and Mesara. Liae's marginal location could have made it slower to follow the other domains in forging close European contacts, but there might also have been other raja clans lost in collective memory. One narrative features Nida Dahi in a far from flattering context which points to an early connnection with Sumba. The Sumbanese accused him of having stolen golden objects from one of their raja's graves. Some time later a Sumbanese force landed at Kolowègu in Liae to take revenge; however, the attack was unsuccessful.

It is not entirely clear who Nida Dahi's successors were. However, the last one was a certain Ama Nguru Kale, a well-attested figure; the VOC records show he was a temukung (genealogical village chief) under the Liae regents in 1682 when a new clan had appropriated the raja title.[122] This circumstance casts an interesting light over the relation between oral and archival data. Tradition has it that *udu* Nanawa lost the raja position as well as Apu Lod'o to the new line, *udu* Napujara. Ama Nguru Kale was an in-law of the new clan, so the transition from one clan to another does not seem to have been very dramatic. The last princely representative of the old family continued as a prominent temukung—Ama Nguru Kale is actually the only temukung mentioned in 1682—and he negotiated with the Dutch together with the new rulers Ama Jami and Riwu Manu. Nanawa was considered older than Napujara and therefore had a formal pre-eminent position, continuing to enjoy some authority. Perhaps more to the point is the *makemone-nakebèni* (uncle-nephew) relationship between Ama Nguru Kale and his nephew Jami Riwu.[123]

The contemporary Apu Lod'o, Lado Lod'o, lost his priest position to Napujara. Of interest is that the event is attributed to female agency—his sister Hota Lod'o was responsible for the transfer. Lado Lod'o went to Raijua and

---

[122] VOC 1375 (1682), dagh-register, dated 7 June 1682. The Dutch spelt the name "Ama Guru Cale".

[123] *Makemone* is the maternal uncle (MB or mother's brother) while *nakebèni* refers to his sister's children (ZC).

Figure 45: Rulers of Liae since VOC times

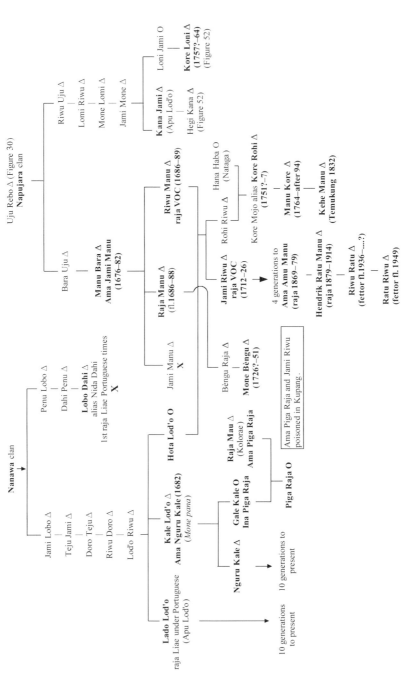

failed to return on time to perform an important ritual; according to other oral sources he failed to conduct a number of rituals. His sister Hota Lod'o felt ashamed of his negligent behaviour and gave the position of Apu Lod'o to her husband's clan, the Napujara.[124] As has been discussed, priest roles are hereditary positions in a lineage. The change of lineage is an exception and can only occur with grave reasons, often the result of quarrels and inter-clan warfare. However, as seen earlier with regards to war alliances, the genealogies of Nanawa and Napujara reveal a *makemone-nakebèni* relationship. Such a situation would be bewildering if encountered in a patriarchal society; however, in Savunese adat there is a particularly strong relationship between a brother and his sister's children. In this context, the transfer of the raja and Apu Lod'o positions makes sense if Ama Nguru Kale, as *makemone*, passed on the rights to his sister's son Jami Riwu, his *nakebèni*, and not to his brother-in-law Riwu Manu. A *makemone-nakebèni* connection is closer than a father-son relationship. Nevertheless, local memory depicts Riwu Manu as the first raja of VOC times. It is probably no longer possible to reconstruct what actually happened. Another narrative detailed further on questions the peaceful relationship between Nanawa and Napujara. Again, this might cast light on the workings of oral tradition; remembering a personal story might provide an alternative to deleting from social memory more complicated inter-clanic relationships, manipulation, disloyalty or even treachery.

The new Napujara clan had a less than auspicious start. After the demise of Ama Jami, the founder, some time in the 1680s, two of his sons began to quarrel violently, as amply attested by the colonial archive. The circumstances show that the VOC system was far from secured and that there were other sources of authority in the eastern archipelago. After Makassar fell to the VOC alliance in 1667, many Muslim seafarers from South Sulawesi were unable or unwilling to live under the restricted conditions imposed by the Bungaya Treaty. The treaty severely curtailed the freedom to undertake long-distance voyages that many people depended on for their livelihood, so smaller and larger fleets roamed the East Indies outside the control of the VOC. They sometimes turned violently anti-VOC and gained influence in areas of the archipelago where Dutch power was weak (Andaya 1995). With little shipping of its own and few VOC visits, Savu was an island where the Makassarese-Buginese seafarers had little to fear. In 1686, four Makassarese ships landed at Liae and the seafarers tried to persuade the local elite to leave the VOC system. The brothers Raja Manu and Riwu Manu shared authority in the domain. Raja Manu had no intention of breaking off relations with the Dutch. However, his younger brother Riwu Manu agreed

---

[124] Interview with Agustinus Moi, Waduwèla (17.05.2006).

with the suggestion. It is unclear what he thought would replace the Dutch-led system, but the Makassarese machinations suited Riwu Manu's own ambitions for power. Thus, he managed to make himself the master of all Liae and drove Raja Manu into exile in Mesara and later Seba.[125]

In spite of his actions, collective memory shows Riwu Manu as the first Dutch-affiliated raja of Liae, presumably as he was the ancestor of most of the later rajas. Any Makassarese influence in the domain can only have been temporary, but for the next few decades there is hardly any information about Liae. A little more can be gleaned from oral sources: Riwu Manu fought an unsuccessful war with Seba, losing the mountain of Lede Pemulu so that Seba stretched far to the south. It was only from 1712 that a continuous sequence of dated rulers commences with Riwu Manu's son Jami Riwu (d. 1726).

In Liae, a narrative remembers Jami Riwu had a tragic death linked to his horse which had badly damaged crops in a rice field owned by Ama Piga Raja.[126] Shortly after, a Sumbanese called Ama Badi Manu visisted Ama Piga Raja. The frustrated Ama Piga Raja told him what had happened and asked his guest to kill Jami Riwu's horse, which the man did. Jami Riwu, enraged by the loss of his horse which at that time must have been a rarity, wanted to report the case to the Dutch authorities in Kupang; so Jami Riwu and Ama Piga Raja sailed to Kupang. As they were staying at the fortress, both died from a poisoned drink and were buried within its grounds. Later on a citrus tree grew on Jami Riwu's grave while a *gèdi* tree grew on the grave of Ama Piga Raja.[127] Jami Riwu appears in VOC documents until 1726, so his death must have happened that year. However, there are no traces of the incident in VOC documents, so local memory might have embellished part of the story.[128]

Succession throughout the 18th and much of the 19th centuries was irregular. The various rajas were not succeeded by their sons, although they are known both from pedigrees and VOC sources to have had offspring. Thus, after Jami Riwu was a distant relative called Mone Bèngu (r. 1726–51) and then a nephew Kore Rohi (r. 1751–57).[129] After him a member of the fettor lineage, Kore Loni (r. 1757–64), took over the position, followed by Kore Rohi's son

---

[125] VOC 8310 (1686–87), dagh-register, dated 2 March 1687.

[126] Raja Mau—alias Ama Piga Raja—of the Kolorae clan was the son-in-law of Ama Nguru Kale of 1682; he was also Jami Riwu's mother's brother (*makemone*).

[127] *Alstonia scholaris* or blackboard tree is a tall tropical evergreen.

[128] Interview with Jami Kaho (Ama J'ari) from Liae (17.06.2012). Perhaps two deaths by poisoning would also not reflect well on the VOC, hence not finding the detail in the reports!

[129] According to the genealogies, he was actually adopted into Liae—being the biological offspring of *udu* Nataga in Seba his initial name was Kore Hana.

Manu Kore (r. 1764 to after 1794). The pattern differs from that in the other domains where over all the rajas regularly succeeded each other and the anomaly might be due to a combination of factors. The VOC reports suggest that a few violent internal crises wrecked Liae during the 18th century and it was also occasionally involved in the political troubles of its neighbours.[130]

Raijua

Raijua, as a separate island, constitutes a domain that followed its own trajectory outside the control of the European powers. While the population is Savunese, they have certain markers that set them apart from the main island. Thus, the naturalist Salomon Müller noted in 1829 that Raijuans wore white textiles which were lighter and less coarse than the black or bluish Savunese cloth (Temminck 1839–44: 292). In spite of being only 36 square kilometres, Raijua appears on some of the early maps, even where Savu itself was omitted. The spelling 'Rendouw' that occurs in some VOC texts seems to go back to an early form of the name—Rai Ndua. VOC reports mention Raijua intermittently from the 1650s but not in a positive sense. The Dutch in Kupang perceived the small island to be a troublemaker of the first magnitude, as Willem Tange depicted in 1688:

> The Island of Savu which is somewhat distant is of the same character [as Rote], and its conflicts emanate from the Island of Raijua attached to the same land. They are by nature a people that is much more quarrelsome and robust, and want to join into the Noble Company enterprise. They frequently meddle into the conflicts of the Savu people, and light-heartedly choose sides against gifts.[131]

The Raijuans also had a long-lasting reputation of colluding with the Makassarese and other seafarers who operated across the vast waters of the eastern region out of the company's reach. This might have partly been a rationale for their reluctance to reach a permanent understanding with the VOC. Sometimes the regents of the small island would make overtures to the 'stranger-kings' in Kupang but, in the end, they tended to their own business.

As in the other five domains, there was a line of rajas in Raijua, but it had no roots in Portuguese times as far as the sources reveal. Unlike the other domains, it is not clear if the Portuguese influence actually reached Raijua.[132] The rajas moved from Ujudima to nearby Tahe Nate Mèngi (sweet, prosperous assembly);

---

[130] See Appendix V for the list of all known rajas and fettors in Savu.

[131] Report by Willem Tange, 1688, H 49u, KITLV Archive.

[132] The rajas have kept a Dutch flag in their Ujudima residence which is now in tatters.

Figure 46: Rulers of Raijua in VOC times

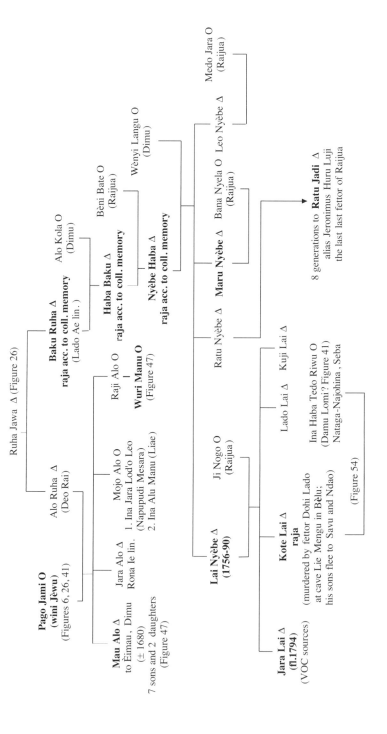

Figure 47: Mau Alo of Raijua and *wini* Jèwu

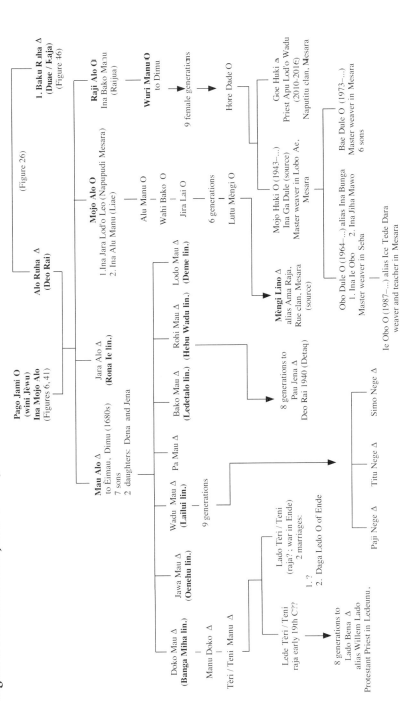

however in everyday language it is simply rendered Ternate. The pedigrees depict the raja Nadaibu clan as having descended from the same original clan as the other rajas, but it is only in Dutch times that it became more than an enumeration of names.

Baku Ruha is the first raja, at a time probably corresponding to the second half of the 17th century. He had ties to powerful Dimu through his Dimunese mother-in-law, but tradition has a few other reasons as to why he was chosen as Raijua's ruler. In one version he challenged his elder brother Alo Ruha to a swimming competition. The first competitor to swim to the company ship and touch the flag would become raja; Baku Ruha was the better swimmer and gained the dignity. The other version repeats the trickster tale known from Dimu and Mesara: Baku served a delicious meal of *babi ma'i besar* (large boar) to the white strangers, food which earned him their gratitude, and consequently they preferred him to his elder brother.[133] However, no VOC source confirms any contact with a Baku Ruha. His elder brother Alo Ruha was Deo Rai of Ketita and therefore might not have been suitable for the political task of raja. There is no specific story about Alo Ruha apart from the swimming contest, but his wife Pago Jami is a well known and respected figure among women of the female lineage *wini* Jèwu on both islands. She created a specific pattern which has since been part of her descendants' heirloom baskets (Duggan 2016: 19).

The VOC sources certainly mention Mau Alo, son of Alo Ruha. Traditions regarding Raijua relate that Mau Alo originally resided in Ketita. He was on bad terms with another chief in Raijua called Hebu Wadu who is called "raja" but is not found in the pedigrees.[134] There was conflict which Mau Alo lost; therefore, he moved to Sumba where he stayed for many years and assisted a ruler of Parede (Rindi) against his enemies. He eventually ventured to return to Raijua and received word that Hebu Wadu's anger had receded. This, however, turned out to be untrue. When Mau Alo was about to bring his perahu into a harbour in order to attend a funeral, Hebu Wadu arrived on the shore and shot an arrow in his direction. It missed Mau Alo but struck his niece Wuri Manu who was pregnant, though she was not killed. Mau Alo left Raijua at once and this time sailed to Dimu. Having arrived at the Liu river estuary, Wuri Manu gave birth to a child who was half blind due to the wound.[135]

---

[133] Interview with Luji Huke (Ma Medo) (09.04.2012).

[134] Interview with Hernimus Leo Riwu (23.04.2013). Hebu Wadu is the name of a lineage descended from Mau Alo's son, Rohi Mau. It is possible that Hebu Wadu died without having a son; therefore his name is remembered in the name of a lineage.

[135] Wuri Manu is his sister's daughter. Here again is the privileged relationship between a *makemone* and his *nakebèni*. She stayed in Rae Awu (Dimu) where she has descendants.

Raijuan as well as Dimunese oral tradition remembers Mau Alo for having helped the raja of Dimu to expel invaders led by a certain Rega Nawi. The exact identity of these invaders is unclear; according to one source the intruders came from the sea, but another said they were from Seba. For his warlike exploits Mau Alo received land from the raja. The place is now known as Èimau, a village next to Menia in the present subdistrict of Sabu Tengah. Mau Alo leaves a positive impression as an important warrior with no details about his demise.

It is instructive to compare these stories with the colonial archive. On 2 May 1680, Dutch records—the Kupang dagh-register—relate some particularities about Savu. Mao (Mau) had been the upper regent of Raijua; however, he had been put to death some months previously as he had mistreated a temukung in Dimu.[136] The laconic passage is both clarifying and confusing. It confirms Mau as a prominent chief from Raijua connected to Dimu. However, the oral stories do not depict him as raja (upper regent) and it is somewhat surprising that his violent end did not make an impression on the collective memory. The omission is all the more remarkable given that he is a recognised figure in Raijua; six of his seven sons were powerful enough to form new lineages.

The Sumbanese connection is also worth attention as other sources confirm Raijuan interference on that island in the late 17th century. This involvement centres on Bali Lai, who received a VOC flag on behalf of the entire Raijua domain. Local Raijuan tradition describes a person called Ama Bali as an early *duae* or leader, who lived 12 generations before the present. He was from the Rohaba clan from which people remember rajas were born in olden times.[137] Collective memory also remembers the rivalry between the Rohaba and Nadaibu clans. Once Toda Baku, the son of Raja Baku Ruha of Nadaibu, tried to seize the Rohaba's drums and gongs but failed to do so as the Rohaba people had already buried them, meaning they had renounced certain ritual rights (*tao leo*). This clan did not own agricultural land as seen in the Ina Ju Deo narrative (chapter 4). Of note is that the Rohaba clan holds a strategic position as its members live on both sides of the Raijua Strait and occupy Kolohaba hill which overlooks the strait and the main harbour, Namo. The Rohaba had similarities with the Kelara clan and they might have served as mercenaries in the region. It has its own council of priests with a ritual arena in Kolohaba where remnants of the houses of origin still exist; one of them is Ama Bali's house. Although Ama Bali is a teknonym that literally means 'father of Bali', a connection with Bali Lai of VOC records is not excluded.

---

[136] VOC 1358 (1679–80), dagh-register, dated 2 May 1680. Considering the number of lineages Mau Alo created for his sons, he must have been a powerful person.

[137] In Raijua, Rohaba is a marginal clan founded by Jèka Wai, a late arrival.

The VOC reports make clear that Bali Lai initiated an approach to the VOC via Dimu and even expressed his wish to see *opperhoofd* Moerman in person in Raijua. Firstly, he wanted the company to intervene in the internal disputes that plagued the small island. And secondly, he wanted to resolve conflict between the Savunese and Sumbanese after the recent massacre of second regent Leko of Melolo and most of his crew on the island. The intiative did lead to contact between *opperhoofd* Moerman and Bali, as a report the following year revealed.

Sumba was a politically fragmented island that was easy prey for foreign powers. The *opperhoofd* Willem Moerman headed an expedition in the fall of 1693 to achieve contracts for sandalwood and slave deliveries. He first went to Savu where he asked Fettor Luji Talo of Dimu to accompany him to Sumba with the local skipper Ambili. Bali arrived and told the Dutchman of his experiences: he said that two years previously Raja Mandi of Mangili (eastern Sumba) had appeared in Raijua telling Bali that he wanted to obtain a Dutch flag and initiate trade in sandalwood with the company. Bali offered to travel to Sumba to assist Moerman in implementing the arrangement. The Dutch official accepted in spite of the Sumbanese massacre in Raijua the previous year.[138] A few days later Moerman, Luji and Bali arrived in Melolo where Ambili had already landed in Luji's perahu. Luji and Bali went ashore and found Ambili who had spoken to Mandi of Mangili and Sama Taka of Melolo and had received positive signals. The timely absence of Portuguese-affiliated traders from Sikka and Larantuka in Flores, who traded with Sumba, assisted the Dutch-Savunese enterprise. According to Ambili, the Portuguese Christians did their best to discourage even the Savunese from keeping with the VOC. They asserted that they would be much better off under Portuguese suzerainty. Moerman commented that this Portuguese slandering could be countered if the VOC-minded Savunese and Raijuans increased travel to Sumba, and pointed to the fact that many Sumbanese were in-laws of his fellow visitors. He specifically mentioned one Raijuan in the expedition as being able to speak "Sumbanese" (more accurately one of several Sumbanese languages).[139]

The rest of the expedition was not entirely positive, however. A Sumbanese Catholic called Pascal Prego and a certain Larantuqueiro visited Moerman's ship at Kambera and related disturbing news that the Larantuqueiro leader António Hornay had officially appointed the Portuguese Francisco de Sousa as "governor of the lands in this place". Moerman, trying to maintain friendly intercourse, asked them if they had water, rice and firewood to sell. The two Catholics replied

---

[138] VOC 1553 (1693–94), dagh-register, dated 3 October 1693.

[139] VOC 1553 (1693–94), dagh-register, dated 5 October 1693, 6 October 1693.

that this was a cursed land where they could not obtain a handful of rice, while the inhabitants had a very bad and murderous character. Later it appeared that the two men had slandered the Dutch as well. They told Raja Kapita of Kambera that the Dutch were a harmful and useless people, though the raja did not quite seem to believe them. A few days later Luji and Bali arrived with Raja Mandi of Mangili, who bestowed a child of three or four years on Moerman, and declared his happiness to meet the company at last. However, he dared not sell sandalwood which he had to deliver to the Christians of Flores that year. The rajas of Melolo and Kambera also changed their minds under the influence of the persuasive powerful Catholics: the VOC's rivals stated that the company would surely implement oppressive methods a few years after they had gained a foothold in Sumba and enslave people. Moerman drew the conclusion that the time was not right to establish a VOC presence on the island. He returned to his vessel and withdrew from Kambera while Bali of Raijua remained there to travel on to Melolo and Mangili in Ambili's perahu.[140]

The circumstantial account seems to show that the enterprise was very much in the interests of Bali and the Raijuans, and that there had been a history of frequent communication and even intermarriage with the inhabitants of Sumba. If Bali could increase his influence by supporting the VOC's aims, it would presumably strengthen his position vis-à-vis the other Savunese domains. Nevertheless, things did not end well for Bali, as can be gleaned from a 1698 report:

> In accordance with You Excellency's orders, no action shall be taken to recover the five iron cannons and two anchors that are said to remain on Raijua. Nor shall there be a quick despatch to the island Sumba for the sandalwood that grows there. And although the sloop *Doradus* might be spared to make the trip from here, we consider, with Your Excellency's consent, that there is not much to commit there, considering that the regent Luji from the negeri Dimu, who lives on Savu, told us in last year that he, after his stay on Sumba (mentioned to Your Excellency in our letter of 5 June 1696) had not received the least news from there. And he would not dare to send his ship there any more, because of the wild islanders who murderously took the life of the Raijuan temukung Baly, who went there with Resident Moerman, afterwards [after the departure of Moerman]. And although the *nakhoda* [shipper] of the aforementioned Luji, called Ambily... assured that about 100 sandal trunks had been put in stock in the *negeri* Melolo (which the Sumbanese asserted that they did not want to deliver to the Portuguese subjects), one may assume that after such a long time, these people, seeing that the wares have not been

---

[140] VOC 1553 (1693–94), dagh-register, dated 6 October 1693, 9 October 1693, 11 October 1693.

picked up by us, would change their minds and make their trade with the
Portuguese subjects as before. For that reason, and as we understood from
the coming of a second sloop from Savu, that Raja Mandi of the *negeri*
Mangili (to whom Resident Moerman bestowed a Dutch flag on his visit
to Sumba) has passed away, we have not been able to speak with the
other regents of the island (due to the vicious practices of the Portuguese
underlings who were there then).[141]

One can only speculate about the sudden Sumbanese hostility towards the
Savunese visitors. After Bali's violent end, little more is said about Raijua for
a number of decades, except for an incident in 1702.[142] The report from 1692
indicates that internal disputes wracked the island and Bali wished to resolve
them by involving the VOC as a 'stranger-king'. Oral tradition asserts that
Upper and Lower Raijua were always at war in olden times. Finally, Raijuans
found a way to avoid the fighting: they transformed the antagonisms into ritual
cockfights, allocating 14 places for such ritual warfare. Otherwise, the oral
material only specifies the number of rajas. Baku Ruha's son Haba Baku ruled
for a time, succeeded first by Nyebe Haba and then Lai Nyebe. It was only
when the Paravicini mission tried to gather the rulers of Timor and the adjacent
islands under a unitary contract that VOC interest in Raijua resumed. While the
contract of 1756 does not mention Raijua, its absence induced the *opperhoofd* to
approach the little island. This was easier said than done; Raijua was inhabited
by "still uncivilised people" (perhaps implying that the Savunese were considered
civilised) and they were hindered from seeking contact with the company by
their "unfounded fear."[143]

In 1758, finally, the ice broke. Lai Nyebe, the brother of the Raijuan ruler,
accompanied the Savunese regents to Kupang. The *opperhoofd* received the prince
in friendship, bestowing a minor gift, and hoped that the raja himself would
soon appear.[144] He was not disappointed. The following year Kupang received a
visit from "the king with the name Leo Nyale from the second main *negeri* there,
called Anadenka" who swore an oath of loyalty and undersigned the Paravicini

---

[141] VOC 1609 (1698), missive, 9 May 1698.

[142] A perahu from Raijua with 18 crew members was stranded at Kupang in 1702. When
they had repaired their craft the crew went in the company of the VOC sloop *Doradus* towards
Savu but capsized in the Semau Strait and the crew went aboard the sloop. The *opperhoofd*
Van Alphen took them to Raijua whose main regents expressed their gratitude and accepted a
VOC flag (VOC 8313 [1702], f. 4–5). However, this gesture did not have lasting diplomatic
consequences.

[143] VOC 8350 (1757), f. 70–1.

[144] VOC 2933 (1758), f. 30–1.

contract.[145] All this complicates current understanding of Raijua's history. VOC records refer to Leo Nyale as raja of Raijua from 1759 to 1761 alongside Lai Nyebe, but their names suggest that they were not literally brothers; it is Lai Nyebe who collective memory describes as the raja.[146] At any rate, Lai Nyebe probably outlived his kinsman in Anadenka and is in the reports up to 1790.[147] Unfortunately, these persons are little more than names with no particular stories related to them. Lai Nyebe must have passed away in the early 1790s; in 1794 Jara Lai was ruling.[148] Oral tradition mentions other names as his successors, namely his brother Maru Nyebe and son Kote Lai. Kote Lai's story heralds the arrival of the post-VOC period in the early 19th century—his dramatic fate is discussed in the following chapter.

Tradition clearly points to far from peaceful connections with Flores as well as Sumba in the late 18th century. Four generations after Mau Alo, probably in the late VOC period, a Lado Tèni conducted a war in Ende. There he married Daga Ledo, presumably a slave, who he took back to Raijua. Lado Rohi, father of the later fettor Dohi Lado (fl. 1807), was involved in warfare in Sumba. There he fell so severely sick that his comrades could not take him home. His son built an enclosure in the forest and left him there to die. The group took several Sumbanese heirlooms back to Raijua.

Savu in the late VOC period

The VOC reports must be read in context, considering the aims and nature of the colonial archive. The point of the missives and dagh-registers was not to inform superiors about the fabric of society, but rather they were to monitor issues of governance and surveillance, and make annotations on trade and tributes. The sheer detail of the data sometimes allows an interesting glimpse of material conditions, hierarchical concepts and cultural values among the local populations of the East Indies, even revealing the voice of the subaltern. The book has sufficiently demonstrated that Savu's strong oral tradition goes back

[145] VOC 8353 (1759), f. 19. "Anadengka" is possibly Nadega which is the name of a clan, not of a settlement. It took place in today's village of Bolua.

[146] VOC 2965 (1759); VOC 2991 (1760); VOC 3024 (1761). Lai Nyebe certainly had a brother called Leo Nyebe, but the archival texts clearly have Nyale rather than Nyebe as the patronymic element.

[147] VOC 3135 (1765), report, dated 20 June 1765; the source states that, besides Lai Nyebe, there was a second regent of Raijua called Tailogai who is actually Tulu Gae (Figure 53).

[148] A document from that year also refers to a second regent (fettor) called Raja Tulu who had succeeded his deceased brother Lomi Tulu (Comité Oost-Indische Handel en Bezittingen, No. 102, 1794–95). See also Figure 53.

hundreds of years, and that the narratives and the colonial reports often elucidate each other. Nevertheless, an analysis of Savunese society suffers from the lack of a third viewpoint from external travellers. The Portuguese had little to say and other European nations were not welcome in these waters. However, there is a small body of texts from the late 18th century that gives the requisite third perspective on Savu. As mentioned earlier, there are the British accounts from the expedition of Captain James Cook in 1770 and an attentive but prejudiced relation by Jean-Baptiste Pelon from about 1778. The former stayed only for a few days in Savu while Pelon, being an engineer in VOC service, built his conclusions on reasonable experience in the area. However, the most information is preserved in the four British accounts: Captain Cook's journal, Joseph Bank's journal, Sydney Parkinson's journal and the lengthy published account by John Hawkesworth.

Pelon characterises Savu as a flat land without any considerable forested areas (Pelon 2002: 61). The statement ignores the fact that the interior is quite hilly but seems to confirm that any dense forest had disappeared by the early-modern period. The Hawkesworth account provides an impression not too dissimilar to that which greets the visitor today: a flat ground by the sea with many coconut trees and areca palms, "and beyond them the hills, which rose in a gentle and regular ascent, were richly clothed, quite to the summit, with plantations of the fan palm, forming an almost impenetrable grove" (Hawkesworth 1773: 681). The text enumerates the crops and fruits they saw or heard about during the brief stay: coconuts, tamarind, limes, oranges, mangos, maize, guinea corn, millet, callevances (a kind of pulse), watermelons and, occasionally, sugar cane. Other bounty considered more of a "luxury" was betel leaves, areca nuts, tobacco, cotton, indigo and some cinnamon. Pelon mentions rice and millet as the most prominent crops (Pelon 2002: 61).

As appears in later ethnographic descriptions, the palm harvest received much attention from visitors. Similar to Rote, an important means of livelihood for the Savunese was the sugar juice extracted from the lontar palm. Pelon, however, was under the impression that the juice did not have as great an importance as it did in Rote. As the British account states:

> The æsculent vegetables and fruits have been mentioned already, but the fan-palm requires more particular notice, for at certain times it is a succedaneum[149] for all other food both to man and beast. A kind of wine, called toddy, is procured from this tree, by cutting the buds which are to produce flowers, soon after their appearance, and tying under them small baskets, made of the leaves, which are so [closely woven] as to hold liquids

---

[149] Meaning 'a substitute'.

without leaking. The juice which trickles into these vessels, is collected by persons who climb the trees for that purpose, morning and evening, and is the common drink of every individual upon the island; yet a much greater quantity is drawn off than is consumed in this use, and of the surplus they make both a syrup and coarse sugar. The liquor is called *dua*, or *duac* [tuak], and both the syrup and sugar, *gula*. The syrup is prepared by boiling the liquor down in pots of earthen ware, till it is sufficiently inspissated; it is not unlike treacle in appearance, but is somewhat thicker, and has a much more agreeable taste: the sugar is of a reddish brown, perhaps the same with the Jugata sugar upon the continent of India, and it was more agreeable to our palates than any cane sugar, unrefined, that we had ever tasted. We were at first afraid that the syrup, of which some of our people eat very great quantities, would have brought on fluxes, but its aperient quality was so very slight that what effect it produced was rather salutary than hurtful. I have already observed, that it is given with the husks of rice to the hogs, and that they grow enormously fat without taking any other food: we were told also, that this syrup is used to fatten their dogs and their fowls, and that the inhabitants themselves have subsisted upon this alone for several months, when other crops have failed, and animal food has been scarce. The leaves of this tree are also put to various uses, they thatch houses, and make baskets, cups, umbrellas, and tobacco-pipes. The fruit is least esteemed, and as the blossoms are wounded for the tuac or toddy, there is not much of it: it is about as big as a large turnip, and covered, like the cocoa-nut, with a fibrous coat, under which are three kernels, that must be eaten before they are ripe, for afterwards they become so hard that they cannot be chewed; in their eatable state they taste not unlike a green cocoa-nut, and, like them, probably they yield a nutriment that is watry and unsubstantial (Hawkesworth 1773: 688).

As for animals, the British mention buffalos, sheep, goats, pigs, fowls, pigeons, horses, asses, dogs and cats. The buffalos were meagre (although this was probably as a result of visiting in the dry season) and had "not an ounce of fat in the whole carcass", but their meat had a good and juicy taste. The sheep, by contrast, did not suit the tastes of the Britons, being "the worst mutton we ever have eaten". The horses were small but good, and the locals rode them without saddle and with only a very simple bridle. The Britons discerned a clear culinary list of preferences among the Savunese: hogs were considered the most delicious over horses, buffalos and poultry. The Britons as well as Pelon write that they ate dogs with good appetite, but there were some ritual restrictions. Thus, the inhabitants of Liae were not to eat dog because their aristocracy descended from the female line of the Dimu rajas; anyone who consumed dog meat would become ill (Pelon 2002: 63). However, Pelon's remarks may be qualified by modern observations: the prohibitions on chicken and dog meat are mnemonic markers for lifelong ties between a married woman and her maternal uncle, and all male relatives who have received part of her bridewealth. This would not apply to all inhabitants of the domain.[150] Breaching the taboo was said to cause a skin disease locally known as *lawija*. The case that Pelon mentions apparently refers to the marriage of the contemporary Liae raja, Manu Kore, to a princess of the Dimu ruling family.

There is little reference in the European accounts to marine products as economic assets. In spite of their proximity to the sea, the Savunese were not primarily a fish-eating people at the time, and lower-ranking people mainly consumed fish. Like most people in the Timor-Flores area the islanders were not seafarers either. The VOC dagh-registers kept by visiting officials seem to confirm this by implying there was a scarcity of boats.

The British accounts describe the Savunese in great detail; such valuable information is rarely part of Dutch administrative reports. People tended to be under European middle size—the men were well-shaped and vigorous with individual facial characteristics. They would remove hair from their armpits and faces, although they sometimes wore short moustaches, and fastened their long lank hair on top of their heads. The accounts describe the women as short and squat with stereotyped countenances, and wore their hair bound in a club at the back of their heads. The British visitors found the style rather unbecoming.

A feature of modern Savunese culture that has received much attention is the weaving traditions. The British account shows that the skill was developed by this time. They noticed spindles, dye vats and back tension looms, and gins for separating the seeds from cotton are also mentioned. However, the latter have disappeared in Savu, although they are still used in Sumba and Flores. Men and women wore locally produced cotton textiles. Male attire consisted of two similarly sized pieces of cloth; one worn around the waist and the other covering the upper part of the body.[151] The material was the same for both sexes, but the women wore the waist-cloth differently, letting the lower edge hang down to the knees. The visitors obviously did not see Savunese women dressing up; otherwise they would have noticed that they wore only one long tubular cloth, tied under the armpits and folded back below the waist. Nowadays, women wear

---

[150] Duggan (2011b: 105–6). However, in Liae some clans have a prohibition on dog meat which is shared with a branch of the Amabi raja clan in West Timor. According to Liae social memory, the founder of the Amabi branch, Hari Juda, is of Savunese origin. He was once defeated and left for dead but was cured through the use of dog parts applied to his body. Since that time, his descendants have not been allowed to eat dog meat.

[151] Joseph Banks remarks that they wore "turbans of the finest material they can procure". Such a turban is depicted in a coloured gravure by Van Oorst (in Temminck 1839–44), but this tradition has vanished entirely and today men wear batik head-cloths. The foreign origin of the male head-dress can be traced in a narrative. See http://genevieveduggan.com/savu-ceremonial-textiles/head-cloths

their sarongs down to the ankles which are pulled up to the knees for certain household activities or if they have to walk some distance.

The first VOC report from 1648 noted that the clothes worn by the local leaders did not distinguish them from the rest of the population. And yet they knew about red imported cloth. More than a century later, important people wore fine linen, and Raja Ama Doko and the old Fettor Manu Jami wore nightgowns of coarse chintz. These imported textiles were probably gifts from the "Noble Company" as seen in the lists of presents in the VOC records. People were keen on adorning their body with girdles and strings of beads, chains, bracelets and rings, and the better off had ornaments made of gold. Tattooing was universal, with parallels to other island societies in the eastern archipelago and Oceania. The British accounts note that men had characters tattooed on their arms that represented their names, perhaps indicating their clans. However, this detail calls for reflection: normally, all the men in one area belong to the same clan, so why then should the name of their clan be written on their arms? Could it be that the Britons actually saw slaves tattooed with the name or mark of their owner? Women had "a square ornament of flourished lines" under their elbow, similar to patterns depicted on the sarongs of the female lineages (*wini*), undeniably a marker of group identification. Interestingly, in the modern era when the fashion for tattoos has developed worldwide, this tradition has ceased completely in Savu. Pelon adds that the islanders applied oils to their bodies, extracted from fragrant wood or nutmeg (2002: 64).

House construction followed a universal layout, although their size might vary between 20 and 400 feet, according to the status of the owner. They were always raised on posts which were about four feet high. The posts supported a floor of wood and on this floor was another set of poles. These poles supported a palm-thatched roof of sloping sides which met in a ridge at the top. Accounts describe the Savunese house as having three apartments—the centre of which was reserved for the women of the household. This is not quite compatible with modern observations which indicate two apartments, male and female; however, ritual houses may have an extra apartment in the female section. A Savunese household, in contrast to several other places in the archipelago, was monogamous; it was only acceptable for a man to marry one woman at a time, even for the elite. This particular detail did not fail to gain the attention of visiting Europeans who found the Savunese to be morally superior to neighbouring island societies. However, slaves were numerous among the well-to-do. Some might possess half a dozen, others up to 500 slaves. The Britons asserted that the price of a slave equalled that of a fat hog, which seems doubtful.

The British visitors admired the cleanliness of the people who seemed to be healthy and long-lived. During the few days they visited the island they saw nobody urinating or defecating and it was a mystery for them where this was done in the densely populated area. On the other hand, the visitors had little regard for the age-old custom of chewing betel nut, saying it was a hateful sight which made the teeth turn black and eventually fall out. The habit wore down the front teeth of men as young as 20 or 30, sometimes almost to the gums. Pelon documents the custom of filing the teeth, often found in Southeast Asian societies. This took place when the children were about ten to twelve years of age (Pelon 2002: 64). The way the islanders managed their lives in accordance with the scarce resources in the dry environment is also nicely illustrated by the British account of how they cooked food:

> The common method of dressing food here is by boiling, and as fire-wood is very scarce, and the inhabitants have no other fuel, they make use of a contrivance to save it that is not wholly unknown in Europe, but is seldom practised except in camps. They dig a hollow under ground, in a horizontal direction, like a rabbit burrow, about two yards long, and opening into a hole at each end, one of which is large and the other small: by the large hole the fire is put in, and the small one serves for a draught. The earth over this burrow is perforated by circular holes, which communicate with the cavity below; and in these holes are set earthen pots, generally about three to each fire, which are large in the middle, and taper towards the bottom, so that the fire acts upon a large part of their surface. Each of these pots generally contains about eight or ten gallons, and it is surprising to see with how small a quantity of fire they may be kept boiling; a palm leaf, or a dry stalk, thrust in now and then, is sufficient: in this manner they boil all their victuals, and make their syrup and sugar. It appears by Frazier's account of his Voyage to the South Sea, that the Peruvian Indians have a contrivance of the same kind, and perhaps it might be adopted with advantage by the poor people even of this country, where fuel is very dear (Hawkesworth 1773: 690).

As could perhaps be expected, early European visitors had little appreciation or understanding of Savunese ritual practices. What is today known as the Jingi Tiu religion was considered "an absurd kind of paganism" where every person chose the deity he wished to worship and even determined the way to perform worship. The result, according to the Britons, was that there were almost as many gods and worshipping practices as there were people on the island. Pelon, likewise, deemed the Savunese to be "extremely superstitious" people who had the custom of killing animals on all manner of occasions for ritual purposes (Pelon 2002: 62). Both the Britons and Pelon noted the existence of sacred stones in Seba. Pelon related that there was a particular stone to which the inhabitants of Seba turned when they wanted to pray about some matter, touching it and swearing oaths. It had the power to kill cheaters. On one occasion, an adulterer whose guilt could not be proven was led to the stone; when he touched it, it split into two and remained in that condition (Pelon 2002: 62).

The British account offers a more elaborate description of Seba's stones, stating that they lie on top of a hill (as they still do today) and that they were situated "in the principal town of Seba" (Photo 3, page 105).[152] If taken literally, this would mean that the main settlement at that time was not near the seashore as it is today, but rather in elevated Namata. Local tradition clearly indicates that the rajas stayed in the house Bèni Keka at Nadawawi on Namata Hill during the period in question. Bèni Keka had a venerable history; it had been used by the Nahipa clan some 250 years previously and stands no more than 50 meters from the large stones. Considering the contemporaneous insecurity of the eastern archipelago with slave raiders and other hostile foreigners, the location is logical. The Britons counted 13 ritual stones as well as some fragments. They marvelled at the locals being able to move the large and heavy stones to their present place. However, as they said:

> the world is full of memorials of human strength, in which the mechanical powers that have been since added by mathematical science, seem to be surpassed; and of such monuments there are not a few among the remains of barbarous antiquity in our own country, besides those upon Salisbury plain [that is, Stonehenge] (Hawkesworth 1773: 695).

While some aspects of Savunese life evoked admiration from the Europeans, there were also aspects that seemed to confirm Savunese irrationality and detachment from the norms of Western civilisation. Perhaps not surprisingly, the accounts are disparaging of ritual practices. As the British wrote with regard to the sacred stones:

> These stones not only record the reigns of successive princes, but serve for a purpose much more extraordinary, and probably altogether peculiar to this country. When a Raja dies, a general feast is proclaimed throughout his dominions, and all his subjects assemble round these stones; almost every living creature that can be caught is then killed, and the feast lasts for a less or greater number of weeks or months, as the kingdom happens to be more or less furnished with live stock at the time; the stones serve for tables. When this madness is over, a fast must necessarily ensue, and the whole kingdom is obliged to subsist upon syrup and water, if it happens in the dry season, when no vegetables can be procured, till a new stock of animals can be raised from the few that have escaped by chance, or been

---

[152] Curiously, there was no major settlement in Dimu in spite of its precedence in Savu. For that reason Seba may indeed be termed the principal settlement (but still a village rather than town).

preserved by policy from the general massacre, or can be procured from
the neighbouring kingdoms (Hawkesworth 1773: 695).

At the time of the Cook expedition, there were still fresh memories of Jara
Wadu's *tao leo* funeral the previous year. However, the idea about the significance
of the stones seems to be incorrect; at least it does not correspond to later
interpretation. A modern survey of Namata's ritual arena recorded the names
of the sacred stones (Figure 24). None of them was meant to "record the reigns
of successive princes". The stones are the responsibility of various priests of the
Namata and Nahupu clans, and have ritualistic purposes. None of the Namata
stones belong to the raja clan. *Udu* Nataga has its own stones at Nadawawi's
kepaka tree. When a stone is named after somebody it is because that person has
disappeared without leaving a trace. In this case the stone acts as a memorial.

With regards the "madness" of feasting, such sumptuous consumption
occurred in other places in the region such as Timor. It finds a parallel in the
famous potlatch occasions among the Native Americans of the northern Pacific
coast. As remarked in the American case, what may seem wasteful irrationality
can to some extent also be seen as a form of redistribution—in the Savunese case
providing the lower strata of the population with the surplus of the elite (Josephy
1968: 75). In that sense it could have a socially binding function.

Pelon on his part wrote about another custom, the significance of which also
seems to have eluded him:

> They have a pastime which is quite peculiar for their land. The subjects
> of the king of Seba assemble once a year on a plain and enter a fight by
> throwing stones, since they are very skilful at that exercise. Those who
> have the luck to be injured are esteemed, and they believe that they will be
> lucky for the rest of their lives, if they do not die. If someone is injured in
> a fight or by accident, he does not take another medicine than a piece of
> fresh lard that he applies on or in the wound; he changes it every day, and
> within short the wound is gone however grave it was (Pelon 2002: 62).

As apparent from later accounts, the *pepèhi* (throwing rocks) is a ritual act
rather than a "pastime". It takes place after an exorcising ceremony before the
start of planting in the last month of the dry season (Bègarae), according to the
Savunese calendar. The ritual lasts until blood falls on the ground. This symbolic
act is a transfer of fertility and prosperity to the earth: it strives to appease the
malevolent spirits which live underground, and bring sickness and calamity.
From that point of view, the custom expresses a ritual collectivity rather than
an irrational violent game. Later, the Dutch colonial authorities prohibited it
as the ritual could degenerate into vicious fighting. This had in fact happened
during Portuguese times. Collective memory remembers the death of Jara Lai.
Apparently, he was so hated by the population that the ritual became a means

to stone him and his six sons to death. However, as his younger brother Bire Lai then took on the position of the Seba raja, it could well be a case of sibling rivalry rather than communal retribution.[153]

On the division into social classes and the governance of the princedoms, the European accounts give vague information. Like the first Dutch visitors in 1648, the Britons had difficulties in recognising social status from outward appearances. The Savunese seem to have generally worn a standard form of dress, but the more wealthy people had the privilege of wearing adornments. This even applied to noble-born children who sometimes wore brass spirals round their arms. According to Pelon, it was expressly forbidden for commoners to wear bracelets and adornments which were reserved for the high-ranking lineages (Pelon 2002: 63–4). Slaves were also a common status marker. When a chief left his house at least two non-free attendants accompanied him: one carried his sword and the other held a bag with betel and tobacco utensils.

Pelon perceptively notes the way that ritual and governance were embedded in each other. Each of the island's domains had a particular entity that applied religion and administered justice. This refers to the Deo Rai, the highest ritual figure in the Savunese system, whose sacral functions restrict his sphere of activities. The priest-cum-judge inspected the entrails of ritually slaughtered animals in order to determine the omens. He also acted as executioner when someone was sentenced to capital punishment. When he appeared in a ceremony he would always carry a sword, the symbol of his dignity, and it engendered great respect (Pelon 2002: 63). Later data show that the 'sword' was in fact a ceremonial knife called an *èku*, which is shorter than a sword. The British accounts imply Savunese deference to the central system of justice—although they identify the chief judicial administrator as the raja rather than the Deo Rai, whose functions they did not quite comprehend. Theft seemed very rare (although people pilfered some belongings from the Britons), and injuries and even murder did not cause people to take justice in their own hands. Instead, they dutifully turned to the princely centre for settling criminal matters (Hawkesworth 1773: 697).

Finally, it appears that the Dutch presence, although marginal, had implications for life on the island. While the rajas delivered certain quantities of maize and rice to the VOC, they gained some advantages in return. Like the other allied rajas of the Timor area, they identified in their letters to the VOC which luxury goods they wished to receive. This included fine cloth, cutlery, arrack, firearms and the like. There was hardly any other way of obtaining such goods, although Makassarese and Bugis 'smugglers' may have supplied occasional merchandise from other parts of the archipelago. Apart from the Britons in 1770

---

[153] Duggan 2011c: 43; Figure 28.

and a French ship in 1792, no Europeans other than VOC personnel seem to have passed through Savu in the 18th century—or at least none that has been documented. The agreements and contracts with the company strictly forbade any dealings with non-Dutch outsiders. VOC Commissioner Paravicini stationed an interpreter in Savu in 1756. At the time of the British visit, the interpreter was a German called Johann Christopher Lange, whose relationship with the unexpected guests oscillated between suspicion and friendship. His white skin and his European dress set him apart from the locals, but otherwise he had largely 'gone native'. He sat on the ground in the fashion of the region, chewed betel and seemed to have adopted the characteristics and manners of the Savunese. His wife was Timorese, unsurprisingly with white women rare in the East Indies at the time. She kept the household in the local tradition, and Lange admitted that he was ashamed of inviting Cook and his men to his house because he could not entertain them any better than the locals did (Hawkesworth 1773: 698).

Lange's role was not entirely symbolic—he toured around the island every second month. On his trips he travelled with 50 mounted slaves, presumably as a token of prestige as much as for practical concerns. During the tour the interpreter visited each of the rajas. His arrival was not altogether unpopular with them because he had the habit of bringing plenty of arrak, a drink that "their principal people never cease to drink, as long as a drop of it remains." (Hawkesworth 1773: 698). The interpreter's primary concern was to check that the plants ear-marked for the VOC were properly cultivated. When the crops were ripe he would ensure that sloops went to pick them up for the storehouses in Kupang.

Besides the interpreter there were two other non-Savunese residents in 1770. One was Lange's aide, a Portuguese mestizo from Timor. The other was a Dutch mestizo called Frederick Craig who instructed young people in the tenets of Christianity and gave basic school education. Dutch clerical sources documented that Christianity had made inroads in Savu by this time. According to the statistics, there were no Reformed Christians on the island by the mid-18th century. However, in 1753 *opperhoofd* Van der Burgh reported that a church and a school had just been built, and a Christian teacher appointed.[154] By 1779, there were 267 baptised persons in Dimu with 51 unbaptised children in Christian families.[155] It was not many for an island population numbering in the tens of thousands, but it was the kernel of a religious congregation that would completely dominate spiritual life in the 20th century. The Savunese

---

[154] VOC 8346 (1753), f. 53–4.

[155] ANRI Timor: 43, Letters from the Church Council of Timor.

congregation paralleled similar ones established in Rote in the mid-18th century. For the Dutch authorities it was desirable to bind the local princedoms in the area to the company through religious instruction.

In sum, the foreign visitors provide a lively picture of Savunese society hardly conveyed in the VOC documents. The question is, of course, how much insight can be expected from temporary encounters. The intricate ritual and social system known from later anthropological research is only hinted at. The brevity of the Cook expedition's stay means that some darker and less harmonious sides of Savunese life might have gone unnoticed by the Britons. The French naval officer, Bruni d'Entrecasteaux, who briefly landed on the island in 1792 during his search for the lost La Pérouse expedition, rightly noted that the rough sea trip that preceded Cook's Savunese visit must have increased the attractiveness of the island in British eyes. D'Entrecasteaux, who visited Savu at the end of the dry season, accuses the Cook expedition accounts of exaggeration:

> The shore, which seemed so agreeable and smiling to that illustrious voyager, had in fact only the merit that it could be approached without danger. Apart from that, the coast does not offer anything but a sandy beach to the eye, and it is only at some distance from the coastline that an inanimate greenness starts, which does not reveal any sign of freshness. The hills that Cook saw rising like an amphitheatre, are only very small heights which have nothing picturesque over them. In general the sight of these islands [Savu and Raijua] is so monotonous that one can hardly distinguish any remarkable points that could be listed (Temminck 1839–44: 291).

Nevertheless, the European accounts of conditions in the 1770s depict an island that had stabilised considerably since the internal turbulence of the 17th and early 18th century. A comparison between the British visitors and Pelon, and various VOC documents indicates that the company-led system was functioning in certain ways, especially in containing disputes between the chiefs and domains. More importantly, the material illustrates the dynamics of Savunese economic and social life, which was able to use scarce resources efficiently to support a dense population.

The genealogical ordering of the past

The importance of the ancestors is clearly visible in the European accounts; according to the Britons, of all the people they had encountered none seemed so interested in their past as the Savunese. However, neither Pelon nor the Cook expedition had much to say about the system of clans and moieties which had formed before the arrival of Europeans. Before leaving the early colonial period, it is helpful to consider once again the genealogical groups and inherited titles, and the capacity the Savunese have for ordering their past according to genealogical models.

In Savu there was no more clan (*udu*) creation during the Portuguese and the VOC period, and the two female moieties (*hubi*) had their beginnings in ancient times. However, the clan division into *kerogo* or lineages continued as did the segmentation of the moieties into *wini*. New *kerogo* appeared with a division of ritual tasks in the council of priests, *Mone Ama*, especially those related to warfare. A number of female lineages (*wini*) began long before European times, such as *wini* Dila Robo, the daughter of Robo Aba of Seba. Some formed just prior to the arrival of the Portuguese: *wini* Ga Lena for the Greater Blossom, and *wini* Jèwu and *wini* Putenga for the Lesser Blossom. Others emerged at the beginning of the Portuguese era; for instance, *wini* Wènyiratu in Raijua and its offspring, *wini* Waratada in Savu. A subgroup of *wini* Putenga, Jingi Wiki, specialised in black magic. Pi'i Robo Tari, full cousin of the first Portuguese raja in Seba Kore Rohi, established *wini* Pi'i. The primary patterns of all these *wini* are abstract and geometrical. *Wini* creation continued during the Portuguese period; for example, *wini* Mèko (Greater Blossom), named after Mèko Lod'o whose father was a goldsmith from Ndao.[156] This *wini* is found in Savu as well as in Raijua and its members tended to marry into the ruling classes on both islands. Interestingly, its primary pattern is probably the first zoomorphic image depicted on a woman's sarong: chickens (or possibly hens). The partly external origin of Mèko Lod'o might explain the choice of a realistic motif.

During the VOC period, Migi Jami, the daughter of Dima Riwu and Jami Lobo of Seba in the first decades of the 18th century, created *wini* Migi. Mamo Tèro, the daughter of Dima Riwu's first marriage, also created an unnamed *wini*. For both *wini* the identifying patterns are more zoomorphic or realistic: *lègu koko* (a rooster turning its head back) for *wini* Migi and *kae baku* (the feet of a bench) for Mamo Tèro (Plate 17). However, the patterns attributed to a contemporary, Ina Loni Dimu of Mesara, are still entirely abstract even when the name refers to a specific action such as *wue jara* (carried on horseback). Ina Loni Dimu's first more realistic pattern is *puru loko* (to go down to the river to bathe) where the fine blue, red and white lines evoke a river. A motif owned by *wini* Putenga clearly depicts a boat and commemorates Toda Wadu's departure when she married in Sumba. Here again, an external influence is certainly at the origin of a more figurative pattern. Besides the patterns owned by each *wini*, there are two trans-*wini* patterns restricted to the ruling classes: one is called patola because it is derived from patterns depicted on the valuable Indian cloth;

---

[156] It is a reminder that the language of Ndao was related to Savunese and that the Ndaoese were well-known in the eastern islands for their skills as goldsmiths.

the second, *lèba* (restricted) suggests two confronting *nagas*—the sacred snakes in South and Southeast Asian mythologies. A traded foreign cloth was certainly the inspiration for the *lèba* pattern. Each *hubi* owns one type of patola motif which still allows for the moiety identification.[157] Various *wini* own a type of *lèba* pattern for the descendants of women who married into a raja house (Duggan 2013 and Plate 17).

It seems that the increase in the number of female lineages corresponded (or was a response) to the spread of male lineages. At the time a *wini* is created, its founder develops at least one textile, the main pattern of which identifies her and her descendants in the community. A deceased person has to wear such a primary motif in order to be identified upon arrival in the ancestral realm. Therefore, the primary purpose of Savunese woven patterns is to act as a group identifier for men and women of the same *wini* and the same *hubi*.

Genealogies undeniably structure Savunese thought and its terminology reveals the type of mental images Savu people construct for their genealogical "sites of memory". The most salient characteristic of Savu society is certainly its ability to memorise long, secret and public genealogies even from a distant past. These are disclosed on certain occasions only when closing a funeral ceremony, a knowledgeable relative recites the entire male and female genealogy of the deceased. The narration of genealogies mainly requires two types of memory. The rhythmic structure of ancestral name recitation involves auditory memory and mental visual images because the name of an ancestor is intimately associated with a place. Sites, places, villages or ancestral houses require essentially visual memory, although the naming of these sites involves both types of memory. The primary mental structure for remembering in Savu is in the form of a genealogy. One of the purposes of remembering genealogies in relation to places is certainly for proving landownership. Two main ideas derive from remembering the path of the ancestors and of the genealogies; one is that of shared origin and the second is that of an order of precedence as a fundamental organising principle, connecting the past and the present. This concept implies that newcomers are either treated as descendants of Savu people who returned to the island or they have been incorporated and their genealogies constructed to fit the general pattern, so it is no longer possible to trace them as newcomers or outsiders.

Both paternal and maternal lines have their ritual houses. Everyone is bound to one ancestral house in his/her male line (*udu*, *kerogo*) and to one ancestress house, *tegida*, in his/her female line (*wini*, *hubi*). The ritual houses of both lines fulfil a number of similar functions, yet they reveal differences related to gender. The ancestral house, *èmu kepue* (house of origin), of a group of people in the

---

[157] http://genevieveduggan.com/savu-ceremonial-textiles/womens-sarongs

Photo 12. Heirloom baskets containing textiles kept in an ancestral house; Seba (2012)

Photo 13. *Tegida* or ancestress ritual house for worshipping Ga Lena; Rae Jo, Seba (2012)

male descent line (*udu*, *kerogo*) and the *tegida*, or ancestral house in the female descent line (*hubi*, *wini*) are both the repositories of heirlooms and the loci of rituals. The leaders of each have the ability to mediate between the ancestors and the members of the group, channelling prayers and blessings. The *èmu kepue* is large, static and generally inhabited; the ritual food is prepared and cooked outside. The head of the house conducts the rituals with his wife only if both are from the same *wini,* recreating the brother-sister pair of origin. If they are of different *wini*, the leader's sister from the house of origin assists him during the ceremonies.

For the *tegida* too the leader, Bèni Hau Tegida, receives her brother's help who is in charge of the building construction. The *tegida* is small, movable and uninhabited, and the ritual food is prepared and cooked inside the building. The *tegida* contains textiles with patterns shared by the members of the *wini*; these are checked on various occasions. The order in which people take the textiles out of the basket must correspond to the chronology of their production: they remove the textile with the oldest pattern first; then the second oldest pattern and so on, visually reproducing the rule of precedence. Later, after being checked and eventually replaced, the textile with the oldest pattern goes back first. A *tegida* is always next to the house of its leader for practical and safety reasons. Women of the same *wini* meet in the *tegida* to plan the production of specific textiles, to prepare the first indigo blue and morinda red dyes of the year, and to store textiles they exclusively own. This meeting place allows a woman who married in another part of the Savu-Raijua archipelago to reunite with members of her own *wini*.

It is remarkable that the genealogical matrix is not only used for the genealogies of people, for the succession of settlements (topogenies) and of houses (domogenies), but also for the successive creation of textiles (textilogenies).[158] Savu people place a great emphasis on the use of a genealogical matrix to manage their society: indeed, ordering everything under the same model represents a distinctive 'economy of knowledge' in Savunese culture. Society has extended the image of the genealogy in a unique way to apply to a number of other important heritable aspects of material culture.

As the chapter shows, Savu in the late 17th and 18th centuries displays a curious combination of stability and turbulence. After the 1676 war, nothing significantly disturbed the VOC diplomatic system set up in 1648. *Opperhoofden* would arrive on the little island when needed in order to resolve local issues and never met with any direct resistance. The increasing importance of the Savunese in the VOC system in this part of the archipelago is obvious: the

---

[158] For the domogenies, see Figure 43. For the textilogeny of *wini* Ga Lena, see Figure 44.

much-feared Savunese cavalry constituted the backbone of the company's striking force in its campaigns against the Larantuqueiros and Timorese. Oral tradition clearly indicates that the company was the ultimate warrant of order, although it was sometimes heavy-handed or easy to fool. On the other hand, the VOC documents and collective memory bear ample witness to the perpetual petty wars that flared up every now and then, often between factions within the domains. These confrontations could be quite gory and even included the slaying of a raja. And yet Savu's division into five domains survived, certainly underpinned by the strong ritual identity in each. The first detailed ethnographic outsider descriptions appear at a time in the late 18th century when the internal chaos had begun to recede; they convey positive images of a frugal but reasonably flourishing society.

Chapter 7 | Savu and the Colonial State, 1800–1900

By the new year of 1800, the Batavian Republic—a client state under revolutionary France—had finally liquidated the debt-stricken VOC, taking over its lands and assets (De Klerck 1938 I: 443–4). The effects on Savu of this organisational change are debatable. In the course of the 19th century, few Westerners visited the island—for long periods probably even fewer than in the days of the company. The essential conditions of life observed by Cook and Pelon were not significantly altered. Nevertheless, Savu was not changeless, if a society can ever be.

The 19th century meant a number of new developments and opportunities for the Savunese, for better or worse. From a political point of view, the Savunese elite was heavily involved in the complicated affairs of Sumba where it constituted a decisive force, mostly in close alliance with the Dutch. Secondly, Christianity, specifically the Reformed Protestants, made inroads after 1870. While initially marginal, the impact of the missionary efforts would increasingly change the islanders' spiritual world. Thirdly, epidemics took a horrendous toll on the population, with ensuing collective traumas as discussed in chapter 8. And fourthly, the Dutch colonial state that formed after 1816 slowly increased its grip even on far-lying islands, such as Savu, favouring elite groups who were the smoothest and most adaptable in their relations with the white man. The Savu that became a Dutch *zelfbesturend landschap* (self-ruling territory) in 1915 was therefore significantly different from the island visited by the last VOC servants in about 1800.

A problem facing anyone wishing to study 19th-century Savu is the sources. The archival material produced by the Kupang post in the 17th and 18th centuries is relatively conscientious, albeit less detailed as the VOC era draws towards its close. However, the data quickly deteriorate in the 1790s with the downfall of the company and the subsequent political changes. For the period 1800 to 1830 there is, as a matter of fact, very little Dutch (and not much Portuguese) material about the internal conditions of local polities in the Timor area. Instead, visitors to these waters, such as Péron (1801, 1803), Freycinet (1818), Reinwardt and Bik (1821), Kruseman (1824) and Müller

(1828–29), wrote long accounts of their experiences which yield valuable ethnographic data, though detail is relatively sparse about Savu.[1] The Batavia authorities reorganised the government of Dutch Timor in the years 1831 and 1832, after which there is regular archival material. Especially after about 1870, the so-called *mailrapporten* (mail reports) give information on a monthly basis. Even so, Savu seldom looms large in the eyes of the Kupang administrators. Luckily, the Protestant missionary archive houses copious letters and reports from the 1870s onwards, detailing the conditions of the elite as well as the general population, along with welcome ethnographic data. In addition, oral tradition retains a central role and opens up many interesting perspectives not touched by administrative records.

Tumultuous days in Kupang

The tempests of the French Revolutionary and Napoleonic Wars spilled over into the colonies. The British navy tended to dominate the sea roads and it carried out a number of seaborne operations with varying success in Latin America, Africa and Asia. British expansionism even afflicted faraway Kupang. An expedition in 1797 captured the town, but local people killed many British soldiers soon forcing their departure.[2] The fighting reduced Kupang to rubble and bands of Timorese subsequently plundered the town. Another British attempt in 1811 was likewise defeated with considerable losses. Only after Janssen's capitulation to the British in Java later in the same year—where Stamford Raffles was then proclaimed lieutenant governor—did the Dutch government in Kupang yield, surrendering in January 1812. A British observer recorded the war-like but ultimately peaceful first contact with the Savunese:

> [T]he people of the Small Isle of Savo ... are said to be almost amphibious in their habits. This is a Warlike Race distinguished for their Nobleness of Mien and independence of character. The chiefs are completely arbitrary and conduct the armed Bands in Flotillas to the neighbouring islands whenever called on to settle internal disputes. One happened to arrive at Coopang with this intent at the time when possession was ... [taken] in the British name. Unacquainted with the motives of this hostile invasion, enquiry was made as to its object; he replied that it was at the requisition

---

[1] For bibliographic information about these travellers, see Sherlock (1980: 19, 171, 249, 266, 273).

[2] The raja of Liae, Ama Raja (identity unconfirmed) and the junior raja Ama Bida (possibly Elias Jara Hili) of Dimu, were present during these events leading 120 and 50 soldiers, respectively (Raad der Aziatische Bezittingen [Council of the Asiatic Possessions], 2.01.27.02, No. 128, missive, 14 April 1798).

of one of the native Chiefs of the island. When the recent events by which the Dutch Power had been supplanted were explained to him and the friendship of the British Government proffered, he hesitated not to accept it on the footing hitherto maintained with the Dutch. On being cautioned to discourage Tumults and disturbances which his followers might perhaps provoke with the Europeans, he replied in an independent tone that he would strike off the head of any of his subjects who insulted an Englishmen and expected the same punishment would be inflicted were they the Aggressors. He invited the British officers to his Island and "when you come", he remarked, "remember your visit is to me. You are my friends.[3]

The Dutch capitulation was followed by four years of British rule.[4] As the quote indicates, the rulers of Savu accepted the change of regime and armed Savunese were present in the town during this period.[5] Their leader was the regent Ama Lomi (Ama Loni?), who might be the same person as the later raja of Seba, Ama Loni Jara (d. 1859).

Being soldiers with a fearsome reputation, the Savunese of Kupang were a proud and self-conscious company. An eyewitness found them quarrelsome and arrogant. In 1795, a Savunese community of some size was involved in an incident with the Timorese of Funai, close to Kupang. One Savunese was killed in the brawl. The "regent of Savu" later arrived to investigate the matter, and the temporary *opperhoofd* Carel Gratus Greving had to mediate between him and the raja of Funai to avert a more serious confrontation.[6] The Savunese ancestral religion served as a cohesive focus outside their home island. An account from the 1820s shows they kept a ritual stone in a building in the centre of Kupang. There they occasionally killed a dog and studied the intestines for auspicious or inauspicious signs (Temminck 1839–44: 294). The British interim rule had obvious difficulties keeping the Savunese in check. On one occasion in 1812, the authorities discovered a theft had occurred and knew who the culprit was. However, his Savunese compatriots absolutely refused to surrender him to the administration. The Resident Knibbe, a Dutchman serving the British, sent armed men to pick up the thief in his house. However, this provoked uproar. The enraged Savunese resisted Knibbe and his men, and forced their return to Fort

---

[3] MacKenzie Private Collection 167–171, William Callbrooke, "Sketches relating to the Range of Islands Connected with the East Coast of Java", 4–5–1812. Thanks to James Fox for the reference.

[4] For the British intervention and rule, see Farram (2007: 458–71).

[5] 'Iets over het Eiland Timor en Onderhoorigheden' (Something about Timor Island and Dependencies), H 245a, KITLV, c. 1819, f. 21.

[6] Raad der Aziatische Bezittingen, No. 128, 2.01.27.02, Nationaal Archief.

Concordia. A British sailor, watching the riot, received a javelin in his buttocks and had to flee to the fort with the Resident (Heijmering 1847: 211–2). The British commanding officer lost his hat, which the aggressors appropriated and defiantly demanded a ransom for it.[7] There is no mention of any punishment being meted out, either for the thief or the rioters. Although those who did not know Savunese ways found them difficult to control, they were quite simply too important for military undertakings to dispense with. The Savunese, whose task was to maintain a semblance of order in the ranks, supervised the large numbers of disorderly auxiliary troops employed by the British and Dutch in Timor. The situation clearly shows the efforts of resource-scarce colonial establishments to use the elements to their advantage: they needed the undisciplined to inspire discipline (Fox 1977: 161)!

One of Knibbe's successors, Joseph Burn (in charge 1812–14), had an even more serious issue to deal with. According to later opinion, he was a drunkard who commanded little respect from the local peoples. Soru, the fettor of the Rotenese domain Dengka, plotted to get rid of the British by persuading his followers to run amuck and divide up the victims' property. Together with the Rotenese staying in Kupang, he managed to inveigle the government slaves and the Savunese under Ama Lomi to participate. Having predetermined the time of the attack, at the last moment a slave told the influential Dutch Eurasian Jacobus Arnoldus Hazaart what was to transpire. Hazaart saw to it that Soru was arrested and restored order in the colony (Heijmering 1847: 213–4). Again, there is no mention of the other plotters being punished. The size of the British forces in Kupang was not large and neither was the white population. The Residents presumably had to maintain a tense balance in the port town as well as they could with the scanty resources at hand. The intricate situation is indicated by the fact that Hazaart was British Resident of Kupang in 1814, although he had fought the same Britons a couple of years previously.

Between the political crises, a few peaceful foreign visits to Kupang occurred in 1801, 1803 and 1818 when French explorers arrived at the port. The French scientists were perceptive and noted many details of life in this part of the East Indies. Although they did not visit Savu, they came into contact with the community staying in Kupang. Péron, leader of the expedition which visited Kupang in 1801 and 1803, made the acquaintance of a "king" from Savu called Ama Dima who stayed at the port. His identity and relationship to the aforementioned Ama Lomi are not clear but the name seems to point

---

[7] Ibid.

to Seba.[8] Péron describes him as a man of medium height, about 45 years old, with an agreeable and lively appearance. As one of the rare early descriptions of intercourse with Savunese persons of a personal and non-official nature, the account is interesting. The reception took place in a chamber where Péron and his colleague were staying, but the occasion was disturbed by the thievish conduct of Ama Dima's accompanying grandees who pilfered objects in the house. Péron commented in his account that theft was a passion among the Malays (meaning the Austronesian peoples of the East Indies). He saw it as a common vice among "savage or little civilised peoples" and pointed out the pivotal role of legislators of any nation to establish property rights as the foundations of social institutions. Péron's views are, of course, highly debatable. An account from the Cook expedition seems to imply that theft in Savu was very rare, but perhaps a foreign visit led to a diversion from the normal code of conduct. Péron then describes an exchange with Ama Dima:

> Of all the objects that I showed the good Ama Dima, it was the phosphor that amazed him the most; its spontaneous inflammation, the rapidity of combustion, the colour of its flame, all this seemed too prodigious to the simple monarch, that he left no stone unturned to persuade me to hand over the flask where I kept a few ounces. After having vainly offered me a large quantity of fowl, hogs and sheep, he made a last attempt… With an air of confidence, he called on one of his grand officers, and was given a beautiful sack of betel, at the bottom of which was a small packet; he took it, unwrapped it and came up with a Spanish piastre[9] which he presented with an air of confidence that was as ridiculous as it was hard to describe. He seemed to tell me: 'At that price you cannot refuse me'. I still refused to his great amazement, and the poor king who could not obtain the flask, was content to only ask for a little bit of the phosphor contained in it. In vain I wanted to tell him about the dangers that such substance would often carry; Ama Dima continued his bid in such an affective way, that I finally agreed in order not to lose his friendship … [He] carefully put it in his beautiful betel sack, kissed me with the nose according to the custom of the land, and disappeared with his numerous suite… We soon saw him again in a state of profound consternation; the phosphor had been set ablaze, as I had predicted; the betel sack of the king was consumed, several of the highest courtiers had their hands burnt…

---

[8] An Ama Dima Lomi was the father-in-law of the well-known Sebanese raja Ama Nia Jawa (r. 1864–68). A modern source, Marthen Heke Medo, linked Ama Dima with Ama Dima Luji, a son of Raja Ama Loni Jara (r. 1830–58). This is implausible for chronological reasons but, as explained previously, Ama Loni Jara's place in the pedigree might have been confused by local tradition.

[9] The term applied to Spanish 'pieces of eight' (originally from the Italian for thin metal plate) used globally by traders for centuries.

> M. Depuch and I could sooth the affliction of Ama Dima with difficulty, offering him a handkerchief as retribution for the royal sack consumed by the phosphor, which then received the name *api takut* [frightening fire (In)] (Péron 1807: 150–1).

Ama Dima often went to see the Frenchmen in the coming days. One day he asked Péron, "Friend Péron, come and eat rice in my house." He then took Péron by the hand and led him to "his palace or his bower (for either name might be applied for this royal habitation)". A large number of slaves were ready as if there was a feast and the women with Ama Dima prepared a slaughtered sheep for the meal. At the dinner table Ama Dima divided up the sheep served with rice, providing Péron and himself each with a piece weighing five to six pounds. "I dared not contest him his appetite and voracity, but I ate as well as I could." After the meal an interesting rite of friendship followed. A slave brought a bottle of rum and Ama Dima poured much of it into a coconut shell, turning to his guest he said, "Man Péron, you are the friend of King Ama Dima; King Ama Dima is the friend of the man Péron. Man Péron, King Ama Dima gives to you his name; would you give yours?" Péron readily agreed, which filled the raja with joy. For the rest of the evening the raja steadfastly addressed his French guest as *Tuan* (Master [In]) Ama Dima and his slaves followed suit. The Frenchman returned the courtesy, though he often forgot and addressed his princely host with his Savunese name (Péron 1807: 161–2).

Péron, a child of the Enlightenment and French Revolution, relates his travel adventures with a rational and slightly ironical edge, and never misses the opportunity to make a good story out of his experiences. He actively sought communication with local aristocrats, not self-evident in travellers of his time. The unfamiliarity of locals with chemical substances is unsurprising—the Dutch had not yet introduced education beyond basic Christian schools. Still, the story indicates the raja's willingness to learn. The custom to exchange names as a sign of friendship is common in Oceania and is also known among Native Americans in North America.

That the Savunese were a small but prominent element in Kupang by this time is demonstrated by the presence of princes such as Ama Lomi and Ama Dami. The sources do not disclose in any detail their motives to stay in Timor for extended periods of time; however, they stress that they were much feared by the Timorese for their martial skills, which the Kupang administrations put to good use in military expeditions towards the interior.[10] However, the sources imply that there were economic networks where the rajas could very well have

---

[10] Kruseman, 'Timor', f. 140, Coll. 271, No. 146, Nationaal Archief.

played a role as overseers.[11] The playwright Jacques Arago, who accompanied the 1817–18 Freycinet expedition, mentions that the women of Kupang wore *kebayas* (traditional women's blouses [In]) over their *kain* (cloth [In]) or sarongs. Almost all the textiles from which these were made were manufactured in Savu, though some originated from the Timorese inland (Arago 1823: 190). As J. Kruseman mentions in his 1824 report, there lay at anchor about 30 perahu in the Kupang Bay, attended by slaves and Solorese sailors. Usually the Chinese managed trading activities. Two of these ships used to depart from Kupang to Savu every year, loaded with iron utensils and Javanese textiles. Arriving in Savu they would barter these goods for tobacco, sheep and a few horses. Kruseman makes no mention of bartering for Savu's famous textiles, however.[12]

In one respect at least, Savu had an economic role that involved the world outside the eastern archipelago and even outside maritime Southeast Asia. Since at least the 17th century, the island was known for horse breeding. However, there is only the barest mention of horse trading during the VOC period.[13] If such trade took place on a grand scale it apparently occurred out of sight of the company. After the Napoleonic Wars, when some new commercial routes emerged, this changed. When the Dutch scholar Reinwardt visited Kupang in 1821 he noted the amazing qualities of the horses. In spite of the rough Timorese terrain, the animals were physically suited to it; the best ones were of Savunese stock (Reinwardt 1858: 342). In his memorandum from 1832, Commissioner Emanuel Francis noted that the Savunese horses were of better quality than those of Rote (Kontrak perjanjian [Contracts/agreements] 2007: 292). Two years later an annual report from Kupang noted that horses from Savu, Rote and, occasionally, Timor were exported to Java, Mauritius and the British colonies in Australia. In the period 1828 to 1833, 661 horses left these islands via ship. The numbers may seem modest but the trade certainly made a difference for a comparatively small and resource-scarce land.[14]

As for Savu's general economic state in these years, there is no mention of the island being afflicted by the infamous eruption of the Tambora volcano in Sumbawa in 1815, which otherwise devastated large parts of the central and

---

[11] In his study of trade and politics in 19th-century Nusa Tenggara, I Gde Parimartha (2002) distinguishes five trading zones in the region, namely Bima-Sumbawa, Lombok, Solor-Alor-Larantuka, Ende-Waingapu, and Timor-Kupang. The last two were the main areas of interaction for the Savunese.

[12] Kruseman, 'Timor', f. 140, Coll. 271, No. 146, Nationaal Archief.

[13] See in particular the memorandum of *Opperhoofd* Fokkens from 1777, VOC 3473 (1777).

[14] ANRI Timor: 68, General report, 1834.

eastern archipelago. Savu was probably just outside the sphere of dense ash fall.[15] For the rest, Savu appears to have been a typical subsistence economy of the kind that was found in most places in the world at the time, including rural parts of Europe. In pre-modern societies affluence is the exception rather than the rule; the relation between population density and the available land and natural resources tends to strike a fragile balance. The Briton John Crawfurd, who collected materials about East Indian geography in the early 19th century, made the following observation on Savu in a brief entry in his *Descriptive Dictionary*:

> In ordinary years … the inhabitants raise a sufficiency of maize, millet and yams, for their own subsistence, and in times of scarcity, obtain a living from the banana, and the sugar of the lontar palm (*Borassus flabelliformus*), both of which are abundant. The island produces a small quantity of tobacco reputed to be of very high quality. The principal domesticated animals of Savoe are the buffalo and horse, both of which are abundant… The women go naked with the exception of a short petticoat, and the men wear no other dress than a piece of cloth wrapped round the loins (Crawfurd 1856: 378).

Crawfurd's picture was largely confirmed in a report from 1851 written by the Dutch Resident Baron van Lijnden—otherwise known as the man behind the first border treaty with Portuguese East Timor. The Savunese cultivated sorghum, millet, sugar cane, green grams, paddy (rice in the husks), sirih (betel leaves) and fruit for their own needs. The list is thus a bit different from Crawfurd's, suggesting that the choice of crops was not constant. In one respect the cultivation of crops was more advanced than in Timor: the peasants replanted the *bibit* (paddy seedlings [In]) as they did in the central islands of the archipelago. Trade was not developed and there were no Chinese on the island. Only the rajas possessed larger sea-faring vessels, and the Kupang and Buton perahus carried whatever commerce there was. The few export items included tobacco, syrup, *tuak* (palm wine [In]), horses, woven textiles and coconuts. The islanders imported cotton, red head-cloth, dyes for the yarn, iron, gongs, ivory bangles, glass pearls, gold coins, shotguns and gunpowder.[16]

Cotton, cloths and dyes are significant items in Savu. Cotton grows on the island as it is a component of offerings where only indigenous ingredients are allowed in rituals. However, as referred to earlier, Jacques Arago reported that many of the textiles seen in Kupang in the early 19th century were Savunese.

---

[15] The ash fall was more than one centimetre thick in places. There were probably consequences for Savu in terms of fluctuations in temperature, etc. See the map of ash fall density in D'Arcy Wood (2014: 23).

[16] Van Lijnden 1851: 403–5.

The local production of cotton might not have been sufficient to cover the demand, so people imported it from neighbouring islands. The late Zadrak Bunga remembered that cotton used in Mesara was imported from Alor at a small landing place near Kabila in exchange for Savunese lontar syrup; a pot of lontar syrup for a pot of the same size tightly filled with cotton buds. Imported red head-cloths were an essential part of the male attire. Red is associated with heat, danger and is eminently male; the image of a Savunese warrior from the mid-19th century shows him wearing head gear combining various cloths; the white and the red cloths seem to be of foreign origin while the cloth with red, black and white stripes looks like a local product (Plate 14). Traditional dyes used in Savu (indigo and morinda) are from the plants on the island. Indigo grows wild during the rainy season, and is linked with secrecy and taboos, while the morinda—possibly of Indian origin—was certainly introduced through trade or migration.[17] The red dye production is less associated with taboos and secrecy than indigo, despite its 'hot' colour, the reason for crediting a foreign origin to this dye.[18] The "dyes for the yarn" on the list must have been twigs, leaves and bark of the *luba* tree (*Symplocos*, a flowering tree genus from tropical regions) which does not grow in Savu but in mountainous areas in Sumba, Flores and Timor. Sold in small bundles and mixed with the dyes, it serves as a mordant for the colour to penetrate the yarns as well as a fixative to make them colour-fast. *Luba* is still sold in the Seba market today. Savu has always been dependant on trade with its neighbours to produce colour-fast dyes.

Commercial activities in Southeast Asia had greatly expanded after the founding of Singapore, but the effects were thus far limited on outlying islands such as Savu. The choice of products was not much different from what was expected in one of the region's island societies in the 17th or 18th century.

Population in the 19th century

The British returned the Dutch assets in the East Indies in 1816. For Timor the change went smoothly; the British had appointed Jacobus Arnoldus Hazaart as Resident in 1814 and he continued at the post after their withdrawal. The long and rather authoritarian rule of Resident Hazaart (1808–11; 1814–18; 1819–32) had its advantages; the Resident was able to make the most of the small means available and played Timorese rulers against each other. He was not always successful in his game of power; the redoubtable Amanuban kingdom

---

[17] *Morinda citrifolia*, the roots of which are used for dyeing, and in Savu is known as *kèbo hida*.

[18] Duggan 2016: 18–20.

resisted him in spite of repeated military expeditions.[19] On the whole, however, he appears (a supposition, given there are few archival reports from his time) to have maintained the prestige of the Dutch tricolour. At any rate, visitors in Kupang, such as Freycinet, Reinhardt and Müller, held Hazaart and his policies in high regard.[20]

The patchy documentation from the first three or four decades of the 19th century significantly afflicts a study of Savu. An account of the politics in the six Savunese domains is therefore heavily dependent on oral tradition, supported by the few extant textual documents. Of these, Commissioner Emanuel Francis's report looms large. After the Java War, Batavia finally had time to consider hitherto ignored outposts and sent Francis to investigate Hazaart's colonial kingdom. On arrival, he found that much had been mismanaged, in particular when it came to economic affairs. A *Landraad* (legal land council) was in operation, whose members were picked from the colonial bureaucracy and various indigenous groups. One of them was the Savunese headman who stayed in Kupang.[21] All this influenced Savu itself only indirectly, but at least Francis drew up a comprehensive demographic survey. There he listed all the princedoms in Timor and the adjacent islands. For those under Dutch suzerainty, he carefully noted down the names of the rajas, fettors and chiefs, and the number of people over whom each of them ruled. As the first survey of its kind, the Savu section deserves attention.[22]

Francis multiplied the number of able-bodied men (*weerbare mannen*) by four in order to obtain the population total. That means there were 28,940 inhabitants in Savu and Raijua. However, there might have been motives for both over- and under-reporting (such as evasion of the anticipated corvée service or prestige), and the demographic figures for Timor do not make a very reliable impression. The number of fit men—7,235—is close to 7,300, the figure given by the Cook expedition. However, the allocation to the various domains is different. The 1832 numbers are much higher for Dimu (1,440 fit men against 800 in 1770) and Mesara (1,010 against 400), and much lower for Liae (1,320 against 2,600) and Raijua (415 against 1,500). Seba stays about the same and the Cook expedition did not count Menia. Whether these fluctuations depend on real demographic

---

[19] Farram 2007: 470–2. Warriors from Savu-Raijua are known to have participated in the struggle against Amanuban, as discussed elsewhere in this book.

[20] Hazaart's career is discussed at some length in Farram (2007). He died in Savu in December 1838 after concluding an official mission to Sumba.

[21] Francis, Dagboek, dated 30 November 1830, H540, KITLV Archive. Such *landraden* existed in all the Dutch possessions in the East Indies.

[22] It is reproduced as part of Appendix IV.

changes or faulty calculations cannot be known, but the two estimations indicate a population that stayed in the vicinity of 30,000 over the decades. Generally, the East Indies fragmentary evidence suggests that the population increase was slight before the 20th century. Crop failure, epidemics, warfare, long-distance slave raiding, natural disasters, and poor knowledge of health and hygiene kept population figures down.

Perhaps the list's most interesting aspect is the choice of villages, the first of its kind. For the most part, it does not include the most prominent settlements found today. Many names are today no more than obscure subunits of larger villages. Francis's data are a reminder that the strongly traditional patterns found in Savu should not be misinterpreted: the settlement structure found in 20th-century records did not reflect a particularly stabile or unchanging pattern over the centuries.[23] The same obviously goes for the choice of genealogical chiefs who Francis counted as "temukungs". In many cases the temukungs can be identified in the genealogies recorded in modern times, but their descent lines were usually abrogated one or a few generations later. This can probably be explained by the devastating smallpox epidemic of 1869, which is discussed later.

Francis's table indicated the number of Christians in the various domains. Outside direct Dutch jurisdiction, there were exceedingly few and in Savu there were none at all. Compared to the VOC period, there seems to have been a serious contraction owing to the lack of preachers and missionaries since the late 18th century. However, the memory of the Christian mission lived on. The missionary Geerloff Heijmering (1792–1867) notes the following in a letter from 31 July 1844:

> … Thus the rajas of the Island of Savu came very recently, and insistingly requested [that Heijmering send Christian schoolmasters]; among other things, they use as an argument the remark that their forefathers, about 150 years ago, already possessed a schoolmaster, as some of them had already been received in Christianity through the holy baptism. It is a pity that I did not fulfil their reasonable request, due to the lack of suitable persons. The less so since, if I had been able to find them, I would expand the good cause on the mainland of Timor in the first place, since it is the time for sowing here, too, and also for harvesting already.[24]

The background to this is the reintroduction of Christian missions in the Timor area by the *Nederlandsch Zendelinggenootschap* (Dutch Missionary Society,

---

[23]   Resident Baron van Lijnden presented another table of villages or hamlets (1851). His list, drawn from an official report, is much longer than that of Francis and does not entirely accord with the settlements known today; see Appendix IV for details.

[24]   Raad voor de Zending, 1102–1: 1403, Geerloff Heijmering, letter, 31 July 1844.

NZG), a pietistic organisation that concentrated its efforts on the East Indies. As previously stated, Protestant missionaries had been active in the area in VOC times, although proselytising was not a company priority. With the company's decline and the tempests of the Napoleonic age, this activity came to a halt. There was no permanent church minister in Kupang after 1775 and it received few visits from ordained Protestant ministers. It was only in 1819 that the NZG, formed in 1797, began to send missionaries there (Aritonang and Steenbrink 2008: 139, 301). As they soon found out, the Timorese were not susceptible to proselytising; they were attached to their traditional hierarchy and lived in scattered settlements. The Rotenese, on the contrary, had a long history of clerical schools and the first missionaries made good progress among them. Many Rotenese rajas were baptised and this seems to have made an impression on their Savunese peers. The rajas' quoted request indicates the presence of Christian schoolmasters by 1700, though they are actually only documented later, in the second half of the 18th century. Nevertheless, the time was still not ripe and the NZG era would only come a quarter of a century later.

Dimu in decline

With the exception of Menia's shifting status, the political division of Savu appears remarkably stable over the centuries. Oral tradition indicates that the five or six domains were formed at an early stage before European arrival, although the position of a raja (*duae*, *mone paji*) was influenced by European demands for a representative with whom to negotiate. In that respect, Savu differs from Rote where the number of acknowledged *nusak* (domains) shifted between twelve and nineteen; and various offshoots emerged in the 18th and early 19th centuries. The contrast with Timor is also stark with its shifting borders and migrations. A brief survey of the political development of the five domains in Savu and Raijua, during the period in question, is therefore necessary.

After the long reign of Hili Haba in the late VOC period, the collective memory of Dimu's history is curiously vague. From the archival records it appears that his son Elias Jara Hili succeeded him in 1798 and ruled until after 1809. He disappeared some time before 1832 when a certain Rewo Daga (that is, Rebo or Riwu Daga) ruled. However, the local tradition in Dimu recorded to date does not recall either of these two figures. Instead, it insists that Hili Haba's son Hede Hili apparently ruled for an extended time. In an adat house in Bodae, a three-pointed spear is preserved among the *pusaka* (heirloom [In]) objects. This spear is attributed to Hede Hili, who is said to have died without issue. At least one of the oral accounts incorrectly asserts that Hede was succeeded by Ama Piga Jara, whose history dates from 1869 to 1910.

That the Savunese account is simplified has already been mentioned. It again provides an interesting perspective on how oral historiography works. While relatively specific data have been preserved over the centuries, names and whole generations of leaders are occasionally left out. The linear time that imprints Western historical thinking is simply absent; the past is marked out by genealogical origins, generations, places and objects.

If indeed he was a raja, Hede must have ruled in the long interval between 1809 and 1832. There are no archival records from the period, and there were at least three intervening rajas between him and Ama Piga Jara. After Rewo Daga, the domain was wracked by internal conflicts. When a new raja was chosen in 1847, such tension arose that the Dutch saw reason to dispatch a brig of war. The arrival of the colonial force calmed down the situation and the brig commander confirmed the raja in his dignity.[25] This person was probably Ama Hili Haba, who is documented in the years 1851 to 1857, and he was followed by Ama Lai Daga from 1857 to 1869. These two rulers are remembered in Savu in modern time, though they are only vaguely part of a historical context.

As the story goes, Ama Hili Haba was involved in warfare with Liae but was taken prisoner and kept in custody at Ege on the south coast. He was later released. Undeterred by his initial failure, he attacked again and managed to gain some land from Liae.[26] It is not clear if his actions have something to do with the succession of 1847. His family background is entirely unknown, though he married a member of the Seba fettor family.[27] His successor Ama Lai Daga is however included in the genealogies as a great-grandson of Hili Haba. He succumbed to the great smallpox epidemic of 1869 which took a very heavy toll on the Savunese elite. The dreaded sickness probably wiped out the old princely lineage, for the next raja had only the most tenuous genealogical connection with his predecessor. Ama Piga Jara belonged to a distant branch of the princely *udu* and would prove to be the last ruler of Dimu.

Dimu's claim to prominence was partly based on it being at the centre of Dutch-Savunese relations. In the time of Hazaart, a Dutch *posthouder* (representative) had a seat in Dimu and received 30 guilders per month from

---

[25] Kartodirdjo 1973: 413; ANRI Timor: 78, General report, 1847.

[26] These were the villages of Lobodei, Bebae, Tada and Eiada. They have a mixture of clans as people from the victorious side moved there after the war. Interview with Wila Hege (15.05.2011).

[27] Ama Hili Haba's consort was Moi Tedo Riwu Gadi, descendant of the well-known fettor Jami Lobo (from first half of the 18th century). Her grand-uncle Wono Gadi was fettor of Seba in 1832 (Francis 1832: table of local princedoms).

the government.[28] Later in the same century he was relocated to Seba. While some European accounts of the mid-19th century still repeat the mantra of the Dimunese position of precedence over the entire island, this was increasingly belied by political and economic developments.[29] Brief reigns and dynastic breaks might have contributed to a relative erosion of prestige, as suggested by the events of 1847. It was rather Dimu's neighbour to the west that emerged as the leading Savunese power: Seba.

There is relatively little evidence of warfare between the Savunese domains after the mid-18th century. In that respect, Savu follows a different trajectory to Rote, which was wracked by intra-island wars far into the 19th century, not to speak of the conflict-enmeshed areas of Solor and Alor Islands, and the Timorese mainland. However, there was one brief incident in 1872 which has received particular attention in both oral and written narratives. It was in fact the last regular war fought between two domains. A comparison between the versions is instructive as the perspectives are so different. A Dutch newspaper article provided the following summary of the events:

> Hostilities took place in Savu between the rajas of Dimu and Seba. In a fight between the subjects of the two princes, caused by several factors, 30 people were killed. In 1859, Dimu handed over a piece of land to Seba that had long been disputed, as satisfaction for 200 horses which two Dimu chiefs had stolen from Seba territory. It seems that the raja of Dimu hatched the plan to make the piece of land into a bone of contention once again; his theft of horses and other animals from Seba territory in September 1872 was attributed to this.

> As negotiations did not lead to any result, both sides took to arms. In a subsequent fight the raja of Dimu was put to flight while the victor claimed a large number of animals. After the Resident summoned the two rajas, he decried the unacceptable and improper manner of their behaviour. As a consequence, the raja of Dimu acknowledged his guilt, while the raja of Seba returned the captured animals as a sign of good will (*De Locomotief* [*The locomotion*], 14 January 1873).

A story recorded in Seba says that a large area of land between the domains of Seba and Dimu was used as common horse pasture. During Ama Hili Haba's rule (1851–57), a case of equine theft occurred when 60 horses from Seba suddenly disappeared. As *udu* Nahipa had the same cattle mark as *udu* Nataga,

---

[28] Kruseman, 'Timor', f. 140, Coll. 271, No. 146, Nationaal Archief. See also Baron van Lijnden's report (1851) which mentions Dimu as the posthouder's permanent place of residency.

[29] ANRI Timor: 145, Report of 5 February 1850: "it is divided in five kingdoms … of which Timoe is the foremost".

it was difficult to prove which horses belonged to whom. The Dutch authorities demanded that the 60 missing animals should be replaced with no fewer than 600, an order which Ama Hili Haba had no means to fulfil. The result was a state of hostility between the two domains; however there was no actual fighting. People in Dimu were not keen to follow Ama Hili Haba.[30]

This story seems to refer to the incidents of the late 1850s, spoken of in the Dutch report. It also reflects the great value of horses when many a steed was exported for a good price. The unpredictable and unreasonable behaviour of the colonial authorities is emphasised as a catalyst for the problems. Another person spoke of a war between Seba and Dimu in the time of Ama Doko Kaho (of Seba, 1868–82). The background was the marriage of the fettor Ama Tanya Luji of Dimu to a Eurasian woman (of Dutch and local extraction). There was a feast celebrating the marriage and Ama Doko Kaho attended with his consort. While the celebration was in full swing Ama Tanya Luji made it clear that the woman marrying Ama Doko Kaho was not as good-looking as his own consort, a Eurasian woman.[31] As could be expected, Ama Doko Kaho reacted furiously to the insult—the reason for the war.[32] Noteworthy here is the association of European blood with ideals of female beauty.

While the Sebanese account does not actually reveal the outcome of the war, this is explicated by a tradition from Dimu. The reason for the hostilities was the aggressive behaviour of the Hurati (Natadu) people in Dimu. They intended to appropriate all the good land which actually belonged to Wolo.[33] In the process of asserting their demands, the Hurati proceeded to burn down Wolo village. Ama Dida Li, the leader of Wolo, therefore asked for Seba's help, negotiating with them in order to defeat Hurati. Seba proved ready to assist. Consequently, the allies besieged the mighty stone fortress of Hurati. The Hurati people were unconcerned about access to water inside the fortress as they had a horse which could magically bring them water. After being under siege for seven days, the Hurati people triumphantly showed off their water containers from the walls. The Sebanese did not think they would be able to take the fortress; however, Ama Dida Li fired an iron bar at the fortress gate—blockaded by stones—which caused a breach. By that time, however, Fettor Ama Tanya Luji had already left

---

[30] Interview with Marthen Heke Medo, Seba (30.06.2012).

[31] Ama Doko Kaho's consort was Eurasian as well as is discussed later in the text. However, according to genealogical tradition, he also had a second wife, a Savunese woman by the name of Wahi Mone.

[32] Interview with Ama Behi, Seba (30.06.2012).

[33] The Wolo, like the Nabe'e, are considered indigenous people of Dimu as they had lived there before the arrival of Hue Dida in the area.

Hurati. Ama Dida Li and the Sebanese were finally able to enter the fortification. They burnt Hurati and it would never again be used in warfare. After the Hurati victory, the Sebanese made Ama Dida Li the *duae* of Dimu, but he only held power for about a year. Apparently, Ama Dida Li did not want to remain king and voluntarily stepped down.[34]

While the Dutch account and the various oral traditions are disparate, they do not entirely exclude each other. In the contemporary European text, it is a case of horse theft which escalates the conflict: in the story from Seba it is a matter of hurt pride and the version from Dimu describes it as an essentially internal affair. Each version of events included aspects to support a particular point of view, spicing it with legendary themes. In one respect at least, the Dimunese version can be corroborated. A Dutch report from 1874 shows that Dimu had temporarily deposed Ama Piga Jara, but they had reinstated him by that year for want of better alternatives (*Mailrapport* 1874: 282). The events highlighted his relatively weak position.

After the war of 1872, Savu remained relatively peaceful. However, resentment caused by the conflict was still simmering a few decades later. On 12 January 1892 a hundred people from Dimu visited Seba and demanded back the territories lost in the war. The reason for the request was not sheer irredentism, but rather that Dimu's rice fields were insufficient to support the local population. While it is not clear how the episode ended, Seba presumably held on to its erstwhile conquests. There was no armed clash recorded from the time.[35]

The rise of Seba

Seba saw a regular succession of leaders throughout most of the VOC era, but this was broken in the 19th century. Unlike Dimu, tradition in Seba preserved a good knowledge of the ruling branches of the *udu* Nataga, the clan providing rajas. Nevertheless, there are obscure points here as well. Doko Lomi, who died after 1794, had two sons—Riwu Doko and Bire Doko who are sometimes accounted for as rajas—but their order and chronology are not clear.[36] Doko Lomi's purported brother Ama Loni Jara encountered difficulties during the age

---

[34] Interview with Ama Dubu, Dimu (30.06.2012).

[35] Raad voor de Zending (1102–1: 1406, H.C. Kruyt, Notebook 3, 1892). According to Resident De Nijs Bik's relation in 1934, there was "almost an eruption" of warfare between Seba and Dimu around 1890 (De Nijs Bik 1934: 187).

[36] A regional list reproduced in Duggan (2001: 107) mentions Riwu Doko and Bire Doko, named after their father Doko Lomi. Riwu Doko's mother Libu Weti was the granddaughter of the troublemaker Ama Bala Nguru in Dimu (who is documented in the 1740s and 1750s).

Figure 48: Fettors of Dimu, Natadu clan in the 19th and 20th centuries

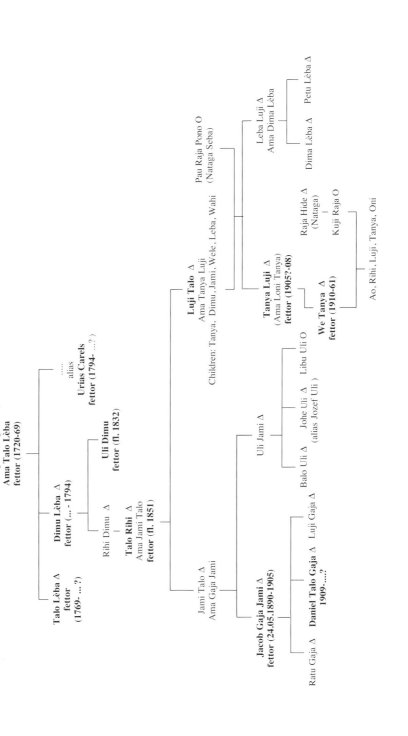

of Resident Hazaart (thus in the interval 1808–32) when his ruling colleagues in Dimu, Liae and Mesara accused him of unspecified shortcomings before the Dutch. He stepped down for a while and his nephew Bire Doko was made temporary ruler in his stead.[37] Later, he returned to power as he is known from Dutch sources between 1830 and 1858.[38] If his place in the pedigree is correct, he was at least 80 years old at his demise as his putative father passed away in 1778. Apart from the rivalry between Ama Loni and his elder brother (described in chapter 6), the only information on this person concerns his two marriages. His first wife Tanya Luji of Dimu committed adultery with Tedo Riwu, the raja's sister's husband, after which Tedo Riwu was killed. Ama Loni Jara later married Hanna Jami Lobo who was from the same lineage as Tedo Riwu (Nataga Najohina).[39]

The fact that a Dutch posthouder was once again stationed in Seba indicates its star was rising. There seems to have been no European representation on the island for long periods, but after the British had left, the colonial authorities took measures to ensure there was at least a minimum of surveillance. In 1819, the Batavia government decided to place posthouders in Sutrana (Ambeno), Naikliu (Amfo'an), Maubara and Fialaran, and on the islands of Rote, Solor, Savu and Pantar.[40] The posthouder in Savu, while residing in Seba, received his means of subsistence from all the domains and did not actually have a salary from the Kupang authorities (Kartodirdjo 1973: 413).

There is a little more detail about Ama Loni Jara's children. The eldest died young, but the second son Ama Dima Talo inherited his father's position and ruled from 1859 to 1864. By this time the *udu* Nataga had become deeply involved in Sumba affairs. In spite of the VOC's belated attempts to establish a toehold on the sizeable island, Sumba had fallen completely below the company's radar by the end of the 18th century. It is possible that a careful collation of oral data may be able to disperse some of the mist that surrounds Sumba in the first half of the 19th century, but it was only in 1845 that substantial contact with the company resumed. In the meantime, the situation in Sumba appears to have persisted as a free-for-all; it was a place which, being neither Christianised nor Islamised, was a tempting object for plunder and slaving (Needham 1983). Apart from seafarers from Sulawesi and the Endenese from Flores, Seba was

---

[37] Raad voor de Zending, 1102–1: J.K. Wijngaarden, notebook, 1890 (Figures 37 and 49).

[38] He is identified as a raja in Sumba in an oral source. On relations with Sumba, see the later discussion.

[39] Raad voor de Zending, 1102–1: J.K. Wijngaarden, notebook, 1890.

[40] ANRI Timor: 44, letter, Batavia to Kupang, 16 December 1819.

another of the contenders. The *udu* Nataga built up positions in eastern Sumba through matrimonial alliances and settlements. Thus, the sister of Ama Dima Talo, Dunga Jara, was married to a raja called Umbu Nggaba Haumara of Melolo (known to have ruled in 1863). The place was one of the Sumbanese domains that the VOC and Raijua had approached in the 1690s. There may therefore have been a tradition of contacts between the Savunese and particular places in Sumba over the centuries, although the voluminous but selective colonial tomes did not record them. Ama Dima's nephew Ama Kuji Bire and the latter's nephew, Ama Luji Dimu, would later acquire a strong position of leadership in Sumba, based in Melolo.

The Dunga Jara dynastic marriage alliance was not a happy one, according to later tradition. While living in Sumba Dunga Jara became mentally ill. After the illness had become more serious, her husband Umbu Nggaba Haumara sent a *koa* bird (a dove) over the sea to her brother in Savu. Tied to the bird's leg was a message written in Savunese and the bird carried her brother's reply back to her husband in Sumba. In the letter he beseeched the raja to send his sister back to Savu and Umbu Nggaba complied. A certain Haba Jeru brought the princess back to her original island. The story presupposes that knowledge of writing had spread by this time. It also indicates at least a minimum of attention to the well-being of aristocratic females. Indeed, the revelation goes further—what is true for the aristocracy is the same for the rest of the population. In the context of Savunese society's close brother-sister relationship, this is actually not surprising; a brother has a life-long responsibility for his sister/s and vice versa.[41]

The original residence of the Sebanese rajas was Nadawawi on Namata hill. The last ruler to stay there was the shadowy Bire Doko. Ama Dima reportedly built a new residence of wood, close to the Teni Hawu Palace of later times.[42] His time was short, though. By 1864, his behaviour became increasingly erratic and he appeared to some observers to be half-crazed. The last straw was an incident where he nearly killed a visitor with his bare hands. A member of the elder branch stepped in and resolutely took charge of the situation. This was Ama Nia Jawa, a son of Bire Doko, who was the acting raja some time before 1830.[43] Over the years he had built up a positive reputation with the Dutch in Kupang. His good command of Malay enabled him to function as an interlocutor in

---

[41] Interview with Marthen Heke Medo, Seba (30.06.2012).

[42] Interview with Ama Bèhi, Seba (30.06.2012).

[43] There is no direct mention of this in contemporary Dutch sources. However, the official annual *Almanak en naamregister voor Nederlandsch-Indië* (Almanac and name register for Netherlands India) says that Ama Loni Jara's (second) reign started in 1830 (possibly a rough approximation made when the listings started in the 1850s) which means that Bire Doko's reign may have ended around 1830.

dealings with the colonials, who regarded him as a "civilised" type according to their own standards. In a swift coup he took power from Ama Dima and was acknowledged as the new raja. A party of Sebanese malcontents tried to foment trouble and plotted against the new ruler. However, the son of the ousted Ama Dima surprisingly chose to back Ama Nia Jawa rather than his own impaired father. He promptly told Ama Nia what he knew about the plans and the uprising was nipped in the bud.[44]

Although he did not enjoy his position for long, Ama Nia Jawa was an important leader after whom the ruling branch acquired the name Jawa. Unlike the previous rulers, there is substantial information about him in oral traditions. The collective memory portrays him as a cultural hero of sorts who changed economic life in Seba. Up to this point, there was no shop or *warung* (stall [In]) in Savu, only traders who bartered goods. Ama Nia Jawa undertook to open up joint trade with Makassar and with Butung, off south-east Sulawesi. The raja bestowed some coastal land on Bugis and Makassar people, and Arab merchants. Tradition identifies the land grants as the reason why some traders near the shore are Muslims to this day. The merchants came to trade horses, buffalos and, later on, goats.

In order to keep the old customary land traditions, Ama Nia Jawa arranged for a special ceremony before planting. Called *pekèdi melaka dobutu*, *pekèdi* means to leave or go away, *melaka* is Malacca—referring to the origin of the foreigners established in Savu—and *do butu* are the Butonese traders. The ritual predating Ama Nia Jawa consists of sending out to sea the bad things foreigners may have brought with them. In Seba during his time the ritual took on a new aspect with its name mentioning newcomers from Malacca and Buton. Today's rendering is *pekèdi mehalah* (*halah* [Sa] meaning bad or wrong).This annual cleansing ritual towards the end of the dry season is held in every domain; first in each village where people burn their rubbish, then the priest Rue holds the ritual for the entire community. In Seba it takes place at the harbour where a small lontar leaf made into a boat containing objects of foreign origin is put out to sea. A sheep is sacrificed. In Dimu, this ritual is known as *penyèro èmu rue* or sweeping/cleaning the house of Rue before the planting season starts.

Furthermore, tradition records a pragmatic stance on religion. In order to maintain good working relations with the foreigners, Ama Nia Jawa enjoined his classificatory brother and vice-raja (*wakil raja* [In]), Ama Alu Bèhi, to convert

---

[44] ANRI Timor: 106, monthly reports, May 1864. The son was presumably Dima Talo of the genealogies. Tradition asserts that he died before his deposed father. No Dutch records in current knowledge state how long Ama Dima lived after the coup.

Figure 49: Rulers of Seba in the 19th century

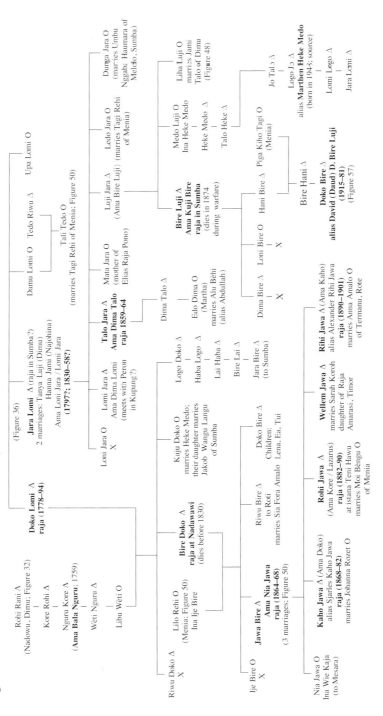

Photo 14. A stone carving representing the ship *MS Sutherland* that capsized off the north coast of Savu in the 1860s. Tourist guidebooks wrongly identified the carving as Captain Cook's *Endeavour*; Nadawawi, Namata hill (2016)

Photo 15. The *Kowa Makaha* (Makassar boat) motif for a man's hip cloth; the unrestricted pattern is a reminder of Makassarese traders settling in Seba at the time of Ama Nia Jawa; Seba (2010)

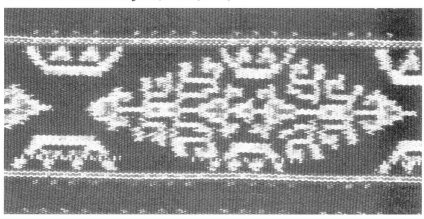

Photo 16. The residence of the rajas of Seba and later of Savu. On the right is the broken mast of the *Peni*, Ama Nia Jawa's boat; Teni Hawu, Seba (2012)

to Islam.[45] His new name was Raja Abdullah. Ama Nia Jawa himself preferred to accept the Christian religion, though he was not baptised. After opening trade with Sulawesi, more Muslims arrived in Savu. A modern source makes the counterfactual observation that Savu might have become Muslim if it had not been for the Dutch missionary project.[46]

Tradition also knows something about Ama Nia's relationship with the Dutch. Interestingly, however, the events are portrayed as being tainted by rivalry and ill feeling. Ama Nia possessed two vessels called *Wilhelmus* and *Peni*—the former named after the Dutch king. A skilled sailor himself, Ama Nia left Seba's harbour on board the *Peni*, with the intention to sail to Kupang. The sea trip turned out to be a race, as his craft departed at exactly the same time as a Dutch ship. Ama Nia's boat arrived in Kupang first—the defeat aroused the anger of the Dutchmen. They took revenge by cutting the *Peni*'s mast. The mast is still to be seen on the terrace at the residence of the Seba rajas.[47] The event is remembered in the form of a verse about the raja's mantra name: "Only *Peni* stands brave enough to challenge the Dutch rule." The tale falls into a category of stories from this part of the archipelago which portrays the whites as competitive, ill-tempered and prone to dirty tricks. While the Arabs, Makassarese and Butungese fall naturally into the socio-economic world of the Savunese, Europeans remain unpredictable outsiders.

It is interesting to contrast this image with the colonial archive. In fact, the Dutch officials never tire of praising Ama Nia Jawa's virtues; he was supposedly the brightest raja in the region and behaved with a European-style politeness. Even before his accession, he possessed a schooner called *Savoe Pakket*—it was the first European-built vessel that a Savunese sailed. It was however lost in a severe tempest in 1863.[48] He actively cooperated with the authorities in Kupang and sold them horses for the armed troops. On one occasion, he picked out six black horses and offered them as a gift to the governor-general in Batavia.[49] The colonial reports confirm the tradition that there were no markets in Savu as late as 1850. Aside from horses, the Savunese also exported some coarse ceramics and tobacco, and imported cotton from the Solor Islands.[50]

---

[45] Ama Alu Bèhi was not actually his brother, according to the extant genealogies, but rather the great-grandson of Raja Wadu Lai (c. 1704–42).

[46] From an interview with Marthen Heke Medo, Seba (30.06.2012), rather than from oral tradition.

[47] Interviews with Ama Bèhi, Seba (19.04.2011) and (30.06.2012).

[48] ANRI Timor: 105, monthly reports, dated April–May 1863.

[49] ANRI Timor: 107, monthly report, September 1865.

[50] ANRI Timor: 80, General report, 1850.

However, Ama Nia Jawa did not report everything to the Dutch authorities. A document kept by the Namata clan shows that he also administered justice when his possessions were under dispute.[51] In 1866, he sold a rice field previously owned by the Teriwu clan to Ama Mako Lai, head of the Namata. This was a time when a series of quarrels between Teriwu and Seba, dating to very early times, were at their peak, so some background information is necessary. Teriwu, as an independent polity, disintegrated before the arrival of Europeans in Savu. The documents indicate that descendants of Hire Wunu from Teriwu lost a war against the Namata and the Teriwu settlement was torched; as a result, Teriwu lost the ritual cockfighting site of Raemoneie. Large parts of Teriwu territory became part of Seba, which acknowledges only the Nada Ae arena with the large megaliths in Namata for ritual cockfights. Teriwu kept its right to ritual cockfights in Liae domain.

Around 1860, members of the Teriwu clan used the ancient unsettled disputes with Seba as an excuse to burn their rivals' fields, destroying the harvest—fields which had previously been part of Teriwu's *tanah suku* (tribal land [In]). These plots of land were then owned respectively by the Namata and Nataga clans. Teriwu people stole cattle, killing some of them, and slaughtered a large number of buffalos personally owned by Ama Nia Jawa. This was akin to a declaration of war. Ama Nia Jawa avowed that the Teriwu should compensate him with 60 animals (horses and buffalos) and allowed them time to meet his demands. Ama Iawu Lomi, then head of the Teriwu, did not comply, so Ama Nia Jawa confiscated a plot of their land instead. The Namata clan offered to give Ama Nia Jawa the 60 animals in exchange for the Teriwu land. According to Savunese adat, they marked the border with stones, and held a ceremony to sacrifice a dog and a red rooster. They placed the rooster's red feathers and the dog's teeth underneath the border stones and pronounced an oath. Ama Wènyi Luji then prepared the transaction to make the deal legal. The parties signed a formal letter establishing ownership of the rice field called Teriwu on 3 February 1866.

None of the Teriwu attended the ceremony because they had already lost ownership of that land. Thus concluded, the Namata and Nataga considered the case closed. They had made statements of landownership both through a traditional ceremony with an oath and binding words, and by signing a written document with an even more binding consequence for the future. Savu had entered the realm of written notary transactions with signatures and legal stamps. Members of the ruling clans educated by the 'stranger-kings' were comfortable with this practice, which was still unknown to the majority of illiterate Savunese.

---

[51] Interview with Dooly [Dule] Koy (08.06.2012).

In the course of time, Teriwu people contested other plots of land located in ancient Teriwu territory then owned by the Namata. A survey dated 21 November 1902, signed by Raja E.L. (Elias Luji Raja Pono) of Seba, Fettor Pawe Rèke and 11 village chiefs, lists 49 plots of land owned by the Namata clan which are located in the Teriwu tribal area. A note indicates that the letter was unsigned and unread by the posthouder. The case was brought several times to the local jurisdiction by both parties until it was definitely settled in 1981. This case does not seem to have reached Dutch records of the time; Raja Ama Nia Jawa of Seba, in charge of the reports to the Dutch authorities, might have considered the affair too parochial to be reported.

> Signatories in 1866:
> Ama Nia Jawa (Nataga Naluluweo, raja of Seba)
> Ama Wěnyi Luji (Nataga); his grandson Saul Haba Jingi is one of the signatories in 1981
> Ama Lomi Dira (Nataga Najohina)
> Ama Alu Bèhi (Nataga); his grandson Ori Hide Lilo is one of the signatories in 1981
> Ama Upa Riwu (Napujara, raja of Liae)
> Ama Pita Dadi (?)
> Kaho Jawa (Nataga; son of Ama Nia Jawa)
> Ama Mako Lai (head of the Namata clan)
> Ama Kati Luji (Dimu)
> Ama Lie Mèno (Dimu)

Ama Nia eventually received a gold medal for his merits.[52] He must have realised the potential in playing the Europeans' game. The eastern parts of the archipelago still consisted of highly traditional societies where most of the leaders probably had a parochial outlook and where the colonial government seldom intervened with force. Perhaps Ama Nia was able to discern the changes that were under way: steamships, weaponry and technological equipment had improved visibly during his lifetime, and Dutch involvement had expanded in nearby Sumba. The raja took the strategic step of placing some of his children with European families in Kupang. This acquaintance with Western culture paved the way for the subsequent Christianisation of the elite.

---

[52] According to *Mailrapport* (1882: 512), the government decided to bestow a golden chain on Ama Nia Jawa, which was later given to his son Ama Doko Kaho. This is probably separate from the medal.

One of Ama Nia Jawa's marriages was to Upa Tagi, whose father was raja of the small but fertile Menia domain. At his demise in 1868, Ama Nia Jawa left at least two daughters and three sons who ruled in turn. They were Ama Doko Kaho (Sjarle Kaho) who ruled from 1868 to 1882, Lazarus Rohi Jawa who held power from 1882 to 1890 and Alexander Rihi Jawa who headed the domain from 1890 to 1901. They inherited at least some of their father's enterprising spirit, and their time saw the expansion of Seba's power and prestige. Through a system of marriage alliances, the *udu* Nataga created a web of contacts with other polities of the eastern region. Marriages outside Savu were not unknown in earlier times, but they appear to have been employed in a systematic way in the 19th century. Alexander Rihi Jawa married a princess from Termanu, the most important domain in Rote. Two of their sons in turn married princesses from Korbaffo in Rote and Amarasi in Timor. Later on, a descendant of Ama Doko Kaho married the raja of Amarasi, while Alexander's eldest son adopted a Termanu princess.

No less conspicuous was the career of Riwu Bire, a brother of Ama Nia Jawa. Modern tradition relates that this prince wished to find a bride of similar aristocratic status. He was, however, unable to find a suitable woman in Savu. For that reason he went to Rote where he met a princess called Sia Fora Amalo. She was the daughter of a Termanu raja who died in the late 1830s and she had an interesting history. Sia seems to be identical to Geertruijda Fora Amalo who is known from Dutch sources. She first married the Protestant missionary Johan Coenraad Terlinden (died 1832) and then a British sailor called Charles Wood—many Britons stayed in Kupang for a time as it was a port of call for ships between Australia and India. Opinions about her character were divided: Terlinden adored her and called her a second Apollonia, while the co-missionary Heijmering called her unclean and boisterous, and noted that she was not a virgin on her first marriage (Hägerdal 2013: 83–5). At any rate, Sia married Riwu Bire in what was probably her third marriage. As her status in Rote was quite elevated, he could not take her back to Savu; instead he stayed with her Termanu kin. Perhaps the circumstances of the marriage were more strategically planned than tradition admits. Termanu had long been the foremost Rotenese princedom, although it had a chequered history, having at least ten rajas throughout the 19th century. The family of Riwu Bire came to dominate Termanu as *wakil raja* (vice-raja) for a number of generations, in effect running the affairs of the reigning Amalo Dynasty.[53] In this way, *udu* Nataga obtained great influence in Savu as well as Rote (and even parts of Sumba and Timor).

---

[53] Thanks to James J. Fox for sharing the information.

There was a Dutch component in this dynastic network. The bourgeoisie of Kupang was dominated by a few old European families, such as Tielman, Vent and Thedens. Due to the lack of white women they usually had indigenous or Eurasian spouses, often Rotenese who were considered fair and attractive in comparison with the dark-skinned Timorese. Being a Christian, Raja Ama Doko Kaho was able to marry the burgher daughter Johanna Rozet. A member of the Rozet family had been posthouder in Savu for a while which might explain the connection.[54] Johanna was Eurasian and used Kupang Malay as her mother tongue; she only had limited knowledge of Dutch (*Mailrapport* 1874: 282). The marriage was less than harmonious. The raja's kinsman Ama Kuji Bire headed a Savunese community in Sumba and was killed during local warfare in 1874. He left a widow by the name of Ina Loni who had illicit relations with the raja even before her husband died. Ama Doko Kaho headed an excursion to the war theatre in Sumba and came back to Savu with lots of golden objects, and Ina Loni as his concubine. This was clearly not acceptable to prevalent Savunese moral standards and certainly not to a Eurasian burgher's daughter. In a letter to the missionary Teffer, Johanna Rozet complained bitterly of her fate:

Honourable Sir,

Through these few lines, I make known to You that my husband has left me and has attached himself to a woman called Ina Loni. He lives entirely with her at home. Already from September 1875 he began to desert me. I patiently endured all until my father came to Savo with the Resident. I then told him everything. As a consequence, my husband Ama Doko (that is the name of Raja Seba) promised to improve. You must not be angry at me, Honourable Sir, if I seem bothersome to You, but Ama Doko has not kept his word. I treat him friendly and good, but he threatens to murder me, and I escaped from the butcher's knife not long ago, as a consequence of which a native woman received a wound. Please help me. So far I endure everything patiently, but what will be my end?

Reverently, Johanna Rozet.[55]

---

[54] Conversely, a Cornelia Raja, possibly a member of the Seba raja family, married the colonial official Johannes Jacob Sick around 1860 (N. Posthumus, Castricum, personal communication; March 2014).

[55] Raad voor de Zending, 1102–1: 1411, letter, M. Teffer to NZG Rotterdam, 24 May 1876. Teffer rendered the Malay letter in a free Dutch translation.

In his letters, Teffer railed against Ama Doko Kaho and the Dutch government which played his game. To the fiery missionary, the raja was a scoundrel who committed innumerable acts of mischief, aside from his appalling treatment of Johanna. And it was not only Teffer who reported Ama Doko's violent behaviour. Similarly, Resident Ecoma Verstege related in 1878 that Ama Doko had difficulties controlling his passions. One of his female subjects, Kunga Lingu, evoked his displeasure on some issue. The raja flew in a rage, pulled the woman off a traditional sofa, and kicked her in the neck and side. Blood gushed from her nose as she passed away from her injuries. The posthouder reported the matter to Resident Verstege. As the details were unclear, he ordered the posthouder to investigate the incident very carefully, to give Ama Doko no reason to think that the Dutch were interfering in Savunese internal business. It was an illustration of non-intervention current in contemporaneous colonial policy.[56] From Teffer's perspective, the Dutch Resident seemed to care nothing about the raja's behaviour as long as he received valuable deliveries of horses. How else, Teffer asked rhetorically, could a native man, a Savunese, keep Kupang in the reins and ridicule the government? His popularity with the colonial authorities "gave him the privilege to marry an honourable girl as an honourable man, in the presence of the official of civil affairs." Teffer satirised Ama Doko's motivations in the first person: "I make the Resident blind and deaf by stuffing a horse in his ear and eye."[57] At any rate, Johanna Rozet survived her violent husband who passed away under "horrible" circumstances in May 1882, as Teffer noted with ill-concealed glee. Officially, Ama Doko died from an illness that spread after a violent cyclone ravaged Rote and Savu in March 1882; however, Teffer vented his suspicion that a certain temukung had helped him to the other side.[58] Johanna soon married a Kupangese burgher.[59]

The horse trade was an important reason for Europeans to keep a good working relationship with Seba. In the year 1876 no fewer than 600 horses arrived in Java from Savu. However, European observers noted with some consternation that this trade was offset by the prevalent ritual practices. In the same year, some 800 horses were slaughtered on festive occasions and when work in the rice fields was to take place. Those responsible for the killings were the settlement

---

[56] Ecoma Verstege (*Mailrapport* 1878).

[57] Raad voor de Zending, 1102–1: 1411, letter, M. Teffer to NZG Rotterdam, 24 May 1876.

[58] Ama Doko Kaho Jawa passed away on 13 May 1882 according to *Mailrapport* (1882: 512). Teffer, angry that the raja had kept imported medicines for himself and his closest kin, obviously had no qualms about sharing his views on the matter (*Ramp op Savoe* 1882: 181).

[59] *Naamlijst der Europeesche inwoonders* (Name-list of European inhabitants) 1889. She married Diederik Marcus Pelt on 1 March 1888.

chiefs. There was a grim rationale behind the practice, though. Not only did the community desire the meat for consumption, but slaughter was often the only solution to the lack of fodder. As the easterly monsoon commenced, vegetation in Savu disappeared under the dry conditions. People could only feed their horses and other domesticated animals lontar palm leaves and some weeds that grew occasionally in the remaining wet areas (*Kontrak perjanjian* 2007: 406–7). In 1877, as the island was beset by a severe drought, Ama Doko Kaho took measures to obtain extra rice for his hungry dependents. He paid a sum of money to visiting traders or agents from Makassar and went there in person on a British schooner. In Makassar he took 350 piculs, some 22,000 kilos, of rice back to Seba. This was obviously made possible by the horse trade, as rajas in the Timor area were usually poor and lacked financial assets. As in many polities of maritime Southeast Asia, the raja acted as the prime trader for his realm. This was not appreciated by the Resident of Kupang, Ecoma Verstege, who believed that a raja in the Timor residency should remain in his territory. He later reprimanded Ama Doko for making extended trips to Sumba and Makassar without notifying Kupang, and for leaving his domain in the care of lesser chiefs (*Mailrapport* 1877: 807). Ecoma Verstege's displeasure forebodes the colonial officials' increasing ambition to keep local affairs under their control. This, however, would only come to fruition a few decades later.

The absorption of Menia

To the north-east of Seba, Menia maintained its autonomy for the greater part of the 19th century under the leadership of the *udu* Kekoro. Being a small place, it was of limited interest to the Dutch, who recorded few facts about it apart from the succession of rajas. After Ama Piga Rehi, who reigned from 1794 to an unknown date, a certain Ama Piga Tagi is recorded in 1832. In May 1842, the rajas of Menia, Dimu, Liae and Mesara went in person to Kupang to be formally confirmed in their positions by Resident Cornelis Sluyter (Kartodirdjo 1973: 413). The new raja of Menia was Ama Gaja Tagi, the son of Ama Piga Rehi.

However, internal conflict in Ama Gaja's immediate family spelled the end of Menia. As related by current tradition, the raja had unresolvable differences with his son. After the death of his wife Ina Gaja Tagi, Ama Gaja Tagi married a younger woman who had a sexual relationship with his son, Gaja Tagi. The raja was profoundly offended, and he went to Ama Kore Rihi Jawa in Seba to whom he gave the Wuihebo land on the condition that his son and descendants would never be able to lay claim to it. A ceremony took place at Bojo Terèjo next to two large black stones; Kuji Lai (Ama Loni Kuji) the raja of Raijua pronounced the oath that the Tagi family of Menia could never again eat the harvest of Wuihebo.

In reality, at a much later date the land would again belong to the Tagi family through D.D. Bire Luji. According to a modern source, Raja Paulus Charles Jawa of Savu, who had no descendants, adopted (*hapo*) D.D. Bire Luji (who became D.D. Jawa) and he received the Wuihebo land from the raja. Later D.D. Jawa, who was related to the Tagi family from Menia through his mother's lineage, returned the Wuihebo land to Menia, thus breaking the oath. The Tagi family could once again cultivate the land and enjoy its harvest, but it is never allowed to sell the land.[60]

At that time, however, Ama Kore's father Ama Nia Jawa agreed to intervene and settle the matter. At one point Ama Gaja Tagi's daughter married Ama Nia, though it is not clear if this happened before or after the intervention. Moreover, the difficulties besetting Menia continued as the raja's son persisted in creating trouble. Eventually, Seba simply took the decision to abrogate traditional autonomy and annex fertile Menia.[61] There was frequent inter-marriage between the aristocracies of the two domains which closely bound them together. There might be another factor at play in the annexation: the great smallpox epidemic that raged in the late 1860s possibly causing the demise of Ama Gaja in 1868–69. One of his other sons, Ama Lena Rihi, took over the weakened Menia, but he was entirely under Seba's control and had to step down in 1873. Henceforth, there was neither raja nor fettor in charge, just a temukung.

The closer circumstances between the two domains are ill-defined. A Dutch report from 1874 asserts that it was not just an internal Savunese affair because Kupang took the final decision. The Resident deposed Ama Lena Rihi because of his uncivilised acts (*woeste handelingen*) and commissioned the governance of Menia to Ama Doko Kaho of Seba. The next Resident, Hendrik Carel Humme, saw no reason to change this arrangement as Ama Doko seemed to handle his new acquisition well. There is no record of protests against the loss of autonomy in either oral or documentary sources. The contemporaneous able-bodied male population, after smallpox had taken its toll, was no more than 60 (*Mailrapport* 1874: 282). That may be compared to the (certainly unreliable) figures from 1832 which state there were 1,150 able-bodied men.

The missionary Johan Frederik Niks toured the island in 1885 and provides his observations of Menia after the Seba takeover. His account deepens the opacity that surround the end of the Menia domain, because he suggests that the reasons for its fall had more to do with Seba's military strategy than any formal agreement:

---

[60] Interviews with Ama Bèhi (10.05.2014); and Marthen Heke Medo (17.05.2014).

[61] Interview with Marthen Heke Medo (30.06.2012). On the marriage alliances between the domains of Seba and Menia, see Figures 49 and 50.

I visited Menia that was previously an independent kingdom and is now annexed by Seba. It is one of the most fertile spots of Savu, with a valley where a river meanders, whose water is used for irrigation of *sawah*s [rice fields (In)] and gardens. The *negeri* is situated on a rock, surrounded by a wall of rock boulders piled up. However, in spite of its favourable situation, that small fortress could not keep its independence since there was no drinking water, which had to be fetched.[62]

Mesara and Liae

To the south-west and south, the minor domains of Mesara and Liae led a comparatively peaceful existence throughout the 19th century. However, there was some conflict-related mobility of a few enterprising people. Oral tradition records that people from Mesara were involved in the Sumba campaigns. Five people enlisted for service with the Dutch troops in Banten, Java where an anti-colonial rebellion erupted in 1888. Dutch sources also refer to Savunese involvement in the same conflict.[63]

Social memory of the Deo Rai clan (Nabèlu) remembers Riwu Ratu (Ama Manu Riwu). He is listed as fettor of Mesara in 1832 in the Francis manuscript in relation to two incidents. First, Ama Manu Riwu quarrelled with Raja Ama Biha Buki Uli over land which, to the present, is still an unresolved matter. Second, the circumstances of his death, which occurred while he was living in Kupang, were murky. He was cutting the beard of a Dutch officer, whom he accidentally wounded, and he fled the scene. People found him some time afterwards under a tree. At first, they did not notice that he was dead because he was sitting with his back against the tree. Apparently, he had committed suicide. The Dutch officer felt sorry for him and arranged for a statue in Pariti near Kupang where this happened.[64] The later fettors of Mesara came from the Naputitu, as did the rajas; one may wonder why a fettor was recruited from the Deo Rai's clan. His wife was however from the raja clan of Mesara.[65]

The position of raja in the *udu* Naputitu was secure; from 1781 to 1914 the rajas succeeded each other from father to son, but they no longer lived in Raepedèro. They were Buki Dimu (1781 until after 1794) who lived in nearby

---

[62] Raad voor de Zending, 1102–1: 1408, J.F. Niks, travel report, 5–29 June 1885.

[63] "The Resident has asked to enroll 20 Christians as soldiers to serve in Bantam. They sign up for three years, receive 40 guilders in cash per person, and 14 guilders per month (Seba 5, Mesara 5, Liaae 4, Timoe 6)" (Raad voor de Zending, 1102–1: 1406, H.C. Kruyt, notebook, c. 1888).

[64] Sources: Ina Ta Bire and Zadrak Bunga (17.05.2013).

[65] See the Francis list in Appendix IV.

Figure 50: Marriage alliances between Menia, Seba and Mesara in the 19th century

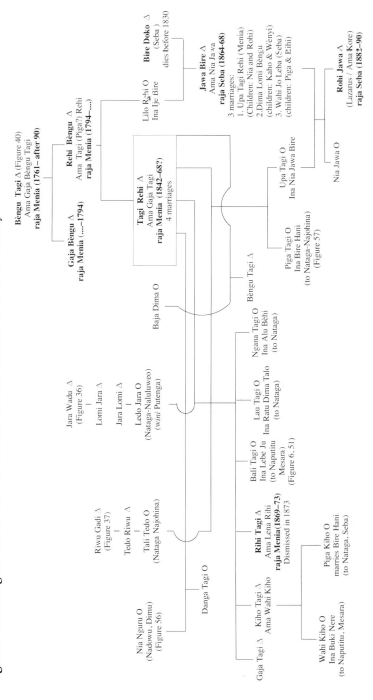

Raemèdi as did Uli Buki (early 19th century); Ama Biha Buki Uli (before 1832 to 1868) moved to Ledemawide where his successor Ama Lebe Ju Buki (1869–93) also lived. Ama Tenga Doko Ju (1893–1914) moved to Ligu, near the sea, where his brother and Fettor Kore Ju had already established himself. The raja's house in the shape of a cross is still standing today. Next to his house the raja opened a weaving centre which no longer exists. However, the building's carved beams ended up in Pedèro as the house was demolished in the late 20th century. Otherwise, there is not much information about these figures in either oral or documentary records.

Social memory in Mesara depicts Uli Buki dying suddenly in what were later interpreted as questionable circumstances. Uli Buki was crushed to death by a tree that he and his son Ama Biha were cutting down. As the tree fell exactly where he had been told to stand, a rumour soon arose that the death was not accidental. The claim was fuelled by the apparent haste in which Ama Biha acceded to the raja position. The Resident referred to Ama Biha as the brightest raja in the region together with Ama Nia Jawa of Seba, already noted as a person who knew how to get along with Europeans.[66] Of interest here is that both rajas were closely related; Ama Biha's son, Kaja Buki, married Ama Nia Jawa's daughter. The missionary Huising devotes a few kind words to the last of the line, Ama Tenga, and his consort. They were tranquil people who enthusiastically welcomed a Christian teacher. He considered the raja to be a great improvement on his deceased father.[67]

By contrast, Liae had a much more irregular history in this period. This was already the case in the VOC era when different branches of the *udu* Napujara took turns exercising power. Memories about the first half of the 19th century centre on a certain Rohi Jami who lived in the village of Ledetalo (Mountain of Talo). For unknown reasons he decided to leave Savu and migrate to Kupang. However, after waiting in vain for months (or years) for a boat to pass by, he gave up his plan and decided to stay in Savu, renaming the place Kotahawu. *Kota* refers here to Fort Concordia in Kupang and *Hawu* is Savu. It is conjecture as to whether the name reflected derision or disillusionment, or perhaps it was simply marking a new start in his life.

Rohi Jami is Ama Lena Rohi, listed in the 1832 Francis document, and his given residence is indeed Kotahawu. Thus, the failed departure and the change of village name occured prior to 1832. Dutch sources are lacking as it was during the period in which they were not visiting the island. What people remember is an

---

[66]   ANRI Timor: 107, monthly reports, June–July 1865.

[67]   Raad voor de Zending, 1102–1: S.J. Huising, report, 20 May 1895.

Figure 51: Rulers of Mesara in the 19th and 20th centuries

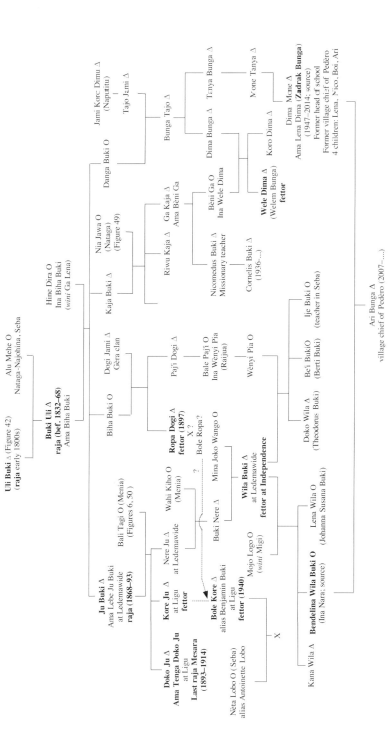

Figure 52: Important figures of Liae from the 18th to 20th centuries

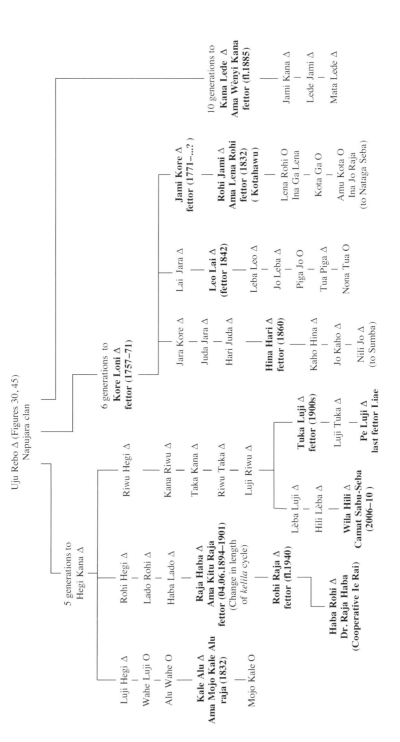

unsuccessful attempt to leave Savu which led to a new place name. A new name is usually an instrument for communicating something significant in the life of an ancestor. What is remembered 200 years later is in fact a non-event. Of interest is that in 2004, after the new *kecamatan* (subdistrict [In]) was created, Kotahawu was divided into two new villages—one carrying on the name Kotahawu and the second reviving the old name Ledetalo.

The Liae raja listed in the Francis manuscript in 1832 is "Ama Moje Keloa".[68] He is presumably Ama Mojo Kale Alu who was related to the *udu* Napujara on the female side. He may have met an untimely end, for in 1848 a certain raja was drowned in an accident—not an uncommon fate for Savunese leaders whose island was situated in the midst of an unpredictable body of water. In January 1851, the Dutch Resident Baron van Lijnden confirmed his successor Ama Ije Jote Robo.[69] From the genealogies, it appears that he was not a member of the *udu* Napujara but rather belonged to the *udu* Nahai, which was only remotely related to the Napujara. According to current tradition, he was only *wakil raja* (vice-raja [In]), thus a temporary figure who led Liae from 1851 to 1857.

More assertive was Fettor Leo Lai, who governed in these years. Appointed by the Dutch in April 1842, he was controversial, identified by the leaders of other domains as a decidedly troublesome figure. Unlike most Savunese aristocrats, he had little regard for the Dutch colonial state. The Savu posthouder had obtained permission to bring some people from Raijua to cultivate two places called Raibala and Kusabi. When the posthouder tried to enact the plan in 1845, Leo Lai impeded him, weapon in hand. For the Kupang administration it was yet another reminder of the colonial state's precarious position in these quarters. Resources were so scarce that the Resident did not care to deal with the issue; he would rather wait for the fettor to appear in Kupang in a not-too-distant future, when the matter could be more closely investigated.[70] The conflict does not seem to have had far-reaching consequences, but it was not isolated. Oral materials imply that another issue occurred around the mid-19th century where Liae clashed with Dimu and eventually lost some land.

Ama Ije was followed by another irregular reign. Ama Baki Bali from the *udu* Gopo held the position of *duae adat* (lord of customary law) between 1857 and 1868. Like others in the Savunese elite he succumbed in 1868–69, probably in the apocalyptic smallpox epidemic that ravaged the island. Then at last a member of the established *udu* Napujara, Ama Amu Manu, was raised to the dignity. He

---

[68] Francis, H 548, KITLV Archive, 1832.

[69] ANRI Timor: 60, Register of the acts and decisions, dated 24 January 1851. His full name was provided in an interview with Marthen Heke Medo, Seba (30.06.2012).

[70] ANRI Timor: 76, General report, 1845.

was the great-great-grandson of the 18th-century Raja Jami Riwu and ruled Liae from 1869 to 1879. There is no explanation in either oral or written sources about why representatives of different clans were chosen; the genealogies identify a number of Ama Ije's sons and brothers who had no known claims to the raja dignity. Competition between the various *udu* and a lack of suitable heirs may account for the variety of clan representatives. Both Ama Amu Manu and his son Hendrik Ratu Manu (1879–1914) were well regarded by the missionaries: Ama Amu Manu, "faithful to his call", established a church, though it was a rudimentary construction that became unserviceable within a few years. Before his death he assembled resources to build a more durable house of God, a task fulfilled by his son.[71] According to J.F. Niks, who visited in 1885, Liae was the smallest domain on the island. Owing to the lack of fertile land it led a troubled existence. Several Liae people left their native island for the arduous life of a "coolie" in Kupang. Many were interested in the Christian creed, and the raja and his wife made as much effort as they could to favour the congregation.[72]

Raijua

The small but important island of Raijua was firmly tied to the VOC from the 1750s. There is more information about its political leaders than some other Savunese domains. Tradition was explicit about the succession of rajas and it is possible to check the details occasionally against the colonial archive. The material shows that the position of raja was usually kept within the same lineage. However, there is not a single example of a son succeeding his father and there are several cases of internal rupture.

The last VOC raja was Jara Lai who passed away after 1794. His uncle Maru Nyebe led for an interim period before the latter's nephew Kote Lai took over the dignity. This individual had a dramatic death that reverberated in colonial reports as well as recorded tradition. In 1807, there was still a Dutch interpreter in Savu who reported to Kupang on the tense situation where the regent of Raijua was at odds with his fettor. The fettor gained the upper hand and burnt the regent's land. As Savu's highest formal raja, the lord of Dimu sent some men to assist the regent of Raijua. When the belligerent fettor heard about the impending action, he made clever use of the profound disunity within the Savunese aristocracy. He invoked the assistance of other Savunese regents who were hostile to Dimu. They

---

[71] Raad voor de Zending, 1102–1: 1411, M. Teffer, letters, 15 April 1879, 9 January 1880. Van Dijk (1925) erroneously merges Ama Amu Manu and Hendik Ratu Manu into one person. Hendrik was baptised in 1874, according to the locally preserved Liae church register.

[72] Raad voor de Zending, 1102–1: 1408, J.F. Niks, travel report, 5–29 June 1885.

readily provided help and dispatched the Dimu troops, forcing them to return to the main island without being able to rescue the raja of Raijua. The fettor then proceeded to arrange his opponent's murder in a treacherous manner, without a care for either the Dutch interpreter or Dimu.[73]

The bloody incident is well remembered to this day. The stories give the impression that the raja in question, Kote Lai, was not entirely an innocent victim. He had a reputation for abusing women. Once he harassed and possibly raped a relative of Fettor Dohi Lado. The latter was so outraged by the transgression that he killed Kote Lai in a cave called Lie Mèngu, situated in Bèlu village. A variant of the story has it that Fettor Dohi Lado did not immediately kill the raja, but let him die of starvation in the cave. Kote Lai's three sons fled respectively to Seba, Ndao and Dimu. The prince who found refuge in Seba was Ama Mehe Tari, who married a Sebanese woman. While it is not confirmed that the raja's sexual predations were the catalyst for his downfall, tradition clearly reveals the ideals of chastity in Savunese society. When a leader of the small Raijuan world committed grave transgressions in this respect, it had terrible consequences for stability in local society. The incident confirms what is known from numerous other cases: the rajas' prerogatives were limited and insufficient when dealing with determined recalcitrant grandees.

Troops from Raijua had a vital role in military enterprises in Timor. In 1807, Raja Louis of Amanuban fell out with the Dutch which set in motion a long series of hostilities. Amanuban was one of the most important kingdoms in West Timor; it fiercely resisted the British and later the newly restored Dutch authorities (Veth 1855: 715). Tradition tells of a renowned Raijuan warrior called Ama Heo Nera who participated in one of the European expeditions. Six generations on, the descendants of Nera Bia still hold vivid memories of their ancestor and are proud of his deeds. He left his hamlet of origin, Boko (Kolorae), with Kana Raga from the same lineage. He did not take his own horse on the boat trip to Timor but found a similarly grey-spotted steed and gave him the same name: Ratu Jawa. During the campaign the Dutch troops besieged a fortified place in Amanuban.[74] Nera Bia managed to penetrate the fortifications and set them on fire, allowing the colonial troops to enter. When he returned to his village, his horse sensed that his master had arrived. The animal jumped from a rock at the edge of Rae Boko to the main road to reunite with its master. The narratives describe the jump as a 'flight'; indeed Rae Boko is about six to eight metres above the fields. Nera Bia brought back five skulls which he buried in front of his house. His warrior

---

[73] ANRI Timor: 14, Report, 30 September 1807.

[74] The troops could also have been British as both countries organised expeditions; however, oral tradition does not specify.

jacket made of plaited leaves is now kept in a house in Bèlu.[75] The story may refer to an expedition in 1814, 1820 or 1822. While colonial troops subdued some Amanuban strongholds during the invasions, none of them achieved their aim to subdue Raja Louis. Amanuban only renewed its ties with the Dutch in the 1860s.[76]

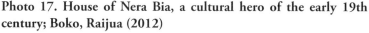

Photo 17. House of Nera Bia, a cultural hero of the early 19th century; Boko, Raijua (2012)

Kote Lai's murder was followed by the reigns of two obscure rajas, Leo Nyebe and Ledo Teni, the latter being related to the 17th-century Raja Mau Alo. Then the Seba-based son of the slain ruler, Ama Mehe Tari, came to power. Dutch sources fix his reign between the years 1830 and 1868. In spite of his long career he was not secure in his position. Like his father before him, he encountered an uprising in 1849; the circumstances suggest there was continuity in the reasons behind the conflict because his main opponent was the fettor. Similar to his father, he received abortive assistance from the main island. The "Fettor of Savu" Ama Jami, probably situated in Dimu, dispatched 14 men on a craft to help settle the affair in Raijua. The dangers of the Savu Sea were immanent in spite of the

---

[75] Interviews with Ama Konga (20.05.2011); Lulu Leba and Rede Hajo (10.06.2012). Tradition now links the jacket to Maja and sometimes to Gajah Mada! It has become a tourist attraction fueling stories about Majapahit times. The jacket is surrounded with sacredness requiring the sacrifice of an animal (or the payment of a corresponding sum) to be able to view the jacket.

[76] McWilliam 2002: 55–60; Farram 2004: 74–9, 90–8.

Figure 53: Melako clan; line of fettors and the genealogy of Nera Bia

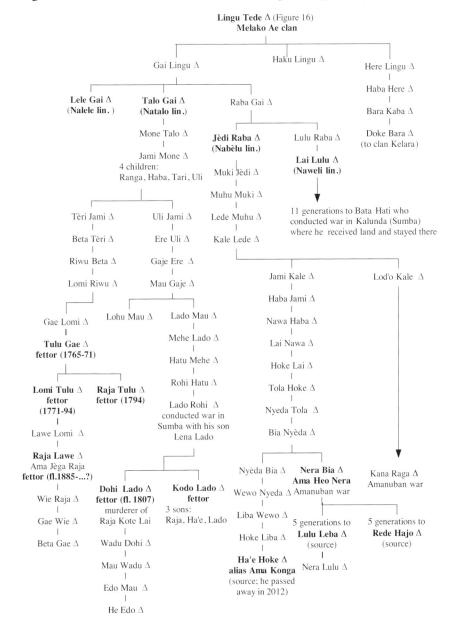

Figure 54: Rajas of Raijua in the 19th and 20th centuries

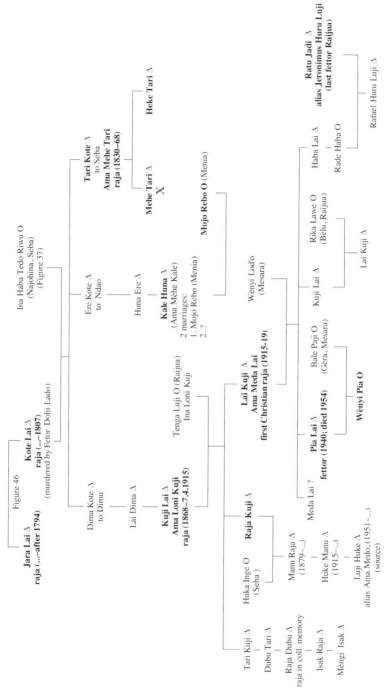

short distance between Savu and Raijua. As fate dictated, adversary winds drove the little expedition northwards. The perahu was stranded at Wanu in Flores where the locals promptly took possession of three copper *lilas* (a type of gun) found in the wreck. The area was still under Portuguese suzerainty. However, the nearby ruler of Sikka helped the sea-wrecked Savunese and provided them with a new perahu to reach Kupang. In the end, it was the lack of boats that impeded further interference in Raijuan affairs.[77] The perils of the sea, even for modest sea trips, were once again highlighted the next year, when in 1850 the then fettor of Seba, Manu Bèhi, drowned off the Raijuan coast.[78]

At length Ama Mehe Tari was able to prevail and enjoyed an extended reign. He probably died during the disastrous smallpox epidemic, as did other Savunese rajas, at the end of the 1860s. Local traditions record the three rajas after him: Mehe Tari, Heke Tari and Kale Huna. No trace of them appears in Dutch records, but they may have died in quick succession, as smallpox made its deadly sweep across the island. What is known is that in 1869 the Kupang authorities acknowledged Ama Loni Kuji, a great-grandson of Kote Lai, and he governed up to his demise in April 1915.

A trait specific to Raijua needs to be underlined. There is no doubt that Melako, the fettor clan, increased its power owing to the contacts with the Dutch, although it is rarely mentioned in VOC reports. The role of Fettor Dohi Lado in Kote Lai's violent death may illustrate this. Melako is Raijua's youngest clan in the order of formation, but it became more powerful than the original clans. It changed the order of precedence, making the display of wealth a new criterion; for instance, demonstrating power through accumulated wealth at *tao leo* ceremonies. Competing displays of wealth seem more obvious in Raijua than in Savu where charisma is still a major reason for staging a *tao leo*.[79] Notable in Raijua is that the female moieties and their subgroups (*wini*) compete in the same manner—displaying a rich collection of cloths challenges the order of precedence; the number and size of heirloom baskets establish the ranking. For example, *wini* Mèko, which is only eight generations old and whose members often marry into the Melako clan, have adopted the same aggressive attitude to achieve power and overthrow the traditional ranking system. The practice is not known in Savu where the *wini* neither display their collections of weaving to other *wini* nor do they question the classifications between them. The Dutch presence influenced

---

[77] ANRI Timor: 58, Register of the acts and decisions, dated 15 December 1849.

[78] ANRI Timor: 60, Register of the acts and decisions, dated 24 January 1851.

[79] *Tao Leo* funerals take place every year in Raijua while they are more seldom in Savu. See Kagiya (2010).

the ranking system in Raijua and local competition to accumulate wealth led to an increase in power. The same is not true in Savu.

Local observers, such as the missionary Mattheus Teffer, discuss Raijua (or "Randjuwa" as he calls it) at some length. It was not the main arena for missionary activities, but Teffer visited there in 1876: he shows a high regard for the locals on the small island. Conditions there were frugal, even more so than in Savu. Water was scarce and the earth was infertile. Nevertheless, Teffer implies that one could call the inhabitants richer than the Savunese. They had achieved a comparatively good level of welfare which immediately struck the visitor and they tended to be more alert than the Savunese. The diligence of the Raijuans made their little island a storehouse of provisions, from which Savu benefited. The houses were more suitable and regularly built than those in Savu, and people tended to dress better. They made a calmer impression and looked the visitor steadily in the eye, unlike the restless Savunese.

Teffer believed that the Raijuans did not seem to have suffered such a horribly bloody history as the Savunese. According to his information, the immigrants to the main island had exterminated the original inhabitants and then engaged in endless fraternal wars. The Raijuans, on the other hand, were believed to be the first inhabitants of their little island and did not roam around the region as the Savunese did. They occasionally sailed to nearby Dana Island (about 30 kilometres south-west of Raijua).[80] Teffer also believed that he could trace some Christian motifs in Raijuan legends, referring in particular to the Ju Deo story discussed in chapter 4.[81]

Teffer's colleague H.C. Kruyt,[82] who had a great interest in ethnological details, provides numerous descriptions of life in Savu and Raijua towards the end of the 19th century. In a note from about 1890 he observes the characteristic embedding of ritual aspects in practical matters:

> Every 6th year, every Kelila [cycle], the Raijuans go to Dana in order to catch goats. One must use two special perahus for that, namely *rebu wudu* and *pugoa* (other perahus can accompany them). The people bring with them 2 pigs in order to sacrifice them in the first hand. If one cannot move forward with the perahus at sea, then the pigs are made to scream at it [the sea]. Furthermore one must bring along a *kabi runai nahoro* (tobacco from Seba). The goats on Dana are wild.[83]

---

[80] Dana has specific sacred significance: it is inhabited only by goats for most of the year except when Raijuan elders visit for cultural purposes.

[81] Raad voor de Zending, 1102–1: 1411, M. Teffer, letter, 3 August 1876.

[82] He is not to be confused with his brother, the more famous missionary-cum-ethnologist Albertus Christiaan Kruyt (1869–1949).

[83] Raad voor de Zending, 1102–1: 1406, H.C. Kruyt, notebooks, 1888–92.

The most notable part of Kruyt's description is that it shows he understood little of what he was told, probably because it was unlikely he would have been permitted to attend the ritual himself. Today, no outsiders can travel to the island without permission from the elders. The ritual journey to Dana, conducted every six years, is to worship the ancestors—two of whom he incorrectly names as boats, Rebo Wudu and Pu Goa. The elders set out in four perahus called *Pelaaji*, *Hurululu*, *Eiledo* and *Maniameni'a*, carrying with them a black boar and a red rooster for sacrifice. Part of the meat is left on sacred stones in Dana. Modern sources for the ritual are unable to clarify what Kruyt may have meant by the "pigs are made to scream at the sea"; perhaps it is simply another example of the second-hand nature of his report. There are no "wild" goats in Dana—other than in the sense there are no shepherds to tend them—as those that live there are from Raijua. The people take their animals there to graze, fetching them back as needed for rituals or for sale. It is, of course, possible that some details of the ritual may have changed since the 19th century. However, of more significance is that Kruyt's record reflects the misinterpretation of Savunese cultural practice common in a number of the written sources, a static one-dimensional representation of a complex tradition.[84]

Kruyt confirms Teffer's impressions that Raijua was more than able to feed itself in spite of its barren character. When the corn harvest failed in Savu in about 1890, it was excellent in Raijua. A lot of people therefore sailed to Raijua to barter for food. Raja Ama Loni Kuji composed a *pantun* (traditional poem [In]) for the occasion in order to shame the Savunese guests: "*Wuru aka Namo/ Meimo rai wonaeki*" (The perahus in the harbour Namo place their hope in a small island).[85]

Rulers and ruled in the Savunese domains

The preceding pages provide an overview of the 19th-century development of the six Savu-Raijuan princedoms, as far as the sources permit. A few general comments are required here. First, the rajas are not as remote or autocratic as the Javanese kings or Malay sultans, or some of the Timorese rulers. The missionaries working on the island in the 1870s found the rajas to be covetous types whose old mores were not so easily changed by nominal conversion to Christianity. They also found the *raja muda*s (the princes) to be the scourge of the land. However, their actual resources were severely limited as one observer notes:

---

[84] Sources Ama Pada Haba Uli and Maria Nalo (18.11.2017).

[85] Raad voor de Zending, 1102–1: 1406, H.C. Kruyt, Notebook 4, c. 1890.

> Savu is a land where no-one is poor as nobody is rich. The Raja of Liae,
> for example, lives on the same [provisions] as the small boys who tend his
> sheep. A few rajas assert that they eat rice every day. Is that true? I realised
> that many smaller princes (*raja muda*) ate rice three or sometimes five
> days a week. So one can easily understand that some are found who never
> eat solid food.[86]

The Dutch visitor, accustomed to conditions in the central parts of the East
Indies, associated the eating of rice with civilised standards, Asian style. The
reverence in which the locals held the rajas was, moreover, not unconditional.
H.C. Kruyt noted down the following incident in about 1892 where a man used
magic against an unnamed raja:

> Ama Huru has accused the raja: Ama Pau Poro has made offerings on his
> behalf to the *duae mone ae*, to get rain. In order that the raja may lose
> the case, he has made an image of the raja, *tao nglu* carved from tuak
> leaves, the head bowing its neck, a thread bound around the mouth (*luwa
> wengu*) (significance: the raja cannot say anything to defend himself, his
> mouth is closed).[87] This small image was placed under a sacrificial stone
> with a stinking egg (not hatched). Just as the egg pollutes the image, it is
> hoped that the person in question is made to stink.[88]

Popular conceptions of the raja's powers may also be gleaned from legends
written down by the missionaries in the 19th century, long before the full
implementation of colonial rule. One such story tells of an ancient raja called
Hakam (a Muslim name) who wished to claim land belonging to a villager in
the neighbouring village. He dispatched his fettor to order the man to give up
his land for 100 rupiah. However, the villager was unwilling because his father
had made him promise not to sell the land to anyone. The raja threatened to
confiscate the land without paying him anything if he remained stubborn.
When the villager again declined the raja told him to pack his belongings and
leave, never to return: the raja claimed the land as his own. The man, filled
with sadness, loaded his belongings onto a donkey and prepared to leave, not
knowing where he would go. However, the village chief heard of his predicament
and promised to help him. He entered the raja's house and told him that the
villager would like to take a sack of earth from his land to remind him of his
ancestors' home. The raja looked troubled but laughed, saying that the villager

---

[86] *Maandberigten van het Nederlandsche Zendelinggenootschap* [*Monthly Reports of the Dutch Missionary Society*] 1875–77: 102.

[87] *Tao* is to make and *nglu* is a spell or curse.

[88] Raad voor de Zending, 1102–1: 1406, H.C. Kruyt, Notebook 3, c. 1892. The context is unfortunately missing. Did Ama Huru accuse the raja of behaving in an un-Christian way? If so, it did not in any way stop Ama Huru from applying pre-Christian magical practices!

could take a thousand sacks if he so wanted. The village head subsequently went to the contested land and filled a sack with earth. He then returned to the raja and asked if he could possibly grant another favour. The raja willingly agreed as he was fond of the village head. The village head asked if he could help him to lift the sack of earth because he could not do it himself. The raja went out and tried, but it was too heavy for him. The village head commented "If one sack is already too heavy, then the more so the thousands of sacks that Milord has taken. Try to think, Milord." The raja finally understood his intention. He changed his mind and gave the land back to its owner together with 100 rupiah as compensation.[89] The story shows that one can expect abuses of power from a raja, but also that relations were quite informal between rulers and village chiefs.

The missionary J.K. Wijngaarden, with his colleagues Letteboer, Kruyt and Niks, came closer to Savunese society than almost any other contemporary white man in the late 19th century. He wrote that succession to the raja position was not an internal dynastic affair. The choice was actually made by the temukungs—genealogical chiefs of the villages—and the *raja muda*s (princes). In Seba the only criterion was that the raja must belong to the lineage of Wadu Lai (d. 1742). The Dutch authorities then formally approved the choice. Wijngaarden relates how the Resident arrived in Seba in 1890 and met the raja in an inauguration ceremony at the posthouder's house. The raja swore two oaths—one Christian and one "heathen". A glass of genever (Dutch gin flavoured with juniper berries) was proffered, with some gunpowder and a bullet poured in it. The Resident drew his state sword and touched the ground with it, then stirred the contents of the glass with the tip. The raja drank the contents and held the bullet in his mouth. He then declared that he deserved to be killed by the gunpowder and bullet if he became disloyal.[90]

There were also checks and balances of princely power at the local level. Savunese society was genealogically defined, but there was also a division into estates or social classes. Wijngaarden distinguished between three such estates, namely *duae* with *anak duae* (leaders and princes), *dou moneaha* (free people) and *dou énnu* (slaves).[91] The temukungs were appointed from the free people, but they belonged to particular families. Thus, the raja's choice was not entirely free as he was bound by tradition.[92] Although he believed that the general free

---

[89] Raad voor de Zending, 1102–1: 725, "Sawoenese fabels en andere teksten" (Savunese fables and other texts), c. 1888. The ruler's Muslim name suggests that the story's prototype might have come from elsewhere, but it is retold in a Savunese setting.

[90] Raad voor de Zending, 1102–1: 1415, J.K. Wijngaarden, letter, 1 April 1890.

[91] Ibid., 3 February 1891.

[92] Ibid., February 1890.

population did not have any influence as such, Wijngaarden had a high opinion of their self-esteem:

> The Savunese character is different from the Javanese. The Savunese does not know the heavy yoke of slavery under which the Javanese have been weighed down for centuries. The Savunese is free and feels that he does not want to be subjected. He is his own lord and master. One has to take this into account [when conducting missionary work in Savu].[93]

Although the passage seems to forget the numerous slaves on the island, Wijngaarden did also comment on slavery. He writes that it did not take much to be declared a slave in olden times. It was sufficient to steal a prince's chicken, behave impolitely to the raja's family or something similar. Although slavery was officially abolished in the Dutch East Indies in 1860, thirty years later the rajas of Liae and Mesara still refused to manumit their slaves. Nevertheless, slavery was less harsh than in earlier times. By the late 19th century a male slave was, in addition to other tasks, expected to bring his lord a jar of syrup each year and a female slave a certain amount of yarn.

In spite of numerous instances of disharmony, it is obvious that conflicts were briefer and less frequent than in the VOC period. The placement of an interpreter and later a posthouder in Dimu or Seba perhaps had a calming effect. While Dimu was noted as the seat of the "*raja besar*" (great raja [In]) far into the 19th century, it did not have the central position to solve conflicts about land disputes, cattle rustling, absconding labour and the like. Rather, the role of the Dutch government as a 'stranger-king' had matured over the centuries. As amply shown in the colonial documents, the Dutch administration had very few resources to interfere outside its immediate jurisdiction in the Kupang area. However, being external to the genealogical and ritual system of Savu, the distant "Company" (as it was still called after 1800) functioned as an ordering force precisely because this was in the interests of the local elite. The system allowed the ruling elite to manage the domains according to inherited precepts while there were very few Europeans living on the island. It was only in the early 20th century that colonial reorganisation of the Dutch East Indies would bring increasing outside control and put an end to a political system that had been in place since at least the 17th century.

The Savunese in Timor

While Savunese society may have seemed 'traditional' and slow-changing, it was not isolated from the currents of the outside world. Migration to other parts

---

[93] Ibid., 3 June 1890.

Photo 18. Daily female activity – using lontar baskets to fetch water; Pedèro (2015)

Photo 19. Daily male activity – tapping the sap of lontar palm trees; Pedèro (2015)

of the region on a small scale had been going on for centuries, as seen by the occurrence of Savunese names among the Mardijkers of Dutch Kupang and the Sabos of Portuguese Oecusse. A general report from the Timor Residency in 1846 reveals that:

> The Solorese people make a living in Kupang by fishing and service as sailors, while the Savunese who stay here are often hired to accompany the Chinese traders going to the mountains; or else they sell the tobacco cultivated on Savu on a modest scale.[94]

Not least their alleged martial prowess was of interest to the Europeans (and Chinese), considering the generally insecure conditions in the residency. The Savunese supposedly possessed more spirit and bravery than their Rotenese neighbours, which made them useful on the sporadic military expeditions (Olivier 1833: 263). It is also known that individual Savunese were occasionally able to marry into the Timorese elite. As such, this feature is not particularly surprising because there were also Chinese and European marriages with local princesses. A case in point is Fettor Baki Koi in the Sonba'i-affiliated domain of Takaeb, a mountainous land to the east of the area under Dutch jurisdiction. His father was a Savunese who married a woman from the Western Kono clan. The Kono lord was, with Oematan, the main lieutenant under the so-called emperor of Sonba'i. Although he was only a Kono on his mother's side, Baki Koi managed to build up a strong position of authority in West Timor from about 1846. His aggressive and generally anti-Dutch policy led the colonial officials to detest him, as they strove to bring a minimum of order to the residency, and he was the catalyst for a military expedition in 1857. Though defeated by the colonial troops, the unruly half-Savunese was never caught nor brought to justice and remained a problem for the Dutch until his death at a ripe age in 1877 (Hägerdal 2013a: 339).

Another case, on a more mundane scale, took place in the multi-ethnic environment of Kupang. The story has survived because a Resident described it in legal proceedings. A certain Savunese called Pyatuh married a woman of the Bekker family, possibly Eurasian. When Pyatuh eventually passed away, his widow administered the household belongings. About six months later she remarried; her new husband was the raja of Amabi, Arnoldus Adriaan Karel Lotty (d. 1834). He was one of the petty rajas who resided close to Kupang, steadfastly loyal to the Dutch government since days of old. The woman's son from her first marriage became a Christian, taking the name Adrianus. She took the goods with her to the princely household in Koinino. However, she told Adrianus that he

---

[94] ANRI Timor: 77, General report, 1846, f. 21.

should not be afraid to take the belongings and move to Kupang if she happened to pass away. Adrianus himself married a sister of his step-father, the widow of another Timorese petty lord.

The story did not end well, though. His stepfather and mother passed away, and Adrianus stayed with his in-laws for a time. Four years after his mother's death he followed his maternal uncle Barnabas Bekker to Savu for unspecified reasons. When he returned to Koinino in 1845 he found that the new Raja Osu had not only taken his inherited goods but also put his wife in custody. The inventory gives an indication of what a wealthy Savunese might possess in the mid-19th century. The goods consisted of 27 Makassarese sarongs, 300 *Spansche matten* (reals), 4 buffalos and various lesser items. Adrianus tried to prove his case against the covetous raja by submitting a complaint to the Resident. After hearing some witness testimony, the Resident decided that there was no proof of his claims, leaving the hapless Savunese to his own devices.[95] Other sources confirm there were close relations between Savu and Amabi; for example, a set of pedigrees provided by a Savunese resident in Kupang suggest a close relationship between the rajas of Amabi and Savunese clans.[96]

At grassroots level Savunese people were sometimes commercially active. A memorandum from 1913 complains that Chinese, Rotenese, Savunese and Endenese buyers made their way inland from Kupang where they fooled the gullible inhabitants and made outrageous profits. However, with closer control by the colonial state around 1900 and the establishment of regular markets, these abuses declined (Rieschoten 1913: 113). The Savunese were also, as previously mentioned, used as escorts on inland trading expeditions. That these escorts could be quite self-willed is seen from an incident in 1851. Many exiles from the central archipelago stayed in Timor at this time, among them was a certain Javanese called Mohammad Moesa who lived in Pariti close to the Kupang Bay. His daughter married a Makassarese trader, Daeng Pambona, newly arrived in Timor. In about July 1851 Pambona and his wife, with another Makassarese called Lababa, embarked on a journey inland, accompanied by four Savunese and two Timorese servants carrying their merchandise. They arrived at Sunleu, a village belonging to Fettor Baki Koi in Takaeb.

At this point, something went awry. In one version a Savunese servant, Ama Toda, was a rebellious and scheming figure. Ama Toda had previously stayed in the West Timorese princedom Amfo'an and behaved improperly towards Raja Willem Manoh's daughter. The raja therefore held Ama Toda prisoner for half

---

[95] ANRI Timor: 55, Register of the acts and decisions, dated 28 June 1845.

[96] The pedigrees, provided to Geneviève Duggan by the late Rehabeam Bengu, are historically somewhat problematic but mention a number of persons known from other sources.

a year. The trader Daeng Pambona bought the Savunese from Raja Amfo'an for 150 guilders. Ama Toda showed no gratitude but rather bore a grudge against his new master. When in Sunleu he went to his half-Savunese compatriot Baki Koi and told him that Daeng Pambona intended to poison Baki Koi. Another version says that Pambona carelessly displayed his valuable goods, gold, silver and coral collars, thus provoking the poverty-stricken Timorese. Neither the rajas nor their subjects were wealthy in Timor, making such behaviour very dangerous. Irrespective of the preamble, their hosts gave the guests a place to sleep, but around nine o'clock the next morning Baki Koi, leading a hundred Timorese, assaulted and seized them: Pambona was so mistreated that he lost an eye. The Timorese bound the guests, but the Savunese managed to escape (or was allowed to go). The Timorese then beheaded Pambona after deliberately insulting him as a Muslim by smearing him with pig's fat. His captors divided up his goods and the emperor of Sonba'i married his widow.[97]

Colonial authorities preserved these snippets of life and death in the eastern region because they were unusual enough to be noted down. The bulk of the Savunese must have led tranquil lives in the shadow of the nascent colonial state. However, the incidents are a reminder of the fragile existence in this era where aristocrats were frequently perpetrators of robberies and gross abuses of their powers. Primordial solidarity between the expatriate Savunese was therefore a strategy that was applied even against the local Europeans. An eyewitness who visited Kupang in about 1819 relates how a certain Savunese insulted a sentry at Fort Concordia. The culprit was taken into custody, but a band of fully armed Savunese compatriots soon appeared and threateningly demanded their comrade back. No end to the story was recorded.[98]

Although the colonial authorities were sometimes sceptical of the self-willed Savunese, they still favoured the transfer of troops from Savu to the area in Timor under Dutch jurisdiction. Since the early years of the 19th century, a community of immigrants settled in the relatively fertile Babau area east of the Kupang Bay. As the story goes, the raja of the Amalo family from Termanu in Rote was oppressive, so the chiefs of two local communities complained to the Dutch. Resident Hazaart found that the situation could be used to his advantage. At this time, right after the British occupation, the inhabitants of the Kupang enclave felt highly insecure. In the highlands to the east, Sonba'i was an unpredictable neighbour and the Dutch did not entirely trust their allies close to the town. The Mardijkers, Papangers and burgher guards had low combat value. In 1816/17

---

[97] ANRI Timor: 60, Register of the acts and decisions, 1851; ANRI Timor: 146, Report on the state of affairs, 1852.

[98] 'Iets over het Eiland Timor en Onderhoorigheden', H 245a, KITLV, c. 1819, f. 21.

and 1818/19, respectively, Hazaart therefore transported many hundreds of Rotenese to Babau where they were joined by contingents from Savu and Solor.[99]

The immigrants were deemed better agriculturists than the Timorese and could also service as a *cordon sanitaire* (a buffer) against the roughshod Timorese lords in the mountainous inland. To be sure, the measure did not prevent hostile incursions, as evident from a few bloody incidents in the 1840s and 1850s. A report from 1865 shows transmigration to have been in the interest of the Resident as well as Raja Ama Nia Jawa of Seba. The raja fully supported the project of taking Savunese to Babau and it was only the lack of steamships in the residency that impeded the plan from being fully carried out.[100] The other reasons for Ama Nia's enthusiasm are a matter of conjecture; the plan would have expanded his net of influence, and the removal of men might have eased pressure on the available land at a time in the 1860s when Savu was suffering from calamities such as drought and failed harvests.

The Savunese in Sumba

Savunese influence can also be traced on the other neighbouring islands. At least a couple of raja families in Rote claim close affinity with Savu. The prominent domain Thie, outmanoeuvred by its enemies on the island, supposedly called for assistance from Savu in the early 18th century. One of the intervening war leaders stayed in Thie and became *manek* (raja) of the domain (Kaho 2005: 15–7). The narrative is historically impossible, but a branch of the Thie raja family is believed to have settled in Savu and has kept occasional contact with kinsmen in Rote ever since.[101] A somewhat better founded case is the ill-fated domain of Landu in eastern Rote which experienced genocide through VOC intervention in 1756.[102] A certain Johannis, of Savunese stock, became fettor of the diminished realm around 1800 and subsequently replaced the old raja family; his line governed until the 20th century.[103]

---

[99] Raad voor de Zending, 1102–1: 1408, J.F. Niks, "De Rottineesche nederzettingen op Timor" (The Rotenese settlements in Timor), 31 July 1887. When the Savunese arrived is not specified but, according to Niks, it happened during Hazaart's governance, thus before 1832.

[100] ANRI Timor: 107, monthly reports, September 1865.

[101] Matheos Messakh, Waingapu (personal communication; March 2014).

[102] The Dutch killed a large number of people and took more than 1,000 as slaves, so it is likely that the domain lost at least half its population.

[103] Lintje Pellu, Kupang (personal communication; February 2012); Leiden University Library, LOr 2238, Letter from the Rotenese regents, 1800. His relation to the old line of rajas is not clear as the Landu genealogical tradition presents an unbroken line of succession, gainsaid by Dutch sources (Pellu 2008).

The presence of Savunese people in Sumba had an impact on quite a different level. The importance of Sumba in Savunese consciousness is clear from the island's religious significance: the divine entity Ama Piga Laga brings the dead's souls to a cape on the north coast of Sumba, Tanjung Sasar. In the 19th century, the Savunese women used to sing a *pantun* (traditional poem) while working in the paddy fields:

> O women, do not go to Sumba!
> For if you go there
> And your breasts are swollen,
> You will become slaves of Rau Wau.

To interpret the cryptic verse, it is important to place Rau Wau, the henchman-spirit of Ama Piga Laga. His task was to take women to his master because Ama Piga Laga had a great demand for the female sex. In the first place Rau Wau chose women with "swollen", that is, full breasts. Once, when he had captured a well-developed young woman and set out for Sumba on his horse, he rode so hard that milk sprouted from her bouncing bosoms. That was the origin of the Milky Way.[104] Thus, Sumba held a somewhat ambiguous place in the popular imagination as a domain of important but also of dangerous spiritual powers.

Trying to reach Sumba could involve loss of life, with or without spirits. When the wind was favourable, it was possible to traverse the Savu Sea and reach the north coast of Sumba in 12 to 15 hours in an ordinary perahu. However, the sea was dangerous for much of the year and unpredictable even in the sailing season. The missionary Letteboer describes an incident that cost the lives of 60 people, men and women, and was certainly not unique:

> On 18 July [1903] the raja of Seba sent a perahu with 70 people to Sumba for some business. As far as the prince knew there were only 72 people on board. When all were aboard the raja, standing on the shore, signaled if everything was in order. He who captained the perahu hoisted the flag as a sign that all was well, whereupon the raja responded that they may depart.… At first all went well, but an adverse wind drove the perahu back so they ended up in the strong current that dominates the strait between Raijua and Savu. It seems that panic broke out on board the perahu. The boat capsized; some were washed away while others held on to the perahu and thus saved their lives. All this took place at night. When some people of Raijua went to the shore to fish the next morning, they saw the perahu turned upside down with people drifting about. Efforts were made to save the shipwrecked. Some corpses drifted ashore on Raijua, others

---

[104] Raad voor de Zending, 1102–1: 1444, J.H. Letteboer, letter, 4 August 1899.

disappeared. But what was now revealed? That 100 rather than 70 people had been on the perahu. Those who were not dispatched by the raja made use of the opportunity to come to Sumba without paying.[105]

In Timor the Savunese were not permitted anything more than a subordinate position within the colonial state; however, the unsettled conditions in Sumba allowed enterprising Savunese aristocrats to wield wide political influence. The island became a colony for the inhabitants of the somewhat over-populated Savu (Wielenga 1926: 6). To explain the context, as mentioned the Dutch in Kupang had very limited resources at their disposal. After the abortive expeditions to Amanuban between 1814 and 1822, colonial troops seldom went beyond the *sespalen gebied* (the stretch of government land near the Kupang Bay). It was only in 1857 that Batavia lost patience with the disturbances in the residency and sent an expedition to chastise the half-Savunese Baki Koi of Takaeb and the raja of Lidak in Bèlu.[106] In the Dutch East Indies, a policy of abstention (*onthoudingspolitiek*) was the norm of the day until the late 19th century, as established by Governor-General van den Bosch in 1833. Troops from the hub in Batavia were expensive and the administration would only dispatch them as a last resort. The Resident of Kupang had to rely on cooperation with the innumerable princes of the regency and he had no power to intervene in the petty wars that often surfaced in this part of the East Indies. The Resident's annual reports often started with a mantra-like assurance that conditions in the residency were satisfactory, which was followed by the terse reservation that raids and killings took place here and there, and were of little concern for the government.

Some chiefs in Sumba had entertained contacts with the company in the 18th century. They were leaders of local *kabisu* (clan [Su]) whom the Dutch liked to regard as rajas who could act on behalf of the population in larger areas. It was a mistaken belief and relations soon broke off. As the Dutch observer Tekenborgh wrote of the self-styled rajas of Mangili and Melolo in 1775: "They promised something that was not in their power, and presented themselves as something they were not" (Couvreur 1915: 17). After the 1770s, the island was left to its own devices and remained a virtual *terra incognita* (unknown land) for several decades. There were trading relations of some consequence with the Makassarese, Endenese and Bimanese but apparently not with Savu to any

[105]   Raad voor de Zending, 1102–1: 1444, J.H. Letteboer, letter, 20 January 1904.

[106]   This expedition is discussed in detail in Hägerdal (2013).

degree.[107] Traders shipped out slaves as well as sandalwood, although there was an alleged ritual taboo on cutting sandalwood in at least some places—the sandal trees were associated with the ancestors (Couvreur 1915: 20)

It is only in 1838 that archival sources shine some light on Sumba. The Endenese on the south coast of Flores, Muslim descendants of immigrants from Sulawesi and local people engaged in a flurry of activity in the eastern archipelago at that time. They haunted the coasts of Sumba in fleets of 50 to 100 small craft, taking slaves by the score whom they sold to white traders from Bourbon Island and Mauritius. Although the slave trade had been prohibited in the Dutch East Indies in 1817, and in 1834 Britain had abolished slavery altogether, this meant very little in practice (Needham 1983). Furthermore, the Endenese impeded trade in the Solor and Alor Islands, and even ravaged the Dutch post in Atapupu on the north coast of Timor. Their foremost rivals and enemies were the Savunese.

The Resident of Kupang's protestations led to a government decision in 1838 to the effect that the navy should take measures to counteract the slave trade in the region, and also to prepare for the occupation and colonisation of Sumba. The latter point may have been motivated by fear that a power other than the Netherlands might gain a foothold. However, the meagre resources allocated to Kupang were not sufficient to allow actions to follow words. Nevertheless, in 1838 Larantuka and Ende suffered an attack from a Dutch squadron in conjunction with three perahus with 100 Savunese (De Roo van Alderwerelt 1906: 243). The event broke at least some of Ende's ambition to be the principal slave emporium of the south-eastern islands. In the following year, an Arab of great standing and prestige settled in Ende as the trading agent of Kupang's Dutch Resident. This was Syarif Abdulrachman Algadri, born in 1807, and a member of the sultan family of Pontianak. The *syarif*[108] was known as a "civilised" type, a forceful personality who spoke some Chinese, English, Dutch and several local tongues. The Resident considered him to be the right man to increase Dutch influence, particularly in light of the strong Endenese presence in Sumba. As in Savu, the key was the horse trade, as large droves of horses had been reported since the 18th century. The *syarif* settled in Sumba in 1843 and

---

[107] A story of biodiversity occurred through Savunese-Sumbanese relations. The missionary Letteboer describes a species of date called *ko* (*Ziziphus jujuba*, commonly called jujube or red date) which originally grew in Sumba. A certain Savunese raja later brought the *ko* to Savu where it was growing everywhere by 1900 (Raad voor de Zending, 1102–1: 1444, J.H. Letteboer, letter, 20 January 1904).

[108] *Syarif* or sharif is a term used for a descendant of the Prophet Muhammad through Fatima, his daughter.

developed Waingapu as the only good seaport on the north coast (De Roo van Alderwerelt 1906: 247).

The nature and origins of modern colonialism are hotly debated by historians. Observations implying that colonial advancement can be seen as defensive, a response to powers that seemed to threaten the metropolitan centre's interests, challenge traditional explanations of active and rational, albeit covetous, reasons for territorial expansion (Ardhana 2000: 4–7). It is certain that a strain of Anglophobia guided the actions of Dutch colonial officials after the Napoleonic age. Fear of foreign encroachment into their claimed sphere of influence made the Dutch meddle in regions where economic opportunities were limited. In the Sumba case, the presence of Syarif Abdulrachman proved to be no guarantee against other influences. British ships visited the island from time to time and carried on a lively trade. Worried by this encroachment, Batavia ordered the Resident of Kupang to go to Sumba as a commissioner and confirm the subordination of the local chiefs to the Dutch colonial state. Sumba was vaguely attributed to the Dutch zone by the London Treaty of 1824 where the Netherlands and Great Britain agreed on their respective spheres of influence in maritime Southeast Asia, but no purposeful diplomatic contacts had taken place for 70 years.

In early 1845, taking two ships the Resident Cornelis Sluyter went to Savu and met Fettor Ama Wono and Prince Ama Riwu, both of Seba. They brought lively complaints about the transgressions committed by their Endenese enemies against their dependents in Sumba. In other words, there was a degree of traffic between Savu and Sumba which was not detailed in the official reports. Accompanied by the two Savunese grandees, Sluyter arrived in Waingapu, the largest town in Sumba. The Resident attempted to summon the persons considered to be rajas, aiming to involve them in a formal contract. Syarif Abdulrachman combed the domains to the west of Waingapu while the Savunese grandees searched for local political representatives in the east. The south of Sumba was left for another time as the syarif characterised people there as too wild to deal with. The mission was only partially successful. While the syarif managed to encourage the lords of Kambera, Kanatang and Kapunduk with their fully armed guards to go to Waingapu, the Savunese had less luck because the eastern lords were occupied fighting each other. Eventually, a sufficient number of lords gathered to enable Sluyter, clad in ceremonial *tenu* cloths for the occasion, to draw up a contract (Couvreur 1915: 34–8).[109]

---

[109] (*Tenu*[n], locally woven cloths [In]). Fine textiles were a marker of nobility in Sumba, explaining Resident Sluyter's outfit. Sluyter thought to honor the Sumba noble men, so he dressed like them as a mark of respect.

Why did the so-called rajas sign the contract and were they rajas of the territories they represented at all? The structure of Sumbanese society, divided into various *kabisu* and the leadership by ritual experts (*ratu*) and genealogical chiefs (*maramba, ama bokul*), left little room for what Europeans would call rajas and kingdoms. The persons who signed may therefore not have been actual rulers of all the lands ascribed to them. Moreover, they may well have been attracted by the gifts the Kupang administration bestowed, rather than seriously pondering the contents of the contracts which they may not have fully understood.

The lack of comprehension was made painfully clear when the Dutch wished to update the contracts in 1860, after 15 years of irregular relations. Once again the Savunese served as intermediaries. Resident Willem Brocx sent the posthouder of Savu, A. Rozet, and the raja of Seba in advance to Sumba where they prepared the ground by gathering the so-called rajas. On this occasion, the Sumbanese lords reportedly understood the contents of the revised contracts "very well". Two years later, however, Brocx's successor Isaac Esser found to his dismay that this was far from the truth. Esser asked Rozet and Prince Ama Nia Jawa if the rajas and sub-regents had actually comprehended the contents of the documents. They replied that they had read out the paragraphs in Malay before the grandees and even translated them to "Sumbanese" (in itself a tricky matter because there is more than one Sumbanese tongue). However, the lords had not actually understood and only said "yes" to everything (De Roo van Alderwerelt 1906: 269)!

Local tradition from Mangili provides a long story about the events leading up to the contracts of 1845 and 1860. Some of the Mangili clans had Savunese origins and a lot of people from Savu stayed in a place called Mau Kawini. Around the middle of the 19th century a clash occurred. Members of two leading *kabisu* greatly disliked a Savunese from Mau Kawini called Ama Luji and conspired to eliminate him. They tricked him into leaving the village, pushed him into a ravine and he died. A Sumbanese, with alliances on both sides, saved Ama Luji's wife by spiriting her away. The murder caused great resentment in Savu and hundreds of war perahus soon set out towards Mangili, armed with skilled stone-slingers. However, Sumbanese on horseback proved to be more than a match for the invaders. They speared the Savunese or trampled them under the horses' hoofs, so they fled to their perahus helter-skelter. That did not save Mangili, however, for the Savunese soon returned with a larger force. They made a successful attack on Pariangu village at night and collected a rich booty. Among the spoils were golden *pusaka* objects. The opportunities for plunder encouraged the Savunese to renew their raids from time to time. The attacks badly disrupted local agriculture and starvation afflicted Mangili (Pura Woha 2008: 120–3).

A gathering of prominent Sumbanese agreed that they must seek peace with the Savunese. Appointing as their envoy a well-considered man called Umbu Mangu Tara Panjang, they arranged a number of modest but well-chosen presents for the Savunese leaders. These included ten pieces of Sumbanese *kain* (sarung), ten *sarung pahudu* (embroidered sarungs for women), ten baskets of *kamba kain* (two-coloured ikat cloths for males), ten baskets of peanuts, ten bundles of *sirih* (betel leaves) and ten wraps of *pinang* (areca nuts). At this time there were, according to the story, ten rajas of Savu (*sepuluh orang raja* [In]): foremost of them were the leaders of Seba—Ama Nia Jawa, Ama Alu Bèhi and Ama Dima Talo. The Sumbanese offered each of them one set of presents, which they willingly received. The ten rajas also agreed to accompany Umbu Mangu to Kupang to meet the Resident. During the meeting the white 'stranger-king' asked the group who was in charge of affairs in Sumba. Umbu Mangu mentioned two leaders of prominent *kabisu* in Mangili—Umbu Dundu Mina and Umbu Ndena Nggaba. The Resident resolved to bestow two *tongkat*s (canes [In]), flags and rifles on these two lords, and thus officially appointed them as Mangili's raja and fettor. Umbu Mangu then sailed back to Savu and, subsequently, to Sumba, accompanied by the ten rajas. Mangili celebrated the news of the settlement; Savunese and Sumbanese alike joyfully feasted, epitomised in the saying "*Humba Humba ndaba, Hau Hau ndaba*" (Sumba is Sumba, Savu is Savu). In other words, the Savunese and Sumbanese were to mind their own affairs without disturbing those of the other.

However, the two *kabisu* leaders did not think it appropriate to become raja and fettor. Rather, the dignity was owed to the ceremonial *tuan tanah* (lord of the land). The latter in his turn declared that the objects bestowed by Kupang could stay in Umbu Mangu's hands (Pura Woha 2008: 123–7). The story of the war and subsequent settlement is not directly confirmed by Dutch sources, but from official papers it appears that Umbu Ndena Nggaba was acknowledged as raja of Mangili in 1845 and Umbu Mangu in 1860, Thus, the events of 15 years have been telescoped into one single incident which, incidentally, highlights the insubstantial grounds of appointing this or that person as the "raja" in regions where monarchy was not part of the power structure. That the position of the Savunese in Mangili was strong by 1860 is certain from the written sources and this is reinforced by the frequent references to intermarriage in local tradition.

Meanwhile, the colonial state found itself entangled in a bitter struggle between the Savunese and Endenese on Sumbanese soil. The honourable Syarif Abdulrachman married the sister of two Endenese princes called Etto and Lawatto, but the union did not stop the Endenese pursuit of raiding and enslaving Sumba's coastal population. Collective memory recalls that impact of the Dutch action against Ende in 1838 was apparently short-lived: in the region, people quickly rebuilt destroyed settlements and colonial surveillance was poor. The Dutch loaded captives on to perahus and took them to Bali and Lombok for the slave market; a number of Endenese grandees who stayed in Sumba oversaw the whole process. Resident Brocx commented:

> It seems to me that the people of Sumba live in a good understanding with the Savunese. The Raja of Seba stated his wish to me, to dispatch some 400 Savunese to Kadumbu [on Sumba's north-east coast] where the land offers extremely good opportunities for agriculture; first, in order to find better means of livelihood, and second, to keep the Endenese in check. The Raja of Kadumbu has made the same request, since he and his people are very fond of the Savunese. I have completely endorsed this proposal, since much good will come out of this (De Roo van Alderwerelt 1906: 263).

In other words, the enterprising Seba elite used the Dutch predicament to undertake a little colonisation project of their own. Four hundred men did, in fact, sail from Savu to Kadumbu in July 1860, led by Raja Ama Dima Talo and Ama Nia Jawa. When they landed, the local raja related that Syarif Abdulrachman and his brothers-in-law had recently arrived. They had demanded that he pay an indemnity for ten perahus, which the Dutch had shelled and sunk in his roadstead. The poor raja had no other option but to pay. It transpired that Syarif Abdulrachman had been playing an interesting double role in Sumba: he was both the agent of the colonial state, and someone who sold munitions to the Endenese and gained a share of the profits from the slave trade.

After a few days in Kadumbu, Ama Dima Talo, Ama Nia Jawa and their men marched towards the Endenese camp, which they found defended with cannonry. Undaunted, the Savunese marched into the fortified camp for a parley and demanded that the marauders give back the goods they had taken from Kadumbu. The Endenese refused, pointed their firearms at their adversaries and as the Savunese responded in kind, a sharp fight ensued. The Endenese Prince Etto and three of his retainers fell, the Savunesae torched the surrounding houses and the Endenese fled to Patawang where the chief was Etto's father-in-law. A second confrontation between the two adversaries was likewise unsuccessful for the Endenese, but then luck ran out for the Savunese. Considerable reinforcements arrived from Ende and the Savunese had to retreat to Melolo, which had family ties with Ama Dima Talo. Adversary winds separated the Savunese forces at sea. Ama Dima's boat was almost trapped by the Endenese fleet and then it drifted to Sumbawa. However, the enterprising Ama Nia Jawa made landfall and, accompanied by troops, marched overland towards Kadumbu. Another round of fighting took place where the two adversaries were each assisted by their respective Sumbanese allies. Over all, Ama

Nia Jawa kept the upper hand. His force took Patawang and he incorporated it into the domain of Melolo: the Endenese fled to Waingapu, Syarif Abdulrachman's domain (De Roo van Alderwerelt 1906: 264–6). Henceforth, they kept mostly to the northern and western parts of the island, leaving the east to the Savunese (Wielenga 1926: 6).

Most of the Savunese returned to their home island after these events. Although they had been victorious, Sumba may not have been quite the agricultural bonanza that they had hoped; the presence of the belligerent Endenese and the ever-unreliable Syarif Abdulrachman made a permanent settlement insecure. Nevertheless, a number of people stayed on. When in 1866 Batavia placed the first two colonial officials in Sumba, one of them settled in Kabaniru at the Kambera River estuary to the south-east of Waingapu, where a number of Savunese lived. The other official eventually settled in Melolo on the east coast, where there was also a Savunese community (Couvreur 1915: 66). In the violence-wracked societies of the Savu Sea, the Dutch leaned on the Savunese elite, considered the most loyal and civilised prop for their authority. While the Endenese problem persisted, the resolute Savunese warriors at least rid Sumba of the worst raiders.

Nevertheless, the action did not guarantee safety for the European officials. In Melolo, the official Van Heuckelum had a brief and ignominious stay. When the local raja heard that he had come to reside permanently, his response was far from welcoming: "I shall speak this over with Ama Nia, the chief of the Savunese there, when he returns from his trip to Savu" (Wielenga 1926: 12). Van Heuckelum asked the Savunese who lived on the coast to assist him building a house. They declined, stating that Ama Nia had forbidden them from doing so and that the local raja had threatened to kill them if they helped him. The increasingly agitated Westerner again spoke to the raja who reiterated that he must speak to Ama Nia, denying that he had threatened the Savunese: he only forbade them to cut wood without his permission. In the following days, the Savunese and Sumbanese persisted in their passive resistance to the demands of the unfortunate Van Heuckelum, who cursed the character of the Savunese settlers. In his words, they were:

> … the scum of their nation, who are more similar to a band of criminals than a peaceful colony. It is only the fear of Ama Nia that prevents the Sumbanese from throwing them into the sea. They make every effort to hinder me and to incite the Sumbanese against me. There are big fights every day. A certain Anna [Ama?] Walu Luji nearly killed a woman. Meanwhile a deserting police servant from Kabaniru clandestinely disappeared. Not long ago he killed yet two people. He was summoned but refused to appear and took refuge with the Raja of Melolo (Wielenga 1926: 13–4)!

Van Heuckelum was happy to get away alive.[110] It appeared that the friendly appearance of the Savunese and Ama Nia Jawa should not be misinterpreted: they had little interest in close Dutch surveillance and were certainly not sorry to see the official leave. What the colonial government had failed to understand was that lone Europeans did not have automatic status in these quarters; the Savunese and Sumbanese followed their own chiefs. They were not keen on obeying the commands of whites who did not know the language or customs and had no military backing. Van Heuckelum subsequently settled in Waingapu which was the focal point for the important horse trade and emerged as the centre of the colonial presence, such as it was (Couvreur 1915: 67–8).

Local Mangili tradition, which makes a relatively trustworthy impression, implies that the Savunese had some further impact in opening up Sumba to the forces of colonial modernisation. When the Savunese leaders returned home after making peace with Mangili, they took with them Prince Umbu Ndena and a boy called Titus Jaja Dene, whose father had saved Ama Luji's wife from being killed. Ama Nia Jawa and Ama Alu Bèhi sent the prince to Kupang for schooling, while Ama Nia Jawa raised Titus himself in Seba. It was, of course, a convenient way for the Seba elite to strengthen their Dutch-backed contacts in Sumba. Titus had an interesting career as a teacher, distributor of the smallpox vaccine and assistant to the Protestant missionaries who spread the Gospel in Sumba. He also married two Savunese princesses in turn, from Mesara and Raijua. The geographical range of his activity included Savu, Kupang, the Lamaholot area and eventually Melolo in Sumba, highlighting the opportunities for resourceful persons within the expanding colonial state (Pura Woha 2008: 130–1).

The *controleur* (local colonial official) Salomon Roos had a luckier career living with the Savunese in Kabaniru than his colleague in Melolo. He stayed in Sumba for six years and was known by the Savunised name Ama Rohi. There was no question of interfering in the internal squabbles between the Sumbanese chiefs and villages, even when the fight raged before his very eyes. When in 1871 the chief of Sudu attacked Pamusukaba village, Roos chose to adhere strictly to the policy of non-intervention:

> All this happened such short distance from the house of the controleur that the attenders there, some 30 forced labourers, and a 100 Savunese, rushed out at the shouting and noise and only waited for a sign from the controleur to support Pamusukaba. Controleur Roos, however, strictly forbade them to meddle, since it was an internal matter between

---

[110] Lulofs 1911: 282. Van Heuckelum's expulsion in 1869 apparently became known to French, British and American traders when they visited Sumbanese ports to purchase horses. Thus, the incident was detrimental to the prestige of the Dutch colonial state in the area.

Sumbanese, and the Raja of Kambera enjoyed self-rule. As a consequence, when all that breathed had been killed off, the kampong was set on fire. The dead and wounded were thrown into the burning houses, and half an hour later Pamusukaba was no more than smoking ruins. 11 corpses were found in the neighbourhood, who were buried by the Savunese (Couvreur 1915: 73).

However, the Savunese were soon to play a major role in political developments in Sumba. Their actions in the following years have an interesting duality. On one hand it was the raja of Seba fighting for land and booty, using the endorsement of the Dutch government; on the other hand it was the Dutch government waging a war of conquest in Sumba, using the raja of Seba as its instrument. The catalyst in this story was Kiritana, a settlement at the upper reaches of the Kambera River in eastern Sumba. By the 1860s, its population was known to shelter bellicose raiders and the neighbouring domains Kambera, Lewa, Taimanu and Kapunduk complained to controleur Roos, who did nothing about the matter. The marauders took or killed thousands of horses and hundreds of buffalos. In 1873 the afflicted Sumbanese lords had had enough and threatened to equip an army with the aim to exterminate the troublesome Kiritana people altogether. The matter was the more worrisome because the lords of Bata Kapedu, Melolo and Tabundung sided with Kiritana.

The new controleur Roskott wished to avoid a bloodbath on the island. The Resident of Kupang approved the arrangement of a grand meeting in October, where both Syarif Abdurrachman and Ama Doko Kaho of Seba were present. All the local chiefs declared that it was a vain effort to negotiate with the Kiritana raiders, and that the only solution was to let the Savunese surround the place and capture the culprits. The controleur nevertheless decided to try softer methods. He first dispatched the old and in this context venerable Syarif Abdulrachman, who was a friend of the mighty Kiritana ally, Umbu Ndai of Bata Kapedu. He soon returned without having achieved his aim.

Next, Ama Doko Kaho of Seba went to parley with Umbu Ndai and the Kiritana chiefs. He was not exactly received with a Sumbanese fanfare. At a meeting with the Savunese raja, Umbu Ndai refused to negotiate with the Dutch government and it appeared that he let the Kiritana chiefs have the last word in the deliberations. On an island that had rarely seen a Dutch soldier, the prestige of the colonial state was close to zero. Ama Doko felt badly insulted by the rude behaviour of the Sumbanese who, furthermore, increased his anger by stealing horses from his brother and retainers. When he returned empty-handed to Roskott, the controleur decided the best solution was to pit the Savunese warriors against Kiritana. A Dutch military expedition was not a good option as the Dutch still clung to the policy of non-intervention (the Aceh War would soon give reason to alter this stance) and "the soup was not worth the cabbage", as Roskott stated (Couvreur 1915: 77–84).

Another controleur, writing in 1915, remarked that Roskott's machinations were unworthy, both in their intrinsic integrity and with an eye to Dutch prestige (Couvreur 1915: 84). However, the colonial policy was ambiguous and Roskott was certainly not alone in his warmongering. Resident Humme came from Kupang in early 1874 and gave Ama Doko Kaho permission to act. Formally, however, it was not a situation in which Ama Doko acted on behalf of the government. Rather, it was officially seen as a personal matter between Ama Doko and the recalcitrant Kiritana. The implication seemed to be that Seba could embark on a campaign of territorial conquest with the muted blessings of an inactive colonial state. Even so, the Resident tried to minimise the anticipated atrocities by making Ama Doko promise to avoid unnecessary killings.

The Sumbanese did not await the attack passively. Bata Kapedu and some of its allies decided to assist Kiritana by launching a general attack on the Savunese on the island and expel them for good. People from Rindi domain leaked the information to the Savunese, however, and auxiliaries from Savu arrived the day before the attack was planned. The Sumbanese strategy was never executed. In June 1874, the Savunese took the offensive, marching a troop inland under the command of Ama Kuji Bire, a nephew of Raja Ama Dima Talo. However, luck was not on their side this time; when they approached Kiritana a bullet killed Ama Kuji and the troops retreated to the coast. As Kiritana was a harder nut to crack than anticipated, Ama Doko Kaho sailed to Kupang the following month to consult Resident Humme. The Resident had no scruples about augmenting the conflict. He readily lent the raja 50 carbines and supplied him with a government vessel to transport more troops from Savu to Sumba. With these reinforcements, Ama Doko Kaho launched a new attack against Kiritana and this time it was successful. They subdued the area in August and took some people captive. The victors, whose losses were limited to three wounded, set a good example by avoiding looting and wanton killings. The bulk of the enemy, however, retreated to Bata Kapedu whose raja showed no sign of extraditing the chief "culprits" (Couvreur 1915: 84–7).

Immediately after these dramatic events, Resident Humme arrived in Sumba. After hearing about what had passed, he tried to arrange a peaceful surrender. When, perhaps inevitably, this failed he could see no other alternative than enjoining the Savunese to attack Bata Kapedu, too. At the end of August, the Savunese warriors closed in on Bata Kapedu, a dry and rather infertile highland area to the south-west of Waingapu. They were met by war cries and gunshots from the defenders. Over the next few days, exchanges of volleys alternated with negotiations, but Umbu Ndai dared not surrender to either the controleur or Ama Doko Kaho. He apparently feared that the raja of Seba would satisfy past injuries by taking his life. At this point, the Savunese cut access from the main village to the nearby river and without water the Sumbanese situation was hopeless: they spontaneously capitulated after an eight-day siege. Two hundred and fifty people left the fortified site after assurances that they would be spared any atrocities. Umbu Ndai and some of his subjects slipped away via the rear side of the village. The Savunese rushed inside and set fire to the place, with a few nearby settlements undergoing the same fate. Some 50 Sumbanese had fallen during the campaign while the Savunese did not suffer any losses (Couvreur 1915: 87–9).

The Savunese had gained in prestige and power, but what about the Dutch colonial state? "To tell the truth", wrote the Resident, "I must declare that the conduct in this matter did not satisfy me, and that the militancy and posture of the Savunese—some of them excepted—did not answer to the demand that was made" (Couvreur 1915: 90). However, at least the enemy had mainly been worsted and Lewa's powerful raja in Central Sumba undertook a treaty of friendship with the Dutch. The Resident also hoped that the campaign would lead to advantageous colonisation by Savunese settlers, possibly augmented with immigrants from Rote—the successful example of Babau in Timor may have been on his mind. Regardless of the minor benefits, the Savunese had cleared a path with fire and sword, as revealed in a report from 1876:

> The valley of the Kambera River is depopulated; all has been plundered and burnt by the Savunese. A glaring lack of basic means of livelihood reigns everywhere. But this is not the only inconvenience. The ruler of Sudu [Lewa], happy that the one from Bata Kapedu has been put to flight, takes the opportunity to pillage and plunder in all directions under the pretext of searching for lost horses, assisted by Savunese and Endenese, the latter of which he receives from Syarif Abdulrachman against promise of deliveries of slaves. The arrogance of the Savunese and the enterprise of the ruler of Sudu frighten the lesser man from working his field. The Savunese openly confess: settle more Sumbanese; we Savunese will harvest your rights (Couvreur 1915: 93).

As to the chaotic politics of Sumba in the following decades, the belligerent posture of the Lewa raja was the main Dutch headache. He created an extensive realm on the island for the first time in recorded history, refused to visit the Dutch officials and routinely referred to the Resident of Kupang as his "younger brother"—a politeness not appreciated by the Dutch official. Lewa was a so-called secondary state in the sense that its rise was a reaction to foreign (Savunese and Dutch) interference, but it never had the time to stabilise into a real kingdom. Dutch action brought an end to the pattern of competing petty realms by 1906,

1. Wadu Mea where the first ancestors arrived (2012)

2. A beach near Koloalo, the site of a VOC shipwreck in 1672 (2015)

3. A ritual house currently inhabited by the priest Kenuhe; Ketita, Raijua (2015)

4. The ritual house of priest Apu Lod'o Wadu; Ledelo, Mesara (2012)

5. An ancestral house with an extended roof ridge; Kujiratu, Dimu (2015)

14. *Voorvechter van het Eiland Savoe* (A warrior from the island of Savu) by P. van Oort, printed by Kierdorff, Leiden, Netherlands between 1839 and 1846 (private collection)

11. A Raijuanese in full attire at the *daba ae* ritual cockfight; Dèiwei, Ledeke village (2013)

12. Two members of the Nadega clan dressed for a ritual cockfight; Bolua, Raijua (2012)

13. *Ledo* dancers at a *tao leo* funeral; Boko, Raijua (2013)

9. Ruins of the Hurati fortress with children's graves on the left (2016)

10. The house of Fettor Dohi Lado; Bogi, Raijua (2012)

6. Deo Rai Gopo of Liae arriving at Kolorame for a ritual cockfight (2015)

7. Deo Rai of Mesara blessing offerings covered with sacred cloths; Kolorae (2011)

8. Villagers of Lobohede building a *kowa hole* (thanksgiving boat) on the beach; Uba Ae, Mesara (2013)

15. The *kowa hole* ceremony or launching a thanksgiving boat; Menia (2006)

16. Shelters for seaweed farm on the southern coast (2017)

17. Selected sarong patterns with historical relevance

Primary patterns for *hubi ae* or Greater Blossom (left) and *hubi iki* or Lesser Blossom (right)

Wini Ga Lena, Greater Blossom, *kobe morena* motif (left), first created in the 16th century
kobe molai motif (centre) created by Mojo Lado, late 16th or early 17th century
wue jara motif (right) created by Ina Loni Dimu, second quarter of the 18th century

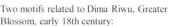

Wini Jèwu, Lesser Blossom
kebèba Raijua motif (left) created by Pago Jami, mid-18th century
kètu pedi motif (second from the left) attributed to Wuri Manu, late 18th century

Two motifs related to Dima Riwu, Greater Blossom, early 18th century:
kae bengku (left) for Mamo Tèro and her descendants,
legu koko for Migi Jami and her descendants (*wini* Migi)

Motifs related to colonial times and imported trading cloths are restricted to women of the ruling classes.
Patola motif, Greater Blossom (left); *patola* motif, Lesser Blossom (centre)
lèba motif for noble women of both moieties (right), reminiscent of confronting *naga*s; each *wini* owns a variation of the motif.

when they entirely abandoned the non-intervention policy (Wielenga 1926: 27–32). The same shift of colonial policy would soon have consequences for Savu itself, though under more peaceful circumstances.

Small colonies of Savunese people continued to exist in eastern Sumba and are present to this day. In particular, Melolo was a Savunese stronghold. A prince from Seba called Ama Luji Dimu, a nephew of the leader killed during the 1874 Kiritana expedition, governed the community as "raja". He was even acknowledged as raja of Melolo for a short time around 1890, when the Dutch were encouraging more immigration from Savu to Sumba.[111] In 1888, the Dutch rewarded Ama Luji for his great services to the colonial state and he received a model of a Turkish curved sabre.[112]

Nevertheless, the Savunese community in Sumba was far from wealthy. Missionaries of the Reformed Church began to appear on the island after 1881 and it was natural that they initially stayed close to the Savunese, who had already been exposed to Christianity. The pioneer missionary J.J. van Alphen made the following observations which, although condescending and racialist, highlight the frugal conditions:

> Though belatedly, we will take a good look at the Savunese kampong, which is only a few minutes away from my house. We do not ride through the entire kampong which is three quarters of an hour in circumference, although it counts no more than 40 houses which are placed in groups without any order. The houses look miserable, we never saw any poorer. They simply consist of some poles on which a roof rests, covered with lontar leaves, and are so low that the two-legged inhabitants, and also the pigs, goats and dogs, have to creep inside. There are no walls, so that one can look inside when bowing a little, and one does not see any house utensils except a few braided baskets, apart from a *bale-bale*, a couch that is used for resting and sleeping. The inhabitants make no more advantageous impression than their houses; their demeanour and clothing as well as their acts hurt our feelings of morality and fill us with compassion. One single sarung is the only piece of clothing for the woman. The girls comb their hair to the front and cut it above the eyes; this and the immodest clothing give these women a lewd look. The few men that we meet (at this time of the day most men are away from home in order to collect *tuak* and sweet liquid from the lontar palm) are more orderly dressed; above the sarung that they have fastened around the waist, several of them have a *baju*, smock; however, their faces show slyness; they really look like bad felons. Among these men you think you can discern two Sumbanese,

---

[111] Van Dijk 1925: 538. This source erroneously alleges that Ama Luji Dimu was the brother of the raja in Seba. The Savunese genealogical tradition should be preferred here.

[112] ANRI Timor: 93, General report, 1888.

judging from their cloths. You are mistaken; they are Savunese who go out
in this guise in order to steal horses (Van den End 1987: 87).

Chapter 7 has followed the events of Savunese society in and outside Savu over
the 19th century. For much of the period the endeavour is hampered by a lack
of written sources. As for internal political history, the first half of the century
would almost have been blank had it not been for the lively oral tradition. The
absence of sources in itself indicates that the new Dutch colonial state saw little
reason to intervene in Savunese affairs. The island was almost an archetypical
example of the colonial *onthoudingspolitiek* (politics of non-interference).
Savu had its share of internal turbulence, though perhaps less so than in the
preceding centuries and, with the exception of Menia, the status of the various
domains was never seriously threatened. The 19th century was marked by an
enormous upsurge of trade in maritime Southeast Asia, fueled by Singapore's role
and the increasing colonial exploitation. Savu played a modest part in regional
commerce with the horse trade and a few secondary export products such as
tobacco and cloth. What is remarkable about Savu in this century, however, is its
ability to use colonial power relations to expand politically and demographically.
The settlements in Timor and, in particular, the "colonies" in Sumba testify to
this. A degree of openness to the outside world facilitated the introduction of
Christianity which marked the inclusion in a European discourse of modernity.
At the same time, the tardy development of the new religion bore witness to the
old ritual system's ability to provide meaning to a small island in the midst of a
sea of changes.

Chapter 8 | Changes in the Late 19th Century

Death and disaster

The 1860s was a time of new economic initiatives in Savu and political expansion in Sumba. However, it was also a time of calamities which descended on the population with full force and made people reconsider their place in the world. In the dry season of 1865 the lontar palm trees did not blossom as usual.[1] As a consequence, people could not tap the sap—extract the sugar liquid by cutting into the tree's crown. Considering that the liquid constituted the basic means of nutrition on the islands, the consequences were indeed dire. To make matters worse, the maize harvest failed in 1864 and 1865, causing a widespread lack of food.[2]

Ama Nia Jawa and the other princes notified the Resident that a number of persons had died of starvation and from consuming bad food. When the Kupang authorities heard the news they sent the official Waleson and an interpreter to Savu on a cruising boat. The craft also brought 335 piculs of rice purchased in Kupang for the low price of eight guilders per picul. The Dutch Government thus showed a degree of responsibility to their faraway client, but it was not for free. The rice delivery required the payment of 20 horses for army use. Even this was not enough to feed the hungry, but Ama Nia Jawa intervened and paid the amount remaining in money. As mentioned in the previous chapter, he was one of the few princes in the region in a strong economic position.

The desperate locals began to devour seaweed and turned to harmful plants for food. As a consequence, a lot of people developed a sickness in the belly which was coupled with high fever. Waleson and the interpreter related that they did not see a single home there without wailing and tears over the death of a

---

[1] At least, this is how the colonial reports described the situation. That the lontar did not blossom seems quite extraordinary (James J. Fox, personal communication; Jan. 2017). For more on the lontar palm see Fox (1977).

[2] *Ministerië van Kolonien*, Supplement, 2.10.03, National Archive, The Hague. Survey of the political condition in Netherlands India, 16 October 1866: 1033.

relative. They encountered houses where those still alive were too sick and weak to bury their dead.

Kupang asked the governor of the Celebes residency *en Onderhoorigheden* (and dependencies) to announce that Savu had a severe food shortage. The idea was that Sulawesi merchants would go to barter food for horses, the people's plight being to their advantage. The misery in Savu, the Dutch said, could not be relieved by the means Kupang had at its disposal. It was not even possible to send the military doctors from the Kupang garrison to administer medicine. Communications between Kupang and the outer world were still primitive, and there was not even a steamship at hand. One potential plan was to send the medical personnel to Savu on a cruising boat, but it would not then be possible to anticipate when they could return.

One calamity was heaped on another. In the same year, another sickness struck Savu that afflicted the throat and claimed many lives. For the Resident of Kupang this was also a strategic disadvantage: sickness and death reduced the surplus population from which he had hoped to colonise the Pariti Plain, east of Kupang in Timor.[3]

By mid-1865 the situation had slightly improved. Most of the lontar palms still had no yield, but a sufficient number blossomed to allow lontar tapping and so abate the worst misery. Kupang sent some medicine to cure the belly sickness, though it was insufficient, and patients with less serious symptoms received gambier extract.[4] Although it did not actually help, the Resident counted on a placebo effect, and the bonds of confidence between the government and the Savunese population would be strengthened accordingly. It is unknown if it had the intended effect.[5]

Worse was yet to come. Smallpox had been a killer in the eastern archipelago since at least VOC times. While it was a dreaded scourge in continental Asia and Europe before the introduction of variolation,[6] resistance in demographically scattered populations at the fringes appears to have been even lower. It is a reminder of the ravages of smallpox in the Americas from the 16th century onwards, which may have decimated the majority of Native American populations in large areas. The missionary W.M. Donselaar, who conducted proselytising work in Timor and Savu in the second half of the 19th century, remarked that

---

[3] ANRI Timor: 107, monthly report, September 1865.

[4] It is a yellow water-soluable resin from a woody vine (*Uncaria gambir*) which grows in the region. It has a medicinal use for its astringent properties, but it usually accompanies chewing betel.

[5] ANRI Timor: 107, monthly report, October 1865.

[6] Vaccination against smallpox

"it seems as if some tribes are more susceptible to the sickness than others" (Donselaar 1871: 104). It appears from VOC records that the Savunese feared the sickness "like [they would] the plague" and with good reason. When the company needed auxiliaries to fight the refractory Sonba'i ruler in 1786 it was exceedingly difficult to make them travel to the Timorese mainland, at the time ravaged by smallpox.[7]

Savu had in the vicinity of 30,000 inhabitants in 1869 when smallpox struck with terrible effect. Three years later, the estimation was that no more than 16,000 remained, Raijua included. If these figures are reliable,[8] the disease took a far heavier toll than the 1348–50 black plague in Europe. The missionaries who visited the island in the following years heard stories of the islanders' suffering. In many families there was only one child left who was entrusted to the village chiefs. A village in Raijua with 300 inhabitants lost its entire population with the exception of one child. In some houses everyone was infected and no one had the strength to bury the dead; those who had not yet succumbed managed only to pull the corpses outside the houses where dogs and pigs devoured them. Some people fled in desperation to seek refuge in caves and other places in the wilderness, though that did not always help. Afterwards, in outlying areas, one could sometimes find groups of four or five bodies—fleeing villagers who had all perished (Donselaar 1872: 291).

As in 14th-century Europe, people searched for all kinds of supernatural causes and remedies for the catastrophe. When sickness occurred, people performed magic rituals, such as making clay pigs and buffalos, and offering them to the spirits.[9] There was reportedly an idea that smallpox could be magically cured by eating stolen horses and cattle, which only increased the chaos and depleted the livestock.[10] The raja of Raijua was in Savu when the epidemic began. He received some money for a horse he had sold to the Resident and a few pieces of furniture from the posthouder. The raja then returned to Raijua which was still not afflicted. Soon after his arrival, unsurprisingly, the disease erupted and the riches he had obtained were seen as a cause. The raja, urged by the people, threw the money and goods into the sea. When the smallpox did not abate, the people decided it was necessary to sacrifice a slave, who was to be drowned in the strait between Raijua and Savu. However, the chief assigned to perform the

---

[7] VOC 3732 (1786), f. 51.

[8] There were no precise demographic statistics at this time, although the Residents of Kupang provided estimates in their reports.

[9] Raad voor de Zending, 1102–1: 1406, H.C. Kruyt, Notebook 2, c. 1890.

[10] *Mailrapport* 1874: 282, Relation of a tour of inspection, 15–26 March.

sacrifice fell ill and died soon after, so the slave lived (Donselaar 1872: 291–2). If this information is correct, it highlights the state of desperation and despair: human sacrifices were, at least according to early 20th-century tradition, reserved for funerals. The favourite slave of important deceased persons followed them to their grave. Alive and tied to a pole, the slaves had their flesh cut from the bones. The flesh was then buried in the same hole as the deceased master (Heyligers 1920: 35).[11]

The disease spared neither high nor low born. In all six domains of Savu and Raijua, the reigning rajas disappeared in 1868–69. Colonial records are strangely reticent about their simultaneous end and the oral traditions found so far say nothing in particular about the way they died. In Seba, Ama Nia Jawa's gravestone states he passed away in 1868, thus before the onset of the epidemic. His son and successor Ama Doko Kaho lost his young wife, leaving him with an infant. For the rest it seems likely that at least some of the elite were victims of the dreaded disease. The raja family of Mesara counted 150 persons before the disaster, but afterwards there were no more than 3 alive.[12] The missionary Donselaar confirms that the raja of Dimu, Ama Lai Daga, succumbed to smallpox and the Dutch man was present at his mortuary feast. As it is the earliest account of such a feast, Donselaar's testimony has considerable interest:

> In the large house a chair is placed in the middle, covered with fine kains or pieces of cloth. On this seat the deceased is imagined to sit, as he was when he was alive and in full health. His relatives and subjects sit around. In their close vicinity, the gold and silver ornaments which belonged to him, apart from a great many costly pieces of cloth, are hanging. Thus the deceased is imagined to amuse himself in the sight of his treasures, relatives and subjects, as in better days. Now a female servant walks forward to the seat and offers the prince refreshments. But alas, the refreshments are not accepted; also, repeated offers are in vain: the prince is no more in the land of the living! A loud and general wailing replaces the tense stillness and, as in despair, some people run to the narrow end of the oblong house which is built on pillars; they kick at the walls as if desperate, and these, already loosened by design, fall down with a crack. For the death of the lord of the house brings his residence to a broken state! This is the beginning of the feast of mourning. Night and day, one hears at intervals the wailing of a number of women who remain in the house during the

---

[11] So far there have been no references to human sacrifices in archival sources, although the practice is mentioned a few times with regard to Rote in the VOC period. In Sumba, sacrificing people declared 'slaves' in connection with high-status funerals reportedly still occurs. Human sacrifice in eastern Indonesia is typically difficult to document, and it is hard to assess the related rumours and traditions.

[12] Raad voor de Zending, 1102–1: 1411, M. Teffer, letter, 7 March 1874.

feast, while guests who come and go beat metal cymbals (gongs) almost
incessantly. Meals and the playing of gongs remain the main ingredients
of the feast until the end (Donselaar 1872: 3, 114–5).

Photo 20. Graves in Ba, settlement of the Dimu rulers (Nadowu clan); the large number attest to the devastating impact of the epidemics from the l860s to the 1880s (2011)

Such an enormous loss of life left deep psychological scars. According to the
Christian missionaries, many people felt their old beliefs were insufficient,
because they no longer provided support and consolation in a time of misery and
loss, and no real hope for the future.

> Where all disasters were seen as the consequences of the wrath of higher
> powers, only fear could reside in their hearts that excluded love. In vain
> were the spirits of the ancestors called, in vain did they try to exorcise the
> wrath of the angry gods through offerings. They must helplessly watch
> the sick succumb; inconsolably they must bring beloved deceased to the
> grave. Then their hearts were severed from the religion which could not
> provide any support and no consolation and no hope for the sufferings
> and hardships of life, and evoked an indeterminate longing for something
> better in their minds (Donselaar 1871: 105).

Was this how the Savunese actually saw their grim situation or was it creative
interpretation? There is little possibility of knowing as the Christian ministers

had a rather limited idea about Savunese spirituality, apparent from Donselaar's comments in 1872:

> It is indeed very difficult to gain a clear understanding of the religious conceptions of the Savunese. I have made all efforts to investigate, and turned to persons who were said to be the most knowledgeable in these matters. I have not been able to obtain the desired information from a single one of those mentioned to be the most judicious in religious matters. There was not a single case where their information agreed. For example, various persons would attribute wholly different properties to the same god. No one could give me a coherent depiction of the whole (Donselaar 1872: 304).

Donselaar attributed the lack of theological coherence to the non-literate character of society and the lack of a separate priesthood. Here he overlooks the ritual priests—Deo Rai, Apu Lod'o and others. Donselaar also perceptively criticised previous Western travellers who had only a fragmentary cultural understanding from their short stays and tried to insert order through their own judgement. Thus, it is questionable whether any 19th-century Western observers, including the early missionaries, had the prerequisites to make conclusions about the attachment to ancestral beliefs. Despite these reservations, it does seem plausible that the magnitude of the disaster could have made some people susceptible to new explanations of their place in the world. At any rate, Donselaar of the Nederlandsche Zendelinggenootschap (NZG, Dutch Missionary Society) landed on the island in August 1870, and his and his associates' activities afforded a new important influence in Savunese life.[13]

The spread of Christianity

When Donselaar set foot on Savunese soil there was already a Malay school in Seba, established in 1862 on Resident Isaac Esser's initiative. The teacher was a good-natured Ambonese Christian called W. Pati who got on well with the local community.[14] Ambon was a centre of Reformed Christianity in the eastern region, and a lot of teachers and clerics propagated Dutch religion and culture in the various outposts of the East Indies. Although the missionaries were quick to find fault with the Ambonese teachers, nevertheless they were able to work closely with local populations in a way that few white clerics could. The teacher Pati provided the sort of knowledge about the outside world that attracted the

---

[13] *Maandberigt van het Nederlandsche Zendelinggenootschap* 1871–75: 65.

[14] W. Pati's compatriot Manuhutu (1862–66) and the Timorese S. Mae (1866–67) preceded him (Fox 1977: 165).

locals. Several, including Raja Ama Doko Kaho, went to listen to his teachings with some regularity, and even attended the religious services that he held for his household and pupils on Sundays.[15] The raja's teenage daughter actually taught in the school and managed the class when Pati was ill with malaria (Fox 1977: 165). With the school accepted by the community, Donselaar's arrival in 1870 was not a radical turn in the spiritual fortunes of the Savunese as the ground had been prepared.

The NZG was not always on good terms with the colonial government. Some of the missionaries in Kupang and Rote in the 1830s and 1840s engaged in verbal battles with a succession of Residents, and these disputes turned inward between the clerics themselves. The Dutch NZG missionaries came from the poorer strata of metropolitan society and were not always well prepared for their roles in a new cultural setting. Poor funding from the NZG centre in Rotterdam, deficient language capabilities and the increasingly secularised outlook of many colonial officials turned their sojourn in maritime Southeast Asia into a series of frustrations, often cut short by premature death—tropical medicine was still in its infancy. The NZG centre wound down the Timor mission in the 1850s due to the lack of real success with the scattered and unreceptive Timorese settlements.[16] A border agreement with the Portuguese in 1859 defined the Dutch sphere of interest, leaving Flores, West Timor and the adjacent island under their (sometimes nominal) influence. However, the treaty also stipulated that Flores, the Solor Islands and Central Timor had to be left to the Catholic mission. The Alor Islands and Sumba were still too insecure to attract NZG clerics, who were seldom candidates for martyrdom. Rather, their proselytising centred on Rote and Savu—islands tied to the Dutch by alliances of hundreds of years and considered relatively well-ordered societies.

Donselaar's first visit only lasted a day but seemed promising enough. The posthouder told him that some Savunese had expressed interest in baptism, including Ama Doko Kaho, most of his chiefs, and their respective families and associates. In the evening he met a crowd of people in the posthouder's house and spent several hours explaining the basic precepts of Christianity in Malay. He did not fail to refer to the recent epidemic and the consolation offered by the new creed. When reading his account of the positive attention he aroused, it is important to remember that representatives of the colonial government accompanied him on his brief trip and foremost was the Resident himself.[17]

---

[15] *Maandberigt van het Nederlandsche Zendelinggenootschap* 1871–75: 67–8.

[16] Hägerdal (2013) detailed the trials and tribulations of the NZG in the Timor area.

[17] *Maandberigt van het Nederlandsche Zendelinggenootschap* 1871–75.

Missionary and colonial interests did not always converge and the two could take quite hostile positions against each other. However, the contemporary Resident Johan Arnoud Caspersz was clearly in favour of the enterprise. Local Savunese tradition believed the two entities to be closely connected—note that the story of the first Dutch expedition to Dimu was, supposedly (and incorrectly), a reaction to the killing of clerical people.

Donselaar's colleague Mattheus Teffer arrived in 1872; by which time there were 250 converts.[18] During the following years he oversaw the rapid dissemination of the Gospel and, by 1874, the number had risen to almost 1,000 (Fox 1977: 165). However, in spite of his long years in Savu, he never really learnt Savunese so could only communicate with the few Malay-speaking locals. Moreover, his interest in teaching was somewhat limited, which was also apparently detrimental to his efforts to bond with the local people (Kruijf 1894: 206). Some of Teffer's successors, such as Niks, Letteboer and Wijngaarden, enabled their task considerably by making the effort at least to learn some Savunese.[19]

Letteboer discovered the awkward consequences of trusting translators before he had learned the language properly. Once, when he gave a sermon in the Seba church, one of the church elders translated his words to Prince Jonathan Doko. Suddenly Jonathan sprang up and yelled "Do not listen to that figure, for he is a whore child himself!" It transpired that the elder had translated wrongly, so it seemed that Letteboer had accused him of being illegitimate by birth before the congregation! Letteboer desperately tried to reconcile with the prince through the mediation of Raja Alexander Rihi Jawa but to no avail. The incensed Jonathan threatened to introduce Catholicism to Seba when he became ruler, perhaps knowing the intense disdain that the NZG brothers felt for their Christian rivals.[20]

The NZG writings reveal a curious mixture of sharp-eyed observations of local society and unabashed Euro-centrism. This is only what can be expected, given the period: their unquestioning acceptance of the superiority of Western civilisation was strengthened by the deference shown to them by most Asian people they encountered. Life in Savu was evidently lonely for them. Several letters from Jan Kornelis Wijngaarden speak of his agony after losing his (Dutch) wife, who fell sick after a short stay in Savu.

---

[18] Teffer lived from 1826 to 1907. In 1894, in his later years, he joined the Catholic clergy (Aritonang and Steenbrink 2008: 696). This, however, was long after his time in Savu.

[19] Kruijf (1894: 206) confirms that Wijngaarden spoke passable Savunese by 1890 and used his skills to teach promising young Savunese.

[20] Raad voor de Zending, 1102–1: 1444, J.H. Letteboer, letter, 26 February 1897.

Work on Savu is hard, full of difficulties and vicissitudes. Several times during the year … I sat down in despair. My wife consoled me. Her calm and trust in God was beneficial for me … I was used to be welcomed by her friendly voice when I come back home from my work—no more now, all is cold and still in my house. And there is no one who understands me. Yes, the Savunese cried with me on the day my wife died. But no more now; the funeral is over and thus the sorrow has also come to an end. The Savunese does not yet know what love is. And who can blame him for that? He is still not sufficiently immersed in Christianity.[21]

It is only the missionary letters which reveal the dynamics of conversion, because oral tradition does not give much insight. Teffer relates an incident in the first half of the 1870s which indicates that conversion to the new creed was sometimes sanctioned by the old ritual practices. The uncle of Seba's raja presided over a mortuary feast. The Jingi Tiu priests slaughtered a lot of animals for the occasion and they carefully scrutinised the beasts' intestines. Hundreds of Savunese flocked around the priests, eager to hear what the future would bring. The royal uncle, related to the priests, asked them why their faces seemed so troubled. "Speak up! What do you see? What does the future spell? Come, share the summary of your investigations with us; come! Hurry up a bit; you see how people are crowding." The priests replied: "The future does not show any good for us. Our cause is lost. Although the Christians are few in relation to us, they will surely triumph." Pondering this, the raja's uncle considered that maintaining the beliefs he was raised with was futile and declared his support for the new religion.[22] While Teffer of course interpreted this as a triumph for the spread of the Gospel, the story also reveals that those involved did not doubt the power of the traditional ritual practices. This syncretistic feature of Savunese Christianity was later noted by colonial officials less passionate than the NZG representatives (Heyligers 1920: 24).

The NZG urgently wanted to gain a foothold in Savu to hold off their rivals. Muslim traders from Makassar and Kupang tried to persuade the rajas and chiefs to accept the precepts of the Prophet, well aware of the way that conversion often works in hierarchical premodern societies: once the elite converts, the majority of the population is likely to follow. The Christian missionaries complained about the Muslims' "base arguments", which they believed the "undeveloped" and "entirely ignorant" Savunese could not gainsay or question. They thought it a worrying sign that Ama Nia Jawa of Seba wore a Muslim *jimat* (amulet) and

[21] Raad voor de Zending, 1102–1: 1415, J.K. Wijngaarden, letter, undated, c. 1890.
[22] Raad voor de Zending, 1102–1: 1411, M. Teffer, letter, 8 February 1875.

refrained from eating pork.[23] It is likely that the Savunese were more than able to balance their ancestral beliefs with influence from Muslims than the missionaries gave them credit. Chapter 7 shows how Ama Nia Jawa's disposition was to promote conversion to Islam to maintain good relations with Muslim traders, clearly with pragmatic results.

A similar balance became apparent between Reformed Christianity and the old religion. The missionaries baptised four rajas on the main island in the 1870s while the Raijua ruler followed in the early 20th century.[24] However, the baptisms did not entail wholesale conversion until far into the 20th century. Statistics assembled by Johan Frederik Niks in 1887 alleged that there were more than 3,000 converts, which is a rapid development from 1870—when the number was almost nil—and 1872, when there were 250 converts.[25] Still, this was only a minor part of the overall population and religious adherence would remain as such until relatively modern times; for example, in 1920 there were still no more than 5,000 Christians out of a total population of 27,311 (Heyligers 1920: 23-4). Niks's 1887 statistics give the following number of Christians in seven places in Savu:

Figure 55: Christians in Savu in 1887

Place	Males	Females	Altogether
Seba	748	787	1,590
Menia	77	83	168
Rai Liu	68	69	139
Liae	257	268	526
Dimu Bodae	152	169	335
Dimu Bolou	65	45	117
Mesara	228	221	450

Although the statistical accuracy is in doubt (the sum totals are not equal to the indicated numbers of males and females), the data show that Christianity had taken root in Seba by the late 19th century and had a small but significant following in the other three domains. It needs to be stressed that it was not the few whites in the field who preserved continuity but rather the non-white

---

[23] Raad voor de Zending, 1102–1: 1397, W.M. Donselaar, letter, 4 November 1870.

[24] This was Paulus Lai (r. 1915–18), the last ruler of Raijua. His Raijuan name is Lai Kuji (Figure 54).

[25] Raad voor de Zending, 1102–1: 1408, J.F. Niks, Statistical table, 3 October 1887; ANRI Timor: 133 (1872).

religious teachers. Their lives were far from affluent; J.F. Niks mentions in a letter from 1887 that a teacher had to survive on vegetables and a little sugar juice because a picul of rice in Savu cost the princely sum of 14 guilders. Niks sent the poor teacher five sacks of rice "in the name of the Lord". By the end of the 19th century, native Savunese took up the torch; in about 1895 a certain Jacob Ribu Dumi was employed as a teacher in one of the congregations.[26]

The missionary letters need to be read with caution when they describe the individual motives for conversion. The missionaries sent the letters to the central NZG authorities in Rotterdam and may have left out some of the more 'awkward' details. As they stand, the letters sometimes claim to quote the locals who came in contact with the mission. In a letter from 1874, Teffer quotes a long conversation with the raja of Liae, Ama Amu Manu (r. 1869–79) whom the cleric believed was 'won' for the new religion before he was even aware of it. On his visit to Liae, Teffer asked Ama Amu how things were—the raja replied:

> With me, matters are not at their best. I suffer much from pain in my body. I can usually not rest, usually not sleep. Neither day nor night do I find respite. As for the weather, alas! This is also in a sorry state. If it goes on like this there will be famine. All the crops are already destroyed. Our priests have already done everything to advance the rainy season, but whatever they try, the rainy season will not come. We are out of counsel; do you perhaps know a way to bring rain?

Teffer asked Ama Amu what exactly they had done to make the rain fall. The raja, otherwise known as taciturn, gave an elaborate reply:

> They slaughtered cattle, cut through the intestines and read out in how many days there would be rain. They have already sacrificed a large number of buffalos, pigs, sheep and chickens, but matters are not in order. First they prophesised in five days, but the five days passed without their prophecy being verified. Then they sacrificed again, and the prophecy said in seven days, but these seven days also passed without any rain. Then they said that they might have been a little mistaken. They again wanted to sacrifice. In nine days there would surely be rain—thus their new prophecy. However, the nine days passed and all remained dry. At the end, counsel was taken to sacrifice once again, increase the offerings and carry out the investigation as carefully as possible. The outcome of all these secretive investigations was in eleven days there would no doubt be heavy rain. However, it only became drier and drier and the sunshine on the already dusty earth was unbearable. The priests were out of their

---

[26] Raad voor de Zending, 1102–1: 1408, J.F. Niks, letters, 13 June 1887; and c. 1895.

minds with shame and they did not dare to make another sacrifice or make prophecies about the rainy season.[27]

Teffer asked the raja what consolation the gods and spirits brought to him. The raja declared that his creed told lies and cheated. It was clear from all the evidence that the gods were powerless and the priests were liars. Next, Teffer installed a teacher, Meester Jacob, in Liae who assisted the locals in various daily matters and was considered the right person for the job. In his letter Teffer may very well have amended the words of the raja to suit his own ideas; it is highly unlikely that he would have categorically denied the divine world of his Jingi Tiu beliefs. Nonetheless, maybe he saw the Christian priests as superior in spiritual power, as hinted when he asked Teffer if he could bring rain. In another letter, written in 1893, a less privileged Savunese told his conversion story to the missionary J.F. Niks:

> I visited Liae, Mesara, Rai Liu and Menia. I was heartily received everywhere and the attendance was excellent. In Seba, where almost 2,000 native Christians live, I naturally spent most of the time. As previously, people treated me cordially. Among other things, I was not without fruit for one single day on the barren Savu. The Raja of Seba, Alexander Rihi Jawa, seemed to me to be a very well-intentioned man. In all matters where I needed his help, such as harvesting debts, erecting a *pagger* [wall] around the churchyard, etc., he assisted immediately. He elevated the road to the church. His wife Anna, a pupil of Father Donselaar, is his good spirit.
>
> Now, let us take just one single example of how true the Gospel and the power of God are to bring salvation. The deacon Hanoch Hede Kore accompanied me on my tour. He is not enterprising and is somewhat fearful. During the trip I asked him, "How was it that you became a Christian?" And he related to me, "When *Pandita* [*pendeta* minister (In)] Teffer arrived I had left the school of *Guru* [teacher] Patti, and was able to spell somewhat. I heard *Tuan* [master] speak, and thought that I must know more about it. I bought an Old Testament for 5 guilders and a New Testament for 2,50 guilders and a *buku serani* [Bunyan][28] for 2,50 guilders. Then I trained myself to read so that I first read Bunyan and then the New Testament. I believed that Lord Jesus was the saviour, and I asked to be baptised. Later I became a member [of the church council],

---

[27] Raad voor de Zending, 1102–1: 1411, M. Teffer, letter, 15 June 1874.

[28] John Bunyan's classic allegoric work *The Pilgrim's Progress*—published in two parts between 1678 and 1684—was often translated by Protestant missionaries as next in importance after the Bible.

and then *Tuan Pandita* said 'Do not let anyone take away your belief, keep it steady.' And behold, *Tuan*, there I stay."[29]

The quotation shows that the intellectual curiosity of a hitherto illiterate people should not be underestimated. The potential of the written word was quickly realised as a work like Bunyan's *The Pilgrim's Progress* resonated with Savunese thought. The passage also confirms that the new religion's acceptance would not have been possible without the Ambonese teachers who lived and worked with the locals. NZG developed a clerical organisation with church councils and schools to serve as the institutional backbone. The missionaries believed that the rapid spread of the Gospel had an immediate and beneficial effect on the Savunese mindset and made the fearsome island warriors less prone to commit atrocities. One missionary wrote:

> My feelings about this were strengthened during the warfare of 1874 in various places in the Timor Residency. How much less frequent were the cruelties committed by the Savunese on Sumba, compared to the cruelties perpetrated by the Timorese? People say 'The Savunese are probably of a milder disposition than the Timorese by nature.' That betrays an utter ignorance of these two peoples. The experience of those who have known the two tribes at close distance, and over a long duration is, that 500 Savunese commit more cruelties and damage than 2,000 Timorese. How briefly had the Savunese known the summons of the congregation of Christ when the leaders of Savu … went to war on Sumba?[30]

Still, the NZG letters cannot hide that there was a degree of resistance to the new ideas. For example, the eastern domain of Dimu meant trouble for the missionary enterprise. Whether this had something to do with its traditional rivalry with Seba, where the mission was centred, is open to debate. Shortly after Raja Eduard Luji Jara's conversion, it came to Teffer's ears that the raja had used force in order to press some people into converting. This practice may not have raised eyebrows in premodern times, but for the pietistic Protestant movement of the 19th century—with its emphasis on personal salvation—a sword mission was abhorrent. Teffer took his time to investigate the matter and gave one victim the choice to remain in the Christian congregation or rejoin his heathen brothers. However, the man replied "Although I was forced to undergo baptism, I later realised that it is better for me to be a Christian."[31] There is no way to know if his reply was honest or conditioned by fear—either of the white minister or the raja.

---

[29] Raad voor de Zending, 1102–1: 1408, J.F. Niks, letter, 7 May 1893.

[30] Raad voor de Zending, 1102–1: 1411, M. Teffer, letter, 9 April 1876.

[31] Raad voor de Zending, 1102–1: 1411, M. Teffer, letter, 8 February 1875.

Eduard Jara Luji seemed to be a serious advocate for the spread of the faith. However, although the raja and his fettor, Ama Tanya, had been baptised and created deacons, their behaviour bewildered and disappointed the European NZG clerics. The two rulers were at odds with each other—not an uncommon situation in Savunese history—and as a result the NZG mission had made little progress by the late 19th century. Some anti-Christian figures burnt down the church and the fettor appropriated the material that would have been used to build a new one. Raja Eduard himself was deemed unsteady in his new faith: he let another person perform the prescribed ancestral offerings in his stead and was suspected of indirectly acting against "the good cause".[32] The raja's behaviour, of course, can also be regarded as an expedient way of striking a balance between religious novelty and tradition. Eduard, formally married, also set a bad example by taking a concubine at the same time. J.F. Niks confronted him on the matter and he promised to improve. Eduard Jara Luji's irreverent posture was made clear when Niks gave a sermon before a 90-strong Dimunese congregation. During the service Eduard negotiated with a Chinese trader about purchasing gunpowder which significantly distracted the worshippers (Kruijf 1894: 202). And so it seems the NZG mission in Dimu was constrained as the congregation declined and the chiefs appeared to work against rather than for the Christian project.[33]

Not even Seba was seen as an example of Christian development. The first baptised raja was Ama Doko Kaho (r. 1868–82), encountered in chapter 7 as an active player in Sumbanese politics and an avid horse trader. Donselaar thought him a young man of good character and intellectual capacity.[34] His relations with Donselaar's colleague Mattheus Teffer, who stayed in Savu from 1872 to 1883, were quite different. Teffer and his European wife seemed to be much revered by the locals and he exercised some influence on the political leadership. The Resident of Kupang thought this was advantageous for the situation on the island.[35] However, Teffer was soon embroiled in a bitter conflict with Ama Doko Kaho, as seen from the frustrated remarks in his letters:

---

[32] Raad voor de Zending, 1102–1: 1408, J.F. Niks, letter, 15 July 1887.

[33] Raad voor de Zending, 1102–1: 1408, J.F. Niks, Travel report, 5–29 June 1885.

[34] Raad voor de Zending, 1102–1: 1397, W.M. Donselaar, letter, 4 November 1870.

[35] *Mailrapport* 1874: 282.

The number of atrocities that this scoundrel has committed since he succeeded to the position, and indulged in since the war on Sumba in particular, is too comprehensive to be accounted for in a simple letter. And this man is celebrated in Timor Kupang, being the cordial friend of the Resident. … Previously, about half a year ago, his child by his true wife passed away. It was an infant son. As for me I was not well at the time. I could hardly walk; but hoping that I would win the heart of the father at the right time, I went to the house of the deceased. However, when Ama Doko saw me, he escaped. I went out in person to search for him, saying "A father must be at the burial of his son" My search was in vain and the child was buried without the runaway father.

And I did not see him any further! I only heard that he is constantly busy on Sumba with all kinds of complications in his life. Thus an entire government was misled and, for a few beautiful Savunese horses, the welfare of the colonies was put at stake by those who should monitor it, with the bestowal of grand allowances; and woe to any missionary who publicly speaks out about what he knows.[36]

Teffer shares his disdain of the raja and the Dutch colonial government; the latter he depicts as irresponsible and greedy. While it has been fashionable in post-colonial literature to include missionaries and colonial writers in a comprehensive discursive formation, or a hegemonic discourse of Orientalism, this requires some qualification. Judging from their comprehensive correspondence, the missionaries in Asia and elsewhere did not oppose the role of the metropolitan centre as an ordering force that made their missionary endeavour possible. Nevertheless, there are many instances where the missionaries denounce the practices of the colonial apparatus in terms reminiscent of Multatuli's novel *Max Havelaar*.[37] In addition, the colonial officials' disinterest and even resistance to the Christian mission certainly would not have improved relations.[38] Just like in *Max Havelaar*, the letters portray the European-backed local Asian leadership as potentially despotic and an impediment to good society.

Racialism in the Dutch East Indies, moreover, was not merely a white-versus-non-white affair. One of Teffer's letters combined indignation at the Resident's behaviour with open anti-Semitism to construct a sympathetic image of the indigenous Christian elite: Salomon Roos was reputedly the son of a Jewess

---

[36] Raad voor de Zending, 1102–1: 1411, M. Teffer, letter, 24 May 1876.

[37] Written in 1860, *Max Havelaar: Or the Coffee Auctions of the Dutch Trading Company* was a satirical novel by Eduard Douwes Dekker—a former controller in North Sumatra—known under the pseudonym Multatuli. The novel, named after the main character, tells of Havelaar's battles against the corrupt Dutch colonial system.

[38] Teffer wrote with disdain about Mohammedan-loving Residents (Raad voor de Zending, 1102–1: 1411, M. Teffer, letter, 2 January 1884).

from Leeuwarden and born out of wedlock. According to Teffer, after Roos was posthouder in Sumba, where he reportedly amassed a fortune of 80,000 guilders by breeding horses, he became Resident in Kupang. He visited Savu in 1883, after a great cyclone had devastated the island, and there he scolded and cursed the local Christians, in Teffer's words:

> just like mean Jews may scold and curse. Nota bene, at the first meeting with rajas—free princes—he refused to give them his hand. It was sad to see them being so insulted, in the midst of calamity, in the midst of their fallen houses and trees, under the sky.[39]

It is at this point that attention can return to the *udu* Nataga, the clan to which Ama Nia Jawa belonged. Some of its members were in fact seen as trusted servants of God. Here it is necessary to consider dynastic conditions that probably went unnoticed by the NZG ministers. When Raja Wadu Lai passed away in the early 1740s, he had two sons: the younger succeeded him and continued the ruling line. The elder son Melo Wadu was made Apu Lod'o and started a lineage that became known as the Raja Pono Family. The principal representative of the lineage in the late 19th century was Elias Luji Raja Pono who married Ama Nia Jawa's daughter. He appears in the NZG sources from the 1880s and always in positive terms. Niks characterised him as one of the most pious and civilised men on the island, and his wife Maria was ordained as a deaconess.

Elias was keen to secure a clerical education for his son Soleman, thus partly transforming the line of Apu Lod'o into a Christian priestly lineage. Niks received the boy in his house when he was six years of age, and praised his mild and attractive character. Soleman became the best playmate of the missionary's children from whom he learned to speak Malay, Dutch and take the first few steps in the school curriculum. In due time he went to school in Kupang where he became the most diligent of his class. He had "nothing of the headstrong and recalcitrant traits of the other native children, so that he very seldom had to receive any reprimand or minor chastisement".[40] However, his best European or Eurasian mate died in his early teens and he began to hang around with ostensibly wayward schoolmates. His school results declined, although the missionaries still had hopes for his capacity to learn. There were plans to send Soleman to the missionary post in Menado in North Sulawesi and even to the Netherlands. Elias Luji Raja Pono was prepared to cover the costs of his son's

---

[39] Raad voor de Zending, 1102–1: 1411, M. Teffer, letter, 25 April 1883.

[40] Raad voor de Zending, 1102–1: 1408, J.F. Niks, letter, 27 November 1887.

travel and maintenance.[41] It was important for the mission to educate sons of powerful elite and provide Christianity in Savu with a solid indigenous base. The paucity of the records does not provide details of Soleman's career, but in an irritated letter in 1892, Niks complained that one of his colleagues, Hulstra, had treated the lad unfairly and thus lost the confidence of Seba's entire raja family. This, Niks remarked, could be harmful to the missionary project.[42] Soleman's father Elias would briefly become the raja of Seba.

What consequences did conversions bring for life in Savu? The NZG clerics alleged that changes in outlook and material culture were already obvious by the late 1870s. Previously, according to Teffer, there were hardly any lamps; even the rajas stayed in darkness in their so-called palaces after dusk. People, including rajas and grandees, slept on mats on the floor. The only thing that distinguished the rulers from the populace, the missionary wrote, was their greater viciousness, slyness, thirst for blood and oppressive character. Christianity had begun to change all this. Such aspects as the way people dressed and the introduction of proper sleeping places were the first modest steps towards Western modernity.[43] J.K. Wijngaarden notes the importance that members of the church council paid to dress. They wore trousers, vests, jackets, hats and shoes on solemn occasions.

> They walk around in [the shoes] with difficulty, but gladly take this discomfort. If such a gentleman enters church wearing shoes, one hears him from afar. At a closer look such a dressed-up native is a repulsive sight. In the first place European cloths do not fit the native. Adding to this, Christianity often sits in a filthy old jacket. It is too sad to speak about. How much better they look with a simple *bajau* with a *kain*.[44]

Wijngaarden's observation illustrates the apparent prestige of adopting European cultural symbols though uncomfortable and ill-suited to Savunese life.

Most important of all was that Teffer believed practising Christian virtues had effects; this distinguished the present from "the abominable past", as he put it. The NZG view of Savunese culture is rather ambiguous. On one hand, the missionaries emphasise the dark sides of traditional life to justify the introduction of the new religion that provided the basis for better social conditions.[45] For instance, there were no wars between the domains after 1872. Raids committed

---

[41] Raad voor de Zending, 1102–1: 1408, J.F. Niks, letters, 24 November 1884, 22 July 1885, 28 July 1886, 27 November 1887.

[42] Raad voor de Zending, 1102–1: 1408, J.F. Niks, letter, 19 September 1892.

[43] Raad voor de Zending, 1102–1: 1411, M. Teffer, letter, 12 September 1877.

[44] Raad voor de Zending, 1102–1: 1415, J.K. Wijngaarden, letter, 24 April 1890.

[45] Raad voor de Zending, 1102–1: 1411, M. Teffer, letter, 12 September 1877.

by kinsmen of the rajas became increasingly rare, as did murders and atrocities. "If one considers what a horrible past the present-day Savunese had according to their own account, then we have reason to be grateful for the effectuation of the Gospels."[46] On the other hand, the same missionaries often express astonishment and admiration for the frugal, efficacious and chaste society, which could feed a substantial population on a relatively barren island.

The NZG representatives took care to exert discipline on the converts' social relations. An obvious focus was marriage and family. While the Savunese were monogamous, the letters complain that divorces took place daily, with the least misunderstanding leading to separation. Teffer knew of a man who divorced a succession of 14 wives—his 15th marriage lasted until his demise as it was an official Christian ceremony in the church. In a letter from 1875, Teffer related in detail his attempts to persuade persons in the Christian congregation to stay with their spouses:

> Of all the marriages that were concluded in the young congregation, there were only three pairs asking for divorce. They began by confronting each other violently and passionately. I asked the arguing spouses to sit down. They were offered tea and some rice cakes. They drank and ate and calmed down considerably. Then I asked them "Who forced you to marry?" "Nobody." "When you married did you, husband, think that your wife was an angel, thousand-fold better than yourself?" "No!" "But when you now disown your wife, do you think that an angel stands ready for you, who shall always do exactly as you want? And do you, perhaps, mean that you are an angel yourself?" "No." "Can you, husband, imagine a single women of your tribe with whom you can live without the least dispute?" "No!" "When considering things a bit, is it then necessary to abstain from this woman? And you, wife, do you think you could find a Savunese man who always treats you so kindly and well that you will never pick a dispute with him?" And without waiting for an answer I provided them each with a small gift. Now tears trickled from their eyes. ... And then their reply was "We did wrong. We wish to acknowledge our foolishness." "If my wife wants to remain with me, I will accept her again." And the wife stated "If my husband does not disown me, then I gladly follow him." Thus the three divorce cases were concluded. All these people were only temporarily overwhelmed by the power of tradition ... Presently all three couples, being youthful Savu Christians, live in a desired state of harmony.[47]

---

[46] Ibid., 8 February 1875.

[47] Raad voor de Zending, 1102–1: 1411, M. Teffer, letter, 8 February 1875.

Bride price (*weli*, *belis*) was an inevitable part of family life in the eastern archipelago where exogenous clans tended to intermarry. And yet this feature was not present in Savu as it did not have the rule of exogamy. In other words, persons of the same clan could marry, with consequences for the economic exchange involved in marriage. For the general population in Savu *weli* was a relatively modest affair by the late 19th century. Missionaries who investigated the marriage system found that *weli* was not really a case of 'buying' a bride; rather, it was compensation for the related marriage costs to the bride's family. A man who travelled to another settlement to propose to a woman had to bring some *pinang* (areca).[48] To marry, the wife's family brought a pig and the husband's family exchanged this with a buffalo. NZG dictates did not easily stop the custom. Through his great authority in Savu, Teffer was able to halt the payment of *weli* among the Christian congregations. However, H.C. Kruyt noticed in about 1890 that some people still practised it. The fettor of Dimu set a 'bad' example by paying *weli* when he married the niece of the raja in Mesara.

Kruyt also related a story that revealed something of the practical benefits of converting. A certain Ama Lobo Kana was still a "Hindu" (by which term Kruyt meant he practised the Jingi Tiu religion). He was about to marry and the siblings of his bride-to-be demanded the payment of *weli*. Ama Lobo had no wish to do so and soon found the solution. He converted to Christianity together with his sweetheart and proceeded to marry under NZG auspices. Consequently, there was no question of paying anything to his in-laws. Kruyt mentions other persons who employed the same strategy, which must have evoked a great deal of local resentment.[49]

Thus, the NZG's activities in Savu, like any missionary project, were a mixture of successes and failures. The uppermost elite converted, the NZG established small but viable congregations and marginalised the Islamic influence. Nevertheless, expansion was slow after the early flurry of conversions and the missionaries did not easily dispense with local adat and beliefs. The NZG publications, the *Maandberigten van het Nederlandsche Zendelinggenootschap* [*Monthly Reports of the Dutch Missionary Society*] and the *Mededeelingen van wege het Nederlandsche Zendelinggenootschap* [*Messages Concerning the Dutch Missionary Society*] brought regular news to their European audience from overseas work in the field, and tended to paint an optimistic picture of progress and heroic efforts. It was vital to persuade parishioners in metropolitan regions

---

[48] H.C. Kruyt notes that the areca was replaced by a *rijksdaalder* (a Dutch silver coin) in Raijua; this was known as *pergi makan* (go eat [In]); see Raad voor de Zending, 1102–1: 1406, H.C. Kruyt, Notebook 4, c. 1890.

[49] Raad voor de Zending, 1102–1: 1406, H.C. Kruyt, Notebooks 2 and 4, c. 1890.

to promote and donate money to NZG activities.[50] A comparison between the published pieces by Donselaar, Teffer and others, and the copious body of letters they wrote in Savu, reveals that the society carefully omitted frustrations and failures from the printed version. Likewise, the publications cut or toned down the frequent verbal attacks on the colonial officials. The archival material therefore presents an unpolished and obviously more genuine image of Savu in the borderland between a premodern and colonial society, between Jingi Tiu and Christianity. And yet just how genuine can it really be? Although the missionaries provide long accounts of material culture and spiritual life, and sometimes quote the locals at length, it is hard to know how the Savunese *really* felt about the religious changes.

At length, the Nederlandsch Indische Protestantische Kerk—the general Protestant organisation in the East Indies—took over the activities of the pioneer missionaries. Letteboer, the last NZG representative, stayed until 1904, although his term ended on a bad note due to conflicts with the local teachers and with the Dutch posthouder.[51] The change of organisation is understandable because the number of Christians had actually decreased in the 1890s, partly through the colonial state favouring migration to Sumba after 1890. The 'traditional' religion was more resilient in Savu than in Rote, probably because the Savunese clans were more localised, with a ritual system that required public ceremonies by a hierarchy of priests (Fox 1977: 172–3). The missionaries, deeply frustrated by their lack of success, searched for other proto-sociological explanations. Wijngaarden compared conditions with Mojowarno in Java where the poor people were usually the first to accept the new faith. In Savu, by contrast, the rajas and their families were the first converts, and this was not the advantage it may have seemed. The general population followed to some extent, not from personal motives but to please their superiors.[52] The explanation complements the fact that the raja institution was relatively recent and not tightly embedded in the ritual system. As long as the cycle of ceremonies and rituals continued, there was little incentive to abandon Jingi Tiu beliefs even if the rajas appeared to do.

---

[50] The *Maandberigten* contains lists of donations made month by month, which indicate the amount of enthusiasm that the reports were able to evoke in the metropolitan area. For example, an anonymous donor in Leiden gave 50 guilders for the church and school in Savu in June 1875 (*Maandberigt van het Nederlandsche Zendelinggenootschap* 1875–76: 96).

[51] Raad voor de Zending, 1102–1: 1444, J.H. Letteboer, letters, 11 November 1901, 15 December 1903.

[52] Raad voor de Zending, 1102–1: 1415, J.K. Wijngaarden, letter, December 1889.

Wijngaarden also criticised colleagues, such as Teffer, who had stayed on the island for twelve years without learning Savunese or giving regular tuition. It was obvious that the little island congregation needed a steady organisational foundation rather than the ad hoc enthusiasm of a few white preachers who barely understood the local language and adat. Under the Indische Kerk, ministers residing in Kupang or in Rote supervised the congregations. The new institution established a teacher from the region called J.H. Tentoea in Seba in 1903 and he was subsequently entrusted with the task of administering the sacraments (Passar 2005: 275). When his term ended assistant ministers regularly visited the island from Rote to tend to the flock. It was only well into the 20th century that the church appointed a native Savunese, Abraham Haba Kore (d. 1932), as assistant minister (Aritonang and Steenbrink 2008: 305; Passar 2005: 124). Only then did Savunese Christianity begin to evolve into a truly indigenous affair.

Christianity comes to Raijua and Sumba

While the rajas of Seba, Dimu, Liae and Mesara were baptised during Resident Caspersz's administration (1869–72), Raijua's geographically isolated position delayed NZG's attempts to missionise. The island's lack of wood to make boats was not conducive to sea travel. Savunese people went to Raijua from time to time, but the Raijuans seldom visited other islands with the exception of the small islet of Dana.[53] The communication with Sumba, documented in the early VOC period, had apparently ceased. Ama Mehe Tari, the raja of Raijua between 1830 and 1868, had experienced at least a minimum of contact with the white man's world. As a young man he went to school in Kupang, apparently in the early 19th century, and was able to read and write. He took a copy of the Bible to Raijua on his return. The sources do not disclose the significance of the event: the book could have been an object of prestige rather than something that he actually read.

Ama Mehe's successor Ama Loni Kuji (r. 1869–1915) showed little interest in Christian matters. However, the missionaries in Savu believed they were able to discern a Raijuan curiosity in the new creed; now and then they arrived in Savu to see for themselves if it had made an impact.[54] Of the locals, Ama Loni's children were actively interested in receiving education from the missionaries. By 1876, the missionaries had converted some 90 persons including the princes.[55] The NZG placed the Ambonese F. Leituhitoe on the island as a teacher, but he was

---

[53] Raad voor de Zending, 1102–1: 1411, M. Teffer, letter, 29 October 1876.

[54] Ibid.

[55] Ibid., 3 August 1876.

not particularly successful. During three and a half years of work, he converted just 35 people. Some of the converts moved to Savu and Sumba, leaving 19 Christians in Raijua by the mid-1880s. When Leituhitoe died in 1884 he left an unpaid debt of 121 guilders, to the great displeasure of Ama Loni Kuji. The raja refused for a while to receive a new teacher and it was only when Resident W. Greve put pressure on him that he accepted a replacement.[56]

In June 1885, J.F. Niks visited Raijua in the company of Seba grandee Elias Luji Raja Pono. He asked to hold a service with the few Christians, but this was denied him. Niks was also forbidden to baptise children. His impression of the island was consequently far less positive than that of Teffer a decade earlier:

> Here one still finds the uncultivated Savunese, since communication with Savu is only possible for five months per year. The chiefs are heathen, who did not receive us … In the evening I arranged a meeting with the raja and fettor, besides the other chiefs. With Elias interpreting, I said that God loved them too and sent his son to make them happy. However I looked up bewildered when the answer came "Ju (son) Deo (God) has been here in person, some 100 generations ago. Ina Ju Deo—the mother of Ju Deo—came from the sky and gave birth here. Ju Deo was wiser than all of us, and our forefathers hanged him one and a half *paal* [miles] from here, on the hill of Ketitah, out of fear that the inhabitants of Raijua would follow him and disown the majority religion. We drowned the mother; we offer *sirih* and *pinang* to her on every trip to Savu and back, so that she may give us a safe trip and not let the great waves swallow us" … Since the raja stood up, further discussion was impossible. I only told him that the teacher would come back here in a year, which he found good. Since there is only one single person here who speaks Malay, and the most of them do not speak Savunese, I understood that [the task of preaching to the Raijuans] was impossible for this man.[57]

Niks, like Teffer, assumed that the Ju Deo myth reflected stories of Maria and the suffering of Christ, deriving from Portuguese visitors and intertwined with the ancient history of Raijua. Various narrative elements had been incorporated into a localised account—"just as with all other uncivilised peoples". The raja apparently never became a Christian.[58] Christianity does not seem to have made a significant impact in Raijua until far into the 20th century, long after the island ceased to be an autonomous domain. In 1920 there was still only one teacher on the island, which at that time had 3,474 inhabitants (Heyligers 1920: 23–4).

---

[56] Raad voor de Zending, 1102–1: 1408, J.F. Niks, letters, 4 July 1884; 15 September 1884; Travel report, 5–29 June 1885.

[57] Raad voor de Zending, 1102–1: 1408, J.F. Niks, Travel report, 5–29 June 1885.

[58] His son Paulus Lai (1915–18) was baptised though.

The contemporaneous Sumbanese religion had parallels with the Savunese Jingi Tiu and with other belief systems in this part of maritime Southeast Asia. Central to this were the *marapu*, the spirits of the dead, especially the ancestors. Rituals for the *marapu* were conducted at sacrificial stones. There was also the highest being who had created everything but who was not regularly worshipped and was not concerned with the fate of humans (Wielenga 1926: 61–2). Small but significant Savunese colonies had arisen in Sumba in the second half of the 19th century. The dissemination of Christianity in Savu meant that some colonists were Christians. Being uprooted from their highly localised clan settings, the Savunese in Sumba were much more inclined to accept Christianity than their compatriots on the home island. In fact, several immigrants had been driven out of Savu because they were Christians and declined to attend the all-important rituals (Fox 1977: 174). Among the aristocrats from Seba who stayed in Sumba were the later rajas, Lazarus Rohi Jawa and Elias Luji Raja Pono.[59] The major proclaimer of Savunese Christianity, Mattheus Teffer, realised that their spiritual needs must be satisfied from Savu. He therefore dispatched an Ambonese man to serve as headman of the Sumba congregations and in 1877 Teffer went in person to oversee matters. The colonial authorities in Kupang were not overly impressed. A controleur wrote in 1883 that the converted Savunese were "just as heathen as before", although *guru jamaat* (teachers of the congregations [In]) were active in both Melolo and Kabaniru (Wielenga 1926: 87). Teffer had no immediate plans for Sumbanese conversion. The highly insecure conditions in Sumba, especially the aggressive stance of the anti-foreign raja of Lewa, impeded such endeavours.

However, by the late 19th century missionary societies had multiplied in the East Indies. The Dutch colonies were extensive, and differences arose over theological perspectives and strategy. One of the new organisations created alongside NZG was the Nederlandsch Gereformeerde Zendingsvereeniging (Dutch Reformed Missionary Association) which disseminated Christianity in Java. Realising that Sumba was a blank or 'white spot' on the missionary map and hardly touched by Islam, the Zendingsvereeniging decided to act. The Leiden-educated Johan Jacob van Alphen arrived on the island in 1881, in the company of the Dutch controleur, with the express order to work among the Sumbanese rather than the Savunese. There was only one problem: the Sumbanese themselves and the low-level violence in their villages. Van Alphen immediately realised that his best chance to remain safe was to stay with the less volatile Savunese in Melolo.

---

[59] For a critical estimation of Ama Kore Rohi alias Lazarus Rohi Jawa, see Van der Felt's description of his visit to Sumba (1871) in Collection Louis Onvlee, Or. 635: 333, KITLV Archive, Leiden.

At the time, the Sumbanese were more in awe of the Savunese and Endenese than of the whites (Wielenga 1913: 133). Soon after his arrival Van Alphen paid a friendly visit to Teffer in Savu. Teffer opined that Sumba was large enough for two missionary societies. With colonial *grandeur*, the two men divided the island into spheres of interest—the NZG would tend to the Savunese while the native Sumbanese were for the Zendingsvereeniging (Wielenga 1926: 88–90).

However, practical concerns soon interrupted their neat plan. Given the unruly conditions across most of the island, with violence and low-scale warfare in the settlements, there was no way that Van Alphen could stay in an ethnic Sumbanese village. The missionary was destined to live in a hut close to the seashore with the Christian Savunese whose needs he was not allowed to address. It was an awkward situation for all involved. By 1883 there were some 1,000 Savunese colonists and of them 376 were baptised—a small number but not negligible in the context of the eastern archipelago.

Dutch opinion of the Savunese colonists, whether Christian or not, was not particularly positive. The reason was no doubt connected to the difficulties in governing them. In every Savunese settlement there was a village chief who received orders from the Dutch officials in Sumba. The problem was that the population did not care in the least about the decrees and that made the position of village chief unenviable. The chronicler of the Sumba mission, D.H. Wielenga, relates how the controleur forced the Melolo colony to elect a chief sometime in the late 19th century. After a long deliberation, a figure called Ama Ale Kote accepted the position. However, it soon transpired that he was low-born, did not know Malay, accumulated debts without paying them back, had an excessive fondness for strong drink, was a dullard and, as a consequence of his non-aristocratic kinship ties, commanded absolutely no respect from the Savunese (Wielenga 1926: 94).

Wielenga also describes the Savunese way of obtaining justice. Fear of *suangi*, witches, was a common feature in the eastern region. Persons who stood accused of witchcraft could find themselves in as serious a predicament as in late medieval Europe. A certain Ama Opa, who had previously plotted the murder of a *suangi*, had two persons living in his household who were both suspected of witchcraft. In order to avoid it being viewed as an internal Savunese affair, which might have consequences with the colonial authorities, he arranged with a Sumbanese chief called Umbu Tanya to dispose of the two unfortunate suspects (Wielenga 1926: 94). A colonial report from 1883 provides a convoluted story of the rather rough justice in the Savunese colonies:

> Ina Bida Wila, the Savunese Nonna [lady], who was already the subject of serious complaints a few years ago when she stayed in Mangili, has still

not improved her life. She was guilty of the following mischief. At the time when Ama Kore (the Savunese village chief) was still in Melolo, she picked a dispute with him over a child. She asserted that the family of that child were her slaves, while Ama Kore said that the slaves belonged to the Sumbanese princess Rambu Hau, who now lives with a Savunese man. I [the controleur] then announced that neither had any right to the slaves and declared them in the presence of everybody to be free people, just like all Savunese on Sumba. Not long ago a complaint reached me that Ina Bida Wila once again had appropriated the child by force while the mother and stepfather were absent. I commanded the village chief to fetch the child from Ina Bida and take it back to the mother. They would not follow my command.

The village chief does not dare to act against her since she now lives with the Sumbanese prince Umbu Talu outside of the *negeri*, and since her cousin Elias Luji Raja (a Savunese prince) is staying in Melolo during the dispute. As well as that, she has appropriated two women with children from Petawang since these women were formerly her slaves. One of these women escaped, hid for five days, and then turned herself in to the village chief. But Elias came and demanded her, and again turned her over to Ina Bida. During my stay in Melolo, Ama Lobo (stepfather of the stolen child) came and complained that Ina Bida fined him 25 guilders, since his wife had said that the posthouder had fined Ina Bida 25 guilders. Since he had no cash he gave two pigs and a *rijksdaalder* [a Dutch silver coin]. They were ordered to give it back but would not do it. I let an *oppasser* [assistant] fetch the child and summon Ina Bida. She did not turn up but did give back the child (Wielenga 1926: 92–3).

While the story testifies to the oppressive methods of the high-born against people with a slave background, decades after the official abolition of slavery in the East Indies, it also gives an interesting case of female agency: the village chief seems to have been powerless against the strong-willed well-connected woman. When Teffer returned to Sumba in 1883 to tend to his Savunese flock, Van Alphen frankly shared his perception of their shortcomings. The initially cordial relationship between the two whites became tense. In contrast with his colleague, Teffer represented a gradualist outlook on conversion: the indoctrination of Christianity took its time and there was no need to rush the process. Teffer asked Van Alphen not to concern himself with Savunese matters, which were his responsibility, but rather to focus on the Sumbanese. He added that Van Alphen's inflexible methods and his strict adherence to Christian protocol explained his lack of success with the native population of Sumba (Wielenga 1926: 97–8).

In his increasing desperation to achieve results, Van Alphen even entertained the idea of buying slave children and raising them as missionary janissaries of sorts.[60] However, his superiors put an immediate stop to the plan; it would give the Sumbanese the idea that their ministry sanctioned the slave trade. Within a short time Van Alphen lost his wife and newborn child, leaving Sumba later the same year, disappointed and grief-stricken. Although he later returned, the mission in the 1880s suffered from a lack of continuity as few missionaries set foot on the disorderly island. Nevertheless, the Ambonese teachers served the daily needs of the Savunese congregations. They were not always models of conduct in the eyes of their European superiors—one was expelled for superstitious and violent behaviour—but they made sure that the Christians at least did not discard their nominal belief. It was only after 1890 that more missionaries arrived and their sphere of activity expanded. They established schools in Waingapu, Kabaniru and Melolo with modest success but not without some setbacks. Their strategy was to use the Savunese colonies as bridges to the Sumbanese audience. Along with Malay, the Savunese usually knew one of the Sumbanese languages; thus the missionaries were able to communicate with Sumbanese areas close to the colonies (Wielenga 1926: 99–134). It goes without saying that it was a tardy process and the Sumbanese were more interested in the whites' rudimentary medical knowledge than the Gospel. It was only after 1904, when the colonial state began to interfere on the island, that the missionaries were sent inland and a more systematic method of conversion began. This process, however interesting, is beyond the scope of this book.

Jingi Tiu versus Christianity—a reflection

The rich body of missionary texts provides a lively view of the first stages of the Protestant religion in the 19th century. However, they do not seem to comprehend the fundamental concepts of the 'pagan' religion, Jingi Tiu. For instance, the missionaries missed the essential gendered pairings that promise peace and cosmic harmony, and the necessary complementarity between sweet and bitter, hot and cold and so on. In rituals, as well as in everyday life, binary associations based on male and female gender were and still are the constant points of reference.

In spite of the vivid assurances of the NZG figures, it is speculation as to whether Christianity provided better answers than Jingi Tiu about existential aspects of human life at its most vulnerable moments: droughts, famines, cyclones, floods, epidemics and death by accidents. Christian ministers rendered

---

[60] The Janissaries were for centuries the elite troops in the Ottoman Empire. Their members were initially recruited from among young Christians in the Balkan who then converted to Islam once accepted into the army.

the *Mone Ama* councils obsolete, bypassing the long chain of ancestors, and instead connected converts directly to God. However, the genealogies formed the backbone of socio-political life in Savu. Indeed, the worship of God eliminated sacrificing animals to ancestors, but these sacrifices were the only occasions where people consumed meat in communal meals. Such ceremonies called *kewèhu* (knots) tied the community together. An essential task of *Mone Ama* priests was to regulate agricultural life through prescriptions and prohibitions in ways that a modern interpretation may consider based on sound ecological concerns. The Christian ministers certainly had to incorporate such aspects, but they did not refer to these matters when writing to their distant superiors.

Although the Jingi Tiu religion has existed for many centuries, the councils of priests evolved over time and the structure of ritual cycles underwent changes. At least that was the case in Seba, Menia and Liae, as previously shown. It is also important to trace the role of *Mone Ama* based on recent observations while listing a few cases, as research in the field does not indicate that current practices are recent innovations.

The *Mone Ama* priests are in charge of ritual calendars based on the lunar cycle and the position of the constellations Antares and the Pleiades. The calendar decides when to start planting, harvesting and performing the thanksgiving ceremonies (*hole*).[61] Deo Rai and more generally the *Mone Ama* safeguard and apply numerous rules whose ecological character is not in doubt. The priests decide at which time of the year animals have to be attached to poles, so they do not disturb plant growth, and when they are allowed to roam freely. People are not allowed to cut tree branches starting in the first month of the rainy season (Ko'oma), the month devoted to clearing the fields and planting. Cutting branches and leaves for roofing is allowed in the first month of the dry season (Wèru a'a) which is the prescribed month for repairing or rebuilding houses. However, people are permitted to feed cattle with freshly cut branches during the entire dry season. In fact people planted *lamtoro* trees especially for fodder after Indonesian independence and these are exempt from the religious/ecological rules.[62]

It is forbidden to cut down trees or even take branches for making *sopi* (or arak, sometimes known as the region's 'rum') obtained from distilling lontar syrup. To boil the lontar sap and to make *sopi* the rules permit people to use the

---

[61] See the knots tables in Appendix II. Chapter 9 discusses when the *hole* ceremony coincided with Good Friday, which caused conflict and a rebellion.

[62] The introduced tree, a legume called *Leucaena leucocephala*, grows well in the tropics. It is high-protein food for cattle, though can be toxic to non-ruminants, and the pods are used in some Javanese dishes.

dead stalks and fan leaves of the lontar tree. It is also forbidden to tap the lontar tree during the rainy season. However, the rule is not related to ecology—it is neither to protect the tree nor to allow its regeneration, because the more the tree is tapped the more sap it produces. In the rainy season the trunk might be slippery and cause accidents for the climbers which are mainly fatal. Besides wet season safety, the sap reduces in quality when mixed with rain water. Strictly speaking, the religion entirely forbids the consumption of *sopi*, but here the priests are more lenient; a number of them indulge in drinking *sopi*. The Jingi Tiu priests generally sanction the balance between humans and nature, and apply fines in the payment of a large animal, such as a cow, buffalo or horse, for those not respecting the rules.

The most evidently ecological regulations, gaining the approval of today's ecologists, concern the seashores and their immediate surroundings. The estuaries of small rivers form lagoons as sandbars block the ever-decreasing flow of fresh water into the sea during the dry season and the remaining water pools cannot be disturbed. For example, when the water volume in the Seba river estuary at Napae starts to decrease, priests hold a ritual there and hang the bladder of a sacrificial animal on a pole. It informs the population that the prohibition on fishing has started, in order to allow small fish to grow until the next rainy season when a high river level breaks through the sand bank, opening up the estuary to the sea once again. It is forbidden to dig holes on the beaches, to take sand away, to cut down any trees (for instance mangrove) or clear any creeper plants covering the sandy beaches, or to remove stones. The same rules apply to the river beds. However, restrictions on the shores are lifted for seaweed towards the end of the dry or 'hungry' season. A similar rule applies for lime which is an essential element of betel chew and making indigo dye. For ten days towards the end of the dry season, at a time when the sea recedes more than during the other months, people can take living coral. Each family can only take coral once, so the rule restricts the amount of damage the coral sustains. The period is delimited by two rituals; the second is called *pepèhi wowadu*, the throwing of stones, referred to in previous chapters. It is forbidden to take specific animals from the sea at certain times of the dry season. In Raijua, the harpooning of manatees (sea cows) is only allowed on one night each year and, during certain rituals, people cannot catch fish on the south-west coast. The introduction of seaweed farming necessitated negotiations with the *Mone Ama* who performed several rituals to incorporate the new situation; they also gave seaweed a local name—*wawi dahi* (sea pig)—because like pigs seaweed grows fast. They then permitted farmers to position poles in the sea from which to fix their cords and to build huts to rest in between the tides. However, the priests forbade seaweed farming during the rainy season, a sensible precaution to prevent people drowning or being swept away in the strong winds and big seas.

The traditional religion also has rules about marriage and adultery. Western visitors noted the custom of monogamy in Savu which was not a Christian import. Indeed, an important element of Jingi Tiu is the taboo on adultery; early ancestor Dida Miha committed the offence by beginning another family in Raijua and a narrative anchors it in collective memory (chapter 1). The priest Rue Iki has the task of punishing adulterers and re-establishing harmony. And yet to Christian ministers, Savu people had the 'shocking' tradition of sexual freedom before marriage. A small hut was built next to the parents' house for a young woman if she wished to have sexual relations before marriage until this was prohibited in 1974. If she became pregnant, the marriage was only celebrated after the birth of the child if this was her wish and her family agreed. A woman who survived the birth of her first child gained significance as she proved herself fertile and gave birth without complications—death in childbirth was far from uncommon. Besides, a child was always a future working hand and enriched the clan of his or her maternal grandfather. Such considerations do not seem to have registered in the minds of the missionaries, as they crusaded to prohibit sexual relationships for females before marriage. However, after the *kenoto* ceremony with the gift of bridewealth, adultery by either spouse was severely punished.[63] In addition, divorce was a relatively easy procedure.

Teffer and Kruyt mention marriage rules in Savu and Raijua, although they do not seem to be aware of the female lineage role. The ideal Savunese marriage is inside the same female lineage, *wini*, and is referred to as *pekale ana ina* (looking for the mother's daughter); there is no bride price, just a *kenoto* ceremony. This requires the gift of a bag especially woven for the occasion (*kenoto*) filled with ingredients for betel chew (Duggan 2017: 3–16). Larger gifts would not make sense as 'the group would be giving a gift to itself'. The members of both families (*peloko nga'a*) share a meal. As the place of residence is patrilocal, the bride leaves her parents' house with a basket of fluffed cotton with which she is expected to weave her husband's first hip-cloth. Furthermore, she also takes a small basket with seeds to plant and a mature sow, if possible pregnant, as a sign of fertility and reproduction. After her marriage, her brother becomes responsible for her and her children's food, while she has to take care of his physical and mental health throughout his life. Such sister-brother ties are representative of societies with strong maternal control, and there are several cases of privileged relationships between a maternal uncle and his nephews and nieces (*makemone-nakebèni*) in previous chapters. However, in Savu and Raijua the residence is patrilocal.

---

[63] For a case of adultery and cleansing the offence in Raijua, see Kagiya (2010: 37–43).

For marriages between *hubi*, as well as the gift of a *kenoto* bag, the rule of bride price (*weli*) applies: this can vary according to the *wini*, and the wealth and status of the bride's family. A remarkable difference between Savu and other islands in the region is the fact that there are no gifts, not even textiles from the bride's family to that of the bridegroom. The bride does not enter her husband's clan; she remains a member of her father's clan. In the case of divorce, the wife has to return to her parents' house before she can become engaged to marry again, otherwise this is considered adultery (Duggan 2011b: 105–6).

Funerals are entirely family matters and the *Mone Ama* priests are not directly involved. It is the women of the deceased's female lineage who play an essential role in death rites. They provide the most essential *wai* cloth—to allow the deceased to come back to life in an unspecified future—as well as textiles with the pattern of their maternal line because the deceased will reunite with his/her maternal-line ancestors; hence of the same *wini*. While men sit outside, women are inside the house and mediate between the realms of the living and the dead through their laments and chants. They call on their ancestors to come down to the place and take their deceased relative. Husband and wife will stay together in the after-world only if they are from the same *wini*; therefore the basic marriage rule for a man, 'looking for the mother's daughter'. At a Christian funeral, a minister officiates—a cross put in the coffin replaces the *wai* cloth, the maternal line becomes irrelevant and women no longer have a role to play. This is a fundamental change introduced by Christianity.

Jingi Tiu is distinctly different from Christianity regarding the burial traditions. Savunese know two categories of deaths; natural (sweet) and unnatural, violent (bitter). In the first case, the deceased husband is buried in a foetal position under the male part of the house; the wife is buried under the female part of her father's or brother's house. However, if a ceremony called *woba ngaka* (to batter the dog to death)[64] is performed when a woman can no longer bear children, both husband and wife are buried underneath their own house—the husband under the male part, the wife under the 'stern' or female part. In the case of a violent death, caused by murder or accident, the deceased cannot be buried in a foetal position but must lie straight and be interred outside, at the head of the house. One might wonder about the stratagems missionaries had to employ for convincing the families of new converts who had a natural

---

[64] If a husband and wife so wish, a four-year cycle of rituals takes place in mid-life: it starts with a symbolically male sacrifice—a dog is clubbed to death, *woba ngaka*, which gives its name to the entire cycle. The more significant aspect of the cycle is that the wife is bonded more closely to her husband's clan. See Duggan (2011b: 103–22).

death to be buried outside the house and, moreover, lying straight. Rarely do the missionaries' letters mention these facts.

The story of Savunese Christianity is largely based on a source material which is both close to and distant from the Savunese people and, therefore, presents particular complications. The voluminous letters of the missionaries provide an intimate and detailed picture of the Savunese world, especially when the authors had some knowledge of the local language. For example, they recorded traditions of distant ancestors which are in part similar to current tradition, testifying to the faithful transmission of oral data.[65] The missionary sources bring substance to people who would otherwise have been little more than a list of names, if that. On the other hand, a careful comparison between their descriptions of life and rituals, and later anthropological recordings, time and again reveals probable misinterpretations and wishful thinking. Whatever impact the Christian precepts may have made on local society, the Western men of God failed to realise the way the new faith was localised, or the resilience and meaningfulness of the old creed. In that sense the letters are both windows to the past and mirrors on colonial culture.

---

[65] One may refer, for example, to the notebooks of J.K. Wijngaarden (c. 1890). His observations, however scattered and unsystematic, accurately support the recently recorded oral traditions of Ie Miha, Ngara Rai, Ga Lena-Ina Tenga, etc. (Raad voor de Zending, 1102–1: 1416, J.K. Wijngaarden, notebooks).

Chapter 9 | The Late Colonial Period

During the 19th century Savu and its colonies in Sumba had largely attended to their own affairs. After 1879, Savu and Rote were formally lumped together in an administrative unit under a *civiel gezaghebber* (civil administrator), but this meant very little in practice. There was never more than a few Europeans or Eurasians staying on the island. All this was in line with the Dutch *onthoudingspolitiek* (policy of non-interference) that Batavia preferred to maintain in its far-flung island realms.

Colonialism, however, changed towards the late 19th century. The international scramble to claim land in Africa and Asia fuelled Dutch concerns to secure their sphere of interest. The Aceh War from 1873 to 1903 was related to this concern, as were a number of other operations such as the Lombok expeditions in 1894 (Van den Doel 2011: 108–12, 120–34). Around the turn of the 20th century, it became fashionable to regard the non-interference line as harmful, both to Dutch interests and to the majority populations. The so-called ethical policy emerged in the 1890s and strove to 'improve' the lot of the 'natives' by ridding their societies of supposedly barbaric or conservative features, and achieve social and economic development (Van den Doel 2011: 150–1). However, in order to make an omelette it was necessary to crack the eggs and the ethical concerns (intertwined with brute power politics) resulted in a lot of bloodshed. In particular, an endless series of campaigns in the early years of the 20th century forced a more directly implemented version of colonial rule on the outer islands of the archipelago.

The operations in the Timor Residency were comparatively small. Resolute naval action in Solor in 1888 reduced the coastal villages of Lamahala, Lamakera and Menanga to ashes to inaugurate closer Dutch control on the islands north of Timor (Taniputera 2013: 1351). Several years later, the colonial troops undertook a mopping-up operation on the West Timorese mainland, at the same time as the Portuguese fought bloody wars in East Timor. The Dutch defeated and captured the formerly prestigious Sonba'i lord in 1905–06, and drawn-out campaigning took place in Flores and Sumba (Taniputera 2013: 1365; Parimartha 2002: 361; Hägerdal 2017). Most of the territories in the residency did not actively resist the colonial encroachment though. However, both Savu and its sister island Rote underwent a number of changes of some consequence.

After they had a secure military grip on the territories within the Timor Residency around 1905–10, the Dutch authorities moved to make governance more effective. They abolished a number of traditional domains and introduced larger administrative units, the *zelfbesturende landschappen* (self-ruling territories). The micro-states the Dutch colonial administration recognised in the 19th century (like many raja states of British India) were often no more than villages with a hinterland, populated by a few thousand, or even fewer, people. The application of colonial governance needed larger areas, ruled by *zelfbestuurders* (self-rulers) with a measure of education or familiarity with western administrative ideas.[1] Thus, the 19 domains in Rote began to merge in 1911 and in 1928 the entire island became a *zelfbesturend landschap* (self-ruling territory) under a member of a fettor family (Taniputera 2013: 1315). Similarly, the five domains which formed a *cordon sanitaire* around Kupang and were attached to Dutch over-lordship merged into a single area called Kupang in 1917. The same happened on the islands of Solor and Alor, in Flores and in the Timor interior.[2]

This chapter examines how the Dutch applied the new colonial organisation in Savu and partly changed the island but not without some resistance. The discussion follows the vicissitudes of the island when in 1942 new Asian overlords briefly replaced the old colonial masters and finally it investigates how the tempests of the Indonesian Revolution affected a minor insular society. In sum, the chapter considers the development over half a century, from near-independence under indigenous rulers to independence under a central government in faraway Jakarta and, in the intermediate period, the level of external interference and enforcement.

Seba takes the lead

In the process of tightening colonial control, Seba had a key role as a relatively reliable ally of the Dutch and the centre of Savunese Christianity. The previous chapters trace Seba's history in the 19th century in some detail. After the rule of activist Ama Doko Kaho (1868–82), his brothers Lazarus Rohi Jawa (1882–90) and Alexander Rihi Jawa (1890–1901) held power in the

---

[1] Bongenaar (2004) considers the evolution of the *zelfbesturende landschappen* in great detail.

[2] The details of these mergers appear in the listings in Van Dijk (1925).

micro-state.[3] Lazarus evoked some negative comments before his elevation to the raja dignity when he ruled the Savunese in Sumba. He had his own way of managing the horse trade and of speaking to European officials, which did not please the colonial authorities. The prince irreverently exclaimed "*Saya tahu, saya tahu!*" (I know, I know!) when asked about something.[4] There is a description of Lazarus by Ph. Bieger from 1888. He was short, bareheaded and barefooted, clad in a *baju* (upper-body clothing [In]) and a sarung. He had short curly hair and his countenance appeared Papuan as he was not pure Savunese. His lips were red with blackish rims—from his preference for *sirih pinang*. He chewed a lot of tobacco and a few tobacco strands were visible between his lips.[5] As a raja he displayed a lukewarm interest in Christianity, did not attend church services for lengthy periods and stayed at home during the Seba church council meetings. This predictably enraged the missionary Niks who opined that the saying "Who wants to be rich falls into many temptations" fitted the raja's character as someone who was unwilling to listen to serious admonitions.[6] His colleague Wijngaarden added that Lazarus was a "true Oriental ruler" who expropriated paddy fields, horses or whatever pleased him against insufficient payment.[7] Colonial officials found the political conditions in Savu favourable during his time but quoted rumours that Lazarus demanded heavy corvée service from his subjects, even to the extent that they could not meet their own daily necessities. He also physically mistreated a subject. However, none of this was sufficient for the Resident to act, because his only concerns were with dispositions contrary to Kupang's interests. Lazarus was a difficult partner in business and repelled the horse traders who otherwise frequented the island. This led to less money circulating in Savu with further economic consequences. The raja also tried to prevent people from migrating to Sumba as it weakened his own power base. Resident De Villeneuve, who appeared to think rajas should be treated like naughty schoolboys, barked at Lazarus in a private meeting and thought his tirade had a favourable effect.[8]

---

[3] After Ama Doko Kaho's death, his foremost temukung and right hand Ama Wengi (Wenyi?) was temporarily made ruler of Seba, assisted by Ama Kore Rohi alias Lazarus (*Mailrapport* 1882: 585). This seems to be the same temukung who Teffer suspected had murdered Ama Doko Kaho (see fn 67 in this chapter). Lazarus acceded to the dignity the same year.

[4] Relation of a trip to Sumba by Van der Felt (1871) in Collection Louis Onvlee, Or. 635: 333, KITLV Archive, Leiden.

[5] Raad voor de Zending, 1102–1: 879, Ph. Bieger, letter, 7 August 1888.

[6] Raad voor de Zending, 1102–1: 1408, J.F. Niks, letter, 15 July 1887.

[7] Raad voor de Zending, 1102–1: 1415, J.K. Wijngaarden, letter, 3 February 1891.

[8] ANRI Timor: 93, General report, 1888.

The missionary Wijngaarden gives a detailed account of Lazarus's untimely end, an event hastened by his own lifestyle. Although he had suffered from pain in the breast for some time, he would not take European medicine, a small amount of which the missionaries administered to their congregations. One day when he was bathing in the river he started to drink genever with tuak (palm wine) and succumbed to a severe fever. He went to bathe again and another fever attack rendered him unconscious. Twenty-four hours later, on 12 February 1890, Lazarus was dead.

The raja's demise triggered a grand amount of wailing where people fell on the corpse in sorrow and despair. A few cannon shots announced the death of Lazarus and errands were dispatched to the other rajas. In the late colonial period, and probably earlier, a ruler could not be buried until the other rajas and their families were present—even if the corpse had begun to decay. Sensitive to the growing odour, Wijngaarden commented that the Savunese obviously had an under-developed sense of smell, as they did not share his discomfort![9] The burial took place three days later and was a mixture of Christian and pre-Christian tradition. The *raja muda*s (princes) carried the coffin from the palace as the cannon fired. Wijngaarden spoke about the ruler in the church, upon which the singing mourners brought the coffin to the churchyard. Three hundred buffalos, pigs and horses were slaughtered and the meat was shared out to the population. Every head of a household received 12,5 pounds of meat and Wijngaarden himself received an entire pig. The generosity accorded to the population is based on tradition. At the funeral of an important person, the blood relationship is calculated as starting nine generations prior to the deceased whose descendants are all considered 'family'; thus, they are entitled to a share of meat. The ancestor Lomi Riwu of the early 17th century represents the ninth generation prior to Lazarus Rohi Jawa. This meant hundreds of families scattered over the island are here described as 'the population' by Wijngaarden.[10]

---

[9] Wijngaarden's remark is, of course, ethnocentric—bearing in mind that sensitivity to smell is cultural. Even today, traditional practice in Nusa Tenggara Timur (NTT West Timor) can delay the burial of the corpse for weeks; relatives of the deceased tolerate the smell as it is culturally determined.

[10] Raad voor de Zending, 1102-1: 1415, J.K. Wijngaarden, letter, undated (1890).

Photo 21. Mrs. Wijngaarden's grave (1868–90); Raeloro (2011)

Photo 22. The grave of Ama Nia Jawa; Rae Jo (2011)

Photo 23. Alexander Rihi Jawa's grave; Raeloro (2011)

While contemporary Dutch documents regarding Raja Lazarus Rohi Jawa are available, such is not the case for his wife. Moi Bèngu survived her husband by 30 years and she is mentioned in local accounts. A particular Savunese tradition ensures that the Nadowu clan of Dimu remembers Moi Bèngu, her mother Nia Nguru and their female descendants. While land is usually passed from father to son, a father or a brother may give land to the daughter or sister which is then inherited exclusively down the female line. This is known as *rai lere* (the land that follows one another—from mother to daughter). Should the female line become extinct, the land has to return to the male lineage that made the initial gift. It is reason enough for male clans to remember the genealogies of their female members.

The Nadowu's *rai lere* started at the time of Wèti Nguru, a descendant of the renowned troublemaker and cultural hero Ama Bala Nguru (discussed in chapter 6). Wèti Nguru made a gift of land to his sister, Nia Nguru, as she married Fettor Bèngu Dimu of Menia.[11] Their daughter Moi Bèngu was born

---

[11] Figures 50 and 56. Rehabeam Bèngu's genealogical book, generously loaned to G. Duggan in 2002, lists the genealogy as follows: Nia Nguru—Moi Bèngu—Nia Rohi—Tali Nia. Nia Nguru, born in 1815, married at 20 to Ama Gaja Tagi, not yet the raja of Menia. A daughter, Danga Tagi, was born. However, the marriage did not last more than five years, and both Nia Nguru and Ama Gaja Tagi remarried. The marriage occurred before the land was given to Nia Nguru, so Danga Tagi is excluded from the inheritance.

in 1842 and married Bèngu Raja Pono of Seba in the mid-1860s. Out of this union came a daughter, Medo Bèngu, who died aged one. Her husband passed away two years after his daughter in 1871 at the venerable age of 75. In the same year Moi Bèngu, then 30 years old, remarried, taking as her husband the abovementioned Lazarus Rohi Jawa who was not yet the raja of Seba. A daughter, Nia, and three sons, Kore, Wele and Jakob, were born from this marriage. Nia Nguru passed away in 1896, at the respectable age of 81, and her land went to her daughter Moi Bèngu. She was by then in her mid-40s and a widow, as Lazarus had died in 1890. By inheriting her mother's land after her husband's death, she was able to keep it—a fortunate chronology given his propensity for claiming other people's property—and she did not remarry. The land is said to be of considerable size; a document owned by the source Rehabeam Bèngu mentions a thousand palm trees of various kinds. The raja's widow Moi Bèngu passed away in 1920, leaving the land to her daughter Nia Rohi (born in 1872), who kept it until her death in 1946. At this stage the inheritance becomes more complicated. Indonesia was struggling for its independence bringing a wind of change to Savu, which questioned ancient traditions, especially female rights to landownership. The next chapter follows how the Nadowu clan retrieved its land in the last year of the 20th century.

The *rai lere* practice, which the colonial documents did not grace with a single word, reveals the importance given to the female line in Savunese society. There are no other similar known cases of female landownership in the islands surrounding the Savu Sea, and it might be a unique trait of the Savu and Raijuan cultures. Moreover, oral accounts mention how some people secretly devised documents at the beginning of the 20th century, at the time of Fettor Pawe Rake. The documents had official seals and transferred plots of land cultivated by a female line to the male line, deliberately bringing the *rai lere* tradition to an end. These cases surfaced only decades after the deaths of the original female owners.[12] Two factors were certainly at work here—Dutch colonial rule and Christianity—both based on patriarchal social organisation.

Lazarus's successor Alexander is relatively well regarded in the missionary writings and in local tradition.[13] The missionary Letteboer described him as a short fat man with large rolling eyes and a friendly helpful disposition,

---

[12] Interview with Beha Lado (11.12.2005).

[13] Compare, however, S.J. Huising's comments after he performed a tour of inspection in 1895 and did not find Raja Alexander compliant enough. The NZG inspector and Alexander had an argument about the size of the classes in Seba's school where the children, according to Huising, sat like packed herrings (Raad voor de Zending, 1102–1: S.J. Huising, report, 20 May 1895).

Figure 56: The Nia Nguru *rai lere* case

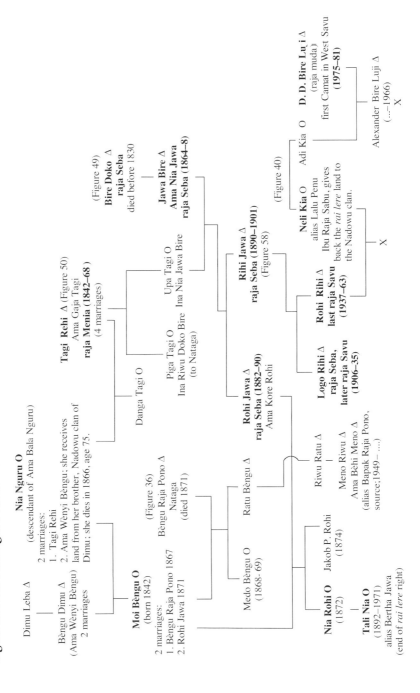

though after the raja's death in 1901 the missionary revealed he could neither praise nor denounce him.[14] Perhaps the ambiguous reaction stemmed from Letteboer's frustration with the raja's lack of control over the princes who did as they pleased. This was particularly the case with the expected heir, his nephew Jonathan Doko, who was the richest of the princes and therefore gained great influence. Jonathan Doko was inclined towards Catholicism and had plans to bring a pastor from Sumba, to the great irritation of the Protestant Letteboer—there was little love lost between missionaries of the two Christian denominations. In 1899, Jonathan committed manslaughter under horrible circumstances. He asked a village man called Liwe Heo to work in his rice fields. When the work was finished, Liwe Heo asked to return home but was instead informed that he would be turned into a slave. The man tried to escape. Jonathan caught him and tied him up: he received 150 blows from a cane, he was burnt with hot glowing tongs and he was then hung upside down over a smoking fire. Two days later Liwe Heo passed away. The Dutch Resident of Kupang was slow to deal with the crime as Raja Alexander was in Sumba at that moment. Shortly after, in the same year, Jonathan mistreated another man and held him captive. His sister sneaked in at night and cut the ropes that bound him. The man then crept to Jonathan's house and, on finding the crown prince asleep outside the door post, stabbed him with a knife. The knife's edge hit a rib bone and did not hurt him fatally. The postholder took the man into custody and there is no information on his ensuing circumstances.[15]

Several activities in the days of Rajas Lazarus and Alexander heralded Seba's political fortunes. The reign of Lazarus Rohi Jawa saw the construction of a new raja palace, replacing the old wooden structure built for Ama Dima Talo. As the story goes, Lazarus once visited Batavia and had the opportunity to admire the governor-general's residence (nowadays the presidential palace in Jakarta). With reference to the services he had provided for the colonial state, he asked the Dutch authorities if he could have a similar palace in Seba. The Dutch gave permission and hired an Ambonese builder along with workers from Liae. They were dissatisfied with their employer who did not pay them properly.[16] The Batavia residence was the template for the shape of the columns while the architectural layout was similar to that of the palace in Termanu. Instead of ordinary cement,

---

[14] Raad voor de Zending, 1102–1: 1444, J.H. Letteboer, letter, 13 June 1896; letter, October 1901.

[15] Raad voor de Zending, 1102–1: 1444, J.H. Letteboer, report, 29 December 1899.

[16] The raja of Seba had confiscated their land, Maluna (Kolo Maka), in spite of a written document that promised to return it, presumably after they had finished work on the palace.

they used *air tali putri*.[17] This is a sap-like substance from a parasitic vine that was boiled with buffalo skin, and mixed with sand and limestone to make excellent cement.[18] The result, the Teni Hawu Palace—"truly a palace built of stone with a zinc roof"—is standing to this day.[19] Although the parallels between the modest residence and the Jakarta palace might demand a stretch of imagination, the emulation of Western symbols of power is typical during this period. Local rulers from all over the archipelago strove to manifest their authority by building their residences in more durable materials on a grander scale, as demonstrated by the existing palaces in Medan, Siak and Ternate.

Local tradition states that the island's principal harbour changed location during Raja Alexander Rihi Jawa's rule. Previously situated in Banyo, Dimu domain, Seba became the site of the primary harbour.[20] This is not confirmed by other sources, which indicate that Dimu was a relative backwater without boats of its own by the late colonial period, but it implies that Seba had definitely taken the preeminent position on the island. As other family members had done before him, Alexander tried to arrange a Western upbringing for one of his children. When the missionary Niks visited him in 1893, he asked Niks to accept his small boy and to raise him in his own house. Niks agreed and promised to do this for free, although he had his own children to take care of. When Niks stayed with the raja, he noted with pleasure how his Rotenese consort, the Termanu princess Anna Amalo,[21] enjoined the people present at the meals to pray before eating.[22] His colleague Letteboer was equally enthusiastic about the queen. On one occasion in 1896 when the missionary needed to transport some planks, nobody in the Christian community assisted. The queen then came with a number of women and retainers, and began to remove the planks. When he heard about it, Letteboer was so moved that he rode to the Seba palace and asked her about

---

[17] *Tali putri* (lit. princess rope) is the Indonesian name for dodder (genus *Cuscuta*), a vine parasitic on many different plants in the tropical and temperate regions.

[18] Interview with Ama Bèhi, Seba (30.06.2012).

[19] The missionary Letteboer's words; see Raad voor de Zending, 1102–1: 1444, J.H. Letteboer, letter, 7 August 1896 (?).

[20] Interview with Ama Bèhi, Seba (30.06.2012).

[21] However, the genealogies say she is Johanna Amalo, undoubtably the same person.

[22] Niks says that he received a portrait of the raja family as a gift. Unfortunately, this photograph cannot be found in any collection, so it probably remained in the area after he returned to the Netherlands (or might be lost).

her altruism. She replied that she could no longer endure the lack of cooperation from the Christians.[23]

The presence of a Termanu princess in the Seba raja's house was no coincidence. A persistent feature of the Jawa family was their ability to network. There were several dimensions to this. One was their efforts to ally with and emulate the white colonials, which included the marriage to a Eurasian burgher's daughter. On another level they entertained relations with elite groups on the neighbouring islands, as seen by matrimonial ties with various Sumbanese and Rotenese princely families, and the influence of their Biredoko cousins in Termanu affairs (cf. Heyligers 1920: 62). After Raja Lazarus's death, his brother-in-law Elias Luji Raja Pono, a favourite of the missionaries, was sent to Maujawa (probably meaning Melolo) in Sumba in order to lead the Savunese community as a 'subraja'. Raja Alexander, the next Sebanese leader, died from beriberi in July 1901 while he underwent medical treatment in Kupang. He was no more than about 35 years old and his three sons were too young to be considered for the raja position. After a long deliberation, the grandees and chiefs decided to reject the raja's unpopular nephew, Jonathan Doko, who they later exiled from the island for his violent acts.

Instead, Elias Luji Raja Pono was offered the dignity. He accepted after some hesitation, encouraged by his missionary ally Letteboer. How Elias could become a raja at all is somewhat unclear. Letteboer alleges that Alexander's forefathers (Jara Wadu and his offspring) had violently usurped the throne while the Pono branch (Melo Wadu and his offspring) was the 'right' one. The Ponos cursed the ruling branch, saying that every raja would die before their tenth year of rule. Although this was not entirely fulfilled, the rajas after the mid-19th century did tend to have short reigns.[24] However, it is also possible that the appointment of Elias was not because he came from a co-lateral branch (Pono Melo Wadu), but mainly because he married Ama Nia Jawa's daughter Maria. In many other regional societies a daughter might succeed her father, but this was not the case in Savu under Dutch rule and so Elias, as Maria's husband, acceded to the dignity. Elias's Christian connections had their advantages. Apart from his Western-educated son Soleman, he had a daughter who married a Dutchman called

---

[23] Raad voor de Zending, 1102–1: 1444, J.H. Letteboer, letter, 7 August 1896 (?). In spite of the couple's Christian profile, there were also pre-Christian aspects to their marriage. When they got married in 1885 Alexander had to agree to pay 4,000 guilders worth of cattle to Anna's Rotenese family as bridewealth. See Raad voor de Zending, 1102–1: 1444, J.H. Letteboer, letter, 14 November 1897.

[24] Raad voor de Zending, 1102–1: 1444, J.H. Letteboer, letter, October 1901.

Gerard Lans.[25] His Christian credentials might have been more pragmatic than the missionaries preferred to think, for he married another daughter to a man from the Muslim island of Butung off Sulawesi. There was an economic aspect to it: on that occasion he received the Butungese perahu *Beni Butu* (Butungese Lady) as part of the bride price.[26]

Unification and resistance

After the death of Elias in November 1906, Soleman[27] had no claim to rule worth staking and Alexander's sons were deemed old enough to exercise power.[28] The eldest, Semuel Thomas Jawa (alias Logo Rihi), was born in 1885. His younger brothers were Welem Jawa and Paulus Charles Jawa (alias Rohi Rihi). Semuel Thomas became raja of Seba and continued his family's policy of bonding with Rotenese royalty, marrying Angelique Manubulu from the Korbaffo domain in eastern Rote. His accession and early years coincided with the vigorous Dutch expansion of power in the regency, and the consequences were soon obvious. The Dutch constructed a colonial administrative centre known as the Skaber around this time in Menia, thus in the Seba domain.[29] Reminiscences from those who remember indicate that the Skaber included administrative buildings, a gaol and houses for the teachers. Of significance was that it had a well that never ran dry.[30]

---

[25] Their son Karel Lans was later killed by the Japanese in Kupang during World War II. Their daughter Wempi (Bertha) Lans went to live in the Netherlands where she died in 1991. Another female descendant of the Seba raja family, Cornelia Raja, was reportedly abducted by a *bestuursambtenaar* (government official) called Johannes Jacob Sick; her descendant still lives in the Netherlands (Nicholas Posthumus, personal communication; 2014).

[26] Interview with Ama Bèhi, Seba (30.06.2012).

[27] According to current oral tradition Elias went back to Sumba and left the kingship to Semuel Thomas Jawa, but Dutch documents indicate that he died in 1906 when there was a change of raja. Soleman stayed in Savu in the vicinity of the raja palace and lived on his inheritance. He married Rika Piga of *udu* Nataga and passed away in the 1930s. Interview with Marthen Heke Medo (27.11.2014).

[28] The well-known Indologist Rouffaer visited Savu in 1910 and met the Dutch-speaking "raja muda of Seba, cousin of the raja of Seba" (Rouffaer, 'Kleine Timor-Eilanden' [Small Timor Island], H 673, KITLV Archive). This may have been Soleman, whose mother Maria was the aunt of the current Raja Semuel Thomas Jawa.

[29] The Skaber was constructed right next to the Kekoro Raepudi clan's village at Kolorato on the slope of Kekoro hill; this clan had provided the line of Menia rajas, but by then this land had had become Seba's territory.

[30] Interview with Petrus Bara Pa (09.05.2014).

Figure 57: The last rulers of Savu

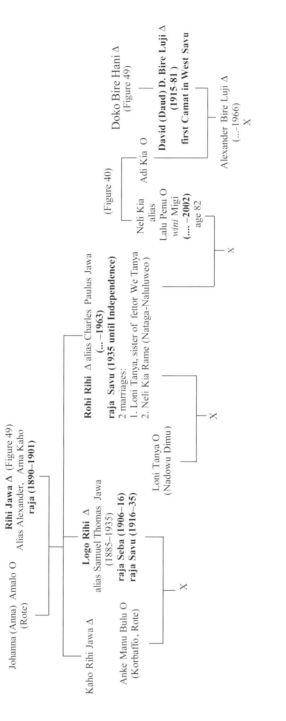

Photo 24. Anna Amalo and her sons, Semuel and Charles (picture taken after 1901, the year her husband died, as she is wearing a *batik* pattern associated with widowhood)
(Photo courtesy of Ibu Tibuludji, Kupang)

Photo 25. Portrait of Semuel Thomas Jawa; Teni Hawu (died 1935)
(Photo courtesy of Bapak Heke Medo, Seba)

Photo 26. Paulus Charles Jawa, the last raja of Savu (died 1963)
(Photo courtesy of Bapak Heke Medo, Seba)

Photo 27. David (also known as Daud) D. Bire Luji, the first subdistrict head of West Savu (died 1981)
(Photo courtesy of Bapak Heke Medo, Seba)

Eduard Jara Luji, the aged raja of Dimu, passed away in August 1910 after more than 40 years in power. Although he had relatives via his sister, they were not deemed eligible. Semuel Thomas Jawa was therefore proclaimed acting raja of Dimu. The fettor family continued to have a strong role in Dimu in the person of We Tanya, an imposing figure who would survive to see an independent Indonesia. The personal union between the two domains was nevertheless confirmed by a governmental decision in September the next year. This set the scene for a series of arrangements to abolish the other three small domains. The raja of Mesara, Ama Tenga Doko, passed away in July 1914. The colonial authorities decided not to replace him, although he had a large family. Mesara was merged with Seba-Dimu and, on 29 December 1916, Semuel Thomas Jawa was officially appointed raja of a new political creation, the landschap of Savu. Shortly after this, in April 1918, the Dutch honourably discharged the two rajas Hendrik Ratu Manu of Liae and Paulus Lai of Raijua from their positions. This was despite Raijua's first and last Christian raja being described by Assistant Resident Van Kempen as "otherwise no Napoleon, [but] is a splendidly impressing figure with sharp and noble facial characteristics and a fiery glance".[31] Meanwhile, a number of measures around 1913 increased direct Dutch supervision. A *civiel gezaghebber* (civil administrator) replaced the former Dutch posthouder position, adding a counterpart local person as a *bestuursassistent* (governmental assistant), both of whom helped the raja of Savu to run administrative affairs. It seems the colonial state did not send forth its best sons when it came to Savu. For example, the Dutch dismissed a gezaghebber in Larantuka called Anten, who did not perform satisfactorily, and relocated him to Savu where he soon proved to be a source of disaster, as the chapter later shows (Rieschoten 1913: 13). Road construction improved infrastructure to connect the four domains on the island, which naturally demanded an extensive use of corvée labour. The raja and the heads of the various districts (the former domains) were entitled to services from the population according to customary law (adat). Thus, the raja had the right to call a 100 people twice in 7 days and the district heads could each request 50 labourers twice in 7 days (Heyligers 1920: 59). Males of 17 years and above were required to pay tax which, according to oral data, could amount to as much as 30 per cent of the harvest.[32] Four per cent of the taxed income went to the landschap treasury and there was also a tax on slaughtering buffalos (Heyligers 1920: 57).

---

[31] Paulus Lai (alias Lai Kuji, Figure 54), the last raja of Raijua (Van Kempen 1917: 60).

[32] *The Savunese (Indonesia): The struggle for the survival of their ethnic culture & religion* (Jakarta: Rai Hawu Foundation, n.d.: 3–4).

Thus, Savu was under the bureaucratic structure that existed across several levels. Immediately under the Batavia government, the Residency *Timor en Onderhoorigheden* (Timor and Dependencies) encompassed the Dutch possessions from Sumbawa in the west to the border of Portuguese Timor in the east. The residency in turn was divided into five divisions (*afdeelingen*), each headed by an assistant resident who had a controleur or gezaghebber by his side. One of the five was the division of South Timor which, in spite of its name, also included the islands of Alor and Wetar to the north. Here Savu constituted a subdivision (*onderafdeeling*) with Seba as the capital (Ardhana 2000: 439–41). In 1921 Savu was merged with Rote into one subdivision.[33] Apart from Wetar, the town of Kupang and some adjacent territory, all the lands in the residency were zelfbesturende landschappen governed by a variety of rajas and sultans of different magnitude: from the extensive realm of the sultan of Bima in Sumbawa to the micro-states of Rote and Savu. At their accession the zelfbestuurders were required to undersign a declaration or contract. Most of them, including those in Savu, signed a tersely-worded version known as the *Korte veklaring* (Short declaration) (Ardhana 2000: 439–41).

Contemporary colonial reports tend to praise the various mergers occurring in the Timor Residency in the early 20th century. They greatly facilitated control and, therefore, the Dutch deemed them advantageous for the island populations. However, the new dispositions had the decided disadvantage of breaking age-old cultural and ritual structures which gave significant meaning to people's lives. For example, Muslim princedoms in Solor suddenly found themselves ruled by the Catholic rajas of Larantuka, their traditional enemies, and highland villages in Alor were expected to obey coastal rajas with whom they were on tense terms. Some of the landschappen in Timor were governed by people who apparently did not have any princely blood, which caused resentment. In Savu, matters did not initially seem too bad with the various rajas, chiefs and grandees reportedly agreeing to the changes. While the socio-political system in Savu was hierarchical and based on clans and lineages, the raja (*duae, mone paji*) institution was less deeply rooted than in many other systems in the eastern region. As previously discussed, the rajas as such were probably appointed after the establishment of European contacts, co-existing with the old system of priestly dignitaries (Apu Lod'o and Deo Rai). A Savunese ruler was not the exalted figure of a Javanese *susuhunan* (monarch), a Balinese raja, or a *liurai* (traditional ruler) of Sonba'i or Wehali. Another factor was that warfare between the domains had been rare since the late 18th century, with unbroken peace since 1872. The enduring tranquil conditions may have lessened resentment to the ascension of the Seba dynasty.

---

[33] Bosch 1938: 32; *Encyclopaedie* 1917–39, Vol. VII: 1365.

Photo 28. Memorial to the 1914 Mone Mola rebellion built in 2013 with donations from the Savunese community in Jakarta; Ledemawide, Mesara (2013)

However, there was one serious incident in Mesara shortly before the Dutch abolished the raja position. There are several accounts of this brief uprising. A few colonial reports and newspaper articles tersely describe it, but there is also a lengthy Savunese account which gives interesting perspectives on the way events in recent history made an impression on posterity. A Protestant minister called Victor Tanya, the son of a former fettor from Dimu, documented the event as a form of oral history.[34] The text was first published in the Indonesian series *Sejarah perlawanan terhadap imperialisme dan kolonialisme* (*History of the Resistance against Imperialism and Colonialism, 1982–1993*); an English version later appeared in a collection of articles from the Rai Hawu Foundation. The official nature of this series, issued at the height of the then President Soeharto's *Orde Baru* (New Order), requires a critical eye concerning the treatment of the account. Nevertheless, the author's father was a leading figure in early 20th-century Savu and would have been in a good position to acquire information about the incident. Tanya interviewed three local men—Ama Tai Junga, son

---

[34] *The Savunese*, n.d.; Interview with Bèngu Bire, Nabèlu clan (27.11.2014). There is also a more recent version, recorded in 2011, from Mèngi Lino (alias Ama Raja), a grand-nephew of the priest Rue (Rohi Wolo) who took an active part in the rebellion. Rohi Wolo died while in custody in Kupang. A memorial slab in Savu details the names of the victims.

of the Deo Rai who participated in the uprising, and Ama Tujo Uju and Ama Rohi Luhu, who had intimate knowledge of the Mone Mola uprising (possibly as eye witnesses). While imprinted with a strong sense of post-independence anti-colonialism, Victor Tanya's account suggests that the administrative changes in Savu engendered considerable dissatisfaction. Corvée service and the payment of taxes were burdensome to the inhabitants of an island marked by material poverty and few natural resources. Failure to pay taxes resulted in fines amounting to ten per cent of the sum and refusal to meet the demands resulted in confiscations, prison or severe physical mistreatment.

Photo 29. Detail of the Mone Mola memorial with a list of the victims (2013)

The direct cause of the uprising, however, was the encroachment on Savunese culture and religion. The dissemination of Christianity and schools began to threaten the adat and traditional ways of life. It also undermined the authority of the priestly councils, *Mone Ama*, which handled the ritual cycles and required their correct application to maintain ecological balance. If these rituals were not correctly performed, adverse natural phenomena would occur as a result: droughts, pests, storms, diseases and so on. This reached a crisis when the Christian authorities, in concert with Semuel Thomas Jawa and the colonial representatives, resolved to discard symbols of the Jingi Tiu religion. In 1914, at the *bègarae* ritual—for cleaning the village and earth at the change of season—the authorities ordered the burning of a number of ritual objects. Supposedly, this was to punish the Sebanese *Mone Ama* which refused to cancel the ritual that took place on a Sunday, the day of Christian worship. Dutch sources confirm that the newly appointed civiel gezaghebber Anten, who through poor performance had been removed from the same position in Larantuka, acted in an entirely confrontational way vis-à-vis the locals. He ordered the teacher Mauo (perhaps Manu?), a relative of the Seba raja line, to stop the ritual cock fighting in Seba on 13 April. The local Sebanese refused to obey Mauo, however. Shortly after, Anten himself arrived and Mauo asked him to confiscate two ritual drums and a *keris* (traditional knife [In]). When the Jingi Tiu priest declined to hand over the *keris*, Anten pointed a revolver at his head and forced the priest to yield the object.[35]

The incident galvanised the *Mone Ama* of Mesara and, at a meeting in the house of the Deo Rai, they decided to oppose any similar sacrilege. The presence of two Christian teachers in Mesara, believed to run errands for the colonials, also aroused local feelings of suspicion. In April 1914 the important *hole* ritual happened to fall on Good Friday. According to Victor Tanya's account, Raja Ama Tenga Doko, who died three months later, recommended that the Jingi Tiu practitioners not disturb a Christian holy day with traditional ceremonies. This caused widespread resentment. In particular, a certain Mone Mola who had previously been punished for his resistance to the new tax demands, became a leader of the resistance (*The Savunese*, n.d.: 5–6).

The contemporary colonial reports and articles do not quite endorse Victor Tanya. However, they say that Anten proceeded to Mesara in order to put an end to the cock fighting, customarily held for the *hole* ritual, which happened to fall on Easter Sunday, 19 April. However, his visit was unsuccessful, for the chiefs and population flatly refused to convene with him. The contemporary Dutch

---

[35] "De opstootjes op Savoe" (The disturbances on Savu), *Het Nieuws van den Dag voor Nederlandsch-Indië* (*Daily News of Netherlands India*), 28 May 1914.

sources do not agree exactly on the sequence of subsequent events. One report says Anten brought 100 Sebanese with him as escort, but they fled on seeing the people's anger, leaving the gezaghebber with a small retinue of police. His small troop retreated to a guest house nearby.[36] The Resident of Kupang, E.G. Th. Maier, later expressed his astonishment over the thoroughly inept behaviour of the gezaghebber (Maier 1918). The discontent spilled over into violence; the community torched the church, the school and the teachers' residence. The teachers barely managed to slip away alive.

According to Victor Tanya's account, the outburst was followed by a meeting where the *Mone Ama* members and traditional leaders from eight villages discussed how to handle the expected Dutch retaliation. They decided to make Kolarae village the hub of resistance and to collect weapons. The fighters were to undergo a war ritual and depart from the Deo Rai ritual house, Due Duru, which is situated on the top of Kolorae hill (*The Savunese*, n.d.: 6–7).

On 20 April the gezaghebber heard that the Mesara people were on their way towards Seba. He therefore went out with a police escort consisting of five armed men and some pro-Dutch forces from Seba under the prince Thomas Nyaila.[37] His aim was to contain the insurgents and, if possible, drive them back. In Mesara territory he first entered Ligu village. People there were not involved in the uprising and the contingent proceeded to the raja's residence, Lederaewawide, where they took up quarters in the guest house. Unbeknown to him there had been a discussion in Mesara the same morning where Christians and relatives of the raja had tried to persuade people to give up their resistance and avoid bloodshed. This was to no avail, however. At noon, just after the officials had encamped, the insurgents, led by Mone Mola, attacked the Dutch and Sebanese from all directions. The Dutch remained inside the post and exchanged fire for a long time. As the Mesarese ran out of ammunition, they attempted to storm the guest house with swords and lances. They broke through a fence and some followers of Mone Mola entered but were quickly dispatched by the Dutch. During the tumult the gezaghebber shot one of the policemen, Leeryck, by accident. Meanwhile, Thomas Nyaila shot Mone Mola in the head. The Dutch subsequently retreated with great difficulty, mounted their horses and headed back to Seba. The insurgents pursued them to the border, but the Dutch shot several people as they fled. Thus was the end of the only Savunese-Dutch military encounter since 1676: four insurgents lay dead and three were wounded. The

---

[36] Ibid.; Maier 1918. Other sources seem to imply that Anten retreated to Seba and that the incident in the guest house took place the following day.

[37] *The Savunese*, n.d.: 7. *Mailrapport*s (1914: 1375 and 1914: 897) say five armed police followed the gezaghebber, but Maier's account says 15.

wounded policeman Leeryck died of his injuries in Seba and was buried there with full honours.[38]

When Kupang received the incident report, the administration dispatched a detachment under the command of a lieutenant of the infantry, together with a brigade of armed police. The colonial reports are in conflict as to whether another armed encounter took place, but a contemporary *Mailrapport* basically agrees with Victor Tanya's detailed account, saying that the Mesarese offered no more open resistance. Similarly, Van Kempen's "Memorie van Overgave" (Memorandum of Succession) states the relief expedition did not encounter any armed opposition (Van Kempen 1917: 140–1).[39] Not all in Mesara favoured continued resistance and the *Mone Ama* felt pressed to negotiate. On the initiative of Raja Semuel Thomas Jawa, the Deo Rai and a war chief arrived in Seba to negotiate with the colonial authorities. The Dutch arrested the envoys and their entourage, ten in all, and subsequently sent them as forced labour to Seba, Alor, Rote and Kupang.

It goes without saying that the rising was doomed from the start and the incident left an impact. The Dutch enforced an agreement which stipulated that the members of the *Mone Ama* council would be replaced and that the Mesara people would pay 500 guilders to replace the loss of the two Christian teachers.[40] On their part, the Dutch undertook not to interfere in Jingi Tiu ceremonies. They also enjoined followers of the old and the new religions to co-exist. Moreover, the administration sacked gezaghebber Anten the same year and sent him to a post in Merauke in Papua—hardly a splendid appointment for a European official, considering the frugal and trying conditions there (*The Savunese*, n.d.: 8–10).

The incident falls into a pattern of discontent that can be seen in other parts of the eastern archipelago. While the increasing presence of the Dutch apparatus might have improved security in the region, locals detested the requirements of corvée labour for public works and the high-handed imposition of new taxes. The discontent sparked religiously laden movements with a millenarian taint. Victor Tanya's account mentions 14 war leaders who headed the attack against the guest

---

[38] *The Savunese*, n.d.: 7–8. Victor Tanya calls him "commander" Leeryck. His grave cannot be identified today.

[39] *Mailrapport* (1914: 1375) agrees with *The Savunese* (n.d.: 9)—the second expedition met with no resistance —while Maier 1918 attributes the four dead and three wounded to a second encounter. Victor Tanya also asserts that more Dutch soldiers than Leeryck were killed, which is not borne out by the colonial sources.

[40] The Deo Rai, Rohi Bire, interestingly, was replaced by his father Bire Junga. The Rue priest died in custody in Kupang, which is not mentioned in the Dutch reports but kept in the memory of the family (information from his grand nephew Mèngi Lino (alias Ama Raja).

house and people believed they possessed supernatural powers, having undergone proper war rituals. Similarly, there was an incident in Alor a few years later, in September–November 1918, where a woman who claimed supernatural power incited highland villages to resist the coastal raja and the Dutch, promising her followers independence from the "Company" (Wellfelt 2011: 170). The following year a woman in Belu, Timor claimed to stand in direct communication with the spirit world, inspiring a movement against taxes and corvée labour, and promoted the idea that a mystic ship would arrive and expel the Dutch (*Mailrapport* 1920: 1895). Colonial troops swiftly suppressed these movements, which may be described as the last attempts of traditionalist resistance before the emergence of Indonesian nationalism in the inter-war period.

Governance in the Savu landschap

The political history of Savu between the process of administrative unification and the Japanese occupation from 1942 is poor in dramatic events. The Mone Mola uprising was really the first and last of its kind. Once the Dutch had succeeded in road construction and people became accustomed to the taxes, colonial rule appears to have been accepted, though perhaps not with a joyful heart. One factor is that the new system did not actually diminish the identity of the traditional domains. Semuel Thomas Jawa governed the island via fettors in Seba, Dimu and Mesara, and *duae* in Liae and Raijua. These people were simply chosen from the old fettor and raja families of the domains. Similar to the traditional system, a son or close relative succeeded a deceased fettor or *duae* and performed an oath; the Resident of Kupang then formally appointed them. In every district (formerly domain) there was also a grand temukung who acted on behalf of the fettor or *duae* when necessary. Under them were the various genealogical heads (*bèngu udu*), initially playing the same role as the Dutch-termed temukungs, who headed a mother village and its satellites (Heyligers 1920: 56, 60). As time passed, persons other than the *bèngu udu*s were appointed temukungs. While the former remained the genealogical headmen, the latter emerged as officials who the Dutch could dismiss from the position if they did not live up to the expectations of the colonial state (De Nijs Bik 1934: 186).

Moreover, the districts or domains preserved their old ritual structure, keeping a priestly council with a Deo Rai and an Apu Lod'o who conducted public rites according to the complex lunar calendar.[41] The interference in Jingi

---

[41] *The Savunese*, n.d.: 16–7. The particularity of the various old domains was still strong, as demonstrated by a minor dispute over the border between Seba and Liae around 1930. However, the issue was solved without much difficulty (De Nijs Bik 1934: 187).

Tiu practices seems to have temporarily ceased after the Mone Mola revolt. It may be noted by 1920 the Christians were no more than 5,000 souls out of 27,311; thus less than 20 per cent of the population. Apart from being a modest minority, they were not particularly interested in discarding the old traditions. Here it is helpful to quote the cynical comment from the gezaghebber Heyligers, bluntly gainsaying the earlier hopeful reports by Donselaar, Teffer and Niks:

> Not much effort comes forth from these [indigenous clerical] leaders! The Christian Savunese is without exception a heathen by heart; he believes in heathen spirits and omens and participates in all heathen customs and feasts, such as the payment of *belis*, the cutting of the hair, etc. There are even several kampongs (villages) in the immediate neighbourhood of the centre of governance which are entirely heathen and where virtually no indigenous teacher is seen, such as the kampongs Bora, Rai Weta, Leomadamu, Leo Geh, Wui Hebo Dai Gama, and Ledetalo (Heyligers 1920: 24).

In spite of his dubious role in the Mone Mola affair, Semuel Thomas Jawa appears to have been relatively well respected, as shown by the many local legal cases that people entrusted to his direct arbitration.[42] According to Heyligers, he communicated with the district heads in an amicable and fraternal way, facilitated by the fact that they were all related to each other through matrimonial or blood ties. Living tradition remembers him as a person who could listen to his subjects. He walked around Seba and shared betel chew with the people he met. Should someone prove unable to pay the taxes, he agreed to reduce the amount. Internally, he was known by the grandiose title Kehe Hawu or Keizer Sabu, though it was not a parallel term to the kaiser of the German *Reich*.[43] In fact, there was an inflated use of imperial titles in the Timor Residency where the Dutch introduced the denomination *Keizer* in the 17th century that could be borne even by minor, low-ranking rulers.

The routines of governance were not overly complicated. Semuel Thomas accompanied the Dutch administrators on their tours around the island. During these tours the fettors and *duaes* received instructions on particular tasks and regulations, and they then forwarded them to the subordinate chiefs.[44] The raja or official controlled the command implementation on subsequent tours.

---

[42] De Nijs Bik 1934: 186. Of the other major chiefs, Resident De Nijs Bik characterised the fettor of Dimu, We Tanya, as a particular powerful lord with a good knowledge of adat.

[43] Interview with Marthen Heke Medo (17.05.2014).

[44] Rajas and fettors of other districts had to keep horses prepared: they rode to Seba to pick up the Dutch official and accompanied him on his inspection tour. Interview with Zadrak Bunga (12.05.2014).

However, the obesity of meat-loving Raja Semuel made him less mobile as time went on. Horses were the only means of transportation and the raja restricted his tours to two or three per year; most of the time the subordinate chiefs would come to his residence for administrative matters.[45] From time to time, a council of the chiefs occurred for the temukungs to gather and deliberate on common concerns. The council handled legal cases under the leadership of the Dutch official. The raja ruled on minor misdemeanours that involved imprisonment of up to three months or fines of up to 50 guilders; however, the Dutch authorities had to approve his sentences.[46] It is clear that the new system pressed the rajas of the Dutch East Indies into a bureaucratic mould in the early 20th century: princely blood no longer compensated for the lack of administrative competence and education. Heyligers also made some interesting comments about relations between the raja and the villagers:

> The population respects their higher chiefs, but do not always carry out the orders or requests willingly! There is no suggestion of the submissive attitude present in, for instance Java! Thus, for instance, people do not take any notice when the prince walks by, remaining in the posture as before he passed, and answer—also on being questioned—in that position, be it sitting or standing or working. There was one lying down when he passed by. All this can be attributed to the lack of manners and not to the reluctant attitude towards the prince or the lower chiefs, since their questions often are like: '*Kako la mi, Muria-Aë*' (Where are you going, Highness?) upon which the prince gives an amicable reply (Heyligers 1920: 60–1).

Oral accounts confirm the rather informal character of the Savunese mode of kingship. The princely household in Teni Hawu consisted of no more than about ten persons, servants included. Although they kept crockery and cutlery in the palace, it was reserved for prominent guests; the family normally ate with their hands from lontar leaves. A lady of the Tanya fettor family who spent her childhood there remembers that she played with village children and basically lived in a similar manner as most of the population. While participating in the traditional feasts, Semuel Thomas reportedly stayed away from the Jingi Tiu rituals but also avoided causing conflicts with the non-Christian believers.[47] His private life was less than harmonious. The raja entertained erotic relations

[45] Interview with Ester Tibuludji, Kupang (17.06.2014).

[46] Karthaus (1931: 55) mentions a '*Savoekas*' (Savu treasury) which had been abrogated by 1931.

[47] Interview with Ester Tibuludji, Kupang (17.02.2014).

with many women apart from his wife, which caused many bitter words between the spouses.[48]

Some statistical data are available which show the amount of government taxes on professions and other incomes in Savu. In the 1910s, the tax burden tended to rise markedly not only in Savu but also in the other *onderafdeelingen* (subdivisions) in the area. Still, the average amount paid per inhabitant was somewhat lower than in Kupang and Rote, and usually lower than in Alor. As a relatively large amount of money circulated in Savu in the late colonial period, the pressure might have been felt less than in places, such as Alor, where there were several anti-tax insurrections in the 1910s. The development over a few years is set out in a simple table:[49]

Figure 58: Revenue in 1914–16

Year	Amount of revenue	Average per taxpayer	Average per inhabitant
1914	15,089: 40 guilders	2: 16 guilders	0: 58 guilder
1915	21,671: 22 guilders	3: 10 guilders	0: 83 guilder
1916	24,636: 69 guilders	3: 53 guilders	0: 95 guilder

A report from 1931 characterised Semuel Thomas Jawa and his chiefs as worthy people, but they displayed little interest in social change. While the Dutch forced populations in Timor into new settlements, the local Savunese elite successfully resisted the imposition. They argued that the existing arrangements were acceptable as they stood, so why force a settlement reorganisation? Resident Karthaus found it unwise to press the matter, as he stated in a curious generalisation:

> On Savu everything always went well, one had no trouble with governance on that island. It paid the taxes, got little or nothing in return since little or nothing was necessary, and continued to bring forth revenue without grumbling (Karthaus 1931: 55).

Semuel Thomas's faculties had declined by the early 1930s and the colonial authorities thought of encouraging him to step down (Karthaus 1931: 55). However, before the Dutch followed their intention, he passed away in September 1935. According to the unanimous testimony of his kinsmen, he did not have children with his Rotenese wife Angelique. Instead, an adoption

---

[48] Leopold Nisnoni, Kupang (personal communication; 2014). Leopold Nisnoni is the son of Semuel Thomas Jawa's adopted daughter.

[49] From Van Kempen 1917, Appendix VI.

ceremony occurred with his Termanu relatives. In 1915, Semuel Thomas and Angelique received the four-year-old princess Adeleida Amalo as their daughter (Passar 2005: 62–3). The thoroughly Savunised Adeleida subsequently married Alfonsus Nisnoni who was the zelfbestuurder of the newly created landschap of Kupang and an able respected politician in Timor.[50] Adeleida was an interesting personality in her own right and an example of the modernising mission sometimes found within the region's aristocracy in the late colonial period. In 1945, she founded the first social women's organisation in Timor, *Pendirian Ibu* (Mother Foundation), concerned with social, educational and cultural issues (Passar 2005: 63). Adeleida's sister was the consort of Joel Simon Kedoh, the zelfbestuurder of the likewise recent landschap of Rote (*Mailrapport* 1933: 348: 18). It reveals the strategic politics of marriage linking the islands' elite in the residency long after the implementation of colonial rule.

An alternative story is that the raja actually had a number of children who settled in Kupang, Sumba and Flores. Semuel Thomas Jawa's extra-marital relations might account for these children, as a number of oral sources clearly state that the raja did not have any biological children with his wedded wife. One of them, Rudolf Louis, born in 1904, was sent first to Ende and later, in his twenties, to Larantuka to work for the Dutch. He died in Flores without ever having had the opportunity to take the zelfbestuurder position; his branch of the Jawas is still in existence.[51]

Of the raja's two brothers, Welem Jawa married a daughter of the important Timorese raja Rasi Koroh of Amarasi (r. 1872–87, 1892–1914). The Amarasi connection is not surprising as some young members of the kingdom's aristocracy grew up in the household of Mattheus Teffer and stayed in Seba for a period. Although Teffer does not write much about it, the Timorese nobles must have met the Jawas frequently. The marriage produced two sons called Alexander and Hendrik Arnold, born in 1902 and 1904, who probably stayed in Savu in their early childhood.[52] As the sons later became rajas of Amarasi (1924–25, 1925–51) the Jawa family network expanded further still. The energetic Hendrik Arnold, moreover, was married to a great-granddaughter of the 19th-century raja Ama Doko Kaho. In spite of their Jawa paternity the brothers were always called by

---

[50] Donald P. Tick, Pusat Dokumentasi Kerajaan2 Indonesia [Central Document Kingdom 2 Indonesia]; Vlaardingen, the Netherlands (personal communication; November 2013).

[51] Mathias Djawa (personal communication; November 2013). The source has reportedly been asked to become the titular raja of Savu.

[52] Welem and his Timorese wife lived in Savu. Interview with Ester Tibuludji (17.06.2014).

the clan name Koroh, not Jawa.[53] The reason was economical: the bridewealth that the Jawas should have provided for the princess was not paid in full, so the children were considered part of their maternal grandfather's lineage. Hendrik Arnold had a controversial role during the Japanese occupation of 1942–45 when he provided the occupiers with *romusha*s (forced labourers) and 'comfort women', but he won praise during the ensuing Indonesian Revolution for his firm anti-Dutch stance.[54]

How long Welem Jawa lived is not precisely known, but it was the youngest brother who succeeded him to rule. This was Paulus Charles Jawa who was chosen by the "people", meaning of course the genealogical heads. The beginning of his rule was not exactly auspicious. Owing to a legal transgression, the Seba council of chiefs sentenced him to exile for one month, transferred into a fine.[55] Resident J.J. Bosch nevertheless installed Paulus Charles as acting raja of Savu in May 1937.[56] At the same time he placed the Rotenese J.J. Detaq as *bestuursassistent* (government assistant). Detaq subsequently enjoyed a political career in independent Indonesia and published a short book on Savunese mythohistory (Passar 2005: 57–8; Detaq 1973). The Resident had great hopes for Detaq who was expected to head a more efficient and constructive governance, and keep the chiefs under closer control. He wrote: "Until now, practically speaking, the work of the head of the *onderafdeeling* Savu only consisted of the arbitration of legal matters" (*Mailrapport* 1937: 935: 5–6). In general, the Dutch colonial reports in these years are brief and portray the situation on the island as harmonious—there was no noticeable political agitation. In sharp contrast with the perennial conflicts in Rote, the relations between the population and their chiefs were generally agreeable (*Mailrapport* 1939: 1146: 5). The second and last raja of Savu governed under the complicated transition of Indonesia from a colony to an independent republic. He was married to Loni We Tanya, the daughter of the

---

[53] Interestingly, the Koroh family has kept the raja of Savu's crown (Loesi Koroh, personal communication; August 1994), palace of Baun.

[54] Passar 2005: 124; Interview with Charles Koroh, Baun (06.01.2004); Fobia 1984: 117–8.

[55] *Mailrapport* 1936: 297: 6–7. The sentence, pronounced in June 1936, was due to his overstepping paragraph 404 (1), W.v.S., but no further details are given.

[56] Oral accounts assert that the two-year interregnum in 1935–37 was due to Paulus Charles Jawa's unsatisfactory character. There was another ruling candidate (possibly Rudolf Louis Jawa?) whose name is not disclosed in the documents and who did not achieve his goal in the end.

Dimu fettor who also ruled as fettor of Seba on a temporary basis.[57] The two leading traditional powers of Savu were thereby bound together. The marriage did not produce any children, however, nor did his later marriage. Opinion about him is divided in oral sources: some have a positive opinion about the raja as having "a high sense of discipline". On the other hand, he was not as close to the people as his brother and predecessor, presumably as his obesity made travel outside Seba problematic.[58] A Resident complained that he "could have been more active" but attributed this to his lack of experience in administrative matters (*Mailrapport* 1938: 901: 7).

Late colonial society

Savunese society has been avidly studied by a number of Indonesian and foreign anthropologists since the late 20th century. These scholars have highlighted the flow of life in terms of the kinship system, ritual, territorial organisation and local economics, usually emphasising the resilient, slow-changing features of society and the ecological balance of the economic system. This begs the question of how the data gathered by recent fieldwork compare to the colonial officials and missionaries' body of knowledge in the late 19th and early 20th centuries. While early visitors, such as Cook and Pelon, had only brief (albeit informative) experience with the Savunese, the picture is different for the late colonial period. There is no denying that the perspectives presented by the NZG representatives and the gezaghebbers were either religious or governed by the ambition to administer the land according to European principles. However, they stayed in Savu for years, mixed with people of different classes and locations, and sometimes even learnt some Savunese. While their observations should be critically scrutinised in the light of modern anthropological research, they provide valuable glimpses of a society that might have been slow-changing, but it was not immutable.

As a people, the Savunese had a favourable nature in the eyes of most visitors. The population had a "good predisposition for development" and were not inferior to the Rotenese in any respect, according to the imagined racial hierarchy of the time. The Dutch administration considered the combined population of Rote and Savu superior to other peoples in the Residency. To quote J.J. Bosch in 1938, "the Rotenese and Savunese form the most energetic part of the population in

---

[57] *Mailrapport* 1939: 1146: 7. The rightful fettor candidate was Gabriel Manu who was too young to take up the fettor dignity in Seba, so Samuel We Tanya governed both Dimu and Seba for a while.

[58] Interviews with Ama Bèhi, Seba (30.06.2012); and Ester Tibuludji (17.06.2014).

these quarters".[59] Missionaries noted with pleasure that people seldom indulged in the use of *laru*, fermented alcoholic lontar juice, unlike the Rotenese. They were generally merry people who lacked the phlegmatic stance of the Javanese. They also displayed a degree of flexibility, were often willing to move to other milieus and adapted well in places such as Kupang. Nevertheless, they kept their Savunese identity even if they married someone from another ethnic group (Heyligers 1920: 19). Quite a few Savunese seemed inclined to follow European models in terms of dress and furniture, if they had the economic means to do so (Iets naders 1872: 155). Visitors also found them restless and compared them to untamed horses—"They sit now here, now there; to sit still is impossible for them" (Teffer 1875: 222).

In the geographical and ethnographic literature of the colonial era, it was common to judge foreign peoples by a balance sheet of characteristics and the Savunese did not escape this. Thus, they were on one hand "gentle and compliant although not slavish or submissive" and possessed "courage, soberness, consensus, calm and moderation—one very seldom hears of drunkenness—and cheerfulness". However, this was contrasted by a number of alleged shortcomings:

> They are mendacious, thievish, lazy, unconcerned. They are very frank which is especially seen in their speech and communication with their chiefs and nobles. The nobles sit down brotherly at the side of the lesser. If he takes in some sirih for himself, the lesser shall also not hesitate to pick some sirih from his higher neighbour without invitation (Heyligers 1920: 17–8).

The list of 'good' and 'bad' characteristics says more about colonial attitudes than complex Savunese realities; indeed, some of the 'minus' traits might be regarded as sympathetic by modern readers. Although the missionaries tended to rank the islanders higher than the Timorese and Rotenese, they wrote ironically about their perceived lack of work ethic:

> We should not forget that we live among a Savunese population whose principal sin is laziness and who, as a former Resident of Kupang had it, 'are too lazy to keep their eyes open'. I readily admit that I am now more of a *mandor* (overseer) than a missionary. I must egg on the people if I want something done. The Savunese are lazy. You may not know the Savunese working day? If not, listen now. Communal work is to be carried out. You agree to start work in the 'morning'. Morning means here something like eleven when the burning sun already sends its rays vertically to the earth. Then, finally, a few sit there. Will they start? No, not yet since a *sobat* (mate) has not yet arrived. Eventually he comes, half

---

[59] Bosch 1938: 33. Again it must be stressed that the interests of the colonial establishment conditioned such generalisations and they lack explanatory value in themselves.

an hour later. Lo, now they are ready, now to work? But behold, first there is another half hour of chit-chatting why the *sobat* came so late. Some talk, some speech, forgetting to hear and see. But finally, now they have sorted it out. Now, quickly to work to make up for the lost hour? No, first wait for the indispensable *mama* (plums). Then (but now at least one and a half hours have passed) they are finally to begin. But behold, they are busy, or number 1 is 'pedoha' (sick), number 2 'mara' (tired), number 3 'pemanga' (hungry), and so on. And finally, well look here, it is so late, and you know, the tuak must be tapped. The best thing is that we now go home and do it tomorrow, and on the day after tomorrow....[60]

Letteboer's comments reveal his ignorance. The men do not only tap the lontar palm in the evening but do the same in the morning, starting before dawn. For this men may walk some distance, and could climb up and down as many as 20 trees. There is no doubt that they would then rest at home before walking to the communal work site; hence, the activity takes place in the hot hours of the day. Again underlining the missionary's lack of knowledge is that *mama* comes from the expression *mama kenana* (to chew betel); it is not related to plums which are not known on the island.

The perceived *mañana* (sometime in the future) attitude to labour was evident when it came to missionary construction work. It says little about the ability to manage the household economy and the 'laziness' is, moreover, gainsaid by some other missionary letters. However, the image certainly says a lot about the Calvinist ethics of work in which the Dutch visitors were grounded. The NZG brother has no qualms seeing himself as the motor attempting to drag the 'natives' out of their inertia. To quote the same missionary voice, "O, how to teach these people: work is blessing, blessing from God, and so on?"[61]

As the missionaries were concerned with the education of the young, they gained a limited insight into Savunese family life and the sphere of childhood. As they put it, children were not particularly susceptible to order and regulation. When at home they acted as they wished, and their fathers and mothers did not have much power over them. The parents might send their children to school, but if this was not to their satisfaction the children stayed at home, whatever the elders said. When asked why they had been absent, they replied "*Ta pana ihi, ta emu, né ta roee*" (approximately, it is not nice). It did not take much to divert them from schooling. If father and mother went to the forest or fields, the children would accompany them, or they might be told to mind younger brothers or sisters. The parents introduced them to the

---

[60] Raad voor de Zending, 1102–1: 1444, J.H. Letteboer, letter, 22 June 1894.

[61] Ibid.

traditional household tasks as early as possible. Small boys kept the buffalos, and girls brought lontar juice to the house and learnt how to weave sarungs. In harvest time, old and young went out to pick green grams and maize, and cut the paddy.[62] For the missionaries, who probably misunderstood the relations between parents and children (as they tended to do with other areas of Savuese life), the contrast between the liberal ways in Savu and the stricter way of child-raising in their European homeland was bewildering. They deplored that the parents were ostensibly ruled by the children.

Gender relations evoked many comments. The 19th-century missionaries noted the existence of male clans and female moieties.[63] Praise for the islanders' strictly monogamous system could not hide the sad fact that syphilis was widespread, suggesting numerous liaisons outside of wedlock (Van Kempen 1917: 91). Women tended to do most of the work in the household, which was attributed to the warlike Savunese past that kept men busy with other matters. At the same time they stood up against their husbands and were often their actual masters. Women bartered items and kept the profits for their own means. Unlike many other societies in the East Indies, men did not have any propensity for handicrafts, which was left entirely in the hands of their wives and daughters (Iets naders 1872: 222–3).

The foreign observers were stunned and not a little impressed by the frugal qualities of life in Savu. Missionaries argued philosophically that there was no scarcity in Savu because people were used to having nothing.

> If it is true what some say, that people who have the least needs are the happiest ones, then the Savunese are undoubtedly the happiest people on the entire earth. Really, no people has been found so far which harbours such small needs.[64]

A small quantity of lontar juice or a spoonful of syrup was enough to keep a person alive for a day. A woman who engaged in a conversation with the European wife of Mattheus Teffer in about 1875 remarked: "This year there is not much syrup." Mrs Teffer replied: "That is quite sad. Then what do you eat?" "*Ei loko* (river water)" was the reply.[65] Some people were able to eat rice or other crops from time to time, but the staple means of nutrition remained the lontar juice. Europeans noted with astonishment how the entire economy hinged on the lontar palm. People fed the liquid to their pigs and dogs. Trunks from the

---

[62] Raad voor de Zending, 1102–1: 1415, J.K. Wijngaarden, letter, 3 February 1891.

[63] Raad voor de Zending, 1102–1: 1406, H.C. Kruyt, Notebook 2, c. 1890.

[64] *Maandberigt van het Nederlandsche Zendelinggenootschap* 1875–77: 102.

[65] Ibid.

tree became beams for the simple houses, and the fan-shaped leaves served as excellent roofing that withstood rain and sunshine much better than other palm leaves. Hats, parasols, sleeping mats, harnesses, baskets and boxes were all made from leaves or the fibres from the leaves. The undivided leaves made excellent water-tight containers. Thus, everything the Savunese needed seemed to derive from this "wonder tree".[66]

All this, of course, presupposed that the lontar trees were in a good state of preservation. However, the forces of nature sometimes threatened this vital means of survival. Major cyclones in the Savu Sea occasionally directly hit Rote and Savu with devastating results. A cyclone in the night between 19 and 20 March 1882 is particularly well documented with the prolific writer Teffer as an eyewitness. The fury of the winds destroyed almost all of the houses and some people were killed under the collapsing buildings. The cyclone ruined the crops and blew down a great many lontar trees. The trunks lay like broken pipes in all directions, having fallen across each other.

> Hopeful and so far never disappointed, the head or natural caretaker of the family leaves his house or hut—whatever it be—in the morning, already before sunrise. Humming and singing in the lontar palm which is mostly 60 to 70 feet high, he does what is necessary to gain the lontar juice. The acquired quantity is usually quite sufficient to feed humans and animals. In the afternoon, around four or five o'clock, one climbs up once again to obtain what is necessary for livelihood on Savu. This morning however, we did not meet a single Savu singer in the crown of the lontar. It was dead still, everything lay on the ground. … The smaller or younger trees, which however were incapable of yielding any foodstuff, had often been able to resist the hurricane without falling to the ground in great number. Others, which might yield the necessary foodstuff, must first be worked on. What was left? Nothing other than acquiring the edible parts of the fallen trees, once again cultivating the remaining lontar palms for acquirement of foodstuff and then have patience until things are once again in balance ("Ramp op Savoe" 1882: 176).

Official reports confirm that thousands of lontar trees fell in Rote and Savu, while the unripe paddy and maize were completely ruined. The foreseeable effect was lack of food which especially afflicted Savu. Raja Ama Doko Kaho of Seba planned to sail to Java with an Arab trader to buy rice for the people, but the

---

[66] Ibid., 103.

cyclone disaster was followed by an outbreak of a serious illness which laid Ama Doko in an early grave before he could set sail.[67]

Considering the enormous value of the lontar palm it is natural that ritual practices evolved around the tree and its relation to people. In his notebooks from about 1890, H.C. Kruyt reports that two men fell from trees in a single day and died from their injuries. As he noted, when such things occurred among the 'heathens' they would hang the equipment of the lontar climber in a tree at Nadagai. From there, people went to Turu Hole by Leo Baka, to wash the cloths belonging to the deceased, and then they walked to Nyiu Geru and Wadu Bekka at Kolorae.[68] After the ritual progress people returned to their homes. There were also regulations for people visiting the dead lontar climbers in their houses.[69] Modern anthropological data, as previously discussed, shows that people who die in accidents are buried lying straight rather than in the foetal position used for natural deaths.

There was modest cultivation of commercial crops by the late 19th century. *Pinang* (or areca) nuts were in high demand in this part of the archipelago because people chewed them with *sirih* (betel) leaves. There were gardens of areca palms in Savu which were considered the only product on the island of a more general value.[70] The gezaghebber Heyligers did not consider the Savunese to be great agriculturists. They planted just as much as they needed. People annually planted rice, maize, millet and green grams, but the produce was usually not enough for an entire year: they needed to import small quantities to make up the shortfall. For example, in 1919, 82 tons of rice and 45 tons of maize were imported (Heyligers 1920: 54). The limited state of agriculture again underlines the island's reliance on the lontar palm. Oral stories speak of the Dutch regulating the rice fields close to Seba to the benefit of the raja.[71] There are also bitter recollections of cleptocratic tendencies; if villagers could not pay

---

[67] *Mailrapport* 1882: 585. As noted earlier, Teffer suspected a temukung "who according to the general feeling helped him to his grave.… Yes! There are also such deaths on Savu. While the Lord had praise spoken through the mouths of the young ones, the man passed away in the prime of his life, without praise on his lips" ("Ramp op Savoe" [Calamity on Savu] 1882: 181).

[68] There is a place called Nadagai under the Rue of Seba which matches the description as Rue is the priest for accidents and disasters. In the list of villages in Van Lijnden (1851), there is indeed a village called Kolorae, indicating that the double deaths took place in Seba.

[69] Raad voor de Zending, 1102–1: 1406, H.C. Kruyt, Notebook 2, c. 1890.

[70] "Ramp op Savoe" 1882: 175. Heyligers does not mention *pinang* in his "Memorie van Overgave" of 1920, so the areca plantations might have decreased in importance from the 1880s, quite possibly as a consequence of the 1882 cyclone.

[71] Interview with Ester Tibuludji, Kupang (17.02.2014).

their taxes or fees, the raja was likely to confiscate their agricultural land. Thus, the raja furthered his personal interests under the umbrella of the Dutch colonial state.[72] An example of this is a dam and an irrigation system that ran along a new paved road from Raeloro to Mèba. When construction was underway around 1930, every owner of a rice field had to pay one guilder as a contribution. The raja claimed the rice fields of those unable to pay and used them for his private enrichment until the owner paid his debt—which could take years. There are instances where, even after independence, the confiscated land remained with the raja family, only to be seriously disputed in the 1990s. After the death of the last raja's widow in 2002, some owners were able to regain their fields after some six decades.[73]

Animal husbandry was of greater importance than crop production. Possession of buffalos and horses was a status marker "and the fieriest wish of anyone who neither possess a horse nor a buffalo, is to once be able to call such animals his own!" (Heyligers 1920: 47–8) Even poor people would usually own at least a sheep, goat or pig. Horses were a mainstay of inter-island trade and visitors noted the extensive areas of the small island devoted to grazing. J.F. Niks conducted a tour of inspection around Savu in 1885 going from Seba via Menia to Dimu:

> On 9 June we departed from Menia to go to Dimu Bodae. After having marched through the splendid valley of Menia, we arrived at a large horse corral, a few hours walk in circumference.[74] On Savu there is a custom, when cultivation of *sawah*s [rice] and *jagung* [maize] fields takes place, to drive the horses into this wide-stretching area of land, entirely covered with rock boulders. This corral, which I partly traversed, constitutes one eighth of the Island of Savu. Thus, one can imagine what work it is to construct this wall, and it proves that there is no lack of stones on Savu. The advantage of all that effort is that they now do not need to fence the gardens and sawahs. We rode on an elevated plain that made a beautiful impression at some places. Here and there along the road one sees stone altars on which the heathens perform their sacrifices when there is lack of rain or it does not occur [at all]; which foremostly occurs in November or December. Then many animals die from lack of grass.[75]

---

[72] Interviews with Elo Lado (Malobo) and Mingu Lutu (19.03.2002).

[73] Interviews with Petrus Bara Pa (18.11.2014) and Marthen Heke Medo (17.05.2014).

[74] This corral is located in Èilode, now in Sabu Tengah. People from all over the island used to take their animals, mainly horses, there during the rainy season, because animals were not allowed to roam freely. In the dry season there is no grass there. Interview with Petrus Bara Pa (18.11.2014).

[75] Raad voor de Zending, 1102–1: 1408, J.F. Niks, Travel report, 5–29 June 1885.

In the 1920s, a Savunese stallion could fetch anywhere between 80 and 600 guilders which was a lot of money in the eastern archipelago. During the year 1919, Savu exported 411 horses worth a total of 55,600 guilders. The horse trade was the sole domain of the aristocracy; the raja and fettor families delivered horses to traders from Australia and elsewhere.[76] In Rote, Savunese steeds largely superseded the small and enduring local horses by the 1920s.[77] It was by far the biggest export product, followed by copra (29,805 guilders), hides (7,654), syrup (520), onions (178) and some minor items (4,635).[78] With an efficiency that must have seemed disturbing to the Savunese, considering butcher fees and export duties, the colonial authorities registered the domestic animals found on the island: 3,860 horses, 3,880 buffalos, 4,595 sheep, 1,180 goats and 4,010 pigs.[79] Chickens, dogs and pigeons were not registered and non-domesticised animals were of little consequence to the household economy. In spite of its insular situation, Savu was not a centre for fishing, as seen by available statistics: in 1920 there were no more than 15 perahus in Savu and 8 in Raijua. The districts Dimu and Liae did not have any boats at all. The Dutch believed that the population was fearful of the sea, even more so than the Rotenese (Van Kempen 1917: 117). The sea fish caught around the island with some regularity included species of sardine and swordfish; the latter could be found in the dry season. Women sometimes combed the water margin at low tide, looking for turtles, octopus, urchins and seaweed. People even ate insects. On a daily basis, children carried swats and canisters made of lontar leaves; they hit the grasshoppers and gathered them in the boxes, eventually roasting them over the fire.[80]

Communication with the outside world was restricted—this was not helped by the small number of boats on the island. It was certainly not a unique Savunese problem. It was only at the end of the 19th century that the regular shipping lines of the Koninklijk Paketvaart Maatschappij (KPM, Royal Packeting Company) linked the Timor Residency's main islands. By the early 20th century

---

[76] Interview with Ester Tibuludji (17.06.2014). Such trading contacts exist today. In December 2002, when the island was experiencing another drought, G. Duggan witnessed the export of dozens of Savunese horses to Mauritius on a Bugis boat.

[77] *Encyclopaedie* 1917–39, Vol. VII: 1365.

[78] Heyligers 1920: 54. The syrup was usually exported to a value of about 5,000 guilders per year, but the lontar palms did not yield the normal amount of sugar juice in 1918.

[79] Heyligers's figures are significantly different from those given by Van Kempen 1917, (Appendix III: 3,242 horses, 3,541 buffalos, 3,410 sheep, 497 goats and 978 pigs). As it is unlikely that such a rise in sheep, goat and pig numbers would have occurred naturally over three years, the 1920 figures illustrate the increasingly fine-tuned means of surveying livestock.

[80] Heyligers 1920: 52. Roasted grasshoppers allegedly go very well with tuak!

two KPM lines visited the roadstead of Seba once a month (Van Kempen 1917: 117). In spite of the recently constructed roads, intra-island communications were also limited. The Savunese did not use horses and buffalos as pack animals because they roamed over large areas and were hard to catch at short notice. The only "pack animals" available were humans—in most cases women. When Philippus Bieger arrived in Savu in 1888 he noted that it was mostly women, seemingly stronger than the men, who carried the heavy chests ashore from his boat.[81] The highly localised society was not conducive to economic change. The only activity approximating a cottage industry was weaving—referred to in the VOC period—and textiles were exported to Timor by the early 19th century. In the late colonial period women produced attractive *kain* (cloth) and sarongs, usually made from foreign yarn, which they imported in some quantity each year—1,280 kilograms in 1919. What the household did not need was sold to the outside world and the popularity of Savunese textiles increased markedly in the early 20th century. The price for *kain* oscillated between 15 and more than 40 guilders, which meant that selling cloth was quite profitable (Heyligers 1920: 48). Data from 1920 give reason to believe that the population was no longer as poor as the NZG missionaries had asserted in the 19th century. There was some money circulating in the local economy. Similar to many pre-modern cultures, the earth itself was a natural safe; people put their coins in earthen pots and buried them. The colonial authorities arranged for an auxiliary bank (*hulpbankje*) to be established in 1916 and persuaded at least the more educated Savunese to keep their savings there (Heyligers 1920: 49–50).

The 19th-century missionaries described the pattern of settlement, albeit in rather vague terms. In contrast with the scattered Timorese villages, the Savunese preferred a more intimate pattern. In Seba people lived in villages which were built close to each other. The main village of Seba was situated on Namata hill, surrounded by gardens with coconut and other useful trees, and served by wells dug at strategic locations (Iets naders 1872: 154). Today, Seba is a coastal settlement; increasingly secure conditions in the late colonial era allowed villages to be close to the shore. The placement of Savunese villages was otherwise not very regular. They were usually situated anywhere between 10 and 80 meters above sea level and could be built either on flat ground, slopes or hilltops. There were also some households positioned apart from the others. A cluster of houses could be oblong, round or square according to the needs. Modern data indicate that clusters generally represented a boat with a 'bow' and 'stern', positioned in

---

[81] Raad voor de Zending, 1102–1879, Ph. Bieger, letter, 7 August 1888. Bieger's opinion of the physical strength of Savunese men was unfavourable: apparently, four Savunese would carry a rice bale with effort that one single Javanese could have handled!

an east-west direction to make the best use of the winds. Walls made of stones and mud most commonly surrounded the villages. About one metre high, the walls were not particularly impressive, but cacti growing alongside increased the desired deterrent effect. In premodern times, the walls had been much higher and thicker, reflecting the generally insecure political situation; the more recent walls were mainly to keep roaming cattle and thieves out. In spite of the highly traditional layout there were some small changes by the early 20th century. Thus, people tended to plant more lontar and coconut palms around the villages (Heyligers 1920: 12–3).

While Christianity made slow progress far into the 20th century, the schools established from 1862 played a part in informing the younger generations of the world outside their island. After the NZG's pioneering efforts, its activities were assumed by the common church organisation of the Dutch East Indies, de Nederlandsch Indische Protestantische Kerk. Nine clerics administered to people in eight places in Savu and Raijua by 1920, usually also serving as schoolmasters. By this time, however, lay education had taken root. A Governmental Indigenous School in Seba accommodated 80 pupils who learned reading and writing, mathematics and a little geography. There were also the Indigenous Popular Schools. By 1913, there were already five schools in place and a further three planned which, seven years later, had increased to ten with more than six hundred students (Rieschoten 1913: 161). As was the norm for 'native' education in the East Indies, Malay was the language of communication, laying the foundations for teaching Bahasa Indonesia long before independence (Heyligers 1920: 50–1). Gezaghebber Heyligers's testimony depicts an island society that had taken up certain forms of Western culture by the inter-war period. Interestingly, while Heyligers gives largely positive images of Savunese traditional culture, his example of hybridity has a slightly sarcastic edge, as of discussing people who try to become something they are not 'supposed' to be:

> The progress to the church on Sunday in Seba offers a nice image. The "gentlemen" and "ladies" then sport their Sunday garb. The gentlemen neatly wear a closed white jacket and white trousers, shoes and a straw hat. It does not matter if the trousers are somewhat too long and too narrow or if the collar and sleeves are somewhat tainted or frayed—it is a white parcel! The ladies are better dressed; they have booties, a pretty sarong and a bright white kabaya with much lacing and a parasol. If the lady is somewhat late she follows after, trotting with closed parasol in one hand and the booties in the other! The more prominent women come with socks and shoes and brightly coloured gowns (not always of the latest fashion); this adds little to it. And last not least the "Tuan" Guru, the indigenous teacher, comes in an old green-and-black sack of cloth, sallow white collar, sometimes also cuffs and a greasy brown-black tie above the collar (Heyligers 1920: 25–6).

The winds of war

When the Dutch colonial historian E.S. de Klerck concluded his two-volume survey *History of the Netherlands East Indies* in May 1938, he breathed a restrained optimism about the future of the colonial overseas realm in spite of the gathering clouds in Europe and East Asia: "It is sufficient to reiterate that [the Netherlands] fulfills her colonial task in a satisfactory manner, a fact that is also readily admitted in well-informed native circles." In view of the impotency of the League of Nations and the poor colonial defenses, he nevertheless found it proper to end the book with a misplaced Shakespeare quotation: "To be or not to be, that is the question" (1938: II: 614).

The answer to the colonial Hamlet's question came within four years. The German invasion of the Netherlands in 1940 left the East Indies a pro-allied territory cut away from the "motherland". The fate of the colony was doomed when Japan decided in November 1941 to acquire resource-rich Southeast Asia. The initial American and British defeats in the Pacific area, Hong Kong and Malaya opened the way for Japanese landings in Sulawesi and Kalimantan in January 1942. Events painfully repeated the British conquest of 1811, highlighting the same syndrome. The Dutch colonial troops were sufficient to keep internal order but had no chance of repelling a well-equipped invader. De Klerck's words four years earlier rang hollow: the bulk of the population did not appreciate the "satisfactory manner" of colonial rule and did nothing to support the defenders. Indeed, many were initially enthusiastic over the supposed liberation from the Dutch yoke (Van den Doel 2011: 311–4). The Dutch jointly defended Timor with Australian troops, who also took position on the technically neutral Portuguese end of the island. The island fell after hard fighting in February 1942, although Australian commandos kept resistance alive in East Timor for some time, supported by the Timorese.

The invaders did not neglect the smaller islands in the vicinity of Timor. As in the rest of the archipelago, the local administrations and zelfbestuurders continued with a Japanese slant. Current tradition remembers the Japanese relationship with Savu through an interesting mythologising edge. When the Imperial forces moved from Batavia towards Kupang in early 1942 they were not able to see the island. They could not determine a location because the locals used rituals to render Savu invisible to outsiders—the effects of magic. The new masters then invited the raja to sail to Kupang for a meeting. Paulus Charles Jawa arrived with his boat *Nge ta d'o ludu* ("Almost not chosen", referring to his belated appointment as raja). In Kupang, the Japanese at first intended to kill him as he had made the island invisible. However, the raja was saved by his big belly. When the Japanese saw his stomach they changed their minds and instead accompanied him to Savu. The story does not explain the Japanese fascination with the ruler's substantial proportions. However, it provides a Savunese rationale for the behaviour of the new overlords.[82]

Thus, Paulus Charles Jawa was able to continue as *syuco* (local regent [Ja]) under the Imperial flag. A small detachment of about 30 Japanese troops was stationed in Savu and positioned all over the island. The Japanese administration occupied Teni Hawu, the palace, while the raja had to move to the Skaber, the Dutch military-administrative establishment near Raepudi, the place of the former Menia rajas. In three and a half years, the newcomers brought important changes to the island. The harshness of Japanese rule on an archipelago-wide scale is well attested and it was motivated by the single aim of the occupation policy: to contribute to victory in the Pacific War. This included forced deliveries of food and other produce, forcibly recruited labour (*romusha*s), and draconic punishments for any kind of opposition. The inhabitants of remote Savu, as elsewhere, experienced some of the darker sides of the Japanese policy.

There were also some positive effects of Japanese rule. First, education progressed during the occupation. In Dutch times few young people had the opportunity of schooling. For the most part it was children of important families and the ruling clans who attended school, and gained proficiency in Malay. For the Japanese it was important to communicate with their new subjects, not least in order to instill in them anti-Western and pro-Japanese thinking. According to the new regulations, all children and teenagers, and even young adults, had to attend school. It was a way to keep control over labour. The students had to study Malay (or Bahasa Indonesia as it is now called) and a minimum of Japanese. Should a child be seen out of school, he and his father would be caned. However, it seems that this was not implemented strictly over the entire island but mainly in Seba and Dimu. People who lived in remote places may not have even seen the Japanese during the occupation.

Second, the Japanese initiated some economic development. They introduced new plants and obliged every household to grow cotton to make cloth. This, however, was for the families' own use and not for the Japanese war effort. Similar to the situation in Timor, the occupiers also forced people to open up new fields such as at Ramo in Mesara. The conditions of forced labour were so hard that the work was known as *kerja mati* (death work [In]). If people were found to be slow workers they were beaten.

Many stories about the Japanese occupation focus on the brutality of the new masters. Similar to everywhere else in occupied Southeast Asia, the Japanese soldiers forcibly abducted local women and girls for their 'comfort'. A number of children resulted from these cases of sexual exploitation, but they did not stay

---

[82] Interview with Marthen Heke Medo (30.06.2012).

in Savu after the war, probably for reasons of social ostracism. Some women used the soot from certain plants to blacken their teeth because the Japanese did not appreciate this feature—hopefully it meant the soldiers left them alone. The juridical system was arbitrary to say the least. If two Savunese had a dispute, the Japanese occupiers believed the first of the contenders who reported the argument to the authorities; arrest and punishment befell his opponent. The Japanese applied severe torture at times; for instance, they would hang from a tree and cane anyone transgressing their authority. If he passed out, the soldiers doused him with buckets of water and continued beating him with the rottan. Japanese soldiers sometimes entered the households and confiscated any available food including chicken, eggs and sorghum. Neither was the elite always spared. The Japanese arrested the imposing Fettor We Tanya (d. 1961), considering him too loyal to the former Dutch masters, and took him to Rote. Nevertheless, he was luckier than most people the Japanese captured. Together with another Savunese he escaped and stole a *sampan* (a flat-bottomed boat with two oars). The two of them managed to row back to Savu and the fettor somehow survived the war years.[83]

There were various measures to defend the small island from allied incursions. In the later stages of the occupation the troops largely consisted of Savunese people who had undergone military training. The ethnic Japanese in Savu were basically the Maidan (military staff). The Japanese established a coast-guard system selecting a number of people living near the seashore to keep watch against any boat arriving from the sea. If the Japanese guards saw the crafts before the local coastguards, the Savunese received beatings and were dismissed. Reportedly, the Japanese forbade the Savunese from lighting fires to reduce their visibility to the Allies. It was a major impediment for people who were used to burning rubbish and setting fire to the fields after harvest.

Allied air raids over the eastern region from Australian bases intensified towards the end of war and cities such as Kupang and Ambon lay in ruins. Not even Savu was entirely spared in spite of its somewhat limited strategic value. The Allies attempted to bomb Teni Hawu, the site of local Japanese command; however, both bombs missed the palace complex and exploded nearby. A third bomb fell in the river estuary in Seba's harbour without exploding. The bombings, however ineffective, facilitated a hasty and inglorious end to Japanese rule in Savu. Immediately after the air attack, the Japanese embarked on a Chinese ship loaded with mother-of-pearl which they presumably wanted to barter on their journey. They also took their so-called 'comfort women' on board the vessel. Thus equipped they left the island, never to return. Japan officially

---

[83] Interview with Petrus Bara Pa (15.11.2015).

capitulated on 2 September 1945. The Allied command decided that Australian troops would occupy the eastern region on behalf of the Dutch. The Japanese occupation had been a traumatic experience for most people, though it may have been less atrocious than in many other parts of the archipelago. It was a historically important four years: the occupation facilitated the opening up of Savunese society to the outside world through education and awakened it to the political winds that blew across the archipelago.

Revolution!

By the time the Allies occupied the Timor Residency, the flames of the Indonesian National Revolution were already engulfing the central and western islands. Leaders of the Indonesian independence movement, Sukarno (soon to be the new nation's first president, 1949–66) and Mohammad Hatta (its prime minister, 1948–50), had already issued their proclamation of independence in Jakarta on 17 August 1945, in defiance of the Allies, sparking over four years of conflict and turmoil. A Savunese man, Riwu Ga, played a role on that seminal August day. He had been a trusted assistant of Bung Karno (as Sukarno was known) during his Dutch-enforced exile in Ende (1933–42) and had followed the leader to Batavia. After Sukarno had read the proclamation, Riwu Ga hired a jeep and drove throughout the streets of Batavia shouting "*Merdeka* (independent)" and disseminated the news (Rohi 2004). Word of the proclamation spread in the following months while actual fighting against the Dutch and Allied troops began in October.

Many people in Java, Sumatra and Sulawesi were sympathetic to the republican cause. However, enthusiasm was considerably less in the outer areas, which were ruled by Dutch-appointed rajas, and still had a rather traditional structure. The mainly Javanese and Muslim character of the revolutionary movement made it less appealing to peoples in the Timor Residency. The Allied takeover of eastern Indonesia in fact went smoothly. A ship with an Australian battalion and a very small Dutch detachment departed from Darwin and reached severely ravaged Kupang on 11 September without meeting the least resistance. The atmosphere among the allies was tense, however: the Australian commander Dyke irritated his Dutch colleague De Rooy by refusing him a place in the talks with the local Japanese and hoisting the Australian flag on landing. De Rooy gained his revenge when the Dutch representatives were enthusiastically greeted by the locals who were "simply crazy from joy".[84]

---

[84] *Rapportage Indonesië*, 02.10.29, No. 757, Report, 15 September 1945.

Nor did the Dutch and Australians meet any armed resistance in the rest of Timor or the adjacent islands. The Allies disarmed 4,000 Japanese troops in Timor and 10,000 in Flores. A Dutch report confirms the oral account that there were no Japanese in Savu at the point of capitulation, nor were there any in Rote.[85] Thus, the Dutch colonial army (NICA) rapidly gained control of the region, although it took some time before the smaller islands around Timor received visits from Dutch or Allied representatives (Farram 2003: 216). Nevertheless, there was much republican agitation from educated persons who had decided that the colonial regime had run its course. The Dutch arranged a conference in Malino, Sulawesi in July 1946 with delegates from Kalimantan and the eastern islands, expecting them to support a continued connection with the Netherlands. However, the delegates' demands for genuine autonomy surprised the Dutch. Meanwhile, several Savunese fought the Dutch in central Indonesia, joining the Paradja battalion. This unit was named after Marthijn Marseha Paradja, a Savunese who had led a mutiny on board the Dutch vessel *De Zeven Provincien* in 1933 and was killed in the process. Among the fighters were Is Tibuludji and El Tari who gained prominence after independence—the former as a senior military leader and the latter as governor of Nusa Tenggara Timur (NTT, West Timor) from 1966 to 1978.[86]

Conditions in Savu were relatively tranquil during the revolution. Raja Paulus Charles Jawa simply went from being a Japanese *syuco* to a Dutch zelfbestuurder and there was no recorded open resistance. The lack of agitation was partly related to the isolated character of the island. The Dutch administration in Kupang arranged a conference in Kefamenanu in West Timor from 21 to 23 October 1946 and almost all of the rajas in the Residency attended. The aim was to stabilise the new Timor Federation through which the colonial regime hoped to maintain power. From a Dutch point of view the meeting was a success. The only raja unable to appear was Paulus Charles Jawa; however, it was not from unwillingness—there was neither a ship going there nor radio communications. The meeting decided to send three delegates to a larger convention in Denpasar, Bali.[87] This was followed by the Dutch proclamation of the so-called federal state of East Indonesia in December. This was a creation that encompassed the five residences—Bali-Lombok, South Sulawesi, North Sulawesi, Maluku, and Timor and Adjacent Islands. Under the last-mentioned were four autonomous regions,

---

[85] Ibid.

[86] Kaho 2005: 29–31; Passar 2005: 205, 277–8. The airport outside Kupang is named after El Tari.

[87] *Rapportage Indonesië*, 02.10.29, No. 749, October 1946.

one of which was also called Timor and Adjacent Islands. Within this region, Savu constituted a *swapraja* (zelfbestuur).

Although the "state" had its own president and cabinet it was obvious to all that it was a Dutch creation. NIT (Negara Indonesia Timur, State of East Indonesia) was jokingly interpreted as *Negara Ikut Tuan* (state following the master). Nevertheless, the Dutch Resident Cornelis Schüller initially found the situation in the Timor region to be favourable (*gunstig*), although he deemed the Javanese in Kupang a possible source of problems. A number of non-governmental organisations evolved in Kupang which the authorities nervously monitored. Of the six in existence by late 1946, at least two had individual or organisational bonds with Savu. Persatuan Demokrasi Indonesia Timur (PDIT, Democratic Association of East Indonesia) had the Savunese intellectual and later national hero Izaak Huru Doko (1913–85) as the chair. Doko had been educated in Kupang as a teacher, was a champion of independence from colonial rule and had a political role during the Japanese occupation. For the Dutch he was an uncomfortable figure. An educational inspector described with consternation how the "notorious collaborator" Doko approached him in a confrontative and challenging way, complaining that "a few Japanese underlings now speak in the name of the Timorese people".[88]

Doko was nevertheless appointed as a delegate to the Denpasar conference which led to the creation of East Indonesia.[89] The other organisation was Serikat Sabu Studiefonds (SSS, Savu Study Funds Union) with A. Rihi as the chair and a board that included Doko and three others. The aim of the organisation was to create a study fund, in the first place for Savunese people. To gauge the number of potential members, the organisation reckoned all the taxable Savunese in the residency willing to contribute a guilder per year.[90] Another interest group, Penabungan Kaum Savu (PKS, Savunese People's Savings) was created in June 1947, the next year. It had parallels to SSS but was geared towards economic and social issues among the Savunese in Savu and Timor. According to its statutes, it was not to meddle in political affairs. Nevertheless, the group arranged an open meeting in Airnona, Timor with S. We Tanya of Dimu's fettor family. I.H. Doko and the Menadonese A. Rotti, members of the parliament of East Indonesia, spoke of their political experiences, as nervously noted in a Dutch report.[91]

---

[88] *Rapportage Indonesië*, 02.10.29, No. 757, Relation, 13 March 1946. For a reverent nationalist biography of I.H. Doko as a national hero, see Manafe (2009). A prominent educationist, he was elevated to the status of national hero in 2006.

[89] *Rapportage Indonesië*, 02.10.29, No. 749, second half of November 1946.

[90] *Rapportage Indonesië*, 02.10.29, No. 749, first half of November 1946.

[91] *Rapportage Indonesië*, 02.10.29, No. 749, June 1947.

One of the members of the PKS was Ruben Rohi Mone who had been working as a lighthouse guard (*lichtwachter*). While the SSS and PKS were connected to the expatriate community in Timor, Rohi Mone created a Savu-based organisation in September 1948 which was explicitly political. This was the reading society Taman Pembacaan whose members eagerly studied the republican paper *Merdeka* and used its content as a basis for their political schooling. Even the isolated island began to feel the powerful dynamics of the revolution, as the Dutch gezaghebber witnessed. When the gezaghebber made an unexpected visit to Savu shortly after the founding of Taman Pembacaan he noted to his irritation a sign hanging at the entrance of the auxiliary hospital. The text made it clear that this was a place where one could speak of *kemerdekaan* (independence).[92]

However, it is apparent that most of the population in the Timor Residency, in Savu as elsewhere, was relatively untouched by the political developments. In a report from January 1949 Resident Verhoef remarked on what little notice people paid to events in Indonesia. In his opinion, people lacked insight into what passed beyond their own little world, what anthropologists term a parochial outlook. This was also the reason why people believed the most outlandish stories, as is clear from the evidence Verhoef provides. A steersman who worked on a KPM ship that travelled to Savu in early January returned with news of a tale that had been circulating on the island. It was said that all the Dutchmen had already left the region and there were no more Dutch ships or airplanes. The currency began to decline in value and prices started going up. The steersman recounted that when the KPM boat arrived in Savu people were astonished to see that a Dutch ship had appeared.[93]

It is not surprising that conditions in resource-scarce Savu were meagre after more than three years of Japanese rule. In 1947, for example, the Kupang authorities had to send paddy plants to the island and there was a decline in the production of lontar syrup.[94] The Dutch and East Indonesian authorities nevertheless entertained hopes of developing Savu at least marginally, in the first place through the export of livestock. They introduced new cattle—as opposed to buffalos—sharing breeding pairs among the populace favouring the 'small man' in order to avoid concentrations among the well-to-do. There were also initiatives to expand the *ladang* (dry field) land. Horses, the traditional export item, were an important part of the plans to develop the local economy. There was a demand for horses in other places of East Indonesia, such as the port town

---

[92] *Rapportage Indonesië*, 02.10.29, No. 749, second half of September 1948.

[93] *Rapportage Indonesië*, 02.10.29, No. 749, first half of January 1949.

[94] *Rapportage Indonesië*, 02.10.29, No. 749, first half of January 1947.

of Menado in North Sulawesi, and in 1946/47 Savu exported 400 animals.[95] At the same time the balance of trade was decidedly to the disadvantage of the Savunese. In 1946, the island's imports amounted to 116,000 guilders while generating only 65,000 in exports.[96]

To achieve any commercial expansion, Savu needed regular communications. However, the tardy facilities of KPM shipping impeded reliable transportation. To improve commercial interaction within the Timor Regency the authorities arranged for a new shipping line in mid-1947. A boat with cargo facilities went via the route Timor–Rote–Savu–Sumba–Sumbawa–Bali–Java once every third week. Towards the very end of colonial rule new technology finally ended Savu's isolation. On 31 August, a new radio installation in Seba made its first transmission amidst much celebration. The former lighthouse guard R. Rohi Mone gave a speech with strong political overtones declaring that "the people are no more for the raja, but the raja is for the people". Paulus Charles Jawa was in the audience and the speech presumably served as a reminder that the Savunese elite lived on borrowed time.

As Rohi Mone delivered his pronouncement, negotiations for Indonesian independence were already underway in The Hague. The inability to stamp out republican resistance and international pressure forced the Dutch to seek a diplomatic solution and relinquish their vast colonial island empire after more than three centuries. In September 1949, before the negotiations were over, the colonial apparatus transferred the governing capacities to the various *daerah* (regions) in East Indonesia. On 28 September, during a ceremony in Kupang, the Dutch devolved power to the College of Delegates for the Region of Timor and Islands. People sang the new national anthem of republican Indonesia, '*Indonesia Raya* (Great Indonesia)', but not the Dutch anthem '*Het Wilhelmus* (lit. The William)'.[97] According to Resident Verhoef's last report, it created an unpleasant atmosphere.[98] The world's biggest island country, the United States of Indonesia, proclaimed itself fully independent in December 1949 and included East Indonesia as a constituent part. By this time, the main political institutions in West Timor generally supported the Republic. It is less clear how readily tiny Savu accepted independence, but the relative lack of Dutch interference on the

---

[95] *Rapportage Indonesië*, 02.10.29, No. 749, July 1947.

[96] *Rapportage Indonesië*, 02.10.29, No. 749, March 1947.

[97] The national anthem about William of Orange, first written down in the early 1570s, is the world's oldest, though the Dutch government did not accept it as the official anthem until 1932. Of note is that it stems from the Netherland's own struggles for independence from the Spanish Empire.

[98] *Rapportage Indonesië*, 02.10.29, No. 749, September 1949. A. Verhoef wrote it in Singaraja, Bali on 30 September.

island may have rendered the old colonial power less oppressive in the eyes of the local elite.[99] The effects of the republican fervor of I.H. Doko and other Kupang-based Savunese in Savu were presumably limited. However, many Indonesians saw the federal aspect of the political solution as illegitimate and entailing a colonial heritage. East Indonesia was eventually dissolved in August 1950 and was included in the unitary Republic of Indonesia.

The period from 1900 to 1950 saw dramatic changes in the archipelago: from the "ethical policy" and the wave of colonial conquests in the first years of the 20th century, through the relatively stable period of the colonial state, the Japanese occupation, the revolution, to eventual independence and the formation of a unitary state. Although the centre of gravity might have been the central and western parts of the archipelago, this chapter has demonstrated that each of these stages left imprints on the small world of Savu. For most people, the life they led in 1950 might not have been too dissimilar to conditions in 1900, but they certainly felt the political and economic changes. The uprising of 1914 followed the implementation of colonial governance that had counterparts all over the outer islands, with increasing demands on the locals to pay for administrative modernity. As in Flores, Timor, Sumbawa and so on, the increasing presence of the colonial state made for brief but easily suppressed resistance. Nevertheless, most of the elite supported or at least accepted the reorganisation of Savu and Raijua into one zelfbesturend landschap, an island-wide monarchy that was a novelty for the two islands. In spite of this stability, it is clear that the system brought tension because Savunese leaders displayed cleptocratic tendencies under the protection of the colonial state. This, too, is closely paralleled by developments in other colonised parts of the world: indigenous ruling structures became bureaucratic but still pursued new ways of appropriating land and resources. Nevertheless, the *Pax Neerlandica* provided a measure of public safety, as well as small advantages in the form of education, modern medicine and regular communications. The winds of war and anti-colonial resistance in the 1940s saw very little physical fighting in Savu, although individual Savunese played a role in the Indonesian Revolution in other parts of Indonesia. The lack of natural resources of industrial value, the near-absence of colonial establishments and the faraway location made the islanders less susceptible to political agitation than societies in Java, Sumatra and Sulawesi. It was left to the new republican government to change the living conditions even for insulated peoples in the east of the new island realm.

---

[99] This is highlighted in Brigitte Raskin's largely documentary novel *Radja Tanja* (1998). The novel depicts reverends and teachers having taught the old fettor (in the novel 'raja') We Tanya respect for the Dutch. We Tanya did not share the republicans' resentment for the colonial regime, as the Dutch left Savu to its own devices and did not establish colonial entrepreneurs on the island (Raskin 1998: 17).

Towards the Tip: Continuity and Change After 1949

As the chapter discusses more recent times, the expression 'towards the tip' both symbolises Savu's primary mental structure for remembering and reflects the newer history of the 'young growth'. It underlines the botanical idiom of growth from the root to the tip which, as a concept, is a constant reference embedded in all aspects of society and, as chapter 3 concludes, an essential matrix for organising time in Savu.

Administrative incorporation

The new Indonesian republic shared an important characteristic with many territories which became independent after World War II. Colonial policy had ultimately defined their territorial extent and they had few 'natural' ethnic or geographical borders. The new nation, whose name had only recently gained popularity, was to manage many hundreds of distinct cultures and languages.[1] Thus, the nationalists, catapulted into positions of power, had to integrate a complex territory across 17,000 islands bequeathed by the colonial state. In spite of all the anti-colonial rhetoric, the fledgling republic made a virtue out of necessity and kept features of the old colonial organisation, and the manner of conducting public affairs, until they were ready to introduce something better (Hoadley 2006: 89–91). This also applied to the innumerable rajas, sultans and *panembahan*s (ruling princes) heading the Indonesian principalities from Sumatra to the Papuan Islands, and where the Jawa raja of Savu was far from an atypical example.

These aristocratic figures continued to lead their territories for the interim, as *kepala daerah swapraja* (headmen of self-ruling regions). However, they were widely seen as feudal and colonial remnants, and the fact that they had tended to support the Dutch during the revolution did not help their case. This was

---

[1] British scholar J.R. Logan first employed the name 'Indonesia' in 1850, replacing the term 'Indian Archipelago' then currently in use, and independence-seeking nationalists adopted it after World War I.

paralleled by the republican mistrust of the *priyayi* (upper class, especially during the colonial period) in Java who had collaborated with the Dutch and was often oriented towards Dutch culture. Such people were kept out of the central organs of the new republic, but in the outer islands with a shorter history of implemented colonial governance, the aristocrats could not be replaced as easily (Hoadley 2006: 91). Beset by a number of serious political and economic problems, including armed uprisings, the new leaders had little option but to leave the hereditary rulers temporarily in position. During the transitional period in the 1950s, central governmental services were functioning on a modest scale, and the state was primarily concerned with overcoming the inner convulsions and problems that arose.

Nevertheless, the Jawas and other princely lineages were living on borrowed time. Administrative changes in the late 1950s and early 1960s brought an end to the petty monarchies. Paulus Charles Jawa remained the headman of Savu until he passed away in 1963, leaving no children. Savu was made a subdistrict under the Kupang Regency (*kabupaten*). Much later, in October 2008, the government announced it was to be a regency of its own. In some parts of Indonesia, such as Timor, North Maluku and Java, there has been a lasting attachment to the defunct principalities with cases of revivalism (or 'sultanism') under the republican umbrella, in particular after the fall of President Soeharto in 1998. There is little to suggest such sentiments existed in Savu. The united *landschap* of Savu was too brief to imprint on the local community. Outside Seba the collective memory of the royal Jawa brothers is weak. Local identity has rather focused on the ritual hierarchies of the traditional domains, just as it has since proto-historical times.

The first independent decade in Indonesia was devoted to a democratic experiment that included one general election before the project was dismantled. The Java-based parties began to attract followers in the Timor area and by 1953 there were nine political parties. As seen in the previous chapter, educated Savunese played a role in local politics during the revolution. I.H. Doko was one of the main figures of PDIT while his fellow islander Max Rihi led the youth wing (Farram 2004: 233–4). Doko was also the minister of education in the cabinet of East Indonesia. After President Sukarno had established the unitary republic in 1950, Doko continued as the head of the provincial education department until 1971. This gave him a vital role in the region's political and social development, underpinned by his association with President Sukarno (Farram 2004: 290). In several publications he wrote about local—and in an Indonesian-wide context—completely unknown historical figures who had resisted the Dutch colonialists and worked for national independence. As did a large part of this genre of historiography, his studies had shortcomings: he tried to portray supposedly nationalistic personalities in the best possible light, but at least they conveyed a degree of knowledge of the Timor area's local history to an Indonesian-speaking audience.

The highlight of the democratic period was the election of 1955, the only one that was free and fair before 1999. The elections were considered a success in the Timor area and obviously served to educate people in political matters on a scale previously unknown (Farram 2004: 292). However, Savu's isolated position made it difficult to assess news about the outside world, as shown by a tragicomic incident. After the end of vote counting in Liae, a police officer called Mone Obo took the results to Seba. When he passed Lede Pemulu, a hill that overlooks the north and the south coasts, he started to shout that foreign military ships were coming. The effect was tremendous: panic seized the population and the news spread rapidly to all parts of the island. People ran to hide in caves, in the forest, or hid at home. The fettor of Mesara put all the recently collected tax money into a bag and ran to a hiding place. *Mone Ama* held ceremonies to render the island invisible. People also killed animals and immediately consumed the meat to prevent the enemy taking it. When it became clear that no foreigners were attacking Savu, people returned home. This period coincided with an epidemic and many cattle died. The *Mone Ama* saw the death of the livestock in relation to the elections and the general panic.[2]

The year of living dangerously[3]*—even on a small island*

Savu in the post-1949 era is generally without dramatic events. There was relatively little bloodshed after the internecine wars stopped in the 19th century and the Japanese interregnum was perhaps harsh rather than atrocious. The contrast is obvious when compared with Savu's unfortunate neighbour Timor and, in particular, East Timor (officially now Timor-Leste). There is however one particular episode that has created a deep trauma which has not been lessened by the silence that has surrounded it until recently. Not surprisingly it is the infamous chain of events in 1965–66. The supposed 'Communist coup' attempt of 30 September 1965, which saw the murder of six generals in Jakarta, resulted in militarist-right-wing retaliation that would eventually bring Soeharto to power and inaugurate the authoritarian New Order regime. A large-scale wave of killings commenced where the victims were Partai Komunis Indonesia (PKI, Communist Party of Indonesia) members as well as anyone suspected of being a communist or associated with them (Ricklefs 2001: 338–42). While most

---

[2] Interview with Petrus Bara Pa (17.05.2014).

[3] Referencing Christopher Koch's 1978 novel of the same name set against the background of 1965 and the overthrow of President Sukarno.

studies of the killings have concentrated on Java and Bali, the province of NTT (West Timor, Flores, Sumba and adjacent islands) and even the small island of Savu were not spared the atrocities. It is of significance to see how events that began in Java were replicated in a local and relatively isolated setting.

As the situation in Savu became tense and insecure, the police trained people in the civil defense corps (Pertahan Sipil or Hansip) to maintain order. Physical violence commenced in 1965 as shops in Seba were torched. The school in Ledemawide and the church near it were also burnt down; the newly built school in Menia was torched and its director, Salmon Bèngu, was falsely accused of the crime. He was nevertheless set free in the end. As is common everywhere in Indonesia, people do not like to talk about this period. The unwritten rule of silence that accompanied Soeharto's New Order regime still prevails. However, in 2010 the Christian Evangelical Church (Gereja Masehi Injili di Timor, GMIT) eventually initiated interviews with the survivors, the widows and children of the victims. The results were published in 2012 under the telling title *Memori-memori terlarang* (Forbidden memories).[4]

It appears that people in Savu, as elsewhere in the archipelago, were taken into custody without having the opportunity to defend themselves. In March 1966 hundreds of people in Mesara were summoned to the fettor's house, spreading fear throughout the population. However, most of them were soon released. Of those arrested were members of the Aelungi clan owing to quarrels over landownership in Lede Ae—in the course of the killings across Indonesia the anti-Communist attacks often overlapped opportunistically with local disputes. In each of the districts those detained and taken to Seba were mainly educated young men and women—teachers and public servants. Teacher Petrus Bara Pa was pulled out of his class and told to keep watch over the prisoners, many of whom were his colleagues and friends. He was told "*pilih mati atau hidup*" (choose to die or to live). The Raeloro health post was turned into a prison and Beha Lado, who lived next to it, had no choice but to guard the prisoners detained there.[5] Late in the evening of 29 March, 34 of the male prisoners, accompanied by their guards, marched to Hanga Loko Pedae[6] where they were executed en masse. Twenty of them were teachers. The bloodbath was such that the guards forced to attend the execution, carried out by a squad from Java, first went to the seashore

---

[4] Kolimon and Wetangterah 2012 (*Forbidden memories* [in English], Monash, 2015). In Savu the Protestant priest Paolina Bara Pa conducted the interviews.

[5] Interviews with Beha Lado (14.12.2005) and Petrus Bara Pa (17.05.2014). See also the Petrus Bara Pa interview in *Tempo Magazine* (1 June 2014: 62–3).

[6] This expression means 'the river valley where a talk took place' and refers to the meeting between Tèro Weo and Jami Lobo after the latter kidnapped Tèro Weo's wife (Chapter 6).

to wash themselves and their clothes before returning home. None of the 22 women arrested were executed, but their heads were shaven and they were taken to Kupang. Sixteen of them were teachers and they were henceforth banned from practising their profession. Needless to say this slaughter was detrimental to the yet-to-be-developed educational system in Savu. As a consequence, even today the lack of trained teachers remains a problem for the young *kabupaten* (regency) (*Memori-memori terlarang* 2012: 180–1).

The name Loko Pedae, already mentioned, has significance in Savu. It is where Fettor Jami Lobo and the raja of Menia held a meeting and talked (*pedae*) before going to war in the early 18th century. However, the prisoners of 29 March were not permitted to speak in their defence, a fact that has a poignant irony in light of the place's name. Among those arrested in March 1966 were two Jingi Tiu followers. A decisive consequence of the 1966 executions was that people converted to Christianity in order to evade persecution or be labelled "Communists". This explains the mass conversions that took place in the 1970s. This closely paralleled developments in other parts of Indonesia where the violence of 1965–66 triggered widespread conversion to the state-approved world religions.[7]

Disaster did not strike just once. If the tragic events of March 1966 were not enough, the notorious Savu Sea also took its toll. On 29 July 1966 the ship *Tangiri* sailing from Savu to Kupang sank in bad weather near Rote. There were no survivors. Among the victims were the subdistrict head of Savu, Ruben Rohi Mone, his son Jara Rohi, as well as Alexander Riwu Doko, the son of the dynastic strongman David (also known as Daud) D. Bire Luji. In the traumatic aftermath of multiple deaths, people explained the calamity as the result of a curse on the island in 1965 and 1966.[8] And there was more evil ahead. The *Tangiri* left Savu at the same time as another ship belonging to the popular and well-known Captain Doko who had two ships to service the route between Savu and Kupang. Although his ship did not capsize, he did not live much longer. Doko was soon arrested and executed in Kupang on suspicion of friendship with PKI members. The charge against him shows that it did not take much to condemn someone during such tumultuous days: he was suspected of delivering rice to party members in Dehla in Rote.[9] He is otherwise remembered positively by the population for his honest character and charisma.

---

[7] The official religions of Indonesia are Islam, Protestantism, Catholicism, Hinduism, Buddhism and Confucianism, ranked in order of decreasing size according to the 2010 Indonesian census.

[8] Interview with Marthen Heke Medo (17.05.2014).

[9] Interview with Pastor Franz Lackner (05.05.2014).

Elite survival

The long rule of Soeharto (1966–98) meant increasing administrative centralisation of Indonesia and an end to the previous relative political pluralism. While almost all traces of princely rule had been abrogated in the region by this time,[10] the old aristocratic lineages occasionally managed to transform their authority into modern ways of wielding power. This was very much the case in Savu. Among the people who were arrested in March 1966 were some who had voiced dissent against the recently deceased raja of Savu. These people asked for the abolition of the rajas' personal landownership. After Raja Paulus Charles Jawa died in 1963, the cases concerning the fields he confiscated remained unresolved. Memories of the raja were not altogether rosy: he had more than regained the five rupiahs or the one guilder owed to him—unpaid debts being the reason for the land seizures. Although he had no sons, there was no lack of family members from collateral branches. David D. Bire Luji replaced Paulus Charles Jawa as the dynastic strongman and became the first subdistrict head of Seba. If any of the owners of the confiscated rice fields were with the 1966 protestors, they obviously had just cause. However, they were not given the opportunity to voice their claims.

The previous chapter considers a case of land passing from mother to daughter, namely the *rai lere* land in Delo which Nia Nguru had received from her brother in 1841. It was passed down to her daughter Moi Bèngu, then to her granddaughter Nia Rohi and finally in 1946 to Tali Nia alias Bertha Jawa. She was married to Daniel Raja Pono, but there were no children from the marriage. The couple lived in Jakarta so Bertha's cousin, who was the raja of Savu Paulus Charles Jawa, administered the land in her name. Later, D.D. Bire Luji took over the task. When Bertha Jawa passed away in 1971, there were no surviving female descendants of Nia Nguru. Therefore, according to adat the land had to return to the Nadowu clan of Dimu which made the initial gift. D.D. Bire Luji ignored the requirement and continued to 'take care' of the plantations until his death in 1981. Moreover, his widow continued to 'take care' of the land until she passed away. Her sister, the widow of Raja P.C. Jawa, decided to keep the land 'caretaker' role. However, the tides were turning in Indonesia and even in Savu the population resented the situation as unfair. Finally, the Nadowu clan received its land back, after compensating Ibu Raja Sabu with nine buffalos—nine being the compulsory number in Seba for matters of adat.

The Nadowu land case underlines the power of the ruling elite during Soeharto times. Nobody dared challenge the subdistrict head or his widow with

---

[10] Some of the rajas (*manek*) in Rote were in charge of their territories up to circa 1970.

their rightful claims. The grip of the raja descendants on the land thus continued after independence. Although the raja position no longer existed, subdistrict leaders—often recruited from the same lineage or clans as the rajas and fettors of colonial times—continued similar practices. It was only towards the end of the Soeharto era, but more particularly after his fall, that things started to change and people began to take the initiative in voicing their claims. Often these were for land rights, plots of land that had been taken from them to become *tanah gerakan* (land which had been moved, in fact, confiscated by the local ruler), so they could pay the taxes demanded by the colonial power.

Religious tradition and Indonesian conformity

As the previous chapters have shown, Christianity made a slow start in Savu. In the first half of the 20th century, most people still adhered to Jingi Tiu beliefs. As in Timor, Christianity became the religion of the majority but only after the Dutch had left.[11] After 1966, anyone associated with traditional practices was considered to be 'without religion' and was therefore potentially dangerous: Communism and atheism were closely associated in the New Order discourse— both were considered subversive. In 1976, the various *Mone Ama* met at Namata in Seba and decided to contact the provincial governor to complain about the threats and brutal treatment experienced by followers of the old religion. An incident at the same time seemed to back their case. A mass baptism was to take place in Seba on 13 September 1976. However, on that day heavy rains fell even though it was the dry season. The river beds flooded and people were not able to reach Seba for the sacrament. Needless to say, the Savunese did not view such coincidences lightly. Some days later, an envoy from the governor arrived with an order that forbade forced conversions. Nevertheless, membership in the Protestant church grew steadily in these decades, from 19,982 souls in 1971 to 36,481 (out of 57,609) in 1987 and 47,692 (out of 63,617) in 1998 (Kaho 2005: 166–7).

While Protestantism made advances in the wake of the 1965–66 bloodshed, another branch of Christianity made modest gains. From 1956 to 1967 the Catholic Church, without a presence in Savu for several centuries, was represented by Pater Piet Konijnsun normally an inhabitant of Rote. He also visited Savu from time to time because three Catholic police from Flores were posted there. In 1967 a young Austrian Jesuit priest, Franz Lackner, arrived in

---

[11] The congregations of the Indische Kerk in the Timor Residency were included in the new Gereja Masehi Injili di Timor (GMIT, Christian Evangelical Church of Timor) on 31 October 1947 (Kaho 2005: 165).

Savu. He was originally posted to Rote but his duties extended to Savu and later to Raijua. On his arrival there was only one Catholic family of mixed Filipino origin on the island. In the course of time he was able to build Catholic primary schools in isolated villages in Mesara (Prema) and Liae (Mehona) for which he recruited some of the teachers who had been banned from practising their professions in 1966. In Mèba a small church was built as well as two boarding houses, one for girls and one for boys. Accommodation was free for high school students of any religion who had to walk long distances to attend classes. The bulk of the students came from Liae, Mesara and Raijua which did not have a high school until the time of *Reformasi* (Reformation) after 1998.[12] Both boarding houses still function at their maximum capacity as some high school students still have to walk up to two hours one way to reach the subdistrict high school. Sometimes they attend for just one or two lessons when the teachers have meetings or complete administrative work. When in 2008 the regency was created, each subdistrict received covered trucks to take children to school; however, this did not last more than two years as the trucks' maintenance costs were too high for the district. These blue trucks were subsequently rented to private persons to transport all sorts of materials but no longer school children. Statistics from 2015 indicate that two per cent of the population is Catholic. The numbers are dwarfed by the 90 per cent who are Protestant and are significantly higher than the figures for Muslims (0.9 per cent), Jingi Tiu (7.24) and "others" (0.01 per cent).[13]

New branches of the Protestant Church—primarily the Adventists and the Bethel Church—arrived in Savu in the 1980s. In October 1999, a Christian prayer team (Bethel Church) from Timor decided to establish a church on the top of Kebuhu hill; it seems one of their followers had had a dream in which God told him to build on the exact place where he found an arrangement of small megaliths. Kebuhu is the second highest hill in Savu and has been known as the 'mast' of the land since mythological times. On this sacred hill the Jingi Tiu priests hold some of their rituals using the stones for their offerings. The place is not the prerogative of one council of priests; rather, it can be worshiped by any *Mone Ama* and any Savunese individual. To proceed with the church construction, the prayer team disturbed the layout of the stones. The act enraged not only Jingi Tiu people but also a number of Savunese Christians who wanted to maintain their ancestors' sacred place as they had left it. One Sunday after mass, people started the arduous walk to the top of the hill. There is no road

---

[12]   See p. 421 for further information on *Reformasi.*

[13]   See Appendix VI.

leading to Kebuhu, no trees to provide shade from the scorching sun and no village nearby.[14] As the gathering turned into a confrontation, outnumbering the New Church members, they had to abandon their plans. The Jingi Tiu priests put the stones back in position, held a ceremony and no church was allowed to be built on the sacred hill. A positive outcome of this event was the population's new awareness of the importance of the traditions. In the first decade of the 21st century people have become more tolerant towards the Jingi Tiu priests as keepers of the island's memory and protectors of the traditions.[15]

Nevertheless, globalisation has had its effect on belief systems. In Indonesia, people are expected to conform to the main tenets of the six officially acknowledged world religions. In today's Savu, a great majority are Christians, mainly Protestant Calvinists. As such, they do not acknowledge or recognise the values of the "*kafir*" (pagan [Arabic] or the ancestral religion, Jingi Tiu) people as the foundations of their culture.[16] Some are more interested in the stories, especially the genealogies, of the Bible than in their own ancestors. Within the next generation it is a very real possibility that the cultural knowledge kept so far by the Jingi Tiu people will die out along with their religion.

The political and judicial systems of modern Indonesia, and the predominance of a monotheistic religion, have influenced the practices and meaning of life-crisis ceremonies. Christians are told that ancestors should no longer play a role in their lives. A number of sacred or mantra texts chanted on such occasions are no longer seen as relevant and are likely to vanish from people's memories. However, the case of the teacher Beha Lado sheds some light on syncretism. In the early 2000s, Beha Lado, then in his seventies, started to prepare for his funeral, building next to his house a family tomb large enough for his ten children and their families. For the first time, he wrote down in a booklet his paternal and maternal genealogies, as well as the mantra names of his children.[17] When he passed away in 2007 his funeral ceremony borrowed from Savunese traditions as well as from Christian practices. A traditional ritual took place in the house with laments and chants before the coffin was carried out to the veranda for the Protestant ceremony. Then those officiating at the ceremony opened the booklet and read aloud Beha Lado's mantra name; it was greeted with a profound silence. The booklet's mantra names for his children also were read out. One of his sons, Elo, had known only part of his own mantra name and was surprised to have

---

[14]   It seems the location was far from practical for the purpose of attracting people to Sunday mass.

[15]   Interview with Elo Lado (Malobo) (26.05.2000).

[16]   The originally Muslim term *kafir* is also used by Christians to refer to the Jingi Tiu religion.

[17]   Once, as he was discussing genealogies with G. Duggan, he revealed the booklet.

received the longest mantra name of his siblings. His father had often disapproved of Elo's lifestyle and their relationship was frequently tense. In giving his son a long and intricate mantra name, the father showed his concern for his son as well as his hope that these powerful words would guide and protect him throughout life. Perhaps his father's decision played a role in his later success as Elo became a member of the People's Regional Representative Council (DPRD, Dewan Perwakilan Rakyat Daerah) in 2014. Most of the children and grandchildren of Beha Lado live on other islands. They returned to their homes after the funeral, all with a copy of the booklet. Hopefully, documenting oral practices, as Beha Lado did, will help to preserve some of Savu's past and traditions, especially for descendants who have migrated to other islands, and provide their children or grandchildren with a sense of the richness and particularity of Savunese culture.

The role women play in modern religions is not comparable to their traditional Jingi Tiu tasks. For example, following custom, women play a predominant role at family funerals, providing the deceased with the prescribed cloth to ensure his/her entrance to the ancestral realms of the same *wini*. In accordance with traditional beliefs women conduct a number of rituals as wives of *Mone Ama* priests. In the specific organisations shaped by the moieties (*hubi*) and the *wini* women also have an important role to play. All villages should have a number of small buildings called *tegida*—for members of a *wini* to meet to worship the group's founding ancestress, asking her to protect the *wini* people and take care of them. Christian women no longer attend meetings at the *tegida*, especially on the night of ritual (*bui ihi*) at full moon in the last month of the adat calendar where the women check their heirloom baskets and gradually replace damaged weavings. A large part of traditions are vanishing owing to the neglect of activities related to the *tegida*. Modern religions do not offer women similar or compensatory roles. Under modern Indonesian law women have arguably fewer rights than with adat law.

However, one tradition has been experiencing a revival among Christian Savunese migrants who pass away overseas. Known as *rukètu* (returning the hair to the home land), this practice originated in a narrative about the remote ancestor Jawa Miha, discussed in chapter 1.[18] After he fled from Savu and was about to die abroad, he asked that his hair be wrapped in his head cloth and returned to Savu. Savunese did not traditionally leave the island without a *wai* cloth woven by their mother or sister. The cloth allowed them to come back to

---

[18] For a literary treatment of the *rukètu* tradition, see Brigitte Raskin's novel *Radja Tanja* (1998).

life on the day of resurrection.[19] Nowadays, relatives of the deceased no longer bring the hair wrapped in a *wai* cloth. Often, when they visit Savu in subsequent decades, community elders remind them that they have not yet held the *rukètu* ceremony for their parents or siblings, depending on who has died. Should they visit Savu several times without complying with the request, the elders scold them. At first reluctant to comply, more and more migrants conform to the tradition. As they do not have hair from the deceased to bring back to Savu, they purchase some cloth to wrap in a Savunese weaving. It is not unusual to see passengers disembarking from the ferry and going straight to the market to purchase cloth, which they then wrap in a Savu weaving as a replacement for the *wai* cloth. A female relative of the same *wini* as the deceased then receives the *rukètu*. The family prepares small offerings to the ancestors and they adopt the deceased's *rukètu* (*hapo rukètu*). To complete the ritual, they share a meal, tell the family's old stories and recall ancestral narratives. This ceremony allows the deceased and those Savunese who live abroad to reconnect with their lineage, their clan and, in sum, with their origins. The ceremony re-affirms the Savunese identity of the deceased and will, according to tradition, allow him or her to resurrect in Savu.[20]

Social and economic change

One characteristic that continues to strike visitors to Savu is its geographical isolation. To visit the island for pleasure or business has always required considerable logistics and this still applies in the 21st century. The north-west monsoon is known for treacherous seas, and the months of January and February are generally avoided for sea travel. Not so well known is that the Savu Sea can turn dangerous at the peak of the south-east monsoon in June and July. Traditionally, the monsoons determine sailing patterns in maritime Southeast Asia and this is very much the case for the Savu area. In the dry season, the common pattern for the Savunese is to sail first to Sumba; from there to the southern coast of Flores, Aimere or Ende; then to the Solor Archipelago; and cross to the north coast of Timor (Amfoan) before returning to Savu. The tour of the Savu Sea would last two months, including the loading and unloading of cargo in each port, which allowed traders to make the journey two to three times during the dry season. Only one day was necessary to sail to Sumba, but crossing

---

[19] On the *wai* cloth and head cloth see Duggan (2001: 65; 2010: 33–40). A *rukètu* ceremony was held in Seba in 2009 for the late governor Piet Tallo who came from Savu (Nataga clan).

[20] On efforts the Christian Church made to revitalise the tradition of *rukètu*, see Paoina Ngefak-Bara Pa (2017).

from Savu to Rote could take two weeks and, as seen previously, the boat did not always reach the island as intended.[21]

Communication and contacts with the world outside Savu evolved slowly. Starting in the 1960s, a Mission plane (Mission Aviation Fellowship, MAF) flew from Kupang to Seba three times a week bringing staff of the GMIT Church and preachers to Savu for the day. The plane returned to Kupang in the evening; it even managed to land in Raijua. When MAF no longer flew to Savu, Merpati Nusantara Airlines (the second Indonesian state carrier) began flying once a week to the island with a 15-seat Casa plane.[22] It was only after the creation of the Sabu-Raijua Regency that a second airline, Susi Air, opened a route to Savu, offering a daily connection to the provincial capital.

For the period from independence to the present, the most important changes kept in collective memory refer to improvements in education and access to water. They are remembered in connection with the name of a subdistrict head, *bupati* (regent) or governor. This is how collective memory works, associating someone with a site, a school here or a pond there, as demonstrated throughout the previous chapters.

Photo 30. School children in Savunese attire; the only person wearing shoes is the teacher, Salmon Bèngu. Seba (1961)

---

[21] Zadrak Bunga (personal communication; 11.05.2013).

[22] Interview with Beha Lado, Raeloro, Seba (14.12.2005).

Education became one of the priorities after independence. More children attended school and the schools recruited teachers locally, at first training them on the island, and later in Rote and Kupang. School children wore home-woven sarongs and blankets, as there were no uniforms, and they sometimes had to walk barefoot for long distances to school. Most villages had newly constructed small ponds (*titi*) which were essential for keeping buffalos throughout the year. However, the roadworks showed less progress—the road around the island built during Dutch times was neglected. The French anthropologist Jeanne Cuisinier, who visited Savu in 1955, mentions that she needed a whole day to reach Liae from Seba (Cuisinier 1956). There were no other improvements in people's lives in the first decades after independence.[23] Anecdotal information shows that people still made their own soap, while bed bugs and sometimes scabies were common inconveniences; only boiling the infested clothes could get rid of the bugs.[24] The local economy was still surprisingly premodern; in the 1950s and 1960s people did not use money. Rather, the traditional system of exchanging goods was valid throughout Savu and Raijua. A pot of lontar syrup was bartered for a pot of sorghum, mung beans, cotton or salt of the same size.[25]

The New Order regime began introducing changes that touched the lives of ordinary people even on small and faraway islands. Its bloodstained inception in 1966 was followed by a strong central concentration of state power. Via the Home Ministry Soeharto controlled the appointment of governors in the provinces, who in turn appointed *walikota*s (mayors) and screened the selection of *bupati*s (regents). Political activity at village level was severely restricted. With a political direction partly inherited from the Dutch colonial state, the Jakarta-based regime expected rural communities to concentrate on economic development and kept them isolated from outside influences (Hoadley 2006: 98–9). Unlike other parts of eastern Indonesia Savu escaped forced village re-locations, but the regime strictly imposed other central initiatives. The Savu population does not positively remember President Soeharto's family planning program instituted in 1978 because it was conducted in a punitive manner. People registered and went to the Seba health post while guarded by soldiers. The population was forced to follow the program; for example, in Mesara men who had a vasectomy were described as '*kebiri*' (castrated, neutered). If a couple did not want to follow the family planning program they were ordered to divorce.[26]

---

[23] Ibid.

[24] Ina Ta Bire (personal communication; 14.05.2013).

[25] Zadrak Bunga (personal communication; 14.05.2013). See the traditional system of exchange in Appendix III.

[26] Interview with Robinson Rohi Mone (18.05.2014).

More constructively, Raja Haba from Liae's fettor family headed a cooperative called Ie Rai (Good Land). It focused on activities considered suitable for both men and women including seaweed farming and hand-woven textiles. The farming developed well in Savu and Raijua and still provides an essential income to villagers living near the coast. Attempts at fish farming and sea-salt extraction were much less successful. In Mesara weaving was the extension of an activity first created at the turn of the 20th century by Raja Ama Doko Ju who built a weaving house next to his house in Ligu. The activity was revitalised in 1981 in Pedèro where weavers grouped together to work. Ie Rai asked the Mesara weavers for their motifs; they sketched these patterns on paper for weavers in other districts. The cooperative gave weavers the option to sell their products through NGOs such as Oxfam. They gathered samples of motifs and everyone was free to transform the structure of the cloth and to weave any pattern independently of her maternal lineage (*wini*). There were neither prescriptions nor prohibitions based on the history of the *wini*. Many traditional aspects of the weaving skill were thus ignored. Everything became possible—from motifs of foreign origin to new creations. By embracing 'modernity' the weavers had a singular goal, namely earning their livelihood.[27] The cooperative, unable to compete with industrially woven cloth from Java, declined in the late 1990s and finally ended after the fall of Soeharto in 1998. A new weaving cooperative called Tewuni Rai (Placenta of the Earth) began in Pedèro village in 2006 to reproduce textiles with heraldic patterns using natural dyes, identical to those kept in the weavers' heirloom baskets, ensuring that weavers can provide for the collectors market without having to sell their heirlooms.

In the last decade of last century, Savu was exposed to more changes. People were conflicted by the attraction of modernity, under the spell of national politics, education, a modern world religion and the media, and the wish to safeguard traditional values. A glimpse of the tensions between urban life and the ways of a Savu villager appears in the story of Apu Lod'o Wadu of Mesara (Ama Pela), a priest responsible for rituals related to the lontar palm tree. He went to Kupang where he attended his grandson's wedding. To his great surprise he noted the monetisation of urban life:

> In Savu I never had to pay for betel chew, water, salt, lontar syrup, rice. In Savu I have everything, syrup, mung bean, buffalos, goats and dogs. Life in Kupang is difficult; here [Savu] wherever I go I get something to eat; there [in Kupang] I can sit for a long time in a house, and wait and wait, nobody gives me anything to eat. Life is boring in Kupang; there I feel like a slave. The houses are small, they do not have gardens, and if they have a yard, they have only one or two trees. There is nowhere I can relieve

---

[27] See Duggan (2004b: 104–7).

myself. It is noisy everywhere from morning until night. To have a burial place, one has to pay Rp. 70.000; here [in Savu] we dig under the house to bury someone. There, when sitting at a funeral wake, people do not feel like relatives but like strangers to each other. They all sit on chairs. One does not have that feeling of intimacy between relatives.

The mothers go out of the house and take their children with them—they have to look for money themselves. Women migrate (to work overseas) and come back with a big belly.

I am not afraid walking through the town. I just wear my Savu cloths [hip cloth and shoulder cloth]. I am not afraid in crowded places. But once while I was walking in town I lost my way. I could not ask anyone; people walk fast, too fast; besides I do not speak Bahasa Indonesia. Fortunately, I met a woman with a lovely face, a Savunese face, a woman from Seba. I asked the way; she did not take me to the house of my grandson; she took me to her house and gave me a large plate of rice with a lot of fish. Yes, she gave me something to eat!

A time of reformation

In spite of the geographical closeness to the Indonesian invasion of the formerly Portuguese East Timor in December 1975 and the ensuing guerrilla resistance, NTT province had few disturbances during the Soeharto era. The frugal, small-scale and increasingly Christianised societies seem to have accepted the New Order as a matter of necessity. Despite the authoritarian and increasingly corrupt nature of the regime there were a few advantages: in line with the *Pancasila* ideology,[28] the government seemed to promise a degree of stability across a sprawling 17,000-island nation with a large Muslim majority. However, as trouble developed in the late 1990s it quickly became apparent that it was a fragile and superficial stability. Moreover, the low level of industrialisation did not save islands on the margins when the developed central regions of Indonesia encountered problems. The national economic crisis of 1997–98, part of the larger meltdown known as the Asian Financial Crisis, hit the isolated Savu archipelago severely. The Savunese have a long history of migrating to other islands to find work, but in the late 1990s many were no longer able to send remittances home, depriving the island of an important source of cash. Even worse, people returned to Savu where they could not find work.

---

[28] In brief, the philosophy underlying the Indonesian state, from the old Javanese words for 'five principles', encompasses: One God; humanity; unified Indonesia; democracy; and social justice.

The Asian Financial Crisis in combination with general public dissatisfaction concerning the abuses and corruption of the New Order marked its doom in 1998. Under the leadership of President Habibie,[29] Indonesia embarked on the rocky path to democracy and civil rights: *Reformasi*.[30] As a reaction to the New Order's over-centralisation, President Habibie granted a high degree of autonomy to the Indonesian provinces through the Regional Autonomy Law (or RAL) of 1999, implemented in 2001. After Raijua became a subdistrict, the population in Savu asked for the creation of more subdistricts, which would allow for closer contact between the population and the administration. The RAL of 2004, especially article 200 (2), gave more autonomy to villages and stipulated that:

> The formation, abolition, and/or merger of villages will proceed with consideration of their origin (*asal-usulnya*) and at the initiative of the community.[31]

As a consequence of these laws, new villages were created by splitting large villages into two. Thus, they could achieve the required number for forming new subdistricts. In that way the four new subdistricts of Seba, Mesara, Liae and Dimu were created in 2004 in concordance with the RAL of 2004 regarding customs and origins (*asal-usul*), because they correspond to the former states of late Dutch colonial times. The islands of Sumba and Rote had also formed new administrative units or regencies (*kabupaten*), something that induced Savu to aspire to similar changes. In order to achieve the required number of subdistricts and to include a sufficient number of villages in them, a new subdistrict called Sabu Tengah (Central Sabu) was created. In the process the subdistrict of Dimu was split into two districts, which made it necessary to create more villages in Dimu and in the new Sabu Tengah subdistrict (see the map section). Kotahawu once again became part of Liae after having been included in Seba after independence. It is noteworthy that Seba did not lose any territory at its eastern border when Sabu Tengah was created. Moreover, it is remarkable that the former state of Menia was not re-created at all. This shows that the last war fought in Savu between Seba and Menia in the 18th century is still a sensitive subject. It is also striking that most of the villages in Seba are larger than in other parts of the island. This reflects the continuing hegemonic grip of Seba over the

---

[29] Bucharuddin Jusuf Habibie, vice-president at the time of Soeharto's resignation after 31 years in power, assumed office in May 1998.

[30] The post-Soeharto period involved changes to government institutions, the judiciary and law enforcement, in response to public calls for a stronger democracy, and allowed more press freedom.

[31] Quoted by Adriaan Bedner and Stijn van Huis (2008: 173).

rest of Savu.[32] All the offices of the new regency were built in Menia, a reminder of its past position, giving the former domain a new importance.

A lesser known consequence of provincial autonomy is that NTT has received fewer subsidies from the central government, although informed people believed it was obvious that the province was unable to sustain itself. In Savu the health posts received less and less medicine. Village health posts (*Posyandu*)[33] closed down because there were not enough personnel. In 2004 and 2006 there was child malnutrition on the island owing to drought and a number of people died of dysentery from the lack of clean water. In villages lacking health services, the statistics did not include cases of child malnutrition and dysentery. Teachers and nurses, who used to be paid by the central government, were no longer replaced by trained staff once they reached retirement age. Liae, which had long struggled with an acute shortage of schools, found its own way to solve the problem after *Reformasi*. A secondary school opened in 1984, but no more schools were built. Its director, Robinson Rohi Mone, saw the creation of the Liae subdistrict in 2002 as an opportunity to improve education. He led the development of Universiti Terbuka (Open University) recruiting local staff to train more teachers. The little university had 36 students who graduated as trained teachers after three years of study and many joined the teaching staff of the recently opened Liae high school in 2010. The majority of school teachers in the regency have been recruited at provincial level, with almost no training and very low salaries. The situation therefore fuelled the demand to establish a new regency. People hoped that more funds from the central government in Jakarta would flow directly to Savu, bypassing the provincial capital in Kupang.

Improved telecommunications and access to electronic media have accelerated the pace of change in Savu society. Mobile telephony reached the town of Seba in 2006. Relays were built and a year later it was possible to reach every district by telephone though not every village. The population, finally connected to the rest of the world, welcomed the development. The fascination with modern ways and Western life styles increased the growing disdain for traditional values among the island's youth. Christianity is also synonymous with modernity. There are different stages of cultural change depending on the degree of exposure to modern Indonesia, to Christianity and to the western world. Many young people leave the island either to seek higher education in Kupang or to find work in Timor, Flores or Java, sustaining their families on the island through

---

[32] The fertility of Menia is underlined by the fact that Sabu Barat, which comprises Menia, produces 1,400 tons of wet rice a year, more than half the total production of the regency.

[33] Pos Pelayanan Keluarga Berencana Kesehatan Terpadu (Post for Integrated Family Planning Health Services).

remittances. The 2010 census shows the Savu population was 75,000 while the 2015 estimation gives 85,000 inhabitants. Figures from 2015 indicate as many as 85,320 people (43,665 male and 41,656 female) work outside the island. The labour migrants usually go to Malaysia, although a few find employment in places such as Brunei and the Middle East.

The new regency of Savu Raijua was officially established under Law 52, dated 26 November 2008. The year is commemorated in the regency's logo which shows 26 grains of sorghum and 11 sheaths of cotton. A regent, Tobias Uli was nominated in 2008 and the first elected regent, Marthen Dira Tome, took office in January 2011.[34] The regency, whose population suddenly increased with incoming civil servants, became a construction site. A new regent's office and a hospital were completed in 2015. Following the creation of the regency each subdistrict was granted a space with internet facilities. However, none of the installations worked for more than two weeks, as the technical equipment provided was not fit for purpose. New schools opened, new roads were built and the widening of the old roads entailed the loss of thousands of trees lining them. The extension of the harbour and the construction of a road around the island have been 'works in progress' for years owing to a lack of money and many wonder when they will be finished. Numerous new ponds have been excavated and old ponds rehabilitated, so people can have gardens and cultivate vegetables all year round. However, a number of them have no water in the last months of the dry season. The statistics of 2012 and 2015 (Appendix VI) reflect this agricultural improvement. While most of the goods consumed in Savu still need to be imported, there is a substantial increase in local production. The traditional trademark of Savunese life, lontar juice, is exported to other islands. Programs have reintroduced cows to Savu, but cattle can no longer roam free and the authorities are allowed to shoot errant animals.

Although there is little real industry to consider, the regency capital Seba now has a small enterprise for industrial salt production. Traditionally, people gathered sea salt in giant clams. In recent years, hundreds of hectares of sandy beaches have been levelled to allow for the construction of large sea beds to produce high-quality salt. However, large-scale projects need proper investment and the management of public money requires skills, which may not be available in newly created regencies such as Savu Raijua. As a consequence, similar to

---

[34] Post-Soeharto politics confirms that the old elite lineages still have influence in local affairs. Tobias Uli is related to Dimu's fettor clan, the Tanyas. One of the candidates for regent in 2011 was a member of Seba's Raja Pono family, a branch of the raja clan (D.P. Tick, personal communication; 20 May 2010). The regent Marthen Dira Tome is from the lineage Nataga-Najohina, from which came the fettors of Seba during colonial times.

other regencies, Savu has had cases of corruption. Three cases were prosecuted in relation to the sea-salt project; two heads of department and one department secretary received sentences of between six to eight years in 2017.[35] Also in 2017, the Regent Marthen Dira Tome was sentenced to three years for corruption surrounding the disbursement of education funds in 2007.[36]

Savu has not been spared the impacts of a recent rise in Islamist extremism. In December 2016 a 32 year-old Javanese man arrived in Savu, selling goods house to house. On 13 December he entered a primary school in Seba and injured seven pupils with a knife before being detained by a soldier from the military station opposite the school. The man was taken to a small nearby police station which had only a few police officers. Social media spread false information about the deaths of school children throughout the island. People boarded trucks and arrived in Seba with knives and machetes. A mob of several hundred people stormed the police station, demolishing the wall of the cell where the Javanese was detained and stoned him to death. The crowd ran unchecked through the market near the harbour and torched shops owned by Muslim traders. After the event, the Muslim traders wanted to leave Savu, but the second regent and the governor of NTT, reflecting the actions of a previous Savu leader, persuaded them to stay. In the mid-19th century, Savu had no market and Raja Ama Nia Jawa, as described in chapter 7, gave land to Muslim traders to settle near Seba's harbour. The number of Muslims on the island is less than one per cent and relations between Christians and Muslims had been peaceful. Sadly, the event marks Savu's entrance into the age of 'fake news' and 'mobocracy' instigated by social media where the truth appears to be dispensable.

The island has also seen some progress in the sphere of cultural protection. In each district, the rebuilding of an ancestral house (*èmu kepue*) or of a Jingi Tiu ritual house receives subsidies. This material aid now extends to the smaller movable *tegida* of the female lineages. In this way the local government offers the population the possibility of preserving these places as markers of ethnic and cultural identity, as well as for tourism as sites of cultural significance. Despite these efforts, the picture in Savu is not overly rosy. Savu Raijua has the highest cost of living in the NTT province and has the largest percentage of officially poor people.[37]

---

[35] Gaudiano Colle, *Pos Kupang*, 01.12.2017.

[36] Djemi Amnifu, *The Jakarta Post*, 31.07.2017. Appeals were lodged in all the 2017 cases.

[37] According to 2015 statistics, Savu-Raijua has 32% of people living at or under the official poverty line of Rp 291,000 (under USD 22) per month, even more than Rote-Ndao (29%).

Whether life in Savu is better or worse today in contrast to a generation ago is a matter of perspective. An elderly man from Dimu expressed the opinion that times passed were more abundant compared to the present. He believed everyone owned more buffalos and pigs, and could grow some rice, though it is difficult to draw conclusions from impressionistic data. However, every year from July to August, epidemics dramatically reduce the numbers of one or more species of domestic animals when access to water and fodder becomes difficult. This is reflected by the fluctuations in animal numbers in the annual statistics. Most epidemics affect chickens, a number of which die from endemic forms of avian flu in Asia.[38]

Island of history

Savu is still coping with the uncertainties and hopes of the post-*Reformasi* era. Time will tell if the Savunese manage to find a balance between the ways of their ancestors, and the demands and attractions of the modern world. It remains to summarise a few themes in Savunese history, and discuss continuities and discontinuities. To scrutinise an island society, such as Savu, it is necessary to look at the larger historiographical picture of Indonesian images. A number of conventions have haunted Indonesian history, partly explained by the Western-derived perspectives or discourses besetting Indonesian scholars, and to a degree conditioned by the lack of real interdisciplinary approaches. These conventions fall within a few different categories. In part they have to do with the problems of positioning local, insular cultures within larger regional or even global perspectives.

As demonstrated in the book, Savu is geographically isolated and keen on preserving or revitalising some of the old socio-cultural structures. The incredible depth of genealogical memory bears witness to the cultural will to anchor familial bonds, hierarchical claims and land rights in local society; for reasons that are not entirely clear, such genealogical identity is much more precise than in the surrounding island societies. Outside Savu, people identify themselves in relationship to their lineage house whose name is publicly known and is often linked to an upper class. Seldom are they able to state the connection to their ancestors.[39] In Savu, clan and lineage houses are not linked to an upper class. The cultural groups certainly have named houses; however, these are not disclosed as the name of the house forms the first part

---

[38] Interview with Eliah Mige Rohi, Dimu (28.06.2012).

[39] Note for instance Clamagirand (1982: 65–9) for the Marobo of Timor; Howell (1995: 156) for the Lio of Flores; Waterson (1995: 55) for the Toraja of Sulawesi.

of its mantra name, which is considered powerful. Instead, people identify themselves primarily with the name of their clan and lineage, and are able to give instantly their link to an early ancestor. Oral traditions and other data indeed suggest an early division in genealogical groups preceded the naming of houses (Figure 43) and this mental process shows remarkable resilience in a society which experienced few disruptive invasions.

At the same time, however, Savu is not atypical when seen against the backdrop of mainstream Indonesian history. The engagement with the medieval Hindu-Buddhist realm of Java and beyond, the Portuguese seafarers and the Dutch merchant-colonialists is chronologically coterminous with processes in other parts of the archipelago. Contact with the trade routes that connected various parts of maritime Asia with or without European presence brought about small but significant alterations in Savunese society. Features, such as slaving, trading in livestock, *merantau* (migration in search of work) and employment as military auxiliaries, brought the Savunese into contact with the outside world and have parallels in a wide range of island societies such as Minangkabau, Ambon, Bali, among others. In such a context, a detailed study of Savu reveals some of the dynamics in the region's history over the last half millennium or so.

The conventional interpretation of Indonesian history by scholars as well as non-academic writers also tends to understate the agency of geographically limited island societies. While few modern historians of Southeast Asia are fooled by the old conventions of changeless premodern cultures, such ideas are nevertheless reified in a number of contexts. In practice, island societies are often seen through an impact-response model. A so-called 'traditional' Indonesian culture might be seen as regulated through a structural model of socio-cultural relationships. Only through external and, in particular Western, impacts are the structures significantly altered. The investigation of Savu's past complicates this. The ritual-political divisions and functionaries of pre-1900 society evidently have roots far back in time, but the system was open to a degree of change. The establishment of rajas in connection with European arrival indicates an ability to create new institutions with (apparently) a minimum of actual Portuguese or Dutch interference, so the old priestly and genealogical figures co-existed with the newly imposed administrative positions. Something similar is valid for religious change: although Protestant missionaries made the first concerted inroads after 1870, real progress occurred after European preachers departed, through Indonesian and local Savunese efforts, thus indigenising the dynamics of conversion.

Another and related convention is the nature of European presence and colonial rule. Here, too, it is still not uncommon to find African and Asian cultures depicted as either passive or resisting victims of European expansionism in the historiography. This has been questioned by some modern historical research and the results are definitely applicable to Savu. European overseas expansion has a 'pull' as well as a 'push' factor and is not only dependent on the perceived economic or political gains of the coloniser. Thus, one must also look at the roots of colonial establishment in African and Asian societies. Colonial enterprises were usually dependent on the interest of certain local groups to accept the Europeans in the neighbourhood, whether for trading opportunities, material gain, security or chances of political ascendency. In the Savunese case, there is little to suggest any deliberate 'anti-colonial' sentiment and this applies to many areas in the archipelago—Indonesian historiography which emphasises the anti-colonial struggle as a central theme, at the same time as taking in Western-derived notions of the nation, is sometimes quite misleading. As seen in chapter 5, the Savunese elite actively forged bonds with the VOC in 1648 and conceived legends about the Dutch arrival and allocation of raja titles that depicted them as stern, foreign but not necessarily unwelcome. The Dutch enjoyed a role as an external ordering force impartial enough to mediate in a conflict-ridden society, what has been called the "stranger kings syndrome" by recent researchers (Henley 2002). Moreover, the Savunese created subsystems of surveillance and influence within the Dutch colonial complex. They went to Flores, exported labour to Timor and even used the Dutch colonial state to launch their own colonising project in Sumba. In the late colonial era, some elite families were astute enough to seek opportunities to have their children educated with the Dutch at schools and with missionaries.

There is an intriguing agency in Savunese history that contrasts with the material poverty of the island. The words of the 19th-century missionary—no one in Savu was poor because nobody was rich—are still valid. As amply observed by visitors through the ages, the islanders have been forced to make the most of very limited resources, where the Jingi Tiu beliefs had a considerable role to play in terms of resource management. Outsiders viewed the Savunese more positively than other groups in the Timor area. In the 18th century they were considered the best soldiers; in the 19th and early 20th they were allegedly more agile and morally upright than their neighbours. Such conventions should only be accepted for what they are, namely expressions of colonial power relations or how the Savunese were useful at certain points to Dutch administrative or religious interests, and have no explanatory value per se. Nevertheless, they convey compelling images of an island society that gained local importance far beyond the shores of the Savu Sea.

Appendix I | Narratives

1. Ama Jawi Rai or God's teachings[1]

This narrative might be the compilation of several narratives, the main protagonists of which are Ama Jawi Rai, his wife Ina Jawi Rai, their son Jawi Rai and Be Lodo, who is Ama Jawi Rai's second wife. Each of them is the main actor in one of the story's four episodes. The first part concerns Ina Jawi Rai and her 'long breasts'; the second part tells of the arrival of a pig which turned into a woman who brought a fire-making technique to Savu; the third part shows God testing Ama Jawi Rai as he teaches him slash-and-burn land clearing; the last part explains why Jawi Rai takes care of all the infants who die before their traditional baptism.

> There was a time when people lived on the land, in the sky or in the sea and were able to go back and forth between these three realms.
>
> On the land lived Ama Jawi Rai, his wife, Ina Jawi, and their son Jawi. Ina Jawi—a 'woman-from-the-sea'—had such long breasts that she carried them over her shoulders on her back.[2] One day, as she was carrying her son Jawi on her back, he asked why she looked so hideous, having such long breasts. He complained that he had to climb on her back to be fed. His mother became angry and told Jawi, "Just stay here!" while she sat him against a pillar of their house. Then she sat on the ground and started to spin herself around very fast, drilling a hole into the earth until she reached the base of the world. She went back to her parents and siblings who lived there. Since this time Ina Jawi has been holding the world in a *patola lai rede* cloth. When she takes her meals, this causes an earthquake.[3]

---

[1] See Figure 3. Elo Lado assisted in combining and translating various recordings in Savunese in November 2003.

[2] The correct expression is 'from-inside-the sea'. A woman with very long breasts is a recurrent theme in Southeast Asia from Vietnam to Malaysia. In Bali, for example, she is called Rangda.

[3] A variation is when she falls asleep and her head drops forward onto her chest; this causes an earthquake. A *patola* cloth is an imported silk cloth from India: traded for spices and sandalwood in Indonesia it was highly valued, sacred and kept by the ruling families in their heirloom baskets.

Ama Jawi and his son were left alone. At that time people did not know about fire; they dug out roots (*ubi hutan* [In]) which they ate raw.

In the sky lived Be Lod'o. However, as she had been suspected of using black magic she was expelled from the sky by Apu Lod'o Liru.[4] He told her, "If you really are a witch, you will fall in a hole. If you are pure you will land at Lokowadu Ae ('the Pond with a Large Stone')."[5] She came down to earth in the shape of a yellow sow not far from the house of Ama Jawi; she soon found a hiding place in a hole left after the extraction of some large roots.

One day, as Ama Jawi and his son were leaving for the forest to look for food, they saw a yellow pig eating grass. They caught the pig and took it home. After tying the pig to the female side of the house, father and son left for the day. When they came back they were surprised to see that someone had prepared the roots they kept in their house. They ate them and were amazed by their smoothness and taste. Over the following days they had similar experiences with baked roots. Ama Jawi decided to discover more about the mystery behind the taste of the roots. The next day he let his son go to look for roots alone while he hid outside the gate of their yard. At once Be Lod'o came out of the pig, grasshoppers combing her hair. They flew down onto the twigs she had gathered and they started to drill holes in the wood to light a fire. This is how people learnt to make fire from wood (*pudu ai*). Be Lod'o carried the wood to the fire and started to cook the roots. Ama Jawi thought "For sure she was sent by Apu Lod'o Liru". He entered the yard, cut the rope tethering the pig, threw it in the fire and it burnt. Be Lod'o no longer could hide in the pig. When Jawi Rai returned, his father told him, "Already caught, it's a woman" [to explain the mystery of the roots and his capture of Be Lod'o].[6]

Be Lod'o was a beautiful woman. Jawi said, "She will be a daughter [-in-law] to you." However, his father replied, "No, let her be your [step] mother as you no longer have a mother." They quarrelled, but Be Lod'o became Ama Jawi's wife. They had two children, Piga Rai and Ngara Rai.

One day Ama Jawi and Be Lod'o left for the forest looking for roots. Jawi stayed at home looking after his young half-siblings; they were quarrelling and crying so he was fed up and said, "Descendants of pigs just annoy people!" They were shocked and stopped crying. When the parents came back, the children repeated Jawi's words asking if they were descended

---

[4] To the Savunese he is God; thus the sky may also be heaven. See below for how the Savunese depict heaven, where access is via a slippery pillar covered with glass splitters, ending in darkness where people are asleep.

[5] Near Teriwu.

[6] For a similar narrative about a pig who changed into a woman, see Clamagirand about the Marobo of Timor (1982: 77–80) and Geirnaert-Martin about the Laboya of Sumba (1992: 43–4).

from pigs. Their mother replied, "It is true; because I came down from the sky in the shape of a pig." Be Lod'o felt ashamed but also angry. She asked Ama Jawi to pick a young red coconut and bring it to her. After her husband had left, she put both children on her lap, Ngara Rai on the right and Piga Rai on the left, and made an incision in the coconut. As the water gushed out of the coconut, she used the spouting force and a whirl wind to climb to the sky with her children.

When Ama Jawi returned he looked for his wife and children but could not find them. He asked Jawi who explained, "The three of them were sitting on the coconut you picked earlier and they disappeared. For sure they returned to the sky." Ama Jawi wanted to look for them in the sky.

The house of Apu Lod'o Liru rested on a slippery pillar covered with buffalo fat and glass splinters. Ama Jawi could not climb and cried.

While he was crying the King of the Flies arrived and asked, "Why are you crying?"

Ama Jawi lamented, "I want to climb up there but I cannot; it is too slippery and sharp."

"This is easy to solve," the King of the Flies replied. "You just have to give me the pus from your wounds and those of your descendants."

Ama Jawi accepted and did as requested. The King called all the flies which came, ate the buffalo fat and covered the sharp splinters by defecating on them. Ama Jawi climbed up to the house of Apu Lod'o Liru. When he arrived there were many people asleep. It was so dark that he could not see his wife and children, and did not know where to look for them. He started to cry again.

A mosquito appeared and asked, "Why are you crying?"

He answered, "My wife and children are here, but I cannot find them; the place is too dark and there are too many people."

The mosquito ordered, "Give me your blood, the blood of your children and their descendants and I will show you your family. Those who move will be your wife and children."

Alas, everybody began fidgeting on hearing the mosquito and Ama Jawi felt betrayed. He cried again.

A bedbug appeared and asked, "Why are you crying?"

He replied, "My wife and children are here, but I cannot find them; the place is too dark and there are too many people."

The bedbug told him, "Let me sip your blood and the blood of your descendants and I will find your family." Having no other choice, Ama Jawi agreed. The bedbug found Ina Jawi Rai, Piga Rai and Ngara Rai who could not stop squirming.

Ama Jawi spoke to his wife and children, "I was looking for you on the land and finally I came here to take you back home."

However, Ina Jawi replied, "What a son you have! His words have offended us too much, so we are not going back."

Apu Lod'o Liru heard the conversation and said, "If you want to take your family back with you, you first have to fell the trees of the forest there." Apu Lod'o took an axe which had cut several stones and gave it to Ama Jawi.

Ama Jawi came back to earth with the axe to cut down the forest near his house. However, he could not cut a single tree; the axe was no longer sharp. He was crying again when Four Winds arrived.

Ama Jawi asked, "Your Highness please—help me cut down the trees growing here because I can't."

"If you reward me with coconut trees which large coconuts, areca palm trees with the biggest fruit and the tallest lontar palm trees, I will fell all the trees in this forest," Four Winds replied. Ama Jawi accepted. Four Winds sent a tornado through the place and all trees in the forest blew down. Ama Jawi reported to Apu Lod'o Liru that he had achieved his task.

"As all the trees are down, now you have to burn them," Apu Lod'o explained, giving him fire. Ama Jawi left and tried to burn the trees. Alas, it had rained so much that the wood would not burn properly. Ama Jawi cried again.

Cyclone[7] arrived and after hearing Ama Jawi's plight he said, "I can help you. Give me the banks of rivers and the slopes that easily collapse as well as coconut trees." Ama Jawi agreed. Cyclone blew on the wood and all trees burnt to ashes. Ama Jawi reported this to Apu Lod'o who said, "Now take a basket of millet (*botok*) and plant the grain all over the burnt area." Ama Jawi scattered the grain across the land and went back to Apu Lod'o showing him the empty basket.

"You did not plant correctly," Apu Lod'o said. "You must go back and pick up the grains to show me." Ama Jawi could not find the grain which was now under the ashes. He cried.

The King of the Birds arrived and Ama Jawi told him his problem. The King of the Birds said, "We birds can pick up the grain but you have to pay for this; you and your descendants will give us the first sorghum of the season." The birds picked up the grain and Ama Jawi took the grain basket to Apu Lod'o. He said, "Some grain is missing, go and bring me the rest."

---

[7] *Angin puting beliung* (In).

Indeed, there was a type of bird that hid the grain at the back of their neck. Ama Jawi beat them behind the neck until the area turned red and they dropped the grain. Today, this type of bird is not allowed to feed on sorghum in the fields—it only feeds on seeds from wild plants. The basket was full and Ama Jawi went to see Apu Lod'o Liru who said, "You have to make holes in the ground and in each hole you put a few seeds. Now you can return home with your wife and children."

Apu Lod'o gave Be Lod'o rice to plant next to the vessel in front of the house where they kept water to wash their feet. Rice is Apu Lod'o's main food staple—the rice people eat with pork meat at *kelila*[8] ceremonial meals. Back on the land Be Lod'o planted the rice near the water vessel.

Ama Jawi asked his son Jawi to accompany him to the forest where he wanted to dig out yam roots which grow deep in the ground. After Jawi had dug a deep hole he said, "I am pulling out this root now." The father asked him to dig deeper so that the root would not break. When Jawi was very deep in the hole, the father started to cover him with soil.

Jawi said, "Wait first, I have to say something! All the infants who die before the *daba* baptism[9] or before cutting the hair will belong to me. The parents who have two children only will have to sacrifice a dog, bitter Jawi (*Jawi hèro*), to me. If you wish Father, bury me, my time has come." Jawi was completely covered with soil. He travelled inside the earth and met the priest Kenuhe. They went to the placenta of the earth (*tewuni rai*). From there Jawi reached the bottom of the world and stayed with his mother, Ina Jawi Rai. So ends the story of Jawi Rai.

Commentary

The narrative is very instructive. It details the connections between God in heaven, humans on the land and the placenta of the world located deep inside the earth. Apu Lod'o Liru gave humans fire, rice and pigs; it is not surprising then that the Apu Lod'o priest in several domains is responsible for the rituals related to rice. It explains why people eat a certain type of rice and pork for the ceremony *kelila*; God gave both foods to humans for accomplishing specific tasks. *Kelila* is a ritual that takes place twice a year in every household: once in the rainy season to ask for enough rain for a plentiful harvest; and once in the dry season to ensure abundant lontar sap. An animal is sacrificed and rice (or sorghum and mung beans) is cooked for the ceremonial meal.

The most informative part of the narrative shows how Ama Jawi learnt slash-and-burn techniques. Yet for this knowledge Ama Jawi Rai had to pay a

---

[8]   See the commentary for explanation and Appendix II.

[9]   See the commentary for explanation.

heavy price, of consequence for future generations. The narrative explains the 'unexplainable' in nature: earth quakes and landslides, cyclones, tornadoes and hurricanes. It justifies why flies take pus from wounds, why mosquitoes and bedbugs suck human blood, and why birds feed on cultivated fields.

The story also indicates a rule of conduct for parents on the death of an infant or a stillborn baby. Jawi Rai refers to the *daba* baptism where the child is presented to the ancestors. The ritual is held on a fixed day in the year for all '*daba*' babies in the month called Daba. While the families hold the ceremony in their houses, the priest Deo Rai holds a ceremony in his ritual house for all of the babies to ensure the ancestral links are strong. The hair is then cut leaving a round space in the hair near the forehead and a triangle at the top of the head.

Jawi Rai has no descendants; his half siblings, Piga Rai and Ngara Rai, committed incest and had a son Miha Ngara (see Figure 3). Piga Rai is attributed the techniques for making pottery—*piga* meaning 'plate'—and from then on food was cooked using earthenware. Ngara Rai or 'Name of the Land' is the name heard in all ritual chants of Savu and Raijua as the diversification in the genealogies started with his descendants.

2.   Horo Nani and the Aelape clan in Lobohede, Mesara[10]

> Horo Nani, from the Lobo clan of Raijua, was a fisherman who came to fish on the shores of Savu's north coast. He stayed at a place called Laiei, not far from the actual town of Seba.
>
> It was at a time of war between Mata Lai the Deo Rai of Seba and Gele Jara the ruler of Dimu,[11] who had a difference of opinion regarding the ownership of land called Tèrupulomi, between Dimu and Seba. As the case could not be solved through negotiations, they decided to look for other means. They asked someone with special knowledge, a wise man, to solve the case. Mata Lay had heard of a man from the island of Raijua, Horo Nani, who could also possibly help. He called him to Namata and Mata Lai presented the situation to Horo Nani.
>
> Horo Nani asked Mata Lai for a four to five day-old chick and a gong. The next day Mata Lay and Horo Nani left for Tèrupulomi. There they dug a hole in which they placed the chick. They decided that during the meeting with Gele Jara the wise man would ask three times standing near

---

[10]   Recorded from Ama Nico Ratu Bunga, Lobohede; October 2000. Tèrupulomi is in today's village of Èilode.

[11]   While Mata Lai is remembered as the founder of Seba's Namata clan as well as holding the priest role of Deo Rai (Lord of the Earth), the name Gele Jara has not been recorded in the Dimu genealogies.

the hole if Gele Jara was the land owner. If the chick stayed quiet, Mata Lai would stamp on the ground with his foot and the wise man would ask Mata Lai the same question three times. Should a sound come from the chick in the ground, this would be a sign that he was the owner of Tèrupulomi. Then they placed the gong above the chick. They closed over the hole and put the grass back so that nobody could see that the hole underneath. Finally, they peed on the place and walked back to Namata.[12]

The following day the wise man arrived in Namata as the sun was rising above the hills. He said that to his knowledge both Mata Lai and Gele Jara claimed ownership of Tèrupulomi and asked "Who is able to give a proof of the ownership?" Mata Lai suggested that they would go to the place and ask the ground itself. "If the ground gives a sign about the ownership, this will be the proof," he added. The wise man agreed.

Accompanied by Horo Nani, Mata Lai and the wise man went to the disputed land. Gele Jara was there too. They stood near the covered hole dug the previous day. The wise man said "If this land has been given by God to the ancestors of Gele Jara, the land should say that it belongs to him". During this time Horo Nani was sitting at a distance, east of the group, busy making a fishing net. The wise man started to talk to the ground "He, Land, Gele Jara says this land belongs to him. Mata Lay says this land belongs to him. There is no proof of land ownership. For this reason we are puzzled and ask you, ground, to tell us the truth". He asked three times "Ground, if you belong to Gele Jara, tell us". No answer came from the ground. Then Mata Lai hit the ground with his foot and the wise man asked "God, if you created this ground for the ancestors of Mata Lai, say that you belong to Mata Lai." Then from the ground came the sound "Mata Lai". The wise man asked a second and a third time, and obtained the same answer. He decided that the ground had spoken in favour of Mata Lai. At that moment Gele Jara fell dead to the ground [from the shock of hearing the news]. For this reason a pond located near the place is known since as Eilobogele.[13]

Mata Lai and the wise man walked back to Namata while Horo Nani walked back to Laiei beach. After a few days of festivities, Mata Lai called Horo Nani to Namata. He asked him to stay in Namata, but Horo Nani refused. Then he offered him land in Leomadamu near the bay of Seba. The place is known as Harta Horo Nani, 'Wealth of Horo Nani'. Then Mata Lai offered him land in Rahihawu, but again Horo Nani refused. He went further west, further than Kolomolie and decided to stay at the place known now as Lobohede. At that time nobody lived there and it was covered by forest.

---

[12]   They urinated on the grass instead of watering it (as they may not have had water) so that the grass did not die.

[13]   *Eilobo* means place with water, thus pond.

Commentary

In collective memory of early times in Savu, people resolved differences through means other than physical strength and material weapons, using ruses and other ploys to mislead the opposite party.

Lobohede is located in Lower Mesara. The name comes from Horo Nani's clan of origin, Lobo, and *hede* means flat land. Place names are more than mere topographical references. Horo Nani is also said to have started a new clan called Aelape; *ae* means great, *lape* probably comes from the name Lape Mata, the son of Mata Lai. Hence, privileged contact was created between both clans. The founding house of Lobohede, called Kèni Bèhi 'Iron Keel', is possibly an offspring of the ritual house Heo Kèni 'Nine Keels' in Namata. A visual link through the house itself and an oral link through its name connected Namata and Lobohede over centuries. Lobohede has a stone called Kebèla Pehere (also *batu sumpah* [In], oath stone). At this stone people of Namata and Lobohede made the oath never to attack each other. The ancestors said "If someone from Namata starts a fight, he will be the victim; and if someone from Lobohede starts a fight he will be the victim too". Indeed, no war is remembered between the Namata and Aelape clans. The spell uttered at the stone was enough to deter people from transgressing the pact.

3.   How Savu women usurped the name Ga Lena

The ancestress Ga Lena, who gave her name to the female line *wini* Ga Lena, is believed to have had magical powers and is still worshipped today. Several women have been associated with the story of Ga Lena whose name they used to achieve their goals; for instance, Dila Nawa of Dimu and Dila Tede of Mesara. The latter is from the Nahipa clan and is said to have lived eight generations after the original Ga Lena. Dila Tede's granddaughter married the first raja of Seba in Portuguese times. The version recorded here is about Ina Tenga Bèngu[14] who took the name Ga Lena and her name is similar to Ina Tenga of 1682.[15] At Wuirai, at the western end of Savu, various place names are connected to Ina Tenga and her husband, Ama Tenga Bèngu, He is attributed a tragic death, falling from a tamarind tree. A coral stone was positioned near the sea as a memorial carrying his name. A channel through the coral between the beach and the sea is

---

[14]   Recorded from Eu Dane, 16 May 2013. She is a descendant of Ga Lena and to her knowledge the ancestress who took the name of Ga Lena was Dila Tede. See Duggan (2001: 42–4) and Figures 6 and 44. She heard the version reproduced here while attending a funeral in 2012.

[15]   See chapter 5 and the version recorded by Teffer.

known as *lahai Ga Lena* (the path of Ga Lena). In the nearby village of Lederaga grows 'the tamarind tree of Ga Lena'.[16] Of note is that the Savunese believe that the great fortress in Solor (fort Henricus or Holo Kota Ga) is actually named after Ga Lena; hence, the narrator refers to Holo Kota Ga Lena—the Great Solor fortress Ga Lena.

> After the death of her husband, the people of Wuirai helped to build two boats for Ga Lena, alias Ina Tenga Bèngu: one was called *Mage Miha Lena do d'o toi lod'o dèka* (Mage Miha Lena who does not worry about the day which will come);[17] the second boat was called *Mage Miha Lena do nga na'i galu gape* (Mage Miha Lena who knows how to make herself attractive). Ina Tenga brought from Ja, her village of origin, bones of animals that resembled human bones. Then she sailed to Kupang with the two boats. She asked to meet the *kumedo* (commander) and showed him the bones and described the war which decimated her village, saying "*Do ke j'ai rèu lai, do ke rewe rèu hape* (the combs of the fighting cocks have been smashed)". She asked him for help. The kumedo said that he had to attend to other urgent matters; he had to fight the raja of Solor first. Then Ina Tenga Bèngu declared that this would be an easy matter for her; yes, she would take care of the raja of Solor herself. "If so, yes, you are welcome to help", the kumedo replied.
>
> Ina Tenga left for Solor. While there she went to Holo Kota Ga Lena, going from place to place as if she did not know her way. When people asked her name she said "Ga Lena". Then she was taken to the raja of Solor who received her in his house and she stayed with him.
>
> [However, the raja was killed].
>
> When she received the raja of Solor's head,[18] Ina Tenga Bèngu took it to Kupang to the kumedo.[19] Ga Lena (Ina Tenga Bèngu) received a flag in Kupang and sailed back to Savu. She took the flag to the Nahipa clan's village of origin in Mesara where there is a stone called *hèla paji*.

---

[16]   Of note is that the area at Wuirai is connected to the Rohaba clan and not the Nahipa.

[17]   A second interpretation was also given: 'Mage Miha Lena does not worry when the boat will arrive'.

[18]   Whether or not she killed the raja and how he died are left to the imagination. In the version recorded by Duggan in 1999, Dila Tede did not kill the raja but married him and did not return to Savu. However, her daughter, Dila Nawa (or Tenga Bèngu) went back to Savu.

[19]   Here the text says "She stayed in Kupang and lived with the kumedo. They had two daughters, Tali Kume and Baki Kume, whose descendants left and vanished from Savu's genealogies". This is an amalgamation of two narratives. There is indeed an ancestress called Tali Kume whose father was a VOC member (thus the name Kume for *Kumedo*), but she lived a few generations later.

Commentary

To the descendants of Dila Tede and to the members of the Nahipa clan who live in the village, the stone is known as *hèla paji Dila*. It is a reddish stone with dead coral attached to it (see Photo 9 on page 168). The stone has a rounded top, but does not have a hole for holding a flag; on one side it has two incised lines which form a cross. This stone could also have been a marker for a grave in European times. The primary pattern of the female line *wini* Ga Lena is based on a cross and could have been derived from a motif on an Indian trade cloth.[20] There is a pattern for a man's hip cloth called *hèla paji* or 'flag's pole' and is owned by the male descendants of Dila Tede in Mesara.

All the narrative versions recorded about Ga Lena show similarities and take place against a background of warfare on the island of Savu. Ga Lena takes bones to another island (Solor or Timor) to gain the support of local rulers. Her deeds brought changes to Savu: the creation of a new maternal line and the gift of a VOC flag.

In the female genealogies Dila Nawa and Dila Tede are said to have both become Ina Tenga Bèngu. There is no information about the husband called Bèngu. Tenga Bèngu married Nguru Tadu of the Kekoro clan of Menia. This places the story of Ina Tenga shortly before the Portuguese arrival; thus one hundred years or more before the queen of Seba, Ina Tenga, who was well known to the VOC representative in the early 1680s.

4.   The marriage of sorghum and mung beans

In Savu sorghum (*terae*) and mung beans (*kebui*) are considered to be a complementary pair; sorghum has male and mung beans have female connotations. For this reason people plant them together. They are symbols of fertility and upon marriage the bride brings both seeds for planting to her husband's house. Nevertheless, sorghum and mung beans were not originally considered as a pair and so were not planted together.[21]

> There was a time when plants, such as [the grain crop] sorghum and [the] mung bean [bush], were able to talk like humans. People planted them on the island and their seeds were the main sources of food in Raijua. They were indeed happy to be useful to the people of the island and pleased to nourish them. However, one day during a prayer at the male pillar of the house (*tèru duru*) for the sorghum and at the female pillar (*tèru wui*) for the mung bean, Sorghum started complaining. "If people are happy to

---

[20]   Duggan 2001: 118–9; Figures 28, 29 and 32.

[21]   Recounted by Daut Paje of Raijua (06.08.2001).

eat me, it is fine with me. If people are happy to eat you, that is also fine. But, I always have to be beaten hard in the mortar from which I come out half dead. The place resounds with the beat of the mortar; I am sick of it!" Mung Bean replied: "Ok, but when you are about to be eaten the whole neighbourhood knows about it. Nobody knows when I am prepared for a meal. There is no indication. It is too bad!"

They continued their argument until they fought each other. As a consequence, they no longer fulfilled the needs of the people of Raijua. If planted, they did not grow; if they grew, they did not bring seeds. In the end, the population became angry with them and turned against Deo Rai, the Lord of the Earth. People did not listen to him anymore. Finally, Deo Rai cried out in great sadness.

He walked around the island thinking of a solution to the problem and finally reached a cave. He had been there for a while when a woman approached him. She told him: "You do not know the way because you do not know that you have to ask *wango*.[22] I can help you. Go and look for an octopus and we will meet on the 16th day of the month of Bègarae. Then I'll tell you more". Deo Rai thanked her and prepared to look for an octopus. On the 16th day of Bègarae he met the woman again at a place called Bèlu. After receiving the octopus the woman gave it back to Deo Rai and requested that he carry it to the top of a lontar tree. After Deo Rai placed the octopus at the top of a lontar tree, it changed into a lontar fruit—those fruit we have in large numbers in Raijua. Then the woman asked him to call all the people. When all people were assembled the fruit was given to the woman.

One pair of lontar fruit was to be used to unite sorghum and mung beans, and to remember their reconciliation. "From now on," she said "plant sorghum and mung beans together. This is my law. In each hole, mix mung beans and sorghum." The following year people planted sorghum and mung beans together, and the harvest was plentiful. After this the woman wanted to leave for the sea. The whole population accompanied her to the sea where she became a fish, *kebèdu*,[23] which people are not allowed to eat otherwise they die.

On land the woman is called Pu Hana. She is remembered every year at the ceremony of *pe'ele* where people make small containers of sorghum and mung beans for her, called *kewore Pu Hana*.

---

[22] For details about *wango* see chapter 1.

[23] It is a poisonous fish; possibly a puffer fish or box fish.

Commentary

The purpose of the narrative is to explain why people have to plant sorghum and mung beans together; the symbiosis is rendered with the metaphor of a married couple. Sorghum grows on long stalks; the grains can be white, yellow, red or black. Mung bean is a short, bushy plant. In the local binary classification, the long sorghum plant received a male gender while the short, round, bushy mung bean plant is associated with the female gender. Sorghum and mung beans exchange nutrients while growing; this symbiosis brings a better harvest than if they are planted separately.

Deo Rai is the highest priest in a council of the traditional religion Jingi Tiu and conducts numerous agricultural rituals especially in the rainy season. In Seba he is responsible for sorghum and mung beans with his wife Bèni Deo who is in charge of the physical act of mixing the grains before planting.

The word *bègarae* means 'to beat the village'—more exactly to beat the ground in the village to expel potential bad spirits. It refers to rituals held at the end of the dry season when houses and villages are cleaned of all external impurities, especially things people might have brought from the sea during the dry season. When people have burned the rubbish in the villages Deo Rai holds the ritual for the entire domain. People then prepare for the planting season on a purified island. At the *pe'ele* ritual, dedicated to the mysterious foreign lady who introduced the knowledge to Savu and facilitated the increase in production, people pray for a good harvest. Pu Hana is the name of an ancestress who changed into a spirit.

5. Jawa Wadu and water for Mesara

In collective memory Ina Hulu Hide married in four domains of Savu. In Mesara she became Ina Ago Rai (chapter 3 and Figure 10). Ago Rai married Ina Jawa Wadu and her son Jawa Wadu is the offspring of his mother's previous marriage.

> Ina Jawa Wadu became severely sick and Jawa Wadu decided to leave the island in order to find special water to cure her. He went to sea as far as Jawa Lai Laju looking for the precious water.[24] When he came back a few drops of water fell at different places in Mesara: Bēlu, Lokoae and Hubu. These are now the main water springs and wells in Mesara. Later, he heard that his mother had passed away. There had been no proper *tao*

[24] No country is known by this name. In Nico Kana's recording the land is "Rai Jawa Hina Wui Wèru" (1978: 505). Jawa and Hina (China) are the two terms commonly found in Savu to designate foreign countries. *Wui wèru* means literally 'stern of the moon'. By extension the stern is the back of the boat; thus *wui wèru* means 'behind the moon'. This metaphor portrays a faraway country.

leo ceremony for her funeral and, instead of gongs, the people beat dried lontar fruit (*wokeke*)—he was both devastated and furious. He rested at the place now called Be'ijawawadu (the sleeping place of Jawa Wadu). Then he went to Menia where he poured out the rest of his water. This is why the abundant water sources of Savu are in the eastern part of the island and why Mesara is so dry. Jawa Wadu left for Kota (now Kupang), in Timor and has no descendents in Savu.

Commentary

A *tao leo* funeral can last from a few days to several weeks depending on the wealth of the deceased. People come from all parts of the island to execute a specific dance, *ledo*, which ideally has to be performed day and night. Animals are slaughtered every day to feed the gathering. People beat metal gongs to mark the rhythm to the *ledo*.

People used dried lontar fruit for Ina Jawa Wadu instead of metal gongs. The narrator considers the absence of metal gongs is a sign of disrespect for her as the wife of an important figure of Mesara, Ago Rai (chapter 3). To some he was the high priest Deo Rai; to others, the ruler of the domain. These positions might not have been clearly defined at that time. Why Ago Rai was not able to organise a better funeral for his wife in unclear as the story does not mention him at all. Had he passed away already? Popular memory recalls that gongs were buried at the death of Rohi Ago who was Ago Rai's son and Jawa Wadu's stepbrother (Figure 19). Events at that time might have been more violent than described in today's narrative. However, in informal interviews people in Mesara explain that before metal gongs were introduced to Savu, people used to beat dried lontar fruit of various sizes and refer to this narrative to make their point. In Raijua people used to beat stones slabs (chapter 2).

Jawa Wadu is remembered as the person who brought limited water to Mesara, but punished the people for not having treated his mother well enough. The line of Ago Rai became extinct with his son Rohi Ago. Jawa Wadu and his mother, as well as Ju Deo and his mother (chapter 4), are worshipped at various places in Mesara.

6.   The war at Liti and the story of Bitu Luji[25]

This dramatic story took place during Portuguese times. One of the protagonists, Luji Jara, is the nephew of Haba Jami, the third raja of Seba

---

[25]   Recounted by Ama Wila Laka of Mesara in Savunese in 2005 and translated into Indonesian with the help of Zadrak Bunga. For the structures of the moiety Lesser Blossom and the formation of *wini* Putenga and its subgroup Jingi Wiki, see Figure 6.

(Figure 28). His second wife, Tenga Ga, is the stepsister of Lobo (Nida) Dahi, the first raja of Liae (Figure 17). As the names of the main protagonists change according to their marital status during the story, some preliminary explanation is needed.

Bitu Luji's maternal grandmother is Medo Rebo (Figure 17) from the Lesser Blossom moiety (*hubi iki*) and is associated with Jingi Wiki, the people who practised black magic. She married four times in three domains of the island, so Bitu Luji's mother, Tenga Ga, has a number of half siblings, among them is Lobo Dahi alias Nida Dahi of Liae. The story begins with Tenga Ga's intrusion into the marriage of Luji Jara alias Ama Hede Luji, expelling his previous wife, Ina Hede Luji, who returned to Dimu with her son Hede Luji. Tenga Ga of Mesara marries Ama Hede Luji who becomes Ama Wènyi Luji after the birth of their daughter Wènyi Luji. Tenga Ga becomes Ina Wènyi Luji and their second daughter is Bitu Luji.

The repudiation of Ina Hede Luji was the cause of a war between Seba and Dimu. Ama Wènyi Luji, Ina Wènyi Luji and their first child Wènyi Luji were murdered in their house at Liti in Seba. Bitu Luji, who was a baby at the time, was the only survivor of the massacre. Bitu Luji becomes Medo Kale after Kale Dari, the founder of the Nakale clan, adopts her. Medo is the name of her maternal grandmother and Kale is derived from Kale Dari.

> War broke out on Liti hill because Tenga Ga expelled Ina Hede Luji from her own house. Later, [for that reason, her son] Hede Luji went back to their house and started a war against his father [Ama Hede Luji]. … Hede Luji's mother was from Dimu. The people of Dimu started a war and Hede Luji's father died … [Ama Hede Luij became] Ama Wènyi Luji [after] Tenga Ga seduced [him], destroying his life, [and they] were murdered. They were there [on Liti hill]: Ina Wènyi Luji, Wènyi Luji, Bitu Luji. A bad smell came from [the] bodies [of] Ama Wènyi Luji, Ina Wènyi Luji and Wènyi Luji who were killed by the people of Dimu.

> Before this war, Nida [Dahi] and Kale Dari [used to] send their dogs with betel nuts attached to their necks [to their half-sister Tenga Ga]. The [dogs] were called Kedeko and Gililau. That was what they used to do before the war. Ama Wènyi Luji received the betel nuts. Then the war broke out; Nida and Kale Dari heard of the war at Liti. When the war was over, they decided to send the dogs with betel nuts [to Liti]. However, Kedeko and Gililau returned to Liae with the nuts still attached to their necks.

> As a result, Nida and Kale Dari from Liae decided to go [to Liti]. "Younger brother, let's go to the hill of Liti to check because the betel nuts were still on the necks of the dogs," Nida said. The elder and the younger brothers from Liae left for Liti. When they arrived at Liti hill, it is true, there was such a stench all over Liti coming from the bodies of Ama Wènyi Luji, Wènyi Luji and Ina Wènyi Luji. There was Bitu Luji on her own trying to

suck milk from the breast of her mother [Ina Wènyi Luji] who was dead. Nida and Kale Dari decided to take Bitu Luji to Liae with the stench all over her and with her heirloom basket which forms one with the body. It is not permitted to leave behind an heirloom basket, because this is the basket that ensures that the line thrives.

Then they left for Liae, carrying [the basket and Bitu Luji] with the stench on her body. They started to walk. They arrived at a valley with a river. They decided to bathe Bitu Luji to rid [her body] of the bad odour. For this reason the river is called Loko Lonye, 'the bathing river', 'the stinking river'; the river where the stench was removed from the child—the stench she had from her mother. They bathed the child in the river; she was free from the stench of her mother.

After she was immersed in the water, after she bathed in the river Lonye, they continued their journey with the child towards a hill, walking one behind the other, carrying the heirloom basket hanging from a sugar cane stick between them. The sugar cane broke as they reached the hill. For this reason, the hill is known as the hill of the broken sugar cane. [From there, only one person] carried on one shoulder the heirloom basket of the Jingi Wiki [people] in the direction of Liae.

They carried the child [carefully] so that her body was not hurt. Then they reached another hill, walking slowly taking great care of the child. [After a rest] they continued their journey towards a hill *ngape ie ana d'i* ... (the hill with the stone)—*Ngapi*—as the hill is called until this day. They continued their journey towards Liae, starting to walk downhill. "I am exhausted. I am thirsty; it is a long journey," the younger brother said. For this reason they stopped and Nida stuck a branch of a *nitas* tree upside down in the ground and laid his spear, *kepoke*, on it. The branch sank into the ground and water sprang out; they gave the child water to drink. After having quenched their thirst, they continued walking. Until this day the spring is known as the spring of Nida, as he was walking down to Liae, towards Daba, towards Raewiu, the village of Nida.

They arrived at Nida's house, on his land; they were on the land of Raewiu, in Liae, in the village of Ina Nida who went to Mesara [and married there]. Then Nida said to Kale Dari: "Let's adopt the child; let's kill a pig, kill a goat and let's have the child named after you. I am someone with a sacred name; the child cannot have my name". Then the child was named after Kale Dari, thus Medo Kale.

[Several years passed: Medo Kale grew up and became a shepherd in Liae.]

One day Ama Rojo Bara from the Nahoro clan of Seba saw the young woman, Medo Kale, looking after her herd. He decided to ask for her in marriage and went to Liae. Nida and Kale Dari agreed to talk about the marriage arrangements. Ama Rojo Bara paid the bride wealth and prepared to take Medo Kale from Raewiu. Nida told Ama Rojo Bara to take the young woman on a day of [the groom's] convenience. He added:

"Take the white locusts you see in the fields there. Take them as a token to your village and your fields". The white locusts were sheep grazing in the fields [depicting an image as they appeared to be white dots on the landscape when seen from a distance].

Then people of Nahoro arrived to take Medo Kale. They also took sheep from the fields. They took her on a horse, as [they did] the sheep,[26] to the house of Ama Rojo Bara. Indeed, since the people of Nahoro in Ledeko went to Liae to carry back Medo Kale, they have a particular cooking place. Medo Kale married Ama Rojo Bara, the 'Big Man' (*duae*) of the Nahoro clan. After arriving in Seba, Medo Kale married Duae Ama Rojo Bara; it was like that.

Then they had children, two daughters, Piga Bara and Raji Bara. Piga Bara married in Dimu. Raji Bara married into the Teriwu-Nad'ara clan. I've forgotten some of the descendants of Raji Bara. I know only that there was a woman called Pago.

Then there were Ina Uju Ga, Rato Ga, Lou Ga, Mare Ga. Mare Ga's descendants are among the people from the sea [from inside the sea]. Lou Ga has descendants among the people of the land.

Lou Ga became Ina Mojo Jami.

Mojo Jami became Ina Loni Aju.

Loni Aju became Ina Wènyi Bire, Dila Bire, both girls. The boys Riwu Bire, Rohi Bire are from the Nataga clan—the clan which was at war with Mesara.[27]

Wenyi Bire is my ancestress. She became Ina Haba Lobo.

Medo Lobo, Ina Neri J'eda

Lage J'eda, Ina Jèda Ra in Mesara

Bida Ra, Ina Tai Jara

Tai Jara, Ina Kai Rona, Hege Rona

Kai Rona, Ina Wènyi Haba

Wènyi Haba, Ina Rihi Dudu

Ngedi Dudu, Ina Bara Uli

Hede Uli, Ina Dila Keraba, and Laka Keraba, Ama Wila Laka—that's my name.

---

[26] Carrying the sheep trussed up on horses was presumably faster than herding them alongside.

[27] The narrator refers to the war between Jara Lomi of Seba and Wele Jami of Mesara (chapter 6).

Commentary

The narrative is a good example of how Savu people recite genealogies. It ends with the genealogy of the narrator, Ama Wila Laka of Mesara, a descendant of Bitu Luji. In this manner he justifies his right to recount the story. Some of the place names in the narrative are repeated several times within one episode, a way for the audience to visualise the places and memorise the names. The story also links the people from several domains of Savu as Bitu Luji's grandmother married in various parts of the island. The names of the main actors are mentioned repeatedly within one sequence, also a way to help the audience to remember the story.

The story underlines the importance of a woman's heirloom basket which could not be left in an abandoned house. Here it is known as Ina Nida's heirloom and contains powerful textiles as she was known to have magical power. A woman's heirloom basket has to accompany her throughout her life. She is then buried with the textiles she has woven which were kept in the basket and had patterns passed on to her from earlier ancestresses. These heraldic patterns will allow her to reunite with them. For this reason the narrator states that the basket containing the textiles forms one with her body. It has to be noted that the terminology used for describing parts of a textile is the same as for the human body. In a weaver's traditional perception the act of weaving a textile parallels the act of creating life.

A branch of *nitas* stuck in the ground upside down seems to be part of the magical act to find a spring; in fact this tree has the particularity to grow well if planted upside down. It plays a role in various narratives in Savu; for example, after Jara Lomi of Seba was defeated by Wele Jami of Mesara, the former was brought back to Nadawawi in Seba on a stretcher supported by two *nitas* branches which then were planted upside down (chapter 6). The spear (*kepoke*) is imbued with power and the first *kepoke* was given to the ancestor Kika Ga by God in the Sky. Its power is demonstrated by the fact that it is able to identify the position of a spring.

When comparing the narrator's genealogies, some information has to be taken with care. According to members of the Nakale clan, one of the protagonists was Mone Bawa not Kale Dari, the founder of the Nakale clan. This happens in other stories too where the clan's name is remembered, in which case the founder of the clan is wrongly remembered as the protagonist in collective memory. However, most of the names in the narrative can be traced in the genealogies, which means the story is plausibly from Portuguese times. The ancestress Loni Aju, who lived four to five generations after Bitu Luji, married Bire Lai of the Nataga clan; he is remembered as raja of Seba in Portuguese times. The son

Figure 59: The war at Liti and the story of Bitu Luji

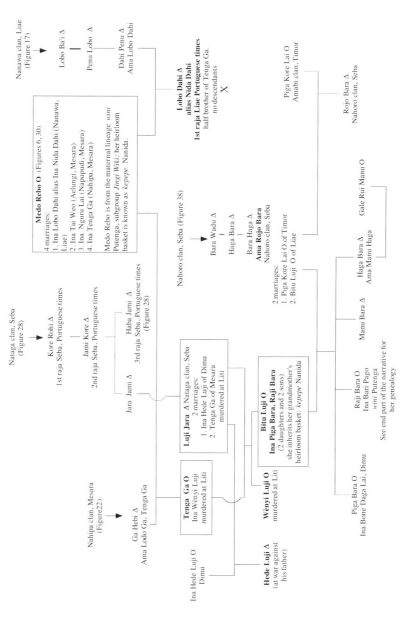

Riwu Bire succeeded his father as the raja of Seba. The names of his grandsons Lai Lomi and Jara Lomi appear in VOC documents between 1684 and 1704 (Figures 28 and 36).

7.   Ceremonial chant (*hoda*) for *pehere jara kelila jola*[28]

This chant is part of the *kelila jola* ceremony dedicated to the ancient settlers, the Jola, who vanished from Savu. *Kelila jola* used to be performed once every 36 years (see Appendix II) and has not been performed for a long time. According to oral tradition, when the Jola people left Savu they made an agreement with the people of Namata (Seba) who expelled them. The latter promised to continue to hold the *jola* cycle of ceremonies to remember the Jola. The priest Deo Mengèru of the Kekoro clan holds this cycle of ceremonies in remembrance of the vanished Jola people.

Every 36 years the ceremonial horse dance *pehere jara kelila jola* is performed at Èikepaka spring which is the traditional ground of the Kekoro-Nadida clan. Deo Mengèru circles the *kepaka* tree[29] (*nitas* [In]), one of the most revered trees in Savu, on his taboo horse.[30] The ceremonial song accompanying the horse dance is partly remembered today. Many people learnt it as a children's song and can still sing it; however, the lines are no longer complete and a meaningful transcription and translation have not been possible. A number of words have different meanings, so the text is open to many interpretations. The root *lila* in *kelila* means to fly;[31] the song has a joyful rhythm and the words 'dancing', 'swinging', 'flying' appear repeatedly. A tentative translation is given below:

1	*Lau le ledo jara lau wa le*	Swing, dance horse, swing west (?) le
2	*Ini bata, Bata Todo*	Lean on Bata, Bata Todo
3	*(i)ni pa lau ledo jara lau wa le*	Lean on to swing, dance horse, swing west, le
4	*Ini ne ini Bata Todo ini lau ya le*	Lean on here, lean on Bata Todo, lean on, swing, ya le
5	*Ledo jara lau ya le.*	Dance horse, swing, ya le
6	*Ele Jola, Jola ya pa ne*	The Jola have disappeared, the Jola from here

---

[28]   The ceremonial circle horse dance for the Jola

[29]   People burned its oil to make light.

[30]   See the commentary for explanation.

[31]   *Lila* is in the word *kapa lila*, 'plane', for example.

7	*Ele ana, ana tudi Jola bèlo*	The blade has disappeared, the blade of the knife [of] the Jola [who have] vanıshed
8	*Pa keo oa ke laga ledi pa lau ya le*	At ....?, swing, ya le
9	*Do jara lau ya le*	Horse swing, ya le
10	*[I]ni ne ini BataTodo ni ka lau le*	Lean on here, lean on Bata Todo, lean, swing le
11	*Ledo jara pa lau le*	Dance horse swing, le
12	*Ledo jara pa lau ya le*	Dance horse swing, ya le
13	*Ele èi,èi hebe kobe hilu leo ledo*	The sarong has disappeared, The sarong with the *kobe*, *ledo* and *hilu* motifs [*leo*?] (or the sarong with the motif *kobe* to wear at the *leo* (?) dance)
14	*La pe pa lila pa lau*	Go on flying, swinging
15	*Ledo jara lau ya le*	Dance horse swing, ya le
16	*Ini bata BataTodo ni pa lau*	Lean on Bata Todo, lean on swinging
17	*Ledo jara lau ya le*	Dance horse swing, ya le

Commentary

The Seba priests think that the chant contains names of the Jola ancestors, for instance Bata Todo, and includes a critique Deo Mengèru addresses to the people of Namata. However, this is not reflected in the tentative translation.

The ceremonial 'dancing' horse is central to the *kelila jola* ceremony. It is taboo as only those with religious power—the Deo Mengèru—can own one; it is forbidden to ordinary people. A taboo horse is born in certain conditions, at a particular time of year and has a specific colour. As soon as a taboo horse dies or becomes too old, it has to be replaced with a horse with the same characteristics. A taboo horse protects the priest; it is imbued with certain powers to enhance the priest's power. In Savu, every priest has a number of taboo animals, including buffalos, roosters and hens. The use of taboo animals, objects and places serves to strengthen social structures, to separate categories and to maintain ideas about the cosmological world.

Line 7 it is not clear whether *bèlo* 'forgotten' or 'vanished' refers to the knife or to the people.

Line 13 seems to contain the names of heraldic motifs on the female sarongs of both moieties. *Hebe kobe* refers to the main motif, Kobe, which is the primary identity marker of *wini* Ga Lena (Figure 44); *hebe hilu* is one of the two main motifs of *wini* Dila Robo (Robo Aba's daughter, chapter 3). Both belong to the Greater Blossom moiety. *Ledo* is the name of the basic motif on female sarongs of the Lesser Blossom moiety (see Plate 17, selected sarongs patterns with historical relevance). However, *ledo* is also the name of a specific dance held at *tao leo*, the highest form of funeral, and *hilu* has a second meaning, 'to wear'. The line is open to two different interpretations. Both moieties existed at the time of the Jola; whether or not heraldic motifs were present at that time cannot be stated.

Some believe that people chased away the Jola at the time of Mata Lai, the founder of the Namata clan. Did Mata Lai chase all the Jola people away? The question remains of why the Jola should be remembered in Seba's ceremonial calendar if there had been a wish to expel or, perhaps, to exterminate them? What seems important to the present-day Savunese is the fact that the Jola left something behind that the people of Savu have cared for—the names of major rituals, *kelila*, and the plants used in those rituals (a certain variety of sorghum, mung beans and yellow rice).[32]

A *kelila jola* ceremony should have taken place in 2004. However, the priest Deo Mengèru of the Kekoro clan in charge of the ceremony had no buffalo to sacrifice and the ceremony was postponed until 2007. This caused a lot of trouble as the priest had to give away his rights to a piece of land to buy the animals he did not have. His relatives (now Christian) were angry with him. The turmoil caused by Deo Mengèru's land sale made people in Seba aware of the ceremony and some of them came to Èikepaka, mainly out of curiosity, not because they were followers of the ancestral religion or because they wanted to support keeping traditions alive.[33]

Theoretically, the next *kelila jola* ceremony will take place in 2034. One may wonder if there will be any member of the ancestral religion left for the celebration. If it is celebrated, it will be interesting to know in which form— whether as a revival of ancient traditions under the leadership of the regency or the Church, as is the case on other islands of the region. However, it is already too late to recover the Jola chant.

---

[32] The missionary Mattheus Teffer's account from 1870 says Mata Lai allied with the western villages inhabited by the original people in order to destroy the eastern villages. Later, he turned on the western villagess as well and captured their populations. At first, they were kept as workers, but they were eventually exported as slaves (Raad voor de Zending, 1102–1: 1411, Mattheus Teffer, report, 1870). A VOC source refers to a population in the interior which was captured and enslaved by the coastal rajas in 1648 (Tiele and Heeres 1886–95, III: 426).

[33] Source: Elo Lado (Malobo). For more information see Duggan (2008: 98–9).

Appendix II | The Knots of the Land, *kewèhu rai*

Introduction

In this appendix, there is first an overview of the lunar calendar (or *kalendar adat* [In]) of all the ceremonial domains (Table 1). For each domain there is a more detailed calendar, either in full for Liae and Dimu or for selected months in Mesara and Raijua (Tables 2 to 5). The annual calendar of Liae reveals how two councils of priests work in parallel. The Dimu calendar shows how two councils work alternating their tasks using the binary opposition 'sweet' (*nèta*) versus 'bitter' (*hèro*) as mnemonic tags. The unique nature of the Mesara calendar resides in the elaborate rituals linked to the lontar palm tree with a 'heating' period (*pepana*), followed by 'cooling' months (*pemeringi*). As Raijua has up to five Deo Rai priests, meaning that there are (or were) five councils of priests, it has been impossible to record them all with accuracy. However, the calendar discloses a clear opposition between Upper Raijua (elder brother) and Lower Raijua (younger brother) shared by all groups and this is best expressed in a month dedicated to ceremonial cockfights alternating between places in Upper and Lower Raijua. The annual calendar of Seba is not included as the information it contains already appears in several publications. See Cuisinier (1956: 111–9), Detaq (1973: 28–37), Fox (1979: 145–73), Kana (1978: 353–420; 1983: 75–104), and Kaho (2005: 92–124) who presented the Seba calendar as representing the entire island of Savu, although it is not the case. Table 6 provides information about the larger cycles called *kelila* which include bigger rituals.

The year is ideally divided into two seasons of six months each: a dry season corresponding roughly to the south-eastern monsoon and a wet season benefiting from rainfall during the north-western monsoon. However, the rainy season does not last more than three months on these islands, so the categories of wet versus dry do not correspond to reality. However, each domain has one ceremony for the entire community called *kelila*, corresponding to each of these two seasons: one is the 'ceremony for rain matters' (*kelila èji lai*) in the rainy season; and the second is the 'ceremony of the stones' (*kelila wadu*) in the dry season. No grass covers the numerous stones which are visible everywhere. In addition, all domains use,

449

to various degrees, the concepts of 'sweet' (*nèta*) versus 'bitter' (*hèro*) and 'hot' (*pana*) versus 'cold' (*meringi*) as classificatory markers for dividing the year and ascribing ceremonial tasks to different groups.

The larger cycles, *kelila ae*, vary from 6 years in Dimu and Raijua, to 49 years in Mesara. The meaning of the word *kelila* is not clear; it contains the root *lila* which means to fly. In collective memory the ancient and vanished Jola people left the name and the tradition of *kelila* for the Savunese.[1] The *kelila* ceremonies which take place at fixed times in the year are called *kewèhu rai*, the 'knots of the land'. The most common meaning of the word *kewèhu* is knot.[2] People commonly refer to these ceremonies as *nga'a kewèhu* to eat the knots as they comprise a festive meal. These rituals bring people together and bind the society over the years. In the past, at funerals, people used to keep track of the gifts brought by the relatives using a fan-shaped lontar leaf. Large cattle were noted by making a knot (or knots) in segments between two ribs of the leaf, starting at one end. For medium-size cattle the knots were towards the centre part of the fan shaped leaf; towards the other end of the leaf a section was reserved to record gifts of textiles and, finally, at the other end of the leaf, gifts of rice, betel ingredients and tobacco were 'knotted' to record them. When at the end of the funeral meat was divided among the guests, each knot was undone as a guest received his share. This is no longer practised.

The idea and use of knots is common in Austronesian societies. Reuter reports that the people in the mountainous area of Bali used in the past a string with knotted bamboo slats for remembering the names and positions of the members in the village organisation. Knotted strings were more practical for keeping track of changes in the particular duties performed at village level than the registers used nowadays (2002a: 58). The Bugis people of Sulawesi used a knotted cord made out of a leaf of lontar palm in relation to warfare. The ruler sent a knotted cord to his allies to summon the warriors to a battle. A specific number of knots corresponded to the number of days until the outbreak of war (Andaya, 2004: 55). The use of knots as mnemonic devices is found in other parts of the world as well. Vansina mentions knotted ropes of different colours and lengths used in Peru (1985: 45). The Yatmul of the Middle Sepik in Papua New Guinea keep in their heirloom a knotted cord which they use in rituals for recounting the migratory journey of the their ancestors, and for remembering totems and objects linked to each settlement (Wassmann 1991: 51).

---

[1] The word *lila* has recently helped to create a new word: *kapa lila,* literally 'flying ship' which refers to a plane.

[2] A hair bun, for example, is called *kewèhu kètu* (*kètu*, head). A second meaning is joint (between two bones). It designates also a joint or node between two segments of bamboo.

1.   Lunar calendar in the traditional domains of Savu and Raijua

In all domains, the lunar calendar (*kalender adat* [In]) year starts with Wèru a'a, the month of the elder sibling, and closes in the month of Bangaliwu during which the largest ceremony of *hole* (thanksgiving) takes place. The name Wèru a'a is the same in all parts of Savu while Raijua has the variant Wèru wadu a'a or month of the elder stone. Other names are shared throughout the islands: these are Bègarae (to clean or purify the village) or Hae rae (to climb to the village of origin for cleansing) before the start of the planting season, Ko'o ma (to clear the fields before planting) and Daba (traditional baptism). The times of the mung bean plant's growth and flowering are very important and are marked in similar ways in the name of a month: Naiki kebui which refers to the young mung bean shoots and Wila kolo corresponds to the blossoming of the plant. In Raijua both names are combined in Leko wila kolo while in Mesara this time is called Penèta (sweet month).

Month	Domain				
	Seba	Mesara	Liae	Dimu	Raijua
April/May	1. Wèru aʾa				
May/June	2. Wèru ari	1. Wèru aʾa	1. Wèru aʾa		
June/July	3. Kelila wadu	2. Wèru ari	2. Wèru ari	1. Wèru aʾa	
July/August	4. Tunu manu	3. Hobʾo	3. Kelila wadu	2. Wèru ari	10. Bègarae ae
August/September	5. Bègarae	4. Wadu ae/Kelila wadu	4. Wadu ae	3. Kelila heole	11. Bègarae ro (no rituals)
September/October	6. Koʾo ma	5. Keʾi ei	5. Haʾe rae	4. Wadu ae	12. Rokoko (rituals for lontar)
October/November	7. Naiki kebui	6. Haʾe rae	6. Koʾo ma	5. Wadu kepete	1. Wèru wadu aʾa
November/December	8. Wila kolo	7. Koʾo ma	7. Naiki kebui	6. Haʾe rae	2. Wèru wadu ari
December/January	9. Hanga dimu	8. Nyale kuja	8. Kelila èjilai	7. Koʾo ma	3. Matina (no rituals)
January/February	10. Daba èki	9. Nyale ae	9. Nyale	8. Naiki kebui	4. Koʾo ma
February/March	11. Daba ae (traditional baptism)	10. Penèta	10. Daba	9. Wila kolo	5. Wari wa/wèru Melolo (rituals for the dead at sea)
March/April	12. Bangaliwu (hole; kowa hole)	11. Daba ae	11. Bangaliwu Kolorae	10. Hanga dimu	6. Leko wila kebui
April/May		12. Bangaliwu (hole; kowa hole)	12. Bangaliwu (hole)	11. Daba	7. Daba/Daba ae (two ritual cockfights)
May/June				12. Bangaliwu (hole)	8. Bangaliwu ae (cockfights)
June/July					9. Bangaliwu ro (kowa Mone Weo; no other rituals)

2.   The knots of the land in Liae

The annual lunar calendar of Liae shows two priest systems at work in parallel. It reveals also the peculiarity of Liae which has two months named Bangaliwu: one for the descendants of the elder brother, the so-called people of the sea; and one for the descendants of the younger brother, the people of the land. It shows clearly the precedence of Deo Rai, the Lord of the Earth (here called respectively Deo Mengèru for the Kolorae clan and the Council of Five Men, and Deo Gopo for the Council of Seven Men), over the other priests (Apu Lod'o for instance), and the precedence of all the priests over the community.

Month	Date; name of ritual	Priest in charge; sacrifice; offering	Description
1. Wèru a'a (June/July) (month for repairing, building houses)			In the first three months, ceremonies are held to nourish and to heat up the earth, the lontar tree and its environment.
	3 peluba (day 3 of a new moon) pedoa bubi due	Deo Gopo and helpers: sacrifice a female goat. Deo Mengèru with Bawa Iri, Rohi Lod'o, Riwu Tadu, Kenue, Doheleo: sacrifice a black hen and a black sow.	The priests ask Deo Woro, Deo Mengèru in all four cardinal directions for the best possible blossoming of the lontar. Place of the ritual for Deo Mengèru: Merèbu hill. Ritual place for Deo Gopo: Ledegopo. One ritual stone at Merèbu is for moto mou rai (the morning star). When people see the star, it is time for them to climb the lontar trees to tap the sap from their blossoms. Another stone is for moto lara lod'o (a star which is not visible after midnight).
	7 pelupa (day 7) ceremony for Maja	Mone Ama and people sacrifice a pig: tèbu wawi Maja	People ask for happiness and wellbeing during the lontar season. If they do not perform the ritual, they will be punished by Maja (wèbe ri Maja): for example, Maja may cause them to fall from a lontar tree.
	between the 7th and 14th day pejej'a alu		Dance performed by the youth while jumping between pieces of wood which are beaten against each other and, while the wood is beaten against the ground, dancers jump between the pieces.
	7 pehape (7 days after a full moon)	beleo bubi due: looking after the lontar blossom	If people could not hold the ceremony for Maja at 7 peluha, they have the possibility to perform it at 7 pehape. Task of Doheleo: in this month people start to cut wood to boil the lontar juice later in the month of Wèru kelila.

Month	Date; name of ritual	Priest in charge; sacrifice; offering	Description
2. Wèru ari (quiet month dedicated to the dead)	*5 peluha* *ami pa ibi duel* (to ask) *ped'oal/pemola ibi duel* (to call)	Deo Mengèru and helpers; Deo Gopo and helpers	A relatively silent month dedicated to the dead. Only one ritual is held to ask for plentiful lontar juice, *ami pa ibi due*. Deo Mengèru holds the ceremony at Merèbu; Deo Gopo at Ledegopo.
3. Wèru kelila wadu	*3 peluha* *pemole ibi duel/pedoa hubi due*	Deo Gopo Deo Mengèru: sacrifice a black sow and a black hen 12 *riwo* (a bundle of three offerings)	The priests ask Deo Woro, Deo Mengèru for the juice to go straight up inside the tree towards the blossoms. The priests ask for a brisk but not too strong a wind; a strong east or south wind reduces the flow of sap. 12 bundles of 3 offerings each are to hang in the tree in all directions (*mad'a ngèla*) for the wind and to lie on the stone (*wadu kebili*) at the bottom of the tree where the basket of juice is placed. To ask for a safe climb (*pa loro jara*) one *riwo* is placed at the first notch carved in the trunk for the climbers' ascent (*pa toba jari rai*), another at the last notch (*pa toba keraba koko*); one *riwo* is placed at the stalk of leaves (*pa para due*), at the blossoms (*pa petae*), at the top of the tree (*kolo*) and for the star (*Pu moto para lod'o*).
	7 peluha *pemole ibi due*	Same ceremony, but for other members of *Mone Ama* and for the people Sacrifice a sheep and/or a chicken	Other members of *Mone Ama* hold the ceremony for themselves as certain tasks related to the lontar tree are not made jointly as in Mesara, for example, but separately.
	same day *Pengia ngapi* (feeding the lontar tool)	The priests perform the ceremony for the community; every family celebrates.	Feeding the tool for pressing the lontar blossoms. On that day it is forbidden to tap the tree (for people who have started before the time of the ceremony or who tap the tree all year round). After Deo Rai/Deo Mengèru has held the ceremony in their ritual house, every tapper holds the ceremony in his own house. Three days after pressing the blossom, the tapping can start.

Month	Date; name of ritual	Priest in charge; sacrifice; offering	Description
	7 pehape *kelila wadu: nga'a kelila*		Ceremony at home for every family. If possible, a larger animal, such as a goat or a pig, is slaughtered; as it is the middle of the dry season, cattle are usually rare. Slaughter of at least one chicken.
	pehere jara Apu Lod'o	Apu Lod'o at the limits between Raewiu and Ledenaboro	Horse dance (*pehere jara*) to ask for strength for the man who will tap the sap, so that he will not fall from the tree. After performing the dance, riding on his taboo horse, Apu Lod'o is followed by the community riding their horses, to ask for a good juice harvest as well as for good quality syrup.
			(Deo Mengèru and his clan do not have the right of *pehere jara*.)
4. Wèru puru hogo	*hiluwara* (full moon) *ketoe ngapi*		Ceremony held at home for hanging up the tool to press the blossoms. It is then time to prepare the cooking place.
	Ke'i rao/hogo due	Deo Gopo/Deo Mengèru	The priests dig out the ceremonial cooking place (*ke'i rao*) for boiling the lontar juice. *Ketupat* (offerings) are placed in the four cardinal directions around the enclosure. If there is not yet lontar juice to boil people have to use coconut juice.
		Deo Gopo/Deo Mengèru	Deo Mengèru digs out the main hole (*ke'i due*) with three smaller holes (*woro ari*) for cooking ritual food (*hogo due, pemole ihi due*).
			As soon as there is a fire in the cooking place, the ceremonies of the second part of the dry season can start for cooling off the earth and the lontar tree.

Month	Date; name of ritual	Priest in charge; sacrifice; offering	Description
	udu ngaʾa making offerings in heaps *Pedoa Ina Naweni* (calling the sister)	Brother and sister are in charge of the *peluna nyiu wo mèngi* ceremony.	A brother and his sister are in charge of the ceremony *udu ngaʾa*. Offerings are of coconut, *peluna nyiu wo mèngi* (sprinkling coconut water mixed with sandalwood and aromatic root: *rukunu*). Brother is in charge of slaughtering an animal. Brother slaughters a sheep for his sister: *ngaʾa nèta* (to give her sweet food).
	All ceremonies are on the same day.	*ngaʾa nèta* Sister responds with 3 chickens.	Sister reciprocates by giving three cooked chickens. Sister is responsible for the safety of the brother. Climbing the lontar tree is a risk, compared to going to war.
5. Wèru liku keruga	*hiluwara* (full moon) *ta wèbe keruga*	Day 1: Bèni Deo Mengèru and Bèni Deo Gopo Day 2: Bèni Pu Mahi Day 3: people	Bèni Deo Mengèru and Bèni Deo Gopo hold the ceremony separately. They both go to the shore and take coral from the sea (*ta wèbe keruga*). Bèni Pu Mahi (Apu Lodʾoʾs wife) takes coral from the sea. Everyone takes coral from the sea; however, each family is entitled to take coral once only.
	14 days after a full moon	Bèni Deo Mengèru/Bèni Deo Gopo	Ceremony for tasting and testing the lime Bèni Deo Mengèru and Bèni Deo Gopo roast the coral, followed by Bèni Pu Mahi and then everyone.
6. Wèru bègarae	1 *peluha* (day 1) *Ke Awunada.* *Menyèru èmu Rue*	Deo Gopo at Gopo Deo Mengèru at Kolo Merèbu, Rue at Kolo Merèbu; sacrifice a male goat	Deo Mengèru goes to kolo Merèbu. Rue goes to Awunada and takes an animal from the community for the sacrifice. The purpose is to clean first the ritual houses and the ceremonial villages; then people clean their own houses and their village, and burn the rubbish into ashes (*aun*).

Month	Date; name of ritual	Priest in charge; sacrifice; offering	Description
	2 *peluba* *Deo Rai pa awu nada.*	One day after Deo Gopo and Deo Mengèru, Apu Lod'o goes to Merèbu too.	Deo Rai at Awunada and Deo Rai's helpers take the sacrificial animal from the community: *padi bad'a.*
	3 *peluba* *peluba ngaʾa rae* *la ke ha'u d'ara nada*	Deo Mengèru at Kolowègu Deo Gopo at Kebuhu Apu Lod'o at Kolomerèbu	Deo Gopo, Deo Mengèru and Apu Lod'o enter the ritual arena (*la ke ha'u d'ara nada*) and clean or 'purify' the place to prepare for the planting season. The village eats (*ngaʾa rae*). In each house people make offerings and eat together the animal they have slaughtered. *Mone Ama* makes offerings and consume the animals slaughtered before the community is allowed to do so.
		Doheleo	All families in all villages of the domain hold the ceremony.
	peloko wango (to curse bad spirits, or to exorcise black magic)		As people have taken coral from the sea, they might have let bad spirits (*wango*) enter the island. Groups of people form; they throw stones (*pekèji*) at each other, protecting themselves with shields. The stones falling on the ground chase away the bad spirits: *bèga mita rae ro.*
	pekèji bagarae (*pepebi*)	Separately, Deo Rai, Deo Mengèru and Apu Lod'o sacrifice a sheep or goat.	Apu Lod'o and Deo Rai Gopo at Kepakahoro go to Eilogo village. Deo Mengèru to Waduwèla at the place called Bègarae.
	purnama (day 14)		The priests provide a protective sweet offering (*mai mènyi*) to Deo Woro/Deo Mengeru by hanging a basket of lontar syrup (*baba donabu*) made of three ribs of lontar leaf (*tèlu lidi*) in the tree. If it rains early, people begin field labour before the end of the dry season. The sweet offering prevents harm to the people from spirits escaping through the wounds in the earth created by working the land.

Month	Date; name of ritual	Priest in charge; sacrifice; offering	Description
	bapu pengo'o (clean the fields)		This is the end of the dry season. The tapping of the lontar sap should come to an end because people begin labouring in their fields. However, people with no other revenue are allowed to tap the trees all year round.
7. **Wèru ko'o ma / kuja ma**	1 *peluha ko'e rai*	Day 1: Deo Rai Gopo and Deo Mengèru	The first part of the month is referred to as *ko'o ma*, or cleaning the fields; the second part, *kuja ma* which means cleaning the tools.
			Deo Rai and Deo Mengèru respectively clear their ceremonial fields, *ko'e rai*.
	5 *peluha kowa* Apu Lod'o	Day 2: Apu Lod'o / Day 3: everyone	Apu Lod'o clears his ceremonial field. / The entire community starts to clear their own fields.
	7 (or) 9 *peluha kowa* Deo Rai	Apu Lod'o launches a ceremonial boat; sacrifice a lamb	Boat is launched at Janga Apu èpa to send away strangers, newcomers. Apu Lod'o slaughters a lamb.
	he'i pehape (day 16)	Deo Gopo/Deo Mengèru: launch their boat; sacrifice a goat, chick and puppy	Deo Mengèru slaughters a goat at his ceremonial place, buries a chick alive on the beach and cuts the throat of a young dog which he throws into the sea (*boro*) to placate the bad spirits.
			The boat for Deo Mengèru is launched: *golo kowa Raja* at Ubahèpu (western part of the bay near Ege); it is filled with cotton, sorghum and *ketupat* to thank Deo Mengèru because they could not launch a boat in the month of Bangaliwu (south-eastern monsoon).
			Deo Gopo launches his boat from the eastern side of the same bay.
	kuja ma / 2 *riuo*		From the first day after a full moon until the end of the month it is planting time. The tools for clearing the fields are hung up with two bundles of offerings. After they finish planting, there is a ceremonial meal: *ngàa jèli ma*.

Month	Date; name of ritual	Priest in charge; sacrifice; offering	Description
		Day 1: Deo Gopo and Deo Mengèru	Deo Gopo/Deo Mengèru plant first, then they slaughter an animal because they have made holes in the earth. Blood has to flow into the ground to heal the earth. Then no animals are slaughtered other than for rituals during the period of growth. No drums should be played in this month—after planting it is silent.
		Day 2: Apu Lod'o Day 3: people	Apu Lod'o plants. People plant. After planting people can also slaughter an animal for the same reason as above.
8. Wèru kelila èj'i lai (no drums, no songs, no gongs in this month)	5 *pehape* (day 5 after a full moon) *kelila èji lai* *pehere jara*	Apu Lod'o *kelila èji lai* *pehere jara èji lai* *wawi kelila* (sacrifice a pig) Deo	Apu Lod'o slaughters a pig (*tunu wawi kelila*) for the ceremony *kelila èji lai*, for rain matters, and asks for the rice to ripen and plants to blossom. He performs the horse dance (*pehere jara*) first; then the community participates in riding dancing horses at the same place.
	7 *pehape* *nyale* (see worms)	Deo Gopo/Deo Mengèru.	The priests collect sea worms.
	9 *pehape* *ngà'a baja kelila*	Apu Lod'o and the population	Apu Lod'o and other priests collect sea worms, followed by everyone who goes to the sea to collect buckets of sea worms to eat at home in a small family feast.
9. Wèru hanga dimu (no drums, no songs, no gongs; no animals sacrificed)	5 *pehape* *po kebui mone à'a*	Apu Lod'o and Deo Rai and Deo Mengèru	*holo kebui mone à'a* (to protect the harvest of mung beans)
	6 *pehape*	and everyone	In the evening people go to the beach to collect the second harvest of sea worms.
	7 *pehape*	*nyale*	Family festival for eating the sea worms at home.

Month	Date; name of ritual	Priest in charge; sacrifice; offering	Description
10. Wèru daba (slaughtering of animals and gongs permitted in this month)			*Daba* is the traditional baptism of the children born in the previous 12 months, followed by two days of cockfighting. Both Deo Rai Gopo and Apu Lod'o take part in the cockfighting; Deo Mengèru never takes part.
	pemape (evening of a full moon)	Day 1: Deo Mengèru Day 2: Deo Gopo and Apu Lod'o	People construct the small hut (*ada manu*) from which the respective clans leave for the ceremonial cockfight area.
	hiluwara (full moon) *Daba ana* (traditional baptism)	Day 3: *èki ada*	Ceremonial cockfight at Kolo Gopo (Deo Gopo and Apu Lod'o); the next day, ceremonial cockfight at Kolorame
	1 *pebape* *peiu manu la kolo Gopo*	Deo Rai Gopo /Apu Lod'o	Both cockfights on the hills of Gopo and Kolorame serve to replace inter-clanic wars, to ask the ancestors to chase away sickness and give strength to the newly 'baptised' children (*ana daba*). The children are introduced to the ancestors.
			Ada mone or *ada bèhi* is located at Daba; *ada rena* at Eiko.
	2 *pebape:* *peiu manu* at Kolorame	*pebelila ru manu*	The first winning cock is offered to the ancestors; its feathers are taken and thrown up towards the sky, towards the ground and towards the sea and later thrown into the sea; the white feathers to the sea, the red feathers to the sky and the black feathers to the ground.
11. Banga liwu Gopo/Banga liwu Kolorae	*peluba–hiluwara:* *pedoa*	*udu* Kolorae, Teriwu and Gopo (*Ratu Mone Lèmi and Ratu Mone Telu*)	Ceremonies for *udu* Kolorae, Teriwu and *udu* Gopo only. From day 1 until the full moon: *pedoa* a circle dance is held from evening until dawn at various places; the rhythm is given through the small baskets (*kedue pedoa*) attached to the feet of the dancers. Dances are accompanied by ritual songs about the past and the ancestors involving segments of genealogies (no drums, no gongs).

Month	Date; name of ritual	Priest in charge; sacrifice; offering	Description
(ritual month only for the clans issued from the former *Ratu Mone Tēlu*, thus for the descendants of Dida Miha)	*kewore delu manu* (day 11) *ngaʾa doka wenyi kenana*	In every household of both clans	Ceremony consists of chewing fresh areca nuts and betel fruit to ask for the health and prosperity of plants.
	kewore kele (day 12) *ngaʾa doka kiʾi Hawu*	Sacrifice a goat.	Asking for fertility, the health of small animals; it involves the slaughter and eating of a goat.
	penupe (day 14) *ngaʾa doka kebau*	Sacrifice a buffalo (or a pig).	Asking for fertility, the health of large animals; it involves the slaughter and eating of a buffalo (or a pig).
	biluwara (full moon) *bui ibi* *pedoa*	Leader of *tegida* Leader of ancestral house	*Bui ibi*: is a silent night of ritual at the ancestress's house (*tegida*) to asking for health and prosperity for humans.
			Circle dances (*pedoa*) all night with chants
			No cockfight, no horse dance (*pehere jara*) this month
12. Banga liwu rame (High month of festivities for the entire community)	*peluba–biluwara* from the first day until the full moon: *pedoa*	Ceremonies for all other clans and for the population	Same rituals and ceremonies as above for all other clans. They are descendants of Ie Miha. *Pedoa* occurs at the ritual place. *Pedoa* dances also take place in Waduwēla, the village of Deo Mengēru, but he conducts no rituals during this month.
	kewore dʾelu manu (day 12) *ngaʾa doka wenyi kenana*	Betel ingredients	Chew fresh areca nuts and betel fruit.
	kewore kele (day 13) *ngaʾa doka kiʾi*	Sacrifice a goat.	Slaughter and eat a goat.
	penupe (day 14) *ngaʾa doka kebao*	Sacrifice a buffalo.	Slaughter and eat a buffalo (or a pig).

Month	Date; name of ritual	Priest in charge; sacrifice; offering	Description
	biluwara (full moon day 15) *peiu manu* *bui ihi* *pedoa*	Deo Rai Gopo, Apu Lod'o	Ceremonial cockfight at Kolorame hill (no gambling) *Ratu Mone Pidu*, thus *udu* Gopo and *do* Nadai (Nahai, Nakale, Nanawa, Napujara, Gopo) and *udu* Teriwu. There is recreational cockfighting at Kepakahoro. No ritual cockfight can take place without Deo Gopo who is part of *Ratu Mone Pidu*. The members of his clan participate too. *Bui ihi*: night of silent ritual at Liae's ancestress houses *Pedoa* dances (at three places: Kolorame, Raewiu and Daba)
	1 *pehape* (day 16) *pehere jara bui ihi*	Apu Lod'o, Deo Gopo: *pehere jara* at Henaha	Horse dance *Hole* is the highest ceremony of the year.
	7 *pehape* (day 22) *hole* *peiu manu hole* *pehere jara hole*	Kenuhe (udu Nahai) at Henaha	*peiu manu*: recreational cockfight; *pehere jara*: recreational horse dance *hole*: offerings of mung beans, sorghum in *ketupat* (coconut leaves woven together [In]), betel (*sirih wangi*, 3 leaves) and areca nuts attached together asking the ancestors to remove the damaged, infertile seeds and to leave the good seeds to plant the following year. The offerings (in *ketupat*) give the earth a good scent (*mènyi rai*) for a profusion of cattle for a plentiful harvest, for Deo Woro who formed the world for humans.
	The closing ceremony of the rainy season.		Instead of launching a boat as in Seba, Menia and Mesara, offerings are simply hung in a sacred tree because the comain overlooks the southern coast, and the current and wind of the south-eastern monsoon would push the boat back to s ore.

3.   The knots of the land in Dimu[3]

There are two councils of priests in Dimu: one derived from the elder brother, Paha Hama Dole; the second from his younger brother, Muhu Hama Dole (chapter 2). Muhu Hama Dole is said to have died tragically before having children. A ritual chant says that Paha Hama gave Hire Ao to the line of Muhu Hama for adoption and he became Hire Muhu. This makes a clear case for the precedence of the Paha Hama Dole line over the descendants of Hire Muhu if people, as happens in other domains, contest the brothers' rank.

The year is divided into two six-month cycles: the dry and rainy seasons with *hèro* (bitter) and *nèta* (sweet) months. The complementarity of sweet and bitter months to ensure cosmic balance is best visible in Dimu's adat calendar. The council of priests of the elder brother's descendants is led by Lado Aga Lou (*lou* means south but also *laut*, sea [In]) or Lado Aga Hèro. The council of priests of the younger brother's descendants is under the leadership of Doheleo of *udu* Napuru who is also known as Lado Aga Nèta, also Lado Aga Rai. He and his two helpers Kiru Lihu and Deo Rai (who has the lowest rank) are in charge of ceremonies to ask for prosperity in the 'sweet' months (*nèta*).

Not only do bitter and sweet months alternate; sometimes a month is also divided into a sweet half and a bitter half, and both councils of priests conduct sweet and bitter rituals. Some months in both cycles are labeled *kètu nèta* (sweet head), while others are known as *kètu hèro* (bitter head); these correspond to a number of prohibitions while the earth is swelling (during the rainy season) and the juice is rising in the lontar trees (dry season).

---

[3] Sources: for Bodae: Mengi Lulu (priest Latia of *udu* Nadowu); Bolou: priest Doheleo (*udu* Napuru at Unuputoka); also Ama Lilo Wadu in Limagu.

Month	Date; name of ritual	Priest in charge; sacrifice; offering	Description
1. Wèru a'a			
Bolou *uèru bèro* for Lado Aga Nèta: only ceremonies related to 'bitter' matters	3 *peluha* (day 3 of a new moon) or 3 *pehape* (day 3 after a full moon) *penyèro èmu* Rue (cleaning the house of Rue)	Rue (*udu* Naju'u) Jèla *penyèro èmu* Rue *hudi b'ada rai* sacrifice a pig, a goat, a dog and a chicken Jèla (*udu* Naju'u)	The year starts with the ceremony for cleaning away mistakes, breaches of taboo, etc. Jèla is the acting priest and the priest Rue follows. The term *rue* also refers to wrongdoing; the task is connected to the people of the sea. The purpose of the ceremony *penyèro èmu* Rue is to clean or wash away all wrongdoing in the domain before the start of the lontar tapping season. The animals are taken from the community, *padi*, (but only from Jingi Tiu followers). Two groups of people participate; one on foot and one on horseback. If there is wrongdoing in the community—cases of 'offenses within marriage'—the priest Jèla is able to wash away the sins and to re-establish harmony. This requires a buffalo. A small and narrow cloth (*uai*) is attached to the right horn (for a man). For a woman a sarong with the motif *uokelaku* or *èi ledo* is attached to the left buffalo horn. The ceremony takes place at Raenaju'u.
Bodae	7 *peluha* (day 7) (or 9 *peluha*)	*keha'o èmu* Rue a chicken	Ceremony for cleaning the house of Rue. If the community has committed no serious wrongdoing, the ceremony takes place on the seventh day of the new moon. People sacrifice a chicken in their own house and roast it. If there has been wrongdoing in the community, the ceremony takes place on the ninth day of the new moon.

Month	Date; name of ritual	Priest in charge; sacrifice; offering	Description
2. Wèru ari			
Bolou			
Lado Aga Nèta: *wèru nèta*	6 *pehape* (6 days after a full moon) *Pedoa gape due*	Kiru Lihu and later Deo Rai sacrifice a chicken. There is also a goat sacrifice the following month.	Ceremony for *gape* (to summon by beckoning): during the ritual the priests symbolically call the lontar sap by waving their hands. Kiru Lihu and Deo Rai conduct the ceremony independently: they sacrifice a chicken, and examine the lines in the liver and the heart for predicting either prosperity or disease. If they read bad signs, a goat is sacrificed to re-establish the balance. For the priest Kiru Lihu it happens at Unuputoka. The two priests have to present themselves to priest Lado Aga Rai who is responsible for the sweetness (*nèta*) of the lontar sap. The ritual takes place in the village of Deo Rai (Dokaiki). He performs the ceremony for the entire domain.
Bodae	1 *pehape*	*para ke dèna*	People start to cut wood for boiling the lontar sap.
3. Wèru kelila			
Bolou (The first half of the month is *nèta*, sweet, for Bolou; the second half is *hèro*, bitter.)	6 *peluba* (day 6) (6 to 8 *peluba*) *hubi due*	1. Lado Aga Nèta 2. Kiru Lihu 3. Deo Rai, followed by the community; they sacrifice a goat (if not already sacrificed the previous month) or a chicken.	Groups of three offerings (*riwo*) are made: one filled with sorghum; the second with mung beans; and the third with rice. They are placed at the bottom of the lontar palm tree where lontar tappers hang the bucket for carrying the juice (*petae*) and at the junction of two branches (*pa telora ru para*) for the safety of the tappers when they go from one tree to the next. One offering contains aromatic roots and is placed at the tip of the youngest branch to ensure the juice is sweet.

Month	Date; name of ritual	Priest in charge; sacrifice; offering	Description
	6 *peluba* Ceremony of *bubi due*; followed by *nga'a kelila*	Every family sacrifices at least a chicken.	Prayer addressed to Deo Mengèru
			Nga'a kelila: ceremonial meal in each family
	On the same day in Bodae: *nga'a kelila are* and *nga'a kelila due* *nga'a kelila due* (see above)	Kiru Lihu and the community sacrifice a chicken, *hogo due*	Ceremonial meal is arranged in each family; the ceremony carries two names—one for rice (*are*) and one for the lontar sap (*due*).
			In the same month people prepare the hearth for boiling the lontar juice (*hogo due*) across the whole domain. In L'imu the priests and the community dig only one hole per hearth.
Bodae For Bodae, ceremonies are in the second half of the month only.	12 *pehape* (day 12 after a full moon)	Kiru Lihu *nga'a gape due* sacrifice a sow, sacrifice a dog; the community sacrifices a chicken and offers betel chew.	Ceremony is arranged for 'calling' the lontar sap; same purpose as above for Bolou. The dog has to be sacrificed with a dagger. Food is prepared by every family.
4. Wèru wadu ae			
Bolou (*wèru bèro* for Bolou)	N/A	N/A	No ceremony for Bolou because it is a 'hot'; thus a dangerous time for the lontar season. There are a number of prohibitions and prescriptions in this month.
Bodae	6 *peluba* (day 6)	Kiru Lihu *petitu rao*	Building the ceremonial hearth for boiling the lontar juice
	7 *peluba*		The following day the community can start to build their own cooking place.

Month	Date; name of ritual	Priest in charge; sacrifice; offering	Description
5. Wèru wadu kepete			
Bodae The first half of the month is *hèro*, for Bolou.	*3 peluba*	Kiru Lihu *dabu rao pana* 3 *kebiha, keduu ai* *bèbu due* *wokepaka*	Close the ceremonial hearth in 3 steps: extinguish the fire, disperse the smoke and cover the ceremonial hearth.
The second half is *nèta* for Bolou.	*3 pehape* *pemenringi rao*	1. Doheleo (Lado Aga Rai) 2. Kiru Lihu 3. Deo Rai	Lado Aga Rai, followed by Kiru Lihu then Deo Rai cool the ceremonial hearth (*rao pana*) with offerings of rice and pieces of dried pork which had been stored from a previous ceremony.
6. Wèru ha'e rae			
Bolou *wèru hèro* for Lado Aga Rai.	*3 peluba* (closing the hearth, if not done the previous month, depending on the start of the tapping season and the wishes of the population)	1. Doheleo (Lado Aga Rai) 2. Kiru Lihu 3. Deo Rai	In the same order as conducted previously: the priests close the ceremonial cooking place for boiling the lontar juice, Doheleo followed by Kiru Lihu, and Deo Rai. People who want to continue to boil lontar juice to make syrup have to dig out a new hearth.
	6 pehape (day 6 after a full moon)	Jèla *penyèro èmu* Rue *hud'i bada rai* sacrifice a pig, a goat, a dog and a chicken.	The purpose of the ceremony *penyèro èmu rue* is to clean or wash away all wrongdoing in the domain before the start of the planting season. The animals are taken from the community, *padi*, (only from Jingi Tiu followers). Two groups of people participate; one on foot, one on horse.

Month	Date; name of ritual	Priest in charge; sacrifice; offering	Description
Bodae *wèru bè'ole*	12 *pehape*	*pengèdu do bèro*	Ceremony held by priests associated with bitterness (*Xèru bèro*): Latia, Bèka Pahi, Rohi Nuha, Rihi Miha. The place where bad things are symbolically thrown is at the border between Dimu and Seba. If a large animal is sacrificed the 'bad things' are brought to Seba and thrown in the sea there.
	N/A	N/A	No further ceremony; this month is added to the calendar every few years as the lunar calendar has 12 months and 10 days.

The ceremony for *pengo'o* and *kuja ma*, which usually takes place the next month, is put forward to the second half of this month respectively on 3 *pehape* and 12 *pehape* for Bocae. |
| **7. Wèru ko'o ma** | | | |
| *Bolou* (*wèru nèta*) | 3 *peluha* (day 3) *hapu pengo'o* (cleaning and sharpening the tools) *loro rai* | 1. Doheleo (Lado Aga Rai) 2. Kiru Lihu 3. Deo Rai, then the entire community | *Ko'o ma* is to clear the fields and it starts with cleaning the tools. In this month it is forbidden to cut lontar branches and to repair houses, work which is done in the first month of the dry season.

For *loro rai*, a chicken is beheaded (*horo*) so its blood flows into the earth. Normally a chicken is killed while bearing the back of its neck so there is no blood flow. |
| | 11 *peluha* *loro rai* | Doheleo (Lado Aga Rai) | The different technique means that the flow of blood compensates for the holes made in the earth while clearing the fields and planting. It also placates bad spirits living underground.

Tool cleaning has to be completed in the first half of the month. If the farmer transgresses the rules s/he has to pay a fine in the form of a cow (or a pig or goat and a pot of sorghum). |

Month	Date; name of ritual	Priest in charge; sacrifice; offering	Description
	12 *peluha* *penèta rai* (to sweeten the village) *huki toka rai* (fencing, closing the village)	Doheleo (Lado Aga Rai) bird *delo* a newborn chick (*na manu do d'o ngaʾe*) *ru helama* (offerings made of lontar leaves)	*B'edo biada*: cattle have to be tethered to poles or kept in fenced fields. People catch a bird known for destroying the harvest (*delo* [Sa]; *burung pipit* [In]) and keep it alive in a jar in the loft at the bow-pillar of the house (*gela d'uru*). The priests conduct *huki toka rai*; to close the gates (*toka*) of the village with young lontar leaves and offerings so that evil influences (diseases) do not enter.
	13 *peluha* *ngaʾa gape*	Doheleo (Lado Aga Rai) and Kiru Lihu and Deo Rai	To call (*gape*) for an abundant harvest
	penupe (day 14) *kuja ma* (planting the fields) day 15 *hiluwara* (full moon) *hepehape* (one day after a full moon)	Sacrifice a goat or a sheep (not allowed to kill a pig). 1. Doheleo (Lado Aga Rai) 2. Kiru Lihu 3. Deo Rai then the community	Doheleo plants first followed the next day by Kiru Lihu. Then Deo Rai plants the day after and the people can start planting. Kiru Lihu plants. Deo Rai followed by the community start planting the fields.
8 Wèru naiki kebui *Bolou* (*wèru nèta*)	5 *pehape* (day 5 after a full moon) *èki kelila èjʾi lai*	Apu Lodʾo at Hurati (*udu* Natadu) Doheleo (Lado Aga Rai) and Kiru Lihu at Unuputoka Apu Lodʾo: sacrifice a boar.	Offerings of young coconut, *ru kengoro*, are brought to the *gèri tèru* pillar in the house. A boar is attached to the *gèri tèru* too. Apu Lodʾo (*udu* Natadu) addresses a prayer to Deo Mengèru for the prosperity of animals and humans. The pig is blessed with coconut oil and slaughtered. Offerings of cooked pork and rice are placed on ceremonial stones and pork meat is divided up between the council of priests.

Month	Date; name of ritual	Priest in charge; sacrifice; offering	Description
			Helpers from the Kolorae clan receive the upper right quarter of the head with an ear and eye (*kètu d'ida*) as a reminder of a sanction against this *udu* for having breached the ru es in a distant past.
	6 *pehape* *ngà'a kelila èj'i lai* *pehere jara* *golo kowa bole*	*Pehere jara* by Apu Lod'o at Hurati and Unuputoka	After the *ngà'a kelila* ceremony, Apu Lod'o's horse per orms the horse dance at Hurati and Unuputoka, then *pehere jara* for the community around the *nitas* tree in Kujiratu village.
		pi'i ladu ai	After *pehere jara*, a boat is launched at sea (*golo kowa role*) filled with *ladu ai*, a coconut shell containing mung bean blossoms. The boat of Doheleo (Lado Aga Rai) is launched at Banyo.
	7 *pehape*	*hud'i manu* sacrifice 5 chickens and a rooster. *pemeringi rae kowa* (*menyeram bawah api* [In])	The ceremony of *hud'i manu* involves the sacrifice of five chickens and a rooster to give to the family of the mair priests. Doheleo (Lado Aga Rai), Kiru Lihu and Deo Rai cool the ritual village of Unuputoka.
Bodae (no rituals)			
9. Wèru wila kolo			
Bolou The first half of the month is *nèta,*	3 or 6 *peluha* (day 3 or 6)	1. Doheleo (Lado Aga Rai) 2. Kiru Lihu 3. Deo Rai and Apu Lod'o	The priests harvest the mung beans in the same order as previously conducted, cook them with rice and grated coconut, and place them as offerings at a particular p llar of their ritual house called *gèri tèru ènu*.
The second half of the month is *hèro*	3 or 6 *pehape*	*hora kaba kebui* Kiru Lihu (*tunu manu*)	Empty pods of mung beans are thrown outside the village gate as a sign of the end of the month; a sacrificed chicken is roasted.

Month	Date; name of ritual	Priest in charge; sacrifice; offering	Description
Bodae	4 *peluha*	Kiru Lihu *hora kaba*	The coconut shell (*kaba*) kept since the ceremony *ngàa gape* is filled with empty pods of mung beans and thrown away outside the village gate, a sign that the harvest has taken place.
10. Hanga dimu			
Bolou	no ceremonies		
Bodae	3 to 6 *peluha*	*Pejedi dèlu*	Ceremony occurs for placing eggs on various sacred stones; the priests have to visit the sacred stones within three days, each time placing an egg on a stone while praying.
11. Wèru daba			
Bodae	*penupe* (day 14)	*daba* *peiu manu*	Traditional baptism for all children of Bodae Traditional cockfight; first as ritual then followed by recreational cockfighting with gambling
	hiluwara (full moon)	*puru loko* at Lokowala	lit. to go to the river to bathe
	4 *pehape* (day 19)	*peiu manu* at Èimadamèda	Second series of ceremonial cockfights
Bolou (*wèru nèta*)	1 *pehape* (day 1 after the full moon or day 16 in the month)	*Daba ana* 'baptism' for children by the council of priests; sacrifice a pig and a goat.	'Baptism' of all babies born since this ceremony took place the previous year The child's hair is cut except for a round spot above the forehead (*pu rei*) and on the crown of the head (*pu kolo*). Animals are anointed and slaughtered; the child's hair is burned, then brought onto a small mat made of lontar leaves *depi be dara*.

Month	Date; name of ritual	Priest in charge; sacrifice; offering	Description
		Daba ana for the community	The child is carried outside to the front of the male ceremonial pillar of the house (*téru*) and is 'bathed' three times. The child receives a mark on the forehead (*bure rei*), and a crown made of six areca nuts and six betel fruit which were kept for the purpose in small containers (*kedue*)'s then placed on its head.
			The child is brought inside the house, placed on the plaited lontar mat (*dépi he dara*) and 'bathed' with the rest of the water to ensure his/her mind and body develop successfully. The child is presented to Rai Bèla.
			The sacrificial pig and goat are carved up on the same mat; the meat is divided into piles (*dindu*) and shared between the family members who brought the animals (from the family of the child's father) and those who brought the rice (family of the child's mother).
	puru loko		Literally 'to go to the river to bathe'. The child is (symbolically) taken to the river (*puru loko*). In fact a boy is swung lying face down, a girl lying face up three times to a certain height (high up) so that his/her head points to Teriwu, the settlement of ancestral origin. Guests receive areca nuts.
2 *pehape* (day 17)	*pedoa*		Two days after *Daba ana*, *pedoa* starts in the village of Deo Rai (Dokaiki) and in the ritual village of Unuputoka. The *pedoa* then begins for the community in Kujiratu aro and the *nitas* trees.
			Pedoa season lasts for four months. In the past there was *pedoa* also in Bolou, but this is no longer the case.

Month	Date; name of ritual	Priest in charge; sacrifice; offering	Description
	4 *pehape* (day 19)	*pedoa*	A circle dance called *pedoa* is performed at night. It starts in the village of Deo Rai (Dokaiki), then in the ritual village Unuputoka and later the *pedoa* dance for the community takes place in Kupjiratu around the large *nitas* tree.
	6 *pehape* (day 21)	*peiu manu at* Dènilobo	Ritual cockfighting begins at Dènilobo in Raeawu (Bodae).
		pereti wo lèpa	Container with the excrement (*wo lèpa*) of the sacrificial animal, its head and a pumpkin are hung at the village gate.
		pehere jara	People throw young buds (*huma leda*) at the horse performing the circle dance (*pehere jara*).
		pedoa ngại pedèka	On the same evening, the *pedoa* dances begin in preparation for the festivities of the next month.
		wobo la terae	Stalks of sorghum (*terae*) are burned with fruits which have a hard skin; they explode while burning. It is meant to make noise to chase away evil spirits.
12. Wèru banga liwu			
Bolou			
(*wèru nèta*)	3 *peluba*	sacrifice a red chicken.	*Pedèka* announces the end of the year. Deo Rai and Kiru Lihu bring a red chicken to Mediri Pili. The chicken is kept there caged for three days.
	ngại pedèka		
	5 *peluba*	*la pejed'i dèlu*	Deo Rai and Kiru Lihu meet again and bring an egg each to Daba Ae. The eggs are placed for a short while on a sacred stone (*wadu mejed'i*); they have 3 days to visit all the sacred stones. The eggs are taken home and placed on the jar containing the small bird (*dèlo*) caught in the month of *ko'o ma*.
	6 to 8 *peluba*		

Month	Date; name of ritual	Priest in charge; sacrifice; offering	Description
	3 *pehape*	*peiu manu* first as a ritual, then recreational *peiu manu* for the community	Ceremonial cockfighting occurs between Bolou and Bodae to replace earlier inter-clanic wars between the descendants of Paha Hama and Muhu Hama. (Deo Rai for Bolou and Kiru Lihu for Bodae)
		pebere jara	The horse dance starts first at Unuputoka with the taboo horses of the three priests, then at Kujiratu for the community.
		pedoa henèbi kebèla jara	Closing *pedoa* dance
Bodae	6 *peluba*	*peiu manu* at Raenalai	Ceremonial cockfighting occurs between Bolou and Fodae (see above).
	4 *pehape*	*peiu manu* at Kolodaba	Ceremonial cockfight at Kolodaba
	6 *pehape*	*peluru ngaka*	There is a dog fight at Eiboa.

4.   Ceremonial calendar for the lontar palm tree in Mesara

The overall structure of the adat year in Mesara is similar to those of Liae and Dimu and is not reproduced here. Instead, the table provides details specific to Mesara with regards the tasks of the priest Apu Lod'o Wadu, responsible for rituals involving the lontar palm tree. If not otherwise stated, Apu Lod'o Wadu performs all the rituals in the following table.

Month	Date; name of ritual	Sacrifice; offering	Description
Wèru a'a (month of the elder sibling)			The ceremonies related to the lontar palm blossom take place in the first part of the month. The general purpose of these ceremonies is to create a propitious situation, to ask for good and great things (*mita wo ie do ae*) for the entire community during the whole of the dry season.
	tèlu peluha (day 3 after the new moon)	*Kedue hubi due*	Plaited lontar leaves in various shapes and sizes are hung in places related to the lontar palm tree and in the lontar palm trees. Apu Lod'o Wadu leaves his village at Ledelo and walks towards the sea to Ub'a Ae.
	hubi due (lontar palm tree blossom)	Sacrifice a white rooster (*manu mola'i wo pudi*).	There he calls while waving his hand, welcomes and 'picks up' the lontar, which people say came to Savu on Talo Nawa's boat.
	gape due (to summon by waving the hand or beckoning)	An offering wrapped in a lontar leaf (*kedue ware* or *ketupat* [In])	The water serves to bathe the sacred stone Lie Dahi at Kepuelie (lit. the coral cave by the sea at the source or origin). This is a sacred cave for the entire island called Liemangau (Kana 1978: 502, 503).
		Offering: a lontar basket filled with water, 3 pieces of dried coconut and grated sandalwood for fragrance (*haba lima baru*)	
	èpa peluha (day 4) *baja wawi wie kowa due*	Sacrifice an intact male pig (not yet neutered).	As the lontar comes from the sea and the priest Apu Lod'o Dahi's duties are related to the sea (*dahi*), he is involved in rituals from the beginning of the lontar season. The pig is sacrificed to ensure the safety of the lontar boat (*kowa due*) and its owner Talo Nawa (*nawa*: wave).

478　Savu: History and Oral Tradition on an Island of Indonesia

Month	Date; name of ritual	Sacrifice; offering	Description
	lèmi peluba (day 5) *Pemuri ra rai pa Ledelo.*	A pregnant goat is sacrificed at the stone *Wadu pemuri ra Ju Deo* (the stone where Ju Deo came back to life).	Ceremony to animate or increase the earth blood in Ledelo, Apu Lod'o Wadu's village. The blood of the earth is red (*ra rai mea*). The stone is said to be where Ju Deo started to show signs of life again. The goat is sacrificed and the unborn goat is buried at the stone. If it is not buried, the fear is that Ju Deo will bring hunger to the island. The stone allows the flow of the earth's blood. A *pedoa* dance reminiscent of Ju Deo's narrative is performed (chapter 4).
	ëna peluba (day 6) *memèngi due* (to give fragrance to the lontar blossom)	At Kepuelie, the cave of origin (near Ub'a Ae) Sacrifices: a white rooster, a grey chicken and a goat Offerings: coconut and sandalwood	The following ceremonies (*memèngi due*) ask for the lontar palm juice to flow, to enrich or improve people's lives while making offerings to the ancestors. The ritual starts at the origin cave, Kepuelie.[1] The animals are caught in the community (*padi*) in the area near the place of worship.
	pidu peluba (day 7)	At Ub'a Ae Sacrifices: a goat, a pig and a white chicken	Asking for an increased flow of lontar sap and for prosperity
	aru peluba (day 8)	At Lielai cave (Ub'a Ae, stones Ro Rai and Naba Rai) Sacrifices: a goat, a pig and a white chicken Offerings: coconut and sandalwood Ceremony at Ledehe	Ceremony held with the priest Kenuhe. The lontar juice is said to have come to Savu by travelling underground. Kenuhe, whose role is dedicated to war, can travel underground to where the conflict is taking place to help and favour his warriors. For this reason, Kenuhe participates in the ceremony at Lielai and asks the lontar juice to travel underground to the roots of the trees, specifically up to the sacred lontar tree of Apu Lod'o in Ledelo.

[1] See Kana for prayers and chants performed at Kepuelie (1978: 502, 503).

Month	Date; name of ritual	Sacrifice; offering	Description
			On the same day, the priests walk from Lielai to Ledehe to worship the stones Lede He and Unu Wo. The meat of the animals sacrificed earlier that day is carried there for worship.
	beo peluhu (day 9)	At Dokadui *wowadu* Hu Lia	Worship at the stone Hu Lia
	tobo d'ara (day 10)	Ceremony at Bela Kejabu and at *wadu be'i* Jawa Wadu	Worship at the stone *be'i* Jawa Wadu (the sleeping place of Jawa Wadu). The stones associated with Ina Jawa Wadu are *wadu* Haga and *wadu* Rao Nalulu (See Appendix 1, narrative 5).
	rèka tud'i (day 11)	Ceremony at Ledenake at *wadu* Rue Rai Sacrifices: a goat, a pig and a black hen	Worship at the stone Rue Rai to remember Rue Rai who is related to Ina Jawa Wadu. (The first Rue office in Mesara was held by a woman. However, her relationship to Ina Jawa Wadu is not clear.)
	wadu bu (day 12)	Ceremony at Ked'èirato at stone *mèngi due* Sacrifices: a chicken, a goat and a pig	The stone *mèngi due* serves to sweeten and add flavour to the juice. The slaughtered hen, offered at the spring *èi mada* Taga Roi (the source of the Taga Roi spring), is for Maja, a spirit related to the lontar's arrival in Savu. Placating the spirit Maja at the source of Taga Roi prevents men falling from the lontar trees; Maja will not disturb their work. Apu Lod'o Liru's sister, Be Lod'o, is said to have married Maja, according to certain sources. Apu Lod'o Wadu uses the oil of *nitas* seeds to heal and quieten the sea. The sea has to be calm during the tapping season as too much wind is not good for the blossoms. At D'èirato, there are also the stones *wadu* Rihi Miha (related to spirits) and *wadu* Mola Uli (the helmsman's stone).

Month	Date; name of ritual	Sacrifice; offering	Description
	kewore (day 13) Èiketadu	Sacrifices: a goat and a white chicken	There is already a lot of lontar juice, but more juice is requested.
	penupe (day 14) *hame ihi, hame donahu*	At Kètumerèga Sacrifices: a pregnant goat, a pregnant sow and a white chicken	Ceremony of the 'belching head' (*merèga* means to belch). At the stone Piga Hina the spoken mantra text is *Piga Hina Deo do pekaro ri kepue Ina Wadu Jawa Ae Rai Bela* (Piga Hina Deo who is radiating from the origin [place of] Ina Wadu Jawa Ae Rai Bèla).
			The foetuses are buried there by digging the hole with a branch of sandalwood. It is a thanksgiving ritual, *hame ihi, hame donahu*, for having received plentiful juice and syrup (*donahu*) and for the 'breath of the land' (*henga rai*) which is the soul of the land present in the wind.
		Ceremony at Hedide Rai Sacrifices: a pregnant sow, a pregnant goat and a dog	On the way back from Kètumerèga, there is a ceremony at Hedìderai in Ledelo.
			The pig is for *penète hogo wie Deo* (to give to God for sweetening the cooking place).
			The goat is sacrificed to God at the sacred lontar tree (*due pana*) which is the tallest tree in Apu Lod'o Wadu's village. The purpose is to prevent people falling from trees.
			The dog is to placate the bad sea spirits which might have entered the island with the lontar. Thus, this sacrifice ensures the wellbeing of the land and its people.
			The purpose of the ritual is to build a fortress for the lontar juice in the sacred village of Apu Lod'o Wadu, so that nothing disturbs the tapping season. As the lontar came from the sea, bad sea spirits may come to the land at that time. Building an invisible fence around the place protects against possible intruders and diseases. The power of Apu Lod'o's place is strong enough to protect the whole domain.

Month	Date; name of ritual	Sacrifice; offering	Description
	petad'a donabu at the house of Rue	Sacrifice a pig.	Each household gives a small pot of lontar syrup (*èru woga*) to Rue Ae, which is saved in the priest's house. People take a pig to Rue's house to safe guard the lontar season. The syrup is used in the ceremony to send back the lontar in Talo Nawa's boat. The pig is slaughtered in the month of Hobo. No further ceremonies for the lontar are held in the month of Wèru a'a.
			There are no ceremonies dedicated to the production of lontar juice in the waning moon.
	7 *pehape* (day 7 after the full moon) *ngai'a wuri kètu*		This ceremony is the closing ceremony of the rainy season. For each season, rituals overlap to avoid breaks in the ceremonial calendar.
Wèru ari (month of the younger sibling)			After the intense activities of the first month, Wèru a'è, there are no ceremonies in the following month of Wèru ari which is dedicated to the dead and is a silent month. People cut wood for boiling the lontar sap later in the season. (In Dimu, this month belongs to the category *hèro* bitter).
Wèru bob'o (month of the buds)	1 *peluba–hiluwara* (from day 1 of the new moon until the full moon) *wèba tadaka*		*Wèba tadaka* (to beat hollow dry lontar fruit) to remember the funeral of Ina Jawa Wadu during which fruit was used instead of gongs and drums
	penupe (day 14) *ngai'a woro hobo*	Sacrifice a chicken or a dog.	*Woro* (bubble), *bob'o* (pollination, germination for plants) Ceremony for the whole community involves family meals and the sacrifice of a chicken or a dog. Dog meat belongs to the category of hot, red.

Month	Date; name of ritual	Sacrifice; offering	Description
	hiluwara (full moon) *ngâ'a bobo ae* (midday) *petuku bobo* (late afternoon)		In the afternoon, after families eat the ceremonial meal, the ceremony of *petuku bobo*, said to replace the inter-clanic wars, follows consisting of group stone-throwing. The purpose is to welcome the lontar juice. If someone is injured by a stone, drawing blood, it is a sign there will be a lot of lontar juice. It takes place at two locations: 1. at Lederaila between upper Mesara (east) and lower Mesara (west) 2. at Ledenyebu (*nyebu* means placenta) between Lede Ae (uphill) and Lie (sea)
	hepehape (day 16) *tèbu wawi dèta*	Sacrifice a pig.	At Raidare, the burial place of Ina Jawa Wadu, in the hamlet of Ledetunu. The pig is sacrificed and carved up, the portions distributed as follows: For Apu Lod'o Wadu: the right half of the head, ribs, (*ru wawi*) and part of the liver For the owner of the dagger used to kill the pig (a member of the Napupudi clan): one back leg Deo Rai: one half leg, the (left) front part which has been pierced with the dagger For Deo Rae in Lede Ae: one half leg (*ha'i*) For Rue: the lower part of the head (*tura kètu wawa*) For Apu Lod'o Muhu: one leg, one *ha'i* For the person in charge of bringing the salt: one small lontar basket of blood (*he kètu ihi*)

Month	Date; name of ritual	Sacrifice; offering	Description
			Apu Lod'o Wadu's share of meat is used for worshipping his stones at home, *wadu Deo, wadu èmu*. The leftovers are saved. Each village has a stone called *wadu* Deo Rai which is worshipped every year by Deo Rai. Each house has a stone, *wadu èmu*, placed on the ground, underneath the house at its centre.
	7 *pehape* (day 22) *pepane rai*		Apu Lod'o Wadu starts the ceremonies for heating the earth, beginning a time of prohibitions: no *pedoa* dance is allowed nor can people make holes in the earth. From that point on people are not to take the following from the sea: *kenege, keka, kai koko* (different kinds of algae that are part of the everyday diet in the dry season) *keroko*, (sea urchins), *woboi* (molluscs).
	wo wadu mare merèmu tule bad'a, jue bad'a (take the cattle to the water place; mark the cattle)	Sacrifice a white chicken.	Ceremony at the stone *mare merèmu* uses a white chicken and a buffalo bone saved from a former *tao leo* ceremony. On the same day, farmers make an incision in one ear of each of their cattle. Each clan has a different mark. (Note: there are also ceremonies for Rue Ae and Rue Iki in this month.)
Wèru wadu ae (month of big stones) *luha* (waxing moon)	*Luha: tuju aj'u hogo due baje pa pehapo*	Offering: lontar leaves	During the first half of the month (*luha*) people cut wood (*tuju aj'u*) for boiling the lontar juice (*hogo due*). Offerings are made and placed on the beam of the house's male pillar (*baje pa pehapo*) so that people do not hurt themselves while cutting wood.

Month	Date; name of ritual	Sacrifice; offering	Description
	3 *peluha* (day 3) *ngapi due*		Apu Lod'o Wadu squeezes the lontar blossoms (*ngapi due*) to allow the flow of juice. The idiom '*due Nalalu Naleto*' (the sap of the orphans) is said about the lontar juice and all activities before the official start of the tapping season. Nalalu is said to have arrived from the sea and travelled over land until she reached Ketu Merega, holding the tool for squeezing the lontar blossom (*ngapi*). She continuously changed her name—Reja, Kahu, Nalalu. Nalalu-Naleto—all names referring to orphans. People who do not own lontar trees can tap the sap of any tree outside the tapping season so that everybody in the community has access to the main staple food in Savu.
			In the month of Weru wadu ae, at the start of the official lontar tapping season, the lontar is called Due Talo Nawa, named after Talo Nawa who brought the lontar by boat to the island. From the moment Apu Lod'o squeezes the lontar blossoms for the first time, only people who own lontar trees can tap their trees. Arrangements can be made between the owner and the previous tapper so that the latter continues to climb the tree for which he made his own footholds and marks, and shares the harvest with the owner.
	kewore (day 13) *ke'i kelaba*		People fetch limestone (*kelaba*) to line the bottom of the cooking place.
	penupe (day 14) *ke'i rao*		Apu Lod'o Wadu digs (*ke'i*) the cooking place (*rao*); four holes for the ceremonial hearth, *rao pana*.

Month	Date; name of ritual	Sacrifice; offering	Description
	hiluwara (full moon) *hogo due pana rao*		Apu Lod'o Wadu boils the first juice at the ceremonial hearth. People are not allowed to squeeze lontar blossoms on that day. If they do so, they have to carry a lontar basket as if they were going to harvest the sap.
	hepehape (day 16 *dao haba due*	Sacrifice a chicken.	Community boils the first juice. People offer pieces of cooked chicken at all corners of the cooking place (all cardinal directions) to call the lontar juice. The first pot of boiled juice has to be stored.
			Apu Lod'o Wadu offers a bone from a previously sacrificed goat kept for the occasion.
After the full moon *pemeringi* (cooling)	*pemeringi dahi*	*kedue* (offerings wrapped in a plaited lontar leaf)	The time of starting to cool (*pemeringi*) what was previously heated: this means the end of restrictions.
			1. Cooling down the sea. Apu Lod'o Wadu (or his wife), followed by all the women from houses involved in lontar production, go to the sea. They bring *kedue* (offerings in plaited lontar leaves) to the sea at Kepuelie, the village of origin. Then they go to Lobolata, Pudimenoka and Ub'adietura.
			After cooling down the sea, they can bring home products from the sea: *keroko, ngahu, woboi, kemege, keka, kai koko.* They are offered to the *rao*, received by the chicken of the *rao* (*hapo ri manu di rao*). People can bring and use *dzuu, deme, worai laka, kai rahi, wue pudi, jega doka, petue aj'u* (all the ingredients for clearing the water, and for poisoning and catching fish, molluscs and octopus).

Month	Date; name of ritual	Sacrifice; offering	Description
	On the same day in the evening: *pemeringi rao*	Sacrifice a black chicken.	2. Cooling the *rao*. The syrup boiled on that day cannot be consumed by the people. It has to be stored in the house loft.
	pemeringi petae (cooling the tools)	Offerings: a lontar basket filled with water, a *kedue* (large offering) and a *riwo kedue* (a bundle of 3 small offerings)	3. Cooling the tools for the lontar activities, cooling the tree and the place where the sap is filtered next to the tree (*petae*) and at home where it is stored awaiting boiling. Everything is sprinkled with water. When in the tree, men are whistling at the same time as sprinkling water to call the good wind, *b'olou dana* (south-eastern wind), which facilitates the flow of a lot of sap.
			The small offerings are placed on the top of the stone to cool the tools (*ud'e di deni wowadu*).
	2 *pehape* (day 17) *pemeringi rai*	Sacrifice a grey chicken.	4. Cooling the earth; a ceremony performed by Apu Lod'o Wadu only
			Chicken is already cooked. The group of three offerings is placed on the stone called *wowadu mola uli* (helmsman's stone).
	peba'e mèti donahu at *wowadu bemuhe*		*Hemuhe* means to inhale. The inhaling stone is located outside the village of Apu Lod'o in the north. The aim of the ritual is to help the lontar juice to climb up to the blossoms and to prevent the earth from inhaling the lontar tree sap.

Month	Date; name of ritual	Sacrifice; offering	Description
Wèru kè'i ei			No special rituals for the lontar palm tree. The month is dedicated to digging wells. There is a sacrifice of a black hen before starting the work. At the end, a goat and a pig are sacrificed for Deo Èi, the god of water.
Wèru Hae Rae (climb to the village)			Note: the ceremonies in the first half of the month are not related to the lontar palm tree.
	3 *pehape* (day 18) *bàja ngaka penèta nada* (to sweeten the arena)	Sacrifice a goat.	Apu Lod'o Wadu asks Rue to hold the ceremony. Rue asks for rain, thunder and lightning at a place called *penèta nada* in the area of Ja (the traditional land of *udu* Nahipa). If the first rain has already fallen, the ceremony is followed by *bàja manu* held by Apu Lod'o Wadu.
	pemawo rao (cooling the cooking place)		The fire in the sacred cooking place is extinguished. Then the cooking place is lit once again from the back and extinguished permanently. (This action reflects the principle that things have to end where they started.) The hearth is cooled down so that the cooking place can be definitively closed on the seventh day after the full moon.
	6 *pehape* (day 21) *ngà'a kelila pa rao pehere jara*		Ceremonial meal made of grilled molluscs (*lengi wobo'i*), fish (*nadu'u*) and octopus (*kepajo*) is prepared. After the meal, *pehere jara*, the horse dance is performed by *udu* Nahipa at Raemèdi. Only *udu* Nahipa is allowed to catch octopus at Gèlanalalu.
	7 *pehape* (day 22) *debu rao pana* (closing the ceremonial cooking place)	Sacrifice a white rooster (*manu molà'i pudi*). Offerings: a coconut cut into small pieces and a small basket with lontar sugar	Ceremony held by Bèni Aji, Apu Lod'o Wadu's wife in the late afternoon (*mada lod'o*); she sacrifices a white rooster saying "*lale rao, dèno rao*" (the hearth is filled with ashes and soil). The leftover wood covers the *rao*.

Month	Date; name of ritual	Sacrifice; offering	Description
			The first syrup boiled and stored in the house loft is taken and used for the ceremony and carried back to the sea; thus it closes the cycle. With a small palm container filled with diluted syrup, Bèni Aji goes to the sea to sprinkle it on various stones. When she is back at the cooking place, she puts the broom (*heboro*) into the hole of the coconut shell so in the coming year there is lontar juice again. A lontar leaf of three ribs and three baskets for covering the juice in the tree (*kebiha*) are placed on the now closed *rao*.
			In this ceremony people ask that their burdens (or diseases) are taken to the sea and what is less troublesome for people stays on the island.
			Then Apu Lod'o Wadu informs Deo Rai that he has closed the *rao*. If people want to continue to boil lontar syrup they have to dig a new cooking place.
			In the late afternoon, Bèni Aji, Apu Lod'o's wife goes to the shore to signal the end of her activities in the lontar ritual, which are all *rao*-related, to say 'goodbye to the lontar'.
	8 *pehape* *ligu keruga* (taking coral from the sea)		In the morning at low tide, Bèni Aji returns to the shore for the start of the ceremony for *ligu keruga*, for taking coral from the sea; she is followed by the community.

Month	Date; name of ritual	Sacrifice; offering	Description
	Puru Pu Lod'o Raja Ub'ad'ara	Sacrifices: a goat, a baby goat, a puppy and a small chicken Offerings: areca blossom and nuts, a bamboo shoot, a yellow leaf of lontar made into a round shape, a *riwo kedue* (bundle of 3 offerings), a large offering in a lontar leaf (*rubelama kewore merai*) and a chicken egg	'Apu Lod'o Wadu comes down [to the sea] (*Puru Pu Lod'o*)'. He sacrifices a goat in his village, in the presence of Deo Rai and Rue. Then they go to Ub'a Ae for the ceremony to 'beat the harbour' (*raja Ubʾad'ara*) at the 'doorstep of the land' (*Kemubunai*) where Rue slaughters a baby goat and a puppy. *Ketupat* are thrown into the sea to appease the marine spirits which are angry because people have cut coral. He sticks two pieces of wood in the ground at the high tide point, where land and sea meet, and places a coconut branch on top to join the wood, forming a gate. Using the *rubelama* offering, he draws two groups of seven lines on the beach parallel to the shore so the sea does not inundate the island. Deo Rai sacrifices the chicken. The egg is thrown into the sea from west to east in the hope that it will break the waves which cause erosion.
		Sacrifice a black hen. Offerings in a basket: 7 pieces of betel fruit (*kenana*), 7 areca nuts (*kelèla*) and a black sarong (*èi wo mèdi*)	As the *rao* is already closed the priests can call for the rain, *buka belu ngelu*, slaughtering a black hen at the stone of Mare Merèmu. This is the signal for the beginning of Deo Rai's rain rituals. Prayer is *puru do maho do bengo* (come down and enter the fire place from the back). Deo Rai is accompanied by Rue Rai, Apu Lod'o Dahi and Bawa Iri. The hen is placed in a lontar basket and, while holding the basket high, the priests call the rain, the thunder and the lightning. After slaughtering the hen, they examine her liver to see how soon the rain will come and if it will be a lot. The basket is beaten against a stone until it breaks. The sarong is soaked in water and beaten against the Mare Merèmu stone; later it is placed on the Deo Rai Hawu stone at the ceremonial arena inside Ledelo village.

Month	Date; name of ritual	Sacrifice; offering	Description
	At Latamoneweo (pandanus tree of Mone Weo)	Sacrifices: an unneutered pig (*wawi do are*) and a black hen (*manu morena wo mèdi*). Offerings: mung beans and sorghum (*kebʼui, terae*) and the tip of a coconut leaf (*ru kolo njiu/ru pengoro*)	The same priests (as above) go to Latamoneweo, to the pandanus tree of Mone Weo. At least a goat or a sheep has to be slaughtered if a pig is not possible. The pig is sacrificed to Talo Nawa, the captain of the boat which brought the lontar. The ceremony takes place at Kepuelie, the cave of origin, where the boat arrived at the beginning of the dry season. The stones Hai Ae, Hai Rai, Liba Lobo and Maja facing the sea, receive offerings. The meat is shared by Deo Rai, Rue, Apu Lodʼo and Bawa Iri. Three stones receive offerings of goat meat, mung beans and sorghum, and *ru pengoro*, the tip of a young coconut. The priests return home and hold a ritual at their respective stones and at the main pillar of their houses. The end of the dry season does not mean the end of Apu Lodʼo Waduʼs role. In the first half of the following month, Koʼo ma, when Deo Rai is in charge of the rituals related to the fields and planting season, Apu Lodʼo Wadu still has rituals to complete as there has to be an overlap of the priests' tasks for both seasons.

5.   The knots of the land in Raijua

There are at least five priests called Deo Rai[4] (Lord of the Earth) in Raijua. There the label *agama suku* (religion according the clan [In]) applies best to Jingi Tiu beliefs.

One month only, Bangaliwu, is reproduced here showing the clearest contrast between Upper and Lower Raijua. Upper Raijua comprises the oldest clans descended from the elder brother while Lower Raijua encompasses the clans descended from the younger brother Ie Miha, among them the clan of the former Raijua rajas.

As in the other domains, Bangaliwu is rich in rituals. Ceremonial cockfights, which have replaced inter-clanic wars, take place daily in the second half of the month and involve a group of Upper Raijua opposing one of Lower Raijua. They start with ritual cockfights, followed by recreational fights. The places where the fights occur are prescribed, and alternate between Upper and Lower Raijua.

---

[4] It seems that every clan had its own council of priests—the Nadega clan's Deo Rai is the most respected.

Weru Bangaliwu ae (bui ihi)	Date; name of ritual	Sacrifice; offering	Description
3 peluba (day 3)	Haga aj'u jami aj'u dab		Ritual to ensure the trees in the forest thrive
5 peluba (day 5)	Lèki kerae oba ana wuri pemau ana		People collect stalks of sorghum from the fields, take them home, burn them and keep the ashes for a later ritual dedicated to the ancestress Bèni Kedo.
6 peluba (day 6)	Bui ihi do made	tèbu ki'i Sacrifice a goat.	Ceremonies commemorate the dead for the families who had a death in the previous 11 months (from day 6 to day 10 in the month).
kewore d'elu manu (day 12)	Kèlu èki bako		Members of the Nadaibu clan bring betel ingredients and tobacco for a ritual at Menanga (north coast). There they beat gongs. On their way home people are allowed to take stalks of sorghum and lontar sap; however, everything has to be consumed before dawn.
kewore kele (day 13)	Ihi bada kebau		Purification ceremony for cattle
pemupe (day 14)	Ihi bada dou / Bui ihi dou		Purification ceremony for people
	Pengi'a dou do èki jara kede kebau	tèbu wawi, tèbu ki'i Sacrifice a pig and goat.	Ceremonial meal, blessing for horses and buffalos
hilu wara (day 15)	Pehere jara kelila pemau rau ana		Horse dance for the community: horses circle the arena; each rider takes either a woman or a child to sit behind him on the horse.
1 pehape (day 16)	Peiu manu kebihu nada Rae Nadega		Cockfight at the arena of the Nadega clan in Bolua (Upper Raijua)
2 pehape (day 17)	Peiu manu kebihu nada Rae Nadaibu		Cockfight at the arena of the Nadaibu clan in Wuirrae (Lower Raijua)
3 pehape (day 18)	Peiu manu kebihu nada Rae Kolorae		Cockfight at the arena of the Kolorae clan in Kolorae (Upper Raijua)
4 pehape (day 19)	Peiu manu kebihu nada Rae Roliu		Cockfight at the arena in Roliu, Ledeunu (Lower Raijua)

Wèru Bangaliwu ae (bui ihi)	Date; name of ritual	Sacrifice; offering	Description
5 *pehape* (day 20)	*Peiu manu kebihu nada Rae Bogi*		Cockfight at the arena of the Bèlu clan in Bogi (Upper Raijua)
6 *pehape* (day 21)	*Peiu manu kebihu nada Rae Ujudima*		Cockfight at the arena in Ujudima (Lower Raijua)
7 *pehape* (day 22)	*Peiu manu kebihu nada Rae Bèlu*		Cockfight at the arena of the Melako clan in Bèlu (Upper Raijua)
8 *pehape* (day 23)	*Peiu manu kebihu nada Rae Kepaka Odi*		Cockfight at the arena in Rae Kepaka (Lower Raijua)
9 *pehape* (day 24)	*Peiu manu kebihu nada Rae Bolua*		Cockfight at the arena in Bolua (Upper Raijua)
10 *pehape* (day 25)	*Peiu manu kebihu nada Hèpa*		Cockfight at the arena in Hèpa (Lower Raijua)
11 *pehape* (day 26)	*Peiu manu kebihu nada Dimu*		Cockfight at the arena in Dimu (Upper Raijua)
12 *pehape* (day 27)	*Peiu manu kebihu nada Leokabi*		Cockfight at the Leokabi arena in Ledeunu (Lower Raijua)
13 *pehape* (day 28)	*Peiu manu kebihu nada Lèba*		Cockfight at the Lèba arena in Bolua (Upper Raijua)
14 *pehape* (day 29)	*Peiu manu nada Watarai begura juli*		Cockfight at the Watarai arena of the Rohaba clan (Lower Raijua)

6.   The large knots of the land, *kelila ae*
Kelila *cycle in Dimu*

As the number six is representative of Dimu, the largest cycle of rituals lasts six years and closes with the ceremony *kelila rae ae*. However, for each year there is a *kelila* celebration which is named after the group of people or clan which is in charge of the ceremony.

Time	Group in charge of ceremony
Year 1	*Kelila j'ari rai*: *Kelila* begins (latest settlers) – *udu* Nabe'e. Although the Nabe'e people are named as ancient settlers, as a clan they are considered newcomers.
Year 2	Subgroup of *udu* Nabe'e
Year 3	*Udu* Woloma (descended from the younger brother). Similarly, although the Wolo people are named as ancient settlers, as a clan they are considered newcomers.
Year 4	*Ketopo* – 'vanished': as there is no 'clan' in charge, there is no ritual.
Year 5	*Lere* (to follow) or *keraha koko nga'a* ('towards the neck', meaning towards the head or the end of the cycle) for the lineages descended from the clans of origin
Year 6	*Kelila rae ae* for all clans of origin (descended from the elder brother)

Ancient and current kelila *cycles in Liae*

The religious organisation of Liae experienced a number of changes throughout the centuries (chapter 3). As seven is the number identifying Liae, the *kelila* cycle was based on the number seven. For the oldest council of priests, *Ratu Mone Tèlu*, *kelila* was only held during the rainy season (*kelila èji lai*). Nowadays, only three clans assume this task. For the remaining years, the groups have vanished and no other groups were appointed to take on the roles. These people are said to have left the island and are remembered as 'people from the sea who returned to the sea'. The *kelila* of the years without ritual are all called *kelila wango*, during which the spirits of the sea are said to hold their own celebrations, sacrificing marine creatures at sea. People on land are not allowed to consume fish or any product from the sea on those days which are now remembered through a 'blank' or an absence of ritual and a prohibition. The Teriwu clan closes the *kelila* cycle. As in Dimu, the precedence among the clans is inverted; the oldest and most revered clans do not come first in the cycle, but they close it with the highest ceremony.

Kelila *cycle of the former council* Ratu Mone Tèlu

Time	Group in charge of the ceremony
Year 1	There is no longer anyone in charge of the land.
Year 2	There is no longer anyone in charge of the land.
Year 3	There is no longer anyone in charge of the land.
Year 4	*Udu* Kolorae
Year 5	*Udu* Gopo
Year 6	There is no longer anyone in charge of the land.
Year 7	*Udu* Teriwu

For most people in Liae, the seven-year cycle is called *heboro*. It is named after a small broom made of a lontar stalk with which men clean the baskets they use for tapping the lontar tree sap. This is the traditional cycle of the Nadai people descended from the younger brother Ie Miha. They formed the Council of Seven Men (*Ratu Mone Pidu*). The cycles of both councils are seven years, so they occurred in parallel to one another.

The seven-year cycle of Ratu Mone Pidu

Time	Group in charge of the ceremony
Year 1	*Udu* Nahai
Year 2	*Udu* Nakale
Year 3	*Udu* Nanawa
Year 4	*Udu* Narebo
Year 5	*Udu* Napulai
Year 6	*Udu* Napuleru/Napuuju
Year 7	*Udu* Napujara: *kelila ae* for *Mone Pidu* or 'Council of Seven Men'

However, Liae used to have the largest cycle, *kelila ae* of 7 x 7 years, or 49 years. In the 19th century, this cycle was shortened at the time of the second regent, Ama Kitu Raja from *udu* Napujara and his younger brother Ama Jami Raja, who were anxious that they might not live long enough to celebrate *kelila ae*.

In an effort to harmonise and unify the religious systems of Liae, a new (now current) cycle combining elements of both cycles runs as follows:

Time	Group in charge of the ceremony
Year 1	*Udu* Nahai
Year 2	*Udu* Nakale
Year 3	*Udu* Nanawa
Year 4	*Udu* Narebo
Year 5	*Udu* Napulai
Year 6	*Udu* Napuleru/Napuuju
Year 7	*Udu* Napujara: '*kelila ae* for *Mone Pidu* or 'Seven Men'
Year 8	*Udu* Kolorae (*Mone Lèmi* or 'Five Men')
Year 9	No ritual is held; this is for the 'people of the sea' (*Wango*).
Year 10	*Udu* Teriwu and *udu* Gopo (*Mone Tèlu* or 'Three Men')

The length of the *kelila* cycle is now no longer seven years but ten. The traditional number seven, found in many Austronesian societies, has been replaced by a decimal system. However, the ancient people known as 'people of the sea' have not been completely removed. They are remembered in the year without ritual which is for the souls of the dead: it is a sign that the concept of *Wango* has a new place and a new meaning. Liae's *kelila* cycle shows the same pattern as Dimu: the order of precedence is inverted. The clans of *do* Nadai, the newcomers (year one to seven), hold their rituals first while the most ancient clans (Teriwu and Gopo) close the *kelila* cycle.

Bawa and kelila ae in Mesara

Like Liae, Mesara follows a *kelila* cycle of seven years called *bawa*, but it still has a larger cycle as well, based on 7 x 7 years or *kelila ae*. For each year a different clan is in charge of the ritual and has to slaughter a pig. *Bawa* refers to the rack or bamboo platform especially built as a place to put the meat from the sacrificial pig. Those who established themselves later in Mesara, coming from Seba, Raijua or Menia, hold the ceremony first. For the seventh year, called *bawa ae*, all clans, both original and newcomers, participate together in the ceremony. The platform used for the first cycle is stored away. A new *bawa* is made and the second cycle of seven years starts. However, the actual observance of the tradition is often different in practice. The table below shows that two years are named *lu*. These are 'blank' years for forgotten or vanished people. The situation in Mesara is similar to that in Dimu and Liae.

Bawa *or seven-year cycle in Mesara*

Time	Group in charge of the ceremony
Year 1	*Kelila jari* or '*kelila* begins': the latest settlers are in charge of ceremony (*udu* Teriwu-Nahire).
Year 2	*Kelila lu*–'Forgotten': as there are no more descendants, there are no more rituals.
Year 3	*Kelila* Bèlu–*Udu* Bèlu is in charge of the ceremony.
Year 4	*Kelila* Haba Dida–*Udu* Haba Dida holds the ceremony.
Year 5	*Kelila* Gèra–*Udu* Gèra is in charge of the ceremony.
Year 6	*Kelila lu*–'Forgotten': as there are no more descendants, there are no more rituals.
Year 7	*Bawa Ae*–all original clans and the newcomer clans celebrate together.

When no clan is in charge of the *kelila* ceremony, consequently there is no *pehere jara* either. Each *bawa* carries the name of a clan. When seven successive *bawa* have been carried out, each carrying the name of one of the seven 'clans', 49 years have elapsed and the largest cycle is complete. The ceremony of *kelila ae* takes place for the entire community with the sacrifice of a buffalo.

The clans have a system of counting *bawa* to remember the passage of time and the ceremonies that tie the community members together. Similarly, the priest Apu Lod'o Wadu, responsible for the rituals related to the lontar palm tree, has his own system based on his ritual hearth, *rao pana*, in Ledelo.[5] It is the only hearth on the island allowed to have four holes for boiling the lontar sap, which gives a particular elongated shape to the place. The hearth is closed at the end of each lontar season, covered with soil forming a mound and is reopened every succeeding year for a total of seven years. Then the *rao pana* is definitively closed. In the following year, a new *rao pana* is dug parallel to the first one and this too is used for seven years. When seven *rao pana* have served seven years each, 49 years have elapsed and *kelila ae* is celebrated the next rainy season at the time of *kelila èjilai*. The seven elongated mounds of closed *rao* visually mark the passing of almost half a century in Mesara. Apu Lod'o Wadu uses different memory tags acting to reinforce memory in the domain.

---

[5]   A *rao* has two openings: the fire is built at one end in the first hole with the hole at the narrower far end drawing the air through—combustion is the most efficient in this manner. A *rao* with four cooking holes gives Apu Lod'o Wadu the right to cook a larger quantity of syrup than the rest of the community. The long *rao* of Apu Lod'o Wadu is reminiscent of a miniature 'dragon' kiln for firing pottery. See Kana on ceremonies for the lontar palm tree, especially the closing ceremony (1978: 370–85; 507–9).

Kelila and jola cycles in Seba[6]

Seba has a unique mechanism for keeping track of the passing years, combining two visual devices. Each year one layer of lontar leaves is added to the roof ridge of Deo Rai's house in Namata. This ritual building is called Bèni Deo, which is also the name of his wife who plays an important role in agricultural rituals. The ceremony for putting a new layer of lontar leaves on the ridge is called *rupelila* (*ru*, leaf; *lila*, to fly) and takes place every year in the last days of the month of Bègarae (September), the last month of the dry season. People at a distance can see the new layer of fresh leaves shining in the sun on the ridge of Bèni Deo; therefore, they are aware that the dry season is coming to an end. When three layers of leaves have been added to the ridge of the roof, all are removed in the fourth year and a new layer is placed on the ridge.

During the following dry season people prepare a new ritual cooking place, *rao pana*, to be used for the next three years to boil the lontar syrup. The hearth is made in the ceremonial field, Rao Ae, which is a 20-minute walk from the ritual village of Namata.[7] On the day after Bèni Deo has closed the ritual hearth, a layer of leaves is added to the ridge of her house. When a *rao* has served for three years, it is closed definitively, although its outline stays visible for years on the ground. The year after a new *rao* is dug parallel to the previous one. When the three layers of leaves have been replaced three times and the cooking place built three times, nine years have passed. This marks the end of a cycle called *kelila Deo Rai*. The passage of time in Seba is measured by the layers of lontar leaves on the roof of the highest priest's ritual house and the ceremonial cooking places for the lontar sap; the latter are the responsibility of his wife.

---

[6]   For the *kelila* and *jola* cycles of Seba, Ama Bawa Iri (alias Ama Lai Helu), the helper of Seba's Deo Rai, was the source of information (October 2000).

[7]   For the historical background of this place, see chapter 6.

Roof of Bèni Deo house	Ceremonial hearth for lontar syrup	Time	Name of ceremony (rainy season)	Name of ceremony (dry season)	Name of large cycle
1st layer	1st *rao*	1 year	*kelila èji lai*	*kelila wadu*	
2nd layer		2 years	"	"	
3rd layer		3 years	"	"	
1st layer	2nd *rao*	4 years	"	"	
2nd layer		5 years	"	"	
3rd layer		6 years	"	"	
1st layer	3rd *rao*	7 years	"	"	
2nd layer		8 years	"	"	
3rd layer		9 years	*kelila Deo Rai*	9 years	
1st layer	1st *rao*	1 year	*kelila èji lai*	*kelila wadu*	
2nd layer		2 years	"	"	
3rd layer		3 years	"	"	
1st, 2nd, 3rd	2nd *rao*	3 years	3 x "	"	
1st, 2nd, 3rd	3rd *rao*	3 years	3 x *kelila èji lai* / *kelila Deo Rai*	"	
				9 years	
1st, 2nd, 3rd	1st *rao*	3 years	*kelila èji lai*	*kelila wadu*	
1st, 2nd, 3rd	2nd *rao*	3 years	"	"	
1st, 2nd, 3rd	3rd *rao*	3 years	"	9 years	27th year *kelila Rae Ae* (Deo Rai)

Roof of Bèni Deo house	Ceremonial hearth for lontar syrup	Time	Name of ceremony (rainy season)	Name of ceremony (dry season)	Name of large cycle
1st, 2nd, 3rd	1st *rao*	3 years	*kelila èji lai* "	*kelila wadu* "	after 27 years (or in 28th year or in 1st year of jola cycle) *hora baja* (Deo Rai)
1st, 2nd, 3rd	2nd *rao*	3 years			
1st, 2nd, 3rd	3rd *rao*	3 years	9 x *kelila èji lai* *kelila jola* (36th year)	9 x *kelila wadu*	*kelila baba* or *kelila muri mada horo baja* (*jola*) (year 1 of new cycle)
			Total	9 years 36 years	

When three times nine years (3 x 3 x 3 *rao*) have elapsed this produces the longest cycle commonly known in Seba as *kelila rae ae* (festival of the great village) and many people do not know any other cycle. However, some sources are familiar with an even longer cycle of 36 years, which combines *kelila rae ae* and another cycle of nine years (3 x 3) known as the *jola* cycle, making up a total cycle of 36 years.[8] Jola refers to people who do not have a fixed home. In everyday speech, Savunese say to someone who does not settle down, does not marry or does not have a proper house—"*helau ou mi Jola*" (you are like the Jola people). This carries the idea of instability, a nomadic life and a lack of possessions. The Jola are said to have been chased away by the people of Seba long before the arrival of the Portuguese on the island. One of the two cycles in Seba carries their name. The *jola* cycle is specialised insider knowledge among the priests; only a few people living near Namata are aware of this phenomenon. Deo Rai is in charge of the 27-year cycle while Deo Mengèru (*mengèru* meaning green, growth) is responsible for the second cycle of what is now nine years. The last ceremony for Deo Rai's cycle is *hora baja* (to give away or to save), which takes place in the first year of the *jola* cycle. Again, the last ceremony for Deo Mengèru is in the first year of Deo Rai's next cycle. This means the two cycles overlap, ensuring continuity. This kind of overlap is quite common in the ceremonial year calendar in all domains. Savunese seem to dislike breaks between the dry and the rainy seasons, the yearly and the *kelila* cycles.

---

[8]   Field research gleaned various details concerning the length of the *kelila* cycle in Seba, with estimations of 27, 36, 48 and even 81 years, until Ama Bawa Iri (Ama Lai Helu) gave the most complete information about both cycles.

Appendix III | Traditional System of Exchange[1]

Background

The system of exchange was based on two essential staples: the areca nut (*keèla* [Sa] or *pinang* [In]), a necessity for betel chew, and syrup from the lontar palm tree (*donahu* [Sa] or *gula Sabu* [In]). Most people consumed these two agricultural products. The syrup could be kept over a period of time only if it was stored in earthenware containers. For historical reasons, Mesara and Liae had the right to produce earthenware (*èru*) but not Seba and Dimu. The Mesara potters previously lived near Namata in Seba at a place called Uduawu (lit. Heap of Ashes); however, they were expelled during the war begun by Mata Lai and his allies known as *muhu kehibo* (encircled by enemies, chapter 3). Seba and Mesara must have made an agreement which gave Mesara the right to make pottery, although there is no ritual text remembered about this. When they moved from Seba, the people took some place names (Tedida) and stones (at Nada Woe) with them to Mesara, as well as their claim to earthenware.

The historical background to Liae's right to pottery making is not known. Mesara and Liae producers of earthenware could sell their pots all over the island and even export them. Earthenware was a necessity not only for boiling lontar sap and storing the syrup but also for producing the indigo blue and *morinda* red dyes for textiles. Pots were also important for general cooking and water storage. It is still possible in the early 21st century to see Liae people in Seba going from house to house selling their pots.

Sea-salt and earthenware production were female undertakings, in addition to the principal female activity of weaving textiles. Women wove textiles exclusively in the dry season when there were no agricultural activities requiring their labour. In Liae, the women who gathered sea salt or made earthenware were not weavers; it was not possible to combine these activities as they are so time consuming. Women collected the sea salt in gigantic clam shells or in lontar-leaf

---

[1] This system of exchange was valid throughout Savu until the 1960s and is still well known among older generations. Sources of information: Zadrak Bunga and Ama Jo Haba (Mesara); Agustinus Moi (Liae); Beha Lado (Seba).

containers, which involved pouring small quantities of seawater into the vessels every day for the slow process of evaporation. Gathering clay and sand to make pots did not require much work, but collecting the horse dung to fire them was time consuming as the pots had to be covered by heaps of dung.[2]

The Savunese used five sizes of earthenware (*èru*) pots and their more or less standard dimensions served as measurement units. Today people use aluminum containers to boil the sap; unlike earthenware, they do not break. To store water and other liquids plastic jerry cans have replaced large earthenware pots. Note that in Liae and Mesara an exchange could not be initiated using a pot of rice as very little rice grew there. Only Seba and Menia people could exchange their rice using this system.

The smallest pot, *èru ketilu*, was used for cooking small amounts of food (it is known as *èru ketodo* in Raijua). The next size up, *èru boga*, was in daily use for storing syrup. It has a volume capacity of roughly 10 litres. The following size, *èru pedako*, equivalent to two *èru boga* (about 20 litres), was used for storing the syrup over long periods of time. In turn, *èru merai*, approximately two *èru pedako*, has a capacity of about 40 litres and also stored syrup. The largest pot, *èru rubi*, is so big (at least 80 litres) that it cannot be transported if it is filled with grains or lontar syrup as it would break.

Areca nuts were the smallest units for exchange. Threaded on strings, they can be stored for months. Strings of areca nuts were necessary, for example, as part of gift giving at funeral ceremonies. One string (*lada* or *lidi*) was made of 16 areca nuts cut in halves. Three strings (3 *lada* or *satu ikat pinang* [In]) corresponded to 48 areca nuts; called *kelake*, it could be exchanged for a baby goat or a piglet. Areca nuts were not part of exchanges involving large animals.

1.   Pot(s) as unit of exchange

1 pot of palm syrup = 1 pot of rice or 1 pot of sorghum of the same size
1 pot of salt = 1 pot of rice or sorghum of the same size
2 pots of mung beans (*èru kebui* – the special size for mung beans) = 1 pot of sorghum
2 pots of syrup (*èru merai*) = 1 baby goat or piglet
1 pot of syrup (*èru merai*) = yarns for one sarong tied and dyed, ready to be mounted on the loom
3 pots of syrup (*èru merai*) = 1 man's hip cloth ready to wear
4 pots of syrup (*èru merai*) = 1 woman's sarong ready to wear

---

[2]   The firing process lasts 12 hours followed by a cooling period of one day. This is different from other areas in Indonesia where firing consists of burning grasses inside each pot; for example, in Lombok.

2.   *Areca nuts*

4 *kelake* (12 *lidi*) = 1 young goat or 1 young pig

3.   *Animals*[3]

2 baby goats = 1 piglet
4 goats = 1 pig
10 goats = 1 water buffalo
4 pigs = 1 water buffalo
10 female sarongs or 10 male hip cloths = 1 water buffalo or 1 horse

In Raijua the system was slightly different. There *èru rubi* corresponded to *èru merai* in Savu and it was worth two goats or a six-month-old pig. A container of syrup equated to two containers of rice or sorghum. Raijuan people received rice from Menia in exchange for strings of fish. A plate (*kerigi*) of sorghum, mung beans or peanuts was worth two fish.

---

[3] This general rule does not take into account the size or age of the animal or if it is neutered, male or female.

Villages of Savu and Raijua from 1832 to the Present

Preliminary information

The village survey includes the colonial lists of 1832 and 1851, as well as more recent data concerning the situation after Indonesian independence in reference to Nico Kana's map of Savu[1] and 2014 field observations. In 1851, the villages were places where the temukungs—genealogical chief of a village or a settlement (and there could be more than one per location)—lived, and it shows that they were recruited from the clans of the rajas and the fettors. In 1832, there were very few temukungs (so it may be that the Francis list is incomplete): in 1851 Dimu had 22 villages/temukungs; Liae 30; Seba 59; Mesara 32; Menia 2; and Raijua 24. Several of the 2014 villages are not on the 1851 list. It is unclear whether certain villages already existed in 1851 or if the land was uninhabited. From independence to 2003/2004, the number of villages shrank consistently, particularly in Liae and Raijua.

It is important to refer to the Indonesian government's 1999 Regional Autonomiy Law (RAL) for decentralisation (see chapter 10). The revised RAL of 2004 had a particular impact on Savu's adminstrative structure. Several new villages had to be created in 2003/04 in order to achieve the necessary number of villages and districts (*kecatmatan*) for the creation of the new regency (*kabupaten*) of Sabu Raijua. In 2014, the Savu-Raijua regency had 48 villages and 5 subvillages; there was no change in the number between 2004 and 2014. Note that the names of several new villages do not appear on previous lists. It is possible that some temukungs (or their clans) had lost their influence after independence, so the villages they had represented were no longer relevant in 2004, revealing a shift in Savunese politics. The political ramifications deserve

---

[1] Kana collected the data from Savu's two district offices in 1974. The map appears first in his thesis (1978: 15) which was then published in 1983. For this reason the date for his village list below is given as 1973.

further fieldwork to discover why villages/settlements disappeared between 1851 and 1973 or, indeed, were permanently removed.[2]

The most 'conservative' villages, those with names that underwent little change, are in Mesara and Seba. Dimu is surprisingly 'unconservative' as there is little continuity in the village names. Historical place names, such as Ba (raja) and Hurati (fettor), were not kept. The name Kujiratu had disappeared from the list of 1973 but resurfaced in 2003. The same happened to Huwaga.

Names of villages

Key to lettering style:

- In **bold** are the village names that have existed continously from 1832 until today.
- In *italics* are the names that existed in 1851 and are still in use.
- *Underlined italics* indicates village names which existed in 1851, disappeared after independence but were re-employed in 2003 or 2004.
- Underlined are names that existed in 1832 and 1851 but are no longer in use; these names were not employed in the creation of villages in 2003 and 2004.

---

[2] In one or two instances, places within 50 metres of another settlement had a change of name; they could conceivably be the same place under a different name.

1. Mesara[3]

In 1832 (Francis list)	In 1851 (Resident Baron van Lijnden)	In 1973 (Kana)	New villages created in 2003/2004	Existing in 2014
Raja Ama Biha Buki Uli, Ledemawide (moved from Raemèdi)	*Pedèro* Tedida Dokaraki *Wadumèdi*	*Pedèro* *Wadumèdi*	Wadumèdi became *Wadumèdi* and *Gurimonearu*.	*Pedèro* Pedèro Pedèro *Wadumèdi*
Temukung Ama Kone Jo, **Lede Ae**	Raemèdi **Lede Ae**	**Lede Ae**	Lede Ae became **Lede Ae** and Ramedue.	Pedèro **Lede Ae**
Temukung Ama Wie Gae, Lenakapa	Lenakapa Ledewunu Ledelo Ledeke Lie Ledejara Hipi Makopo *Molie* *Tanajawa*	*Molie* *Tanajawa*	*Tanajawa*	Lede Ae Lede Ae Lede Ae *Pedèro* Ramedue Lede Ae Tanajawa Lederaga *Molie* *Tanajawa*

<hr>

[3] The 1851 list makes no distinction between villages ruled by a raja and those under a fettor; both positions were filled by people from the Maputitu clan.

1. Mesara

In 1832 (Francis list)	In 1851 (Resident Baron van Lijnden)	In 1973 (Kana)	New villages created in 2003/2004	Existing in 2014
Temukung Ama Nani Ratu, **Lobohede**	**Lobohede** Wuirai Ienungaka? (Lienaka) Kolotede *Gurimonearu* Lederaila Ledekepaka Êimadakebo Ledetadu Raerepa Raekewowo Raemabido Raetigi Ledeko Kebila Tadahege	**Lobohede** Dèieko	Lobohede became **Lobohede** and Lederaga. Total number of villages: 10	**Lobohede** Lederaga Molie Molie *Gurimonearu* Lobohede Lobohede Lederaga Pedèro Pedèro Pedèro Lede Ae Lede Ae Lobohede Dèieko ?

2. Seba

In 1832 (Francis list)	In 1851 (Resident Baron van Lijnden)	In 1973 (Kana)	New villages created in 2003/2004	Existing in 2014
Raja Ama Lomi Jara, **Nadawawi**	(under the raja) **Nadawawi**	**Nadawawi**	Nadawawi became **Nadawawi** and Delo.	**Nadawawi**

2. Seba

In 1832 (Francis list)	In 1851 (Resident Baron van Lijnden)	In 1973 (Kana)	New villages created in 2003/2004	Existing in 2014
	Nahoro			Nadawawi
		Raeloro	Raeloro became Raeloro and Roboaba.	Raeloro
Temukung Ama Upa Jami, Raedana	Raedana			
Temukung Ama Homa Taja, **Raemude**		Ledeana	Ledeana became Ledeana, Ledekepaka and Jadu.	**Ledeana**
	Raemude	**Raemude**		**Raemude**
	Ledetalo			Raenyale
	Raenyale	**Raenyale**		**Raenyale**
Temukung Ama Haba Lai, Raemadake	Raemadake			Raenyale
		Mêba	Mêba became Mêba and Raemadia.	Mêba
	Raedewa	*Raedewa*		*Raedewa*
		Kotahawu	(Kotahawu is no longer part of Seba.)	
	Lederai			Raeloro
	Raejo			Raeloro
	Raeraja			Raeloro
Temukung Ama Rohi Jami, **Ledeana**	Eilata			Raeloro
	Ledeana			**Ledeana**
	Ledeana (new)			**Ledeana**

2. Seba

In 1832 (Francis list)	In 1851 (Resident Baron van Lijnden)	In 1973 (Kana)	New villages created in 2003/2004	Existing in 2014
	Hèla			Ledeana
	Kololie			Ledeana
	Èimadadida			Depe
	Ledemanukoro			Depe
	Kepakamenenge			?
	Nadamanumara			Raeloro
	Raemapau			Raeloro
	Raeiki			Raeloro
		Raekore		Raekore
	Keduli Are			Raeloro
	Èikehero			Raeloro
	Kehaleba			Raeloro
	Tadurèi			?
	Luiana			Nadawawi
	Dènirae			Nadawawi
	Loborengi			Nadawawi
	Raebawa			Raeloro
	Lobowèga			Raeloro
	Jaraèji			Raenyale
	Daidoro			Raedewa

2. Seba

In 1832 (Francis list)	In 1851 (Resident Baron van Lijnden)	In 1973 (Kana)	New villages created in 2003/2004	Existing in 2014
	Kolorai			Raenyale
	Ěiko'o			Raenyale
	Lederaijojo			Raenyale
	Wadumêdi			Nadawawi
	Nadaleba			Raeloro
	(under the fettor)			
	Raipurudida			Nadawawi
	Railorowawa			Raeloro
	Namata			Raeloro
	Loboke			Raeloro
	Raeburu			Raeloro
	Lederaipu'uju			Raeloro
	Depe	*Depe*		*Depe*
	Raeputuka			Depe
	Dokawawi			Raeloro
	Raedete			Raedewa
	Nadadi?			Raeloro?
	Raetala			Raeloro
	Dekapulu			Raeloro

2. Seba

In 1832 (Francis list)	In 1851 (Resident Baron van Lijnden)	In 1973 (Kana)	New villages created in 2003/2004	Existing in 2014
Fettor Wono Gadi, Bodo	Tuleika/Tulaika			Mèba
	Bododeki			Mèba
	Luiwega			Raeloro
	Leodelu			Raeloro
	Leobaka			Raeloro
	Raemawènyilai			Raeloro
		Menia		Menia
		Raenalulu	Total number of villages: 17 and 1 subvillage	Raenalulu
		Teriwu		Teriwu

3. Liae

In 1832 (Francis list)	In 1851 (Resident Baron van Lijnden)	In 1973 (Kana)	New villages created in 2003/2004	Existing in 2014
Raja Ama Mojo Kale Alu, Daba or Ege?	(under the raja) *Ege*			*Waduwèla*
	Kaedupa			Waduwèla
	Waduwèla	*Waduwèla*		*Waduwèla*
Fettor Ama Lena Riwu, Ledewègu	Wègu			Dèinao
	Bagarae			Waduwèla
	Ledeke	*Ledeke*	*Ledeke* became Ledeke and Loborai.	Waduwèla
				Ledeke

3. Liae

In 1832 (Francis list)	In 1851 (Resident Baron van Lijnden)	In 1973 (Kana)	New villages created in 2003/2004	Existing in 2014
	Raiwadu			Ledeke
	Kekawu			Ledeke
	Ledemediri			Èilogo
	Daba	Èilogo		Èilogo
			Èilogo became Èilogo and *Hèlapaji*.	Èilogo
Temukung Ama Mèje Mana, Raepuleba	Raepuleba			Ledeke
	Mabau			Ledeke
	Bolou			Waduwèla
	Raekanawadu			Mehona?
		Mehona	Mehona became Mehona and Èikare.	Mehona
	Lededahi (under the fettor)			Ledeke
	Kolorame			
Temukung Ama Tèru Liu, Raewowiu.	Gopo			Èilogo
	Raewowiu			Èilogo or Ledeke?
	Ledekeli			Ledeke
	Helapaji			Èilogo
	Raepula			*Helapaji*

3. Liae

In 1832 (Francis list)	In 1851 (Resident Baron van Lijnden)	In 1973 (Kana)	New villages created in 2003/2004	Existing in 2014
	Ledemediri			Êilogo
	Raetebo			Êilogo
	Raejara			Êilogo
	Dokarae			Helapaji
Temukung Ama Bunga Bèngu, *Kotahawu*	Ledewèga			Waduwèla
	Kotahawu			Helapaji
	Raetigi			*Kotahawu*
	Êiko			Êilogo
	Êiheu			Helapaji
				Helapaji
Temukung Ama Lutu, Lede Raewuri	Lede Raewuri	Dèinao	Dèinao became Dèinao and Raerobo.	Ledetalo[4]
		Deme		Dèinao
		(Kotahawu still exists but as part of Seba, not Liae.)	*Kotahawu* became Kotahawu and Ledetalo.	Deme
			Total number of villages: 12	

---

[4] Local sources said Ledetalo was renamed Kotahawu by Ama Lena Rohi before 1832. The lists of 1832 and 1851 corroborate the local sources.

4. Dimu[5]

In 1832 (Francis list)	In 1851 (Resident Baron van Lijnden)	In 1973 (Kana)	New villages created in 2003/2004	Existing in 2014
Raja Riwu Daga, <u>Ba</u>	(under the raja) <u>Ba</u> Banyo Mediriae Ledeunupu Eioni Dokadowu Raeawu Raekoli Bodjorae *<u>Kujiratu</u>* Balidida	Bodae	Bodae became Bodae, Keliha and *<u>Kujiratu</u>*.	Bodae Bodae Bodae Bodae Keduru *<u>Kujiratu</u>* Kujiratu Kujiratu Kujiratu *<u>Kujiratu</u>* Keduru
Fettor Uli Dimu Luji Tanya, <u>Hurati</u>	(under the fettor) <u>Hurati</u> Bara Ae Nadahuru Tutu (Wolotu?)	Bolou	Bolou became Bolou, Loborai and Keduru.	Bolou Bolou Bolou Keduru Loborai?

[5] According to the 1832 list, the Napuru clan was under the raja; this clan provided neither rajas nor fettors but had the second highest number of temukungs in 1851. Kujiratu, the centre of Napuru, disappeared as a village after independence, but the name was chosen again in 2004.

4. Dimu

In 1832 (Francis list)	In 1851 (Resident Baron van Lijnden)	In 1973 (Kana)	New villages created in 2003/2004	Existing in 2014
	Nadanguru			Limagu
Temukungs Lomi Djo and Line Ije, **Limagu**	**Limaguwawa**	**Limagu**		**Limagu**
Temukungs Ama Uju and Ama Daba, <u>Kalui</u>	<u>Kalui</u>			Limagu
Temukungs Laga Kêtu and Laga Kone, <u>Telorarai</u>	*<u>Huwaga</u>*			*Huwaga*
Temukungs Leo Doko and Loni Radja of Dêni	Lobohei (Lobodei?)	Lobodei	Lobodei became Lobodei, Êiada and *Huwaga*.	Lobodei? Êiada?
		Jiwuwu[6]		Bolou
		Êilode	Jiwuwu became Keliha.	Keliha
		Êimadake	Total number of villages: 8	
		Matei	2 subvillages (Bolou and Limagu)	

---

6   Jiwuwu, Êilode, Êimadake and Matei are no longer part of Dimu but are now in Sabu Tengah.

5. Sabu Tenggah

In 1832 (Francis list)	In 1851 (Resident Baron van Lijnden)	In 1973 (Kana)	New villages created in 2003/2004	Existing in 2014
		All are former villages of Dimu (see above).	Êilode became Êilode and Êimau. Êimadake became Êimadake and Loboaju. Matei became Matei and Tada. Bebae became Êiada and Bebae. Total number of villages: 8	Êilode Êimadake Êimau Loboaju Matei Tada Êiada Bebae

6. Menia

In 1832 (Francis list)	In 1851 (Resident Baron van Lijnden)	In 1973 (Kana)	New villages created in 2003/2004	Existing in 2014
Raja Ama Piga Tagi, Didarae		Menia is part of Seba.		Raeloro (Seba)
Fettor Ama Wênyi	Wawarae			Menia (Seba)
Temukung Ama Manu Jami, Wawarae	Wawarae			Menia (Seba)
Temukung Ama Rohi Lobo, Didarae	Jamikolo			Menia
Temukung Ama Doko Luji, Daba	Kongkordia			Roboaba (Seba)

7. Raijua

In 1832 (Francis list)	In 1851 (Resident Baron van Lijnden)	After independence	New villages created in 2003/2004	Existing in 2014
Raja Ama Mehe Tari, Ujudima	Ujudima			Ledeunu
Temukung Eni Dadi, Nakai	Dèmuae			Ledeunu
Temukung Eni Miha, Kolohaba	Kolohaba			Ledeunu
	Dokamahana?			Ledeunu?
Temukung Ratu Bèngu, **Ledeke**	**Ledeke**	**Ledeke**	**Ledeke**	**Ledeke**
Temukung Mika Weo, **Bèlu**	**Bèlu**	**Bèlu**	**Bèlu**	**Bèlu**
Temukung Penu Uju, Lobowalu	Nadaae			Ledeke
	Einehu			Ledeunu
	Ledetalo			Ledeunu
	Watarai			Ledeke
	Koro? Eimadakoro			Ledeunu
	Nakai			Ledeunu
	Nadega			Ledeke
	Ramelako			Bolua
	Dènidelo			Bolua
				Ledeke

7. Raijua

In 1832 (Francis list)	In 1851 (Resident Baron van Lijnden)	After independence	New villages created in 2003/2004	Existing in 2014
	Kolorae	*Kolorae*		*Kolorae*
	Ketita			Bolua
	Raematola			Bolua
	Deimêlo?			Ledeke
	Lokowalu			
	(Lobowalu?)			*Kolorae*
	Ledeunu	*Ledeunu*	*Ledeunu*	*Ledeunu*
	Boko			Bolua
	Bogi		The villages: Bolua, Bèlu and Kolorae	Bèlu
		Bolua	The sub villages: Ledeke and Ledeunu	Bolua

List of Rajas and Fettors

Here are the rajas and fettors (executive regents) of the six domains of Savu and Raijua. Some are known from oral tradition, while others appear in the colonial sources. Their exact dates are sometimes impossible to ascertain and the same is true for the genealogical affiliations of certain rulers. Indicated in brackets at the end of each entry is the person's relationship to the entry above (if known), unless otherwise stated.

Dimu

Rajas

Luji Talo 16th century (Natadu clan)

Tuka Hida (Nadowu clan)

(Unclear succession from Tuka Hida to Talo)

Talo fl. c. 1636–45 (descended from Tuka Hida)

Ama Rohi before 1648–78 (son)

Rohi Rani 1678–1731 (son)

Hili Haba 1731–98 (grandson)

Elias Jara Hili 1798 to after 1809 (son)[1]

Hede Hili early 19th century (brother)

Rewo Daga fl. 1832

Ama Hili Haba 1851–57

Ama Lai Daga 1857–68 (descended from Hili Haba)

Ama Piga Jara (Eduard Jara Luji) 1869–1910 (from another branch)

---

[1] In 1801–03, F. Péron mentions a certain Ama Dima (born c. 1755)—"king of the island of Savu" but residing in Kupang—as being the younger brother of a Jara, born in c. 1751. It is not clear if Jara was Elias Jara Hili or if the brothers came from Seba.

Fettors

Ama Talo (Leo Kana) fl. 1648 (Nadowu clan)
Talo Leo fl. 1672–c. 1695 (son)
Luji Talo c. 1696–1720 (son)
Leba Luji (Ama Talo) 1720–69 (son)
Talo Leba 1769–? (son)
Dimu Leba (Ama Luji) ?–1794 (brother)
Urias Carels 1794–? (brother)
Uli Dimu fl. 1832 (son of Dimu Leba)
Ama Jami Talo fl. 1851 (nephew)
Ama Dila fl. 1860
Luji Talo (son of Ama Jami Talo)
Jacob Gaja Jami before 1890–1905 (nephew)
Th. T. Luji 1905–08 (son of Luji Talo)
We Tanya 1910–61 (son)

Liae
Rajas

Nida Dahi 16th century (Nanawa clan)
Kale Lodo 17th century (son of Lodo Riwu)
Ama Jami Manu Bara fl. 1676 (father-in-law; Napujara clan)
Raja Manu fl. 1686–88 (son)
Riwu Manu fl. 1686–89 (brother)
Jami Riwu Manu before 1712–26 (son)
Mone Bengu 1726–51 (grandson of Raja Manu)
Kore Rohi 1751–57 (grandson of Riwu Manu)
Kore Loni 1757–64 (descended from an uncle of Ama Jami Manu Bara)
Manu Kore 1764 to after 1794 (son of Kore Rohi)
Ama Raja fl. 1797
Ama Mojo Kale Alu before 1832–48 (from a collateral branch)
Ama Ije Jote Robo 1851–57 (Nahai clan)
Ama Baki Bela 1857–68 (Gopo clan)
Ama Amu Manu 1869–79 (descended from Jami Riwu Manu)
Hendrik Ratu Manu 1879–1914 (son)

Fettors

Kore Lone 1757–71 (Napujara clan)
Jami Kore 1771–? (son)

Ama Lena Rohi fl. 1832 (son)
Leo Lai fl. 1842 (first cousin)
Ama Hina Hari fl. 1860 (great-grandnephew of Jami Kore)
Ama Wenyi Kama fl. 1885 (from another branch)
Raja Haba fl. 1894–1901 (from another branch)
Tuka Luji c. 1900s (from another branch)
Riwu Ratu fl. 1936 (son of Hendrik Ratu Manu)
Rohi Raja fl. 1940 (son of Raja Haba)
Ratu Riwu fl. 1949 (son)
Pe Luji late 20th century (grandson of Tuka Luji)

Menia
Rajas

Ama Tenga Gae fl. 1648 (Kekoro-Raepudi clan)
Tero Weo (nephew)
Tagi Lado fl. 1718 (nephew)
Jami Tero before 1746–60 (son of Tero Weo)
Manu Jami 1760–61 (son)
Ama Gaja Bengu Tagi 1761 to after 1790 (son of Tagi Lado)
Gaja Bengu ?–1794 (son)
Rehi Bengu 1794–? (brother)
Ama Piga Tagi fl. 1832 (perhaps, similar to the next raja, also a son of Rehi Bengu)
Ama Gaja Tagi 1842–68 (son of Rehi Bengu)
Ama Lena Rihi 1869–73 (son)

Fettors

Kore Rohi ?–1794
Dimu Kore 1794–? (son)
Ama Wenyi fl. 1832

Mesara
Rajas

Lod'o Ga Hebi 16th century (Nahipa clan)
Naha Lulu (Napupudi clan)
Lodo Leo (father's brother)
Lai Lomi (nephew)
Ama Reba Rohi (brother of Naha Lulu)

Rohi Lulu (brother)
Lado Rohi (son)
Reba Rohi (grandson)
Jami Riwu (grandson of Lado Rohi in the maternal line; Naputitu clan)
Ama Weo fl. 1682 (Aelungi clan)
Kana Jami fl. 1688–99 (son of Jami Riwu)
Ama Tenga Wele Jami before 1708–51 (brother)
Kore Wele 1752–56 (son)
Ama Loni Dimu Kore 1756–60 (son)
Rugi Dimu 1760–64 (son)
Jega Riwu 1764–81 (from another lineage of Naputitu)
Buki Dimu 1781 to after 1794 (son of Ama Loni Dimu Kore)
Uli Buki early 19th century (son)
Ama Biha Buki Uli before 1832–68 (son)
Ama Lebe Ju Buki 1868–93 (son)
Ama Tenga Doko Ju 1893–1914 (son)

Fettors

Ama Manu fl. 1832 (Napupudi clan)
Ama Lebe Ju fl. 1869
Pono Tanya fl. 1885
Ropa Dogi fl. 1897
Kore Ju (brother of Ama Tenga Doko Ju)
Bole Kore fl. 1940 (son)
Wila Buki Nere (son of a cousin)
Wele Dima (descended from Ama Biha Buki Uli)

Raijua
Rajas

Baku Ruha (Nadaibu clan)
Mau Alo ?–1680 (nephew)
Bali Lai before 1692–98 (from another clan)
Haba Baku (son of Baku Ruha)
Nyebe Haba (son)
Lai Nyebe fl. 1756–90 (son)
Jara Lai fl. 1794 (son)
Maru Nyebe (son of Nyebe Haba)
Kote Lai ?–1807 (son of Lai Nyebe)

Leo Nyebe (son of Nyebe Haba)
Ledo Teni (descended from Alo Ruha, brother of Baku Ruha)
Ama Mehe Tari 1830–68 (son of Kote Lai)
Ama Loni Kuji 1869–1915 (great-grandson of Kote Lai)
Ama Meda Lai 1915–18 (son)

Fettors

Leo Nyale fl. 1759–61 (Melako clan, Natalo lineage)
Tulu Gae before 1765–71
Lomi Tulu 1771–94 (son)
Raja Tulu 1794–? (brother)
Dohi Lado fl. 1807 (from another branch, also Natalo lineage)
Kodo Lado (brother)
Ama Jaga Raja fl. 1885 (grandson of Lomi Tulu)
Pia Lai 1940–54 (son of Ama Meda Lai)

Seba
Rajas

Kore Rohi (Nataga clan, Naluluweo lineage)
Jami Kore (son)
Haba Jami (son)
Lai Haba (son)
Jara Lai (son)
Bire Lai (brother)
Ama Lomi (Riwu Bire) fl. 1648 (son)
Lomi Riwu (son)
Ina Tenga before 1675–83 (sister)
Lai Lomi 1684–c. 1687 (son of Lomi Riwu)
Jara Lomi c. 1687–c. 1700 (brother)
Wadu Lai c. 1704–42 (son of Lai Lomi)
Jara Wadu 1742–69 (son)
Ama Doko Lomi Jara 1769–78 (son)
Doko Lomi 1778 to after 1794 (son)
Riwu Doko (son; position on the list is uncertain)
Ama Loni Jara (Jara Lomi) early 19th century (uncle)
Bire Doko ?–c. 1830 (brother of Riwu Doko)
Ama Loni Jara (Jara Lomi) 1830–58 (second time as raja)
Ama Dima Talo (Talo Jara) 1859–64 (son)

Ama Nia Jawa (Jawa Bire) 1864–68 (son of Bire Doko)
Ama Doko Kaho 1868–82 (son)
Lazarus Rohi Jawa 1882–90 (brother)
Alexander Rihi Jawa 1890–1901 (brother)
Elias Luji Raja Pono 1901–06 (brother-in-law; descended from Wadu Lai)
Samuel Thomas Jawa (Logo Rihi) raja of Seba, 1907–15; raja of Savu, 1915–35
(son of Alexander Rihi Jawa)
Paulus Charles Jawa (Rohi Rihi) raja of Savu, 1937–63 (brother)

Fettors

Luhi Weo fl. 1693
Jami Lobo fl. 1707–40 (Nataga clan, Najohina lineage)
Manu Jami before 1760–89 (son)
Mehe Manu 1789–? (son)
Wono Gadi fl. 1832 (possibly son of Ama Wono)
Ama Wono fl. 1845 (descended from Jami Lobo)
Ama Tali Manu ?–1850 (grandson of Mehe Manu)
Tali Manu 1851–? (son)
Pawe Rake before 1885–1908 (descended from Jami Lobo)

Appendix VI | Savu Raijua in Statistics[1]

Background

The total surface area of the Savu-Raijua regency is 460.47 square kilometres and together the islands have about 1,000 kilometres of coastline. Sabu Barat (West Savu [In] or Seba) is by far the largest district with 40.2 per cent of the total area.

According to the last census in 2010, the total population was 75,000 inhabitants. The same census shows the population density was 139 people per square kilometre; the estimation in 2015 was 187 people per square kilometre. In 2015 the estimated population was 85,000. See Table 1 below for the population and density figures for each district.

In 2015 there were 43,665 Savunese males working overseas, mainly in Malaysia, and 41,656 females working outside Savu, the majority of whom were in Malaysia, Singapore and the Middle East.

In 2015, 54 per cent of the households did not have electricity; 33 per cent had power from the State Electricity Corporation (*Perusahaan Listrik Negara*, PLN); and 13 per cent used other sources of electricity, for instance, solar panels.

The poverty line was determined at Rp 291.000 (USD 22) per month in 2015.[2] Thirty-two per cent of the population earned less than the recommended monthly minimum, making the regency the pooorest in the NTT (East Nusa Tengara) province. However, at the same time the cost of living in Savu Raijua made it the second most expensive regency after Rote Ndao (see Table 7 for commodity prices).

---

[1] Sources: Sabu Raijua *dalam angka* (Sabu Raijua in figures). *Kupang: Badan Data dan Statistik Kabupaten Sabu Raijua* 2013, 2015 and 2016. Data statistics Kabupaten Kupang 2001.

[2] Currency conversion calculated as of 1 June 2015.

Table 1: Population, area and density in 2015 per subdistrict

Subdistrict	Population	Total area /sq. km	Density /sq. km
Raijua	9,016	39.05	231
Sabu Barat (Seba)	31,105	185.16	168
Hawu Mehara (Mesara)	18,138	62.81	289
Sabu Timur (Dimu)	8,652	37.21	233
Sabu Liae	10,441	57.62	181
Sabu Tengah	8,618	78.62	110
Total of Sabu Raijua	85,970	460.00	187

Table 2: Religion in 2015[3]

Religion[4]	Catholic	Protestant	Islam	Jingi Tiu
Percentage	1.95	89.95	0.95	7.24

Table 3: Education

School (with staff and pupils)	2012	2015
1. Primary school (*Sekolah Dasar*, SD [In]): public and private	76	79
Pupils	11,927	14,200
Teachers	485	619
2. Junior high school (*Sekolah Lanjutan Tingkat Pertama*, SLTP [In]): public	19	27
Pupils	4,900	5,400
Teachers	173	196
3. Senior high school (*Sekolah Menengah Umum*, SMU [In]): public and private	9	10
Pupils	2,660	3,075
Teachers:		
Civil servants	99	155
Temporary teachers (honour teachers)[5]	149	129

---

[3] Source: Ministry of Religious Affairs, Kupang Regency Office.

[4] Hinduism was not represented and Buddhism did not reach 0.1%.

[5] There were no separate figures for the numbers of temporary teachers in primary and secondary schools.

Table 4: Agriculture

Product in tonnes (t) or quintal (q)/year	2012	2015
Rice (t)	3,000	4,200
Corn (t)	8,400	9,900
Cassava, sweet potato, taro (t)	730	790
Peanut (t)	1,900	2,500
Areca nut (*pinang*) (t)	11	52
Cashew nut (t)	140	280
Mung bean (*kacang hijau* [In]) (t)	4,880	4,600
Sorghum (t)	1,050	1,100
Coconut (t)	776	856
Kapok (t)	8	21
Lontar syrup (*gula Sabu* [In]) (t)	234	246
Banana (q)	14,000	12,700
Mango (q)	17,000	16,000
Papaya (q)	21,000	18,000
Jackfruit (q)	5,000	4,700
Watermelon (q)	9,000	3,800

Table 5: Livestock

Livestock	2012	2015
Buffalo	7,900	7,800
Cow	2,900	4,700
Horse	5,500	5,500
Goat	33,000	34,000
Sheep	13,000	12,000
Pig	28,500	36,000

Table 6: Sea resources

Resource	2012	2015
Households involved in seaweed farming	1,230	2,000
Production of seaweed in tonnes	860 (?)	9,450
Fish in tonnes	394	724

Table 7: Commodity prices[6]

Commodity	2000[7]	2012	2015
Rice /kg	2.800	9.000	11.000
Corn /kg	2.000	5.000	6.000
Sugar /kg	4.000	14.000	15.000
Cooking oil /l	3.000	18.000	19.000
Beef /kg	N/A	60.000	90.000
Petrol/gasoline /l[8]	2.500	10.000	6.700
Diesel /l	N/A	5.000	6.700
Cement /sack	22.000	63.000	55.000
Corrugated zinc /sheet	20.000	43.000	50.000
Rebar (6 mm)	N/A	30.000	29.000

Table 8: Transportation[9]

Number of vehicles	2012	2014	2015
Motorbikes	N/A	12,000	14,000
Cars	N/A	190	286
Mini buses	14	41	47
Pickups/ mini trucks	42	80	89
Trucks	153	270	283

[6] Prices are in Indonesian rupiah. In 2012, 1 USD was worth IDR 9.500 and in 2015 it was worth IDR 13.500. A significant proportion of goods consumed in Savu is imported.

[7] Data for the year 2000 are from the Kabupaten Kupang statistics; at that time, Savu was still part of the Kupang Regency.

[8] These are the prices government officials pay, not market prices. As there is no state-run fuel supplier in Savu (Pertamina), most people buy petrol by the bottle; one litre costs IDR10.000. However, a litre can reach as much as IDR50.000 when the boats delivering fuel are delayed by bad weather or technical problems.

[9] The majority of cars are owned by government officials (cars with red number plates) and most of the trucks are the property of the regency government. The comparison between privately and publicly owned motorbikes and pickups is more equitable.

Glossary of Selected Savunese Words

Preliminary information

The Hawu language has no /s/; it has implosive and explosive consonants (/b'/, /d'/, /g'/, /j'/ and /b/, /d/, /g/, /j/). The spelling throughout the text takes into account recent research in linguistics and the remarkable work by Charles E. Grimes (http://e-kamus2.org/Hawu). However, for an English-speaking, non-specialised audience, some simplifications have been made in the text. For instance, the distinction between implosive and explosive consonants has been kept only when the sole differentiation in pronunciation occurs through such consonants; for example, *d'ara* (inside) and *dara* (mark), *d'ue* (two) and *due* (lontar sap), and *lod'o* (sun) and *lodo* (to go). The spelling, respectful of modern linguistic conventions, is in square brackets after the simplified term; for example, aba [ab'a]. There are intermediary stages between the vowels /e/ and /a/ in Savu's various domains; /è/ corresponds to a short accentuated vowel between /e/ and /a/. A number of Savunese verbs have two forms: one form for the verb used in a general manner in the present tense and for a near future; a second to indicate the plural, emphatic, passive and the imperative forms (Walker: 1982). For example, verbs with two forms are given as follows—*ami, ame*: to ask. Many thanks go to Pastor Lackner for the loan of his handwritten, 4,000-word dictionary.

a'a	elder sibling
aba [*ab'a*]	to protect, to shelter; Aba Mone (Man Protector) is the name of an ancestor.
ada manu	small hut built for ritual cockfighting for each party taking part
ade	liver; *dèniade* (lit. on the liver) is the site of emotions.
ad'o	no; *d'o*: not
adu	strong, hard; *lumu* antonym: soft
ae	many, much, great, big; Bawa Ae (Great Helper) is the name of an ancestor.

ahli	original; *udu ahli*: original clan
aji	ritual functionary in ancient times; also a personal name
aju [*aj'u*]	wood; *aju kola*: its dense wood is used for building ritual houses in Savu (*Bischofia javanica*).
alu	fine, refined; also a personal name
ama (*ma*)	father
ami, ame	to ask
ana	child; *ana anu*: slave; also *ana niki*
ao	lime taken from white coral, an essential ingredient for betel chew and in the indigo dye process
apu (*èpu*)	grandfather, grandmother, grandchild; *pu*: ancestors
are	rice on a stalk
ari	younger sibling
aru	eight
A Wonga	ancestor of mythical times at the origin of humanity
awu	1. ash; Raeawu, the name of several villages in Savu, means that they were previously destroyed by fire; 2. grey colour
baba [*b'ab'a*]	short; low
bada [*b'ada*]	cattle
bali, bale [*b'ali, b'ale*]	to return, to go home
Banga liwu	twelfth month of the adat calendar (April in Seba; May in Mesara and Liae; May–June in Dimu and Raijua); eleventh month of the adat calendar in Liae
Banga liwu rame	twelfth and last month of the adat calendar in Liae with the ceremony of *hole*
bani [*b'ani*]	courageous, fearless
banyo [*b'anyo*]	1. mantra chant at *tao leo* funerals; 2. Banyo is the person in charge of ritual songs at a funeral; 2. the harbour in Dimu; in popular memory it means *Spanyol* (Spanish).
bèhi [*b'èhi*]	iron; also a male personal name
bèka [*b'èka, b'èke*]	to cut
bela	to halve
bèla	large, wide
belis (*weli*)	bride price

bèlo [*b'èlo*]	to injure, to wound
bèlu	to forget; *lu* (forgotten) is the name of the years in the Mesara ceremonial calendar when no ritual is held (as if it is forgotten).
bèni	woman; also a female name; *èpu bèni* (*apu bèni, ina apu*): grandmother; a female ancestor; Bèni Aji is the wife of a priest in the ancestral religion; Bèni Deo is the wife of the priest Deo Rai (Dimu, Seba); Bèni Pu Mahi is the wife of the priest Apu Lod'o (Seba).
bodae [*b'od'ae*]	north; Bodae is the name of a village in Dimu.
bojo [*b'ojo*]	hill
boko	to gather; Boko is the name of a village in Raijua.
b'ole	do not; indicates a prohibition
bolou [*b'olou*]	south; Bolou is the name of a village in Dimu.
bui [*b'ui, b'ue*]	to pour, to sprinkle; *b'ui ihi* (to sprinkle the body), the most important ceremony in female lineages, is a night of silent ritual in and at the ritual house of the lineage (*tegida*). The content of heirloom baskets is checked and damaged weaving is replaced.
buki [*b'uki*]	to write; literate; Buki is the name of a raja in Mesara in the 18th century.
Dadi Lai	personal name
d'adi lai	orchid
dae [*d'ae*]	north; Bodae is the name of a village in Dimu.
dahi	sea, ocean; also *dahi ae*: ocean (lit. big sea); *lale dahi*: flood; also tsunami
d'ai	1. to arrive; 2. until; 3. up to
d'a'i	below, bottom; *kolo* or *dida* antonym: up, tip, top; *ru d'a'i*: bottom leaf (the first leaf, the nearest to the ground, thus the oldest)
Dana	island of Dana; *pedane*: to bury someone
dao	indigo
dara	1. mark; incision in a lontar leaf; 2. brand mark for cattle; *pidu dara pidu kewèhu*: seven marks for seven ceremonies in Mesara; 3. spur (for a rooster)

d'ara	in, inside; *dou d'ara dahi*: people inside the sea or people of the sea
dari	string, cord, rope; *dari èhu*: umbilical cord
dèi [*d'èi*]	1. to like, to want; 2. at, in, passing through
dèja [*d'èja*]	to kick, to stamp; *wowadu dèjarai* is the name of the stone on which the ancestor Ago Rai stood defining the border between Mesara and Seba.
dèka	to come, to arrive
delo	small bird known for feeding on the fields before harvest (*burung pipit* [In]); Delo is the name of a village in Sabu Tengah.
dèpi	mat
dere [*d'ere*]	drum
dèu (*dau, dou, do*)	person, people
di	we, us (inclusive: *kita* [In])
dida [*d'ida*]	up, above; *d'a'i* antonym: down, below
Dila [D'ila]	personal female name; Dila Robo was the daughter of Robo Aba, ruler of Seba; *wini* Dila Robo is the name of a female lineage.
dilu (*wodilu*)	ear
dimu	east; Dimu is the name of a district in East Savu.
do	1. people; *do kepai*: adult, grown up; *do Nadai*: Nadai people, the proto clan descended from Ie Miha in Liae; 2. who, which; *dou do baba, do bèla dilu*: people who are short [and] have large ears
d'o (*ad'o*)	not; no
doa [*d'oa*]	prayer; *pedoa* [*ped'oa*]: to pray, to call; also the name of a ceremonial circle dance
donahu	syrup made from the sap of the lontar palm tree; *rai donahu*: the land of the lontar syrup which is an image to describe Savu
dou (Mesara)	people; *dou d'ara dahi*: the people inside the sea or the people of the sea; *dou d'ara rai*: people inside the earth, also the people of the land; *dou d'ara liru*: the people inside the sky or the people in the sky or heaven
dou rai	ordinary people
duae (*dou ae*)	a title; aristocrat, king (lit. Big Man)

due	1. lontar palm tree; 2. lontar sap
d'ue	two
duru [*d'uru*]	bow, prow; the boat terminology is applied to the house; *d'uru èmu*: the prow of the house or the male front part of the house; *tèru d'uru*: the prow pillar or the male pillar of the house; *d'uru tèlu* is the hearth made of three stones (related to cosmology, the three stones stand for Liru Bèla: Large Sky; Rai Bèla: Large Land; and Dahi Bèla: Large Sea)—it is outside the house, at the head or bow of the house; *wui* antonym: stern
ege	1. to remember; 2. Ege is the name of a settlement in Liae, supposedly visited by English seafarers; *Ege: Inggris* (In)
èhu	navel; *dari èhu*: umbilical cord; *èhu rai*: navel of the land located at Merèbu and Wadu Mea
ei	water; *ei lobo*: pond (lit. place with water); *ei loko*: drinking water (lit. water from the river); *ei mada*: source, well
èi	tubular cloth for women, tube skirt; sarong
èji [*èj'i*]	rain; *kelila èji lai* is a ceremony in the middle of the rainy season to ask for more rain, allowing a plentiful harvest.
èki (*tali, iu*)	to tie, to bind, to connect; *èki kelila* is the ceremony whose purpose is to bind the community together; *tali* is used for tying yarns to create a pattern; *iu* is used when tying a cockspur.
èla, èle	already accomplished; used to indicate that an action is complete; *èla ke ya penga'a*: I have already eaten.
èmu *èmu rukoko*	house; *èmu kepue*: house of origin; *èmu rukoko*: traditional house with extended ridges; ritual house for a priest also ancestral house of the paternal line; *èmu tegida*: ancestral ritual house of the maternal line; *èmu kobe* is the name of the ritual house of *wini* Ga in Depe.
èru	earthenware container; *èru hogo*: cooking pot; pots of various sizes were used for storing water or lontar syrup and for storing grains.
èu (*ou*)	you

feto (*weto*)	second regent; derived either from the Portuguese *feitor* (supervisor) or from *feto* (female) in Dawan language. The Portuguese and later the Dutch used the title for the second highest ruler of a domain; he is generally from the same clan as the first regent or raja.
ga [*g'a*]	great, magnificent; Kika Ga is the name of an ancestor of the publicly known genealogies.
g'èdi	evergreen tree from the tropics, commonly called blackboard tree (*Alstonia scholaris*)
gèla	mast; Gelanalalu is the name of a village in Mesara linked to the ancestor Nalalu whose boat was stranded there.
golo (*lulu*)	to roll and to unroll a sail; *golo kowa hole* is a ceremony for launching the ceremonial boat at *hole* in Dimu.
guri	1. hill; 2. murdered, slaughtered; Gurimonearu (lit. eight dead men) is the name of a village in Mesara.
haba [*hab'a*]	bucket made of a lontar leaf; *haba tèlu lidi*: a bucket made of three ribs of a lontar leaf
ha'e	to ascend, to climb; *rae ha'e* is a ceremony at the end of the dry season when people climb to their village and house of origin to clean and purify the place before planting.
hanga	1. space, gap; valley; 2. strait; Hangaraerobo is the name of one of the settlements of the ancestor Robo Aba; Hanga Raijua: Raijua Strait
hape	sappanwood, a flowering legume tree native to tropical Asia (*Biancaea sappan*)
hapo	to receive, to adopt; *hapo ana* is a ceremony conducted shortly after birth during which the father gives his name to the newborn.
hari	with, together with; Nadahari is the name of a public ceremonial place in Pedèro where part of the thanksgiving ceremony *hole* takes place.
Hawu	Savu; Rai Hawu is the island of Savu.
he (*èhi*)	one
hèb'a	mouth, orifice; estuary

Hèba	Seba (the main harbour of Savu)
heboro	small lontar broom used to clean the lontar basket left in the tree; by extension it symbolises a male heirloom.
hekene	woven cloth with no seam; *hekene hi'i* is to describe people who are very close, such as the ancestors Wara Wai of Liae and Kole Wai of Mesara.
hèku	ceremonial knife
helama	blessing; *ru helama* is the name of a small offering.
heleo	to see; *doheleo* (overseer) is the name of a religious office.
heliru	evergreen tree commonly called milkwood, used for medicine and wood; this tree is linked to the lineage *wini* Jèwu as the ancestress Jèwu Liru climbed down to earth from a *heliru* tree (*Alstonia spectabilis*).
hemanga	soul, spirit; *hemanga* lives on for a limited period after a person dies.
henga	soul; *henga* is the soul that never dies.
heo	nine; *heo pad'a liru*: nine levels in the sky
hèpa	to inhale; *kolo hèpa rai* (lit. the tip that inhales the land) is the mantra name for Teriwu.
hepaka	flowering evergreen tree commonly called the champak (*Michelia champaka*)
hèpo	to sever, to cut
hèro	bitter; *nèta* antonym: sweet; Wèru hèro is the name of a month for ceremonies which alternates with Wèru nèta, a sweet month in Dimu; bitterness has no negative meaning, but it is necessary for complementing sweetness; Lado Aga Hèro is the name of a priest in Dimu corresponding to the role of *doheleo* (overseer) in other domains.
heru, here	to go in circles; *pehere jara* is the name of a ritual horse dance performed by one or more priests while circling a sacred tree or a specific area; *pehere jara mokebara* is a ritual for preventing invasions of locusts. Priests perform the ritual in the morning and the community does so in the afternoon in a public place; horses with bells around their necks and ankles demonstrate dancing steps revealing the riders' skills and children take short rides sitting behind the horsemen.

hèru	spindle; *menyèru*: to spin (cotton); *hèru kebèla* is land inherited from mother to daughter in Raijua (in Savu it is known as *raɪ lere*).
hi	1. lasso; 2. spur (in cockfighting) made of a rib of a lontar leaf
hi'i (*hig'i*, *hij'i*)	man's loin cloth (also shoulder cloth)
hika	1. spotted (black and white dots); *terae wo hika* is a variety of sorghum (black and white); 2. *hika* is the name of a bird (dotted black and white).
hila (*ngada*)	high, tall; also the names of ancestors in mythical times who severed the sky from the earth
hili	chili pepper; Hili Haba is the name of a ruler in Dimu in the 18th century.
hiluwara	fifteenth day of the moon cycle (full moon); Hilu is a personal name sometimes given to girls born on that day of the lunar month.
hod'a	sacred chant; mantra text for rituals at harvests, cockfights, marriages and funerals
hogo	to boil; *hogo due*: to boil the lontar sap into a syrup; *hogo nga'a*: to cook food (generally rice); Wèru hogo is the name of a month where the main activity is to boil the lontar sap.
hoiwe	divination technique to find the root of a problem. A chicken is beheaded, allowed to run and the direction the chicken takes indicates where the problem originates.
hole	1. to send away; 2. *hole* is the name of the most important ceremonies in all domains in the month of Banga liwu, the last month of the lunar calendar; *kowa hole* is the ceremonial raft loaded with offerings for the ancestors and launched for the occasion.
holo	1. cover, wrapper; 2. Holo is the island of Solor; *holo hege*: clove (came to Savu through Solor); *holo lakan*: rattan (came to Savu through Solor)
hora, *hore*	to throw; *hore tenaga*: to throw the anchor
horo	grove; *due horo*: a grove of lontar trees
horo, *hore*	to slaughter by cutting off the head of an animal; *horo kebau*: to sacrifice a buffalo for a ritual; *horo manu* is the name of a ritual in Dimu during which the sacrificial

	chicken is not beaten behind the head, as is usual, but its throat is cut so blood flows to the ground.
hubi	1. palm flower; 2. *hubi* is the name of the female descent lines (moieties); *hubi ae*: Greater Blossom; *hubi iki*: Lesser Blossom
hud'i, hud'e (Dimu)	to catch an animal in the community for sacrifice; this technique is known as *padi* in Seba, Mesara and Liae.
huhu (*kewadu*)	1. milk (*susu* [In]); *kewadu*: mother milk; 2. *huhu*: to pile up; *huhu kebie*: to recite a genealogy (lit. to pile up beams or logs); *huhu kebie loro kolo*: to recite a genealogy without interruption (lit. pile up the beams straight to the top); *huhu raiti d'a'i, huhu d'èi d'ida*: an expression used for reciting a complete genealogy (lit. pile up from the bottom, pile up to the top).
ia (*i'a*)	to be able
ibu	together; *peibu*: to assemble; *ibu nyale*: to gather sea worms in the rainy season
ie (*ij'e*)	good; Ie Miha is the name of an ancestor, the younger brother of Dida Miha.
ihi	1. content also to fill up; 2. body
iki	small; *ae* antonym: big
ila, ele	to vanish, to disappear; *ele* Jola: the Jola people have disappeared.
ina (*na*)	mother
iu	to attach; to tie; *peiu manu*: cockfight (lit. to attach [the spur] to the rooster's leg)
jami [*j'ami*]	forest; Jami is a personal name.
jara	horse; *pehere jara* is the ceremonial dance with horse(s) circling a sacred tree or a ritual arena.
jari [*j'ari*]	to start, to begin
jawa [*j'awa*]	foreign; also a personal name; *li jawa*: the Indonesian language
jawi	one year; Jawi Rai is the name of an ancestor; *ana Jawi*: a one-year old child (not yet entitled to a normal funeral, thus belonging to the ancestor Jawi Rai)

jèla	foot; also the name of a clan and a priest position in Dimu
j'i	we, us (exclusive: *kami* [In])
jingi, jinge	to carry away, to loot, to rob; Jingi Tiu is the name of the traditional ancestral religion based on ancestor worship. Jingi Tari is the name of an ancestor, son of Rohi Tari and uncle of Kore Rohi, the first raja of Seba in Portuguese times; Jingi Wiki is the name of a group of people in the maternal line Putenga who practice black magic. They have special motifs for women's sarongs and men's loin cloths.
jola [*j'ola*]	people who do not have a fixed place or who do not have a residence (nomadic people); Jola is the name of ancient settlers who lived near Seba. They disappeared or were chased away.
ka	branch, stalk (qualifier); *ka nyiu*: a branch of coconut palm; *ka terae*: a stalk of sorghum
kaba [*kab'a*]	1. coconut shell; 2. a bowl made of coconut shell; *kab'a keb'ui*: pods of mung beans; *kab'a terae*: husks of sorghum
kale	to look for; also a male personal name
kare [*aj'u kare*]	tall tree—its wood is used for the pillars of the ancestress house (*tegida*); the *kare* tree has to be planted next to the *tegida* or can be used as the *tegida* in place of the building for women of the same *wini* to meet (*Erythrina variegate* var. *orientalis*).
katapa nga'i	Indian almond tree (*Terminalia catappa*)
kebau	buffalo
kebèla	large; *rai hèru kebèla* is heirloom land in a female moiety and inherited from mother to daughter.
kebèli, kebèle	to turn over; *wowadu kebèli*: (lit. stone overturned); mini dolmen; a flat stone is placed on three or four erected stones, leaving a cavity for placing a small stone or offerings.
kebie	1. beam; 2. genealogy; *huhu kebie*: to recite genealogies (lit. to pile up beams)

kebihu	temporary groupings of men for ritual cockfighting purposes in Raijua; every few years new *kebihu* are formed to avoid tensions between the clans; the term is reminiscent of *kabisu* in Sumba which translates as clan.
kèbo hida	tree, sometimes known as the beach mulberry, is a member of the coffee family (*Morinda citrifolia*) (*mengkudu* [In]); the tree's roots provide the red dye for traditional weaving; *kèbo memo*: the roots from this tree give a lighter shade of red dye (*Morinda tomentosa*).
kebui [keb'ui]	mung beans
kedue	plaited container for offerings; *kedue hole*: an offering made for the thanksgiving ceremony; *kedue hubi due*: an offering for the lontar palm tree ritual when the tree is blooming
keèla (kelèla)	areca nut palm, for betel chew (*Areca catechu*); *keèla kenana*: betel chew
kehabe	lac tree grows well in the dry season (also *kesambi* [In]) (*Schleichera oleosa*).
ke'i	to dig; *ke'i ei*: to dig for water; the name of a month in the dry season when people dig new wells; *ke'i rao*: to build the hearth for boiling the lontar sap
kelaga	terrace, veranda on the longer side of the house
kèli	arrow; *rukèli*: lontar leaf
kelila	important ceremony for every household which occurs once in the middle of the rainy season to ask from more rain to allow a plentiful harvest and once in the middle of the dry season for an abundant flow of lontar sap; *kelila ae* is the ceremony that takes place at the end of large cycles of several years.
kenana	betel; *kepepe kenana*: a box to store the ingredients for betel chew
kèni	1. keel of a boat; 2. the ridge of a house roof; Heo Kèni (Nine Keels) is the name of the ritual house of the priest Maukia in Namata; Kèni Bèhi (Iron Keel) is the name of ritual houses in Namata and Lobohede (Aelape clan).
kenoto	1. ceremonial betel-nut bag or box; 2. a handwoven bag for the bridewealth gifts which contain the ingredients and presents brought by the groom for the bride's family; also the name of the ceremony

kepaka	Java olive tree, called *nitas* in Rote and Timor (*Sterculia foetida*); the oil contained in its seeds was used to produce light and to soak threads before they were dyed.
kepepe	heirloom basket containing the textiles of a maternal lineage; *kepepe bra*: an heirloom basket that can be opened at any occasion; *kepepe pana*: a sacred heirloom basket that can be opened only on certain occasions, for instance at the ceremony *bui hi'i*
kepete	hot (from the sun); Wèru wadu kepete (lit. hot stones) is the name of a month.
kepoke	1. ceremonial spear; 2. a straight blade for cockfighting; *ke'i kepoke*: to stick the spear into the male pillar of the house for divination purposes
kepue	1. trunk of tree; tree; 2. base, origin, source; *èmu kepue*: house of origin
kerigi	plate made of plaited lontar palm leaves; *kerigi nga'a* is a plate for ceremonial meals as only indigenous products and tools are allowed in rituals and ceremonies.
kerogo	1. basket to hold sacrificial meat to be shared by members of the same paternal lineage; 2. a lineage in the paternal line, that is, all the people sharing the same sacrificial meat
keruga	white coral for producing lime for betel chew and the dyeing process; *wèbe keruga* is the name of a ceremony for breaking coral once a year.
ketadu haba	kind of cither with bamboo 'strings' and whose resonance body is made of a large lontar palm leaf; *ketadu mara*: a music instrument with metal strings
ketopo	forgotten; the name of years in the Mesara ceremonial calendar where no ritual is held (as if it is forgotten)
kètu	head; *rukètu*: human hair; it is also the name of a ceremony for bringing back the hair of a deceased person to his/her island of origin.
kewèhu (kewahu)	1. knot; 2. a hair bun; 3. a joint (bones), also said for bamboo; *kewèhu rai* (lit. knots of the land) are the ceremonies of the adat calendar; traditions, a calendar of rites which refers to all the festivals which repeat at fixed times in the adat calendar; *nga'a kewèhu* (lit. to eat the knots) is part of a ritual or a ceremony which comprises a ceremonial meal.

kewore	small container for offerings (*ketupat* [In])
ko (*kom*)	wild jujube (*Ziziphus mauritiana*)
kodo	torso, back; *apu kodo*: a beheaded ancestor who could not have a normal burial
kola	wood used for building ritual houses in Savu but not in Raijua (*Bischofia javanica*).
kolo	tip, end, top; *kolo lai*: the top of the sail
ko'o, ko'e	1. to clean; *ko'o ma*: to clear the fields before planting; 2. the name of the month in the adat calendar where field clearing takes place
kopo	room, quarter
koro	pigeon, dove; also a male personal name
kota	1. fortress; 2. Kupang, West Timor (popular); Kota Ga (Great Fortress) is the name of the fort in Solor known in the narratives.
kowa	boat; *kowa Deo*: boat of God; *kowa hole*: the ceremonial boat for the thanksgiving ceremony; *rae kowa*: fenced traditional village, built in the shape of a boat
kuja	to plant; *kuja ma*: to plant in the field; also the name of part of a month in the adat calendar
la	1. to, towards (away from the speaker); *kako la ni*: to walk there; *ma* antonym: to, towards (towards the speaker); *èbe ma d'e*: bring here!; 2. a small branch, stalk, twig; *la are*: a stalk of rice; *la j'u'u*: a blade of grass
lado	crown; also a male personal name; *lado moto*: comet (lit. crowned star)
lai	1. case, purpose, matter; 2. a sail; *lai kowa*: the sail of a boat
lakai	thorny creeping plant which grows on sandy beaches
lale dahi	big flood coming from the sea; a tsunami
lara	1. yellow; 2 gold; 3. purulence; Kelara is the name of a clan in Seba.
lari (Seba)	hill; *kolo lari*: top, summit of a hill
lata	pandanus tree; its leaves are used for weaving mats.
latia	thunder; also the name of a priest position
lau (*helau*)	1. together; 2. the sea (*laut* [In])

lèba	1. prescription, restriction; 2. a crown; 3. the name of a weaving pattern restricted to the ruling classes
lede	mountain; *kolo lede*: the summit of a mountain
ledo	traditional dance performed in pairs day and night during the highest form of funeral, the *tao leo*—the male dancers wear swords.
lere	to follow; *rai lere*: land inherited from mother to daughter(s) (lit. to follow one behind the other)
li [*lii*]	text, words; *li Hawu*: the Savuvenese language; *li Jawa*: the Indonesian language; *li pana*: hot words; mantra knowledge for rituals and black magic
lie (*pahi*)	1. coral; *wowadu lie*: coral stone; 2. submerged; 3. cave; *roa lie*: the space inside a cave
liru	sky; Apu Lod'o Liru is God in the Sky or heaven.
lo (*lou, lau*)	south; also sea
lobo	1. place of residence, of activities; 2. a rice field
lodo	to go
lod'o	1. sun; 2. day; Apu Lod'o (Descendant of the Sun) is the name of priest position generally from the same clan as the ruler.
loko	river; *ei loko*: water from the river or drinking water
lole	wind; *lole wa*: west wind
lu (from *bèlu*)	forgotten; to describe years without rituals because the clans in charge of rituals those years have vanished
luha	crescent, days of the waxing moon; *hepeluha* is the first day of the lunar month; *hape* antonym: days of the waning moon
luji	support; a measure; *nga'a luji*: portion of food; *luji ae*: eagle; Luji Ae is the name of a mythical ancestor.
lumu	soft; *adu* antonym: hard; Lumu Lutu is the name of an ancestor of the Kolorae clan in Liae.
lungi	whale; Iwa Lungi: mythical whale, goddess of the sea; Lungi Rai is the name of the Aelungi clan's founding ancestor in Mesara.
ma	1. field; 2. to, towards the speaker; *mari ma d'e*: come here!

mada (*namada*)	eye; *ei mada*: spring (lit. eye of the water)
made	dead; *dou do made*: deceased
Maja (Maja Muri)	name of an unpredictable spirit of the category Wango; in collective thought, the name Maja is often associated with the Majapahit era; *niki niki Maja* (the children of Maja) is the name given to the inhabitants of Raijua.
makemone (*ama kemone*)	mother's brother (MB); he has an important responsibility towards his sister and her children who are his *nakebèni*.
manu	chicken; *manu la'i ae*: rooster; *manu la'i mea*: red rooster; *manu la'i bèla*: rooster with a large comb (taboo rooster); *manu rena*: hen
mara	1. copper; *raja mara*: to hammer copper; also the name of the first house built in Namata; 2. tired; 3. to recede; *mara dahi*: low tide
mata, mate	to wait; Namata is the name of Seba's ritual centre and it refers to a narrative where Robo Aba's children waited to catch a wild pig.
mea	red
mèdi	black; *pudi* antonym: white
Mehara	Mesara is the name of a traditional domain in west Savu which is today called Hawu Mehara.
mejedi, mejede [*mejed'i, mejed'e*]	1. to sit; 2. to rule over
mela	precious metal; *mela lara*: gold; *mela pudi*: silver
menanga	estuary, bay; Menanga is the name of a small landing place in Raijua.
menganga	hungry, starving; *awe menganga*: the hungry season (dry season)
mengau	to swear, to make an oath.
mengèru	green (plant, nature), by extension fertility, prosperity; Deo Mengèru: God of growth, prosperity, fertility; it is also the name of a priest position.
mèngi	1. perfume, sweet aroma, fragrance; 2. good luck, prosperity; *aju mèngi*: sandalwood
Merèbu (Merabu)	sacred mountain in Liae; the first settlement of the ancestors
meringi	cold, cool; *pana* antonym: hot, dangerous

metana	birth; to be born
miha	itself, on its own; the only one; Miha is a personal name; Miha Ngara is the name of a key ancestor; Dida Miha (On his own up) and Ie Miha (Good on his own) are the names of two siblings at the origin of male clans in Savu and Raijua.
mone a'a	elder brother; Mone Ama (lit. Men-fathers) is the name of the council of priests in the traditional religion Jingi Tiu; Mone Weo (Magnificent Man) is the name of an early ancestor in Raijua who is said to have left when Maja arrived.
moto	star; *moto mou rai*: morning star
mu'u	banana
muhu	enemy; war
muri	life, to live; Deo Muri: God (lit. the always Living God); Wènyi Muri: (lit. the always Living Lady); refers to Mary mother of Jesus in Raijua (Catholic)
nada	arena, place where people gather for rituals; Nada Ae: the name of the ceremonial place in Namata with large megaliths; Nadawawi (Arena of the Pig) is the name of the Nataga clan's settlement of origin on Namata hill; the name was used for a village recently created in the lowland of Seba.
nakebèni	relationship between a man and his sister's sons (ZS) and his sister's daughters (ZD)
nangi	to swim; Nangi Lai is the name of an ancestor in Liae.
nau	1. sea urchin; 2. a plantation, grove; *nau due*: lontar grove
nawa	wave (which breaks on the shore); Talo Nawa (Big Wave) is the name of an ancestor who brought the lontar palm tree to Savu.
nga'a, nga'e	to eat; *penga'a*: to feed; *èla ke penga'a*: already eaten
ngahu (*ngèhu*)	mortar; also a personal name
ngaka	dog; *woba ngaka* (lit. to club a dog to death) is the name of a ceremony conducted when a marriage no longer produces children.

ngara	name; Ngara Rai (Name of Land) is the name of an important ancestor.
ngèlu	wind
ngèru	young; *wèka* antonym: old
ngi'u	body
nida	plant, sometimes known as fishberry, and used for curing epilepsy (*Anamirta cocculus*); Nida Lobo Dahi is the name of an ancestor who was cured by the plant and the first raja of Liae during Portuguese times, according to collective memory. Na Nida is the mother of Nida Lobo Dahi and she is at the origin of the Jingi Wiki group which practised black magic; *kepepe Nanida* is the name of the group's heirloom basket.
nidu (*wango nidu*)	Satan; wango: an unpredictable spirit since mythology; *dou do nidu*: sorcerer; *penidu*: to put a curse (a spell) on someone
nitas (Roti/Kupang)	Java olive tree (*Sterculia foetida*)
pahi	coral, coral stone
pai	to burn; *pai huru* refers to the way people used to make light by burning torches made of twisted palm leaves soaked in the oil gathered from the *kepaka* tree's seeds (*Sterculia foetida*).
pana	hot; *meringi* antonym: cool, cold; *li pana* [*lii pana*]: hot text; sacred language or mantra text
patola	Indian trade cloth that became part of heirloom baskets; *patola lai rede* (lit. full sail cloth) is the name of a highly regarded Indian patola cloth.
pèda	sick, sickness
pedai, pedae	to talk
pedoa [*ped'oa, ped'oe*]	1. to call someone (vocally) as opposed to *gape* (to summon by waving the hand or beckoning); to pray or call the ancestors or God; 2. a ritual dance accompanied by chants, which recall events of ancient times, performed at night during the last two months of the ceremonial year; no gongs or drums are allowed; *kedue ped'oa*: small baskets attached to the dancers' feet to provide the rhythm

pehami	taboo (*pemali* [In]); *jara pehami* is a taboo horse belonging to a priest which protects him and his activities; *manu pehami*: taboo chicken which protects its owner
pehape	days of the waning moon; *peluha* antonym: days of the waxing moon
pehere jara	ceremonial dance which one or several horses perform at various times in the year
peiu manu (*piu manu*)	ceremonial cockfighting to replace war between the clans; *iu*: to tie, to attach
peluha	days of the waxing moon; *pehape* antonym: days of the waning moon
piga	plate; *Piga Hina*: (Chinese Plate) a personal name which also appears in the mantra chants; Piga Rai (Plate of the Land) is the name of an ancestress.
pu (*apu*, *èpu*)	root, origin, ancestor
pudi	1. white; 2. a fence surrounding a *rae* (traditional village) made from pieces of coral, which is initially white.
puru	to come down; Napuru is the name of a clan in Dimu; Pururede (Come down full) is the name of an ancient settlement in Seba with ceremonies dedicated to the lontar palm tree.
ra	blood; every being has three types of blood corresponding to the humours, the bodily fluids in ancient and medieval times: *ra mea* (red), *ra pudi* (white) and *ra mèdi* (black).
rae	traditional fenced settlement; *rae kowa*: a traditional village in the shape of a boat
rahi	meeting place; Rahihawu is the name of a place in Namata.
rai	land, island, region; realm; refers to a spatial category; Deo Rai: Lord of the Earth; the highest priest position; *heo rai*: the nine realms between the earth and the place of God (Deo Muri Mara); Rai Ae (Great Land) is the name of an early ancestor; Rai Bèla (Large Land) is the name of an ancestor in the mantra genealogies who has two siblings—Liru Bèla (Large Sky) and Dahi Bèla

	(Large Sea); *rai lere*: land transmitted from mother to daughters until the extinction of the female line; *uku rai*: adat law; *uru rai*: early realms; ancient times.
raja	to hammer; *raja mara*: to hammer copper; the name of the place where the oldest ancestral house in Namata was built
raja	regent; the title given by the Portuguese and later the Dutch to the main ruler of a domain previously known as *Duae Rai* (Big Man of the Land).
rao	cooking place (one hole) dug in the ground; clay hearth; *rao pana* is the ritual hearth for boiling the lontar sap under the responsibility of a priest; it has three holes, except for that of the priest Apu Lod'o Wadu in Mesara, which has four holes.
ratu	council; a socio-political and religious organisation in pre colonial times which has survived in some areas until recently; *Ratu Mone Tèlu*: Council of Three Men in pre colonial times in Liae, descended from the elder brother Dida Miha; *Ratu Mone Lèmi*: Council of Five Men in Liae, descended from the elder brother (Kolorae clan); *Ratu Mone Pidu*: Council of Seven Men in Liae, descended from the younger brother Ie Miha
Re	constellation of Antares; important in agriculture; Re Babo [B'ab'o] is the name of a mythical ancestress who committed incest with her brother, Wunu Babo.
rede	full, complete; Rede Dida is the name of a key ancestor in Liae.
rihi	own, on its own; Perihi is the name of a mountain in Mesara, important in Savunese history.
ru	narrow and long; *rujara*: road; *rukètu*: human hair; also the name of a related ceremony where relatives bring back the hair of the deceased to the place of origin; *rukoko*: feathers of the neck; also the extended ridge of an adat house; *rulai*: tail; *rumanu*: chicken feather; *rumehai*: seaweed; *runa'i*: tobacco leaf; *ruwèngu*: cotton plant
rue	name of a priest position linked to violent and unnatural deaths, and the breaching of taboos (adultery, incest)

talo	big, high; Talo Hawu is the name of ancestor who brought the lontar palm to Savu.
tao	to make, to build; *tao leo*: 1. to build a house (poetry); 2. the name of the highest form of funeral, lasting at least nine days, for which a dwelling is built made of pillars and a flat roof of coconut leaves. The ground is covered by a large mat on which the guests dance day and night.
tegida	ritual house of a female lineage where women of the same maternal line assemble three times a year—for the first indigo dye, the blessing of the heirloom basket and for the red dye (*morinda*).
tèlu	three
tèni	to meet, to assemble; Tèni Hawu is the name of the Savunese rulers' residence in Mèba, Seba (from the 1870s).
terae	sorghum; *terae Hawu*: indigenous sorghum; *terae jawa*: corn, maize
Teriwu	name of the ancestors' second settlement; as a polity it had been absorbed by adjacent domains in pre-European times; Koloteriwu: summit of Teriwu hill
tèru	bow, also a pillar of the house; *tèru d'uru*: the male (bow) pillar in which a spear is stuck for divination purposes; *tèru wui*: the stern (female) pillar of the house
titu	to stand up, to erect; Titu Hawu is the name of the founding ancestor of the Naputitu clan in Mesara; *petitu rao*: to build the hearth for boiling the lontar sap in Dimu
toka	village gate; there is one gate for each of the four cardinal directions.
tule	to comb hair towards the back of the head; Tuleika is the name of the Seba settlement of the Kelara clan (though an 1851 Dutch manuscript has it as Tule Ikan).
tunu	to roast, to grill; *tunu manu* is the name of a ritual where a sacrificial chicken is roasted; the name of the month in the ceremonial calendar in which the ritual occurs

uba [*ub'a*]	mouth, opening, bay; Uba Ae is the name of the bay in Mesara from which the ceremonial boat *kowa hole* is put out to sea; *ubadara* [*ub'ad'ara*]: a harbour
udu	1. heap, pile, stack, mound; 2. a male clan
uhu	millet
uku rai	adat law
uli	1. rudder; 2. the person operating the rudder; helmsman; a personal name
wadu (*wowadu*)	stone; *wadu turu*: a stone for receiving offerings during rituals; *wowadu kebèli*: an upside-down stone; dolmen
wai	belt for ceremonies and rituals; *wai labe*: a narrow cloth for wrapping the corpse at funerals; *wai mea*: a sacred red cloth previously worn by men going to war and woven by their mothers or sisters; *wai wake*: a belt (worn by men) to hold the loin cloth and the knife; *mane wai*: a ceremony for weaving a funeral cloth; Wai Wèka (Old Belt) is the name of a key ancestor descended from the younger brother.
Wango	unpredictable spirit (often feared as bad spirit) which can be placated with offerings; Christians identify him as Satan.
wata	limit, border; *wowadu wata*: border stone
wawi	pig; *wawi Maja*: a sacrificial pig for the spirit Maja at the ceremony *hapo*, which takes place shortly after birth; *wawi wie Deo*: sacrificial pig to ask for prosperity
wèga (*woga*)	banyan tree; Wègamengèru (Prosperous Banyan Tree) is the name of a place in Seba.
wèka	old; *ngèru* antonym: young
weli	1. to buy (using money); 2. bride price when the bride and groom are not from the same maternal line
wènyi	1. areca palm tree (for betel chew); 2. a female name
weo	bright, magnificent; Mone Weo is the name of an important ancestor in Raijua who fled when Maja arrived.

wèru	1. moon; 2. a lunar month; Wèru a'a: the first month of the year (lit. month of the elder sibling); Wèru ari: the second month of the year (lit. month of the younger sibling)
wiki	more; Jingi Wiki is the name of a group of people who practised black magic.
wila	flower, blossom; also a personal name
wini	1. seed; 2. the name of a branching group or lineage in a female moiety
woana kapa	dugout canoe for fishing along the shore; also used for carrying passengers from the beach to large ferry boats
woba (*wèba*, *wèbe*)	to strike, to hit; *woba lèmi*: five o'clock
woka	1. tip of a fishing hook or harpoon; 2. a cockspur
wolo	1. verdict; 2. to judge; Wolo Manu is the name of an early ancestor; Wolomanu is the name of a ritual place for cockfighting in Liae.
womèngeru	name of a place important in cockfighting matters (lit. the prosperous [place]); *mengèru*: green, thus linked to the idea of nature, fertility, prosperity
Wunu Pidu	constellation of Pleiades
Wunu Babo [B'ab'o]	name of an ancestor who committed incest with his sister Re; he was changed into the star Wunu Pidu and she was changed into the star Antares which never appear in the sky at the same time.

Bibliography

Unpublished sources

Arsip Nasional Republik Indonesia (ANRI, National Archives of the Republic of Indonesia), Jakarta

ANRI Timor, various years, access number K.43.

Bourgois, Alonce. 1619-28. "Memorije van de persoonen die alhier [in Solor] gedoopt en in den houwelijken staat bevesticht" [Memorandum of the Persons who were Baptised and Confirmed in the Married State Here (in Solor)]. Transcript provided by Diederick Kortlang, Nationaal Archief, The Hague.

"Doopboek Timor" [Timor Baptismal Book]. 1669-1732. Transcript provided by Diederick Kortlang, Nationaal Archief, The Hague.

VOC. *Hoge regering 1702-79* [*Supreme Government 1702-79*]. Vol. 02873-04120.

(The) British Library, London

Callbrooke, William. 1812. "Sketches Relating to the Range of Islands Connected with the East Coast of Java." MacKenzie Private Collection 167-171, Book 82. Asian and African Studies.

KITLV (Royal Netherlands Institute of Southeast Asian and Caribbean Studies) Archives, Leiden

Francis, Emanuel. 1832. "Verslag van den Kommisaris voor Timor" [Report by the Commissioner for Timor]. H 548.

Held, G.J. 1955. "Sumbawa – geschiedenis" [Sumbawa – History]. H 1220: 28.

Rouffaer, G.P. 1910. "Kleine Timor Eilanden" [Smaller Timor Islands]. Vol. I. H 673.

Tange, Willem. 1688. "Dertooghen standt der saeken van 't eylandt Rotti, Timor en Solor" [State of Things in the Islands Rotti, Timor, and Solor]. H 49 u.

Nationaal Archief (National Archives), The Hague

Archive of the Vereenigde Oost-Indische Compagnie (VOC, Dutch East India Company). 1602-1799, access number 1.04.02.

Bosch, J.J. 1938. "Memorie van Overgave van de Residentie Timor" [Memorandum of Succession for the Timor Residency]. Ministerie van Kolonien [MMK, Ministry of the Colonies] 345, Open Collection microfiches.

Comité Oost-Indische Handel en Bezittingen [Committee of East Indian Trade and Possessions]. 1794–95. No. 102.

Heyligers, A.H.J.M. 1920. "Memorie van Overgave van het onderafdeeling Savoe" [Memorandum of Succession for the Subdivision Savu]. Koninklijk Instituut voor de Tropen [KIT, Royal Institute for the Tropics] 1273. Open Collection microfiches.

Karthaus, P.F.J. 1931. "Memorie van Overgave van den aftredend Resident van Timor en Onderhorigheden" [Memorandum of Succession by the Outgoing Resident of Timor and Dependencies]. MMK 343.

Kempen, C.J. van. 1917. "Memorie van Overgave van de Afdeling Zuid Timor en Eilanden" [Memorandum of Succession for the Division South Timor and Islands]. KIT 1278.

Kruseman, J. 1824. "Timor". G.J.C. Schneither Collection, No. 131, access number 2.21.007.57.

Maier, E.G.Th. 1918. "Memorie van Overgave van de Residentie Timor" [Memorandum of Succession for the Timor Residency]. Le Roux Collection, No. 5-6.

Nijs Bik, E.H. de. 1934. "Memorie van Overgave van de Residentie Timor" [Memorandum of Succession for the Timor Residency]. MMK 344, Open Collection microfiches.

Politieke verslagen en berichten uit de buitengewesten [Political Reports and Relations from the Outer Possessions]. Timor. Open Collection microfiches.

Raad der Aziatische bezittingen [Council of the Asian Possessions]. 1798–1800. No. 131.

Rapportage Indonesië [Reportage on Indonesia] 1946–49, 02.10.29.

University Library (UB), Leiden

Letters from indigenous princes, late 18th/early 19th century. LOr 2238.

Letters from indigenous princes, late 18th/early 19th century. LOr 2242.

(Het) Utrechts Archief (The Utrechts Archives), Utrecht

Raad voor de zending der Nederlandse Hervormde kerk [Council for the Mission of the Dutch Reformed Church]. 1102-1.

Published sources

Alderwerelt, J. de Roo van. 1906. "Historische aanteekeningen over Soemba (residentie Timor en Onderhoorigheden)" [Historical Notes about Sumba (Timor Residency and Dependencies)]. *Tijdschrift voor Indische Taal-, Land- en Volkenkunde* [*TBG, Journal of Indonesian Linguistics and Anthropology*] 48: 185–316.

Almanak en naamregister voor Nederlandsch-Indië 1826–63 [Calendar and Name Register for the Netherlands Indies]. Batavia: Lands-Drukkerij.

Amnifu, Djemi. 2017. "Sabu Raijua Regent Jailed for Graft." *The Jakarta Post* 31.07.2017. Available at http://www.thejakartapost.com/news/2017/07/31/sabu-raijua-regent-jailed-for-graft.html [accessed 5 March 2018].

Andaya, Leonard Y. 1993. *The World of Maluku: Eastern Indonesia in the Early Modern Period.* Honolulu: University of Hawai'i Press.

_____. 1995. "The Bugis–Makassar Diasporas." *Journal of the Malaysian Branch of the Royal Asiatic Society* 68 (1): 119–38.

_____. 2004. "Nature of War and Peace among the Bugis–Makassar People." *South East Asia Research* 12 (1): 53–80.

_____. 2010. "The 'Informal Portuguese Empire' and the Topasses in the Solor Archipelago and Timor in the Seventeenth and Eighteenth Centuries." *Journal of Southeast Asian Studies* 41 (3): 391–420.

_____. 2016. "Applying the Seas Perspective in the Study of Eastern Indonesia in the Early Modern Period." In *Early Modern Southeast Asia, 1350–1800*, ed. Oei Keat Gin and Hoang Anh Tuan, 69–87. London and New York: Routledge.

Arago, Jacques. 1823. *Narrative of a Voyage Round the World, in the Uranie and Physicienne Corvettes, Commanded by Captain Freycinet….* London: T. Davison and Howlett and Brimmer for Treuttel and Wurtz, Treuttel jun. and Richter. Available at https://archive.org/details/narrativeavoyag00araggoog [accessed 5 March 2018].

Ardhana, I Ketut. 2000. "Nusa Tenggara nach Einrichtung der Kolonialherrschaft 1915 bis 1950" [Nusa Tenggara after the Introduction of Colonial Rule, 1915–50]. PhD diss. Universität Passau, Bavaria, Germany.

Aritonang, Jan Sihar, and Karel Steenbrink. 2008. *A History of Christianity in Indonesia.* Leiden: Brill.

Arndt, Paul. 1951. *Religion auf Ostflores, Adonare und Solor* [Religion in East Flores, Adonara and Solor]. Studia Instituti Anthropos, Vol. 1. Wien-Mödling: Verlag der Missionsdruckerei St. Gabriel [Publishing house of the mission printer St Gabriel].

Arsip Nasional Republik Indonesia. 2007. *Kontrak perjanjian wilayah perbatasan Republik Indonesia, Jilid II: Wilayah Laut Andaman, Selat Malaka, dan Laut Sawu, Timor* [Contracts and Agreements of the Borderlines of the Republic of Indonesia, Volume II: The Regions of the Anaman Sea, Melaka Strait, and Savu Sea, Timor]. Jakarta: ANRI.

Atja, and Saleh Danasasmita. 1981. *Carita Parahiyangan: Transkripsi, terjemahan dan catatan* [Tale of Parahiyangan: Transliteration, Translation and Notes]. Bandung: Proyek Pengembangan Permuseuman Jawa Barat [West Java Museum Development Project].

Badan Pusat Statistik. 2001. "Kabupaten Kupang statistik" [Statistics of Kupang Regency]. Kupang: Badan Pusat Statistik [Central Bureau of Statistics].

_____. 2014–17. "Kabupaten Sabu Raijua dalam angka" [Savu Raijua Regency in Figures]. Kupang: Badan Pusat Statistik.

Bankoff, Greg, and Sandra Swart. 2007. *Breeds of Empire: The 'Invention' of the Horse in Southeast Asia and Southern Africa 1500–1950.* Copenhagen: NIAS Press.

Banks, Joseph. (1770) 2004. *Some Account of Savu.* (State Library of New South Wales, Transcription.) Available at http://southseas.nla.gov.au/journals/banks_remarks/311.html [accessed 5 March 2018]

Barber, Elizabeth Wayland, and Paul T. Barber. 2004. *When They Severed Earth from Sky: How the Human Mind Shapes Myth*. Princeton: Princeton University Press.

Barnes, Robert, H. 1974. *Kédang: A Study of the Collective Thought of an Eastern Indonesian People*. Oxford: Clarendon Press.

_____. 1987. "Avarice and Iniquity at the Solor Fort." *Bijdragen tot de Taal-, Land- en Volkenkunde* [*BKI, Journal of the Humanities and Social Sciences of Southeast Asia and Oceania*] 143 (2/3): 208–36.

_____. 1995. "Time and the Sense of History in an Indonesian Community: Oral Tradition in a Recently Literate Culture." In *Time: Histories and Ethnologies*, ed. Diane Owen Hughes and Thomas R. Trautmann, 243–68. Ann Arbor: University of Michigan Press.

_____. 1996. *Sea Hunters of Indonesia: Fishers and Weavers of Lamalera*. Oxford: Clarendon Press.

Beaglehole, J.C., ed. 1955. *The Journals of Captain James Cook on His Voyages of Discovery*. Vol. I, *The Voyage of the Endeavour 1768–1771*. Cambridge: Published for the Hakluyt Society at the University Press.

Bedner, Adriaan, and Stijn van Huis. 2008. "The Return of the Native in Indonesian Law: Indigenous Communities in Indonesian Legislation." *BKI* 164 (2/3): 165–93.

Bellwood, Peter. 1979. *Man's Conquest of the Pacific: The Prehistory of Southeast Asia and Oceania*. New York: Oxford University Press.

_____. 1985. *Prehistory of the Indo-Malaysian Archipelago*. Sydney: Academic Press.

Bellwood, Peter, James J. Fox, and Darrell Tryon, eds. 1995. *The Austronesians: Historical and Comparative Perspectives*. Canberra: Research School of Pacific Studies, ANU.

Bintarti, D.D. 1985. "Prehistoric Bronze Objects in Indonesia." *Bulletin of the Indo-Pacific Prehistory Association* 6: 64–73.

Bongenaar, Karel E.M. 2006. *De ontwikkeling van het zelfbesturend landschap in Nederlandsch-Indië* [The Development of the Self-ruling Territory in the Netherlands Indies]. Zutphen: Walburg Pers.

Boxer, C.R. 1947. *The Topasses of Timor*. Amsterdam: Koninklijke Vereeniging Indisch Instituut [Royal Society of the Indies Institute].

Brumann, Christoph. 1999. "Writing for Culture: Why a Successful Concept Should Not Be Discarded." *Current Anthropology* 40 (Supplement): S1–S27.

Caldwell, Ian, and David Henley, eds. 2008. *Stranger-Kings in Indonesia and beyond* theme issue of *Indonesia and the Malay World* 36 (105). Available at https://www.tandfonline.com/toc/cimw20/36/105?nav=tocList [accessed 5 March 2018].

Chambert-Loir, Henri, and Anthony Reid, eds. 2002. *The Potent Dead: Ancestors, Saints and Heroes in Contemporary Indonesia*. Honolulu: University of Hawai'i Press.

Clamagirand (Renard-), Brigitte. 1980. "The Social Organization of the Ema of Timor." In *The Flow of Life: Essays on Eastern Indonesia*, Harvard Studies in Cultural Anthropology 2, ed. James J. Fox, 134–51. Cambridge, MA: Harvard University Press.

_____. 1982. *Marobo: Une socièté ema de Timor* [Marobo: An Ema Society in Timor] (Langues et Civilizations de l'Asie du Sud-Est et du Monde Insulindien No. 12) [Languages and Civilizations of Southeast Asia and of the Insulindian World]. Paris: Société Etudes Linguistique Anthropologiques de France.

Clifford, James. 1986. "Introduction: Partial Truths." In *Writing Culture: The Poetics and Politics of Ethnography*, ed. James Clifford and George E. Marcus, 1–27. Berkeley: University of California Press.

Clifford, James, and George E. Marcus, eds. 1986. *Writing Culture: The Poetics and Politics of Ethnography*. Berkeley: University of California Press.

Colle, Gaudiano. 2017. "Kasus Tambak Garam Sabu: Lewi dan Niko Divonis Enam Tahun Penjara" [The Savu Salt Pond Case: Lewi and Niko Sentenced to Six Years in Prison]. *Pos Kupang*, 01.12.2017. Available at http://kupang.tribunnews.com/2017/12/01/kasus-tambak-garam-sabu-lewi-dan-niko-divonis-enam-tahun-penjara [accessed 5 March 2018].

Connerton, Paul. (1989) 1998. *How Societies Remember*. Cambridge: Cambridge University Press.

Coolhaas. W.Ph., ed. (1639–1729) 1964–97. *Generale Missiven van Gouverneurs-Generaal en Raden aan Heren XVII der Verenigde Oost-Indische Compagnie* [General Correspondence of the Governor Generals and Council to the Seventeen Gentlemen of the United East India Company]. Vols 2–8. Den Haag: Martinus Nijhoff.

Crawfurd, John. 1856. *Descriptive Dictionary of the Indian Islands and Adjacent Countries*. London: Bradbury and Evans.

Cubitt, Geoffrey. 2007. *History and Memory*. Manchester: Manchester University Press.

Cuisinier, Jeanne. 1956. "Un calendrier de Savu" [A Calendar of Savu]. *Journal Asiatique* 244: 111–9.

_____. 1999. *Journal de voyage: Malaisie (1933), Indonésie (1952–55)* [A Travel Journal: Malaysia (1933), Indonesia (1952–55)]. Extracts edited by Daniel Perret, Cahiers d'Archipel 31. Paris: Musée de l'Homme.

D'Arcy Wood, Gillen. 2014. *Tambora: The Eruption That Changed the World*. Princeton: Princeton University Press.

"De opstootjes op Savoe" [The disturbances on Savu]. 1914. *Het Nieuws van den Dag voor Nederlandsch-Indië* [Daily News of Netherlands India]. 28 May 1914. Batavia (Jakarta).

Detaq, Yakob Y. 1973. *Memperkenalkan kebudayaan Suku Bangsa Sabu* [Introducing the Culture of the Savu People]. Ende: Nusa Indah.

Dijk, L.J. van. 1925; 1934. "De zelfbesturende landschappen in de Residentie Timor en Onderhoorigheden" [The Self-ruling Territories in the Residency Timor and Dependencies]. *Indische Gids* [*Indian Guide*] 47 (I): 528–40; 47 (II): 618–23; 56 (II): 708–12.

Doel, Wim van den. 2011. *Zo ver de wereld strekt De geschiedenis van Nederland overzee vanaf 1800* [As Far as the World Reaches: The History of the Netherlands Overseas until 1800]. Amsterdam: Bert Bakker.

Donselaar, W.M. 1871. "Eene geopende deur op Savoe" [An Open Door in Savu]. *Maandberigt van het Nederlandsche Zendelinggenootschap* [Monthly Report of the Dutch Missionary Society] 5: 65–73.

_____. 1872. "Aanteekeningen over het eiland Savoe" [Notes about Savu Island]. *Mededeelingen van wege het Nederlandsche Zendelinggenootschap* [Messages Concerning the Dutch Missionary Society] 16: 281–332.

Duggan, Geneviève. 2001. *Ikats of Savu: Women Weaving History in Eastern Indonesia*. Bangkok: White Lotus.

_____. 2004a. "Woven Blossoms, Seeds of History." *Hali* 134: 110–4.

_____. 2004b. "Woven Traditions, Collectors and Tourists: A Field Report from Savu." In *Performing Objects: Museums, Material Culture and Performance in Southeast Asia*, ed. Fiona Kerlogue, 103–18. London: Horniman Museum.

_____. 2008. "Processes of Memory on the Island of Savu." PhD Diss. NUS, Singapore.

_____. 2011a. "Introduction. Memoryscapes: Traditions and Contemporary Experience in Indonesia." In *Memoryscapes in Indonesia* theme issue of *Indonesia and the Malay World* 39 (113): 1–6.

_____. 2011b. "Commensality and Food Prohibition: Mnemotechniques on the Island of Savu, Eastern Indonesia." In *Memoryscapes in Indonesia* 39 (113): 103–22.

_____. 2011c. "Modes of Remembering and Transmitting Knowledge: A VOC Report of 1682 and Local Recollections, Island of Savu, NTT." In *Tradition, Identity and History-Making in Eastern Indonesia*, ed. Hans Hägerdal, 26–67. Växjö and Kalmar: Linnaeus University Press.

_____. 2013. *Woven Stories: Traditional Textiles from the Regency Savu Raijua*. Jakarta: Museum Tekstil.

_____. 2015. "Tracing Ancient Networks: Linguistics, Hand-Woven Cloths and Looms in Eastern Indonesia." In *Ancient Silk Trade Routes: Selected Works from a Symposium on Cross Cultural Exchanges and Their Legacies in Asia*, ed. Qin Dashu and Yuan Jian, 53–83. Hackensack, NJ: World Scientific Publishing.

Duggan, Geneviève and Ice Tede Dara. 2016. "Heritage Weaving: Tense Present and Uncertain Future." *Textiles Asia* 7 (2): 16–24.

Durand, Frédéric. 2006. *Timor: 1250–2005: 750 ans de cartographie et de voyages* [Timor 1250–2005: 750 Years of Cartography and Voyages]. Toulouse: Arkuiris.

Echols, John M., and Hassan Shadily, eds. 1990. *Kamus Indonesia–Inggris: An Indonesian–English Dictionary*. Third edition by John U. Wolff and James T. Collins with Hassan Shadily. Jakarta: Gramedia Pustaka Utama.

Ellen, Roy. 2003. *On the Edge of the Banda Zone: Past and Present in the Social Organization of a Moluccan Trading Network*. Honolulu: University of Hawai'i Press.

Encyclopaedie van Nederlandsch-Indië. 1917–39 [Encyclopaedia of the Netherlands Indies]. Vols I-IX. 's-Gravenhage: Martinus Nijhoff.

End, Th. van den. 1987. *Gereformeerde Zending op Sumba (1859–1972)* [Reformed Mission in Sumba (1859–1972)]. Oegstgeest: Alphen aan den Rijn.

Erb, Maribeth. 1987. "When Rocks Were Young and Earth Was Soft: Ritual and Mythology in Northeastern Manggarai." PhD Diss. State University of New York, Stony Brook, NY.

_____. 1999. *The Manggaraians: Guide to Traditional Lifestyles*. Singapore: Times Editions.

Farram, Steven. 2004. "From 'Timor Koepang' to 'Timor NTT': A Political History of West Timor, 1901–1967." PhD Diss. Charles Darwin University, Darwin, Australia.

_____. 2007. "Jacobus Arnoldus Hazaart and the British Interregnum in Netherlands Timor, 1812–1816." *BKI* 163 (4): 455–75.

Feld, Steven, and Keith Basso, eds. 1996. *Senses of Place*. Santa Fe, NM: School of American Research Press.

Fentress, James, and Chris Wickham. (1992) 1994. *Social Memory*. New Perspectives on the Past. Oxford: Blackwell.

Finnegan, R. 1996. "A Note on Oral Tradition and Historical Evidence." In *Oral History: An Interdisciplinary Anthology*, ed. David K. Dunaway and Willa K. Baum, 126–34. Walnut Creek, CA: Altamira Press.

Forshee, Jill. 2001. *Between the Folds. Stories of Cloth, Lives, and Travels from Sumba*. Honolulu: University of Hawai'i Press.

Forth, Gregory. 1998. *Beneath the Volcano. Religion, Cosmology and Spirit Classification among the Nage of Eastern Indonesia*. Leiden: KITLV.

_____. (2008) 2010. *Images of the Wildman in Southeast Asia: An Anthropological Perspective*. London: Routledge.

Fox, James, J. 1977. *The Harvest of the Palm: Ecological Change in Eastern Indonesia*. Cambridge, MA: Harvard University Press.

_____. 1979. "The Ceremonial System of Savu." In *The Imagination of Reality: Essays on Southeast Asian Coherence Systems*, ed. A.L. Becker and A.A. Yengoyan, 145–73. Norwood, NJ: Ablex Publishing Corporation.

_____. 1980. "Models and Metaphors: Comparative Research in Eastern Indonesia." In *The Flow of Life: Essays on Eastern Indonesia*, Harvard Studies in Cultural Anthropology 2, ed. James J. Fox, 327–33. Cambridge, MA: Harvard University Press.

_____. 1993. "Memories of Ridge-Poles and Cross-Beams: The Categorical Foundations of a Rotinese Cultural Design." In *Inside Austronesian Houses: Perspectives on Domestic Designs for Living*, ed. James J. Fox, 145–82. Canberra: Anthropology, RSPS, ANU.

_____. 1995. "Origin Structures and Systems of Precedence in the Comparative Study of Austronesian Societies." In *Austronesian Studies Relating to Taiwan*, Symposium Series 3, ed. P.J.K. Li, Cheng-hwa Tsang, Ying-kuei Huang, Dah-an Ho and Chiu-yu Tseng, 27–57. Taipei: Institute of History and Philology, Academia Sinica.

_____. 1996. "The Transformation of Progenitor Lines of Origin: Patterns of Precedence in Eastern Indonesia." In *Origins, Ancestry and Alliance: Explorations in Austronesian Ethnography*, ed. James J. Fox and Clifford Sather, 133–48. Canberra: Anthropology, RSPS, ANU.

_____. 2000a. "Maritime Communities in the Timor and Arafura Region: Some Historical and Anthropological Perspectives." In *East of Wallace's Line: Studies of Past and Present Maritime Cultures of the Indo-Pacific Region*, ed. Sue O'Connor and Peter Veth, 337–56. Rotterdam: A.A. Balkema.

_____. 2000b. "'For Good and Sufficient Reasons': An Examination of Early Dutch East India Company Ordinances on Slaves and Slavery." In *Slavery, Bondage and Dependency in Southeast Asia*, ed. Anthony Reid, 246–62. St Lucia: Queensland University Press.

_____. 2008. "Installing the 'Outsider' Inside: The Exploration of an Epistemic Austronesian Cultural Theme and its Social Significance." In Caldwell and Henley, eds, 2008, 201–18.

_____. ed. 1980. *The Flow of Life: Essays on Eastern Indonesia*. Cambridge, MA: Harvard University Press.

_____. ed. 1993. *Inside Austronesian Houses: Perspectives on Domestic Designs for Living.* Canberra: Anthropology, RSPS, ANU.

Fox, James J., and Clifford Sather, eds. 1996. *Origins, Ancestry and Alliance: Explorations in Austronesian Ethnography.* Canberra: RSPS, ANU.

Fraassen, Christiaan Frans van. 1987. "Ternate, de Molukken en de Indonesische Archipel. Van soa-organisatie en vierdeling: een studie van traditionele samenleving en cultuur in Indonesië" [Ternate, Maluku and the Indonesian Archipelago. About Soa Organization and Quadripartition: A Study of Traditional Society and Culture in Indonesia]. Vols I–II. PhD Diss. Leiden University, the Netherlands.

Geirnaert-Martin, Danièle C. 1989. "Textiles of West Sumba: Lively Renaissance of an Old Tradition." In *To Speak with Cloth: Studies in Indonesian Textiles*, ed. Mattiebelle Gittinger, 57–80. Los Angeles: Fowler Museum of Cultural History, UCLA.

_____. 1991. "The Snake's Skin: Traditional Ikat in Kodi." In *Indonesian Textiles* Symposium 1985, ed. Gisela Vögler and Karin von Welck, 34–42. Cologne: Ethnologica Neue Folge, on behalf of the Rautenstrauch-Jöst Museum.

_____. 1992. *The Woven Land of Laboya: Socio-Cosmic Ideas and Values in West Sumba, Eastern Indonesia.* Leiden: Centre of Non-Western Studies, Leiden University.

Glover, Ian, and Peter Bellwood. (2004) 2006. *Southeast Asia: From Prehistory to History.* London: Routledge.

Goor, Jurrien van, ed. (1729–37; 1737–43) 1989; 2004. *Generale Missiven van Gouverneurs-Generaal en Raden aan Heren XVII der VOC* [*General Correspondence of the Governor Generals and Council to the Seventeen Gentlemen of the VOC*]. Vols 9; 10. Den Haag: Martinus Nijhoff.

Grave, Jean-Marc, de. 2001. *Initiation rituelle et arts martiaux; Trois écoles de kanuragan javanais* [Ritual Initiation and Martial Arts: Three Schools of Javanese Kanuragan]. Paris: Archipel/ L' Harmattan.

Haga, A. 1882. "De slag bij Penefoeij en Vendrig Lip" [The Battle of Penfui and Ensign Lip]. *TBG* 27: 389–408.

Hägerdal, Hans. 2010. "Cannibals and Pedlars: Economic Opportunities and Political Alliance in Alor, 1600-1850." *Indonesia and the Malay World* 38 (111): 217–46.

_____. 2012. *Lords of the Land, Lords of the Sea: Conflict and Adaptation in Early Colonial Timor, 1600–1800* (VKI, Verhandelingen van het Koninklijk Instituut voor Taal-, Land- en Volkenkunde 273) [Monographs of the Royal Institute for Linguistics and Anthropology 273]. Leiden: KITLV Press.

_____. 2013a. "Lay Atjien Liok and the Lidak War of 1852: Chinese Networking, Indigenous Agency and Colonial Intrusion in Eastern Indonesia." *Indonesia and the Malay World* 41 (121): 322–47.

_____. 2013b. "The Native as Exemplum: Missionary Writings and Colonial Complexities in Eastern Indonesia, 1819-1860." *Itinerario* 37 (2): 73–99.

_____. 2015. "Eastern Indonesia and the Writing of History." *Archipel* 90: 75–97.

_____. 2017. "Timor and Colonial Conquest: Voices and Claims about the End of the Sonba'i Realm in 1906." *Itinerario* 41 (3): 581–605.

Hall, Kenneth R. 2011. "Sojourning Communities, Ports-of-Trade, and Commercial Networking in Southeast Asia's Eastern Regions, c. 1000–1400." In *New Perspectives on the History and Historiography of Southeast Asia: Continuing Explorations* Essays in Honor of John K. Whitmore, ed. Michael Arthur Aung-Thwin and Kenneth R. Hall, 56–74. London and New York: Routledge.

Hawkesworth, John. 1773. *An Account of the Voyages Undertaken by the Order of His Present Majesty for Making Discoveries in the Southern Hemisphere...* in Three Volumes. London: W. Strahan and T. Cadell.

Heijmering, G. 1847. "Bijdragen tot de geschiedenis van Timor" [Contributions to the History of Timor]. *Tijdschrift van Nederlandsch-Indië* [*Journal of the Dutch East Indies*] IX (3):1–62, 121–232.

Henley, David. 2002. *Jealousy and Justice: The Indigenous Roots of Colonial Rule in Northern Sulawesi*, Comparative Asian Studies 22. Amsterdam: VU University Press.

Hicks, David. 1984. *A Maternal Religion: The Role of Women in Tetum Myth Ritual*, Monograph Series on Southeast Asia, Special Report No. 22. DeKalb, IL: Center for Southeast Asian Studies, Northern Illinois University.

_____. 2016. "Impaling Spirit: Three Categories of Ontological Domain in Eastern Indonesia." In *Animism in Southeast Asia*, ed. Kaj Arhem and Guido Sprenger, 257–76. London: Routledge.

Hill, Jonathan D., ed. 1988. *Rethinking Myth and History: Indigenous South American Perspectives on the Past*. Chicago: University of Illinois Press.

_____. 1996. *History, Power, and Identity: Ethnogenesis in the Americas, 1492–1992*. Iowa City: University of Iowa Press.

Hoadley, Mason C. 2006. *Public Administration: Indonesian Norms v. Western Forms*. Yogyakarta: Graha Ilmu.

Hoskins, Janet. 1997. *The Play of Time: Kodi Perspectives on Calendars, History, and Exchange*. Berkeley: University of California Press.

_____. 1998. *Biographical Objects: How Things Tell the Story of Peoples' Lives*. London: Routledge.

Howell, Signe. 1990. "Husband/Wife or Brother/Sister as the Key Relationship in Lio Kinship and Socio-Symbolic Relations." *Ethnos, Journal of Anthropology* 55 (3/4): 248–59.

_____. 1991. "Access to the Ancestors: Re-constructions of the Past in Non-literate Society." In *The Ecology of Choice and Symbol* Essays in Honour of Fredrik Barth, ed. Reidar Grønhaug, Gunnar Haaland and Georg Henriksen, 225–43. Bergen: Alma Mater.

_____. 1995. "The Lio House: Building, Category, Idea, Value." In *About the House: Lévi-Strauss and Beyond*, ed. Janet Carsten and Stephen Hugh-Jones, 149–69. Cambridge: Cambridge University Press.

Jacobs, Hubert. 1984. *Documenta Malucensia* [Malukan Documents]. Vol. III 1606–82. Rome: Institutum Historicum Societatis Jesu.

Josephy Jr, Alvin M. 1968. *The Indian Heritage of America*. New York: Alfred A. Knopf.

Kagiya, Akiko. 2010. *Female Culture in Raijua: Ikats and Everlasting Witch Worship in Eastern Indonesia*. Tokyo: Japan Publications.

Kana, Nico L. 1978. "Dunia orang Sabu: satu lukisan analitis tentang azas-azas penataan" [The World of the Savunese: An Analytical Depiction of the Principles of Organisation]. PhD Diss. University of Indonesia, Jakarta.

_____. 1980. "The Order and Significance of the Savunese House." In J. Fox ed., 1980, 221–30.

_____. 1983. *Dunia orang Sabu* [The World of the Savunese]. Jakarta: Sinar Harapan.

Kartodirdjo, Sartono. 1973. *Ikhtisar keadaan politik Hindia-Belanda tahun 1839–1848* [Overview of the Political State of the Netherlands Indies, in the Years 1839–48]. Jakarta: ANRI.

Keegan, John. 1993. *A History of Warfare*. New York: Alfred A. Knopf.

Klerck, E.S. de. 1938. *History of the Netherlands East Indies*. Vols I–II. Rotterdam: W.L. & J. Brusse N.V.

Kolimon, Mery, and Lilya Wetangterah. 2012. *Memori-memori terlarang: perempuan korban & penyintas tragedi '65 di Nusa Tenggara Timur* [Forbidden Memories: Female Victims and Survivors of the '65 Tragedy in East Nusa Tenggara]. Kupang: Yayasan Bonet Pinggupir.

Kruijf, E.F. 1894. *Geschiedenis van het Nederlandsche Zendelinggenootschap en zijne zendingsposten* [History of the Dutch Missionary Society and Its Missionary Posts]. Groningen: J.B. Wolters.

Kuipers, Joel C. 1990. *Power in Performance: The Creation of Textual Authority in Weyewa Ritual Speech*. Philadelphia: University of Pennsylvania Press.

Lansing, J. Stephen et al. 2007. "Coevolution of Languages and Genes on the Island of Sumba, Eastern Indonesia." *Proceedings of the National Academy of Sciences USA* (PNAS): 104 (41): 16022–26. Available at http://www.pnas.org/content/104/41/16022.full [accessed 5 March 2018].

_____. 2011. "An Ongoing Austronesian Expansion in Island Southeast Asia." *Journal of Anthropological Archaeology* 30(3): 262–72. Available at https://www.sciencedirect.com/science/article/pii/S027841651100033X [accessed 5 March 2018].

Leach, E.R. 1961. *Rethinking Anthropology*, LSE Monographs on Social Anthropology, No. 22. London: University of London, Athlone Press.

_____. (1964) 1977. *Political Systems of Highland Burma: A Study of Kachin Social Structure*, LSE Monographs on Social Anthropology, No. 44. London: University of London, Athlone Press.

Leach, Edmund, and Alan D. Aycock. 1983. *Structuralist Interpretation of Biblical Myth*. Cambridge: Cambridge University Press.

Leeming, David, and Margaret Leeming. (1994) 2009 (online). *A Dictionary of Creation Myths*. Oxford: Oxford University Press.

Leitão, H. 1948. *Os Portugueses em Solor e Timor de 1515 a 1702* [The Portuguese in Solor and Timor from 1515 to 1702]. Lisboa: Tip. da Liga dos Combatentes da Grande Guerra [Typographer of the League of Combatants of the Grand War].

Lewis, Douglas E. 1988. *People of the Source: The Social and Ceremonial Order of Tana Wai Brama on Flores* (VKI No. 135). Dordrecht: Foris Publications.

_____. 1996. "Origin Structures and Precedence in the Social Orders of Tana'Ai and Sikka." In J. Fox and C. Sather, eds, 1996, 157–77.

_____. 2003. "Ritual, Metaphor, and the Problem of Direct Exchange in a Tana Wai Brama Child Transfer." In *Framing Indonesian Realities: Essays in Symbolic Anthropology in Honour of Reimar Schefold* (VKI 209), ed. Peter Nas, Gerard Persoon and Rivke Jaffe, 27–51. Leiden: KITLV.

_____. 2010. *The Stranger-Kings of Sikka: With an Integrated Edition of Two Manuscripts on the Origin and History of the Rajadom of Sikka* (VKI No. 257). Leiden: KITLV Press.

Lijnden, D.W.C. Baron van. 1851. "Bijdrage tot de kennis van Solor, Allor, Rotti, Savoe en omliggende eilanden, getrokken uit een verslag van de Residentie Timor" [Contributions to the Knowledge of Solor, Alor, Rote, Savu and Surrounding Islands, Drawn from a Relation of the Timor Residency]. *Natuurkundig Tijdschrift voor Nederlandsch-Indie* [*Physics Journal for the Netherlands Indies*] 2: 317–36; 388–414.

Lulofs, C. 1911. "Toepassing en resultaten van de nieuwere beginselen van politiek beleid in de Residentie Timor en Onderhoorigheden" [Adaptation and Results of the More Recent Beginnings of Political Guidance in the Residency Timor and Dependencies]. *Tijdschrift voor het Binnenlandsch Bestuur* [*Journal for the Domestic Government*] 40: 281–308.

Lysaght, A.M., ed. 1980. *The Journal of Joseph Banks in the Endeavour.* Guildford: Genesis Publications.

McWilliam, Andrew. 2002. *Paths of Origins, Gates of Life: A Study of Place and Precedence in Southwest Timor.* Leiden: KITLV Press.

Manafe, Aco. 2009. *Pahlawan nasional I.H. Doko: Perjuang hingga akhir* [The National Hero I.H. Doko: Fighter to the End]. Kupang: Artha Wacana Press.

Matos, Artur Teodoro de. 1974. *Timor Português 1515–1769: Contribuição para a sua história* [Portuguese Timor 1515–1769: Contribution to Its History]. Lisboa: Instituto Histórico Infante Dom Henriqe, Faculdade de Letras da Universidade de Lisboa.

Middelkoop, Pieter. 1968. "Migrations of Timorese Groups and the Question of the *kase metan* or Overseas Black Foreigners." *Internationales Archiv für Ethnographie.* L1: 49–141.

Mills, J.V. 1930. "Eredia's Description of Malaca, Meridional India, and Cathay." *Journal of the Malay Branch of the Royal Asiatic Society* 8: 1–288.

Monk, Kathryn A., Yance de Fretes, and Gayatri Reksodiharjo-Lilley, eds. 1997. *The Ecology of Nusa Tenggara and Maluku.* Jakarta: Periplus.

Müller, Salomon. 1857. *Reizen en onderzoekingen in den Indischen Archipel, gedaan op last der Nederlandsche Indische Regering, tussschen de jaren 1828 en 1836* dl 1 [Travels and Explorations in the Indies Archipelago, done by order of the Dutch East Indies Government from 1828 to 1836]. Vols I–II. Werken van het Koninklijk Instituut voor Taal-, Land- en Volkenkunde II [Work for the Royal Institute of Linguistics and Anthropology II]. Amsterdam: Frederik Muller.

Nederlandsche Zendelinggenootschap. 1872. "Iets naders over het eiland Savoe" [Something More Precise about Savu Island]. *Maandberigt van het Nederlandsche Zendelinggenootschap* [*Monthly Report of the Dutch Missionary Society*] 10: 153–8.

Nederlandsche Zendelinggenootschap. 1882. "Ramp op Savoe" [Calamity in Savu]. *Maandbericht van het Nederlandsche Zendelinggenootschap* 11: 173–85.

Needham, Rodney. 1983. *Sumba and the Slave Trade*, Centre for Southeast Asian Studies, Working Paper No. 31. Melbourne: Monash University Press.

Newitt, Malyn. 2005. *A History of Portuguese Overseas Expansion, 1400–1668*. London: Routledge.

Ngefak-Bara Pa, Paoina. 2017. *Tradisi Ru-Kètu: Suatu Kajian Budaya dan Refleksi Theologis* [The Ru-Kètu Tradition: A Cultural Study and Theological Reflection]. Bandung: Majelis Sinode Gereja Kristen Pasundan [Assembly of the Christian Synod of Pasundan].

O'Connor, Sue, and Peter Veth, eds. 2000. *East of Wallace's Line: Studies of Past and Present Maritime Cultures of the Indo-Pacific Region*. Rotterdam: A.A. Balkema.

Olivier, Johannes. 1829; 1833. *Land- und Seereisen im Niederländ. Indien* [Travels by Land and Sea in the Netherlands Indies]. Vols 1–2. Weimar: Verlag des Landes-Industrie-Comptoir.

Oppenheimer, Stephen. 1998. *Eden in the East: The Drowned Continent of Southeast Asia*. London: Weidenfeld and Nicolson.

Parimartha, I Gde. 2002. *Perdagangan dan politik di Nusa Tenggara 1815–1915* [Trade and Politics in Nusa Tenggara, 1815–1915]. Jakarta: Perwakilan KITLV dan Penerbit Djambatan [representative of KITLV and publisher Djambatan].

Passar, Kanis, ed. 2005. *Ensiklopedi mereka & karya, untuk generasi berlanjut NTT* [Encyclopaedia of Them and Work, for the Coming Generations of NTT]. Kupang: Yayasan Cinta Flobamora Abdi.

Pélissier, René. 1996. *Timor enguerre: Le Crocodile et les Portugais (1847–1913)* [Timor during war: The Crocodile and the Portuguese (1847–1913)]. Orgeval, France: Pélissier.

Pelon, Jean Baptiste. 2002. *Description de Timor occidental et des îles sous domination hollandaise (1771–1778)* [Description of West Timor and the Islands under Dutch Domination (1771–78)]. Ed. Anne Lombard-Jourdan, Cahiers d'Archipel No. 34. Paris: Association Archipel.

Pelras, Christian. 2002. "Ancestors' Blood: Genealogical Memory, Genealogical Amnesia and Hierarchy among the Bugis." In Chambert-Loir and Reid, eds, 2002, 195–217.

Péron, F.A. 1807. *Voyage de découvertes aux terres Australes exécuté par ordre de sa majesté l'Empereur et Roi sur les corvettes Le Géographe, le Naturaliste…* [Voyage of Discovery in the Southern Lands Undertaken by the Order of His Majesty on the Corvettes, *Le Géographe, le Naturaliste…*]. Vol. I. Paris: L'Imprimerie impériale.

Pigafetta, Antonio. 1923. *Relation du premier voyage autour du monde par Magellan, 1519–1522* [Relation of the First Voyage around the World by Magellan, 1519–22]. French edition from the Paris and Cheltenham manuscripts by J. Denucé. Anvers and Paris: Gust Janssens and Ernest Leroux.

Prescott, Andrew. 2008. "The Textuality of the Archive." In *What are Archives? Cultural and Theoretical Perspectives: A Reader*, ed. Louise Craven, 31–51. Aldershot: Ashgate Publishing.

Ptak, Roderich. 1983. "Some References to Timor in Old Chinese Records." *Ming Studies* 17 (1): 37–48.

Raskin, Brigitte. 1998. *Radja Tanja*. Leuven & Amsterdam: Van Halewyck & Balans.

Reid, Anthony. 1988. *Southeast Asia in the Age of Commerce 1450–1680* Vol. I: *The Lands below the Winds*. New Haven, NJ: Yale University Press.

_____. 1993. *Southeast Asia in the Age of Commerce 1450–1680*, Vol. II: *Expansion and Crisis*. New Haven, NJ: Yale University Press.

_____. 2000. "Introduction: Slavery and Bondage in Southeast Asian History." In *Slavery, Bondage and Dependency in Southeast Asia*, ed. Anthony Reid, 1–43. St Lucia: Queensland University Press.

Reid, Anthony, and David Marr, eds. 1979. *Perceptions of the Past in Southeast Asia*, Asian Studies Association of Australia Southeast Asia Publications Series, 4. Singapore: Published for ASAA by Heinemann Educational Books (Asia).

Reinwardt, C.G.C. 1858. *Reis naar het oostelijk gedeelte van den Indischen Archipel in het jaar 1821* [Travels to the Eastern Part of the Indian Archipelago in the Year 1821]. Werken van het Koninklijk Instituut voor Taal-, Land- en Volkenkunde II [Work for the Royal Institute of Linguistics and Anthropology II]. Amsterdam: Frederik Muller.

Reuter, Thomas. 2002a. *The House of Our Ancestors: Precedence and Dualism in Highland Balinese Society*. Leiden: KITLV.

_____. 2002b. *Custodians of the Sacred Mountains: Culture and Society in the Highlands of Bali*. Honolulu: University of Hawai'i Press.

Ricklefs, M.C. 2001. *A History of Modern Indonesia since c. 1200*. Third edition. Stanford: Stanford University Press.

Riwu Kaho, Robert. 2005. *Orang Sabu dan budaya* [Savu People and Culture]. Yogyakarta: Jogja Global Media.

Robson, Stuart. 1995. *Deśawarnana (Nagarakrtagama) by Mpu Prapañca* [Explanation about Villages (Land of Sacred Tradition)] (VKI No. 169). Leiden: KITLV Press.

Roever, Arend de. 2002. *De jacht op sandelhout: De VOC en de tweedeling van Timor in de zeventiende eeuw* [The Hunt for Sandalwood: The VOC and the Bipartition of Timor in the Seventeenth Century]. Zutphen: Walburg Pers.

Sá, Artur Basilio de, ed. 1956. *História de Maluco no tempo de Gonçalo Pereira Marramaque e Sancho de Vascincellos ... 1636. Fundação das Primeiras Cristandades nas Ilhas de Solor e Timor, 1624–25* [History of Maluccas in the Time of ... 1636. Foundation of Early Christianity in the Islands of Solor and Timor 1624–25]. (Documentação para a história das missões do padroado português do Oriente Insulindia,. Vol. 4 (1568–79) [Documentation for the History of the Missions of the Portuguese Patronage in the East Indian Islands]. Lisboa: Agencia Geral do Ultramar.

Sahlins, Marshall. 1985. *Islands of History*. Chicago: Chicago University Press.

Santa Catarina, Lucas de. (1733) 1866. *Quarta Parte da História de S. Domingo* [Fourth Part of the History of St. Dominic]. Lisboa: Panorama.

Savunese, The. n.d. *The Savunese (Indonesia): The Struggle for the Survival of Their Ethnic Culture & Religion*. Jakarta: Rai Hawu Foundation.

Schooneveld-Oosterling. J.E., ed. (1743–1750) 1997. *Generale Missiven van Gouverneurs Generaal en Raden aan Heren XVII der VOC* [General Correspondence of the Governor Generals and Council to the XVII Gentlemen of the VOC]. Vol. 11. Den Haag: Institut voor Nederlandse Geschiedenis.

Schulte Nordholt, H.G. 1971. *The Political System of the Atoni of Timor* (VKI No. 60). The Hague: Martinus Nijhoff.

Sher Banu A.L. Khan. 2017. *Sovereign Women in a Muslim Kingdom: The Sultanahs of Aceh, 1641–1699.* Singapore: NUS Press.

Sherlock, Kevin. 1980. *A Bibliography of Timor: Including East (formerly Portuguese) Timor, West (formerly Dutch) Timor and the Island of Roti.* Canberra: RSPS, ANU.

Sparkes, Stephen, and Signe Howell, eds. 2003. *The House in Southeast Asia: A Changing Social, Political and Economic Domain.* London: Routledge Curzon.

Sperber, Dan. 1985. "Anthropology and Psychology: Towards an Epidemiology of Representations." *Man* 20 (1): 73–89.

_____. 1996. *Explaining Culture: A Naturalistic Approach.* Cambridge, MA: Blackwell Publishers.

Spivak, Gayatri Chakravorty. 1988. "Can the Subaltern Speak?" In *Marxism and the Interpretation of Culture.* ed. Cary Nelson and Lawrence Grossberg, 271–313. Urbana: University of Illinois Press.

Stoler, Ann Laura. 2009. *Along the Archival Grain: Epistemic Anxieties and Colonial Common Sense.* Princeton: Princeton University Press.

Tajib, H. Abdullah. 1995. *Sejarah Bima Dana Mbojo* [*History of Bima Dana Mbojo*]. Jakarta: Harapan Masa.

Taniputera, Ivan. 2013. *Kerajaan-kerajaan Nusantara pascakeruntuhan Majapahit: Hikayat dan Sejarahnya* [The Kingdoms of the Archipelago after the Fall of Majapahit: Folklore and History]. Jakarta: C.V. Gloria Group.

Tarling, Nicholas, ed. 1992. *The Cambridge History of Southeast Asia.* Vols I–II. Cambridge: Cambridge University Press.

Tefa Sa'u, Andreas. 2013. "Kure': Sebuah tradisi religius di Kote-Noemuti" [Kure': A Religious Tradition in Kote-Noemuti]. In *Kebudayaan: Sebuah agenda* [Culture: An Agenda], ed. Gregor Neonbasu, 107–26 . Jakarta: Gramedia Pustaka Utama.

Teffer, M. 1875. "De Savoe-eilanden. De oorsponkelijke en tegenwoordige bewoners. Voornaamste middel van bestaan" [The Savu Islands. The Original and Present Inhabitants. Foremost Means of Maintenance]. *Mededeelingen van wege het Nederlandsche Zendelinggenootschap* 19: 205–33.

Temminck, C.J., ed. 1839–44. *Verhandelingen over de natuurlijke geschiedenis der Nederlandsche Overzeesche Bezittingen* [Treatises about the Natural History of the Dutch Overseas Possessions]. Vol. 3. Leiden: La Lau.

Therik, Tom. 2004. *Wehali, the Female Land: Traditions of a Timorese Ritual Centre.* Canberra: Anthropology, RSPAS, ANU: Pandanus Books.

Tiele, P.A. and J.E. Heeres, eds. 1886–1895. *Bouwstoffen voor de geschiedenis der Nederlanders in den Maleischen Archipel* [Materials for the History of the Dutch in the Malay Archipelago]. Vols I–III. 's-Gravenhage: Martinus Nijhoff.

Traube, Elizabeth G. 1980. "Mambai Rituals of Black and White." In J. Fox ed., 1980, 290–314.

_____. 1986. *Cosmology and Social Life: Ritual Exchange among the Mambai of East Timor.* Chicago: Chicago University Press.

Tryon, Darrell T., ed. 1995. *Comparative Austronesian Dictionary: An Introduction to Austronesian Studies*, Trends in Linguistics, Documentation 10. Berlin and New York: Mouton de Gruyter.

Tumonggor, Meryanne K. et al. 2014. "Isolation, Contact and Social Behavior Shaped Genetic Diversity in West Timor." *Journal of Human Genetics* 59: 494–503. Available at https://www.nature.com/articles/jhg201462 [accessed 5 March 2018].

Vansina, Jan. 1985. *Oral Tradition as History*. Madison: University of Wisconsin.

Verheijen, J.A.J. 1990. *Dictionary of Plant Names in the Lesser Sunda Islands*, Pacific Linguistics: Series D, No. 83. Canberra: ANU.

Veth, P.J. 1855. "Het eiland Timor" [The Island of Timor]. *De Gids* [*The Guide*] 8 (1): 545–611; 8 (2): 55–100.

Vischer, Michael P. 1994. "Black and Red, White and Yellow: Palu'é Textiles as Representations of Socio-Cosmic Ideas." In *Gift of the Cotton Maiden: Textiles of Flores and the Solor Islands*, ed. Roy W. Hamilton, 246–68. Los Angeles: Fowler Museum of Cultural History, UCLA.

_____. 2003. "Substitution, Expiation and the Idiom of Blood in Ko'a Sacrificing." In *Framing Indonesian Realities: Essays in Symbolic Anthropology in Honor of Reimar Schefold* (VKI209), ed. Peter Nas, Gerard Persoon and Rivke Jaffe, 53–69. Leiden: KITLV.

_____. ed. 2009 *Precedence: Social Differentiation in the Austronesian World*. Canberra: ANU E Press.

Walker, Alan T. 1982. *Grammar of Sawu*. Jakarta: Universitas Atma Jaya: Badan Penyelenggara Seri NUSA (Linguistic Studies in Indonesian and Languages in Indonesia) [Organising Committee for NUSA Series].

Wassmann, Jürg. (1982) 1991. *The Song to the Flying Fox: The Public and Esoteric Knowledge of Important Men of Kandingei …*. Apwitihire 2. Boroko, Papua New Guinea: National Research Institute.

Waterson, Roxana. 1990. *The Living House: An Anthropology of Architecture in South-East Asia*. Singapore: Oxford University Press.

_____. 1995. "Houses and Hierarchies in Island South-East Asia." In *About the House: Lévi-Strauss and Beyond*, ed. Janet Carsten and Stephen Hugh-Jones, 47–68. Cambridge: Cambridge University Press.

_____. 1997. "The Contested Landscapes in Myth and History in Tana Toraja." In *The Poetic Power of Places: Comparative Perspectives on Austronesian Ideas of Locality*, ed. James J. Fox, 63–90. Canberra: Anthropology, RSPS, ANU.

Wellem, Fred. Djara. 2005. "Karya Nederlands Zendeling Genootchap di kepulauan Sabu, Nusa Tenggara Timur, Indonesia (1871–1901)" [The Work of the Dutch Missionary Society in the Savu Islands, East Nusa Tenggara, Indonesia (1871–1901)]. In *Een vakkracht in het koninkrijk: Kerk- en zendinghistorische opstellen* [A Professional Skill in the Kingdom: Essays of Church and Missionary History], ed. Chr. G.F. de Jong, 329–47. Groen: Heerenveen.

Wellfelt, Emilie. 2011. "Malielehi – Freedom Fighter or Mad Murderess?" In Hägerdal, ed., 2011c, 149–82.

Wielenga, D.K. 1926. *Soemba* [*Sumba*]. s'-Gravenhage: Algemeene boekhandel voor inwendige- en uitwendige zending [General Bookshop for Inner and Outer Mission].

Wijngaarden, J.K. 1896. *Sawuneesche Woordenlijst* [Savunese Word List]. Leiden: KITLV.

Winichakul, Thongchai. 1994. *Siam Mapped: A History of the Geo-Body of a Nation*. Honolulu: University of Hawai'i Press.

Woha, Umbu Pura. 2008. *Sejarah, musyawarah dan adat istiadat Sumba Timur* [History, Deliberation and Customs: East Sumba]. Kupang: Cipta Sarana Jaya.

Wolff, Eric R. (1968) 1982. *Europe and the People without History*. Berkley: University of California Press.

Wouden, F.A.E. van. (1935) 1968. *Types of Social Structure in Eastern Indonesia*. KITLV, Translation Series 11. Translated by Rodney Needham with Preface by G.W. Locher. The Hague: Martinus Nijhoff.

Wurm, Stephen, and Basil Wilson. 1975. *English Finder List of Reconstructions in Austronesian Languages*, Pacific Linguistics: Series C, No. 33. Canberra: ANU.

Index